THE VICTORIA HISTORY OF THE COUNTIES OF ENGLAND

A HISTORY OF ESSEX

VOLUME VII

THE VICTORIA HISTORY OF THE COUNTIES OF ENGLAND

EDITED BY C. R. ELRINGTON

THE UNIVERSITY OF LONDON
INSTITUTE OF
HISTORICAL RESEARCH

Oxford University Press, Walton Street, Oxford OX2 6DP

OXFORD LONDON GLASGOW
NEW YORK TORONTO MELBOURNE WELLINGTON
IBADAN NAIROBI DAR ES SALAAM LUSAKA CAPE TOWN
KUALA LUMPUR SINGAPORE JAKARTA HONG KONG TOKYO
DELHI BOMBAY CALCUTTA MADRAS KARACHI

ISBN 0 19 722720 1

PRINTED IN GREAT BRITAIN BY
ROBERT MACLEHOSE AND CO. LTD
PRINTERS TO THE UNIVERSITY OF GLASGOW

Romford Market Place in the late 19th century, from the south-east

INSCRIBED TO THE

MEMORY OF HER LATE MAJESTY

QUEEN VICTORIA

WHO GRACIOUSLY GAVE THE TITLE TO

AND ACCEPTED THE DEDICATION

OF THIS HISTORY

A HISTORY OF THE COUNTY OF ESSEX

EDITED BY W. R. POWELL

VOLUME VII

PUBLISHED FOR
THE INSTITUTE OF HISTORICAL RESEARCH
BY
OXFORD UNIVERSITY PRESS
1978

Distributed by Oxford University Press until 1 January 1981
thereafter by Dawsons of Pall Mall

CONTENTS OF VOLUME SEVEN

LIST OF ILLUSTRATIONS

The painting of Warley Camp is reproduced by gracious permission of Her Majesty the Queen. Thanks for the loan of illustrations, and for permission to reproduce them, is due also to Aerofilms Ltd., Mr. N. Carter, Mr. P. H. Clark, Mr. R. Edwards, Essex County Council, Mr. A. S. Frith, Mr. A. F. Kersting, Mr. D. Lipson, the London Borough of Havering, Murex Ltd., the National Monuments Record, Mr. R. R. Squire, and Thurrock Local History Museum. The coats of arms were drawn by Patricia Tattersfield. The photographs dated 1977 and not otherwise attributed are by A. P. Baggs.

LIST OF ILLUSTRATIONS

LIST OF MAPS AND PLANS

Unless otherwise stated all the maps and plans are based on the Ordnance Survey, with the sanction of the Controller, H.M. Stationery Office, Crown Copyright reserved, and were drawn by K. J. Wass, of the Department of Geography, University College, London, from drafts by D. R. Ransome.

EDITORIAL NOTE

THIS volume of the *Victoria History of Essex* is the sixth to be published under the co-operative system described in the editorial note to Volume IV. The contributing Local Authorities have continued, and have substantially increased, their grants. It is to be added that the Essex County Council, which had for many years been giving practical help, in 1977 took over from the District Councils the payment of contributions for the administrative county. The councils of the Greater London Boroughs of Barking, Havering, Newham, Redbridge, and Waltham Forest, continue to furnish contributions for their own areas.

The Essex Victoria County History Committee, formed mainly of representatives of the Local Authorities, has continued to survey the progress of the work under the chairmanship of Sir William Addison. Mr. Donald Forbes, Honorary Treasurer of the committee from 1955, and also Honorary Secretary from 1967, retired in 1975. He was succeeded as Honorary Secretary by Mr. William H. Liddell, and as Honorary Treasurer by Mr. Geoffrey J. Clements. Mr. Kenneth H. Sleat has continued as Honorary Assistant Secretary. The University of London expresses its thanks to these gentlemen and to the other officers and members of the committee, and to the participating Local Authorities (listed below) for their generous grants. During the preparation of the present volume the assistant editorship was held by Dr. David R. Ransome (1973–6), and by Miss Vanessa A. Harding (from 1977). Mrs. Beryl A. Board has continued as senior editorial assistant, and in 1977 Mrs. W. Stubbings was appointed as an editorial assistant. Secretarial help has been given in the preparation of this volume by Mrs. D. Maclaine, Mrs. M. Reeve, and Mrs. K. Caddy.

The structure and aims of the *Victoria History* as a whole are outlined in the *General Introduction* to the *History* (1970). As in Volumes IV, V, and VI the brief descriptions of the earlier parochial registers of each parish, commonly included in the topographical volumes of the *History*, have not been considered necessary, because of the publication by the County Council of *Essex Parish Records, 1240–1894* (1950; revised edn. 1966).

The compilers have again received help from many persons, whose kindness is acknowledged in the text of the volume and in the lists of illustrations and of maps. Especial thanks are due to the Warden and Fellows of New College, Oxford, and their Archivist, Mr. F. W. Steer, for providing access to the college records and for allowing their Liber Niger (MS 9744) to be taken to Chelmsford for microfilming; to the late Mr. F. Lewis for the loan of his manuscripts and cuttings; and to Mr. K. G. Farries for much information on windmills. Mr. E. A. Bird, Mr. G. J. Clements, the Revd. H. Johnson, archdeacon of Sheffield, Mr. C. J. Whitwood, and Havering public libraries provided information and read drafts. Valuable services of many kinds have been rendered by the Essex Record Office, and the early death of the County Archivist, Mr. K. C. Newton, in March 1978 is a great loss not only to the office but also to the *Victoria History of Essex*. The Department of the Environment has continued to allow the use of its unpublished lists of buildings of architectural or historical interest. The Greater London Council, Historic Buildings Division, has furnished information on the buildings in Havering London Borough. A gift of £350 from Dr. Marc Fitch, to pay for the frontispiece, is gratefully acknowledged.

ESSEX
VICTORIA COUNTY HISTORY COMMITTEE

As at 1 March 1978

LIST OF CLASSES OF DOCUMENTS IN THE PUBLIC RECORD OFFICE

USED IN THIS VOLUME WITH THEIR CLASS NUMBERS

Clerks of Assize
- Assizes 35 — Indictments

Chancery
- C 1 — Proceedings, Early
- C 60 — Fine Rolls
- Inquisitions post mortem
  - C 132 — Series I, Henry III
  - C 136 — Richard II
  - C 137 — Henry IV
  - C 138 — Henry V
  - C 139 — Henry VI
  - C 142 — Series II

Court of Common Pleas
- C.P. 25(2) — Feet of Fines, Series II
- C.P. 40 — Plea Rolls
- C.P. 43 — Recovery Rolls

Department of Education
- Ed. 2 — Elementary Education, Parish Files
- Ed. 21 — Elementary Education, School Files
- Ed. 49 — Elementary Education, Endowment Files

Exchequer, King's Remembrancer
- E 134 — Depositions taken by Commission
- E 179 — Subsidy Rolls, etc.

Exchequer, Augmentation Office
- E 301 — Certificates of Colleges and Chantries
- E 317 — Parliamentary Surveys

Exchequer, First Fruits and Tenths Office
- E 331 — Bishops' Certificates of Institutions to Benefices

Exchequer, Lord Treasurer's Remembrancer and Pipe Offices
- E 351 — Declared Accounts (Pipe Office)

Home Office
- H.O. 67 — Acreage Returns
- H.O. 129 — Ecclesiastical Census Returns

Board of Inland Revenue
- I.R. 29 and 30 — Tithe Apportionments and Maps

Justices Itinerant, Assize and Gaol Delivery Justices, etc.
- J.I. 1 — Eyre Rolls, Assize Rolls, etc.
- J.I. 3 — Gaol Delivery Rolls

Court of King's Bench (Crown Side)
- K.B. 9 — Ancient Indictments

Office of Land Revenue Records and Enrolments
- L.R.R.O. 1 — Maps and Plans

Ministry of Agriculture, Fisheries, and Food
- M.A.F. 68 — Agricultural Returns, Parish Summaries

Maps and Plans
- M.P.F. 19 — Map of Rainham (formerly S.P. 13/Case G. 23)

Prerogative Court of Canterbury
- Prob. 11 — Registered Copy Wills

Special Collections
- S.C. 2 — Court Rolls
- S.C. 11 — Rental and Surveys (Rolls)

State Paper Office
- S.P. 1 — State Papers Domestic and Foreign, Henry VIII, General Series
- S.P. 14 — State Papers Domestic, Jas. I

LIST OF CLASSES OF DOCUMENTS IN THE ESSEX RECORD OFFICE

USED IN THIS VOLUME WITH THEIR CLASS NUMBERS

County Council of Essex

C/DP	Deposited Parliamentary Plans
C/M	Minutes
C/ME	Education Committee Minutes
C/MH	Highways Committee Minutes
C/T	Title Deeds of General Properties
C/TE	Title Deeds of School Properties
C/TS	Title Deeds of Small Holdings
C/W	War Records

Deposited Records

D/AB	Bishop of London, Commissary in Essex and Herts.
D/AE	Archdeacon of Essex
D/AX	Archidiaconal Records, Composite Books
	Diocesan Records
D/CC	Consecrations
D/CE	New Parishes, etc.
D/CF	Faculty Papers
D/CP	Deeds
D/CT	Tithe Apportionments and Maps
D/D	Estate and Family (many sub-classes, D/DA to D/DZ)
D/F	Business
D/NB	Nonconformist, Baptists
D/NC	Nonconformist, Congregationalists
D/P	Parish Records
D/Q	Charities
D/SH	Commissioners of Sewers, Havering Levels
D/SR	Commissioners of Sewers, Rainham Levels
D/Z	Miscellaneous Archives

Education Records

E/ML	School Log Books
E/MM	School Managers' Minutes
E/P	Plans of New Schools
E/Z	Schools (Miscellaneous)

Poor Law Guardians

G/Bi	Billericay Union
G/Or	Orsett Union
G/R	Romford Union

Lieutenancy

L/DI	Ilford Sub-division

Court of Quarter Sessions

Q/AB	County Bridges
Q/ALc	County Lunatic Asylum
Q/APr	County Police, Distribution Returns
Q/AX	Exempt Jurisdictions
Q/CR	Clerk of the Peace, Parliamentary Returns
Q/HF	Havering Liberty, Sessions Files
Q/HM	Havering Liberty, Sessions Minutes
Q/HR	Havering Liberty, Parliamentary Returns
Q/HZ	Havering Liberty, Miscellaneous
Q/RDc	Inclosure Awards
Q/RHi	Highways Diversion, Closure, Widening
Q/RLv	Alehouse Recognizances
Q/RPc	Parliamentary Electors' Lists
Q/RPl	Land Tax Assessments
Q/RPr	Parliamentary Electors' Registers
Q/RRp	Papists' Estates, Registers
Q/RSg	Gamekeepers' Deputations
Q/RSr	Charities
Q/RSw	Workhouses
Q/RTh	Hearth Tax Assessments
Q/RUm	Public Undertakings, Plans of Schemes
Q/SBa	Sessions Bundles, Early
Q/SBb	Sessions Bundles, Later
Q/SO	Order Books
Q/SPb	Process Books of Indictments
Q/SR	Sessions Rolls

Transcripts

T/A	Originals in public repositories
T/B	Originals in private custody
T/G	Genealogical material
T/M	Maps
T/P	Material for parish histories
T/R	Parish Registers
T/Z	Miscellaneous

Some of the foregoing classes contain sub-classes which are denoted by additional letters, not shown here, but fully cited in footnotes in this volume. The group called 'Transcripts' includes all forms of copies or catalogues of documents of which the originals are elsewhere, or notes and extracts taken from them.

NOTE ON ABBREVIATIONS

Among abbreviations and short titles the following may need elucidation:

B.L.	British Library
C.C.L.	Chelmsford Cathedral Library
C.D.L.	Chelmsford District Library
Cal. Wills Husting	*Calendar of Wills proved in the Court of Husting, London*, ed. R. R. Sharpe (2 vols. 1889–90)
Ch. Bells Essex	C. Deedes and H. B. Walters, *The Church Bells of Essex* (1909)
Ch. Chests Essex	H. W. Lewer and J. C. Wall, *The Church Chests of Essex* (1913)
Ch. Plate Essex	G. M. Benton, F. W. Galpin, and W. J. Pressey, *The Church Plate of Essex* (1926)
Chancellor, *Sep. Mons. Essex*	F. Chancellor, *The Ancient Sepulchral Monuments of Essex* (1890)
Chelmsford Wills	*Wills at Chelmsford*, ed. F. G. Emmison (British Record Society, 3 vols. 1958–69)
D.P.L.	Valence Library, Dagenham
Davids, *Nonconformity in Essex*	T. W. Davids, *Annals of Evangelical Nonconformity in Essex from the time of Wycliffe to the Restoration* (1863)
E.A.T.	*The Transactions of the Essex Archaeological Society*
E.C.U.	Essex Congregational Union
E.J.	*The Essex Journal*
E. Nat.	*The Essex Naturalist*
E.R.	*The Essex Review*
E.R.O.	Essex Record Office
Essex Par. Recs.	*Catalogue of Essex Parish Records*, 2nd edn., ed. F. G. Emmison (1966)
Feet of F. Essex	*Feet of Fines for Essex* (Essex Archaeological Society; issued in parts: vol. i, 1899–1910; vol. ii, 1913–28; vol. iii, 1929–49; vol. iv, 1964)
Fisher, *Forest*	W. R. Fisher, *The Forest of Essex* (1887)
G.L.C. (in footnote references)	Greater London Council Record Office
H.R.L.	Havering Reference Library
Hale, *Precedents*	W. H. Hale, *Precedents and Proceedings in Criminal Causes, 1475–1640* (1847)
Hart, *Early Chart. Essex*	C. Hart, *The Early Charters of Essex* (2 vols. 2nd edn. 1971)
Hist. Essex by Gent.	*A New and Complete History of Essex by a Gentleman* (6 vols. 1769–72)
Horn. Docs.	*Hornchurch Priory: a Kalendar of Documents*, ed. H. F. Westlake (1923)
Lewis, *Rainham*	F. Lewis, *A History of Rainham, with Wennington and South Hornchurch* (1966)
Lysons, *Lond.*	D. Lysons, *The Environs of London* (4 vols. 1795–6)
Map of Essex (1777)	J. Chapman and P. André, *A Map of Essex from an actual survey taken in 1772, 1773, and 1774* (1777) [Sections of the map are reproduced in this volume.]
Morant, *Essex*	P. Morant, *The History and Antiquities of Essex* (2 vols. 1768)
Newcourt, *Repertorium*	R. Newcourt, *Repertorium Ecclesiasticum Parochiale Londinense* (2 vols. 1710)
Norden, *Essex*	J. Norden, *Speculi Britanniae Pars . . . Description of Essex, 1594*, ed. Sir H. Ellis (Camden Soc. [1st ser.], ix)
Ogborne, *Essex*	E. Ogborne, *The History of Essex* (1814)

NOTE ON ABBREVIATIONS

P.N. Essex	P. H. Reaney, *The Place-Names of Essex* (English Place-Name Society, xii, 1935)
Perfect, *Village of Hornchurch*	C. T. Perfect, *Ye Olde Village of Hornchurch* (1917)
Pevsner, *Essex*	N. Pevsner, *The Buildings of England, Essex* (2nd edn. 1965)
R.C.H.M. *Essex*	The Royal Commission on Historical Monuments (England), *An Inventory of the Historical Monuments in Essex* (4 vols. 1916–23)
Salmon, *Essex*	N. Salmon, *The History and Antiquities of Essex* (1740–2)
Smith, *Eccl. Hist. Essex*	H. Smith, *The Ecclesiastical History of Essex under the Long Parliament and Commonwealth* [*c.* 1931]
Smith, *Havering*	H. Smith, *History of the Parish of Havering-atte-Bower* (1925)
Strat. Expr.	*Stratford Express* [newspaper]
Terry, *Romford*	G. Terry, *Memories of Old Romford and other places within the Royal Liberty of Havering-atte-Bower* (1880)
Thorne, *Environs Lond.*	J. Thorne, *Handbook to the Environs of London* (1876, reprinted 1970)
Trans. E.F.C.	*The Transactions of the Essex Field Club*
Visit. Essex (ed. Howard)	*A Visitation of the County of Essex, 1664–8*, ed. J. J. Howard (Harleian Society, 1888)
Visit. Essex (Harl. Soc.)	*The Visitations of Essex, 1552–1634*, ed. W. C. Metcalfe (Harleian Society, 2 vols. 1878–9)
W.A.M.	Westminster Abbey Muniments
Wright, *Essex*	T. Wright, *The History and Topography of the County of Essex* (2 vols. 1836)

THE LIBERTY OF HAVERING-ATTE-BOWER

THE MANOR and liberty of Havering-atte-Bower, in south-west Essex, was conterminous with the ancient parish of Hornchurch.[1] It stretched north from the Thames marshes for about 8 miles to the wooded village of Havering-atte-Bower, where there was a royal house from the 11th century to the seventeenth. Romford, a market town from the 13th century, was in the centre of the liberty. South of Romford was Hornchurch village, where there was a medieval priory. Havering-atte-Bower village and Romford, both ancient chapelries, became separate parishes in the 1780s and 1849 respectively.

The suburban growth of Romford and Hornchurch began in the 19th century. Among the few older houses still surviving are the mansions of Bower House, at Havering, Langtons and Bretons, both at Hornchurch. The grounds of Gidea Hall, Romford, were developed in 1910 as the Gidea Park garden suburb. Dagnam Park, Romford, was demolished *c.* 1948, when the London county council built the great Harold Hill estate.

Since the Second World War the Phoenix Timber Co. has developed the east side of Hornchurch marshes, and the Ford Motor Co. has built a foundry on the west side, adjoining its Dagenham works. There is light industry along the Southend Arterial road, and in a few other areas. Romford has become one of the main shopping centres of Greater London. In other respects Hornchurch and Romford are mainly residential. Havering-atte-Bower, which lies in the Green Belt, retains its ancient village green.

The liberty of Havering lost its privileged status in 1892, but the whole area which had comprised it was re-united in 1965, when Romford municipal borough and Hornchurch urban district were merged to form the London borough of Havering.

The manor of Havering belonged to the Crown from the 11th century to the 19th; from the 13th to the later 17th century it normally formed part of the queen's dower.[2] Havering was in Becontree hundred in 1086. It is usually held to have become a separate liberty by charter of Edward IV in 1465. Even before 1465, however, it was occasionally referred to as a liberty,[3] and for administrative purposes was sometimes treated separately from Becontree hundred.[4] Here, as in other royal manors, tenants could invoke the little writ of right close, which initiated procedure in the manor court, often followed by a final concord, for settling proprietory disputes or for agreed conveyances.[5] That procedure, recorded from the mid 14th century in the surviving manor court rolls,[6] had been established for contentious cases by 1235, and for all purposes by 1253.[7] From the late 15th century the court rolls of the manor also include enrolments of

[1] This article was read in draft by Dr. M. K. McIntosh, who made some helpful comments.

[2] See pp. 11 sqq.

[3] e.g. in 1269: *Cal. Chart. R.* 1257–1300, 119.

[4] Cf. *Rot. Hund.* (Rec. Com.), i. 149, 152; *Feud. Aids*, ii. 135, 175–6, 224–5; E 179/108/107; *Cal. Pat.* 1321–4, 61; *Cal. Inq. Misc.* 1307–49, pp. 314–15.

[5] Cf. Pollock and Maitland, *Hist. Eng. Law*, i. 383–8; R. S. Hoyt, *Royal Demesne in Eng. Cons. Hist.* 94–9, 195.

[6] Havering court rolls: S.C. 2/172/25–40 (dated 1352–1509); 173/1–5 (dated 1509–1622); E.R.O., D/DU 102/1–128 (dated 1382–1773); E.R.O., Acc. 4612 (court bk. 1732–70).

[7] M. K. McIntosh, 'The privileged tenants of the English ancient demesne,' *Viator*, vii. 1.

common recoveries or real recoveries, initiated like the final concords by the little writ of right close.

Before 1465 three different courts were being held for the manor of Havering. The three-weeken court was a court baron.[8] The general court, for baron and leet business, met at Easter and Michaelmas. Fines and recoveries might be enrolled either in the

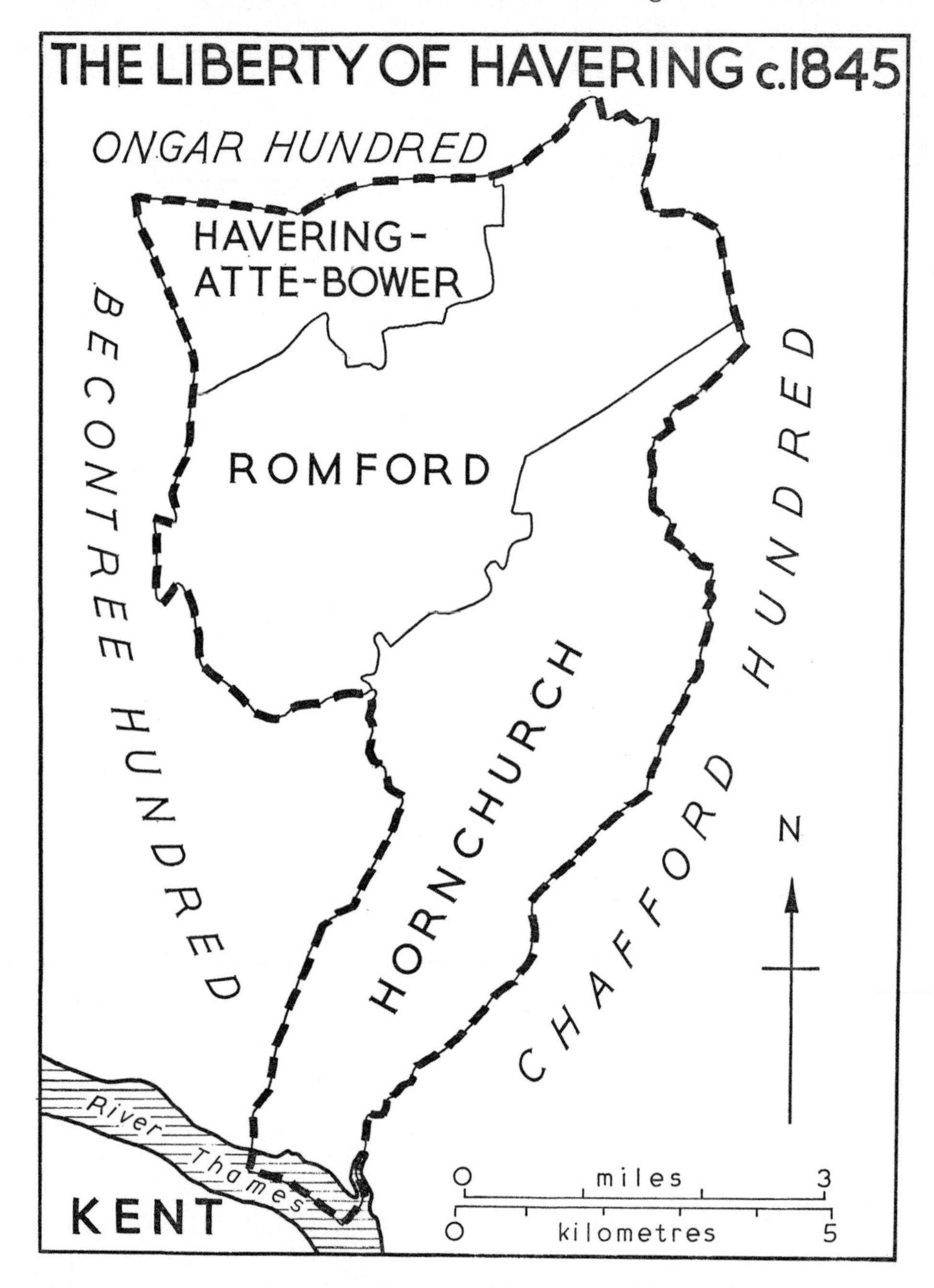

three-weeken court or in the general court. The view of frankpledge, usually held on Whit Tuesday, had leet jurisdiction. From *c.* 1446 the manorial constables, aletasters, woodwards, and other officers were appointed at the view.[9] The manor had a gaol, at Romford, which was in existence by 1259, and seems to have continued, in various forms, until the 19th century.[10] Within the manor of Havering were many tenements, some of which came to be styled manors.[11] By 1274–5 the lords of three of those sub-

[8] Usually referred to simply as the *curia*.

[9] E.R.O., D/DU 102/34, m. 20d.; ibid. 102/38, m. 19d., and later rolls. A few earlier appointments of officers were made in the three-weeken court, e.g.: S.C. 2/172/32 m. 23 (date 1444–5).

[10] See below.

[11] See pp. 11, 31, 64.

ordinate manors, Bedfords (in Havering), Dovers, and Suttons (both in Hornchurch), were claiming the view of frankpledge; Bedfords and Suttons also claimed the assize of bread and ale.[12] In 1285 the lord of Suttons claimed the right of gallows.[13] The lords of the associated manors of Hornchurch Hall and Suttons continued to hold courts leet and baron at least until the mid 17th century.[14]

The tenants of the manor of Havering enjoyed quittance from tolls throughout the realm, according to ancient custom, as was confirmed in 1368 and on several later occasions.[15] Between *c.* 1230 and 1246 they were accounting directly to the Exchequer for the farm of the manor.[16] Such privileges often accompanied borough status. Havering did not become a borough, but the charter of 1465 confirmed and extended its exceptional privileges.

It has been plausibly suggested that (Sir) Thomas Urswick, lord of the manor of Marks in Dagenham and Havering, was instrumental in obtaining the charter of 1465, and that the boundary between Dagenham and Havering was at that time altered to include the manor-house of Marks within the liberty.[17] As a prominent Yorkist, and recorder of London, Urswick was certainly well placed to exert influence; and there is no doubt that in the 15th century the manor of Marks, originally a free tenement of the manor of Barking, was enlarged to include lands in Havering.

The charter of 1465 provided that no tenant of Havering was to be compelled to plead in any court other than that of the manor.[18] The steward and suitors of the manor court could determine all civil pleas, and the sheriff of Essex was to be excluded except on a writ of error or false judgement. The steward, and one man chosen by the tenants from their own number, were to be justices of the peace, with all the authority of justices elsewhere in the county, save that the king's special mandate was necessary before they determined cases of treason or felony. The tenants were to have an annual fair, with a court of piepowder, though there is no record of the court being held. No royal or other purveyor was to take goods or victuals in the manor without the tenants' consent. The rights to appoint justices and hold fairs were new. The other privileges in the charter already existed before 1465.

The charter of Edward IV was confirmed by Henry VII, Henry VIII, and Mary.[19] Mary (1554) also provided that in future the deputy steward of the manor should be a justice of the peace, along with the steward and the elected justice. The charter was twice confirmed by Elizabeth I.[20] Her second charter (1588) constituted a corporation under the name of 'The tenants and inhabitants of the lordship of the manor of Havering-atte-Bower in the county of Essex', with a common seal.[21] The exemption from purveyances was extended to protect horses and carts. The queen also licensed the tenants to found a hospital for the poor, sick, and aged; but nothing seems to have come of that. The charter was confirmed without further amendments by James I, by Charles I, and by Charles II in 1664.[22] About 1664 the government considered making Havering a borough, but did not do so,[23] and the constitution of the liberty was not further changed until the 19th century.

The royal charters always refer to the 'lordship or manor' of Havering, not to the

[12] *Rot. Hund.* (Rec. Com.), i. 152.

[13] *Plac. de Quo Warr.* (Rec. Com.), 232.

[14] Court roll of Suttons, 1298: New Coll. Oxford MS. 9812; Ct. rolls of Hornchurch Hall and Suttons, 1340–1650 (gaps): E.R.O., T/A 168/2 and 3 (microfilm from New Coll. MSS.).

[15] *Cal. Pat.* 1367–70, 119; *Cal. Close* 1381–5, 314; 1399–1402, 9.

[16] *Pipe R. 1230* (P.R.S. N.S. iv), 162; *Pipe R. 1242* (ed. H. L. Cannon), 224; *Cal. Lib.* 1245–51, 57.

[17] *V.C.H. Essex*, v. 275–6.

[18] *Cal. Chart. R.* 1427–1516, 204–6. For a summary of the charter, and the administration of the liberty after 1465, see Smith, *Havering*, 265–88.

[19] *Cal. Pat.* 1553–4, 224–5.

[20] *True Copy of the Charter of Havering-atte-Bower* (Romford, 1820).

[21] For the costs of obtaining the charter of 1588 see E.R.O., D/DU 102/84, Whit. Tues. 1590.

[22] *True Copy of the Charter* (1820). For the costs of obtaining the charter of 1664 see E.R.O., D/DMs O34.

[23] Smith, *Havering*, 267.

'liberty'. The latter style, which seems to have arisen by prescription, was often used from the 15th century onwards, and by the 18th century was well established in the official records of Havering.[24] A common seal was in use by 1573, fifteen years before it was authorized by Elizabeth I.[25] It was oval, and measured 1⅝ in. by 1⅛ in. The device was a castle or gatehouse above a ring. The legend, in Roman lettering, read SIGILLVM MANERII DE HAVERYNG ATTEBOWRE. The same seal was still in use in 1622 and 1635.[26] A later version of it, in use in the 19th century, was almost identical, but measured 1¾ in. by 1¼ in. and, in the legend, used the spelling HAVERING.[27] No matrix is known to exist.

The charter of 1465 had the effect of creating a court of quarter sessions, the functions of which overlapped with those of the older manor courts. The chief officers of the liberty were the high steward, appointed by the lord of the manor, the deputy steward, the justice of the peace, the coroner, and the high bailiff; the last three were elected in the manor courts.[28] There is no regular series of Havering quarter sessions records until the 18th century.[29] From the 15th century, however, the work of the justices occasionally figures in the records of the manor court leet. In 1489, for example, two tenants stood bail in the manor court for a defendant to appear before a justice of the peace when required.[30] In the same year two men suspected of felony were remanded in custody by the manor court to await 'the sessions of the peace and general court with leet to be held on 1 October'.[31] This suggests that, then as later, the quarter sessions and the general court were holding joint meetings. A little information on the work of the Havering justices in the 16th and 17th centuries can also be found in government records and private papers.[32]

In the years after 1465 the tenants of the liberty were jealous of their privileges. In 1467, for example, the homage accused a royal official of delivering a citation from the bishop of London to the vicar of Hornchurch, and in the following year they complained that the bailiff of Waltham Holy Cross was distraining upon some Havering tenants, in both cases contrary to their charter.[33] This attitude persisted, as in 1560, when the homage, while conceding that the archdeacon of Essex might hold his courts within the manor, stipulated that he should do so only during the pleasure of the manor court.[34] Havering's exemption from purveyances seems to have been maintained.[35] The fair granted by the charter of 1465 was held at Romford.[36]

In relation to the central government Havering's status was similar to that of the hundreds of Essex. From the late 16th century the liberty was a separate unit for tax assessment and for musters.[37] In 1586, when the county was split into six divisions for administrative purposes, Havering was included in the southern division, along with the hundreds of Becontree, Barstable, and Chafford.[38] During the Civil War the southern division was placed under a Parliamentary committee meeting at Romford.[39] From 1644 to 1650 there was a dispute between Havering liberty and Becontree hundred concerning their respective assessments to the county rates.[40]

[24] S.C. 2/172/35 m. 9 (date 1489); *Acts of P.C.* 1558–70, 250; *Cal. S.P. Dom.* 1547–80, 257, 380, 450; 1625–6, 521; E.R.O., Q/RTh 5; E.R.O., Q/HM 1.

[25] E.R.O., D/DM T46.

[26] E.R.O., D/DYw 3 and 9.

[27] E.R.O., D/DSa 94; Ogborne, *Essex*, 150.

[28] See below.

[29] The records were in confusion as early as the 16th century: S.C. 2/173/4 m. 3d.; S.P. 1/245(1) f. 98; *L. & P. Hen. VIII* Add 1(2), p. 580. Even the original charters of the liberty have been lost. For the later records see below.

[30] S.C. 2/172/35 m. 7d.

[31] Ibid. m. 9d.

[32] e.g. *Cal. Pat.* 1563–6, 245; E.R.O., D/DM O8; E.R.O., D/DMs O30–40.

[33] E.R.O., D/DU 102/51 (Whit. week 1467); D/DU 102/50 (25 Feb. 1468).

[34] Ibid. 102/66 (18 Apr. 1560).

[35] Hist. MSS. Com. 6, *7th Rep., Lowndes*, p. 540*b*.

[36] See p. 75.

[37] e.g. *Cal. S.P. Dom.* 1595–7, 292 (Taxation); *Acts of P.C.* 1558–70, 250; *Cal. S.P. Dom.* 1547–80, 257, 380, 450 (Musters). In 1565, however, Havering successfully insisted on its right to hold its own musters: *Acts of P.C.* 1558–70, 250.

[38] B. W. Quintrell, 'The Divisional Committee for Southern Essex during the Civil Wars' (Manchester M.A. thesis, 1962), 2, 155.

[39] Op. cit., *passim*.

[40] E.R.O., D/DMs O32.

After 1465 the manor courts continued along the same lines as before. The three-weeken court, which became known as the court of ancient demesne, dealt increasingly with conveyances by fine and recovery. The officers of the manor court were elected, as before, at the Whitsun leet. From 1481 the court rolls record the election of the justice of the peace for the liberty, the high bailiff, and the clerk of the market, along with a varying number of constables, woodwards, verderers, marshwardens, and aletasters; Hornchurch and Romford each had a high constable.[41] The appointment of a coroner of the liberty is first recorded in 1489.[42] After 1617 the surviving series of rolls records only the three-weeken court. There are no regular records of the general court or the Whitsun leet between 1617 and 1730. The main series seems to have been lost before 1824,[43] but there are a few leet papers for 1670–5.[44]

The minute books of Havering quarter sessions survive for 1730–1803 and 1835–92.[45] There are sessions files for 1771–1892, special sessions books 1770–1832, and various other papers.[46] Some of the records of the liberty have been lost since 1925, including those of the court leet (1830–96), and the court of ancient demesne (1770–1838).[47] Extracts from the missing sessions minutes for 1803–35 have, however, been preserved.[48]

Havering court of quarter sessions survived until 1892, when it was merged with the Essex sessions. The court of ancient demesne continued at least until 1891. By the late 18th century it was electing the justice of the peace.[49] It seems to have been in decline at the beginning of the 19th century, but to have revived in the 1820s and 1830s, when it was dealing with real actions and personal pleas, including debt; judgement could be levied on body, lands, and goods.[50] The Whitsun court leet was held for the last time in 1894, after which it lapsed for lack of support.[51] In the 19th century, as in earlier periods, it continued to elect the manorial officers, and also, until 1892, the high bailiff and the coroner of the liberty.[52] Until 1770 the Easter and Michaelmas quarter sessions were combined with courts leet; in that context the leets were no doubt the relics of the old courts general. After 1770 leets were held only at Whitsun.

The functions of Havering quarter sessions in the 18th and 19th centuries[53] were like those of the county sessions in miniature. Judicial work was minimal; the area was still largely rural, and there was little crime.[54] Serious offences, including grand larceny, were normally sent to the assizes. In 1828 legal experts advised the Havering justices to continue sending larceny cases involving more than 5*s.* in value to the assizes, even though the Larceny Act (1827) had abolished the distinction between grand and petty larceny.[55]

The administrative work of the justices was more considerable. It included licensing of all kinds, the regulation of highways, apprentices, and Romford market, and the supervision of parish government.[56] Presentment by grand jury was a normal procedure, mainly concerned with public nuisances. The liberty rate was levied by the high constables of Romford and Hornchurch, and the rating returns were prepared for the

[41] S.C. 2/172/33 m. 11. The high bailiff had earlier been appointed by the lord of the manor: Smith, *Havering*, 269, 287–8; *Cal. Pat.* 1436–41, 67, 161.

[42] S.C. 2/172/35 m. 7. For the work of the Havering coroner see: E.R.O., T/A 428 (Cal. Queens' Bench Indictments, K.B. 9, for 1558–1603); *Cal. Pat.* 1566–9, 412.

[43] E.R.O., Q/HR 2.

[44] E.R.O., D/DMs O36 and 37.

[45] E.R.O., Q/HM 1–3.

[46] E.R.O., Q/HF 1–414; Q/HR 1–5; Q/HZ 1–6; E.R.O., Acc. 4612. Unless otherwise stated the following account of the liberty, 1730–1892, is based on these records.

[47] Smith, *Havering*, 266–88.

[48] E.R.O., T/P 71/1 (Thos. Bird's antiquarian notes).

[49] Smith, *Havering*, 271–2; E.R.O., Acc. 4612 (court book 1730–70).

[50] For its work in the 1820s and 1830s see: E.R.O., Q/HZ 2/1 and 2; *Rep. Com. Mun. Corp.* [116], p. 132, H.C. (1835), xxiii and p. 2879 (1835), xxvi.

[51] Smith, *Havering*, 277; E.R.O., T/P 67/3, no. 1629.

[52] Smith, *Havering*, 269–70.

[53] Well described by Smith, *Havering*, 268 sqq.

[54] In 1841–9, for example, the annual number of prisoners brought before the liberty quarter sessions varied from 7 to 18.

[55] E.R.O., Q/HR 2.

[56] For parish government see pp. 21, 42, 76.

different wards by the petty constables. The rate was made in petty sessions, which after 1734 were held twice a year.[57]

In one respect Havering was very different from the county. The number of justices was never increased after 1554, and the same three men constituted petty sessions as well as quarter sessions. This was inconvenient for administrative purposes[58] and it sometimes led to difficulties over appeals. In 1845, for example, a highway surveyor appealed from petty sessions to quarter sessions. If that had happened in the county the justices originally involved would not have heard the appeal, but the Havering justices were advised by counsel to let the case go forward.

The existence of a liberty within the county produced conflicts of jurisdiction. Responsibility for the maintenance of bridges on the Havering boundaries was sometimes at issue.[59] A typical dispute over highway repairs occurred in 1667.[60] Hornchurch parish had been presented in Essex quarter sessions and fined for failing to repair the road to Upminster.[61] The sheriff of Essex returned part of the fine to the Hornchurch surveyors, but kept the rest for his fees and court costs. In 1658 and 1663 rating disputes at Romford were taken to the Essex sessions.[62] At the beginning of the Seven Years War Havering was for a short time making militia returns to the county sessions, but in 1761 refused to continue that practice.[63] The liberty did, however, contribute towards the building of the county gaol (1775) and the shire hall (1789), both at Chelmsford.[64] By that time Romford gaol was little used, and the liberty found it convenient to send long-term prisoners to Chelmsford.[65]

The most serious disputes between the liberty and the county occurred at the end of the 18th century. In 1792 Havering complained that the county had infringed its privileges by proceeding against a Romford constable accused of failing to follow up a case of assault. The county thereupon drew up a list of 14 prosecutions of Havering men at Essex quarter sessions between 1748 and 1787.[66] There was more trouble in 1801, when ten butchers were prosecuted at Essex quarter sessions for forestalling the market at Romford.[67] All the defendants refused to accept the jurisdiction of the court. The county was advised by counsel that if no prosecutor appeared a case could be quashed; otherwise it could be removed by writ of *certiorari* to the King's Bench.[68] Four of the butchers eventually had their cases removed by that writ. One stood trial and was acquitted and another died. The other four maintained their privileges as inhabitants of the liberty, and their cases were quashed.[69] In the same year, however, the Essex sessions sentenced one Romford man to imprisonment for coining, and remanded another, accused of grand larceny, to the assizes.[70] No protest from the liberty about the last two cases has been found. It seems that there was an uneasy compromise between the two benches of quarter sessions at this time.

The legal and administrative changes of the 19th century made it increasingly difficult to justify the existence of a small liberty like Havering. The sale of the manor in 1828 transferred to a private person the right to appoint the high steward, who was *ex officio* a justice of the peace, and left the Crown with no say in the appointment of the justices of the liberty.[71] The Hornchurch and Romford Inclosure Act (1811) left little scope for inclosure through the court leet.[72] Havering's court of ancient demesne also

[57] E.R.O., Q/HM 1, f. 49.

[58] Smith, *Havering*, 276.

[59] e.g. Paynes bridge, 1567 (E.R.O., Q/SR 23/25) and Dagenham Beam bridge, 1568 (ibid. 26/26).

[60] E.R.O., D/DMs O35.

[61] For similar presentments at different periods: E.R.O., Q/SR 128/44, 232/30 and 548/28.

[62] E.R.O., D/DMs O43 and O44.

[63] *E.R.* xxviii. 17 (quoting E.R.O., L/DIm).

[64] E.R.O., Q/HM 1, 10 July 1775, 2 June 1789.

[65] Smith, *Havering*, 274.

[66] E.R.O., Q/AX 1/1/3; cf. ibid. Q/SPb 14, 15 and 16. Punishments had ranged from fines to transportation.

[67] E.R.O., Q/AX 1/1/3; Q/SR 904 (14 Apr. 1801).

[68] E.R.O., Q/AX 1/1/4.

[69] E.R.O., Q/SPb 17.

[70] E.R.O., Q/SR 905; Q/SPb 17.

[71] *Rep. Com. Mun. Corp.* [116], p. 271, H.C. (1835), xxiii and pp. 2877–82, H.C. (1835), xxvi.

[72] 51 Geo. III, c.187 (Local and Personal act).

lost one of its functions by the establishment in 1846 of county courts for the recovery of small debts.[73] In 1836 the liberty became part of Romford poor-law union, which extended from Barking to Wennington. On the establishment of the Essex constabulary in 1840 the liberty was included in the Brentwood district, with police officers at Romford, Hornchurch, and Havering.[74] Romford local board of health, formed in 1851, became responsible for the urban centre of the liberty.

In spite of these anomalies the liberty survived until the end of the 19th century. It escaped the provisions of the Municipal Corporations Act (1835) and the mandatory provisions of the Municipal Corporations Act (1883). The Act of 1883 did, however, stipulate that at any future date Havering could be united with the county by Order in Council, on application by either authority.[75]

Under the Local Government Act (1888) Havering was placed for administrative purposes under the newly formed Essex county council. Henry Holmes, the first county councillor for Romford, was also the last elected magistrate of the liberty.[76] Little remained of the privileges of the liberty except its separate criminal court, and in 1892 Havering was merged, by agreement, with the county.[77] The offices of clerk of the peace and the high bailiff of the liberty were abolished; the justices were transferred to the Essex bench and the liberty coroner became a county officer.

In the 19th century the court house and gaol of the liberty were on the south side of Romford Market-Place, at the corner of South Street.[78] There had been a gaol of some kind at Romford since the 13th century. The king's gaol of Havering was mentioned in 1259.[79] It was probably at Romford, where malefactors were being imprisoned in 1279 and later.[80] In *c.* 1355 the cotland tenants of the manor of Havering were responsible for maintaining the gaol and guarding the prisoners by day; the virgators had to provide night guards.[81] The 'court hall' in Romford Street (probably the Market Place) was mentioned in 1484.[82] In the mid 16th century the gaol at Romford was called the Round House.[83] The tenants of the liberty claimed in 1650 that the town gaol ought to be maintained by the government.[84]

The court house and gaol were rebuilt by the Crown between 1737 and 1740, but in the following years the gaol was often said to be insecure.[85] In 1747 the liberty quarter sessions set apart one room in the gaol as a house of correction.[86] The gaol and court house were again repaired by the Crown in 1767–8.[87] It became increasingly clear, however, that the gaol was inadequate: in 1790 there were no cells, nor any provision for the sick.[88] An undated drawing, probably of *c.* 1800, shows the court house as a two-storey building of seven bays, with a roof pediment and a cupola. The central five bays of the lower storey were open and were supported by Doric columns.[89] By 1815 the gaol and court house were dangerously dilapidated, and quarter sessions resolved to rebuild them.[90] It was stated about 1816 that the court house was then being rebuilt, with a gaol and cage under it[91] but it is possible that this work was no more than a major restoration, for rebuilding, met mainly by a liberty rate, was carried out in

[73] Small Debts Act, 9 & 10 Vic. c.95.

[74] Smith, *Havering*, 274; B. Tabrum, *Hist. Essex Constabulary*, 30; E.R.O., Q/APr 1.

[75] E.R.O., Q/HM 3, 11 May 1882, 5 July 1883; Municipal Corp. Act, 1883, 46 & 47 Vic. c.18.

[76] *Kelly's Dir. Essex* (1890), 11; Smith, *Havering*, 273.

[77] E.R.O., Q/HM 3, 6 Aug. 1891; *Lond. Gaz.* 1892, p. 2793; Smith, *Havering*, 275–7.

[78] *Kelly's Dir. Essex* (1866), 164; E.R.O., Pictorial Coll. (Romford).

[79] *Close R.* 1256–9, 408.

[80] J.I. 3/35B m. 49; *Cal. Pat.* 1301–7, 90; 1485–94, 278.

[81] New Coll. Oxford MS. 9744, f. 168.

[82] E.R.O., D/AER 1, 54v.

[83] E.R.O., D/DU 102/63, m. 2; E.R.O., T/A 428, f. 1.

[84] E.R.O., D/DSa 63.

[85] *Cal. Treas. Bks.* 1735–8, 386, 557; 1739–41, 325; E.R.O., Q/HM 1, ff. 79, 99 sqq.; E.R.O., T/P 71/1 (extracts relating to gaol etc.).

[86] E.R.O., Q/HM 1, f. 173.

[87] E.R.O., D/DBe O2; ibid. T/P 71/1; ibid. Acc. no. 4612 (Havering Anct. Dem. Ct. Bk., 2 June 1768).

[88] E.R.O., Q/HM 1, 16 Jan. 1790; Smith, *Havering*, 274.

[89] Terry, *Romford*, ed. I. G. Sparkes, f. p. 48.

[90] E.R.O., T/P 71/1; Smith, *Havering*, 275.

[91] Ogborne, *Essex*, 128.

1826.[92] In 1831 the court house was depicted as a tall two-storey building of five bays.[93] Its position, jutting awkwardly out into the Market Place, suggests that it stood on an ancient site. The liberty quarter sessions continued to meet there until 1870, when they moved to the county court in South Street.[94] The gaol, comprising four cells on the ground floor of the court house, remained in use until the new police station, also in South Street, was opened in 1894.[95] Romford gaol seems always to have been very small. In the 19th century long-term prisoners were sent to the county gaol at Chelmsford or the house of correction at Little Ilford.[96] When the liberty came to an end in 1892 the court house was sold by Mrs. McIntosh, lady of the manor, to Romford local board.[97] It was used for offices by the board, and its successor the urban district council, until 1931; it was demolished in 1933.[98]

The gallows of the liberty stood on Romford Common, near the place still known as Gallows Corner.[99] Occasional executions seem to have been carried out there down to the 17th century.[1] In 1791 the court leet resolved to remove the gallows to a more convenient part of the common.[2] The gallows still survived, apparently disused, in 1815.[3]

Each of the three main centres of the liberty had instruments of punishment. In 1670 the court leet ordered that a cage, stocks, and whipping post be set up at Hornchurch.[4] The cage, which obstructed the street, was torn down by rioters in 1675, but was replaced, and was not finally removed until *c.* 1860.[5] In the 19th century it stood in North Street near the junction with High Street. The stocks still existed in 1732.[6] At Romford the cage, stocks, and ducking stool, all in the market-place, survived until the early 19th century.[7] At Havering Green the double stocks and the whipping post still existed in 1976. In 1966, after damage by vandals, Havering borough council replaced most of the woodwork, while preserving the existing ironwork. Most of the cost of those repairs was met by an anonymous local donor.[8]

[92] E.R.O., T/P 71/1 (extracts re gaol, 24 May 1825); H.R.L., 'Notes of Romford Town Centre *c.* 1908 from Cornell MSS.', p. 6; Smith, *Havering*, 275.

[93] Wright, *Essex*, ii, f. p. 435. For later views see: E.R.O., Pictorial Coll.; H.R.L., Pictorial Coll.

[94] H.R.L., 'Notes of Romford Town Centre', 8.

[95] Ibid. 7; Smith, *Havering*, 275.

[96] E.R.O., Q/HM 2 and 3 *passim.*

[97] H.R.L., 'Notes of Romford Town Centre', 8.

[98] Inf. from Mr. W. H. Mott of Havering L.B.C.

[99] *Map of Essex* (1777); O.S. Map, 6″, Essex, LXVI (surv. 1862–71); Terry, *Romford*, 119.

[1] Smith, *Havering*, 268.

[2] E.R.O., Q/HM 1, Whitsun 1791.

[3] Smith, *Havering*, 268.

[4] E.R.O., D/DMs O36.

[5] Ibid. O37; C. T. Perfect, *Village of Hornchurch*, 24.

[6] E.R.O., Q/HM 1, f. 33.

[7] E.R.O., T/P 71/1 (extracts from *Essex Times*, 1869); H.R.L., 'Notes of Romford Town Centre', 2, 3, 22; Smith, *Havering*, 280.

[8] Inf. from Havering L.B.C. For earlier repairs see Smith, *Havering*, 251; *E.R.* xxxvi. 160; *Romford Times*, 19 Oct. 1949. The stocks have often been illustrated: E.R.O., Pictorial Coll.; Barking Ref. Libr., Parish Envelope (Havering).

HAVERING-ATTE-BOWER

HAVERING-ATTE-BOWER, about 3 miles north of Romford, forms the northern part of the London borough of Havering.[1] It is still mainly rural, with a suburban fringe in the south-west.

The ancient manor and liberty of Havering-atte-Bower, which was conterminous with the parish of Hornchurch, was divided into eight wards. Havering-atte-Bower ward, in the north-west corner of the manor and parish, contained 2,093 a., bounded west by Dagenham parish, and north by Lambourne, Stapleford Abbots, and Navestock.[2] In the 16th century Havering-atte-Bower ward, which was also a chapelry, was subject not only to Hornchurch parish but also, for some purposes, to Romford chapelry. By the late 17th century, however, it was virtually independent for civil purposes, and in the 1780s it became a separate parish. In 1934 Havering-atte-Bower was annexed to Romford urban district. It became part of Havering L.B. in 1965.[3]

Havering is on a ridge of rising ground between Romford and the river Roding. The soil is mainly London clay, with Bagshot Beds in the centre of the parish where the village is, and patches of Boulder Clay farther east. The village is about 350 ft. above sea-level, with wide views west towards Hainault forest. Until the 17th century the royal Havering House stood beside the village green with its 1,300-acre park stretching north and west. The Bourne brook flows through the NW. of the parish, continuing as the river Rom into Romford. Another stream flows south from the village past Chase Cross to Rise Park in Romford. There are ponds and springs in many parts of the parish. Others formerly existed.[4]

Excavations in 1972 and 1975 revealed remains of Roman agricultural and industrial activity over a wide area in fields about ½ m. west of Havering village.[5] Finds consisted mainly of pottery, but included a complex of gullies and ditches associated with metal-working. A group of cremation burials was found, and much building rubble. There was clearly a Roman settlement at Havering.

Legend and local tradition link the manor of Havering with Edward the Confessor.[6] He was depicted in ancient stained glass in Hornchurch parish church, and in the old chapel at Romford, which was dedicated to him.[7] The Romford glass, probably inserted in 1407 when the chapel was being built, bore an inscription commemorating the return to Edward of the ring which he was supposed to have given to St. John the Evangelist. A chronicle of *c.* 1436 names Havering as the place where the ring was returned. That well-known legend has been traced from the 12th century, but the earlier versions do not mention Havering. According to another legend, first recorded in the 17th century, Edward's devotions at Havering were disturbed by nightingales, and he prayed, successfully, that those birds might be for ever banished from the park.

Although there is no contemporary record of Edward the Confessor's connexion with Havering, the legends strengthen the probability that he was the predecessor there of Earl (later King) Harold. The manor passed to William the Conqueror, and remained with the Crown until 1828. From the 13th to the 17th century it usually formed part of the jointure of the queen consort or dowager, from which came the suffix 'atte-Bower.'[8] There was a royal house there, with a park, by the early 12th century, and they were visited by successive kings and queens until 1638. About 1536 a smaller park was made at Pyrgo, north-east of the village, by the king's steward, Sir Brian Tuke, from whom it soon passed to Henry VIII himself. From *c.* 1536, therefore, about 80 per cent of the parish was park-land. In the early 17th century settlement in Havering was restricted mainly to the village and the adjoining area to the east, between Broxhill Road and Lower Bedfords Road.[9] During the Interregnum Havering House became derelict, and its park was permanently cut up into farms, but Pyrgo park remained, and by the later 18th century there were also smaller parks south of the village at Bower House and Bedfords. John Heaton, owner of Bedfords from 1771 to 1818, was a progressive landowner who promoted inclosure, endowed the living, and rebuilt the vicarage.

About 1850 David McIntosh, whose father had bought the manor of Havering from the Crown in 1828, built the mansion of Havering Park on the site of Havering House, and laid out a park of 250 a. adjoining it. About the same time a new mansion was built at Pyrgo, and the park there was extended. Several other big houses were also built in the parish in the mid 19th century by wealthy men attracted by the scenery and easy access to London. A writer commented in 1838 that gentlemen's seats were 'thickly strewn' there.[10]

With so much park-land it is not surprising that Havering was sparsely populated. There were only 22 taxpayers in 1523, and 38 houses in 1670.[11] In 1801 Havering had 188 inhabitants, occupying 36 houses.[12] The population climbed steadily, to 427 in 1841, but for the next 80 years remained near that level. In 1931, the last year for which separate figures are available, there were 591 inhabitants. By that time the Havering Park and Pyrgo estates had been broken up, and large areas were being bought by developers, but their plans were soon halted by the Green Belt policy, and since 1931 there has been little building in the parish except in North Road, and in the extreme SW., in the triangle bounded by St. John's Road, Clockhouse Lane, and Kingshill Avenue.

About 1618, and no doubt earlier, Havering's

[1] O.S. Map 2½", sheets TQ, 49, 59. This article was completed in 1976.

[2] For the Dagenham (Barking manor) boundary see *E.R.* lix. 3.

[3] For the remainder of this article the ward or parish of Havering-atte-Bower is referred to for convenience simply as Havering.

[4] E.R.O., D/DU 162/1 (map *c.* 1618): 'the great pool' and 'the new pond' in the park.

[5] O.S. TQ 500930: inf. kindly supplied by Passmore Edwards Museum. For earlier Roman remains in the village: *V.C.H. Essex*, iii. 144.

[6] Smith, *Havering*, 1–4; *E.A.T.* N.S. xvi. 187–9; Morant, *Essex*, i. 58–9.

[7] See pp. 47, 85.

[8] Smith, *Havering*, p. ix.

[9] E.R.O., D/DU 162/1 (map, *c.* 1618).

[10] *Robson's Dir. Essex* (1838), 65.

[11] E 179/108/150; E.R.O., Q/RTh 5.

[12] *Census Reps.* (1801 sqq.).

communications depended mainly on the lane running north–south through the village, now North Road, continuing as Orange Tree Hill and Havering Road.[13] To the north this led via Stapleford Abbots to the Abridge–Ongar road. To the south it ran via Chase Cross to Romford. At Chase Cross it intersected a track, now Chase Cross Road and Lower Bedfords Road, running west to Collier Row and east to Noak Hill. Another lane, now Broxhill Road, ran east and south from the village to Romford common, now Straight Road. All these roads survive, but others have disappeared. About 1618 Newbury Lane skirted the E. edge of Pyrgo park. Another lane ran from North Road through Pyrgo park to Broxhill Road, while a third ran from Broxhill Road south past Bedfords to Lower Bedfords Road. Newbury Lane, which took its name from a small medieval manor merged in Pyrgo park in the 16th century, had apparently disappeared by *c.* 1777.[14] The lane past Bedfords was apparently closed *c.* 1775 by John Heaton, owner of that estate.[15] A few years later Edward Howe, owner of Pyrgo, closed the lane through his park, and an attempt in 1812 to re-open it failed for lack of support.[16] Wellingtonia Avenue was laid out in the mid 19th century, as part of Havering park. Except for a few houses at its eastern end it has been little altered.

No medieval buildings remain in Havering. There were manor-houses on six sites, but all had been demolished or rebuilt by the 19th century, including Havering House, which fell down *c.* 1700. Only one of the sites is still occupied by a manor-house: Earls, now Upper Bedfords, rebuilt *c.* 1771. The medieval vicarage was rebuilt in 1786, and the church in 1878. The oldest surviving building in the parish is Blue Boar Hall, Orange Tree Hill, a timber-framed house of the earlier 17th century, with later additions including a 19th-century brick front. It was an inn in 1712, but was no longer licensed in 1762.[17] Rose Cottage, a timber-framed and weatherboarded house in North Hill, may have been built in the 17th century, partly with re-used medieval materials.[18]

The Bower House, Orange Tree Hill, is a small Palladian mansion built in 1729 by John Baynes (d. 1737), serjeant-at-law, from plans by Henry Flitcroft.[19] The staircase is decorated with paintings by Sir James Thornhill, which in 1976 were boarded over. An inscription in the entrance hall states that remains of the royal house were used in the building, and a stone corbel with the arms of Edward III is preserved in the hall. Charles Bridgeman, named in the inscription as designer, presumably laid out the grounds. About 1800 wings were added to east and west. In the mid 19th century the main room in the east wing was fitted with panelling in 17th-century style, with an original fireplace, dated 1659. In 1976 the house was a conference centre belonging to the Ford Motor Co.

The Round House, Broxhill Road, is a three-storey house built for William Sheldon in the 1790s.[20] It stands on the crest of the ridge, with views north and south. The plan, which is elliptical, is similar to that of Ickworth (Suff.). Most of the original fittings survive, and some early-19th-century wallpapers. The house was long the home of the Revd. J. H. Pemberton (d. 1926), the rose-grower.

The Hall, Broxhill Road, which adjoins the Round House, is a large brick double-fronted house of three storeys, built in 1858 or 1859 by W. Pemberton-Barnes.[21] It replaced an earlier house which can be traced from the 18th century. The 19th-century mansions of Havering Park and Pyrgo have disappeared, though some of their out-buildings, lodges, and home farms survived in 1976, notably the Bower Farm and Park Farm.[22] Havering Court, Havering Road, was previously called Rose Court, and originally Cromwell House. It was built *c.* 1858 by John Gladding, and was enlarged by (Sir) Herbert Raphael (Bt.), tenant in the 1890s.[23] It was damaged by fire in the 1930s, and in 1976 it was derelict and partly demolished.[24]

A few other houses of the 18th or early 19th centuries survive. Bellevue, Lower Bedfords Road, is a late-18th-century timber-framed and weatherboarded house. Fairlight, Bower Farm Road, and Ivy Holt, North Road, date from the early 19th century. On the north side of the Green is a late-18th-century row of four timber-framed cottages. The cottage at the east end, with an extension, was formerly a forge. The cottages adjoining this row to the west date from the mid 19th century. There is a row of early-19th-century cottages west of the Green. Elizabeth Row, North Road, demolished in 1967, was originally called Abraham's Place, and later Jew's Row. It was built *c.* 1800, probably by Benjamin Abrahams.[25]

The earliest known inn was the Blue Boar, already mentioned. In 1762 there were two inns in the parish, the Royal Oak and the Orange Tree.[26] The Orange Tree, which gave its name to Orange Tree Hill, continues in a modern building.[27] The Royal Oak, recorded from 1744, gave up its licence in 1792.[28] A later house of that name, in North Road, has been trading since *c.* 1920.[29]

Havering green, in the centre of the village, was preserved when the other commons and greens were inclosed in 1814.[30] On it stand the double stocks and whipping post, rebuilt in 1966.[31] The water tower, Broxhill Road, a prominent landmark, was built by the South Essex Waterworks Co. in 1934.[32]

Havering's long association with royalty has already been mentioned. Among other prominent families with local connexions were the Greys, the Cheekes, and the Archers, successive owners of Pyrgo between the 16th and the 18th centuries.[33] John Heaton (d. 1818),

[13] E.R.O., D/DU 162/1.
[14] Ibid.; *Map of Essex* (1777); O.S. Map 1", Essex (1805 edn.); O.S. Map 6", Essex, LXVI (surv. 1862–71).
[15] Ibid.; Smith, *Havering*, 113.
[16] Ibid. 113.
[17] Smith, *Havering*, 248; E.R.O., D/DHt T225/6.
[18] Inf. from G.L.C., Historic Bdgs. Division.
[19] S. D. Pomeroy, *About Bower House* (1970); Smith, *Havering*, 125–33; *Country Life*, xcv. 464, 508. See below, plate facing p. 16.
[20] Ogborne, *Essex*, 122; Smith, *Havering*, 138–41. See below, plate facing p. 49.
[21] Smith, op. cit. 133–9.
[22] See below, p. 14.
[23] Smith, op. cit. 141.
[24] Inf. from Mr. C. Rowland.
[25] Smith, op. cit. 250; *Havering Recorder*, 3 Mar. 1967.
[26] E.R.O., D/DHt T225/6.
[27] For deeds of the Orange Tree: E.R.O., D/DNe T1.
[28] Smith, op. cit. 248.
[29] *Kelly's Dir. Essex* (1922 and later edns.).
[30] See p. 19.
[31] See p. 8.
[32] Inf. from Essex Water Co.
[33] Smith, op. cit. 77–106. See also below.

James Ellis (d. 1845), and Collinson Hall (d. 1880), were notable agriculturists.[34] Havering's historian was the Revd. Harold Smith (d. 1936), who lived at Fernside, Broxhill Road.[35] Its best-known eccentric was Elizabeth Balls (fl. 1815), who shared a cottage near the Green with a large company of goats.[36]

MANORS AND OTHER ESTATES. Before the Conquest the manor of *HAVERING*, comprising 10 hides, was held by Earl (later King) Harold.[37] It had probably been granted to him by Edward the Confessor, whose legendary connexion with Havering is mentioned above.[38] The manor had outlying appurtenances in Leyton, Loughton, and Fyfield.[39] In 1086 it was held in demesne by William I. By then the Leyton and Fyfield outliers had been lost. The one at Loughton was still linked with Havering in 1086, but no later references to it are known.

The manor of Havering, based on the royal house and park at Havering village, included the whole of the ancient parish of Hornchurch. It was a royal liberty, confirmed by charter in 1465. The manor remained with the Crown until 1828. It came to include, in addition to the royal demesne, many tenements, some styled manors, but all subordinate to the manor of Havering. Among them were four manors originally held in serjeanty: Earls, Romford, and Gooshayes, the tenants of which were custodians of the royal woods, and Redden Court, the tenant of which had to furnish reeds for the king's chamber at Havering. The tenement called Cely's (later Havering Grange) was held in the 16th century by custody of the south gate of Havering park. The lands given by the Crown to Hornchurch priory in the 12th century appear to have become the manor of Hornchurch Hall and Suttons. Among the priory's later acquisitions were Newbury and Risebridge. All the priory's manors passed to New College, Oxford, but Newbury was acquired by the Crown in the 16th century and was thrown into the new park of Pyrgo. The manor of Marks, in Havering and Dagenham, has been treated in a previous volume.[40]

Until 1197 the manor of Havering seems always to have been administered by the sheriff. In 1198–9 Hornchurch priory was custodian, and during the following years the manor was often farmed out.[41] In *c.* 1230–46 the tenants of the manor jointly had custody.[42] In 1262 Henry III granted the manor to Queen Eleanor.[43] From then until the early 16th century it usually formed part of the jointure of the queen consort or dowager.[44] After Jane Seymour's death in 1537 it was kept in the king's hands, and was not granted to Anne of Cleves or her successors.[45] In 1619 James I granted the manor to Charles, prince of Wales (later Charles I), who later assigned it to Henrietta Maria.[46] Courts baron were held there in the queen's name as late as 1647.[47] In 1650 the manor was surveyed by commissioners appointed under a recent Act for the Sale of Crown Lands.[48] The demesne included the manor-house, the park (1,312 a.), three lodges, and two farms, Wolves (71 a.) and Joyes (27 a.). Montagu Bertie, earl of Lindsey, had before the war been tenant of the park by virtue of his office of lord warden of the forest of Essex,[49] but he had suffered sequestration as a royalist,[50] and in 1650 the tenants of the park were two regicides, Col. (later Admiral) Richard Deane (d. 1653)[51] and Lt.-Gen. Thomas Hammond (d. before 1652).[52] Wolves and Joyes farms were held on leases granted before the war.

The commissioners recommended that the park should be split into four sections, to be sold separately. It was actually sold in two sections, in 1652.[53] The eastern division, of 497 a., with the manor-house, was bought by the previously mentioned Admiral Deane, in association with John Sparrow the elder, and John Sparrow the younger, who may have been related to Deane.[54] The western and larger division was bought by John Grove, Edmund Chittenden, Thomas Chamberlayne, Samuel Dale, and Joseph Sabbarton. Under its new owners the park was cut up into farms. Some further changes of ownership, the full details of which are not known, occurred before 1660.[55]

The manorial rights were separated from the demesne, and in 1652 were bought for public use with funds raised by subscriptions from the manorial tenants. The purchase had been negotiated by a committee including Laurence Wright of Dagenhams, Carew Hervey Mildmay of Marks, and Joachim Matthews of Gobions.[56]

In 1660 the manor was restored to Henrietta Maria (d. 1669), and it was subsequently granted by Charles II to Catherine of Braganza (d. 1705), who appears to have been the last queen to hold it.[57] After the Restoration Havering was never again a royal residence, and the fragmentation of the park was maintained, both divisions being leased. The eastern division, often described as a quarter of the park and later known as Bower (or Manor) farm, was restored to the earl of Lindsey, whose family continued as lessees until 1769.[58] In 1757 it comprised 417 a., adjoining Havering Green to the west,

[34] Smith, op. cit. 68–9, 122. See also below.
[35] *E.R.* xlv. 183–4 (obit.).
[36] Ogborne, *Essex*, 122; *E.R.* xlv. 16–18, 112, 195.
[37] *V.C.H. Essex*, i. 429–30, cf. 497, 545–6.
[38] Ibid. 336.
[39] For Leyton see *V.C.H. Essex*, vi. 185.
[40] *V.C.H. Essex*, v. 275.
[41] *Pipe R.* 1198 (P.R.S. N.S. ix), 126; ibid. 1199 (P.R.S. N.S. x), 103. See also: later pipe rolls; *Rot. Lit. Claus.* (Rec. Com.), i. 347, 612; *Pat. R.* 1217–24, 117, 455.
[42] *Pipe R.* 1230 (P.R.S. N.S. iv), 162; ibid. 1242 (ed. H. L. Cannon), 224; *Cal. Lib. R.* 1245–51, 57.
[43] *Cal. Pat.* 1266–72 (appendix), 736.
[44] The grants of jointure were entered on the patent rolls, e.g. *Cal. Pat.* 1317–21, 115; ibid. 1401–5, 259; 1485–94, 77. See also E.R.O., D/DU 102 (Havering court rolls). When there was no queen consort or dowager the manor might be farmed out e.g.: *Cal. Pat.* 1396–9, 60; S.C. 2/172/29 and 30. See also below, p. 66.
[45] *L. & P. Hen. VIII*, i (1), 94 (35); vii, 552; xii (2), 975.
[46] *Cal. Treas. Bks.* 1689–92, 1954–5; ibid. 1710, 329; E.R.O., D/DU 102/111–14.
[47] E.R.O., D/DU 102/114–17.
[48] E.R.O., D/DSa 63. For the Act and its results see S. J. Madge, *Domesday of Crown Lands*, 78 sqq.
[49] Cf. W. R. Fisher, *Forest of Essex*, 119.
[50] *Cal. Cttee. for Compounding*, 1502–3; *Cal. Cttee. for Money*, iii, p. 1294.
[51] *D.N.B.*
[52] Ibid. s.v. Hammond, Rob.
[53] Smith, *Havering*, 61; Ogborne, *Essex*, 116.
[54] Deane's sister was wife of Drue Sparrow: *D.N.B.*, Deane, Ric.
[55] Smith, *Havering*, 61–2.
[56] E.R.O., T/A 259/36 (Cal. of Hants R.O. 15 M50/298).
[57] *Cal. Treas. Bks.* 1689–92, 1954–5; ibid. 1693–6, 25.
[58] Ibid.; *Manuscripts of House of Lords* (N.S.), viii. 302; Smith, *Havering*, 62; E.R.O., D/DNe E2; Morant, *Essex*, i. 60; *Hist. Essex by Gent.* iv. 314.

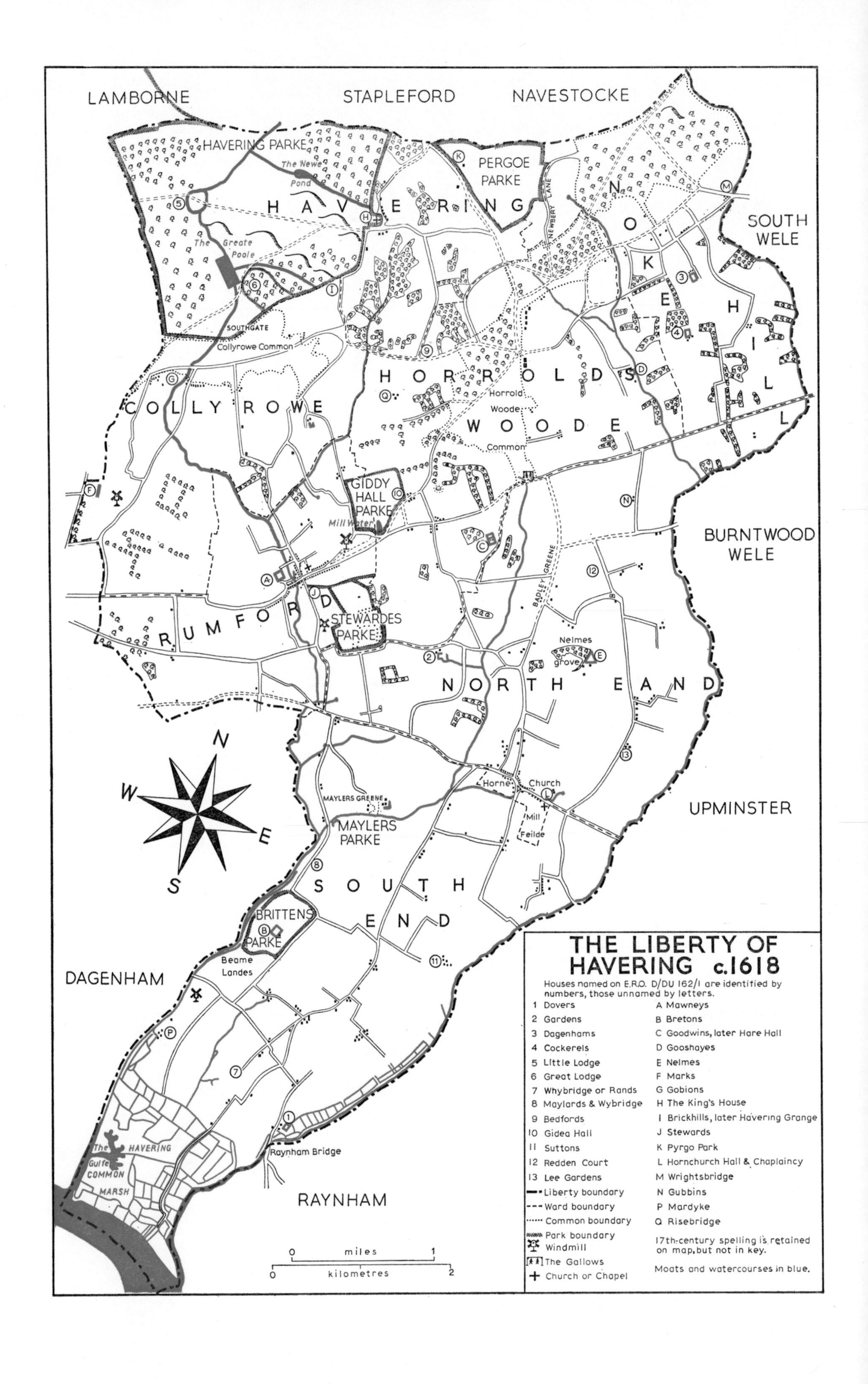
LAMBORNE
STAPLEFORD
NAVESTOCKE
HAVERING PARKE
The Newe Pond
PERGOE PARKE
HAVERING
NEWBERY LANE
NOKE HILL
SOUTH WELE
The Greate Poole
SOUTHGATE
Collyrowe Common
HORROLDS
Horrold Woode
Common
WOODE
COLLY ROWE
GIDDY HALL PARKE
Mill Water
BURNTWOOD WELE
RUMFORD
STEWARDES PARKE
BADLEY GREENE
Nelmes grove
NORTH EAND
N
W
E
S
Horne
Church
Mill Feilde
MAYLERS GREENE
MAYLERS PARKE
UPMINSTER
SOUTH END
BRITTENS PARKE
Beame Landes
DAGENHAM
The Gulfe
HAVERING COMMON MARSH
Raynham Bridge
RAYNHAM
0 miles 1
0 kilometres 2
THE LIBERTY OF HAVERING c.1618
Houses named on E.R.O. D/DU 162/1 are identified by numbers, those unnamed by letters.
1 Dovers
2 Gardens
3 Dagenhams
4 Cockerels
5 Little Lodge
6 Great Lodge
7 Whybridge or Rands
8 Maylards & Wybridge
9 Bedfords
10 Gidea Hall
11 Suttons
12 Redden Court
13 Lee Gardens
A Mawneys
B Bretons
C Goodwins, later Hare Hall
D Gooshayes
E Nelmes
F Marks
G Gobions
H The King's House
I Brickhills, later Havering Grange
J Stewards
K Pyrgo Park
L Hornchurch Hall & Chaplaincy
M Wrightsbridge
N Gubbins
P Mardyke
Q Risebridge
Liberty boundary
Ward boundary
Common boundary
Park boundary
Windmill
The Gallows
Church or Chapel
17th-century spelling is retained on map, but not in key.
Moats and watercourses in blue.

north-west, and south-west; it was sublet to two tenants.[59] In 1769 the Berties sold the lease to (Sir) Richard Neave (Bt.), who about that time was tenant of the neighbouring Bower House.[60] Neave sold the lease in 1776 to John C. Sole, from whom it was bought in 1779 by George Masterman.[61] Masterman (d. 1798) was succeeded by his son William, who bought a new lease from the Crown.[62] William Masterman (d. 1825) was succeeded as lessee by his sister Mrs. Elizabeth Taylor.[63]

The western division, described as three-quarters of Havering Park, and later as Havering (or Lower) Park farm, was in 1662 leased for 21 years to John Gauden (d. 1662), bishop of Exeter, whose widow Elizabeth secured an extension of the lease for a further 13 years.[64] By 1670 Mrs. Gauden's lease had come into the possession of Sir William Ayloffe, who was subletting to three tenant-farmers.[65] In 1696, when that lease expired, the western division passed to Isabella Fitzroy, duchess of Grafton, under a reversionary lease granted to her father, Henry Bennet, earl of Arlington (d. 1685).[66] The duchess also secured a further reversionary lease of 99 years, running from the death of Catherine of Braganza (1705).[67] The duchess and her second husband, Sir Thomas Hanmer, Bt., sold the lease to Richard Holdrich, a director of the South Sea Company.[68] On Holdrich's forfeiture in 1721 the lease was sold to Richard Ladbroke, in whose family it descended until 1819.[69] Richard Ladbroke (d. 1765), nephew of the previous Richard, seems to have been the only Crown lessee who lived at Havering.[70] The other lessees sublet the estate.[71] In 1819 a new Crown lease was bought by James Ellis, a hop-grower.[72]

The manorial rights seem to have been leased separately from the demesne after the Restoration,[73] though no lessees' names have been noted before Sir John Eyles, Bt. (d. 1745), who was already high steward of Havering liberty when he was granted a lease of the manor in 1741.[74] Eyles's son and heir Sir Francis Eyles-Stiles, Bt. sold the lease in 1746 to Charles Benyon (d. before 1751) from whom it passed to his brother Richard Benyon of Gidea Hall.[75] The lease of the manor, periodically renewed, descended in the Benyon family until 1819, when Richard Benyon (later Benyon de Beauvoir) sold it to Sir Thomas Neave, Bt., of Dagenhams.[76]

In 1828 the Crown sold the manor, including the demesne, to Hugh McIntosh, a contractor who had built the East India and London Docks.[77] The manorial rights were still on lease to Sir Thomas Neave, Bt., but were resumable at will.[78] The demesne comprised 1,530 a., small parts of which lay in neighbouring parishes.[79] The western division, then containing 1,101 a., comprised Havering Park farm, Havering Little Park farm, and Hainault Lodge farm, all leased and occupied by James Ellis. The eastern division (Bower farm, 431 a.) was still on lease to Mrs. Taylor. Collinson Hall, her son-in-law, later took over Bower farm, and after James Ellis's death in 1845 Hall appears to have occupied the whole of the Havering manor estate until both leases expired in 1849.[80]

Hugh McIntosh (d. 1840) was succeeded by his son David (d. 1881), who about 1850 settled at Havering and built a mansion on the site of the old Bower Farm.[81] Charlotte McIntosh, David's widow, lived there until her death in 1923.[82] In 1924 the estate, then 1,551 a., was bought from the McIntosh trustees by Allen Ansell of Romford, who in the same year sold Fairlight farm (about 100 a. in the north-eastern corner) to a farmer.[83] Ansell (d. 1933) was succeeded by his son John W. Ansell, a contractor, who in 1937 sold most of the remainder of the estate to T. F. Nash Properties Ltd.[84] Since 1937 there has been building development in the south and south-west of the estate, but some 400 a. in the north and north-east, including Bower and Fairlight farms, were in 1938 bought by Essex county council to facilitate their preservation as part of the Metropolitan Green Belt.[85]

There was a royal house at Havering, with a park, by the early 12th century.[86] Building was in progress there in the early and mid 13th century, and by that time the house was already extensive, with a 'great chamber', apartments for both the king and the queen, two chapels, and various out-buildings.[87] The great chapel, later the parish church, was rebuilt between 1374 and 1377, but after that most of the recorded expenditure was on repairs, and the replacement of service and park buildings. Substantial repairs, including new stone doors and windows in the presence and privy chambers and elsewhere, were carried out in 1573–4.[88] In 1576–7 a new block of lodgings was built between the privy kitchen and the park gate.[89] It was a long timber building of two storeys, with 26 rooms. At that time, however, the main building was still basically medieval, with an irregular plan, and with most of the important rooms on the first floor.[90] The great chamber lay

[59] E.R.O., D/DQa 3.
[60] *Hist. Essex by Gent.* iv. 313.
[61] E.R.O., D/DNe E3; D/DU 70/22.
[62] Smith, *Havering*, 68; E.R.O., D/DU 70/27.
[63] Smith, *Havering*, 68–9; E.R.O., Sage Coll., *Sale Cats.* vi. 2.
[64] *Cal. Treas. Bks.* 1689–92, p. 1954–5. For Gauden see *D.N.B.*
[65] E.R.O., D/DU 572/3; D/DAc 135.
[66] *Cal. Treas. Bks.* 1689–92, 1925, 1954–5; ibid. 1693–6, 25.
[67] Ibid.
[68] Morant, *Essex*, i. 60; *Complete Peerage*, vi. 44.
[69] Ibid.; Smith, *Havering*, 62, 69.
[70] Smith, op. cit. 62, 69.
[71] Ibid. 69.
[72] Ibid.; E.R.O., Sage Coll., *Sale Cats.* vi. 2.
[73] E.R.O., D/DU 102/118–27 (Court rolls, which usually refer to the 'farmers of the manor.').
[74] E.R.O., D/DBe T2; *Burke's Ext. & Dorm. Baronetcies* (1844), 190.
[75] E.R.O., D/DBe T2.
[76] E.R.O., D/DBe E3 and D/DNe E11. Richard Benyon (de Beauvoir) had sold Gidea Hall in 1802.
[77] Smith, *Havering*, 65, 70; inf. from Tower Hamlets Public Libraries.
[78] E.R.O., Sage Coll., *Sale Cats.* vi. 2.
[79] Ibid.
[80] Smith, *Havering*, 68–70; I.R. 29/12/62.
[81] E.R.O., C/T 397.
[82] Ibid.
[83] E.R.O., C/T 397 cf. 395.
[84] Ibid.
[85] E.R.O., C/T 395–7.
[86] Unless otherwise stated the account of this house is based on: Smith, *Havering*, 1–64; H. M. Colvin, *King's Works*, ii. 956–9; iii. 79, 99. Mr. Colvin has also kindly provided additional information in an unpublished draft prepared for a later volume of *King's Works*. For Havering House see also: A. W. Clapham and W. H. Godfrey, *Some Famous Buildings and their story*, 145–50.
[87] For the chapels see p. 22.
[88] E 351/3208, 3209.
[89] E 351/3212.
[90] B.L., Lansdowne Roll 18; Hatfield House, Cecil Papers, Map 2/21.

north-south, with the great chapel at its southern end, and the royal apartments to the north and north-west.

Very little seems to have been spent on Havering House in the following years. It was in a poor condition in 1596.[91] James I often used it as a hunting-lodge.[92] Charles I was rarely there, and visited Havering for the last time in 1638.[93] In 1650 the Parliamentary surveyors reported that the house was 'a confused heap of old, ruinous, decayed buildings.'[94] At the Restoration Havering House, as it was then called, was leased with the eastern division of the park to Montagu Bertie, earl of Lindsey (d. 1666). He was occupying the house in 1662, when it had 50 hearths.[95] Between 1662 and 1678 he and his successor, Robert Bertie, earl of Lindsey, carried out considerable repairs.[96] In 1670 Havering House, then unoccupied, had 58 hearths, which suggests that it had been enlarged or partly rebuilt.[97] In 1686, after it had been damaged by storms, the earl petitioned the Treasury for funds to repair it.[98] No further action seems to have been taken, however, and in 1719 the house, said to have been built of freestone and leaded, was in ruins and uninhabitable.[99] The remains may have been robbed *c.* 1705–9 to repair Havering chapel, and in 1729 to build the Bower House.[1] By *c.* 1740 some of the walls were still standing, but not enough to show the form and extent of the house.[2] Pieces of walling still remained in 1796, but none was visible *c.* 1816.[3]

By the later 18th century Bower (or Manor) Farm had been built on part of the site of the royal house.[4] Soon after 1849, when the leases fell in, David McIntosh laid out the eastern part of the estate once again as a park. He demolished Bower Farm, and on the site built for himself Havering Park, an Italianate mansion of brick with a tower.[5] The name Bower Farm was transferred to a new house about ½ m. NW., built about the same time. Havering Park, which stood due west of the church, was demolished *c.* 1938,[6] but the stable block, north of the church, still survived in 1976. Bower Farm, with its extensive out-buildings and farm cottages, also survived. The southern and eastern sides of David McIntosh's park had been built on, and the northern side restored to farm use, but a few copses and plantations survived.

On the western division of the Havering estate there were two houses in the later 18th century: Havering (later Lower) Park Farm, and Havering Park (later Clock House).[7] In 1869 David McIntosh built Park Farm about 600 yd. north of Lower Park Farm.[8] Park Farm, which still survived in 1976, is a striking example of a model farm from the heyday of 19th-century farming. The buildings, grouped round a courtyard, included several large brick barns, workers' cottages, and an original engine house. Nothing then survived at Clock House, and only out-buildings at Lower Park Farm.

The manor of *BEDFORDS* and *EARLS* (or *NEARLES*) comprised two adjoining tenements, lying south-east of Havering village, which were amalgamated in the 15th century. Bedfords was in 1412 part of the Gidea Hall estate, then held by Robert Chichele.[9] It probably took its name from the family of John Bedford, who was holding land in the area in 1362.[10] Earls originated as a tenement which in the early 13th century was held by the serjeanty of guarding the king's outwood of Havering. John Derewin, who held it in 1212, suffered forfeiture for homicide, after which king John gave the land to William d'Aubigny, earl of Arundel (d. 1221).[11] In 1227 it was held, still in serjeanty, by Hubert de Burgh, earl of Kent, the justiciar, as guardian of Hugh d'Aubigny, earl of Arundel (d. 1243), then a minor.[12] In 1240 the king remitted to the earl of Arundel his offence in not paying the sparrow-hawk which he owed each year for his land at Havering.[13] There is no reference then, or later, to tenure in serjeanty, which seems to have lapsed soon after 1227. The same earl granted the tenement in fee to Richard, son of Reynold Elms (de Ulmis), who in or before 1245 gave it to the abbey of Stratford Langthorne.[14] In 1253 it comprised 100 a. land, 15 a. wood, and 5 a. meadow.[15] In the 13th and 14th centuries it was apparently known as Beaurepeir.[16] The name Earls, though not recorded until the 15th century, clearly refers to the brief association with the Arundels. In 1445 Stratford Abbey gave Earls to Thomas Bernewell and William Hulyn in exchange for land in West Ham.[17] By 1452 the 'manor or messuage' of Earls had been acquired by Thomas Cooke, who in that year also bought Bedfords, as part of the Gidea Hall estate.[18] Bedfords and Earls descended with that estate until 1659, when Richard Emes sold them to Joachim Matthews, lord of Gobions in Romford.[19]

Sir Philip Matthews, Bt., son of Joachim, sold Bedfords and Earls in 1668 to Simon Rogers and his wife Sarah, from whom they were bought in 1678 by Robert Woolley (d. 1695).[20] At that period Bedfords comprised about 110 a. and Earls 120 a.[21] John Woolley, son of Robert, sold the combined manor in 1707 to Robert Bristow.[22] In 1710, after

[91] B.L. Lansdowne MS. 819, f. 28 (survey by Samuel Foxe): printed in Ogborne, *Essex*, 114.
[92] Smith, *Havering*, 48–51.
[93] Ibid. 51–3.
[94] E 317/Essex 13, f. 4.
[95] E.R.O., Q/Rth 1.
[96] *Cal. Treas. Bks.* 1660–7, 409; ibid. 1667–8, 338, 481, 490; 1669–72, 59, 216, 325; 1676–9, 902.
[97] E.R.O., Q/Rth 5.
[98] *Cal. Treas. Bks.* 1685–9, 657.
[99] E.R.O., T/P 195/2 (Holman MSS.), Hornchurch, f. 46c.
[1] See pp. 24, 10.
[2] Salmon, *Essex*, 243.
[3] Lysons, *Lond.* iv. 184n.; Ogborne, *Essex*, 112.
[4] Smith, *Havering*, 64, 68.
[5] Ibid. 69–70; O.S. Map 6", Essex, LXVI (surv. 1862–71).
[6] *Kelly's Dir. Essex* (1929, cf. 1933, 1937); inf. from Mr. J. Bentall.
[7] *Map of Essex* (1777); O.S. Map 6", Essex, LXVI (surv. 1862–71); Smith, *Havering*, 68.
[8] Date on building.
[9] *Feud. Aids*, vi. 442.
[10] E.R.O., D/DJg T12.
[11] *Bk. of Fees*, i. 276, 345; ii. 1348; *Complete Peerage*, i. 236–8.
[12] *Bk. of Fees*, ii. 1348.
[13] *Close R.* 1237–42, 250.
[14] *Horn. Docs.* pp. 18, 41.
[15] *Cal. Chart.* 1226–57, 415.
[16] *Rot. Hund.* (Rec. Com.), i. 149. The form 'Deaurepayr' (in *c.* 1355) (New Coll. MS. 9744, f. 161) may be a miscopying.
[17] *Cal. Pat.* 1441–6, 395.
[18] Ibid. 1446–52, 517. For Gidea Hall see below, p. 67.
[19] Lysons, *London*, iv. 189; E.R.O., D/DHe T1.
[20] E.R.O., D/DHe T1; E.R.O., D/DC 27/88–91; Ogborne, *Essex*, 119.
[21] E.R.O., D/DU 572/2.
[22] E.R.O., D/DC 27/92–3. John Woolley was then living in Constantinople.

Bristow's death, his executors sold Bedfords and Earls to Wight Woolley, whose relationship to the previous Woolleys is not clear.[23] Wight Woolley conveyed the manor in 1737 to his son Houlton Woolley (d. 1752), who devised it to his cousin Nathaniel Houlton.[24] The lords of the manor from Simon Rogers to Nathaniel Houlton were all London merchants or tradesmen, and none of them is known to have lived at Havering.

In 1771 Nathaniel Houlton sold the manor to John Heaton, who enlarged the estate, lived there until his death in 1818, and was prominent in local affairs.[25] He was succeeded by his grandson Charles Heaton Ellis, who in 1846 held 537 a. in Havering.[26] C. H. Ellis let the estate to a succession of tenants until 1854, when he sold it to James W. Hawkesley.[27] Hawkesley sold Bedfords and Earls in 1865 to Charles Barber, whose mortgagee sold the estate in 1870 to Henry R. Stone (d. 1876).[28] Henry J. Stone, son and heir of H. R. Stone, sold part of the estate, including Earls (or Upper Bedfords), about 1920.[29] H. J. Stone died in 1931, and in 1933 his widow Emma, who had remarried, sold Bedfords to Romford urban district council for use as a public park.[30]

Bedfords house was rebuilt by John Heaton, probably soon after 1771, as a two-storey brick mansion, rendered with cement.[31] It was altered and enlarged by Charles Barber between 1865 and 1867.[32] James Theobald (d. 1894), M.P. for Romford, lived there for some years before his death.[33] Romford U.D.C., after buying the estate in 1933, opened the house to the public.[34] During the Second World War Bedfords was occupied by the National Fire Service.[35] After the war it lay empty, was damaged by vandals, and in 1959 was demolished.[36]

Earls (Upper Bedfords) was also rebuilt by John Heaton after 1771, in a crenellated style, including a tower which has often caused it to be mistaken for a church.[37] It still survived in 1976.

The tenement known as *CELY'S PLACE* or *PARKER'S* later as *BRICKHILLS*, and finally as *HAVERING GRANGE*, lay on the south side of Havering Park.[38] In the early 16th century it was held *ex officio* by George Cely, keeper of the south gate. In or about 1537 the keepership and the tenement were transferred from Cely to Thomas Cromwell.[39] (Sir) John Gate or Gates was keeper from 1545 until his execution in 1553.[40] He was succeeded by Sir Edward Waldegrave, who was deprived of his offices on Elizabeth I's accession.[41] In 1559 the keepership was granted for life to Sir Anthony Cooke (d. 1576) of Gidea Hall.[42] Sir Robert Cock, who was holding Cely's Place or Brickhills from *c.* 1618 until his death in 1635, was the husband of Penelope, daughter of Sir Anthony Cooke of Gidea Hall (d. 1604).[43] Penelope, who later married Sir Francis Sydenham, died in 1650. Brickhills was later occupied by her grand-nephew John Davys (d. 1659).[44]

About 1661 Brickhills was acquired by Robert Rich, earl of Holland and later also of Warwick, who had other properties in Havering.[45] In 1695 Edward Rich, earl of Holland and Warwick, sold Brickhills to Christopher and Elizabeth Batt.[46] Christopher Batt (d. 1738) was succeeded by his son Christopher, who died childless in 1756. Brickhills then passed to John Mayne (d. 1785), nephew of Christopher Batt the younger. Mayne, also childless, was succeeded by William Batt (d. 1792), grandson of Christopher Batt the elder. John Thomas Batt, nephew and heir of William, sold Brickhills in 1807 to Margaret, Lady Smith-Burges of the Bower House, who was already the lessee. The property then comprised 92 a., of which 65 a., including the farm-house, lay west of the road to Romford (Orange Tree Hill) and the remainder east of the road.[47] Lady Smith-Burges sold Brickhills in 1808 to Daniel Ximenes, but apparently retained the fields west of the road, which even before 1807 had been thrown into the grounds of the Bower House.[48]

William Hewson owned Havering Grange in 1814.[49] It was occupied in the 1830s by Major Anderson.[50] In 1846 the owner was Mr. Dalmaine, who occupied the house and 16 a., and let the remaining 104 a.[51] Stephen Hope, who was leasing the property from Mrs. Delamare in 1848, later bought it.[52] He died in 1871.[53] His son remained at Havering Grange until *c.* 1920, when it was bought by Lawrence Leefe.[54] Leefe was listed as occupier until *c.* 1929.[55]

Havering Grange house is said to have been rebuilt in 1842.[56] It was burnt down *c.* 1935 after being unoccupied for some time.[57] In 1963 Essex

23 E.R.O., D/DC 27/95–6.
24 Ibid. 27/97–100; D/DHe T9.
25 Lysons, *London*, iv. 189; *Hist. Essex by Gent.* iv. 320; Smith, *Havering*, 121–3; E.R.O., D/DHe E16, T1, 9.
26 I.R. 29/12/162.
27 E.R.O., D/DHe E16; Smith, *Havering*, 123–4.
28 Smith, *Havering*, 124; E.R.O., Sage Coll., *Sale Cats.* vol. ix. 3–5; *Kelly's Dir. Essex* (1855–70); *White's Dir. Essex* (1863), 591; *Burke's L. G.* (1914), p. 1796.
29 Smith, *Havering*, 124; E.R.O., *Sale Cats.* A55, 55A.
30 Burke, *Land. Gent.* (1937), 2165; *Hist. Havering* (1965), 11.
31 Ogborne, *Essex*, 121; Smith, *Havering*, 114, 122; H.R.L., Pictorial Coll.; E.R.O., Pictorial Coll.
32 E.R.O., Sage Coll., *Sale Cats.* vol. ix. 3. For later views see E.R.O., *Sale Cats.* A55, A55A.
33 *E.R.* iii. 84; *Kelly's Dir. Essex* (1882–94).
34 *Romford Record*, vii. 34.
35 *Romford B.C. Mins.*, Parks cttee. 24 April. 1946.
36 Havering L.B. *Recreation and Amenities Division* (1970).
37 Smith, *Havering*, 122; E.R.O., *Sale Cat.* A55.
38 A tenement called Selyceland, recorded *c.* 1355, appears to have lain farther west, at the south-west corner of the park: New Coll. MS. 9744, f. 161, cf. *Cal. Inq. Misc.* iii, pp. 24–5.
39 *L. & P. Hen. VIII*, xii (2), p. 466; xiv (1), p. 63; xvi, p. 603. There are several earlier references to the keepership, but none of them mentions the tenement: e.g. *Cal. Pat.* 1436–41, 75, 193, 250; ibid. 1461–7, 110. For George Cely see also *V.C.H. Essex*, iv. 224.
40 *L. & P. Hen. VIII*, xx (2), p. 322; *D.N.B.*; cf. *V.C.H. Essex*, iv. 199.
41 *Cal. Pat.* 1553–4, 392–3; *D.N.B.*
42 Ibid. 1558–60, 33.
43 C 142/527/74; Smith, *Havering*, 120, 140, 260; E.R.O., D/DU 162/1 (Map of Havering Liberty, *c.* 1618).
44 Smith, *Havering*, 140.
45 E.R.O., D/DB T916; *Complete Peerage*, vi. 540; xii (2), 416–17; E.R.O., D/DAc 134; D/DU 265/5.
46 E.R.O., D/DB T916 (abstract of title 1692–1811) and D/DU 544/1 (deeds 1692–1795): on which the rest of this paragraph is based.
47 E.R.O., D/DHe E14.
48 Ibid.; E.R.O., D/DB T916; Smith, *Havering*, 129, 140.
49 E.R.O., T/M 86.
50 Smith, *Havering*, 141; *Gent. Mag.* 1839 (2), 323.
51 I.R. 29/12/162.
52 *White's Dir. Essex* (1848), 373; Smith, *Havering*, 141.
53 *Fragmenta Genealogica*, ii (1894), 57.
54 Smith, *Havering*, 141; *Kelly's Dir. Essex* (1885–1922).
55 *Kelly's Dir. Essex* (1926, 1929).
56 *White's Dir. Essex* (1848), 373.
57 Ex. inf. Mr. J. Bentall.

county council built Havering Grange special school on the site.[58]

The manor of *PYRGO* lay on the northern edge of Havering, extending into Stapleford Abbots and Navestock. The name, originally Portegore, is recorded from the 14th century.[59] Until the 16th century it appears to have been applied to a district rather than a particular estate. By 1518 the manor was occupied by (Sir) Brian Tuke, a royal official, who in that year leased from New College, Oxford, the adjoining manor of Newbury.[60] In 1530 Tuke acquired from Henry Rede and Alice his wife, daughter and heir of Thomas Roley, an estate at Pyrgo comprising 2 virgates, 5 a. 1 rood, and 8 day-works of land.[61] The earlier history of Thomas Roley's estate has not been traced. It may have been identical with a tenement called Garnetts, which seems to have been named from the family of William Garnet (fl. 1322).[62]

Sir Brian Tuke was appointed steward of the manor of Havering in 1536, and in 1537 was licensed to empark 300 a. of his lands in Havering, Stapleford Abbots, and Navestock.[63] He continued to live at Pyrgo until about 1541, when the king acquired the manor, possibly in exchange for that of Stapleford Abbots.[64] Henry VIII completed the emparking of Pyrgo, in which Newbury was then permanently merged.[65] Pyrgo was managed by a succession of stewards, including Sir John Gate (1545–53) and Sir Edward Waldegrave (1553–8), both of whom were also keepers of Cely's Place and the south gate of Havering Park.[66]

In 1559 Elizabeth I granted Pyrgo in tail male to Lord John Grey (d. 1564), brother of Henry Grey, duke of Suffolk (d. 1554), and uncle of Lady Jane Grey.[67] Lord John was succeeded by his son Henry, later Lord Grey of Groby (d. 1614).[68] Henry's heir was his grandson Henry Grey, Lord Grey, later earl of Stamford, who in 1621 sold Pyrgo to Sir Thomas Cheeke (d. 1659).[69] The manor passed successively to Sir Thomas's sons Robert (d. *c.* 1670), and Thomas Cheeke (d. 1688), lieutenant of the Tower of London.[70] The last Thomas was succeeded by his son Edward (d. 1707). Edward's infant son Edward died in 1713, and his widow Ann in 1723. Pyrgo then passed to Ann (d. 1728), daughter of Thomas Cheeke (d. 1688), and wife of Sir Thomas Tipping, Bt. Lady Tipping left two daughters, of whom the younger succeeded to Pyrgo: she was Katherine (d. 1754), wife of Thomas Archer (d. 1768), who in 1747 was created Lord Archer of Umberslade.[71] Thomas Archer's son Andrew, Lord Archer, died in 1778, leaving four daughters as coheirs.[72] In 1790 the trustees of the Archer estates sold Pyrgo to Edward R. Howe.[73]

In 1828 E. R. Howe sold Pyrgo, then comprising 460 a., to Michael Field (d. 1836), a member of the Stock Exchange, who was succeeded by his brother Robert (d. 1855).[74] Robert Field's trustees sold Pyrgo in 1857 to Joseph Bray, a railway contractor.[75] Bray sold it in 1873 to Maj.-Gen. Albert Fytche, formerly chief commissioner of British Burma.[76] Fytche later bought Wolves and Joyes farm and other neighbouring properties, thus enlarging the estate to over 600 a. His purchases were soon followed by the agricultural depression, and in 1887 the estate was sold by order of the mortgagees to William E. Gibb.[77] In 1901 Gibb sold it to Alice Mary (d. 1921), the rich widow of Thomas O'Hagan, Lord O'Hagan.[78] Lady O'Hagan further enlarged the estate: when put up for sale in 1919 it comprised 824 a.[79] None of it seems to have been sold then, but after Lady O'Hagan's death it was sold piecemeal by her son Maurice Towneley-O'Hagan, Lord O'Hagan.[80] Of the larger sections Asheton farm (284 a.) and Standish farm (95 a.) were both sold in 1922. Pyrgo Park house, with 158 a., was bought in 1925 by Herbert J. Mitchell, who sold it in 1935 to a group of estate developers.[81] In 1937, however, the property was bought from the developers by Essex county council, to facilitate its preservation as part of the Metropolitan Green Belt.[82] The county council also bought Standish farm in 1938, and Asheton farm in 1939.[83]

The site of the early house at Pyrgo was north-west of the surviving farm buildings. The terracing of the gardens could still be seen *c.* 1921, and was partly excavated in 1972.[84] The house was repaired for Henry VIII in 1543.[85] In 1594 it was described as 'a fair house'.[86] It is depicted on a map of *c.* 1618 as a large gabled building.[87] In 1670 it had 30 hearths.[88] It had a small chapel in which were the tomb of Thomas Grey (d. 1564) marquess of Dorset, and floor slabs to Anne (d. 1513) wife of George Lovekyn, clerk of the stables to Henry VIII, several members of the Cheeke family and their descendants, and Walter de Bounstede, an unidentifiable canon.[89] Under the will of Lord Archer (d. 1768) all the Cheeke remains were removed to the parochial chapel of Havering.[90] Between *c.* 1771 and 1778 the chapel and the wings of Pyrgo house were demolished by Lord Archer (d. 1778).[91] The

[58] E.C.C. List of Schools, 1963.
[59] E.R.O., D/DU 102/4 (Ct. Apr. 1389); 102/6, m. 15; 102/30, m. 7; 102/42, m. 6; 102/47, m. 8.
[60] New Coll. MS. 2957.
[61] S.C. 2/173/4, m. 6.
[62] *Cal. Close*, 1318–23, 615; E.R.O., D/DJg T12; S.C. 2/172/35.
[63] *L. & P. Hen. VIII*, x, p. 419; xii (1), p. 514.
[64] Ibid. xiii (2), p. 195; xiv (1), p. 488; *V.C.H. Essex*, iv. 224; Smith, *Havering*, 75–6.
[65] *L. & P. Hen. VIII*, xviii, p. 131.
[66] Ibid. xx (1), pp. 674–5; xx (2), p. 322; *Cal. Pat.* 1553–4, 392–3. For Cely's Place see above.
[67] *Cal. Pat.* 1558–60, 82; *Complete Peerage*, iv. 420–1.
[68] C 142/141/41; *Complete Peerage*, vi. 135; Smith, *Havering*, 77–87 (the Greys at Pyrgo); Morant, *Essex*, i. 60.
[69] C.P. 25(2)/296/19 Jas. 1 East; Smith, *Havering*, 87 sqq.; Morant, *Essex*, i. 60–1.
[70] For Thomas Cheeke see *E.R.* xxxii. 66–71. For Robert see E.R.O., Q/RTh 5.
[71] Morant, *Essex*, i. 61; E.R.O., D/DHe T9 and E16.
[72] *Complete Peerage*, i. 188.
[73] E.R.O., D/DXp 1; D/DHe T1/36.
[74] E.R.O., D/DXp 8, 9, 13; Smith, *Havering*, 113.
[75] Smith, *Havering*, 113; E.R.O., D/DXp 29.
[76] E.R.O., D/DXp 40 and 43; *E.R.* i. 149.
[77] E.R.O., Sage Coll., *Sale Cats.* vol. vi. 8; vi. 10 (attached letters to E. J. Sage); E.R.O., D/DXp 60.
[78] E.R.O., C/T 380; *Complete Peerage*, 44–6.
[79] E.R.O., *Sale Cat.* B12.
[80] E.R.O., C/T 380.
[81] Ibid.; *Kelly's Dir. Essex* (1926–33).
[82] E.R.O., C/T 380.
[83] Ibid.
[84] R.C.H.M. *Essex*, ii. 126; E.R.O., Libr. Folder, Rep. on Excavation (1972) by Mrs. E. Sellers.
[85] *L. & P. Hen. VIII*, xviii, 124.
[86] Norden, *Essex*, 34.
[87] E.R.O., D/DU 162/1.
[88] E.R.O., Q/RTh 5.
[89] E.R.O., T/P 195/2, p. 47 sqq.
[90] *Hist. Essex by Gent.* iv. 316–18.
[91] E.R.O., D/DE T112; Smith, *Havering*, 112.

Bower House in 1797

Pyrgo Park in 1867. Demolished *c.* 1940

HAVERING

UPMINSTER: High House in 1895

HORNCHURCH: Nelmes in 1904. Demolished 1967

CRANHAM: Old Church in 1872

HAVERING: Old Church in 1876

monuments of Walter de Bounstede, Anne Lovekyn, and Lord Dorset probably disappeared at that time. Pyrgo continued in use for a short time, but the remainder of the house had been apparently demolished by *c.* 1814.[92]

Robert Field, who succeeded to the estate in 1836, lived in a farm-house which had been built to the south-east of the old house. In 1851–2 he demolished it and built Pyrgo Park on the site, to the designs of Anthony Salvin, completed in 1852 by the firm of Cubitt.[93] The next owner, Joseph Bray, enlarged the house in 1862 to the designs of E. M. Barry.[94] Pyrgo Park was a mansion in the 'Classic Italian' style, faced with Suffolk white bricks, with dressings and columns of Portland stone. In 1863 Bray employed Edward Kemp to landscape the grounds. In 1867 Pyrgo Park was advertised for sale as fit for 'a gentleman of rank and wealth, or for a merchant prince.'[95] It then had its own gasworks, and a private chapel had been built at Tysea Hill, on the northern side of the park.[96] Lady O'Hagan added a picture gallery to the house *c.* 1905.[97] Pyrgo Park was demolished *c.* 1940.[98] A large symmetrical stable-block, and the north and south lodges, all of the later 19th century, remain, as well as parts of the Victorian gardens. The present Home Farm, which lies immediately south of the site of the Tudor house, dates from the later 18th century, but was enlarged before 1867.[99]

The manor of *REYNS*, later *NEWBURY*, adjoined Pyrgo to the east. It appears to have originated as a tenement of ½ virgate and ¼ virgate which Adam de Reyns in 1222 granted in fee to William Dun.[1] Dun later granted it in fee to Richard son of Osbert.[2] In 1243 Richard Newman, who was probably identical with Richard son of Osbert, joined with Margery his wife to convey to Hornchurch priory the reversion, after their deaths, of a 40-acre estate held of the fee of William Dun.[3] These and later records, when collated, show that the prior's demesne of Reyns had belonged to Richard Newman, and that it became known as Newbury.[4] Reyns was probably not the only property acquired by the priory from Newman. About 1240 Geoffrey son of Robert confirmed Richard Newman's grant to the priory of a tenement which was of Geoffrey's fee.[5] That was probably the property conveyed, about the same time, by Geoffrey son of Robert to Richard son of Osbert.[6] Newbury first occurs under that name in 1306.[7] In *c.* 1355 the priory's tenement 'called Reyns and now called Newbury' comprised ½ virgate and $\frac{3}{16}$ virgate.[8] In 1376 the priory leased its manor of Newbury for 6 years to John Cullynge of Havering.[9] The property included a grange called Otberne (oat barn), and tithes of hay from several tenements in the north-east of the parish, including Dagenhams and Cockerels, and Gooshayes. A new lease of the manor, for 15 years, was granted in 1385 to Nicholas Longe of London.[10]

Newbury, with the priory's other manors, was conveyed to New College, Oxford, in 1391.[11] In 1518 the college leased Newbury, then comprising 47 a. in five fields, to (Sir) Brian Tuke.[12] Tuke, a prominent servant of Henry VIII, lived for many years at Pyrgo.[13] In the 1540s, when Henry VIII acquired Pyrgo, he also took over the lease of Newbury. When the lease expired in 1549 Edward VI took permanent possession of Newbury, for which New College eventually received in exchange lands in Gloucestershire; by 1555 Newbury was part of Pyrgo Park.[14] Newbury field and Upper Newbury field, on the eastern edge of the park, appear on a map of 1828.[15] North of them was Lower Ley field, which was probably identical, in whole or part, with the Leffeld of 1306.[16] Newbury had no separate identity after the 16th century, though Newbury Lane, which had linked it with Navestock (north) and Noak Hill (south) still existed in 1650.[17] Nothing is known about Newbury manor-house, which probably disappeared before the 16th century.

ECONOMIC HISTORY.[18] In 1086 the manor of Havering, rated at 10 hides, included the whole of Havering, Romford, and Hornchurch, which in the 19th century comprised 16,100 a.[19] In relation to the area the number of hides was remarkably low. This was probably because the Havering hide was unusually large.[20] In Essex the hide normally comprised four virgates, each of 30 acres, making a total of 120 a.[21] In Havering, however, the virgate was normally 120 a., which would give a hide of 480 a.[22]

In 1066 the manor contained 41 villeins, 41 bordars, and 6 serfs, with 2 demesne plough-teams, and 41 belonging to the tenants. There was woodland for 500 swine, and 100 a. of meadow. In 1086 there were only 40 villeins, and 40 tenants' plough-teams; the other figures were unchanged. The

92 Smith, op. cit.; Ogborne, *Essex*, 118; E.R.O., Sage Coll., *Sale Cats.* vol. vi. 6.
93 M. Browne, *Records of Pyrgo*, 137, 146. For descriptions of Pyrgo, 1867–1919, see also E.R.O., Sage Coll., *Sale Cats.* vol. vi. 7–10; E.R.O., *Sale Cat.* B12.
94 Browne, op. cit. 145.
95 See plate facing p. 16.
96 For the chapel: *V.C.H. Essex*, iv. 230.
97 Smith, *Havering*, 113.
98 Ex. inf. Mr. G. J. Clements.
99 E.R.O., Sage Coll., *Sale Cats.* vol. vi. 6, 9.
1 *Feet of F. Essex*, i. 60.
2 *Horn. Docs.* no. 347. It was then said to have belonged to Robert de Reins.
3 Ibid. nos. 42a, 460; *Feet of F. Essex*, i. 144.
4 *Horn. Docs.* nos. 265, 313, 347, 403–4; *Rot. Hund.* (Rec. Com.), i. 149, 152; New College MS. 9744, f. 162.
5 *Horn. Docs.* no. 476.
6 Ibid. 313; cf. 348 which implies that Geoffrey son of Robert was a tenant of William Dun.
7 Ibid. no. 404.
8 New College MS. 9744, f. 162.
9 *Horn. Docs.* no. 14.
10 Ibid. no. 386.
11 Ibid. no. 5; *Cal. Pat.* 1388–92, 417.
12 New Coll. MS. 2957.
13 See p. 16.
14 New Coll. MS. 4623; *Cal. Pat.* 1554–5, 69.
15 E.R.O., D/DXp 9.
16 About 1618 that area was called 'the New Layes'; E.R.O., D/DU 162/1.
17 E.R.O., D/DSa 63; cf. ibid. D/DU 162/1.
18 This section, except for the last paragraph, relates to the agrarian history of the whole manor of Havering, i.e. including Romford and Hornchurch.
19 *V.C.H. Essex*, i. 429; ii. 348.
20 Cf. Waltham, with Epping and Nazeing: 55 hides to 20,000 acres; Barking: 30 hides to 19,000 acres: *V.C.H. Essex*, v. 156, 214.
21 *V.C.H. Essex*, i. 334 n.; H. C. Darby, *Domesday Geog. East. Eng.* 220.
22 New Coll. Oxford MS. 9744, Queen Philippa's Domesday of Havering (16th-cent. copy of extent of *c.* 1355). This extent, discovered during the present work, states the acreages of the virgate tenements.

stock then comprised a rouncey, 10 beasts, 160 swine, and 269 sheep, and there was a mill. It was stated that the manor had been valued at £36 in 1066, and at £40 in 1086, but that the sheriff of Essex received from it £80 rent and £10 in fines. These figures show Havering as a prosperous manor, with a well-balanced system of farming. It was not unlike the neighbouring manor of Barking.[23] Both manors extended north from the Thames, with successive belts of alluvium, valley gravel, and London clay. Barking was somewhat larger, in area and in population, and had a much higher proportion of arable and woodland. Havering had more than twice as many sheep.

The most striking feature of Havering's Domesday economy is perhaps the fact that it was being rack-rented at twice its assessed value. This indication that the manor had a considerable productive capacity is borne out by its development during the next two centuries. In *c.* 1355 Havering contained some 430 messuages or cottages.[24] The total included former buildings that had been demolished, but there is no indication that there were many of those, and it thus seems likely that between 1086 and the earlier 14th century the number of households had increased fivefold. That had been made possible by the more intensive farming of the older tenements, by colonization of forest and waste, and by the alienation of the royal demesne.

The extent of 1250–1 states that there were 40 virgates, but actually lists 40¼, divided among 116 tenants.[25] That of *c.* 1355 states that there were $43\frac{17}{24}$ virgates, but lists a total of just under 40,[26] divided among 87. It is possible that the original 40 virgates represented the holdings of the 40 villeins of 1086.[27] The later history of the tenements of the Domesday bordars is more obscure. In 1250–1 there were seven tenants holding one cotland apiece. In *c.* 1355 there were 4 tenants holding one cotland each, and 7 with ½ cotland. Two of the cotlands comprised 60 a., one was 23½ a., and one 20 a. Four of the ½ cotlands were 20 a., and three were 10 a. The cotlands in Havering were thus no more than half a virgate, and usually less. They probably represented the holdings of some of the Domesday bordars.[28] If so the other holdings of the bordars must have lost their identity by 1250–1.

The system of virgates had survived in Havering largely because it was used in assessing the tenants' obligation to repair the pale of Havering park. In other respects it was out of date by the 13th century, but the detailed descriptions of it in 1250–1 and *c.* 1355 help to reveal a remarkable pioneering enterprise, sustained until the Black Death and stimulated by the Crown, which from the 12th century used the manor mainly for hunting and timber, while freely arrenting the demesne and the woodland waste. By 1250–1 the king had in hand, besides the park, only 223 a. of arable and 38 a. of meadow and pasture. There were altogether 272 chief tenants, of whom 42 were also subtenants, and 129 other subtenants, making a total of 401 landholders, apart from the king. 'New purprestures', totalling 975 a., were held by 184 of the chief tenants, of whom 136 held no other tenements. By *c.* 1355 the whole of the demesne farm had been arrented and the royal plough had gone out of use. Most of the larger farms consisted mainly of virgates, consolidated or fragmented, to which 'new lands' had been added by assarting and by arrenting the demesne. The most important exceptions were Hornchurch Hall, Suttons, and Redden Court, in Hornchurch, and Earls in Havering, which contained no virgates, but consisted entirely of former demesne or assarts. In all there were 1,748 a. of 'new lands', including 87 dwellings. Of the 'new lands' 1,089 a. were attached to the older virgate tenements, but the remainder had been formed into separate smallholdings, on which were 70 of the dwellings. Some of the 'new lands', in small parcels totalling about 256 a., had come from the royal demesne called Beryland. A few of the parcels were near Marshalls at Romford, and one or two others at Oldchurch. Most of the 'new lands', comprising about 1,491 a., had, however, been reclaimed from the waste. With 1,154 a. in the park Queen Philippa was still the largest occupier, but there were three other large estates. Hornchurch priory held about 900 a., mainly at Hornchurch.[29] Dagenhams comprised about 611 a., and Gidea Hall about 506 a. The whole manor of Havering, excluding the royal park and the commons, contained some 11,850 a. Of that cultivated land some 7,885 a. were held by chief tenants, and 3,965 a. by subtenants ('undersettles'). There were 190 chief tenants, of whom 100 were also subtenants, and 356 other subtenants, making a total of 546 landholders, apart from the queen.[30]

The above figures show that between 1250–1 and *c.* 1355 the 'new lands' had increased by 773 a., of which about 500 a. had been taken from the waste and the remainder from the demesne. The cultivated land had thus increased by about 4½ per cent. The number of chief tenants had fallen by 30 per cent, but the number of landholders of all kinds had risen by 36 per cent. It is clear that the manor was being much more intensively cultivated in *c.* 1355 than it had been a century earlier, and that the larger tenants were consolidating their holdings. Economic growth had recently been halted by the Black Death: it was stated in *c.* 1355 that because of the great mortality caused by the plague no one wished to take up an assart from the queen. In the long run, however, assarting was stimulated, from the 14th century onwards, by the exclusion of Havering from the forest of Essex.[31]

There are indications that Havering, like Barking[32] may have had open fields. Selions or strips, 40 perches long, lying in fallow fields in the manor, were mentioned in 1250–1,[33] and in *c.* 1355 holdings were in scattered parcels rather than compact blocks. Further evidence is provided by the field name Manland (common land), which in *c.* 1355 occurred in two places within the manor of

[23] *V.C.H. Essex*, v. 214–15.
[24] New Coll. Oxford MS. 9744.
[25] S.C. 11/189 (trans. in E.R.O., Q/HZ 2/4). The exact total of listed virgates is $40\frac{21}{80}$.
[26] The exact total of listed virgates is $39\frac{1378}{1440}$.
[27] Cf. Maitland, *Domesday Bk. and Beyond*, ed. E. Miller, 66: 'Perhaps in general we may endow the *villanus* of Domesday Book with a virgate, or a quarter of a hide . . .'
[28] Cf. Maitland, op. cit. 66.
[29] See p. 31.
[30] The statistics from the extents of 1250–1 and *c.* 1355 were worked out by Mrs. B. A. Board.
[31] New Coll. MS. 9744, f. 172v.
[32] *V.C.H. Essex*, v. 215.
[33] S.C. 11/189.

Havering, both identifiable from later records. One was near Marshalls in Romford,[34] the other at Noak Hill.[35] In the early 17th century both of them were small inclosed fields. By that time, indeed, no open arable still survived anywhere in the manor of Havering.

In the south of the manor, at Hornchurch, marshland commons survived at least until the mid 19th century. In 1735 Havering level included 4 commons in the marshes: Smith Mead (21 a.), the Hassock (69 a.), Woolley Mead (30 a.), and Great Common (67 a.).[36] In 1850 the total area of common marshland was almost exactly the same, although there had been minor changes in the areas of the individual commons. The commons then contained 83 strips, divided among 14 owners, of whom the two largest between them held 54 strips, containing about 140 a. out of the total of 187 a. No common marshes remained in 1975.[37]

In addition to the common arable and common marshes there were the common woodlands or 'outwoods', which are more fully described elsewhere.[38] At the time of Domesday these must have covered much of the northern half of the manor. In the following centuries they were steadily reduced by the assarting already mentioned, and by the early 19th century they had dwindled to open commons at Collier Row, Harold Wood (the present Straight Road area), and Noak Hill. In 1814 those commons, comprising a total of 1,060 a., were inclosed under an Act of 1811.[39] Several small greens were inclosed at the same time. Most of those were in Hornchurch, and they included Redden Court green, Ardleigh green, Squirrels Heath, and two unnamed greens near the present Gaynes Parkway. The greens, with many roadside verges also inclosed, comprised 95 a. Havering green was allotted to the Crown, as lord of the manor, with the proviso that it should remain open for public use. After the break-up of the manor estate it was bought by Dr. Harold Smith, who gave it to Romford borough council in 1935.[40]

In Havering, as in Barking, the existence of these three types of ancient common combines with the Domesday particulars to show the early pattern of local agriculture. The ancient settlements in the centre of the manor, probably with arable fields near, were flanked on the north by forest pastures, and on the south by marshland pastures. Also in the north was Havering park, which existed by the mid 12th century,[41] and by Henry III's reign was playing an important part in the economy of the manor, in supplying bacon, venison, timber, and fish.[42] In *c.* 1355 it was stated that 550 beasts had anciently been pastured in the park, and that there were now 300.[43] In 1650 the park contained 200 deer.[44]

The labour services due from the tenants and subtenants of the manor of Havering were listed in detail in 1250–1.[45] For all the services a cash value was added, which suggests that commutation was not unusual. By *c.* 1355 all labour services seem to have been commuted, and most of them had disappeared from the record. This reflects the alienation of the royal demesne which has already been mentioned.

Mixed farming, without strong specialization, continued to be the pattern in Havering until the 19th century. Before the 15th century arable seems to have predominated on the larger estates, even on the lowlands of the manor, near the marshes.[46] In and after the 16th century the proportion of meadow and pasture was higher than before, and on some Hornchurch estates exceeded arable.[47] There is no evidence of large-scale commercial grazing in the 16th century. One reason for this was the survival of commons rights in the marshes, and the large numbers of small holdings there.[48] No less important was flooding, from which Hornchurch suffered almost as severely as Dagenham.[49]

In the early 17th century Havering had much parkland, not only in the royal park, but also at Pyrgo, Gidea Hall, Stewards, and Bretons.[50] The royal park was cut up into farms in the 1650s, and Stewards before 1696, but several other parks were formed in the 18th century.[51] While the main function of the parks was to provide a pleasant setting for country houses, they were a valuable source of timber. In 1748, for example, the timber on the Dagenhams estate was valued at £2,456,[52] and in 1815 that on the Gidea Hall estate at £5,335.[53]

Between 1770 and 1850 Havering was transformed into a region of intensive and scientific farming, by the enterprise of men like John Heaton (d. 1818) of Bedfords, James Ellis (d. 1845) of Havering Park farm, and Collinson Hall of Bower farm.[54] Heaton was prominent in promoting the inclosures of 1814. The new farm-land taken in then was rapidly exploited. About two years later it was already 'in a high state of cultivation, and great crops of corn and green food for cattle have been obtained'. Many buildings had been erected on the inclosures, and plantations made, and the improvements were thought to have caused Havering 'to assume an entirely new character.'[55] Heaton himself obtained much of Harold Wood common, and built there the model farm of Heaton Grange. Ellis and Hall both farmed land that had once belonged to Havering park, and had the advantage of being tithe-free. They were tenants of Hugh McIntosh, a rich contractor who had bought the Havering manor estate in 1828, and who in the following years carried out many farming improvements.[56] Ellis, who also farmed in Kent, is said to have become the largest hop-grower in the world.[57] His hop plantations at Havering were maintained until his death, but were ploughed up

[34] E.R.O., D/DU 162/1 (Map of Havering liberty *c.* 1618).
[35] Ibid., cf. *Cal. Pat.* 1416–22, 301.
[36] E.R.O., D/SH 25; see below, p. 42.
[37] Inf. from Havering L.B.
[38] See p. 21.
[39] 51 Geo. III c.187 (Local and Personal); E.R.O., T/M 86; Ogborne, *Essex*, 148–9.
[40] *Romford Charter Souvenir* (1937).
[41] See p. 13.
[42] *Close R.* 1234–7: see index s.v. Havering forest, and park; and later vols.
[43] New Coll. MS. 9744.
[44] E.R.O., D/DSa 63.
[45] S.C. 11/189.
[46] As at Dovers: *Cal. Inq. p.m.* iii, p. 388 (date 1299); *Feet of F. Essex*, iii. 254 (1409); and at Bretons: E.R.O., D/DU 102/46 m. 4 (1427).
[47] As at Bretons: *Cal. Close*, 1500–9, 82–3 (in 1503); Gubbins: S.C. 2/173/2, m. 19*d* (1517); Mardyke: E.R.O., D/DHt T383/1 (1624).
[48] For Hornchurch marshes see p. 42.
[49] Cf. *V.C.H. Essex*, v. 282.
[50] E.R.O., D/DU 162/1.
[51] *Map of Essex* (1777).
[52] E.R.O., D/DNe E9.
[53] E.R.O., D/DBe E62.
[54] Smith, *Havering*, 68–9, 122.
[55] Ogborne, *Essex*, 149.
[56] E.R.O., Libr. Folder, Newscutting *c.* 1848.
[57] Smith, *Havering*, 69.

soon after. Collinson Hall, who was at Bower farm in the 1830s and 1840s, pioneered the use of the steam-plough, and was one of the first local farmers to provide milk for the London market.[58]

Farther south, at Hornchurch, the soil was especially suitable for market-gardening. Potato-growing had begun there by 1807,[59] and was well-established by 1830, when some of the farmers were involved in a bitter dispute over potato tithes with John Bearblock of Hornchurch Hall, lessee of the great tithes.[60] Bearblock was himself a large vegetable grower with a London connexion.[61]

Older types of farming, including large-scale grain growing, continued alongside market-gardening. In 1846 the titheable land in Havering and north Romford, which comprised about seven-eighths of the total area, included 3,129 a. of arable, 3,710 a. of meadow and pasture, 174 a. of woods and plantations, and 113 a. of orchards.[62] In 1849 the titheable land in Hornchurch and south Romford, comprising about nine-tenths of the total area, included 4,606 a. arable, 2,179 a. meadow and pasture, 44 a. wood, and 37 a. reeds.[63] At the date quoted Havering and north Romford had 34 farms of over 50 a.; 13 of those were between 50 a. and 100 a., 12 between 100 a. and 200 a., and 9 over 200 a. The largest of all was occupied by Collinson Hall, who by that time had acquired the tenancy of the whole of the Havering manor estate, comprising 1,339 a. In Hornchurch and south Romford the farms tended to be smaller. There were 49 over 50 a., including 15 between 50 a. and 100 a., and 7 over 200 a. The largest was Suttons farm, of 406 a.

Farming remained the main occupation in Havering until after the First World War. Market-gardening, especially in Hornchurch and south Romford, continued to be important, and during the later 19th century came to include fruit and flowers.[64] At that period George Rawlings, whose nurseries lay south of Romford station, was a dahlia-grower well known throughout Europe,[65] and the Revd. J. H. Pemberton of Havering was a noted rose-grower.[66] As late as 1917 market-gardening was still being carried on on a large scale at Hornchurch, which also had fine grain crops.[67] It could be said then 'the chief industry of Hornchurch remains on the soil,' but during the next twenty years most of the farm-land there and in south Romford was built over. In north Romford development was slower, especially in the Noak Hill area, where about 1,500 a. of farm-land survived until the Harold Hill estate was built after the Second World War. At Havering, where development was halted by the Green Belt policy, there are still several farms.

The industries of Hornchurch and Romford are treated under those places. In Havering village there was some tile-making in the 15th century and later, and in the 19th century there were brickfields in Broxhill Road.[68] There was a tanner at Pyrgo in 1441.[69] Some vanished industries are indicated by field names. In *c.* 1618 Mill field lay about ½ m. north of Bedfords.[70] In 1846 Windmill hill was on the boundary between Havering and Stapleford Abbots; Hopkiln hill was roughly where Hillrise Road is now; Brick Kiln corner was in Orange Tree Road.[71] An informal pleasure fair, held in the village on Ascension Day was in existence by 1771.[72] It was abolished in 1877, under the Fairs Act, 1871.[73]

FOREST.[74] The forest of Essex, as defined in 1225, 1228, and 1301 included the whole of the royal manor of Havering.[75] The perambulation of 1301 recorded the Havering boundaries in detail.[76] In 1305 all the demesne lands of the Crown within the forest were declared to be free chases or warrens, reserved for royal use.[77] Even before that, however, Havering was in some respects separate from the rest of the forest. There had been a royal park there at least since 1157.[78] Until the later 13th century the custody of the park was held in fee by the steward of the forest of Essex.[79] In 1262 Henry III granted the park, with the manor of Havering, to his queen Eleanor.[80] Thomas of Clare, who bought the stewardship of the forest in 1267, was deprived of the custody of the park, apparently about 1280, for an offence committed against the queen by one of his parkers. The park was then appropriated by the queen, and was entrusted to one of her officials.[18] In 1306 Gilbert of Clare, son and heir of Thomas, tried to regain custody.[82] He seems to have failed, and no later steward of the forest is known to have had the custody until the 17th century.[83] At the forest eyre of 1324 a separate justice was nominated by Queen Isabel, who then held Havering manor, to hear pleas relating to 'Havering forest'.[84] The queen was to receive all the income from Havering pleas.

As a result of these developments between *c.* 1280 and 1324 Havering seems to have been disafforested and to have acquired the status of a forest purlieu. The inhabitants of the purlieus were not represented at the forest courts and they were exempt from all the forest laws except those protecting the king's game.[85] Those conditions existed at Havering by 1489,[86] and in 1594 its inhabitants were explicitly stated to be 'dwelling in the purlieus.'[87] Havering

[58] Smith, *Havering*, 68.
[59] A. Young, *Gen. View Agric. Essex*, i. 201, 382.
[60] E.R.O., D/P 115/28/8.
[61] Ibid. 115/28/2.
[62] I.R. 29/12/162.
[63] I.R. 29/12/177.
[64] *V.C.H. Essex*, ii. 476, 480.
[65] H.R.L., Cornell MSS.
[66] E.R.O., Libr. Folder (Havering), obit. of Revd. J. H. Pemberton.
[67] Perfect, *Village of Hornchurch*, 10.
[68] E.R.O., D/DU 102/36, m. 7 (date 1448); ibid. 102/45 (Whit Tues. 1455); Assizes 35/20/5 (July 1578); *White's Dir. Essex* (1848), 374; *Kelly's Dir. Essex* (1866, 1886); O.S. Map 6", Essex, LXVI (1881 edn.).
[69] E.R.O., D/DU 102/30, m. 7.
[70] E.R.O., D/DU 162/1.
[71] I.R. 29 and 30/12/162.
[72] *Hist. Essex by Gent.* iv. 318.
[73] *Lond. Gaz.* 31 Aug. 1877, p. 5041.
[74] This section relates to the whole of the manor and liberty of Havering, including Romford and Hornchurch.
[75] W. R. Fisher, *Forest of Essex*, 21 sqq.
[76] Ibid. 393–5.
[77] *Statutes of the Realm*, i. 144: Ordinance of the Forest, 33 Edw. I.
[78] Smith, *Havering*, 6 sqq.
[79] Ibid. 9–12; Fisher, *Forest*, 114–15.
[80] *Cal. Pat.* 1266–72, 736.
[81] *Rot. Parl.* (Rec. Com.), i. 205*a*; Fisher, *Forest*, 116–17.
[82] *Rot. Parl.* i. 205*a*.
[83] Fisher, *Forest*, 118–19, 127; *Cal. S.P. Dom.* 1603–10, 22.
[84] Fisher, *Forest*, 16, 109; E.R.O., D/DU 403/22, pp. 80 sqq.
[85] Fisher, *Forest*, 33–4, 161; *Manwood's Treatise of the Forest Laws* (1717 edn.), 291.
[86] E.R.O., D/DU 403/22, pp. 44 sqq.
[87] E.R.O., D/DU 403/22 (swainmote court).

purlieu is nowhere defined. It presumably included the whole manor of Havering.

In the earlier 17th century the Crown tried to bring Havering back into the forest. James I, soon after he came to the throne, began to levy retrospective fines on those holding unauthorized inclosures in the forest.[88] When he extended those claims to Havering he met strong, and apparently successful resistance from the local landowners.[89] The widespread resentment roused by such exactions led to a statute of 1624 which restricted the king's right to 'concealed' lands by providing that he must prove that he had title to them within the past 60 years.[90] This left unresolved the question of the forest boundaries, and in 1634–5 the Crown, by intimidating the jury at the forest eyre, extended the boundaries to take in much of Essex, including Havering.[91] In the following years, at least until 1640, Havering was treated as part of the forest,[92] and was apparently included in West Hainault 'walk', of which Sir Robert Quarles was keeper.[93] In 1641, however, the previous boundaries were restored by Act of Parliament,[94] followed by a perambulation which recorded, among other landmarks, the ancient boundary stones on the eastern side of the forest.[95] Those stones, or some of them, were renewed in 1642.[96] In 1908 they were repaired and re-fixed. Six of them were on the Havering boundary. Four of those are known to have been moved at some time, before or after 1908, but in 1975 all six survived, more or less in their ancient positions.

In 1086 Havering had woodland sufficient to feed 500 swine.[97] That figure, though considerable, is not large enough to indicate a high density throughout the manor, and it is likely that then, as later, the woodland lay mainly on the northern uplands. Throughout the Middle Ages Havering park, which formed the NW. corner of the manor, was well wooded.[98] South and east of it lay the outwoods (*bosci forinseci*): West (or Lowe) wood, Harold's wood, and Crocleph (or East wood). These provided common pasture for the tenants of the manor, and also for those of Navestock, Stapleford Abbots, and South Weald. Remnants of them eventually became open commons, which survived until 1814.[99] West wood, which lay south of Havering park, became Collier Row common. Harold's wood became Romford common, which extended north from the present Gallows Corner. Crocleph (later Havering wood) became Havering plain, at Noak Hill. During the three centuries after Domesday there was much clearance of woodland.[1] Romford wood, which in the early 13th century was providing pasture for the king's cattle, became the nucleus of the manor of Romford, or Mawneys.[2] By 1306 most of that manor was arable or pasture, and the wood was devastated.[3] Forest clearance was systematically exploited by the Crown, which granted assarts from the outwood on payment of rent.[4] It also occurred in other ways. In 1389 the farmer of Hornchurch rectory was found to have caused waste during the past three years by felling some 500 trees at Beam Land.[5] That reference is also notable in showing that there was then woodland within half a mile of the marshes.

By the early 17th century no large woods survived in Hornchurch, though there were several groves and many individual trees.[6] A small part of Harold's wood remained at the northern end of Romford common. Collier Row common, formerly West wood, was by then open grassland, but Havering wood survived at Noak Hill, where there were also several smaller woods. At that time Havering park was still partly wooded, but during the Interregnum it was cut up into farms, which were allowed to remain at the Restoration. By the later 18th century little ancient woodland survived in Havering liberty, though there were several post-medieval parks.[7]

LOCAL GOVERNMENT. The manorial government of Havering has been treated above.[8] Havering, like Romford was originally a chapelry of Hornchurch.[9] In the 16th century it was treated as one of the wards of 'Romford side',[10] but by the early 17th century its chapel vestry seems to have been largely self-governing in civil, as distinct from church matters.[11]

There are vestry books for 1677–1748, and 1786–1926, together with chapelwardens' accounts, 1705–1811, and bills, 1745–1836, overseers' accounts, 1683–1836,[12] and a few other records.[13] Further information is provided by the vestry books of Romford, 1660–1849, which include extracts from earlier books, 1489–1660.[14]

In the late 17th century the vestry usually met only once or twice a year. From 1706 the frequency tended to increase, often reaching three or four, and occasionally, as in 1747, six a year. Meeting places are rarely stated. Attendances, as indicated by signatures to the minutes, were usually between 5 and nine. In 1727 it was agreed that expenditure on

88 Fisher, *Forest*, 325.
89 S.P. 14/94, 99, 109, 201–3.
90 Act against Pretences of Concealment, 21 Jas. I, c.2.
91 Fisher, *Forest*, 37 sqq.
92 As shown e.g. in the licensing of forest inclosures: E.R.O., D/DMs O49/39, 44, 45.
93 *Cal. S.P. Dom.* 1637–8, 328; cf. Fisher, *Forest*, 384.
94 Act for the Certainty of Forests, 17 Chas. I, c.16.
95 Fisher, *Forest*, 50, 400 sqq.
96 For the Forest boundary stones see: H.R.L., Loc. File 28/5; *E.Nat.* ix. 1–10; xv. 126–9; xxx. 164; *Triton* (Royal London Insurance Soc.) (1964), no. 130, p.33, no. 131, p. 31. Mr. H. de Caux kindly examined all the stones in November 1975. The Warren stone was not moved to Valence House in 1960 as wrongly stated in *Dagenham Digest*, Sept. 1964, 2, 12, 13; the pair of stones illustrated (from grid ref. 485887) have no name: inf. from Mr. J. Howson.
97 *V.C.H. Essex*, i. 429.
98 See p. 12.
99 Smith, *Havering*, 19–20, 254; E.R.O., D/DU 162/2/1 and 2.

1 See p. 18.
2 See p. 64.
3 *Cal. Inq. p.m.* v. 291.
4 New Coll. MS. 9744, *passim*.
5 *Cal. Inq. Misc.* 1387–93, pp. 153–4.
6 E.R.O., D/DU 162/1 (map of Havering liberty *c.* 1618).
7 *Map of Essex* (1777).
8 See p. 1.
9 See pp. 22, 82.
10 See p. 76.
11 See p. 23.
12 E.R.O., D/P 64/8/1 (vestry bk. 1677–1748); 64/5/1 and 2 (wardens); 64/12/1–11 (overseers); vestry bks. (1786–1926) in custody of vicar of Havering. Unless otherwise stated the following account is based on the above records. For extracts from Havering parish records see: Smith, *Havering*, 157–79, 211–15, 225, 239–57; *E.R.* xxv. 144–50.
13 See *Essex Par. Recs.* 131–2.
14 E.R.O., T/A 521/1–3.

refreshments at meetings other than the Easter vestry should be limited to 4*d.* a head. In the early 18th century the vestry was paying a small salary to its clerk, who was once (1731) instructed to collect it 'from house to house'. From 1731 the chaplain of Havering, Mark Noble, was acting as clerk; in 1743, after his death, his daughter succeeded to the post.

In the 16th and early 17th centuries there seem to have been two chapelwardens[15] By the later 17th century, however, there was only one, and that remained the normal custom until 1849.[16] From 1596 the Romford vestry was appointing a warden for Havering.[17] Havering later controverted that practice, but in 1683 Romford's right to enforce it was upheld in the archdeacon's court.[18] After that time the same man was usually appointed as sole warden by agreement between the two vestries, though there were occasionally rival candidates.[19] Romford did not nominate after 1790.[20]

A collector of the poor for Havering was appointed by Romford vestry in 1561.[21] In the earlier 17th century Romford was nominating an overseer of the poor for Havering,[22] while the Romford surveyors of highways had joint responsibility for the whole of Romford side, including Havering.[23] From *c.* 1680, however, Havering nominated its own overseer and surveyor, for formal appointment by the justices of the liberty. A petty constable for Havering ward was appointed under ancient custom in the court leet.[24] By 1677, however, that appointment also was apparently initiated by nomination in the vestry.

From the later 17th century separate church-rates and poor-rates were being levied, but there was much overlapping between the churchwarden's and the overseer's accounts. In the early 19th century there were separate constable's rates. They included the liberty rates, which sometimes, as in 1816–17, amounted to as much as a fifth of all parochial charges.

Poor-relief in this small village followed a simple pattern. In 1709 the vestry was renting a house at Havering Green, and one at Collier Row, for lodging the poor. 'The little house, lately Wrights'' was in similar use in 1713. In 1740 the vestry leased a house at Havering for £4 a year. For the next 50 years the rent, probably for the same house, remained the same.[25] In 1792 a cottage was leased from Thomas Neave, and it was used as the poor-house, sometimes called the workhouse, down to 1836.[26] It had five rooms and a kitchen.[27]

From the 17th century to the early 19th the vestry was paying weekly doles to the aged poor, the sick, widows, and orphans. The total number receiving doles at any one time during that period was usually between 4 and 7 until 1818, after which it rose to 10 or more. Out-relief was also given in kind, by payments for rent or lodging, medical care, apprenticing orphans, or buying the tools of trade. In the 19th century the vestry had a regular contract with a succession of doctors for treating the poor. In 1736 it resolved that a poor child should be lodged on the 'roundsman' system, and in 1745 it passed a general resolution to the same effect. In 1800 and the following years small payments were made to the poor for spinning. In 1813 the vestry paid the large sum of £20 to meet the fine and gaol fees of a man charged with killing a deer.[28]

Before 1700 the total annual cost of poor-relief varied from about £15 to £25. It later rose, with considerable fluctuations, to reach about £60–90 in the 1740s, and to an average of £188 in the years 1783–5.[29] After 1800 it kept fairly steady, usually between £200 and £300.[30] These figures, in relation to the population, suggest that there was less poverty in Havering than in the other parts of the liberty, or in neighbouring parishes like Stapleford Abbots or Stapleford Tawney.[31] The parish records contain little information concerning the work of the surveyor of highways, for which the records of the liberty quarter sessions are a better source.[32] Statute highway labour was still being performed in the 18th and early 19th centuries.[33] Havering, like other places in the liberty, made an annual payment to the Middlesex and Essex turnpike trust for mending the main London–Colchester road.

Havering became part of Romford poor-law union in 1836, and was later in Romford rural district until 1934, when it was annexed to Romford urban district.[34]

CHURCHES. The earliest references to the 'church of Havering' concern St. Andrew's, Hornchurch, which is treated elsewhere.[35] From the 13th century onwards, however, there were also, in Havering village, two chapels attached to the royal house. Both appear on a plan of 1578.[36] The smaller chapel, dedicated to St. Edward, fell down with the rest of the house about 1700.[37] It was probably identical with the chapel, of similar dimensions, built for Queen Eleanor in 1253–60, to replace an earlier one.[38] The larger chapel stood on the site of the present parish church of Havering. It probably originated as the king's chapel, to which there are references from 1201.[39] In 1274 Queen Eleanor, now lady of the manor of Havering, provided that in future Hornchurch priory, owner of the parish church of Hornchurch, should appoint the chaplain of Havering

[15] *E.A.T.* N.S. iii. 36; Smith, *Havering*, 210.
[16] For the chapelwardens see Smith op. cit. 210–14. They were styled churchwardens from 1830.
[17] E.R.O., T/A 521/1, rev. ff. 16v–22v.
[18] E.R.O., T/A 521/1, 27 Sept. 1683.
[19] E.R.O., T/A 521/1, *passim.* For disputes see e.g. 19 May 1708, 20 Apr. 1767.
[20] E.R.O., T/A 521/1 and 2, *passim*; Smith, *Hist. Havering*, 212.
[21] E.R.O., T/A 521/1 rev. f. 16.
[22] Ibid rev. f. 17.
[23] Ibid. ff. 2 sqq.; rev. ff. 17–21v.
[24] See p. 5.
[25] E.R.O., D/P 64/12/2E and 11.
[26] Ibid. 64/18/4–6.
[27] Ibid. 64/18/5: inventory of poorhouse, *c.* 1816.
[28] E.R.O., D/P 64/12/33.
[29] E.R.O., Q/CR 1/1.
[30] In the six years 1816–21 the average was £240: E.R.O., Q/CR 1/12.
[31] *V.C.H. Essex*, iv. 231, 238.
[32] E.R.O., Q/HM 1, *passim.*
[33] Ibid. 12 Jan. 1732, 3 Jan. 1737; E.R.O., D/P 64/21.
[34] Essex County Review Order, 1934.
[35] See p. 46.
[36] A. W. Clapham and W. H. Godfrey, *Some famous buildings and their story*, 149; E.R.O., T/M 229 (photo of map in Cecil MSS.).
[37] H. M. Colvin, *King's Works*, ii. 959; Newcourt, *Repertorium*, ii. 338; Smith, *Havering*, 146, 153.
[38] *Cal. Lib. R.* 1245–51, 372; Colvin, *King's Works*, ii. 957.
[39] *Pipe R.* 1201 (P.R.S. N.S. xiv), 58; Colvin, *King's Works*, ii. 956–7; *Cal. Lib.* 1245–51, 372; ibid. 1251–60, 119. Some references distinguish the 'upper' and 'lower' chapels.

chapel and pay his stipend.[40] That arrangement, in conjunction with the other evidence, suggests that from the late 13th century St. Mary's chapel was used for public worship, while St. Edward's chapel continued to be reserved for the private use of the royal household.

St. Mary's chapel continued to be dependent on Hornchurch until the 18th century. From the 15th century, however, Havering paid chapel-rates to Romford, and buried its dead there.[41] By an arbitration award of 1529 Havering and Romford became virtually exempt from contributions to the repair of Hornchurch church, unless that had suffered catastrophic damage.[42] No similar concession was made by Romford in its demands on Havering, but in the early 17th century Havering began to withhold payment of Romford chapel-rates.[43] Havering's struggle for independence, which involved its civil as well as its ecclesiastical status,[44] gathered pace after the Civil War. In 1650 it was proposed that Havering, with Noak Hill, should become a separate parish.[45] That came to nothing, but Havering chapel was keeping separate registers of baptisms by 1657, of marriages by 1692, and of burials by 1699.[46]

As late as 1749 Romford vestry was still claiming chapel-rates from Havering.[47] It had won a series of lawsuits against Havering ratepayers, but seems at last to have tired of the struggle,[48] and from 1750 Havering was omitted from the list of wards in Romford side assessed to chapel-rate.[49]

Havering remained subordinate to Hornchurch until the 1780s, when a separate perpetual curacy was endowed.[50] The terms of the endowment also provided that Havering, unlike Hornchurch, should be subject to the bishop's jurisdiction. Havering thus became an independent parish, though its status was still puzzling lawyers in 1803.[51]

The chaplain of the public chapel of Havering continued to be appointed and paid by Hornchurch priory, and later by New College, Oxford, until the late 15th century, from which time the college seems usually to have delegated those functions to the vicar of Hornchurch, reserving the right to remove the chaplain.[52] In 1784 the advowson of the perpetual curacy was vested in John Heaton of Bedfords, who had contributed much of the endowment.[53] The advowson passed with Bedfords to Heaton's grandson Charles Heaton Ellis, who presented in 1834.[54] It was subsequently acquired by William Pemberton-Barnes (d. 1872) of the Hall, in whose family it remained until 1919, when the Misses Emily and Amy Pemberton-Barnes conveyed it to the Church Pastoral Aid Society.[55]

In the earlier 13th century the chaplain of the king's chapel of Havering was paid 50*s.* a year from the Exchequer.[56] In 1274 the stipend, to be paid by Hornchurch priory, was fixed at 46*s.* a year.[57] In *c.* 1355 the chaplain was receiving £5 6*s.* 8*d.*[58] By the early 17th century the stipend was £6 13*s.* 4*d.*, paid out of the Hornchurch vicarage.[59] In 1645–6 the chaplain was receiving £50 a year from the impropriate rectory of West Ham, which had been sequestrated from its royalist owners.[60] That augmentation had lapsed by 1650, when the chaplain's only income was £20, allowed by the government out of the small tithes of Havering.[61] At the Restoration the stipend reverted to £6 13*s.* 4*d.*, but in the 18th century, as no doubt earlier, it was supplemented by voluntary subscriptions.[62] In the 1780s the perpetual curacy was endowed with £1,000, producing about £80 a year, furnished by Queen Anne's Bounty with the aid of local contributions.[63] A further £7 10*s.* a year was to be paid by the vicar of Hornchurch in respect of the ancient stipend.

In Queen Eleanor's agreement with Hornchurch priory in 1274, already mentioned, it was provided that the chaplain of Havering should always dwell in the manor.[64] In 1322 Joan Stonard granted to Hugh of Latton, chaplain of Havering, a house abutting south on Havering Green.[65] In 1326 Latton conveyed the house to his successor to hold in free alms.[66] The chaplain's house was said in 1575 to be in great decay.[67] Substantial repairs were carried out by Thomas Mann, vicar of Hornchurch 1632–48, and by a later vicar in 1717.[68] In 1786 the parsonage was rebuilt, largely at John Heaton's expense. Henry Ward, vicar of Havering 1784–1834, enlarged and improved the house,[69] which is a plain yellow-brick building with a parapet to the front, standing in North Road opposite the Green.

The names of several chaplains of Havering occur between 1201 and 1272.[70] A few others are recorded in the 14th and 15th centuries.[71] From the late 16th century the list seems to be fairly complete.[72] Until 1784 the living was so poor that few chaplains stayed long. A notable exception was Mark Noble, who served for 30 years, in two separate periods, 1689–98 and 1721–42.[73] Henry Ward, presented in

[40] *Horn. Docs.* no. 200.
[41] E.R.O., T/A 521/1 (Romford vestry mins.), reverse f. 15; Smith, *Havering*, 217.
[42] New Coll. MS. 4592.
[43] Smith, op. cit. 220 sqq.
[44] See also p. 22.
[45] Smith, *Eccl. Hist. Essex*, 249–51, 348.
[46] Smith, *Havering*, 156.
[47] E.R.O., T/A 521/1, 27 Mar. 1749.
[48] Smith, *Havering*, 151, 220 sqq.; E.R.O., T/Z 13/59.
[49] E.R.O., T/A 521/1, 28 Sept. 1750.
[50] Smith, op. cit. 160–1; New Coll. MS. 3424; Ch. Com. Offices, Q.A.B. Mins. 1782–6, pp. 144–6.
[51] E.R.O., T/P 71/2 (Hornchurch v. Romford church rate case).
[52] Smith, *Havering*, 147–8, 153; *Hist. Essex by Gent.* iv. 315.
[53] New Coll. MS. 3424.
[54] Smith, *Havering*, 191–2.
[55] Inf. from C.P.A.S.: H. Smith, op. cit. 192, states that it was left to the C.P.A.S. by the will of W. H. Pemberton-Barnes.
[56] *Pipe R.* 1202 (P.R.S. N.S. xv), 257; *Cal. Lib.* 1245–51, 136.
[57] *Horn. Docs.* no. 200.
[58] New Coll. MS. 9744, f. 186.
[59] Smith, *Havering*, 152–3.
[60] Ibid.
[61] Ibid. 155.
[62] *Hist. Essex by Gent.* iv. 315.
[63] Ogborne, *Essex*, 107; Ch. Com. Offices, Q.A.B. Mins. 1782–6, pp. 144–6; Smith, *Havering*, 160–1.
[64] *Cal. Pat.* 1281–92, 378.
[65] *Horn. Docs.* no. 422.
[66] Ibid. 423.
[67] Smith, *Havering*, 150.
[68] Ibid. 153, 159; E.R.O., D/P 64/8/1.
[69] Smith, op. cit. 160.
[70] Ogborne, *Essex*, 107; Lysons, *Lond.* iv. 184 n.
[71] *Pipe R.* 1201 (P. R. S. N.S. xiv), 58; *Rot. Litt. Claus.* (Rec. Com.), ii. 48; *Horn. Docs.* no. 155; *Cal. Lib.* 1245–51, 138; ibid. 1251–60, 364, 533; ibid. 1260–7, 101; *Close R.* 1268–72, 519.
[72] *Horn. Docs.* nos. 422–3; C.C.L., J. L. Fisher, 'Essex Incumbents', f. 200–1; E.R.O., D/DU 102/28, m. 12*d.*
[73] Smith, *Havering*, 193–210. There is no list for Havering in Newcourt, *Repertorium.*

1784, held the living for 50 years.[74] After 1818 he rarely resided, and employed an assistant curate, John Wiseman, 1819–34, who was also a local farmer.[75] Richard Faulkner, vicar 1834–73, was energetic, pugnacious, and controversial.[76] He enlarged the church and rebuilt the school.

The old parish church of *ST. MARY*, later of *ST. JOHN THE EVANGELIST*, demolished in 1876, stood west of Havering Green, on the site of the present church.[77] The survival of a 12th-century font suggests that the chapel of St. Mary may have dated from that period. During Henry III's reign the king's chapel was often repaired and improved, but it is unlikely that much of the 13th-century structure survived after 1374–7, when the 'great chapel' was rebuilt at a cost of over £600.[78] In 1578 the chapel was 45 ft. long and 16½ ft. wide. There was a doorway on the north side leading to the 'great chamber' of the royal house, and another on the west leading to the other chambers behind.[79] As depicted in 1814 the church had a south doorway and a small western belfry, weatherboarded, with a shingled spire.[80] In 1818 it measured 56 ft. by 22½ ft.[81] It thus seems that between 1578 and the early 19th century it was lengthened, widened, and otherwise altered. The lengthening may be accounted for by the addition of the belfry, which in 1818 measured about 14 ft. by 19 ft. at the base.[82] Basil Champneys, who surveyed the church in 1874, thought it had been largely rebuilt in brick about 100 or 150 years earlier, but that the base of the tower was of heavy ancient masonry, indicating that a stone tower had been planned.[83] Another writer suggested that this masonry came from the ruins of the king's house,[84] and in general it is not unlikely that the reconstruction of the chapel was carried out in the early 18th century, to fit it better for parochial use after the house had become derelict. Repairs and alterations to the chapel were certainly in progress between 1705 and 1709, including the removal of the communion table to the east end.[85] The weatherboarding and shingles of the belfry were repaired in 1743.[86] A gallery was first mentioned in 1745.[87] Substantial repairs were carried out in 1808–11.[88] In 1836 the church was enlarged by the addition of a structurally separate chancel, and the gallery was rebuilt.[89]

A church organ was procured for the first time in 1856; before that the singing was accompanied by an orchestra.[90] A new organ, given in 1863, was transferred to the new church and served until 1902.[91] In 1552 the chapel had two small bells.[92] It was stated in 1608 that one bell had been taken away by a churchwarden during a dispute over his accounts.[93] Whether it was recovered is not clear, but in and after the late 18th century there was only one bell.[94] That was probably the one bought in 1725, which may have been recast from an earlier bell or bells.[95] It was removed to the new church, where it served until 1897.[96] The church plate all dated from the early 19th century.[97] The sepulchral monuments, which included several of the late 17th and 18th centuries, were also removed to the new church. The first burial in the chapelyard is said to have been in 1671.[98] The yard was then very small, but was enlarged in 1732, 1833, and 1878.[99]

The church of *ST. JOHN THE EVANGELIST*, consecrated in 1878 on the site of St. Mary's, was designed by Basil Champneys in the Decorated style.[1] It is of brick, faced with flint, and comprises chancel, nave, north aisle, organ chamber and vestry, and an embattled south-west tower. Much of the brick came from the old church. The building cost £5,276, towards which the main subscribers were David McIntosh, lord of the manor of Havering, and Mrs. Pemberton-Barnes. During the Second World War the church was slightly damaged by bombing.[2]

The font, which dates from the late 12th century, has an octagonal bowl of Purbeck marble.[3] In 1836, after long disuse, it was replaced in St. Mary's church.[4] Its base, of Bath stone, was added when the font was removed to the new church.[5] A new two-manual and pedal organ was installed in 1902.[6] The peal of 6 bells, replacing the one old bell, was cast in 1897 by Warner & Son.[7] Three were given by Mrs. Charlotte McIntosh, one each by Mrs. Pemberton-Barnes, Mrs. Emily Matthews of the Bower House, and G. P. Hope of Havering Grange. The church plate includes a silver cup and two patens, all given by John Heaton in 1818, a silver flagon given by Mrs. Pemberton-Barnes in 1897, and a silver spoon of 1847.[8]

Among monuments[9] brought from the old church are two of marble, to John Baynes (d. 1737), serjeant-at-law, and Sir John Smith-Burges, Bt. (d. 1790), both occupiers of the Bower House.[10] A marble slab on the north side of the chancel arch

[74] Smith, op. cit. 201.
[75] Ibid. 204. Wiseman had previously been lecturer at Romford.
[76] Smith, op. cit. 204–7.
[77] See plate facing p. 17. The original dedication, to St. Mary, was used in Havering at least until 1836: *Cal. Close R.* 1259–61, 61; Smith, op. cit. 168, 248. Salmon, *Essex* (1740), 244, gave the dedication as St. John, and was followed by later county historians. That dedication had apparently been adopted locally by 1847: *Ch. Plate Essex*, 13.
[78] Colvin, *King's Works*, ii. 956–9.
[79] E.R.O., T/M 229.
[80] Ogborne, *Essex*, 105.
[81] Smith, *Havering*, 158.
[82] Ibid.; cf. 172.
[83] Ibid. 156, cf. 171.
[84] Ibid. 157.
[85] E.R.O., D/P 64/8/1: 19 Jly. 1705; 20 Oct. 1707; 27 Sept. 1709.
[86] Ibid. 5 Apr. 1743.
[87] E.R.O., D/P 64/5/1.
[88] Smith, *Havering*, 163.
[89] Ibid. 166–8, 192 (illus.); photographs of the old church (interior and exterior) in the present church of St. John.
[90] Smith, op. cit. 169.
[91] Ibid.
[92] *Ch. Bells Essex*, 289.
[93] *E.R.* li. 148.
[94] *Hist. Essex by Gent.* iv. 315; Ogborne, *Essex*, 105; Smith, op. cit. 176.
[95] Smith, ibid.
[96] Ibid.
[97] *Ch. Plate Essex*, 13.
[98] Smith, *Havering*, 156.
[99] Ibid. 159, 161–2, 175, 183–90.
[1] Ibid. 173–5; E.R.O., D/CF 15/3 (Faculty); E.R.O., D/P 64/6/1A (Specification).
[2] C.C.L., Bp. Inskip's Recs. iii. 67; inscription in east window.
[3] R.C.H.M. *Essex*, ii. 126.
[4] Smith, op. cit. 145, 168.
[5] Ibid. 145.
[6] Ibid. 177.
[7] Ibid. 176–7; *Ch. Bells Essex*, 288–9.
[8] *Ch. Plate Essex*, 13.
[9] For the monuments: Smith, op. cit. 179–83; cf. Ogborne, *Essex*, 105–6.
[10] Smith, op. cit. 127, 130. For Sir J. Smith-Burges see also *V.C.H. Essex*, vi. 14.

commemorates Collinson Hall (d. 1880), the agriculturalist. It includes the mourning figure of Agriculture, a harvest scene, and a steam plough. There are several gravestones to the Cheekes of Pyrgo, 1688–1712, which were once in the private chapel at Pyrgo, from which they were removed to Havering chapel about 1770.[11]

Calvary mission church, Firbank Road, was opened in 1940.[12] It was a wooden building erected with the aid of contributions from Miss Pemberton-Barnes, to serve the northern part of Collier Row. It was closed in 1954, and was succeeded by St. James's church, Collier Row.[13]

NONCONFORMITY. None known.

EDUCATION. Dame Tipping Church of England primary school, North Road.[14] In 1724 Ann, Lady Tipping of Pyrgo (d. 1728) built a free school for 20 poor children on Havering Green.[15] By her will she endowed it with an annuity of £10 charged on Pyrgo Park.[16] In 1771 the schoolmaster was the curate.[17] By 1808 the school was ruinous and had closed.[18] It remained so until 1818 when it was pulled down and a new school was built in North Road from accumulated funds.[19] In 1833 the school had 21 boys and 16 girls. Michael Field of Pyrgo Park clothed the 20 charity children, and provided their books.[20] The new school was badly built, and in 1837 it was replaced, on the same site, by a National school for 60 children, provided by subscriptions, and grants from the government and the National Society.[21] At that period a few Havering children had free places at St. Edward's National school, Romford.[22] In 1874 a class for 25 infants was opened in a cottage on the Green. It moved in 1881 to a new classroom in the National school. In 1891 the school was rebuilt for 112. Under a Board of Education order of 1905 half Lady Tipping's annuity became payable to the local education authority; the other half was to be retained by the school managers.[23] The school was reorganized in 1936 for mixed juniors and infants.[24] In 1953 it was awarded Controlled status by Essex county council.[25] In 1964, when the teacher's house was sold, it was said that the annuity had not been paid for many years.[26] Since 1965 the school has been administered by Havering L.B.C.

CHARITIES FOR THE POOR. Joachim Matthews of Gobions in Romford, by will proved 1659, gave 20 marks to each of the five wards of Romford side.[27] The charity did not become effective until 1687, when Havering received £20 as its share of the capital and interest. The money was placed on bond with Edward Cheeke (d. 1707) of Pyrgo, whose heirs continued to pay interest on it at least until 1747, and probably until 1778. By 1787 payments had ceased, and there is no evidence that they were resumed.

Lady Tipping's gift for the school is treated elsewhere.[28]

HORNCHURCH

HORNCHURCH, about 12 miles east-north-east of the city of London, forms the southern part of the London borough of Havering.[1] It was a large industrial village until the 1920s, when it rapidly became a dormitory suburb.

The ancient parish of Hornchurch, which was conterminous with the royal manor and liberty of Havering, contained 16,100 a., divided into eight wards. 'Romford side', comprising the five northern wards, became independent of Hornchurch, gradually forming the separate parishes of Romford (four wards) and Havering. 'Hornchurch side' comprising the three (later two) southern wards, with 6,783 a., remained under Hornchurch parish vestry, and from the earlier 19th century constituted the parish of Hornchurch. The following account is restricted to that smaller area, with a few obvious exceptions. Hornchurch parish became an urban district in 1926. The district was extended in 1934 and 1935 to include Upminster, Rainham, Wennington, Cranham, and parts of Great Warley and North Ockendon, all of which were in Chafford hundred. In 1965 the urban district was united with Romford M.B. to form the London borough of Havering.

Hornchurch adjoins Dagenham to the east, extending from the Thames north-east for about 6 miles. The ancient parish church stands in a commanding position 4 miles from the river, on a hill 100 ft. above sea-level. Hornchurch village grew up on the gravel terrace below and west of the church. South of it were Hornchurch marshes, to the north the heavy London clay. The north-east corner of the parish comprising the manors of Gubbins and Redden Court, became known in the later 19th cen-

[11] *Hist. Essex by Gent.* iv. 316.
[12] C.C.L., Bp. Inskip's Recs., ii. 128.
[13] Inf. from Mr. W. S. Moore of Collier Row, who has a photograph of the mission church. For St. James's church see below, p. 87.
[14] Unless otherwise stated this account is based on Smith, *Havering*, 229–38.
[15] Ogborne, *Essex*, 108; *Hist. Essex by Gent.* iv. 315; E.R.O., Q/HM 1.
[16] *Rep. Com. Char.* [1087], p. 723 (1837–8), xxv (1); Smith, *Havering*, 229.
[17] *Hist. Essex by Gent.* iv. 315–16.
[18] E.R.O., D/AEM 2/4.
[19] *Rep. Com. Char.* (1837–8), p. 723; Smith, *Havering*, 232, 234.
[20] *Educ. Enquiry Abstract*, H.C. 62, p. 278 (1835), xli; *Rep. Com. Char.* (1837–8), p. 723.
[21] *Essex Standard*, 30 June 1837.
[22] *White's Dir. Essex* (1848), 380.
[23] Ed. 49/2123.
[24] Inf. from Essex Educ. Dept.
[25] E.R.O., C/ME 47, p. 254.
[26] Char. Com. Files.
[27] Smith, *Havering*, 245–7; see below, p. 97.
[28] See above.
[1] O.S. Map 2½", sheets TQ 48, 58, 59. This article was completed in 1976.

tury as Harold Wood, from the railway station there. It must be distinguished from Harold Wood ward of Romford side, which lay farther north. The river Rom, continuing as the Beam, flows south to the Thames, forming Hornchurch's western boundary.[2] South-west of the old village it is joined by the river Ravensbourne, formerly Bolles or Bowles brook, coming from Gidea Park, in Romford.[3] The river Ingrebourne, which also flows south to the Thames, is Hornchurch's eastern boundary, with Upminster and Rainham. It was sometimes known in the Middle Ages as the Bourne or the Haveringesheth.[4] It is joined at Harold Wood by Paine's brook, coming from Harold Hill, in Romford.[5]

Roman remains, sufficient to prove a settlement, have been found at Mardyke farm, south Hornchurch.[6] In 1086 the name Havering was applied without distinction to the whole of that large manor, and it is not until the middle of the 12th century that the records begin to show the pattern of settlement in fuller detail. By the 1150s the king's house stood in its park by Havering Green.[7] In *c.* 1158 Henry II gave land at Havering, i.e. Suttons in south Hornchurch, and by 1163 also the church of Havering, i.e. Hornchurch, to the hospice of St. Nicholas and St. Bernard, Montjoux (Valais, Switzerland): that was the origin of Hornchurch priory, which was built beside Hornchurch church.[8] Since the parish church was already there, Hornchurch village was probably a well-established settlement by *c.* 1158. The name Hornchurch was first recorded in 1222.[9] From the 13th century onwards Hornchurch was a flourishing community, with at least 10 subordinate manors, several other farms, and a leather industry.[10] In 1522–3 it contained 156 taxpayers, of whom 56 were in the 'town' ward, 73 in South End, and 27 in North End.[11] Over the whole area that represents one taxpayer to 43·5 acres, a density only a little lower than in Romford side, where the corresponding figure was 42·35. The town ward, i.e. Hornchurch village, had a very small area, and thus a relatively dense population.[12] In 1670 the three wards contained a total of 185 houses, compared with 364 in Romford side.[13] This suggests that between 1523 and 1670 Hornchurch did not grow much, and was far outstripped by Romford. It was, however, more populous in 1670 than Dagenham, a neighbouring parish of similar area.[14] In 1801 the population was 1,331.[15] It rose slowly to 2,186 in 1831, but then remained almost stationary until the 1870s. It increased to 3,841 in 1891, 9,461 in 1911, and 28,417 in 1931. Later figures were for the enlarged urban district: 90,800 (estimated) in 1938,[16] 104,082 in 1951, and 131,014 in 1961. At each of the last two dates about 70 per cent were in Hornchurch parish.[17]

In the Middle Ages the main street of the village was Pell (now High) Street, probably named from the leather industry.[18] At the east end of the street, nearly opposite the church, a hoard of 448 silver pennies of *c.* 1223–60, with a few contemporary Scottish and Irish coins, was found in 1938.[19] The dissolution of Hornchurch priory in 1391 had little effect on the topography of the village. The priory buildings seem to have been adapted to serve as the Rectory (Hornchurch Hall), east of which the Vicarage was built in the year 1399–1400. In *c.* 1618 most of the houses in the village were concentrated in that street, but there were a few others in Billet Lane, North Street, and Suttons Lane.[20] There were hamlets south of the village at Hacton and South End, north in Hay Street (now Wingletye Lane) and at Hardley (now Ardleigh) Green, west at Maylards Green, and north-west at Havering Well.[21] The hamlet at Havering Well already existed in the later 13th century.[22] There was still a well there in *c.* 1777.[23] Among other topographical features in *c.* 1618 were the park at Bretons, about 2 m. SW. of the village, a large area of inclosed and common marsh, and Havering gulf, an inlet created by a recent breach in the east bank of the river Beam.[24]

From the 17th century to the 19th Hornchurch was a residential area much favoured by the gentry, for whom many of the older houses were improved or rebuilt, and some new ones built.[25] Otherwise the settlement pattern changed little until the early 19th century, when agricultural prosperity tended to attract farmers rather than gentry, and at the same time a brewery, and an iron-foundry making farm machinery, were opened.

Hornchurch village was at first by-passed by the railways, but Harold Wood lay on the Great Eastern main line, and the first suburban building in the parish was there. In 1866 300 a. of Gubbins farm were bought by a group of developers led by Hugh Campbell, M.D., of Margaretting, W. R. Preston, a Brentwood solicitor, and A. G. Robinson, of Warley Place, Great Warley.[26] The Harold Wood Estate Co. was formed to build a new town there, and contracted with the Great Eastern Railway for the building of a station in Gubbins Lane, on the main London–Colchester line. In February 1868, when the station was opened, the King Harold public house had been built, new roads laid out between the station and Colchester Road, the London Eastern District Land Co. had bought 40 a. of the estate, under covenant to build large villas worth not less than £1,000 each, and a site had been reserved for a church. Harold Wood grew much more slowly than

[2] *P.N. Essex*, 3; J. G. O'Leary, *Dagenham Place Names*, 5.
[3] *Horn. Docs.* no. 438: Bollesbroke (date 1303); *Map of Essex* (1777) (Bowles brook).
[4] *P.N. Essex*, 7; *Cal. Chart. R.* 1226–57, 320.
[5] *P.N. Essex*, 9, 116.
[6] *V.C.H. Essex*, iii. 148; Lewis, *Rainham*, 3.
[7] See p. 13.
[8] *V.C.H. Essex*, ii. 195; and see below, p. 31.
[9] *P.N. Essex*, 112. For its meaning see below, p. 48.
[10] *Horn. Docs. passim*; S.C. 11/189 (extent of Havering 1250–1); New Coll. MS. 9744 (extent of Havering, *c.* 1355).
[11] E 179/108/150.
[12] The town ward lost its identity in the 18th century, and its area is not known exactly.
[13] E.R.O., Q/RTh 5.
[14] *V.C.H. Essex*, v. 267.
[15] *Census*, 1801 sqq.
[16] *Hornchurch Official Guide* (1938).
[17] Exact calculations are impossible because of boundary changes.
[18] *Horn. Docs.* nos. 2, 157, 435, 406; see below, p. 40.
[19] *Brit. Numismatic Jnl.* xxiii (3rd ser. iii), 274; *Romford Recorder*, 19 Aug. 1938.
[20] E.R.O., D/DU 162/1 (map). This map marks but does not name streets.
[21] For Hay St. see: E.R.O., D/DU 102/38, m. 12 (date 1438); *Map of Essex* (1777). For Hardley Green see *P.N. Essex*, 115.
[22] J.I. 3/35B, m. 49: *P.N. Essex*, 115.
[23] *Map of Essex* (1777).
[24] See p. 42.
[25] Houses shown on: *Map of Essex* (1777); O.S. Map 1″, Essex, sheet 1 (1805 edn.); O.S. Map 6″, Essex, LXVII, LXXIV, LXXV (surv. 1862–7); see below, p. 30.
[26] Paragraph based on: *Essex Weekly News*, 7 Feb. 1868. For Campbell see *Kelly's Dir. Essex* (1870). For early buildings at Harold Wood: plate facing p. 129.

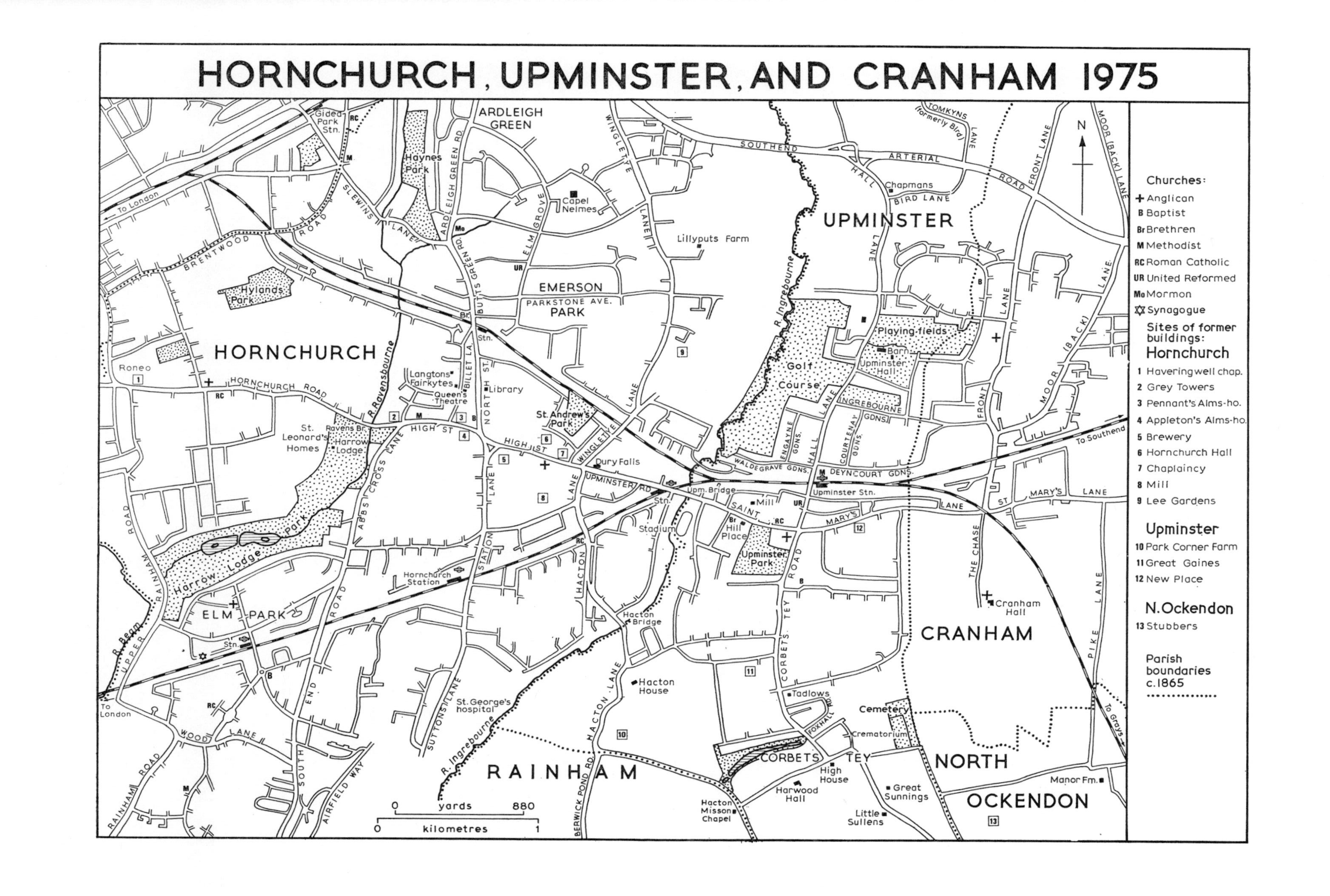
HORNCHURCH, UPMINSTER, AND CRANHAM 1975
Churches:
+ Anglican
B Baptist
Br Brethren
M Methodist
RC Roman Catholic
UR United Reformed
Mo Mormon
✡ Synagogue
Sites of former buildings:
Hornchurch
1 Haveringwell chap.
2 Grey Towers
3 Pennant's Alms-ho.
4 Appleton's Alms-ho.
5 Brewery
6 Hornchurch Hall
7 Chaplaincy
8 Mill
9 Lee Gardens
Upminster
10 Park Corner Farm
11 Great Gaines
12 New Place
N. Ockendon
13 Stubbers
Parish boundaries c.1865
HORNCHURCH
UPMINSTER
CRANHAM
RAINHAM
NORTH OCKENDON
ARDLEIGH GREEN
EMERSON PARK
ELM PARK
CORBETS TEY
Gidea Park Stn.
Haynes Park
Hylands Park
Capel Nelmes
Lillyputs Farm
Chapmans
TOMKYNS (formerly Bird) LANE
BIRD LANE
SOUTHEND ARTERIAL ROAD
HALL LANE
FRONT LANE
MOOR (BACK) LANE
BRENTWOOD ROAD
SLEWINS LANE
ARDLEIGH GREEN RD.
BUTTS GREEN RD.
ELM GROVE
WINGLETYE LANE
PARKSTONE AVE.
Roneo
HORNCHURCH ROAD
R. Ravensbourne
R. Ingrebourne
R. Beam
Langtons
Fairkytes
Queen's Theatre
BILLET LA.
NORTH ST.
Library
St. Andrew's Park
Dury Falls
HIGH ST
St. Leonard's Homes
Ravens Br.
Harrow Lodge
Harrow Lodge Park
ABBS CROSS LANE
STATION LANE
UPMINSTER RD
Upm. Bridge
Stn.
Stadium
Hornchurch Station
HACTON LANE
Hacton Bridge
Hacton House
St. George's hospital
SUTTONS LANE
UPPER RAINHAM ROAD
RAINHAM ROAD
WOOD LANE
SOUTH END ROAD
AIRFIELD WAY
BERWICK POND RD.
To London
To Southend
To Grays
Golf Course
Playing fields
Barn
Upminster Hall
INGREBOURNE GDNS.
ENGAYNE GDNS.
COURTENAY GDNS.
WALDEGRAVE GDNS.
DEYNCOURT GDNS.
Upminster Stn.
Mill
Hill Place
Upminster Park
SAINT MARY'S LANE
ST MARY'S LANE
CORBETS TEY ROAD
THE CHASE
Cranham Hall
PIKE LANE
Tadlows
FOXHALL RD.
Cemetery
Crematorium
High House
Harwood Hall
Hacton Misson Chapel
Great Sunnings
Little Sullens
Manor Fm.
0 yards 880
0 kilometres 1
N

intended, however, and until the First World War was hardly more than a village. There was little local employment. Prosperous commuters, whom the developers had hoped initially to attract, could find pleasanter suburbs nearer London like Wanstead, Woodford, and Loughton, while poor clerks could choose between the thousands of terrace houses of Stratford, Leyton, or Manor Park.[27] The original development soon petered out. In 1877 the estate was bought by John Compton, who built the Grange as his own residence, and played the part of the local squire, while promoting further building, mainly to the south of the railway.[28] Among his tenants was one of the original developers, W. R. Preston, who *c.* 1868 had built the mansion of Harold Court, on the Upminster side of the parish boundary, and later had become the sewage farmer of Brentwood town. The last enterprise ended in Preston's bankruptcy and flight in 1881.[29]

In 1876 Hornchurch was a 'large and busy-looking' industrial village.[30] When the railway station was opened there in 1885 the village was brought within a half-hour journey of London. This was expected to 'open up a new field for the speculative builder'.[31] It did not happen immediately, but in 1895 William Carter, of Parkstone (Dors.), bought the southern part of the manor of Nelmes, comprising 200 a., and some adjoining land, and began to build the Emerson Park estate.[32] Carter, a large developer in several counties, is thought to have named Emerson Park and its roads from his personal associations. By *c.* 1905 his company, then Homesteads Ltd., had built over 200 houses in Ernest and Herbert Roads, Parkstone Avenue, and adjoining roads.[33] Emerson Park was planned as an exclusive garden suburb, with many plots of an acre or more. The original prices ranged from £300 to £1,000. In 1901 the northern 241 a. of Nelmes was sold for similar development, which by 1904 was taking place in Elm Grove and Woodland Avenue, to the designs of Clare & Ross, architects.[34] By 1914 building was also in progress west of Emerson Park in Walden Road and Wickham Avenue, south of the village in Station Lane and adjoining roads, and also in Harrow Drive, north of Hornchurch Road.[35] Meanwhile Hornchurch was being affected by the expansion of Romford, southwards from Brentwood Road.

In the 1920s and 1930s there was rapid building throughout the central and northern parts of Hornchurch. At Harold Wood estates were laid out in the Church Road area, at Redden Court, and to the west of Gubbins Lane. New suburbs sprang up around the old village, at Ardleigh Green, and in the west of the parish at Elm Park, where a new railway station was built. By 1939 north Hornchurch formed a continuous built-up area with Romford. In south Hornchurch there had also been some building between Rainham and New Roads. After the Second World War large housing estates were built at Elm Park and south Hornchurch, and there was large-scale industrial development on Hornchurch marshes. By 1965 the only large area of open land was the former R.A.F. station at Suttons. That had been in military use almost continuously from 1915 to 1963, when it was put up for sale. By 1976 the western side of it was being built on, and gravel-digging was in progress on the remainder.

Most of the houses built since 1918 are semi-detached or in short terraces. Those in the north of the district were sold mainly to owner-occupiers. At Elm Park and south Hornchurch a large proportion of those built since 1945 are council houses. At Harold Wood, where land was cheap, and the shrinkage of the heavy clay tended to damage two-storey houses, a number of small bungalows were built in the 1920s and 1930s. Large detached houses continued to be confined mainly to Emerson Park and Nelmes. During the past 15 years flats have become more common, notably at Mardyke, where the council built a group of tower blocks.

In the Middle Ages Hornchurch's communications with London seem to have depended mainly on the road running west from the village, on the line of the present Hornchurch and Rush Green Roads, to Becontree Heath, in Dagenham, thence by Green Lane to Ilford. That was the road often described, in and after the 13th century, as the road from Hornchurch to London, or from Hornchurch to Ilford.[36] The main London–Colchester road formed the NE. boundary of the parish. In the 17th and 18th centuries travellers towards Colchester could join it via Ardleigh Green, by Hay Street (Wingletye Lane), and Gubbins Lane, or by Upminster and Brentwood.[37] Hay Street, mentioned in 1438, took its name from the Hay (enclosure) and Hay Green, near Lilliputs Farm; its present name probably came from Wingletye Hill.[38] Gubbins Lane, named from the manor, was mentioned in 1601.[39] In the south of the parish there were lanes leading west to Dagenham and Barking, and east to Rainham and Tilbury. About 1810 the Tilbury Fort turnpike trust shortened and improved that route by building New Road through Hornchurch.[40] The spinal N–S road in that part of the parish left Hornchurch Road at Abbs Cross (mentioned 1514),[41] and followed the course of the present Abbs Cross Lane and South End Road. The lane leading south from the village to Suttons, now Station Lane and Suttons Lane, seems to have been known in the 13th–15th centuries as Lake Street.[42] The lake from which the street was named existed in 1297 and 1320.[43] It may have been on the site of the railway sidings south of Hornchurch station, which is marshy ground several feet lower than the adjoining road.[44] Modern growth

27 Cf. *V.C.H. Essex*, iv. 111–12; v. 1–63; vi. 47, 49, 164, 181–2, 320, 338.
28 E.R.O., *Sale Cat.* B1086; *Strat. Expr.* 31 July 1886, 25 Oct. 1890; see below, p. 35.
29 Wilson, *Upminster* (1881), 197–8; *Strat. Expr.* 5 Nov. 1881. For Harold Court see below, p. 146.
30 Thorne, *Environs Lond.* (1876).
31 Perfect, *Village of Hornchurch*, 119.
32 Ibid. 119–20; E.R.O., Sage Coll., *Sale Cats.* vol. ii. 5 and 8; *Sale Cat.* A150.
33 E.R.O., T/P 67/5 (extract from *St. James's Review, c.* 1905).
34 E.R.O., Sage Coll., *Sale Cats.* vol. ii. 8; E.R.O., *Sale Cat.* A150.
35 O.S. Map 1″, sheet 107 (rev. 1914); *Kelly's Dir. Essex* (1914).
36 *Horn. Docs.* nos. 271, 300 etc.; *E.A.T.* N.S. xvi. 180; E.R.O., D/DU 162/1 (map, *c.* 1618); cf. *V.C.H. Essex*, v. 186.
37 J. Ogilby and W. Morgan, *Map of Essex, 1678*; *Map of Essex* (1777).
38 E.R.O., D/DU 102/28, m. 12; *P.N. Essex*, 115; O.S. Map 6″, Essex, LXVI and LXXIV (surv. 1862–71).
39 E.R.O., Q/SR 153/14.
40 *V.C.H. Essex*, v. 268.
41 *P.N. Essex*, 113.
42 *Horn. Docs.* nos. 338, 410, 448.
43 Ibid. 261–2.
44 O.S. Map 2½″, TQ 58.

has, in the main, preserved the lines of the old roads, but there are exceptions. The Southend Arterial road, opened in 1925, ran through the north-east corner of the parish, severing Ardleigh Green Road and Wingletye Lane, the northern ends of which became Bryant Avenue and Redden Court Road respectively.[45]

Dagenham Beam bridge, which carried the old road to Dagenham, and Beam bridge, carrying New Road, have been mentioned elsewhere.[46] So have Red (or Rainham), Hacton, Upminster, Cockabourne, and Putwell bridges over the Ingrebourne, and Paine's bridge over Paine's brook.[47] Wye or Bowles bridge, carrying an ancient lane, now upper Rainham Road, over the Ravensbourne, is the successor to a bridge dating from the 13th century or earlier.[48] Ravens bridge, mentioned in 1777, carries Hornchurch Road over the Ravensbourne.[49] Noreyses bridge (1325)[50] probably carried Suttons Lane over the stream, a tributary of the Ravensbourne, which runs just south of High Street.

In 1769 a stage-coach ran through Hornchurch to London on five days a week.[51] There was still only one coach a day in 1838.[52] Many other coaches could be boarded at Romford.[53] Romford railway station, on the Eastern Counties (later Great Eastern) main line was opened in 1839. Harold Wood station (1868) mentioned above was on the same line. Squirrels Heath (later Gidea Park) station (1910), also on the Great Eastern line, was in Romford parish but was convenient for dwellers in Ardleigh Green. The London, Tilbury & Southend line from Barking to Upminster was opened in 1885, with a station at Hornchurch, continued to East Horndon in 1886 and Pitsea in 1888.[54] Elm Park and Upminster Bridge stations, on that line, were opened by 1937.[55] Emerson Park station, on the London, Tilbury & Southend branch between Romford and Upminster, was opened in 1909.[56]

Postal services have always been provided through Romford.[57] Hornchurch had a receiving house by 1838.[58] There was a telegraph office by 1874.[59] By 1922 there were a few Hornchurch subscribers on the Romford telephone exchange.[60]

Most of old Hornchurch has disappeared during the past 50 years.[61] In 1923 there were thought to be 25 houses in the parish built before 1714.[62] Nine of them had gone by 1953, but there were still at least 50 built before 1800.[63] In 1976 only 16 of the 50 survived. Destruction has been the greatest in the village, which has become a shopping centre. It was stated in 1917 that the village 'may generally be described as of the 17th century.'[64] In 1953 at least 32 pre-19th-century houses remained there, but in 1976 only 10.

During the Middle Ages there were manor-houses on 12 sites. Hornchurch Hall was in the village. Suttons, Bretons, Dovers, Mardyke, Maylards Green and Wybridge, and Whybridge (Rands) were south of the village, Gubbins, Lee Gardens, Nelmes, and Redden Court north of it. In 1976 only two former manor-houses survived: Bretons, dating from the late 17th century, and the Grange, built in 1884 to replace Gubbins. Nelmes, a fine manor-house dating from the 16th century, was demolished in 1967, but one of its out-buildings remains as Capel Nelmes, a 16th-century structure much remodelled in the present century. Of the other large domestic buildings known to have existed before the 19th century only six survive. Albyns, Dury Falls, and Lilliputs date from the 17th century, Langtons, Fairkytes, and Harrow Lodge from the eighteenth.

Albyns, South End Road, takes its name from the Albyn family, recorded in the 13th century and later.[65] The east end of the present building is part of a timber-framed house of the 17th century. The initials TC and the date 16 [20?] are scratched on the plaster of the first-floor landing. The main, south range appears to have been reconstructed and given a a brick front in the 18th century. Dury Falls, Upminster Road, was named from the family of Doryval alias Alwy, who lived in that part of Hornchurch from *c.* 1230 to *c.* 1380.[66] It is an early-17th-century timber-framed house extended and altered in the 19th century.[67] Lilliputs, Wingletye Lane, is a 17th-century timber-framed house encased in brick in the early 18th century. An embanked pond SW. of the house is probably an early-18th-century canal. The present name is first recorded in 1777, but a building there is shown as 'new house' *c.* 1618.[68] The site seems to have been part of a tenement called Mayland alias Drywoods in the Lane, which can be traced from 1345.[69] An old house called Drywoods, adjoining Lilliputs to the SE., was demolished some years before 1917.[70]

Langtons stands on an ancient site in Billet Lane. In 1489 it was also called Marchauntes, a name previously recorded in 1446.[71] It was rebuilt early in the 18th century as a red-brick mansion of three storeys and five bays. Some of the original rooms survive behind the south front. Later in the 18th century canted wings of two storeys were added to the east and west. By 1777 Langtons had a landscaped park stretching down to High Street.[72] The central part of that is preserved as a public garden. Among the ancillary buildings of the 18th century are a stable-

[45] Min. of Transport, *Opening of London–Southend Road.* (1925).
[46] *V.C.H. Essex*, v. 268.
[47] See pp. 60, 126, 146.
[48] *P.N. Essex*, 114.
[49] Ibid. 115.
[50] *Horn. Docs.* no. 387.
[51] E.R.O., D/P 115/28/8.
[52] *Robson's Dir. Essex* (1838).
[53] See p. 60.
[54] Perfect, *Village of Hornchurch*, 116–18; *Havering Hist. Rev.* i. 5.
[55] *Kelly's Dir. Essex* (1937).
[56] K. A. Frost, *The Upminster Branch*, 13–14.
[57] See p. 60.
[58] *Robson's Dir. Essex* (1838).
[59] *Kelly's Dir. Essex* (1874).
[60] Ibid. (1922).
[61] For the topography of the old village: *Havering Hist. Rev.* vi. 2; vii. 2.
[62] R.C.H.M. *Essex*, iv. 71–4.
[63] Inf. from Dept. of Environment.
[64] Perfect, *Village of Hornchurch*, 20.
[65] *Horn. Docs.* (index). For deeds of Albyns: E.R.O., D/DB T1076/17; D/DU 296 and 651/116.
[66] *E.A.T.* N.S. xx. 279.
[67] Cf. R.C.H.M. *Essex*, iv. 72; Perfect, *Village of Hornchurch*, 45. See also: E.R.O., D/DNe 736; D/DU 651/122; Sage Coll., *Sale Cats.* vol. ii. 4.
[68] *Map of Essex* (1777); E.R.O., D/DU 162/1 (map).
[69] *Horn. Docs.* no. 46; E.R.O., D/DHt T362/1; ibid. D/DSx 162; D/DC 41/185; D/Dx T44, T258; D/DC 23/390; D/DU 544/3.
[70] Perfect, *Village of Hornchurch*, 54.
[71] S.C. 2/172/35; E.R.O., D/DU 102/35.
[72] *Map of Essex* (1777).

block, an orangery, and a gazebo.[73] In the later 18th and early 19th centuries Langtons belonged to the Massu family, silk merchants of London.[74] The house was remodelled early in the present century, when the south front was rebuilt, part of the ground floor was opened into a staircase hall, and a large billiard room was added to the west. In 1929 Langtons was given to Hornchurch U.D.C. by Varco Williams and his daughter Mrs. E. V. Parkes.[75] It was used as the council offices from 1929 until 1965. In 1976 it was occupied by the superintendent registrar for Havering.

Fairkytes, Billet Lane, was recorded from 1520.[76] The present house of five bays, with two storeys and attics, was built in the mid 18th century and has an original staircase with turned balusters. It was refronted and enlarged in the 19th century. Thomas Wedlake lived there in the early 19th century, and opened an ironworks on the opposite side of Billet Lane.[77] Joseph Fry, son of the prison reformer Elizabeth Fry, lived at Fairkytes from *c.* 1870 until his death in 1896.[78] Fairkytes was a public library from 1953 to 1967.[79] In 1976 it was Havering Art Centre.

Harrow Lodge, Hornchurch Road, is a stuccoed building of two storeys with a slate roof, said to have been built in 1787.[80] It was damaged by fire in 1858.[81] It was a public library from 1936 to 1967. In 1944 it was damaged by a flying bomb.[82]

Among the oldest houses which have disappeared in the present century, were the Chaplaincy,[83] Bush Elms, Hacton Farm, Mount Pleasant Farm, and the White House. Bush Elms, Hornchurch Road, was probably named from the family of William le Busch (fl. 1269).[84] In 1923 some 13th-century glazed tiles were still preserved in an out-building there.[85] Deeds of the property survive from 1612.[86] Hacton Farm, Hacton Lane, which must be distinguished from Hactons in Upminster,[87] is thought to have been rebuilt in the late 16th century.[88] In 1594 it was one of the principal houses of Hornchurch, the seat of John Jackman.[89] John's father Edward Jackman (d. 1569), alderman of London, had bought it in 1561, and it remained in the Jackman family at least until 1634.[90] Mount Pleasant Farm, Southend Arterial Road, which has been demolished since 1953, was a timber-framed house dating from the 16th century, extended in the 18th century, and greatly altered in the 20th century.[91] It was called Wingletye in the 19th century, and it was probably identical also with North House, recorded from 1384.[92] North House was bought in 1502 by John Barrett and descended throughout the 16th century with Belhus in Aveley.[93] In the late 16th and the early 17th century the North House estate included the neighbouring tenements of Gowells, to the NW. and Hubbards, to the south.[94] No later record of Gowells has been found, but Hubbards Farm survived until the present century and gave its name to Hubbards Chase.[95] The White (formerly Grosvenor) House, North Street, was a weatherboarded house of the 16th or early 17th century.[96] It was demolished in 1957.[97]

Suttons Gate, Suttons Lane, was the country house of Sir Francis Prujean (d. 1666), physician, and remained in his family for over a century.[98] It was probably rebuilt in the 18th or earlier 19th century.[99] It was demolished in 1936.[1] Little Langtons, Billet Lane, dating from the late 17th or 18th century, was pulled down in 1961.[2] Wych Elm, Wingletye Lane, which has also disappeared, was thought to be one of the oldest houses in the parish, but its symmetrical front, of three bays with attics, was probably not older than the 18th century.[3] Grey Towers, a crenellated mansion in Hornchurch Road, was built in 1876 by Henry Holmes, owner of Hornchurch brewery.[4] Standing near the village, in a 50-acre park, it was the last country house built at Hornchurch, and it had only a short life. During the First World War it was occupied by the Army, eventually as a New Zealand base camp.[5] It was demolished in 1931, and the site became Grey Towers Avenue.[6]

Hornchurch had 8 inns in 1762, of which 4 were in the village.[7] In 1848 the corresponding numbers were 9 and five.[8] Of those existing in 1762 only the King's Head, High Street, still functions in its ancient buildings, which are timber-framed, and date from the 17th century.[9] The Bull, High Street, which in 1923 was thought to be a 16th-century building, extended south in the 18th century,[10] had been rebuilt by 1953.[11] The White Hart, High Street, said to have been of great age, was destroyed by fire in 1872 and since then has been twice rebuilt.[12] The

[73] For the orangery see E.R.O., Pictorial Coll.
[74] Perfect, op. cit. 38; E.R.O., D/DCm 1/11 (letters of Mrs. M. Massu).
[75] *E.R.* xxxix. 46; *Havering Hist. Rev.* iv. 30.
[76] *P.N. Essex*, 115; E.R.O., D/DQ 14/91. See plate facing p. 113.
[77] Perfect, op. cit. 41; see below, p.40.
[78] Perfect, op. cit. 43; *E.R.* vi. 17.
[79] See p. 45.
[80] Perfect, op. cit. 56.
[81] E.R.O., D/DU 651/174; H.R.L., Romford L.B. Mins. 11 Feb. 1858.
[82] E.R.O., C/W 1/2/59.
[83] For the Chaplaincy see p. 47.
[84] *P.N. Essex*, 115.
[85] R.C.H.M. *Essex*, iv. 73.
[86] E.R.O., D/DK T228/9–12; D/DU 544/1, 567/13, and 721/1–45.
[87] See p. 145. For the name: *P.N. Essex*, 132.
[88] R.C.H.M. *Essex*, iv. 73.
[89] Norden, *Essex*, 32 and map; cf. E.R.O., D/DU 162/1 (map, *c.* 1618).
[90] C.P. 25(2)/126/1614; C 142/153/35; E.R.O., D/DC 23/384; E.R.O., T/P 67/5, p. 117; *Visit. Essex* (Harl. Soc.), 426; *Genealogist*, iv. 229.
[91] Inf. from Dept. of Environment; Nat. Mon. Rec.
[92] E.R.O., D/DL T1/220; D/DU 102/27, m. 2, 102/28, m. 9*d*, 102/29, m. 10*d*., 102/35, m. 2. For Wingletye see O.S. Map 6″, Essex, LXVI (surv. 1862–71).
[93] *Cal. Close* 1500–09, 118; S.C. 2/172/40, m. 15*d*.
[94] E.R.O., D/DL M18, M19; E.R.O., D/DU 162/1.
[95] O.S. Map 6″, Essex, LXVI (surv. 1862–71); *Kelly's Dir. Essex* (1902–26), s.v. Wheaton, Geo., farmer. *Map of Essex* (1777) names this farm North House, but the 16th-century documents show that North House and Hubbards were not identical.
[96] R.C.H.M. *Essex*, iv. 73; Perfect, *Village of Hornchurch*, 20; inf. from Dept. of Environment.
[97] Inf. from Hornchurch library.
[98] Perfect, op. cit. 47; *D.N.B.*; Morant, *Essex*, i. 72; E.R.O., D/DK T44; *Map of Essex* (1777).
[99] Perfect, op. cit. 46 (photo).
[1] Inf. from Hornchurch library.
[2] Ibid.
[3] Perfect, op. cit. 51–2.
[4] Ibid. 48–51.
[5] Perfect, *Hornchurch during the Great War*.
[6] Inf. from Hornchurch library.
[7] E.R.O., D/DHt T225/6.
[8] *White's Dir. Essex* (1848), 376.
[9] Perfect, *Village of Hornchurch*, 20; R.C.H.M. *Essex*, iv. 72; *Havering Hist. Rev.* iii. 27; vi. 32 sqq.
[10] R.C.H.M. *Essex*, iv. 72.
[11] Inf. from Dept. of Environment.
[12] Perfect, *Village of Hornchurch*, 22.

present house, dating from *c.* 1935, is a large house dominating the island site at the junction of High Street and Station Lane. The Crooked Billet, Billet Lane, was closed *c.* 1870. The building, thought to be about 300 years old, had been demolished by 1917.[13] The Harrow, a thatched and weatherboarded house in Hornchurch Road, was rebuilt in 1894.[14] The Crown, Hornchurch Road, Havering Well, which claimed to date from 1433, had been almost entirely rebuilt by 1923.[15] The Cherry Tree, Rainham Road, recorded in 1773, was rebuilt in 1935.[16] The Albion, Dovers Corner, formerly the Canteen, was built *c.* 1880 to serve the London Rifle Brigade volunteers whose firing range was near.[17]

St. Leonard's, Hornchurch Road, formerly called Hornchurch Children's Home, was built in 1889 by the poor-law guardians of the parish of St. Leonard, Shoreditch, to the design of F. J. Smith.[18] It was designed as an improvement on the barrack type of home, and comprised 11 'cottages', each originally for 30 children, with school, workshops, bakery, swimming bath, infirmary, and other buildings, on an 80-acre site. It was extended between 1893 and 1895. The home was taken over by the L.C.C. in 1930, and in 1965 by the London borough of Tower Hamlets.

Hornchurch Rifle Volunteers were formed in 1860, and a drill hall was built by subscription in 1866.[19] Hornchurch Artillery Volunteers were formed in 1882.[20] In 1892 Henry Holmes of Grey Towers built a drill hall in High Street for them, but they were disbanded by 1898.[21] R.A.F. station Hornchurch originated in 1915, when a military airfield, to defend London from Zeppelins, was opened at Suttons farm.[22] That was closed in 1919, but reopened in 1924. During the Second World War fighter squadrons from Hornchurch were prominent in the Battle of France and the Battle of Britain. Flying ceased there in 1944, but the station was retained by the R.A.F. for other purposes until 1963, when the site was sold.[23]

Hornchurch cinema, Station Lane, was opened *c.* 1914, and closed in 1935.[24] The building, later the Queen's theatre, still survived in 1976. The Towers, later Odeon, cinema, High Street, was opened in 1936.[25] It became a bingo club *c.* 1972.[26] The Queen's civic theatre was opened in 1953 by Hornchurch U.D.C., which had bought the old cinema in Station Lane, and had formed a repertory company.[27] Management was vested in the Hornchurch Theatre Trust Ltd., which continues to receive grants from Havering L.B.C. and from the Arts Council of Great Britain. A new theatre, built to the design of R. W. Hallam, borough architect, Havering L.B.C., was opened in Billet Lane in 1975.[28]

Hornchurch was an early sporting centre. An annual wrestling match, held in Mill field on Christmas day for the prize of a boar's head, is said to have lapsed, but to have been revived in 1824.[29] It was last held in 1868.[30] Mill field was also being used for cock-fighting in 1769, and for prize-fighting in 1785.[31] Trotting races were being held in Whybridge park, south Hornchurch, in the 1860s.[32] Hornchurch cricket club, formed in 1783, was playing successfully in the following year.[33] Early in the 19th century the Hornchurch club was outstanding.[34] At that period home matches were played in Langtons park. A new Hornchurch club, formed in 1889, played in Grey Towers park up to the First World War.[35] In 1974 some 45 sports clubs were meeting in Hornchurch.[36] At that date there were also about 45 cultural and recreational societies. Those numbers did not include clubs and societies meeting in Romford, many of which were available to Hornchurch people. Hornchurch historical society, founded in 1959 has been publishing a journal since 1970, and has helped Havering borough council to open Upminster windmill and Upminster hall barn.

Among notable persons living in Hornchurch was Thomas Witherings (d. 1651), chief postmaster of Great Britain.[37] John Meyrick (d. 1599), vicar of Hornchurch, was later bishop of Sodor and Man.[38] A later vicar was the Puritan William Whitaker.[39] Sir Francis Prujean (d. 1666) is mentioned above. Augustine Garland (fl.1666), regicide, had an estate at Hornchurch.[40] Richard Morris (d. 1894),[41] philologist, and Sir Joseph Broodbank (d. 1948),[42] member of the Port of London Authority, lived at Harold Wood. John Hopkins (d. 1732), owner of Redden Court, was a miser of whose costly funeral Pope wrote:

> When Hopkins dies a thousand lights attend
> The wretch who living saved a candle's end.[43]

MANORS. All the manors in Hornchurch were subject to the manor of Havering.[44] The manors of *HORNCHURCH HALL* and *SUTTONS* formed the original endowment of Hornchurch priory, made by Henry II in two grants early in his reign.[45] One charter, probably of 1158, gave the priory land in Havering worth £25.[46] That was later known as Suttons, which lay about a mile south of Hornchurch

[13] Ibid.
[14] Ibid. 22–3.
[15] R.C.H.M. *Essex*, iv. 73.
[16] Lewis, *Rainham*, 114.
[17] Ibid. 113.
[18] Paragraph based on: inf. from St. Leonard's; Perfect, *Village of Hornchurch*, 126–31. See plate facing p. 49.
[19] Op. cit. 111–12.
[20] Ibid.
[21] Ibid.; *Strat. Expr.* 26 Nov. 1892; *Kelly's Dir. Essex* (1894, cf. 1898).
[22] Perfect, *Hornchurch during the Great War*; H. T. Sutton, *Raiders Approach: R.A.F. Hornchurch.*
[23] E.R.O., *Sale Cat.* B2874.
[24] *Havering Hist. Rev.* viii. 2; *Kelly's Dir. Essex* (1914); *Greater London Arts Assoc. Newsletter*, Feb. 1968.
[25] Inf. from Mr. L. Rose and Mr. K. Gasper; *Kelly's Dir. Essex* (1937).
[26] *Havering Official Guide* (1971, cf. 1973).
[27] *Greater London Arts Assoc. Newsletter*, Feb. 1968.
[28] Inf. from Havering L.B.C. See plate facing p. 32.
[29] *E.R.* iii. 140.
[30] Perfect, *Village of Hornchurch*, 14.
[31] Ibid. 15–16; E.R.O., D/P 115/28/8.
[32] Lewis, *Rainham*, 88.
[33] Perfect, op. cit. 135.
[34] Ibid. 137–9; E.R.O., D/P 115/28/8.
[35] Perfect, op. cit. 136, 140–1.
[36] *Havering L.B. List of Organisations* (1974).
[37] C. R. Clear, *Thomas Witherings and the birth of the Postal Service*; Terry, *Romford*, 178–9.
[38] *D.N.B.*
[39] Ibid.
[40] Ibid.
[41] Ibid.; *E.R.* iii. 162.
[42] *D.N.B.*
[43] *Poems of Alex. Pope*, ed. J. Butt (1963), 575 n., 582 (*Moral Essays*, iii, ll. 291–2); Lysons, *Lond.* i. 534.
[44] See p. 11.
[45] *E.A.T.* N.S. vi. 1–7; *Horn. Docs.* nos. 168 and 78.
[46] This grant is recorded in *Pipe R.* 1159 (P.R.S. i), 4, and later rolls.

village.[47] By the second charter, of the same date or a little later, the king endowed the priory with the church of Havering [i.e. Hornchurch] and its appurtenances. The priory itself was built on the north side of the church.[48] The rectorial glebe, around the church, became the nucleus of the manor of Hornchurch Hall.

During the 13th century the priory also acquired the manors of Newbury, at Havering, and Risebridge, at Romford. It also acquired various smaller properties at Hornchurch, of which the most important was a ½ virgate, lying south of Bretons, which in the earlier 13th century had belonged to Osbert de la Beme, from whose family it was known as Beme (or Beam) Land. In 1249 Osbert's daughter Beatrice, and her husband Thomas Gernet, granted Beam Land in fee to John Waleys.[49] It later passed to Robert Waleys, John's brother, who about 1260 granted it to Richard of Havering.[50] In 1270, or shortly before, Richard Elms (de Ulmis), who was probably identical with Richard of Havering, granted the tenement to Hornchurch priory.[51]

On the dissolution of the priory in 1391 all its Hornchurch estates were bought by William of Wykeham, bishop of Winchester, as part of his endowment of New College, Oxford.[52] In the 16th century the manor of Newbury was conveyed to the king and was merged in Pyrgo Park. The other estates remained with the college.[53] Hornchurch Hall, which was in effect a rectory manor, was from the 14th century usually leased along with the great tithes.[54] In 1663 its demesne comprised 306 a., of which 184 a. lay around the church and the remainder in scattered parcels elsewhere.[55] Suttons comprised 379 a., and Beam Land 58a. Including Risebridge (90 a.) and two fields near Wybridge (6 a.), the college then held 840 a. in Hornchurch. In 1846–9 New College's estates in the parish comprised 930 a., of which the largest parts were Hornchurch Hall (280 a.), and Suttons (406 a.).[56]

Hornchurch Hall was leased in the later 16th and earlier 17th century by the Legatt family,[57] in the later 17th century by the Thorowgoods,[58] and in the earlier 18th century by the notorious John Ward.[59] In the earlier 19th century it was for many years leased by the Bearblocks.[60]

New College sold Beam Land to Romford U.D.C. in 1895.[61] During the First World War part of Suttons was used as a military airfield.[62] After the war it was returned to farm use, but in 1924 the Air Ministry bought 129 a. of the farm and re-opened the airfield.[63] The college sold more of Suttons to the Air Ministry in 1931, smaller parts to Romford poor-law union (1922, 1929), Essex county council (1932–3) and Mrs. J. W. Standon (1930), and the last part to Mr. R. W. Beard in 1934.[64] They sold all the Hornchurch Hall land for development between 1927 and 1931.[65] Part of it was bought by Hornchurch U.D.C. for the Village recreation ground. Among several other purchasers were the British Land Co. and Mr. R. W. Beard.

The manor-houses of Suttons and Hornchurch Hall both occupied medieval sites. Suttons was extended between 1397 and 1400, when New College built a new kitchen and carried out repairs.[66] In 1917 the house was said to be entirely modern.[67] The last farmer, Thomas Crawford, occupied it until *c.* 1933.[68] It was later demolished. Hornchurch Hall, known before the 16th century as the Rectory, stood in High Street, opposite the church, and immediately west of the Vicarage. It was probably part of Hornchurch priory. When the Vicarage was built, between 1399 and 1400, it was divided from the Rectory by a wall.[69] In *c.* 1923 Hornchurch Hall was described as a 16th-century house with a 17th century chimney and a large modern addition on the south front.[70] Other evidence suggests that the south front was built in the later 18th or the earlier 19th century.[71] The house was damaged by bombing in 1940, and was demolished in 1941.[72]

The manor of *BRETONS* or *DANIELS* or *PORTER'S FEE* lay beside the Beam river, about 2 miles south-west of Hornchurch village. It probably took its first name from the Breton family, which lived at Hornchurch from the 12th century to the 14th.[73] Daniels and Porters seem to have been originally separate tenements, also named from families, which became attached to Bretons.[74] Daniels was held along with Bretons by 1446, but Porter's fee was still separate in the later 15th century.[75] William de Northtoft of Finchingfield, who was holding Bretons in 1355, was said to have acquired it from Richard de Stamyngden.[76] In that year John de Cokefield and William Spalding unsuccessfully conspired to gain possession of the manor by force, and by fabricating evidence to show that Northtoft was an illicit coiner.[77] In 1361 Northtoft conveyed Bretons to William Buckingham, chaplain, probably in trust.[78] The manor was later held by John Newmarche, from whom it passed by successive convey-

47 Cf. New Coll. MS. 9744, f. 162.
48 *Horn. Docs.* p. vi and no. 375.
49 *Horn. Docs.* nos. 54–6.
50 Ibid. no. 156.
51 Ibid. nos. 91, 506, cf. 505, 497; *Cal. Chart. R.* 1257–1300, 148.
52 Ibid. nos. 5, 20, 135; *Cal. Papal Reg., Letters,* iv. pp. 440–1.
53 For leases of Suttons in the 15th and 16th cents. see E.R.O., D/P 115/28/7.
54 New Coll. MS. 9744, f. 186; ibid. MSS. 2301 and 2302; E.R.O., T/M 153 (map dated 1663); E.R.O., D/P 115/28/7.
55 E.R.O., T/M 153.
56 I.R. 29/12/162 and 177.
57 E.R.O., Q/SR 30/32; E.R.O., D/DU 23/51; *Acts. of P.C.* 1626, 328; Perfect, *Village of Hornchurch,* 32.
58 Perfect, op. cit. 34; *E.R.* v. 30.
59 E.R.O., D/P 115/8/1A, 4 June, 3 Sept. 1716; D/DU 651/119: sale 1756 on Ward's bankruptcy. For Ward see *V.C.H. Essex,* v. 286–9.
60 Perfect, op. cit. 34; I.R. 29/12/177.
61 Inf. from New Coll.
62 H. T. Sutton, *Raiders Approach,* 19, 46.
63 Ibid. 63; inf. from New Coll.
64 Ibid.
65 Ibid.; E.R.O., Sage Coll. *Sale Cat.* A25.
66 New Coll. MSS. 6391, 6392, 6394.
67 Perfect, *Village of Hornchurch,* 35.
68 Sutton, *Raiders Approach,* 19, 46, 60, 63; *Kelly's Dir. Essex* (1933 cf. 1937).
69 New Coll. MS. 6394.
70 R.C.H.M. *Essex,* iv. 72.
71 Perfect, op. cit. 33 (photo); I.R. 30/12/177 (plan).
72 Inf. from Hornchurch Library.
73 *P.N. Essex,* 115; *Horn. Docs.* nos. 21, 136, 142, 232–3, 334, 377.
74 For the Daniel and Porter families see *Horn. Docs.* index.
75 *Cal. Inq. p.m. Hen. VII,* i. pp. 38, 515; and see below.
76 *Cal. Pat.* 1358–61, 232, 444. For the Northtoft family see also *V.C.H. Essex,* v. 199.
77 *Cal. Pat.* 1358–61, 232, 444.
78 *Cal. Close,* 1360–4, 250.

Hornchurch: Queen's Theatre

Little Warley: Ford Motor Co. Offices

North Ockendon Church: Canopy above tomb of Sir Gabriel Poyntz (d. 1608)

Hornchurch: Bretons, late-17th-century staircase

Upminster: Smock Windmill, Upminster Hill

ances, to Richard de Batheleye, to John Bredeford, and then, in 1373, to William, son of Geoffrey Chisleden.[79]

Sir Richard Arundel (d. 1419), was holding the manors of Bretons, Baldwins (Lee Gardens), and Mardyke in 1417, when he made his will before going to France with the army of Henry V.[80] He devised Bretons to his wife Alice for life, but after his death his executors were involved in a long struggle for possession of the manor against Joan, daughter of Sir John Newenton and widow of Roger Swinnerton.[81] She had inherited the manor of Redden Court. Her title to Bretons is not clear, but she may well have vindicated it, for in 1446, shortly after her death, the manor was conveyed to Thomas Scargill by trustees including Richard Newenton, presumably a relative of Joan.[82] Scargill was also holding Daniels by 1446.[83] He died in 1476, having directed that if his daughter died without heirs the manor should be sold.[84]

In 1501 Christopher Throckmorton conveyed Bretons to William Ayloffe (d. 1517), in whose family it remained for about 150 years.[85] Sir Benjamin Ayloffe, Bt., a prominent royalist during the Civil War, sold Bretons to meet the costs of sequestration imposed upon him by Parliament.[86] The purchaser was John Winniffe, who was holding the manor by 1659.[87] Winniffe soon sold Bretons to John Austen, alderman of London, from whom it descended to his son of the same name.[88] John Austen the younger was holding the manor in 1720. It was stated in that year that the entail had been cut, and that after Austen's death Bretons would pass to another family.[89] By 1742 the owner was John Hopkins, who also held Redden Court.[90] He died in 1772, leaving both manors to John Dare.[91] Bretons descended like Redden Court until 1858, when parts of the Hall-Dare estate were sold.[92] Bretons remained in the possession of the Hall-Dares until 1869, when it was bought by Romford local board for use as a sewage farm.[93] In 1976 the farm was being developed by Havering L.B.C. as a youth centre and sports ground.

The earliest surviving buildings at Bretons are the walls of a 16th-century barn, which formerly had a roof of nine bays, and other buildings south-east of the house.[94] Associated with these is some garden walling with bee boles, and the original house may have stood in the same area. The present house is of late-17th-century origin, and has some panelling and a fine main staircase of that date. It was much reconstructed by John Hopkins in the mid 18th century, when the external walling was rebuilt, most of the rooms were panelled, and the staircase was extended to the second floor, which was probably added then.[95] About the same time the walled garden was enlarged and the forecourt of the house was enclosed by a clairvoyée with central gates.

The manor of *DOVERS* or *NEWHALL* was beside the river Ingrebourne, opposite Rainham village. It was built up in the earlier 13th century by Richard of Dover, yeoman in the service of Robert Passelewe, deputy treasurer of England.[96] In 1235 Adam le Moigne and Agnes his wife, William Gilbert and Denise his wife, conveyed to Richard of Dover in fee a virgate of land, 7 a. meadow, and a mill in Havering.[97] This property was possibly identical with the virgate and mill said to have been given to Dover by Sir Hamon Passelewe, brother of Robert, in marriage with Hamon's daughter Alice.[98] Passelewe's relationship to the le Moignes and the Gilberts is not clear. Perhaps he had been their tenant. In 1247 Henry III confirmed to Richard of Dover $2\frac{5}{12}$ virgates and a water-mill, which Dover held of the king, $\frac{1}{4}$ virgate which Geoffrey Gernet once held, 95 a. new purpresture, and two fleets of water: the Mardyke (Beam) and Haveringsheth (Ingrebourne).[99] Richard of Dover, who also acquired Gooshayes in Romford, died in or before 1254.[1] The wardship of his young son John was given to Sir William of St. Armine.[2]

John of Dover died in or before 1299, leaving Newhall, so named for the first time, to John his son.[3] The latter died in 1334 leaving Newhall to his brother Philip (d. 1335), whose heir was his young son Richard of Dover.[4] Richard of Dover seems to have been the last of his line at Newhall. In *c.* 1355 the manor was held by Richard of Sutton, who had married Dover's widow Agnes.[5] By 1377 it had passed to Ralph Tyle.[6] In 1388 Tyle conveyed the manor to John Fresshe, mercer of London, who died holding Dovers, so named, in 1399.[7] Fresshe's trustees still held the manor in 1409, but it passed by 1412 to William Waldern, also a London mercer, and later to his widow, Margaret (d. 1428).[8] Richard Waldern, William's son, succeeded Margaret, and held Dovers until his death in 1454.

Richard Waldern left as coheirs his sisters Elizabeth, Joan, Eleanor, and Margaret.[9] One of them probably died without issue, for the youngest, Margaret, later wife of John Brewster, conveyed a third of the manor to Avery Cornburgh (d. 1487).[10] Cornburgh, who also held Gooshayes in Romford, left as heirs his sister Agnes Chambre and his nephew

[79] Ibid. 1369–74, 604.
[80] *Collectanea Topographica et Genealogica*, vi. 1–20. His infant son Henry had died in 1412: J. Weever, *Ancient Funerall Monuments*, 647.
[81] *Cal. Pat.* 1416–22, 274; *Cal. Close*, 1419–22, 97, 101; E.R.O., D/DU 102/46.
[82] E.R.O., D/DU 102/34, m. 5*d*; cf. Morant, *Essex*, i. 64.
[83] E.R.O., D/DU 102/35, m. 2.
[84] Terry, *Romford*, 58–9; *P.C.C. Wills* 1383–1558, ii. 469; *E.A.T.* N.S. xi. 323.
[85] S.C. 2/172/39, m. 24; *Cal. Close*, 1500–09, 82–3. For the Ayloffe pedigree see Morant, *Essex*, i. 69–70.
[86] Morant, *Essex*, i. 71; cf. *Cal. Cttee. for Compounding*, 849.
[87] E.R.O., T/P 195/2, ff. 22, 28–9.
[88] Ibid. f. 22.
[89] Ibid.: letter from William Blackburn explaining why his wife, daughter of Austen, would not inherit Bretons.
[90] Salmon, *Essex*, 255.
[91] *Gent. Mag.* 1772, 543; Ogborne, *Essex*, 146.
[92] See p. 38.
[93] H.R.L., Romford L.B. Mins. 27 Oct. 1868 sqq.; see below, p. 78.
[94] R.C.H.M. *Essex*, iv. 73.
[95] Morant, *Essex*, i. 71.
[96] *Close R.* 1237–42, 423. For Passelewe see *D.N.B.*
[97] *Feet of F. Essex*, i. 113.
[98] *Cal. Inq. p.m.* i, p. 295.
[99] *Cal. Chart. R.* 1226–57, 320: cf. *P.N. Essex*, 3, 7–8.
[1] *Cal. Inq. p.m.* i. p. 78.
[2] Ibid.; *Cal. Pat.* 1247–58, 398. St. Armine later held the manor of Dagenhams and Cockerels.
[3] *Cal. Inq. p.m.* iii. p 388.
[4] Ibid. vii, pp. 410, 455; *Cal. Close*, 1333–7, 382.
[5] New Coll. MS. 9744, f. 161v.
[6] *Rot. Orig.* (Rec. Com.), ii. 352; *Cal. Pat.* 1377–81, 140.
[7] *Cal. Pat.* 1385–9, 406; ibid. 1396–9, 198, 250, 403; *E.A.T.* N.S. xiv. 31.
[8] *Feet of F. Essex*, iii. 254; *Feud. Aids*, vi. 442; C 139/36.
[9] *Cal. Pat.* 1422–9, 534; C 139/152.
[10] *Cal. Inq. p.m. Hen. VII*, i. p. 104.

John Crafford. His third of Dovers evidently passed to Crafford.[11] The descent of the other two thirds after 1454 is not clear. In 1519 one third was settled on John Rodys and his wife Margaret.[12] The Craffords probably acquired the whole of the manor. Thomas Crafford (d. 1508) left a widow Alice, who was holding Dovers in 1510.[13] Richard Crafford (d. 1544) was probably Alice's heir.[14] Another Richard Crafford, and his wife Anne, who were holding Dovers in 1572, conveyed it in 1596 to Peter Collett, a London merchant.[15]

Collett (d. 1607) was succeeded by his daughters, Hester wife of Sir Anthony Aucher, and Sara wife of Sir Peter Hayman.[16] Mrs. Elizabeth de la Fontaine brought Hester's half of the manor in 1612, and in 1614 she also acquired an 80-year lease of Sara's half.[17] Mrs. de la Fontaine or one of her successors seems to have redeemed the lease, and by 1684 or earlier the whole manor was passing as freehold. In 1649 Dovers comprised about 350 a.[18] Mrs. de la Fontaine was apparently dead by then. The manor passed to Sir Erasmus de la Fontaine (d. 1672) whose executors sold it in 1684 to Robert Cowley (d. 1694).[19] At that period the manorial rights included quitrents from some 40 tenants, waifs and strays, fishing and fowling.[20] Robert Cowley devised the manor to his wife Grace (d. 1720). Under her will, and a previous settlement, the manorial rights and Great Dovers farm passed to her son Edmund Cowley, while Little Dovers farm, 104 a., passed to her grandson Robert Nash.[21]

The manorial rights and Great Dovers descended to Edmund Cowley's daughter Elizabeth, who in 1741 married the Revd. Thomas Durnford. Little Dovers passed on the death of Robert Nash (1752) to his brother James, who in 1769 bought the manorial rights and Great Dovers from Durnford. James Nash (d. 1786) was succeeded by his daughters Mary and Martha. Mary Nash, who outlived her sister and inherited the whole estate, died in 1797, leaving it to the Revd. Thomas Durnford the younger, son of the previous Thomas. In 1798 Durnford sold Dovers to Thomas Page (d. 1815). Page left it to his niece Ann Bayley, who in 1816 married Richard Reynolds. In 1849 Reynolds's Dovers estate comprised 298 a.[22] In 1862, after his death, it was put up for sale.[23] It was subsequently acquired by Edward Blewitt, who occupied Dovers *c.* 1870–95, and then let the farm to John Poupart.[24] The Poupart family later bought the freehold and held it until 1937, when Dovers, by then reduced to 69 a., was put up for sale after the death of Alfred Poupart.[25] The farm-house and grounds were bought in 1938 by the Roman Catholics as the site of the church of Our Lady of La Salette.[26]

The ancient manor-house of Dovers stood within a moat, part of which still survived in 1976, east of Rainham Road.[27] It was depicted in 1649 and *c.* 1750 as a substantial house with a central gabled porch.[28] In the 17th and 18th centuries it was called Great Dovers to distinguish it from Little Dovers, which had been built west of the road.[29] By 1849 the old manor-house had been demolished, and Little Dovers had been renamed Great Dovers.[30] In 1862 Great Dovers was said to be a 'modern built gentlemanly residence.'[31] In 1938 it became the Roman Catholic presbytery, and a 19th-century brick barn adjoining served as the temporary church.[32] The presbytery was rebuilt in 1968, but the barn still survived in 1976 as a church hall.[33]

The tenement or manor of *GOBYONS* or *GUBBINS* lay south of the Romford–Brentwood road, in and around Gubbins Lane, Harold Wood. It must be distinguished from Gobions or Uphavering[34] and from a house called Gobions on the east side of Collier Row common, though it probably took its name from the same family, Gobion. In 1507 the tenement of Gobyons was conveyed by Richard Fisher to Robert Matthew, and then by Matthew to William Fisher.[35] In 1517 Richard Fisher conveyed to Robert Matthew an unnamed tenement of some 200 a., including 10 a. marsh.[36] Robert Matthew, whose will was proved in 1542, was holding the manor of Gobyons when he died.[37] The manor was later held by Thomas Legatt (d. 1549), and descended to his son Thomas (d. 1556),[38] who also held Dagenhams in Romford.[39] In *c.* 1618 Gubbins was held by John Legatt, a younger son of the same family.[40]

Gubbins later passed in succession to the families of Bulkeley and Gould.[41] John Gould, who held it about the middle of the 18th century, was succeeded as owner by Thomas Hill (d. 1781).[42] Hill left a life interest in Gubbins, then a farm of 180 a., to his housekeeper, Mrs. Elizabeth Bayley, commonly called Hill (d. 1784). After her death it passed to Hill's niece Ursula (d. 1816) wife of William Perkins. In 1819 Mrs. Perkins's children sold the farm to Richard Reynolds, who had recently acquired Dovers by marriage to Ann Bayley. Whether Ann was related to Elizabeth Bayley is not clear. Reynolds owned and occupied Gubbins, comprising 169 a., for many years.[43] In 1862, after his death, it was put up for sale.[44] The farm-house, then called Great Gub-

[11] Cf. *L. & P. Hen. VIII*, i (1) (2nd edn.), p. 236.
[12] Ibid. iii (1), p. 95.
[13] P.C.C. 8 Bennett; *L. & P. Hen. VIII*, i (1), p. 236.
[14] E.R.O., D/AER 6, f. 157v.
[15] C.P. 25 (2)/129/1649; C.P. 25 (2)/138/1746.
[16] Wards 7/47/38.
[17] S.P. 14/202; E.R.O., D/DU 162/1.
[18] E.R.O., D/DU 186/1.
[19] E.R.O., D/DNe T19 (abstract of title to Dovers, 1662–1825, on which the following descent is based). For Sir Erasmus see *P.C.C. Wills* 1671–5 (Index Libr.), 62.
[20] E.R.O., D/DU 527/2.
[21] Cf. E.R.O., D/DU 186/1 (map of Dovers 1649, copied 1739 with added inf.).
[22] I.R. 29/12/177.
[23] E.R.O., Sage Coll. *Sale Cats.* vol. ii. 3.
[24] *Kelly's Dir. Essex* (1870 sqq.); H.R.L., Cornell MSS.
[25] *Kelly's Dir. Essex* (1899 sqq.); E.R.O., *Sale Cat.* B23.
[26] Lewis, *Rainham*, 77; see below, p. 140.
[27] E.R.O., D/DU 162/1 (map, *c.* 1618).
[28] E.R.O., D/DU 186/1 (map, 1649); cf. 186/2 (map, *c.* 1750).
[29] E.R.O., D/DU 572/2; *Map of Essex* (1777).
[30] I.R. 29 and 30/12/177.
[31] E.R.O., Sage Coll. *Sale Cats.* vol. ii. 3.
[32] Lewis, *Rainham*, 77.
[33] Inf. from Rainham R.C. church.
[34] See p. 69.
[35] S.C. 2/172/40, m. 24.
[36] S.C. 2/173/2, m. 19*d.*
[37] *E.A.T.* N.S. vi. 317.
[38] C 142/88/47; C 142/105/44.
[39] See p. 66.
[40] E.R.O., D/DU 162/1. There were several Johns in the family: cf. *Visit. Essex* (Harl. Soc.), 592; C 142/105/44.
[41] Ogborne, *Essex*, 133: where this information is wrongly linked with Gobions *alias* Uphavering.
[42] E.R.O., D/DNe T19: abstract of title 1781–1819.
[43] I.R. 29/12/177.
[44] E.R.O., Sage Coll. *Sale Cats.* vol. ii. 3.

bins, was on the site of the present Harold Wood hospital, but most of the fields lay east of Gubbins Lane. In 1866 most of the farm was bought by a group of developers, who proposed to lay out there the new town of Harold Wood.[45] The Eastern Counties railway (1840) had cut the farm in half. Harold Wood station was opened at that point in 1868.[46] Development was much slower than intended, however, and much of Harold Wood remained farmland until after the First World War. In 1877 the estate was bought by John Compton of Aldgate (Lond.), a retired Army tailor.[47] He and his successor, Henry Compton, lived at Harold Wood *c.* 1880–94.[48]

The manor-house of Gubbins was sufficiently important to be named on a county map in 1594.[49] It was probably the house, with 16 hearths, occupied in 1670 by John Grosvenor.[50] It seems to have been demolished early in the 18th century; according to a later description it was a large building with turrets at the corners 'in the ancient style'.[51] The farm-house which replaced it was in turn succeeded by the Grange, a large red-brick house built in 1884 by John Compton, which is now part of the hospital.[52]

The manor of *LEE GARDENS*, formerly *BALDWINS*, was on the east side of Wingletye Lane.[53] It must be distinguished from (Great) Gardens at Squirrels Heath.[54] Baldwins was named after a family recorded in the parish from the 13th century.[55] Sir Richard Arundel (d. 1419) devised Baldwins in trust to be sold to pay the balance of the purchase price of his manor of Mardyke.[56] Baldwins was said in 1446 to have belonged formerly to Ralph Uphavering.[57] In 1455 John Gobion conveyed it to Stephen Wylet and Joan his wife.[58] It was later held by William Malle, whose son Robert conveyed it in 1572 to John Legatt (d. 1607), who later bought Redden Court.[59] Legatt's heir was his son Thomas (d. 1623).[60]

In or about 1626 Thomas Legatt, probably son of the previous Thomas, conveyed Lee Gardens, by then so called, to William Hudson of Gray's Inn (Mdx.).[61] It was conveyed by Hudson in 1630 to William Harrison of London, and by Harrison in 1635 to Sir Henry St. George, also of London, who appears to have been related by marriage to the Legatts.[62] In 1649 Thomas St. George sold it to Christopher Hoddesdon (d. 1660).[63] Hoddesdon's son and heir, also named Christopher, appears to have died some time after 1669. Under a settlement made by him in 1666 Martha, wife of Cecil Fihers and sister of Christopher Hoddesdon the younger, eventually succeeded to a life interest in Lee Gardens. She was still living in 1709, but apparently died without issue in or before 1714.[64] She apparently sold her life-interest to George Lewis, a painter.

After Mrs. Fisher's death there was for some years confusion concerning the ownership. The settlement of 1666 had created successive remainders, in tail male, to Richard Langhorne and his brother Thomas, who were apparently Mrs. Fisher's cousins. Richard Langhorne had been attainted and executed in 1679 for alleged complicity in the 'Popish plot.'[65] That seemed to give the Crown a claim on the estate, but it was eventually proved that Richard Langhorne's property had been restored to his family by the Crown in 1679. Meanwhile, however, George Lewis had kept control of the estate, claiming that he had a life interest in it. He was challenged by Richard Langhorne, eldest surviving son of Thomas, and in 1732 an agreement was reached over the ownership of Lee Gardens. Langhorne was to have half the property immediately, and the reversion, on Lewis's death, of the other half. In 1735 Richard Langhorne sold his interest in the estate to John Hopkins, later surnamed Probyn.

In 1747 John Probyn sold it to William Dawson. At that time part of Lee Gardens was occupied by John Higgs, under a 21-year lease granted in 1733, and part by George Lewis.[66] The Higgs family later acquired the freehold of the estate, and appear to have held it until *c.* 1815.[67] In 1849 Lee Gardens was owned by the trustees of William Leverton, and occupied by John Mitchell.[68] Mitchell remained there until 1869, when the farm, then 112 a., was bought by Thomas Woodfine.[69] In *c.* 1908 Lee Gardens, owned by Mrs. Woodfine, was being worked as part of the neighbouring Lilliputs farm.[70] In 1919 it was put up for sale as an estate of 167 a.[71] Part of it was subsequently developed for housing in Wingletye Lane, Lee Gardens Avenue, and neighbouring roads, and later in Rayburn Avenue. After the Second World War Hornchurch grammar school was also built on the farm-lands, but a few fields to the south of it were still being cultivated in 1976.

In 1594 Lee Gardens was shown on a county map, and listed as 'a proper house.'[72] In 1771 it was said to have been 'once a remarkable place', and that the house was newly built.[73] It was then a gentleman's residence, occupied by Capt. Joseph O'Hara.[74]

[45] *Essex Weekly News*, 7 Feb. 1868.
[46] Ibid.
[47] E.R.O., Sage Coll. *Sale Cats.* vol. iii. 3; *Strat. Expr.* 17 Sept. 1881; 23 Jan. 1884.
[48] E.R.O., Sage Coll. *Sale Cats.* vol. iii. 3 and 5; *Kelly's Dir. Essex* (1886 and later edns.).
[49] Norden, *Essex*, map.
[50] E.R.O., Q/RTh 5.
[51] Terry, *Romford*, 170 n., where this information is wrongly linked with Gobions *alias* Uphavering.
[52] *Strat. Expr.* 23 Jan. 1884.
[53] O.S. Map 6", Essex, sheet LXXV (surv. 1865–6).
[54] Ibid. LXXIV (surv. 1862–7); *P.N. Essex*, 114. There are many references to (Great) Gardens, from the 14th cent. onwards, e.g.: New Coll. MS. 9744, f. 163; E.R.O., D/DU 102/32, m. 5; S.C. 2/172/40, m. 14*d.*; *Cal. Close*, 1500–09, 279. Morant, *Essex*, i. 69, confuses (Great) Gardens with Lee Gardens.
[55] See e.g. *Horn. Docs.* nos. 194, 343, 459.
[56] *Collectanea Topographica et Genealogica*, vi. 4–5, 10–12.
[57] E.R.O., D/DU 102/35, m. 2.
[58] Ibid. 102/45, m. 4*d.*
[59] E.R.O., D/DYw 1.
[60] C 142/513/51; New Coll. MS. 2985 (Notes on Lee Gardens, 1664).
[61] Unless otherwise stated this and the next paragraph are based on E.R.O., D/DYw 1–55 (deeds of Lee Gardens 1572–1747).
[62] E.R.O., D/DSx 154; *Visit. Essex* (Harl. Soc.), 592–3.
[63] E.R.O., D/DSx 157; D/DYw 17 and 18; *P.C.C. Wills*, 1661–70, ed. J. H. Morrison, 125.
[64] Cf. E.R.O., D/DU 23/62 and D/DYw 36.
[65] See also *D.N.B.*
[66] E.R.O., D/DYw 13; D/DB T1080/7.
[67] Ogborne, *Essex*, 146; E.R.O., Q/RPl 474–96.
[68] I.R. 29/12/177.
[69] Perfect, *Village of Hornchurch*, 36: E.R.O., Sage Coll. *Sale Cats.* vol. ii. 13; H.R.L., Cornell MSS.
[70] H.R.L., Cornell MSS.
[71] E.R.O., *Sale Cat.* A 576.
[72] Norden, *Essex*, 32.
[73] *Hist. Essex by Gent.* iv. 331. 'John Hills' said in that account to be the owner, may be an error for John Higgs.
[74] *Map of Essex* (1777).

When Thomas Woodfine bought the farm in 1869 he found the house beyond repair, and therefore demolished it.[75] A small new farm-house, built *c.* 1890, survived in 1919, but was later demolished.[76]

The manor of *MARDYKE* lay on the edge of the marshes, about ½ mile south of Dagenham bridge. It originated in ½ virgate of land which, early in the 13th century, Gillian daughter of Ellis carried in marriage to William of Mardyke.[77] About 1240 William and Gillian leased it for 40 years to Reynold Rous.[78] Rous later sold the lease to Richard Elms, to whom, about the same time, William and Gillian of Mardyke granted the ½ virgate in fee.[79] Elms was holding it in 1250–1.[80] By *c.* 1300 it had passed to Richard of Barking.[81] In *c.* 1355 Mardyke was held by Joan Vaud, widow of William atte Tey.[82] It subsequently escheated to Queen Philippa, who granted it for life to Joan St. Leir, with reversion, confirmed in 1367, to Joan's daughter Mary St. Leir, the queen's damsel.[83] Mary St. Leir was confirmed in possession of the manor on 1391.[84] In or shortly before 1414 Mardyke was bought from William Pomfret by Sir Richard Arundel (d. 1419), who also held Bretons and Baldwins.[85] Arundel left Mardyke for life to Katherine Kirketon, with remainder to his wife for life. His executors appear to have sold the manor in 1438 to Thomas Rawley.[86]

In 1515 Richard Dryland and Joan his wife conveyed Mardyke to Guy Myrfyn.[87] The manor was subsequently acquired by Sir James Harvey (d. 1583), ironmonger and lord mayor of London, from whom it passed to his son Sir Sebastian Harvey (d. 1621), also ironmonger and lord mayor.[88] Sir Sebastian was succeeded by his brother James Harvey (d. 1627), who left Mardyke to his younger son Samuel.[89] In 1652 the manor was mortgaged to William Denis of London by John Harvey of Wangey in Dagenham, and John Harvey of Lincoln's Inn (Mdx.), who were probably Samuel's brother and son respectively.[90] Denis eventually foreclosed, and later sold the manor to Simon Rogers, merchant tailor of London; Rogers in 1662 sold Mardyke, comprising 140 a. and a mill, to Mary Rudstone.[91]

In or soon after 1702 the manor was bought by Mary (d. 1713), widow of John Fanshawe (d. 1699) of Parsloes in Dagenham.[92] She left it to her son Thomas Fanshawe, who in 1734 sold it to Robert Tyler (d. 1757).[93] Robert was succeeded by his nephew John Tyler (d. 1775), whose heir was his own nephew John Tyler (d. 1807). In 1823 John Tyler, son and heir of the last named, conveyed his interest in Mardyke to his nephew, another John Tyler. In 1849 the farm, comprising 177 a., was put up for sale by the last John Tyler, and seems to have been divided among at least four purchasers.[94] Perhaps as a result of that sale the southern portion was made into a new farm called Little Mardyke.[95] In 1918 Mardyke farm comprised 122 a. and Little Mardyke farm 72 a.[96] Much of Mardyke farm has since been dug for gravel or used for housing.[97] The tower blocks of the Mardyke housing estate, built in the 1960s, occupy part of the farm-land, at the western end of Frederick Road.

Mardyke, the seat of (Sir) Sebastian Harvey, was an important house in 1594.[98] There is no suggestion that any of that building survived in Mardyke farm-house which was demolished before 1966.[99]

The manor of *MAYLARDS GREEN* and *WYBRIDGE* was about a mile south-west of Hornchurch village. It comprised two ancient tenements, lying respectively north and south of Bowles brook, also called Wybridge river, a tributary of the river Beam.[1] The name Maylards was corrupted in the 19th century to Maylands, a form preserved in Maylands Avenue, Elm Park. It must be distinguished from Drywoods in the Lane or Maylands, in Wingletye Lane (formerly Hay Street).[2] Maylands was probably named from the Maylour family, which was recorded in Hornchurch in the 13th and 14th centuries.[3]

Wybridge must be distinguished from Whybridge or Rands, which lay farther south, on the edge of Hornchurch marsh.[4] The name Wybridge, or Bowlesbridge, was probably used first for an ancient bridge over Bowles brook, but by the 13th century was being applied to the area through which the brook flowed.[5] Its survival as a manorial name seems to have been due to its association with a family called Wybridge. In 1237 Hornchurch priory quitclaimed to Walter of Wybridge ½ virgate of land in Hornchurch, in return for which he granted the priory 25 a. at Wybridge.[6] The 25 a. lay south of Bowles brook and east of Abbs Cross Lane. It comprised several small fields, one of which was known as 'Bowle Brooke' as late as 1663.[7] Early in the 13th century the priory also acquired a four-acre grove called Waterbrook, which lay on the Dagenham boundary, north of the confluence of Bowles brook

75 Perfect, *Village of Hornchurch*, 36.
76 *Kelly's Dir. Essex* (1894) s.v. Tho. Woodfine; H.R.L., Cornell MSS.; E.R.O., Sage Coll. *Sale Cats.* vol. ii. 13.
77 The manor was probably named from the Mardyke family and not, as Reaney (*P.N. Essex*, 113) supposed, from the Mardyke river.
78 *Horn. Docs.* no. 275.
79 Ibid. 331.
80 S.C. 11/189; cf. E.R.O., Q/HZ 2/4.
81 New Coll. MS. 9744, f. 163; cf. *Horn. Docs.* no. 121.
82 New Coll. MS. 9744, f. 163.
83 *Cal. Pat.* 1367–70, 4.
84 Ibid. 1388–92, 447.
85 *Collectanea Topographica et Genealogica*, vi. 1–20.
86 Ibid.; E.R.O., D/DU 102/28, m. 7.
87 S.C. 2/173/2, mm. 4*d*, 5*d*, 6*d*.
88 J. P. Shawcross, *Hist. Dagenham*, 2–5; E.R.O., D/DU 162/1.
89 Shawcross, *Dagenham*, 206; *Visit. Essex* (Harl. Soc.), i. 416; E.R.O., D/DHt T383/1. The Harveys also held Wangey House in Dagenham: *V.C.H. Essex*, v. 280–1. Samuel Harvey married a daughter of John Donne, the poet.
90 E.R.O., D/DC 41/182.
91 Ibid.
92 H. C. Fanshawe, *Hist. Fanshawe family*, 323.
93 E.R.O., D/DNe T97 (abstract of title 1734–1847, on which the remainder of this paragraph is based). In 1722 Fanshawe had leased Mardyke to Christopher Tyler: E.R.O., D/DB T1078/7.
94 E.R.O., Sage Coll. *Sale Cats.* vol. iv. 27 (with MS. annotations).
95 O.S. Map 6", Essex, LXXIV (surv. 1862–7); cf. I.R. 29/12/177.
96 Lewis, *Hist. Rainham*, 123.
97 Ibid. 121, 123.
98 Norden, *Essex*, 33.
99 Lewis, op. cit. 123.
1 *Map of Essex* (1777); cf. E.R.O., T/M 153, ff. 2 and 8.
2 O.S. Map 6", Essex LXXIV (surv. 1862–7); E.R.O., D/DC 23/390 and 41/185.
3 *Horn. Docs.* nos. 31, 38, 118, 143, 191, 300, etc.; New Coll. MS. 4744, f. 163.
4 See below.
5 *Horn. Docs.* nos. 400, 486; *P.N. Essex*, 114.
6 *Horn. Docs.* no. 400; cf. 486.
7 E.R.O., T/M 153, f. 2; cf. E.R.O., D/DU 186/1.

and Beam river.[8] This land was beside the grove of Walter of Wybridge on the north, between Dagenham and the public way towards Walter's gate. The abuttals suggest that Walter's house was on or near the site of the later Wybridge Farm. Waterbrook was later known as Wybridge mead.[9] Walter of Wybridge died in 1251, holding three tenements within the manor of Havering, of 1 virgate, ¼ virgate, and ⅛ virgate.[10] Nicholas (fl. 1315), son of John Wybridge, was Walter's descendant in blood and title.[11] In *c.* 1355 John, son of Richard Wybridge held 1 virgate, ⅓ virgate, and ⅛ virgate, representing a total of 155 a.[12]

Sir Anthony Browne (d. 1567) appears to have been holding the manor of Maylards and Wybridge at his death, for in the same year his widow, and John Fowler, conveyed it to Robert Charnock and William Fawkener.[13] William Pennant, who occupied Maylards, died in 1594.[14] In *c.* 1618 Peerce Pennant was the owner of Maylards, but Wybridge was in the possession of William Sterne.[15] By 1659 Maylards had passed to (Sir) James Rushout (Bt.) (d. 1698), who was succeeded by his son Sir James Rushout, Bt. (d. 1711).[16] Elizabeth (d. 1733), daughter of the second Sir James, carried the manor in marriage to (Sir) Paulet St. John (Bt.) of Dogmersfield (Hants).[17] After her death Maylards was sold to John Bamber, M.D. (d. 1753).[18] It subsequently descended like Bifrons in Barking to the Gascoynes, and then to the Gascoyne-Cecils, marquesses of Salisbury.[19] By 1799 the estate again included Wybridge as well as Maylards.[20] In 1849 Maylards farm comprised 165 a., and Wybridge farm 276 a.[21] Both farms survived until the Elm Park area was developed after the First World War.[22] The farmhouses have been demolished. Maylards, which in 1594 was an important house,[23] stood near the present boating lakes in Harrow Lodge park. It had 17 hearths in 1670.[24] Wybridge, which stood in Upper Rainham Road, dated from the 16th century.[25]

The manor of *NELMES*, formerly *ELMS* or *TYLLE*, lay about a mile north-east of Hornchurch village. It took its name from the family of Elms (de Ulmis) which was prominent and widespread in Hornchurch during the 13th and 14th centuries.[26] In 1250–1 Richard Elms held 8 separate tenements totalling over 2½ virgates, i.e. some 300 a.[27] About 1355 William Elms held an estate of 235 a.[28] Thomas Tyle succeeded to the messuage or manor of Elms or Tylle on the death of his father Nicholas in 1433.[29] In 1491 the manor was settled on Thomas Herde and his wife Elizabeth.[30] In 1499 Richard Herde appears to have conveyed Nelmes to William Lawrence of London.[31] In 1514 Lawrence conveyed it to Thomas Otley, a London grocer, but by 1515 the manor had come into the possession of William Wakerfield, a London brewer, and his wife Elizabeth, who in 1517 sold it to (Sir) William Roche.[32] At that period there was much litigation concerning Nelmes, involving Lawrence, Otley, the Wakerfields, and Roche.[33]

Sir William Roche, who became lord mayor of London, died in 1549 holding the manors of Gobions, in Romford, and Nelmes.[34] The two manors descended together[35] until the 1620s, when Thomas Roche sold Nelmes to Sir Robert Naunton.[36] Naunton, master of the Court of Wards and a former Secretary of State, died in March 1635 leaving Nelmes for life to his wife Penelope, with remainder to his brother William.[37] William Naunton died in July 1635, leaving Robert as his son and heir.[38] Lady Naunton was still living in 1646.[39] As a royalist she was then in financial difficulties, and about that time Nelmes was sold to the Witherings family. Thomas Witherings, postmaster of Great Britain, died in 1651 on his way to worship in Hornchurch church.[40] His nephew and heir William Witherings was holding Nelmes in 1659,[41] and was living at Hornchurch in 1662 and 1670.[42]

Sir Godfrey Webster (d. 1720) left Nelmes to his son Sir Thomas Webster, Bt., of Copped Hall, Epping.[43] The Websters had been living at Nelmes at least as early as 1700.[44] Sir Thomas (d. 1751) was succeeded at Nelmes by his younger son (Sir) Godfrey Webster (Bt.) (d. 1780).[45] Sir Godfrey Webster, Bt., son of the latter, sold Nelmes in 1781 to the trustees of the will of Richard Newman, who were evidently acting for Newman's grandson and heir, Richard Harding, later Newman.[46] Richard Harding Newman, a notable huntsman who also held the manor of Romford or Mawneys, was succeeded on his death in 1808 by his son Thomas H. Newman (d. 1856).[47] In 1849 T. H. Newman's Hornchurch estate comprised 573 a.[48] His son and heir was the Revd. Dr. Thomas H. Newman (d. 1882), fellow of

[8] *Horn. Docs.* nos. 143, 457, 496; cf. E.R.O., T/M 153, f. 8 and D/DU 162/1.
[9] E.R.O., T/M 153, f. 8.
[10] S.C. 11/189; *Cal. Pat.* 1247–58, 107.
[11] *Horn. Docs.* no. 486.
[12] New Coll. MS. 9744, f. 163.
[13] Morant, *Essex*, i. 69 n.
[14] Norden, *Essex*, 33; *E.A.T.* N.S. vi. 317 n.
[15] E.R.O., D/DU 162/1.
[16] Morant, *Essex*, i. 69; E.R.O., D/DU 572/1.
[17] Burke, *Peerage* (1913), p. 1349.
[18] Morant, *Essex*, i. 69.
[19] *V.C.H. Essex*, v. 193–4; H.R.L., Cornell MSS.
[20] E.R.O., T/M 454/10.
[21] I.R. 29/12/177.
[22] *Kelly's Dir. Essex* (1922); Lewis, *Rainham*, 118.
[23] Norden, *Essex*, 33.
[24] E.R.O., Q/RTh 5.
[25] R.C.H.M. *Essex*, iv. 73.
[26] *Horn. Docs.* (index).
[27] S.C. 11/189. In Havering the virgate comprised about 120 a.
[28] New Coll. MS. 9744, f. 162v.
[29] E.R.O., D/DU 102/24.
[30] S.C. 2/172/36, m. 7*d.*
[31] S.C. 2/172/39, m. 8.
[32] C 1/370/89; S.C. 2/173/2, 5 Oct. 1514 and 12 Feb. 1517.
[33] C 1/330/27; C 1/370/89; C 1/440/19 and 21; C 1/454/19; C 1/455/2; C 1/576/45.
[34] C 142/9/91; Morant. *Essex*, i. 63; *Visit. Essex* (Harl. Soc.), i. 477.
[35] See p. 69.
[36] E.R.O., T/A 259/2: Parchment Bk. of Carew H. Mildmay of Marks, *c.* 1650–75; Morant, *Essex*, i. 68.
[37] C 142/481/1; *D.N.B.*
[38] C 142/484/148.
[39] *Cal. Cttee. for Money*, p. 188. Mention is made there of her son Sir Robert Naunton; the person referred to was probably her husband's nephew, Robert Naunton.
[40] *E.R.* v. 31: transcript of Witherings's monumental inscription; *Year Bks. of Probates in P.C.C.* 1650–1, ed. J. and G. F. Matthews, 330.
[41] E.R.O., T/P 195/2, ff. 28–9; *Visit. Essex* (Harl. Soc.), ii. 619; *Visit. Essex, 1664–8*, ed. J. J. Howard, 104.
[42] E.R.O., Q/RTh 1 and 5.
[43] *Misc. Gen. Her.* 4th Ser. ii. 209.
[44] *V.C.H. Essex*, v. 122.
[45] Morant, *Essex*, i. 68; Burke, *Peerage* (1913), p. 1970.
[46] E.R.O., D/DHs T51.
[47] Burke, *Land. Gent.* (1914), p. 1395.
[48] I.R. 29/12/177.

Magdalen College, Oxford. Dr. Newman's heir was his nephew Benjamin H. Newman, who sold the southern part of the estate in 1895 for development as the Emerson Park estate.[49] In 1901 the northern part of Nelmes, including the manor-house, was put up for sale, and development began there also.[50] The house, with a garden of about 3 a., was bought *c.* 1903 by Alfred Barber, who sold it in 1925 to John H. Platford.[51] On J. H. Platford's death in 1966 it passed to his nephew Mr. Roy Platford, who demolished it in 1967.[52]

Nelmes house, Nelmes Way, was timber-framed, with an east wing, originally a single-storeyed hall, built in the 16th century.[53] Later in the 16th century the hall was subdivided and a chimney-stack was inserted in the east wall, probably by John Roche, who inherited the manor in 1549 and held it for about 40 years. He was living at Nelmes in 1594, when it was listed as an important house.[54] In the 17th century it was extended to the north, and a kitchen wing, later demolished, was built to the east. Those improvements were probably completed by *c.* 1650, when Nelmes was said to be in good repair, with many conveniences lately added.[55] Nelmes had 15 hearths in 1670.[56] The south front was re-faced *c.* 1720. Further additions were made in the 19th and 20th centuries. The main staircase, dating from the late 17th century, was lavishly panelled and carved.[57]

A former out-building of Nelmes, about 100 yd. SW., survived in 1976 as part of a house called Capel Nelmes, in Sylvan Avenue. The brick range on the north side of this house is thought to be of the 16th century, extensively remodelled.[58] It was converted into a dwelling *c.* 1870.[59] Early in the present century Christian Jensen enlarged the house and inserted in the east range a 17th-century staircase taken from Nelmes.[60] Further extensions were carried out in 1939 by Mr. P. Bates, to the designs of Reginald Ross.[61]

A red-brick tower in the garden of no. 3, Sylvan Avenue, is thought to date from the 17th century, and to be part of a conduit house supplying Nelmes. A water conduit certainly existed *c.* 1650.[62]

The manor of *REDDEN COURT* extended west from the river Ingrebourne, on both sides of Squirrels Heath Road, Harold Wood. It originated in a tenement which William the Fleming held in 1212 by serjeanty of finding reeds for the king's chamber at Havering.[63] This suggests that Redden here means 'growing with reeds'.[64] Henry III granted the tenement, then 120 a., in 1235 to William of Havering, and in 1246 confirmed it in the possession of William's son Richard.[65] By 1274 it seems to have passed to Richard of Havering's widow Lucy.[66] It remained in the same family until 1380, when Sir Richard of Havering sold it to Sir John Newenton.[67] In 1413 the 'manor of Reden', so styled for the first time, was held by Newenton's daughter Joan, widow of Roger Swinnerton.[68] Joan, elsewhere described as heir to her brother Thomas Newenton, held the manor until her death in 1445.[69]

In 1469 Redden Court was acquired by Sir Thomas Cooke, and thus became part of the Gidea Hall estate.[70] It was still part of Gidea Hall when Sir Anthony Cooke died in 1604,[71] but was subsequently sold to John Legatt (d. 1607), who left Redden Court and Lee Gardens to his son Thomas.[72] Thomas Legatt sold Redden Court to William Comyns in 1612.[73] The Comyns family were still living in the district in 1662.[74] In 1710–20 Redden Court was apparently held by John Evered and Jane his wife.[75] It was later bought by John Hopkins (d. 1732), who was succeeded by his nephew John Hopkins (d. 1772), who also bought Bretons.[76] Redden Court and Bretons descended together like the manor of Theydon Bois[77] until 1857, when parts of the Hall-Dare family's estate were put up for sale. At the time of the sale Redden Court comprised two farms: Old Redden Court, with 109 a., stood north of Squirrels Heath Road, and New Redden Court, with 142 a., was on the south side.[78] The manor was bought in 1858 by Alfred Douglas Hamilton.[79] In 1894 Hamilton put up for sale Old Redden Court, with 106 a.[80] It was stated *c.* 1908 that the manor of Redden Court had been held until recently by Adam Roper.[81] Both Old and New Redden Court farms were developed for building between the two world wars.

The ancient manor-house of Redden Court stood *c.* 1618 south of Squirrels Heath Road, on the site occupied in 1976 by Redden Court school.[82] It was possibly the house with 10 hearths listed in Harold Wood ward in 1662.[83] By 1777 the old house was apparently called Readnalls, and the name Redden Court had been transferred to a smaller house, built since *c.* 1618, on the north side of Squirrels Heath Road.[84] In the 19th century the smaller house was called Old Redden Court, and the larger one, on the ancient site, was called New Redden Court.[85] About 1900 New Redden Court was enlarged and partly

[49] Burke, *Land. Gent.* (1914), p. 1395; Perfect, *Village of Hornchurch*, 119; E.R.O., Sage Coll. *Sale Cats.* vol. ii. 5.
[50] E.R.O., Sage Coll. *Sale Cats.* vol. ii. 8; Perfect, *Village of Hornchurch*, 30–1.
[51] Inf. (1964) from Mr. J. H. Platford.
[52] *Daily Telegraph*, 28 Aug. 1967.
[53] R.C.H.M. *Essex*, iv. 71; inf. from G.L.C., Historic Bdgs. Div.; Perfect, *Village of Hornchurch*, 27–31; A. B. Bamford, *Sketches in the Liberty of Havering*; H.R.L. Pictorial Coll.; see below, plate facing p. 17.
[54] Norden, *Essex*, 33.
[55] E.R.O., D/DAc 133.
[56] E.R.O., Q/Rth 5.
[57] R.C.H.M. *Essex*, illus. f. p. 71.
[58] Ibid. iv. 72.
[59] Perfect, *Village of Hornchurch*, 53.
[60] Ibid.; *Kelly's Dir. Essex* (1912 and later edns.).
[61] Inf. from Mr. P. Bates.
[62] E.R.O., D/DAc 133.
[63] *Bk. of Fees*, i. 345.
[64] Cf. *English Place Name Elements* (E.P.N.S. xxv), i. 264.
[65] *Cal. Chart. R.* 1226–57, 211, 305.
[66] *Rot. Hund.* (Rec. Com.), i. 149, 152.
[67] *Cal. Pat.* 1377–81, 498.
[68] Ibid. 1413–16, 103.
[69] Morant, *Essex*, i. 64; cf. *Cal. Close*, 1419–22. She seems also to have held the manor of Bretons.
[70] E.R.O., D/DU 102/54, m. 4*d*.
[71] Morant, *Essex*, i. 64. For Gidea Hall see below, p. 67.
[72] C 142/513/51. For Lee Gardens see above.
[73] E.R.O., D/DU 102/105, m. 1; cf. E.R.O., D/DU 162/1.
[74] E.R.O., Q/RTh 1.
[75] E.R.O., D/DU 102/126 and 127.
[76] Morant, *Essex*, i. 64; *Miscellanea Genealogica et Heraldica*, 5th ser. vii, app. p. 6.
[77] *V.C.H. Essex*, iv. 252.
[78] E.R.O., Sage Coll. *Sale Cats.* vol. ii. 2.
[79] Ibid. vol. iii. 5; Burke, *Peerage* (1913), p. 924.
[80] E.R.O., Sage Coll. *Sale Cats.* vol. iii. 5.
[81] H.R.L., Cornell MSS.
[82] E.R.O., D/DU 162/1 (map).
[83] E.R.O., Q/RTh 1.
[84] *Map of Essex* (1777); cf. E.R.O., D/DU 162/1.
[85] E.R.O., Sage Coll. *Sale Cats.* vol. ii. 2.

refronted, and in 1906 the older part of it was rebuilt.[86] It was demolished before 1939, when Redden Court school was completed. Old Redden Court, which probably dated from the late 17th or the early 18th century, was demolished *c.* 1954, and the site was developed as Court Close.[87]

The manor of *WHYBRIDGE* or *RANDS* was at south Hornchurch, about a mile east of Mardyke.[88] Whybridge probably took its name from the Wybridge family, which in the 13th and 14th centuries held several tenements in Hornchurch.[89] It must be distinguished from Wybridge adjoining Maylards, farther north.[90] In *c.* 1355 Jordan Wych held a tenement of 168 a.[91] This was probably Whybridge, the past owners of which, as mentioned in 15th-century documents, included Jordan Wych and Hugh Wych.[92] Before 1455 Whybridge was split into four, no doubt between coheirs, but in that year all the quarters were acquired by John Rand, from whose family the manor took its second name.[93]

John Rand also held Beredens in Cranham,[94] and both manors descended to (Sir) William Rand, who in 1523 sold them to William Roche.[95] In the same year Roche sold Whybridge, then 276 a., to John Knapp, brewer.[96] Knapp, by his will proved in 1526, devised Whybridge to his daughter Margaret Kirkeby.[97] In 1559 John Bedell conveyed the manor to John Coker.[98] It later passed to Edmund Butt, from whom it descended in 1577 to his daughter Audrey.[99] In 1616 Whybridge was held by Sir William Ayloffe, Bt., of Bretons, who had bought it from Robert Tyte and William Butt.[1] Sir Benjamin Ayloffe, Bt., son of Sir William, sold the manor in 1627 to George Thorowgood, draper of London.[2] Edward Thorowgood, merchant, was holding Whybridge by 1659 and at least until 1670.[3] Stephen Thorowgood sold the manor in 1699 to Robert Hammond, the mortgagee.[4]

Robert Hammond, by his will proved in 1704, left Whybridge for life to his grandson-in-law Christopher Crowe, with reversion to his right heirs.[5] In 1719 the manor was settled on Joseph Newdick and Mary his wife, and Thomas Fowler and Anne his wife.[6] Mary and Anne appear to have been sisters, and they, or their husbands, were coheirs to the estate.[7] Thomas Fowler was dead by 1744, when Joseph Newdick, who was a London fletcher, bought the reversion of the half of the manor held by Mary Fowler.[8] Joseph Newdick (d. 1762) was succeeded by his son Henry (d. 1771) a London wax-chandler.[9] Henry's son and heir, Joseph Baden Newdick, sold Whybridge in 1786 to his brother-in-law Christopher Tyler, whose family appear to have been tenants of the manor at least since 1737.[10] Tyler, who was a prominent local figure, died in 1830.[11] In 1849 Whybridge (312 a.) was owned by Harriet Tyler.[12] The Mashiters, who then occupied the farm, were related by marriage to the Tylers, and probably succeeded to the ownership of Whybridge, as well as other property, in the later 19th century.[13] Farming continued there until the 1930s, when the farm was cut up for development.[14] The house, which was then demolished, had probably been built in the 18th century.[15] In the 1860s trotting races were held in Whybridge Park.[16] The site has been used for houses in Hubert and Nelson Roads.

ECONOMIC HISTORY. Until the 19th century the occupations followed in Hornchurch were mainly those connected with agriculture or with the small crafts and trades of a village. Agriculture is treated in another section, for Havering and Romford as well as Hornchurch.[17]

There were three ancient corn-mills in Hornchurch. The oldest was probably the water-mill on the manor of Dovers, recorded from 1235 to 1614.[18] There was a windmill on the manor of Mardyke *c.* 1240.[19] A later Mardyke windmill is recorded from 1564.[20] In 1613 a man was indicted for damaging it.[21] It was depicted *c.* 1618 as a post mill, on a mound, standing near the river Beam, immediately south of the present Dagenham Road.[22] It still existed in 1722, but had disappeared by 1777.[23]

Another windmill, first mentioned in 1262, was in Mill field, Hornchurch.[24] It was probably the predecessor of Hornchurch mill, which in 1494 was leased by New College along with the rectory.[25] In 1564 William Legatt, then the lessee, contracted with the miller and a firm of wheelwrights to rebuild the mill, according to the pattern of Mardyke windmill.[26] John Legatt, by his will dated 1607, devised the lease of Hornchurch mill to his son Thomas.[27] The mill had apparently disappeared by *c.* 1618, when Mill field, immediately south of the church, had no buildings on it.[28] It was rebuilt shortly before

86 H.R.L., Cornell MSS.
87 Personal knowledge.
88 E.R.O., D/DU 162/1; O.S. Map 6", *Essex*, LXXIV (surv. 1862–7).
89 S.C. 11/189; New Coll. MS. 4744, f. 163.
90 See Maylards and Wybridge, above.
91 New Coll. MS. 4744, f. 163.
92 E.R.O., D/DU 102/45, m. 5; ibid. 102/47.
93 E.R.O., D/DU 102/45, m. 5. The conveyances were made by trustees.
94 See below.
95 E.R.O., D/DU T586.
96 E.R.O., D/DB T1076/8.
97 *E.A.T.* N.S. vi. 316.
98 C.P. 25 (2)/126/1607.
99 E.R.O., D/DB T1076/11.
1 E.R.O., D/DL T1/708.
2 E.R.O., D/DB T1079/27.
3 E.R.O., T/P 195/2; E.R.O., D/DB T1076/14.
4 E.R.O., D/DB T1080/8.
5 E.R.O., D/DU 182/52.
6 Ibid. 102/127.
7 For the relationship between the Newdicks and the Fowlers see also E.R.O., D/DB T1080/10.
8 E.R.O., D/DB T1080/6.
9 Ibid. T1080/10 and 11.
10 Ibid. T1082/17 and 18; cf.: T1080/2 and 3; T1078/12 and 13.
11 Lewis, *Rainham*, 118.
12 I.R. 29/12/177.
13 Ibid.; *White's Dir. Essex* (1848), 376; ibid (1863), 594; Perfect, *Village of Hornchurch*, 56.
14 *Kelly's Dir. Essex* (1886 and later edns.): J. Blows (1886–1917), H. Barker (1922); Lewis, *Rainham*, 118.
15 Lewis, op. cit. 118 and plate facing p. 119.
16 Ibid. 88.
17 See p. 17.
18 *Feet of F. Essex*, i. 113; *Cal. Inq. p.m.* iii. p. 388; *Cal. Pat.* 1385–9, 406; *Cal. Close*, 1422–9, 438; C.P. 25 (2)/294 Hil. 11 Jas. I.
19 *Horn. Docs.* no. 406.
20 *E.A.T.* N.S. xxi. 339.
21 E.R.O., Q/SR 204/98 and 122.
22 E.R.O., D/DU 162/1.
23 E.R.O., D/DHt T383/1; D/DC 41/182; D/DB T1078/7; *Map of Essex* (1777).
24 *Horn. Docs.* nos. 57, 59.
25 Ibid. 309.
26 *E.A.T.* N.S. xxi. 339.
27 Ibid.
28 E.R.O., D/DU 162/1.

1666, and continued to operate until 1912.[29] It was burnt down in 1921.[30] In its closing years, and no doubt earlier, it was a post mill.[31] The adjoining Mill Cottage, which still survives in 1976, is a timber-framed building, probably of 17th-century origin, reconstructed in a picturesque style early in the 19th century, when some rooms were panelled. It stands in the Dell, a wooded site on the edge of an old gravel-pit, only ¼ mile from the town centre, but completely secluded. A millstone and some beams from the mill are preserved in the garden.

Hornchurch was an early centre of the leather industry, from which Pell (now High) Street, recorded from the 13th century, probably took its name.[32] There are occasional references to cordwainers in the 13th century.[33] A cordwainer of Havering, mentioned in 1436, came from Holland.[34] There were tanners at Hornchurch from the 16th century onwards.[35] The last tannery, that of Bright & Beardwell, in High Street, closed *c.* 1846.[36] The last fellmonger, James Fry, of North Street, closed *c.* 1870.[37]

A brewery called 'the Fan' existed *c.* 1200, when Robert de Courtenay granted it to Hornchurch priory.[38] The brewer was Baldwin of Hackford, who paid 8*d.* a year rent. Later brewers are mentioned in 1583 and 1606.[39] Men engaged in the woollen industry included a clothworker (1613) and a stapler (1621).[40] There was a collar-maker in 1665.[41] Among those in maritime trades were a waterman (1514), a wharfinger (1572), and two sailors (1610).[42]

Brickworks existed at different periods in at least three places in Hornchurch. Brick Clamps fields, mentioned *c.* 1650, were part of the manor of Nelmes.[43] That may have been the site, on the west side of Wingletye Lane, which in 1849 was called Kiln field.[44] Another site lay west of the village, between the present Elmhurst Drive and Windsor Road. In 1849 two fields there, Brick Clamps and Hither Brick Clamps, were both cultivated as arable.[45] The third site was behind Red House, in High Street, opposite Grey Towers Avenue. The brickworks there, which also made pottery, are said to have been established early in the 18th century.[46] In 1838 the owner was Charles Cove.[47] Later owners were listed until 1886.[48] In 1917 it was stated that the works had been carried on until recently, and that their remains could still be seen.[49]

In the 19th century Hornchurch's agricultural prosperity was accompanied by the growth of industries linked with farming.[50] The most important was Fairkytes ironworks, established by the brothers Thomas and Robert Wedlake.[51] They appear to have come to Hornchurch *c.* 1780, and at first traded as millwrights. In or before *c.* 1810 they opened a foundry at Fairkytes, Billet Lane, specializing in agricultural implements.[52] The Wedlakes were inventors as well as industrialists.[53] At their peak of prosperity they employed 80 or 90 hands at a dozen forges. They won a high reputation among local agriculturists, who in 1833 subscribed for a presentation to Thomas Wedlake.[54]

When Thomas Wedlake died in 1843 the firm was continued by his widow Mary (d. 1846), with her daughter and son-in-law, trading as Mary Wedlake & Co. Thomas's brother Robert Wedlake left Fairkytes and, with a partner, set up the rival firm of Wedlake & Thompson, at the Union foundry, High Street.[55] By 1855 the Union foundry had been taken over by Richard Dendy, in partnership with Thomas W. Wedlake, son of Robert; Fairkytes foundry had by then gone out of business.[56] Walter Dendy, son of Richard, later joined T. W. Wedlake at the Union foundry, but their partnership seems to have ended *c.* 1894, when Wedlake set up the Hornchurch Ironworks in North Street.[57] T. W. Wedlake & Co. continued in North Street until 1937 or later.[58] Walter Dendy transferred the Union foundry to Barking in 1902.

In the later 19th century there was a blacksmith's forge in High Street.[59] It was taken over *c.* 1872 by Thomas Pearce, who developed an ironmonger's business adjoining it. In *c.* 1902 the premises were rebuilt, and the firm became Pearce & Son. The forge seems to have survived until the First World War. The ironmongery was transferred to Station Road in the 1930s.

Frost Bros., wheelwrights and coachbuilders, originally in High Street, seems to have been founded *c.* 1860 by Jonathan Diaper.[60] Charles Frost, who married Diaper's daughter, took over management in the 1870s. In its early years, the firm specialized in heavy wagons for market-gardeners and traders, but by *c.* 1904, when a new finishing shop was added in North Street, it was building several kinds of road vehicles, including motor-car bodies. In the 1930s

[29] New Coll. MSS. 5738 (leases, 1666–1741) and 5740 (lease 1776); O.S. Map 1″, sheet 1 (surv. 1799–1800); Perfect, *Village of Hornchurch*, 11–14.
[30] *E.R.* xxxiii. 98.
[31] Perfect, op. cit. (illus.).
[32] *P.N. Essex*, 113; *Horn. Docs.* nos. 2, 157, 435, 406.
[33] *Horn. Docs.* nos. 332, 333 (Thomas the cordwainer). Gervase the cordwainer (ibid. 271, 287), who was an alderman, presumably plied his trade in London.
[34] *Cal. Pat.* 1429–36, 545.
[35] E.R.O., Q/SR 79/99; E.R.O., D/DSx 160; E.R.O., Q/SR 416/84.
[36] Perfect, *Village of Hornchurch*, 6.
[37] Ibid.; *Kelly's Dir. Essex* (1866, 1870).
[38] *Horn. Docs.* no. 180. For the date see *Complete Peerage*, v. 72–3.
[39] E.R.O., Q/SR 84/63, 64, 66; Q/SR. 178/69.
[40] E.R.O., Q/SR 204/19; 235/20 and 144.
[41] Ibid. 405/121.
[42] *L. & P. Hen. VIII*, i(2), p. 1400; Assizes 35/14/4 and 35/51A/H.
[43] E.R.O., D/DAc 133.
[44] I.R. 29 and 30/12/177, no. 1057.
[45] Ibid. nos. 860, 858, O.S. Map 6″, Essex, LXXIV (surv. 1862–7).
[46] Perfect, *Village of Hornchurch*, 9, 79.
[47] *Robson's Dir. Essex* (1838), 63; I.R. 29 and 30/177, no. 646.
[48] *White's Dir. Essex* (1848), 376, *Kelly's Dir. Essex* (1866 to 1886).
[49] Perfect, op. cit. 9.
[50] Cf. Thorne, *Environs Lond.* (1876), 360.
[51] This account of Wedlake is based mainly on: Perfect, op. cit. 6; J. Booker, *Essex and the Industrial Revolution*, 15–18.
[52] Mary Wedlake & Co., *Priced List of Farming Implements* (1850) states that the factory had been founded upwards of 40 years; H.R.L., Newscuttings, Small Bk. p. 63, 18 Feb. 1900, 'Iron Founding in Essex', states that the Wedlakes first cast iron at Hornchurch in 1785.
[53] *E.R.* lvi. 78, 81, 115.
[54] E.R.O., D/P 115/28/8.
[55] Cf. *Kelly's Dir. Essex* (1845); I.R. 29 & 30/12/177, no. 813.
[56] *Kelly's Dir. Essex* (1855).
[57] Ibid. (1894); E.R.O., T/P 67/10, p. 48 (obit. of T. W. Wedlake); ibid. 67/5, Cutting from *St. James's Review* [*c.* 1905].
[58] *Kelly's Dir. Essex* (1894 to 1937).
[59] *Kelly's Dir. Essex* (1864 to 1937); E.R.O., T/P 67/5, *St. James's Review* [*c.* 1905].
[60] *Kelly's Dir. Essex* (1866 to 1937); *White's Dir. Essex* (1863), 594; E.R.O., T/P 67/5, *St. James's Review* [*c.* 1905].

Frost Bros. concentrated on motor bodies, at the North Street workshops. The firm was still there in 1974 as motor salesmen and repairers.[61]

The Old Hornchurch Brewery, High Street, was founded *c.* 1789 by John Woodfine (d. 1811).[62] It passed in direct succession to his son (d. 1853) and grandson, both named Thomas Woodfine. The younger Thomas Woodfine sold the business in 1874 to Henry and Benjamin Holmes. They sold it *c.* 1889 to Charles Dagnall, who formed the Old Hornchurch Brewery Co. The company failed, and in 1892 the brewery was bought by Philip Conron. The business continued in the Conron family until 1925, when they sold it to Mann, Crossman & Paulin Ltd.; it then included some 40 public houses. The new owners immediately closed the brewery, which was demolished in 1930–1.

James and George H. Matthews Ltd., millers and seedsmen, Gubbins Lane, Harold Wood, originated in 1895, when James Matthews opened a small shop supplying animal food to dairy farmers. In 1905 he built a mill beside Harold Wood station.[63] He was joined in 1906 by his brother George, and in the following years the firm expanded steadily, opening several branches in Essex and Suffolk, and trading also in fertilizers, seeds, and coal.[64] The firm was taken over in 1963 by Unilever Ltd.; the Harold Wood mill was closed in 1968 and demolished soon after.[65]

Matthews, though traditional in its products, was modern in its choice of location: at the end of the 19th century Harold Wood was a township with good railway communications and cheap land. Other industries tried to exploit these advantages.

Harold Wood Brickworks, Church Road, were established by 1878.[66] The founder was probably John Compton, later of the Grange, who acquired the site in 1877. The brickworks were sold in 1887 by Compton's widow and son to Alfred Rutley. By 1894 the business had been let to George King (d. 1919), a Northamptonshire farmer. King, who was advised and financed by his brother William (d. 1901) a London solicitor, bought the freehold in 1896. By that time the brickworks had its own siding at Harold Wood station. George King extended the works and built four cottages adjoining; but by 1902 the works had been closed. The site was subsequently used for cattle grazing until 1928, when the trustees of the King family sold it to Hermann Noppel, a Swiss. The brickworks seem to have been re-opened by 1929, but to have been closed again by 1933. In the early 1940s a lake, which had formed in the excavations, was the haunt of wildfowl.[67] After the Second World War the brickfield was redeveloped as an industrial estate.[68]

Henry Brock & Son, later Charles T. Brock & Co., opened a fireworks factory at Harold Wood *c.* 1886.[69] It was about ½ mile south of the railway station, in the area of the present Prospect Road.[70] The factory was managed by John R. Brock (d. 1906), and seems to have closed soon after his death.[71]

In the late 19th century attempts were made to develop industry on Hornchurch marshes. The Rock Portland Cement Co., Mud Island, was formed in 1880.[72] It was sold by the liquidator in 1883 and later became the Rainham Portland Cement Co. The works were rebuilt in 1895. The company was taken over in 1900 by Associated Portland Cement Manufacturers Ltd., and the works seem to have been closed by *c.* 1906. During the 1890s there was also a chemical factory on Mud Island, owned by H. Button & Co.[73] It also was short-lived.

One of the principal industries founded before the First World War was the Neostyle Manufacturing Co., Hornchurch Road, now Roneo Vickers Ltd., which makes office equipment. It was just inside the Hornchurch boundary, but is usually associated with Romford, and is therefore treated under that place.[74]

Since the First World War there has been a moderate growth of light industry, including engineering, chemicals, clothing, cabinet-making and food processing, in several areas near the main roads.[75] At Gallows Corner there are factories along both sides of the Southend Arterial Road, in Bryant Avenue, and in Stafford Avenue. In Bryant Avenue residential development seems to have started just before the street was severed by the Arterial Road, and a few houses survive as factory offices. Among the older firms in the area is Lacrinoid Products Ltd., plastics manufacturers, founded in 1920 as the London Button Co., and moved to Stafford Avenue in 1936.[76] At Harold Wood the old brickfield, Church Road, was redeveloped by Thomas Bates & Son, builders, after the Second World War.[77] At South Hornchurch there are factories in the New Road area.

On Hornchurch marshes there was apparently no further development until 1946, when the Phoenix Timber Co., established in 1927, moved to Frog Island, Manor Way.[78] By 1962 the company was occupying over 60 a. adjoining Rainham creek.[79] A floating jetty, built in 1948, made it possible to bring in large cargoes of timber by river. On the west side of the marshes the Ford Motor Co. built a large foundry in the 1950s.[80] It occupies over 200 a. adjoining the company's Dagenham works.

A fair at Hornchurch, held on the feast of St. Andrew (30 November) was recorded in 1633.[81] In

[61] *Telephone Dir.* (1974).

[62] Perfect, *Village of Hornchurch*, 8; L. A. Aves, 'Old Hornchurch Brewery,' *Havering Hist. Rev.* v. 11–16; vi. 14–37; E.R.O., T/P 67/5, *St. James's Review* [*c.* 1905].

[63] *Kelly's Dir. Essex* (1906).

[64] *Hornchurch Official Guide* (1960–1), 103, E.R.O., T/P 67/5, *St. James's Review* [*c.* 1905].

[65] Inf. from Jas. & Geo. H. Matthews Ltd.; *Who Owns Whom* (U.K. edn. 1975–6), i. 659.

[66] For the brickfield, 1877–1928: E.R.O., D/DB E58; *Kelly's Dir. Essex* (1878 to 1933).

[67] Inf. from the late Revd. W. H. May; O.S. Map 2½", TQ 59 (1948 edn.).

[68] Personal knowledge.

[69] *Kelly's Dir. Essex* (1886 to 1906).

[70] O.S. Map 25", Essex, LXVII. 13 (1896 edn.).

[71] H.R.L., Newscuttings, Small Bk., p. 15, Obit. of John R. Brock.

[72] For this cement co. see: *V.C.H. Essex*, ii. 493; *Strat. Expr.* 31 Oct. 1883; *Kelly's Dir. Essex* (1886 to 1906); E.R.O., D/SH 5, 4 Apr. 1884; O.S. Map 25", Essex, LXXXII. 3 (1897 edn.).

[73] *Kelly's Dir. Essex* (1894 to 1898).

[74] See p. 74.

[75] For the leading firms *c.* 1955 see *Hornchurch Charter Petition*, 8.

[76] *Hornchurch Official Guide* (1960–1), 101.

[77] Personal knowledge.

[78] *Hornchurch Official Guide* (1962–3), 121.

[79] For an air view of Phoenix: H.R.L., Pictorial Coll. (*Hornchurch Echo* 28 July 1970).

[80] *Hornchurch Official Guide* (1962–3), 113; inf. from Havering L.B.

[81] E 134/24 Chas. I East. 9.

the 19th century a pleasure fair was held on Whit Monday in High Street until 1878, when it was abolished by statutory order.[82]

MARSHES AND SEA DEFENCES. In 1510 the Hornchurch marshes comprised 590 a., whose owners shared the responsibility for land drainage and sea defences.[83] The Havering 'level', as defined in 1600, comprised 522 a. in Hornchurch marshes, including an inlet called Havering gulf, which branched east out of Dagenham creek about 100 yd. north of the Thames.[84] It was under the jurisdiction of a court of sewers whose area extended from West Ham to Mucking. Havering level remained almost unchanged in extent until 1883, when it was united with Dagenham level.[85]

It is difficult to account for the apparent loss of some 70 a. marsh between 1510 and 1600. That may have been no more than a reduction of the jurisdictional area, but it is possible that the cause was flooding, to which Havering and Dagenham levels were then notoriously liable.[86] In both places the flood defences were hampered by the local pattern of land tenure. In 1510 there were no fewer than 60 landowners in Hornchurch marshes.[87] Much of the marshland lay in strips in four commons, which as late as 1850 comprised over a third of the total area.[88] When serious floods occurred the divided responsibility for repairs made reclamation difficult. In such cases the commissioners of sewers usually employed contractors to do the work, and levied rates to pay them. Such rates, at a time when the landowners had lost their incomes from the marshes, often provoked opposition or evasion. As a last resort the commissioners might 'decree' or sequestrate the lands of defaulting ratepayers, and that happened more than once.

In 1591 floods caused a breach in Dagenham creek, through a wall belonging to William Ayloffe of Bretons.[89] That was the origin of Havering gulf.[90] In 1594 the commissioners of sewers ordered Dagenham creek to be 'inned': Ayloffe was to pay £500 of the cost, the other landowners in Havering level £700, and those in Dagenham level £265.[91] Some of the landowners, including Ayloffe, apparently refused to pay their rates, and the work was eventually entrusted to John Legatt of Hornchurch, to whom the commissioners granted leases of decreed lands. Legatt had completed the work by 1597, not without obstruction from Ayloffe.[92]

In 1613 the Thames river wall was breached at Leeson mead, about 350 yd. east of Dagenham creek.[93] During the following months it was rebuilt farther north, leaving a small permanent inlet.[94] In 1621, after another breach in Dagenham creek, (Sir) Cornelius Vermuyden was employed to carry out repairs.[95] The great breach of 1707, which has been described elsewhere in connexion with Dagenham,[96] also caused flooding in Hornchurch marshes, and enlarged Havering gulf.[97] The breach was not finally closed until 1721, and its effects were felt long after that. In 1735 no less than 220 a. of Hornchurch marshes remained under decree.[98] At that time rates were still being levied on account of the breach of 1707, and it was stated in 1737 that the tenant of Suttons had so far paid £440, though he had received no rent from his marshland for 30 years, and much of the land was still under water.[99]

There seems to have been no serious flooding at Hornchurch after 1707, and in the 19th century it was at last possible to reclaim Havering gulf. In 1737 the gulf was said to be deep enough to anchor the largest ship.[1] It still existed in 1800, but by 1867 most of it had been filled in.[2] During the present century Hornchurch marshes have been converted to industrial use.[3] That process was facilitated by the consolidation of holdings. In 1850 there were only 17 owners, of whom 3 held about half the total area.[4] In 1975 most of the marshland was occupied by the Ford Motor Co. and the Riverside sewage works of the G.L.C.[5]

FOREST. The history of the forest is treated under Havering.[6]

LOCAL GOVERNMENT. The manorial government of Hornchurch is treated above.[7] Hornchurch parish originally comprised the whole of Havering manor, but by the 16th century the five northern wards, forming 'Romford side' had become largely self-governing for civil purposes.[8] 'Hornchurch side', which remained under Hornchurch parish vestry, contained Hornchurch town, North End, and

HORNCHURCH URBAN DISTRICT. *Argent, on a saltire between three roses gules barbed and seeded proper, and in base a human heart of the second, a martlet or.*

[Granted 1948]

[82] Perfect, *Village of Hornchurch*, 17; *Lond. Gaz.* 2 Apr. 1878, p. 2319.
[83] New Coll. MS. 9744, ff. 186*v*–187*v*.
[84] E.R.O., T/M 126.
[85] E.R.O., D/SH 25 (map, 1735); D/SH 3A (presentment, 1850); D/SH 4 (rates assessment, 1855); D/SH 5 (minutes 11 Dec. 1883).
[86] *V.C.H. Essex*, v. 285–8; H. Grieve, *Great Tide*, 12–28.
[87] E.R.O., T/M 126.
[88] For the common marshes see p. 19.
[89] W. Dugdale, *Hist. Embanking and Draining* (1722), 81; K.B. 9/684 (2).
[90] J. Perry, *Stopping of Dagenham Breach* (1721), map: 'here was a breach about 120 years since.' Cf. E.R.O., T/M 126: Wm. Ayloffe had land at the mouth of the gulf.
[91] Dugdale, op. cit. 81.
[92] *Acts of P.C.* 1597, 304–5.
[93] New Coll. MS. 182; E.R.O., D/DU 162/1.
[94] Ibid.; J. G. O'Leary, *Dagenham Place Names*, map 17.
[95] *V.C.H. Essex*, v. 285–6; L. E. Harris, 'Sir Cornelius Vermuyden', *Trans. Newcomen Soc.* xxvii. 7–18.
[96] *V.C.H. Essex*, v. 286–9.
[97] O'Leary, *Dagenham Place Names*, map nos. 15, 17; New Coll. MS. 206.
[98] E.R.O., D/SH 25.
[99] New Coll. MS. 206.
[1] New Coll. MS. 206.
[2] O.S. Map, 1", sheet 1 (1805 edn., surv. 1799–1800); O.S. Map 6", Essex, LXXIV (surv. 1862–7).
[3] See p. 41.
[4] E.R.O., D/SH 3A.
[5] Inf. from Havering L.B.
[6] See p. 20.
[7] See p. 1.
[8] See p. 76.

South End wards.[9] In or about 1722 Hornchurch town ward disappeared, having been divided between North End and South End.[10]

The first churchwardens' book for Hornchurch, 1590–1722, records appointments not only of churchwardens and sidesmen but also, for parts of the period, those of surveyors, overseers, and vermin destroyers.[11] It includes a few vestry minutes, and also, in the churchwardens' accounts, information on poor-relief. There is a vestry order book, 1707–30,[12] and a volume of churchwardens' accounts, 1820–60, also includes some vestry minutes.[13] The minutes of the select vestry cover the years 1826–36.[14] Overseers' accounts survive for the periods 1655–67 and 1701–1836,[15] and apprenticeship indentures for 1700–73.[16]

In 1641 Hornchurch parish vestry resolved to hold monthly meetings, to be attended by the churchwardens, constables, and ten named vestrymen. No later references have been found to this committee, which was tantamount to a select vestry; but it is clear from the overseers' accounts that monthly meetings were firmly established by 1655. There are few indications of numbers attending the monthly meetings. At the Easter vestry the attendance, as indicated by signatures to the minutes, was usually between 8 and thirteen. The vicar was usually present and signed first. Michael Welles, vicar 1658–86, and Thomas Roberts, 1696–1721, are notable for regular attendance over long periods.

Hornchurch had two churchwardens, each normally serving for two years. In 1651 the vicar, William Whitaker, nominated one warden, but with that exception both wardens were elected by the parishioners until the early 19th century, when the vicar established his right to nominate one. By 1615 three sidesmen were being elected each year, normally from the gentry, and each representing a ward; from 1657 the number was reduced to two. The annual election of two vermin destroyers and two surveyors of highways was recorded from 1623, and the nomination of three overseers of the poor, one for each ward, from 1658. In 1693 the number of surveyors was increased to three. They continued to be elected by the vestry until 1696, when a short list of nine, three for each ward, was drawn up for the guidance of the liberty quarter sessions in making the appointments. A high constable for 'Hornchurch side', and four petty constables, two for the town, one each for North End and South End, were appointed under ancient custom in the court leet of Havering manor.[17] Minor officials included the beadle, who in the early 18th century had charge of the poor under the churchwardens and overseers, and who sometimes acted also as vestry clerk.[18]

Throughout the period covered by the parish records there were separate church-, poor-, highway-, and constables' rates. The church-rates, besides meeting church expenses, were also used, in Hornchurch as often elsewhere, to provide casual poor-relief. In the early 17th century the rates were assessed not only on land values, but also on the 'ability' of the taxpayers. The second method, which sounds like a local income tax, was used at least until 1642.

By the 17th century Hornchurch was well provided with charities, including two sets of alms-houses.[19] The parish also owned several houses and lands, the income from which was placed to the churchwardens' account. Parish relief, at that period, was rarely required except for the old, the sick, widows, or orphans. It usually took the form of doles, rent subsidies, or lodging allowances. Those on regular relief rarely numbered more than 15 or 20 at a time. Such arrangements appear to have sufficed until 1720, when the vestry, after a year in which the costs of relief had risen sharply, decided to build a workhouse on the site of Pennant's alms-houses in High Street, Hornchurch.[20] The contract was awarded to Col. Joseph Bennet, who a few years earlier had been associated with the notorious John Ward of Hackney (Mdx.) in an unsuccessful attempt to repair Dagenham Breach.[21] Ward himself was lessee of Hornchurch Hall at that period.[22] The original estimate for building the workhouse was £300. In borrowing the money the vestry incurred great trouble and expense, including a Chancery suit which was not settled until 1734.[23] At one stage they borrowed from John Ward to pay their debts to the builder.[24]

The workhouse came into use early in 1721.[25] All the parish pensioners were ordered into it, but some refused, leaving no more than 13 or 14 to be carted there. It remained in use until 1836.[26] In 1800 it had some 40 inmates, half of them children.[27] After 1836 the premises reverted to use as Pennant's alms-houses.

Out-relief was not completely abolished after the building of the workhouse. Casual payments were often required, and by the mid 1730s the number of regular pensions was again rising. The apprenticing of poor orphans appears to have declined sharply after 1721, but rose again in the 1740s. The surviving indentures show that some 86 per cent of the children were apprenticed within the parish.[28] Some 78 per cent of the boys were bound as farm workers and at least 74 per cent of the girls as domestic servants. Ten per cent of the boys were apprenticed as fishermen, mainly at Barking, and 7 per cent as blacksmiths.

In the early 19th century the number of poor receiving regular out-relief was usually about 20 to 25.[29] The costs of relief were then rising much faster in Hornchurch than in the other parts of the liberty.

[9] E.R.O., D/P 115/5/1.
[10] E.R.O., D/P 115/12/4.
[11] Ibid. 115/5/1. Unless otherwise stated the following account is based on the records mentioned in this paragraph.
[12] E.R.O., D/P 115/8/1A.
[13] Ibid. 115/5/2.
[14] Ibid. 115/8/1–3.
[15] Ibid. 115/12/1–12.
[16] Ibid. 115/14.
[17] See p. 5.
[18] E.R.O., D/P 115/8/1A.
[19] See p. 54.
[20] E.R.O., D/P 115/8/1A; G. Hardwick, 'The Hornchurch workhouse, 1785–1835' (Brentwood Coll. Educ. thesis, 1971: copy in E.R.O., T/Z 38/120).
[21] *V.C.H. Essex*, v. 286.
[22] See p. 32.
[23] E.R.O., D/DU 651/106.
[24] E.R.O., D/P 115/8/1A, 7 Feb. 1725.
[25] In 1721, also, the vestry granted the builder, Col. Bennet, a 61-year lease of three parish houses: E.R.O., D/P 115/8/1A.
[26] E.R.O., D/P 115/12/4–12; Perfect, *Village of Hornchurch*, 24–6.
[27] E.R.O., D/P 115/16.
[28] The series, 1700–73, contains the indentures of 72 boys and 35 girls. In a few cases the details are incomplete or ambiguous.
[29] E.R.O., D/P 115/12/11.

In the three years 1783–5 the average annual cost of relief was £579 in Hornchurch compared with £211 in Havering and £1,296 in Romford.[30] In the six years 1816–21 the average poor-rates were £1,772 in Hornchurch, £239 in Havering, and £1,495 in Romford.[31] The rate increase in Hornchurch was, however, slower than that in the neighbouring Thames-side parish of Dagenham.[32]

A select vestry, under the Second Sturges Bourne Act, was set up for Hornchurch in 1819.[33] In 1826, when its first surviving minute book starts, the select vestry was meeting fortnightly under the chairmanship of the vicar.[34] It had 16 members in 1827, and the number was later increased to the statutory limit of 20. In 1830 there was a sharp rise in petitions for poor-relief, attributed to the closure of a local benefit club. During a cholera scare in 1831 the select vestry appointed a health committee and issued sanitary regulations.[35]

Hornchurch became part of Romford poor-law union in 1836, and was later in Romford rural district. A parish council was set up in 1894 with 13 members representing four wards.[36] In 1905 the number of councillors was increased to 15. The parish council became responsible for the fire brigade, street lighting, and footpaths, and successfully put pressure on the rural district council to provide main drainage and build council houses. Council offices were built in Billet Lane in 1915.

In 1926 the parish became an urban district, with 4 wards and 13 councillors.[37] In 1929 Langtons, an 18th century mansion in Billet Lane, was given to the council by Varco Williams and his daughter Mrs. E. Varco Parkes.[38] The house became the main offices of the U.D.C., and the fine gardens were opened to the public. The urban district was extended in 1934 to include the civil parishes of Rainham and Wennington, and the altered civil parishes of Cranham, Great Warley, and Upminster; the membership of the council was then increased to 21, representing 8 wards.[39] In 1935 part of the parish of North Ockendon was also transferred to Hornchurch urban district.[40]

The membership of the council was further increased to 27 in 1948 and to 30, representing 9 wards, in 1952.[41] In 1959 the number of wards was increased to 10, still with 30 councillors.[42] Hornchurch applied for a borough charter in 1956.[43] With an estimated population of 110,000 it was then the second largest urban district in England. Its petition was, however, shelved pending the general reorganization of London government, and in 1965 Hornchurch became part of the London Borough of Havering.

Until the Second World War the urban district council was dominated by the Hornchurch Ratepayers' Association.[44] After the war control swung between the Labour party, 1946–8, 1954–5, 1956–60, and the Conservatives, 1949–54, 1955–6. The Ratepayers' Association disappeared from the council in 1951, but became active a few years later, and from 1961 to 1965 was the largest group on the council. During that last period no party had a controlling majority. The Labour party held second place, while the Conservatives lost ground, partly to the Liberals, who won two seats in 1962.

Hornchurch U.D.C. had to administer a large and diverse area with a rapidly increasing population. In its early years it bought much land for public parks.[45] After the war it launched a large municipal housing scheme, built a swimming pool, and joined with Romford B.C. and Thurrock U.D.C. to build a crematorium.[46]

PUBLIC SERVICES. The Romford Gas and Coke Co. extended its mains to Hornchurch about 1872.[47] In developing its services there the company benefited from the late arrival of electricity: in the early 1920s new houses were still being fitted with gas lighting.[48] In 1949 Hornchurch, with Romford, was transferred to the North Thames gas board.

Shortly before the First World War a small company, without statutory powers, was supplying electricity to a few streets adjoining Harold Wood station, but that undertaking soon ceased.[49] In 1913 the County of London Electric Supply Co. was given statutory powers to supply much of south Essex, including Hornchurch. The company could not make full use of those powers before the First World War, and Hornchurch did not receive electricity until shortly after Barking power station was opened in 1925.

Until the later 19th century Hornchurch still depended for its water supply on wells and springs.[50] The South Essex Waterworks Co., founded in 1861, was supplying parts of the parish by 1901.[51]

In 1886 Romford local board agreed to allow the use of its main sewers to drain part of Hornchurch.[52] A main drainage scheme for Hornchurch village, the north-west ward, and Harold Wood, was carried out by Romford R.D.C. between 1898 and 1903.[53] In 1934 the urban districts of Hornchurch and Romford formed a joint sewerage committee, and during the following years Romford's sewage works at Bretons farm, south Hornchurch, were enlarged to serve both districts.[54] The Riverside sewage works, at Rainham Creek, in Hornchurch, built by Romford

[30] E.R.O., Q/CR 1/1.
[31] Ibid. Q/CR 1/12.
[32] Cf. *V.C.H. Essex*, v. 293.
[33] E.R.O., D/P 115/12/11.
[34] Ibid. 115/8/1 (select vestry 1826–30).
[35] Ibid. 115/8/2.
[36] For the parish council see: Perfect, *Village of Hornchurch*, 97–105.
[37] Hornchurch (Constitution of Urban District) Order, 1926. For the U.D.C., see *Hornchurch Charter Petition* (1956).
[38] *E.R.* xxxix. 46.
[39] Essex Review Order, 1934.
[40] Essex Review Order, 1935.
[41] County of Essex (Hornchurch U.D.C. Alteration of Number of Councillors) Order, 1948; County of Essex (Hornchurch U.D. Wards and Councillors) Order, 1951.
[42] J. Cantwell, *Hornchurch, a political survey, 1926–65*, 46.
[43] *Hornchurch Charter Petition* (1956).
[44] This paragraph is based on: J. Cantwell, *Hornchurch, a political survey, 1926–65*. [Duplicated TS, 1965.]
[45] See p. 45.
[46] See p. 45.
[47] E.R.O., T/A 521/4, Romford Vestry Mins. 18 Dec. 1873; Gas and Water Orders Conf. Act. 1874, 37 & 38 Vict. c. 87 (local act). For the Romford Gas Co. see below, p. 79.
[48] Personal knowledge.
[49] This paragraph is based on: F. D. Smith, *Hist. Electricity in Romford and S.W. Essex*. [Duplicated TS, 1956]; *V.C.H. Essex*, v. 47, 75.
[50] Perfect, *Village of Hornchurch*, 17–20, 99.
[51] J. C. Thresh, *Rep. on Water Supply of Essex* (1901), 69 and map after p. 62.
[52] H.R.L., Romford L.B. Mins. 14 Sept., 4 Oct. 1886.
[53] Perfect, *Village of Hornchurch*, 104.
[54] See p. 81.

R.D.C. in 1924, served part of south Hornchurch as well as Dagenham, for which it was mainly designed.[55] In 1965 responsibility for sewage disposal passed to the Greater London council, and the treatment of sewage from Hornchurch was subsequently transferred to the Riverside works, the Bretons farm works being closed in 1969.[56]

In 1929 the newly formed Hornchurch U.D.C. took over Park Lane recreation ground, of 5 a., from Romford R.D.C.[57] Parks in Upminster and Rainham were similarly acquired when the urban district was enlarged in 1934. In its early years the U.D.C. bought land for many other parks, and by 1956 owned 471 a. of public open spaces, of which 313 a. were within the ancient parish of Hornchurch. The largest park was Harrow Lodge, 120 a., in Hornchurch Road and Upper Rainham Road. Grenfell Park, 27 a., was given to the council before the Second World War by an estate developer, Thomas England. The Hornchurch athletics stadium, Upminster Road, was opened in 1956.[58] It lies east of the river Ingrebourne, in Upminster parish. Hornchurch swimming pool, in Harrow Lodge park, was also opened in 1956; it cost £160,000.[59] In 1970 there were 478 a. of public open spaces in Hornchurch, including the former sewage farm at Bretons.

Hornchurch parish vestry bought a fire-engine in 1830.[60] The parish council, soon after its formation, took over from the vestry an old manual engine which had been housed at the Hornchurch Brewery, High Street, and removed it to the old Drill Hall, Billet Lane, and in 1898 a uniformed voluntary fire brigade was formed. A new engine was bought in 1900, and a fire station, built in Billet Lane, was opened in 1907. The brigade was eventually taken over by Hornchurch U.D.C., which in 1936 reorganized it on a full-time basis. Essex county council, which took over the brigade after the Second World War, built a new station in North Street in 1963.[61]

In 1913 Romford R.D.C., prompted by Hornchurch parish council, undertook to build 18 municipal cottages in Abbs Cross Lane.[62] These, with 446 houses built by the R.D.C. after the First World War, passed to Hornchurch U.D.C.[63] The U.D.C. itself built about 150 houses before the Second World War. About half the council houses built in the district up to 1939 were in Hornchurch parish, most of the remainder being in Rainham.[64] After the Second World War the U.D.C. launched a large-scale housing programme, and by 1965 had completed over 3,000 new dwellings, mainly in Hornchurch parish.[65]

Harold Wood hospital, Gubbins Lane, was opened in 1909 by West Ham county borough council as the Grange convalescent home for children, in connexion with Plaistow fever hospital.[66] The Grange had been a private house, built in 1884 by John Compton, owner of the Gubbins estate.[67] The convalescent home was maintained by West Ham until the Second World War, when it served as an emergency hospital. After the war it became a permanent hospital, and in the 1960s was greatly enlarged.[68] St. George's hospital, Sutton's Lane, Hornchurch, was built by Essex county council and opened in 1939 as an old people's home called Suttons Institution.[69] During the Second World War it was used to house airmen from R.A.F. Hornchurch. In 1948 it was taken over by the Ministry of Health as a hospital and was given its present name. It has over 400 beds, used mainly for geriatric cases. The Ingrebourne Centre, which is an independent part of the hospital, provides psychiatric treatment for 20 resident and many day patients.

Hornchurch cemetery, 9 a., which adjoins St. Andrew's church in Upminster Road, was opened by the U.D.C. in 1932, and has been several times enlarged.[70] It includes a special section for members of the armed forces. The South Essex crematorium, opened in 1957 by Hornchurch U.D.C. in conjunction with Romford B.C. and Thurrock U.D.C., is at Corbets Tey, Upminster.[71]

Until 1965 all Hornchurch's public libraries were provided by Essex county council.[72] The first, and main branch for the urban district, was opened in 1936 at Harrow Lodge, Hornchurch Road. Other branches were opened in the same year at Upminster and Rainham, in 1937 at Harold Wood, and in 1939 at South Hornchurch.[73] In 1953 the main Hornchurch branch was transferred to a more central position at Fairkytes, Billet Lane. Harrow Lodge continued in use to serve the north-west corner of the urban district. In 1956 another branch was opened in St. Nicholas Avenue, Elm Park. New branches, built for the purpose, were opened in Avenue Road, Harold Wood (1960), and Rainham Road, South Hornchurch (1962), to replace small 'shop' branches. In 1965 Hornchurch libraries were taken over by the London Borough of Havering. A new Hornchurch branch in North Street, planned by Essex, was completed by Havering in 1967. Fairkytes and Harrow Lodge libraries were then closed.

PARLIAMENTARY REPRESENTATION. In 1945 Hornchurch, previously in the Romford division, became a separate county constituency, coincident with Hornchurch urban district.[74] It was constituted a parliamentary borough in 1948. With an electorate which rose from 66,000 in 1945 to

[55] *Hornchurch Charter Petition* (1956), 23; *V.C.H. Essex*, v. 393.
[56] L.B. of Havering, *News Release* (*Bretons Farm Allotments*) 16 Aug. 1974.
[57] This paragraph is based on: *Hornchurch Charter Petition* (1956), 19; L.B. Havering, *Recreation and Amenities* (1970).
[58] *Hornchurch Official Guide* (1962–3), 46.
[59] *Municipal Jnl.* 4 Jan. 1957; *Architects Jnl.* 27 Nov. 1958.
[60] This paragraph is based on: *Hornchurch Charter Petition* (1956), 29; Perfect, *Village of Hornchurch*, 102.
[61] *Essex Co. Co. Mins.* (1962), p. 729; (1963), p. 1191.
[62] Perfect, *Village of Hornchurch*, 103.
[63] *Hornchurch Charter Petition* (1956), 17–18.
[64] Ibid.
[65] *Hornchurch Official Guide* (1962–3), 35; *Havering Official Guide* (1966–7), 32.
[66] *V.C.H. Essex*, vi. 111.
[67] See p. 35.
[68] Personal knowledge.
[69] Inf. from St. George's hospital.
[70] *Hornchurch Charter Petition* (1956), 15–16; L.B. Havering, *Recreation and Amenities* (1970); E.R.O., D/CC 83/9, 88/8, 92/3, 98/9, 104/6A.
[71] See p. 155.
[72] Paragraph based on inf. from Mr. L. Rose and Mr. K. Sleat of Havering Libraries.
[73] For the later history of the Rainham and Upminster branches see pp. 129, 156.
[74] This section is based on J. Cantwell, *Hornchurch, a political survey, 1926–64.* [Duplicated TS, 1965]; *Hornchurch Charter Petition* (1956), 9; *Dod's Parliamentary Companion* (1966 and later edns.).

100,000 in 1970 Hornchurch was one of the largest constituencies in the country. It had a Labour member from 1945 to 1955 and from 1966 to 1970, and a Conservative from 1955 to 1966 and 1970 to 1974. Boundary changes, which took effect in 1974, created three constituencies for the parliamentary borough of Havering: Hornchurch, Romford, and Upminster.

The new Hornchurch constituency was won by Labour in February 1974 and held in November 1974.

CHURCHES. The 'church of Havering', i.e. St. Andrew's, Hornchurch, existed by 1163, when Henry II gave it to the newly-founded priory of Hornchurch.[75] When the priory was dissolved in 1391 its possessions in Hornchurch were bought by William of Wykeham, bishop of Winchester, as part of the endowments of New College, Oxford.[76] In 1392 a vicarage was for the first time ordained.[77] That regulation was revoked in 1398,[78] but the college, following a precedent already set at Romford, made voluntary arrangements in some ways similar to those of a normal vicarage. Each successive incumbent, styled a vicar or chaplain,[79] held office on a long lease. Fifteenth-century leases were conditional upon the vicar's good behaviour, efficient service, personal residence, and sometimes his payment of a small rent; he was entitled to oblations, small tithes, and to allowances of clothing, corn, hay, and fuel.[80] By the early 19th century the vicar was receiving a stipend from the college instead of tithes and allowances.[81] Leasing continued until 1926–7, when the college endowed the vicarage.[82] New College still has the advowson.

Hornchurch priory probably exercised peculiar jurisdiction in the parish, but no details of it are known. New College certainly did so, though its jurisdiction in Hornchurch seems to have been narrower than in the college's other Essex peculiar of Writtle and Roxwell.[83] The bishop of the diocese never instituted to Hornchurch before the 20th century.[84] In 1410 his authority was invoked to confirm the agreement concerning the new chapel at Romford,[85] but in the 18th century he formally disclaimed jurisdiction in the parish at least twice.[86] The archdeacon of Essex never inducted the vicar, but, at least up to the 18th century, the wills of persons from Hornchurch, Romford, and Havering were usually proved in his court.[87] In 1427 and 1532 the archdeacon was involved in lawsuits concerning his rights in Hornchurch.[88] Under Elizabeth I and James I several cases relating to Hornchurch were heard in the archdeacon's court, including a long dispute between Romford and Havering over chapel-rates.[89] When the chapel-rate issue recurred in 1660 the church courts had not yet been revived after the Interregnum, and for that reason no further action was taken.[90] In 1682–3 a similar case, and another concerning the election of a chapelwarden for Havering, were heard and decided by the official of the archdeacon acting as 'the judge of this peculiar and exempt jurisdiction' (of Hornchurch).[91] That formula indicates that the archdeacon was acting only as the agent of New College, and at the archdeacon's visitation of 1683 the vicar of Hornchurch formally denied the archdeacon's right to enter the church, though later admitting him by courtesy.[92] In 1740 Romford vestry resolved to ask New College 'to establish an ecclesiastical court in this peculiar jurisdiction,'[93] and this was evidently done soon after: its earliest records date from 1748. The commissary of the peculiar, appointed by New College, issued marriage licences, granted probates, and conducted visitations.[94] He also confirmed church-rates levied within the peculiar.[95] By 1876, however, the archdeacon's visitation included Hornchurch,[96] and in 1903 the vicar of Hornchurch was instituted by the bishop.[97]

About 1355 the church of Hornchurch, with its chapels, was valued at 100 marks.[98] The rectory became the manor of Hornchurch Hall, the descent of which is treated elsewhere.[99] In 1650 the rectory was valued at £800, out of which the vicar of Hornchurch received £55 in small tithes, and the chaplains of Romford and Havering £45 and £20 respectively.[1] In the 1840s the rectorial tithes of Hornchurch, Romford, and Havering were commuted for £4,272.[2] Over 900 a. land, also belonging to New College, were then tithe free. The vicarage was valued at about £280 in 1791.[3] In 1846 the vicar's income included £5 from lands formerly in Havering park.[4] That payment had probably replaced an ancient right to a buck and a doe from the park.[5] In

[75] H. E. Salter, *Facsimiles of Oxford Charters*, nos. 34 and 35; *V.C.H. Essex*, ii. 195; *E.A.T.* N.S. vi. 1–7; *Horn. Docs.* no. 78. For general accounts of the church see: C. T. Perfect, *St. Andrew, Hornchurch* (1923); Anne V. Worsley, *Hornchurch Parish Church* (1964).

[76] *E.A.T.* N.S. xviii. 17; New Coll. MS. 9744, f. 162; *Horn. Docs.* no. 5; *Cal. Pat.* 1388–92, 262. As an alien priory Hornchurch had been in the king's hands since 1385: *Cal. Fine R.* 1383–91, 128, 168, 261, 301, 304, 322; *Cal. Inq. Misc.* v, pp. 153–4.

[77] *Horn. Docs.* nos. 311–12. In 1315 parishioners had taken legal action against the priory for not presenting a vicar, but had lost the case: *Horn. Docs.* no. 137. Ralph de Longley, chaplain of Hornchurch, occurs in 1257: ibid. nos. 392, 512.

[78] Ibid. no. 315 *b*.

[79] For a list of vicars see Worsley, *Hornchurch Par. Ch.* 31. The style 'chaplain and vicar temporal' is still used for official purposes.

[80] E.R.O., D/P 115/28/7; Smith, *Havering*, 147–8. See also Smith, *Eccl. Hist. Essex*, 249–50.

[81] *Gent. Mag.* (1828), i. 305.

[82] Inf. from New College; E.R.O., D/CP 8/61.

[83] For the records of the peculiar of Writtle and Roxwell see *Essex Parish Records* (2nd edn.), 242.

[84] Perfect, *St. Andrew*, 29–30.

[85] See p. 82.

[86] See e.g. E.R.O., T/A 521/1 (Romford Vestry Mins.) 9 Sept. 1715, 23 Apr. 1750: bishops of London disclaim jurisdiction over Romford chapel.

[87] *Wills at Chelmsford* (Brit. Rec. Soc.), vols. i–iii; E.R.O. D/P 115/28/6.

[88] *Horn. Docs.* nos. 8, 231.

[89] Hale, *Precedents*, 149, 151, 163, 184, 186, 188, 191–2, 200; E.R.O., T/Z 13/59.

[90] E.R.O., T/A 521/1, f. 54.

[91] Ibid. 27 Sept. 1683.

[92] *E.A.T.* N.S. xix. 265.

[93] E.R.O., T/A 521/1, 4 Mar. 1740.

[94] New Coll. MS. 186 (visitation papers 1766–80); 187 (appointment of commissary, 1765, 1767); 190–6 (marriage licences etc. 1748–1841); 213, 1179, 3430 (probates etc., 1753–1839).

[95] E.R.O., T/A 521/1, 3 May 1768.

[96] E.R.O., D/AEM 1/2.

[97] Perfect, *St. Andrew*, 30–1.

[98] New Coll. MS. 9744, f. 162.

[99] See p. 31.

[1] Smith, *Eccl. Hist. Essex*, 249–50.

[2] I.R. 29/12/162 and 177. For disputes concerning tithes in 1830–1 see E.R.O., D/P 115/28/8.

[3] New Coll. MS. 2985.

[4] I.R. 29/12/162.

[5] Cf. E.R.O., D/DSa 63 (survey, 1650).

1851 the vicar's stipend was £700, with a further £30 from fees.[6]

The ancient Vicarage, known in its later years as the Chaplaincy,[7] stood on the north side of High Street opposite the church. It was built by New College in the financial year 1399–1400, and at the same time was divided by a wall from the Rectory (later Hornchurch Hall).[8] Those arrangements suggest that the new owners were adapting the priory site for parochial use. The Vicarage was a timber-framed building, originally comprising an aisled hall with a solar wing to the west, and possibly a similar wing to the east.[9] In the later 17th century the whole house except the west wing was demolished and replaced by a two-storey timber-framed structure with an eastern cross-wing, and a separate gabled compartment on the north front housing the main staircase. Minor alterations were made to the east wing in the 18th century, and in the later 19th century two short parallel wings of brick were built at the east end of the south front. The building went out of use in 1969.[10] In 1970, when it was awaiting demolition, a fire revealed substantial remains of the original structure.[11] When it was demolished parts of the framework of the west wing were removed and stored by the London borough of Havering. The present Chaplaincy, formerly called Wykeham Lodge, is a modern house immediately west of the church.

Simon Abenach, by his will proved in 1307, gave houses in London to maintain a chaplain at the altar of St. Peter in Hornchurch.[12] There may have been a connexion between that chantry and the guild of St. Peter, mentioned in 1479.[13] The guild of Jesus or the Holy Trinity, and that of St. Mary, also existed in the late 15th century.[14] In the early 16th century they used the south and north chapels respectively.[15] The Jesus guild survived until its dissolution in 1548, when it had an income of £5 5*s*., and was employing a priest; it was said to have been founded by William Baldwin.[16] The 'Trinity house' still survived in 1708.[17]

The vicars of Hornchurch have usually been members of New College, and this tradition is still strongly maintained.[18] Thomas Duke, vicar 1531–40, was suspected of plotting against Henry VIII.[19] John Meyrick, 1570–4, was later bishop of Sodor and Man.[20] William Lambert, vicar 1574–92, became involved in a long dispute with John Leche, whom he accused of conducting an Anabaptist conventicle and school at Hornchurch.[21] Thomas Mann, vicar from 1632, appears to have been sequestrated about 1645, though he remained in the parish until his death in 1648.[22] John Hoffman was acting as minister from 1645 to 1648.[23] He had four successors during the Interregnum, of whom the last was Michael Wells, vicar 1658–86.[24] Few references to assistant curates have been noticed before the later 19th century,[25] when the first mission churches were opened. During the past 50 years Hornchurch, with a tradition of 'central' churchmanship,[26] has become one of the most populous and flourishing parishes in the diocese. In 1973 the staff included two curates, a deaconess, and a lay reader.[27]

The church of *ST. ANDREW*, which stands on the hill at the top of High Street, consists of chancel, north and south chapels, four-bay nave, north and south aisles, north porch, and west tower.[28] It is built of septaria and ragstone, with some brick, and limestone dressings. The present building originated in the 13th century, but during the 15th century the aisles and chancel were rebuilt and the north and south chapels, clerestorey, porch, and tower were added. The south aisle and chapel were rebuilt in 1802.

Nothing now survives of the church granted to Hornchurch priory in 1163: it seems to have been completely rebuilt in the 13th century. Work was in progress in 1228, and possibly by 1220.[29] The nave arcades and the triple sedilia in the chancel survive from the 13th century. Soon after New College bought the benefice further work was put in hand. Between 1405 and 1408 the chancel was rebuilt and its windows filled with 167 sq. ft. of glass, which no longer survives.[30] The aisles were rebuilt about the same time. Later in the 15th century the chapels, clerestorey, and north porch were added and the chancel floor was probably raised. The east window of the north chapel contains a few fragments of 15th-century glass, including the arms of Deyncourt and a royal figure, probably Edward the Confessor.[31] The tower, planned by 1476, was completed *c.* 1491–2.[32] It is of 3 stages, with embattled parapet and turrets, and recessed spire. One parapet bears the letters RF in stone,[33] and until 1921 the letter M, or a reversed W, appeared in stone on the west wall of the tower.[34]

[6] H.O. 129/7/197.

[7] The name was in use by 1917: Perfect, *Village of Hornchurch*, 66.

[8] New Coll. MS. 6394 (detailed building accounts).

[9] E.R.O., T/Z 116/1 (G.L.C. Hist. Bdgs. Div. Rep. on the Chaplaincy, 1971).

[10] Inf. from Vicar of Hornchurch.

[11] *The Times*, 13 Oct. 1971.

[12] *E.A.T.* N.S. xiii. 258.

[13] E.R.O., D/AER 1, f. 12v.

[14] E.R.O., D/AER 1, ff. 12v., 55, 75, 101v., 137, 145.

[15] *E.A.T.* N.S. vi. 316; Prob. 11/16 (P.C.C. 8 Bennett, will of Tho. Crafford, 1508), cf. Worsley, *Hornchurch Par. Ch.* 26.

[16] E 301/19/19; E 301/30/23; cf. *Cal. Pat.* 1549–51, 261–2.

[17] E.R.O., D/AER 29, f. 95.

[18] See e.g. E.R.O., D/P 115/28/7; *Misc. Gen. Her.* 3rd ser. ii. 20; *Crockford's Cler. Dir.* and Foster, *Alumni Oxon. passim.*

[19] *L. & P. Henry VIII*, v, p. 293; xi, p. 587.

[20] *D.N.B.*

[21] Hale, *Precedents*, 184, 186, 188, 191–2, 200; Assizes 35/32/H. For Leche's school see below, p. 53.

[22] H. Smith, 'Sequence of Parochial Clergy in Essex, 1640–64.' (TS in E.R.O. Libr.), i. 15–16; Smith, *Eccl. Hist. Essex*, 122, 193.

[23] Ibid.

[24] Ibid.

[25] For an earlier example see Guildhall MS. 9553, f. 29 (curate licensed 1781).

[26] C.C.L., Bp. Inskip's Recs. ii. 136; personal knowledge.

[27] *Hornchurch Parish Dir.* (1973–4).

[28] The following description is based mainly on: Anne V. Worsley, *Hornchurch Parish Church*. The use of Miss Worsley's research notes, including historical material collected by the archdeacon of Sheffield, the Ven. H. Johnson, formerly vicar of Hornchurch, is also gratefully acknowledged. For earlier accounts of the chuich: R.C.H.M. *Essex*. iv. 68–71; *E.R.* v. 18–40; C. T. Perfect, *St. Andrew, Hornchurch*.

[29] *Cal. Close*, 1227–31, 42; *Rot. Lit. Claus.* (Rec. Com.), i. 441.

[30] New Coll. Oxford MSS. 6402, 6404, 6405.

[31] Ogborne, *Essex*, 139 and pl. f. p. 151. The Deyncourts held land in Hornchurch as well as Upminster: *Cal. Inq. Misc.* vii, p. 159.

[32] Terry, *Romford*, 58–9; E.R.O., D/AER 1, f. 12v (will of Ric. Parson, 1479); *N. & Q.* 5th ser. xi. 285–6 (will of Jn. Turke, 1484); E.R.O., T/A 521/1 (church rate for steeple, 1491–2.)

[33] R.C.H.M. *Essex*, iv. 70.

[34] Perfect, *St. Andrew*, 9 n.

On the west face of one turret is the stone figure of a seated bishop.[35]

The roofs of the chancel, north chapel, nave, and north aisle, seem to date from *c.* 1500 and to have been planned by 1486.[36] Those of the chancel and nave were then painted in a red and black chequered design, with gold quatrefoils superimposed.[37]

In 1716 the church was 'pewed and beautified'.[38] The work then carried out created a rich interior described by one writer as like those in Wren's city churches, and including a richly carved wooden pulpit, a reredos in the style of Gibbons, a panelled chancel, and a west gallery.[39]

In 1802 the south aisle and chapel were rebuilt in brick and the spire was clad with copper, replacing lead.[40] The architect was probably John Johnson (d. 1814), the county surveyor.[41] In 1826 the east window, long blocked, was re-opened.[42]

Between 1869 and 1871 the church was heavily restored.[43] A new east window was inserted, the chancel and south chapel arches were rebuilt, the sanctuary raised, the chancel ceiled, and the Georgian fittings removed. In 1913 a choir vestry was made beneath the south chapel, and in 1921 the eastern gable of the chancel was rebuilt.[44] In 1954–62 the tower was strengthened and the roofs were repaired, the chancel was unceiled, the sanctuary floor was again lowered, and new east and belfry windows were inserted.[45] In 1970 a new church hall was opened on the south side of the church, to which it is connected by a covered way.[46]

On the eastern gable of the chancel is the carved stone head of a Highland bull with hollow copper horns.[47] It was first mentioned in 1824, though 'points of lead fashioned like horns', apparently in the same position, can be traced back to 1610.[48] The place-name 'Horned church' occurs by the 13th century. The church may have had horn-like gables, or have been surmounted by features resembling horns, possibly associated with the local leather industry.[49] When the horns became associated with a bull is not known. A bull's head appears on the seal of the prior of Hornchurch in 1384–5,[50] and by 1719 New College was providing an annual feast of 'bull and brawn'.[51]

In 1719 there was a marble font with a black-letter inscription.[52] It may have survived until 1817, when it was replaced by a stone one.[53] which in turn was replaced by a wooden one in 1970.

A bequest to the priest of the Holy Trinity guild in 1479 on condition that he could play the organ implies the existence of an organ then.[54] In 1552 there were two organs, both broken.[55] A barrel organ was erected in the west gallery in 1833.[56] A two-manual organ replaced it in 1861 and a three-manual one, in the south chapel, in 1913.[57]

There were five bells in 1552. They were recast into six by Mears & Co. in 1779, and two more, by the same firm, were added in 1901.[58] Two large earthenware pitchers, dated 1731 and 1815, and formerly used to hold beer for the bell-ringers, are in the church.[59] There was a church clock by 1674, when it was replaced. A new clock was installed in 1814.[60]

In 1385 the church had 3 cups and 3 grails.[61] The plate now includes 2 silver gilt cups and patens of 1563 and 1733, 2 silver gilt patens of *c.* 1690 and 1719, a silver flagon of 1699, an alms-dish of 1716, and a golden cup given in 1948.[62] The parish chest dates from the 18th century. Earlier chests, which no longer survive, were mentioned in 1552 and 1668.[63]

The church has many monuments.[64] There are brasses, or parts of brasses, to Thomas Scargill (d. 1476), Thomas Crafford (d. 1508) of Dovers, Catherine Fermor (d. 1510), George Reede (d. 1531) vicar, Peerce Pennant (d. 1590) the alms-house founder, Thomas (d. 1591), Humphrey (d. 1595), and William (d. 1602) Drywood, and brass indents for Boniface de Hart,[65] canon of Aosta and probably prior of Hornchurch (in 1327), and Philip of Dover (d. 1335), lord of Dovers. An altar-tomb commemorates William Ayloffe (d. 1517) of Bretons.[66] There are other monuments to Francis Rame (d. 1618), Richard Blackstone (d. 1638), Thomas Witherings (d. 1651) of Nelmes, Sir Francis Prujean (d. 1666), and one to Richard Spencer (d. 1784) by John Flaxman. A floriated coffin-lid, probably of the 13th century, survives. Some of the earlier brasses were mutilated in 1644–6, when their 'superstitious inscriptions' were removed by Parliamentary order.[67]

There are two charities for the maintenance of the church.[68] Church field, comprising 6 a., part of Gibbs

[35] *E.A.T.* N.S. vi, pl. f. p. 200.
[36] E.R.O., D/AER 1, f. 75 (will of Tho. Capron, 1486).
[37] Revealed when the later ceilings were removed in 1957.
[38] E.R.O., T/P 195/2, f. 150; E.R.O., D/P 115/8/1A, 4 June, 3 Sept 1716 (church rate of 18*d.* and £50 from Jn. Ward, lessee of Hornchurch Hall).
[39] *Chelmsford Chron.* 4 Nov. 1852 (copy in E.R.O., T/P 196 (King MSS.), Eccl. Hist. Essex, iv, f. 21 sqq.).
[40] *E.R.* v. 21 n.; Ogborne, *Essex*, 148.
[41] E.R O., Libr. Folder (Ecclesiology), newscutting *c.* 1808; inf. from Miss N. R. Briggs,
[42] *Gent. Mag.* (1828), i. 305–6.
[43] Perfect, *St. Andrew*, 11; E.R.O., Sage Coll. no. 503.
[44] Perfect, *St. Andrew*, 12, 16–17.
[45] E.R.O., D/P 115/28/15.
[46] *Havering Recorder*, 6 Feb. 1970.
[47] Worsley, *Hornchurch Par. Ch.* 29–30, cover, frontispiece; Perfect, *St. Andrew*, 58; see plate facing this page.
[48] *Gent. Mag.* (1828), i. 305; Camden, *Brit.* (1610 edn.), 441; J. Weever, *Ancient Funerall Monuments*, 646; E.R.O., T/P 195/2 (Holman MSS.), Hornchurch, f. 1; Salmon, *Essex*, 242; *N. & Q.* 2nd ser. i. 520.
[49] *P.N. Essex*, 111–12; cf. E. Ekwall, *Oxford Dic. Eng. P.N.* s.v. Hornchurch. High St. was called Pell St. in the 13th cent.
[50] *Horn. Docs.* p. vi; Worsley, *Hornchurch Par. Ch.* f. p. 21.
[51] E.R.O., T/P 195/2, Hornchurch, f. 4.
[52] Ibid. f. 150.
[53] E.R.O., Sage Coll. nos. 502–3.
[54] E.R.O., D/AER 1, f. 12v.
[55] *E.A.T.* N.S. iii. 42.
[56] Perfect, *St. Andrew*, 16; H. Bevington, *Psalms and Hymn-Tunes as set on the new organ . . . in Hornchurch* [n.d., *c.* 1837: Copy in H.R.L.].
[57] *White's Dir. Essex* (1863), 592; Perfect, *St. Andrew*, 16.
[58] *Ch. Bells Essex*, 300; Perfect, *St. Andrew*, p. vii.
[59] Perfect, *St. Andrew*, 17–19.
[60] Ibid. 17–20; *Ch. Bells Essex*, 300–1.
[61] *Horn. Docs.* 28.
[62] *Ch. Plate Essex*, 14; Worsley, *Hornchurch Par. Ch.* 27.
[63] *Ch. Chests Essex*, 142.
[64] These have been described in print, with others now lost: R.C.H.M. *Essex*, iv. 70–1; *E.R.* v. 29–38; *E.A.T.* N.S. ix. 27–8; x. 204–6; xi. 321–34; Salmon, *Essex*, 253–4; Worsley, *Hornchurch Par. Ch.* 25–7.
[65] Cf. *V.C.H. Essex*, ii. 197.
[66] Chancellor, *Sep. Mons. Essex*, 327–9; A. B. Bamford, *Sketches in Royal Liberty of Havering*, no. 4.
[67] E.R.O., D/P 115/5/1. There was further spoliation in the 19th cent.: *E.A.T.* N.S. xi. 321.
[68] Unless otherwise stated this and the following paragraph are based on: *Rep. Com. Char.* [108], p. 724 (1837–8) xxv (1); E.R.O., D/P 115/5/1; Char. Com. Files; inf. from Mr. F. C. Hamlyn and Char. Com.

Hornchurch: St. Andrew's Church

Little Warley: The Essex Regiment Chapel

South Ockendon: St. Nicholas's Church in 1820

Romford: St. Andrew's Church, built 1862

Hornchurch: St. Leonard's Homes, built 1889

Havering: The Round House, built *c.* 1795

at Perrys farm, Romford, was given in 1563 by William Talbot, vicar of Rainham. The rent from it was £2 13s. 4d. in the period 1623–36, £5 in 1656, and £20 in 1837. In 1934 the land, then 7 a., was sold for £1,646. In 1975 the income from stock was £100. Shipman's croft, later called Gogneys, comprised 2 a. in South End Road, Hornchurch. It seems to have been given in or before 1570 by Agnes Shipman. In 1624 it was said to be for the poor, but in 1627, when it was leased to William Gogney for 15s. a year, the rent was to be used to repair the church. In 1837 the rent was £4 4s. The land was sold in 1938 for £900. In 1975 the income from stock was £31.

Mildred Bearblock, by her will of 1865, gave £111 in trust for the most regular attendants at church. In 1874 the vicar, who had distributed the charity for two years, refused to do so any longer, and by a Scheme of that year the income was to be used for Sunday school prizes. By 1917 Bearblock's charity was said to be combined with that of Whennell, the total income of about £10 being used to buy Sunday school prizes, books, and furniture.[69] In 1975 the income from Bearblock's charity was £7.

St. Andrew, Hornchurch, had two ancient chapelries, Romford and Havering. During the Interregnum an unsuccessful attempt was made to form them into separate parishes.[70] Havering eventually became independent for ecclesiastical purposes in the 1780s, and Romford in 1848–9.[71] Since 1849 six new churches, all originally missions of St. Andrew, have been built in Hornchurch. Two of them remain under St. Andrew: the church of *ST. GEORGE*, Kenilworth Gardens,[72] built in 1931, and that of *ST. MATTHEW*, Chelmsford Drive (1956).[73] Of the others three have been given their own parishes, and one has been transferred to Rainham.

The mission church of *ST. JOHN*, South Hornchurch, South End Road, was opened in 1864 and enlarged in 1882.[74] In 1954 it was transferred to Rainham.[75] A new church, dedicated to *ST. JOHN AND ST. MATTHEW* was built on an adjoining site in 1957.[76]

The church of *ST. PETER*, Harold Wood, Gubbins Lane, originated in 1871, when an iron building was erected in Church Road.[77] In 1939 a permanent brick church was opened in Gubbins Lane with the help of contributions from James and George H. Matthews, local millers. A separate parish, taken out of St. Andrew's, was then formed, the advowson of the vicarage being vested in New College, Oxford. Under Bernard Hartley, priest-in-charge and later vicar, 1913–46, St. Peter's developed a strong evangelical tradition. When the Harold Hill estate was built after the Second World War the eastern part of it was transferred from the parish of Romford to Harold Wood,[78] and the new church of St. Paul, Harold Hill (1953) was a mission of St. Peter's until a separate parish was allotted to it in 1956.[79] A single-storey annexe was added to St. Peter's church in 1963.[80]

The church of *THE HOLY CROSS*, Hornchurch Road, originated in 1920, when a hut, formerly a chapel in the army camp at Grey Towers, was re-erected at the corner of Malvern Road and Park Lane, to serve as a mission church and social centre for north-west Hornchurch.[81] The mission was at first run jointly by the Church Army and the vicar of Hornchurch, but in 1922 the vicar assumed complete responsibility. A new parish, taken out of St. Andrew, was formed in 1925, the advowson of the vicarage being vested in New College and the bishop alternately.[82] In 1933 a permanent church was built on a new site at the corner of Hornchurch Road and Park Lane.[83]

The church of *ST. NICHOLAS*, Elm Park, St. Nicholas Avenue, originated in 1936, when a temporary building was erected.[84] A permanent church was opened in 1956.[85] In 1957 a separate parish, taken out of St. Andrew, was formed, the advowson of the vicarage being vested in the bishop.[86]

ROMAN CATHOLICISM. There are a few references to Hornchurch recusants in the late 16th century.[87] During the late 17th and early 18th centuries several members of the Prujean family, of Suttons Gate, were papists.[88]

The church of *ST. MARY*, Hornchurch Road, which serves north-west Hornchurch, was built in 1931 and consecrated in 1933.[89] There are junior and infant day-schools attached. At Elm Park a separate parish was formed, and a church hall built in 1939.[90] The church of *ST. ALBAN*, Langdale Gardens, was built in 1960.[91] It is served by the Verona Fathers. A parish was formed for east Hornchurch in 1955, and the church of *THE ENGLISH MARTYRS*, Alma Avenue, was then opened.[92] South Hornchurch is served by the church of Our Lady of La Salette, which is treated under Rainham.[93]

PROTESTANT NONCONFORMITY.[94] Havering Well Presbyterian, later Independent meeting, Hornchurch Road, was first mentioned in 1691, when its minister, Mr. Dod the elder, had to leave after a stay of three years because the congregation was to poor to support him.[95] He was probably Robert Dod, who had been ejected in 1662 from the

[69] Perfect, *Village of Hornchurch*, 108. For Whennell see below, p. 55.
[70] Smith, *Eccl. Hist. Essex*, 249–50, 348.
[71] See pp. 23, 83.
[72] *E.R.* xli. 52.
[73] Foundation stone.
[74] Perfect, *St. Andrew*, 52.
[75] E.R.O., D/CPc 320.
[76] E.R.O., D/CC 108/1.
[77] Paragraph based on: W. G. and M. M. Budner, *Faith at Work . . . the church of St Peter, Harold Wood, 1871–1971*. See also: E.R.O., D/CPc 278 and 288; D/CC 90/6; D/CP 8/28.
[78] E.R.O., D/CPc 318.
[79] See p. 87.
[80] Foundation stone.
[81] Perfect, *St. Andrew*, 52–4.
[82] E.R.O., D/CPc 194.
[83] E.R.O., D/CC 84/6; *E.R.* xlii. 200.
[84] *Kelly's Dir. Essex* (1937).
[85] E.R.O., D/CC 107/5; ibid. D/CP 5/7.
[86] E.R.O., D/CPc 348.
[87] *Cath. Rec. Soc.* xxii. 50; *Essex Recusant*, i. 53, 77.
[88] *Cath. Rec. Soc.* xix. 372 n. 373 n; *Essex Recusant*, ii. 11; vi. 54; xii. 74; Perfect, *Village of Hornchurch*, 47.
[89] *Cath Dir.* (1973); G.R.O. Worship Reg. 53470, 54370; Foundation stone.
[90] *Cath. Dir.* (1973); G.R.O. Worship Reg. 59058.
[91] G.R.O. Worship Reg. 67806.
[92] Ibid. 65042; *Cath. Dir.* (1973).
[93] See p. 140.
[94] This section was written in 1975.
[95] A. Gordon, *Freedom after Ejection*, 40, 43. Unless otherwise stated this paragraph is based on: W. W. Biggs, *Cong. Ch. Romford*, 11; J. P. Longstaff, *Romford Cong. Ch.*, 30–1, 39–40.

rectory of Inworth.[96] By 1698, when Thomas Wight was minister, a large meeting-house, with a graveyard, had been built at the expense of Thomas Webster, whose family about that time acquired Nelmes. Samuel Wilson, who was minister for some years up to his death in 1727, lived at Dagenham, from which some of his congregation probably came.[97] His successor, William Sheffield, left in 1732. The minister of Romford Independent church then took over the pastorate of Havering Well. Havering Well continued as a dependency of Romford until 1819, when it was demolished, and the materials were used in the building of the new meeting-house in North Street, Romford. The Havering Well graveyard was preserved, and interments there continued until the later 19th century. In 1973 about a third of the graveyard, on the south side, was ploughed up and paved in preparation for road widening.[98]

Hornchurch Baptist church, North Street, seems to have originated in 1859, when Hermon Independent chapel, High Street, was registered for worship.[99] Hermon was probably identical with the mission which during the 1860s and 1870s was supported by Romford and Upminster Congregational churches.[1] In 1877 the members of the mission formed a church, but having found it difficult to get Congregational preachers they sought the help of Spurgeon, who sent students from his Baptist college at the Metropolitan Tabernacle.[2] In 1880 the church adopted a Baptist constitution, and in 1882 the present building was erected in North Street, on land given by John Abraham of Upminister. Spurgeon preached at the stone-laying and gave £100 to the building fund.[3] The first settled pastor came in 1890. A schoolroom was added in 1885. The church itself was enlarged in 1903. Between 1931 and 1936 it was further enlarged and modernized, and new schools were built. North Street was for long the leading nonconformist church in Hornchurch, and founded three other churches.

Ardleigh Green Baptist church, Ardleigh Green Road, originated in 1914 as a mission of Hornchurch.[4] In 1932 it joined the Essex Baptist Association.[5] A new school-chapel was built on the same site in 1933.[6]

Harold Park Baptist church, Harold Court Road, was founded in 1930, and joined the Essex Baptist Association in the same year.[7] In 1932–3 the church was regretting the departure of the Association 'from old paths' and its 'dabbling in the Oxford Group movement'.[8] By 1959 it had joined the Fellowship of Independent Evangelical churches.[9] The building was extended in 1960.[10]

Elm Park Baptist church, Rosewood Avenue, originated in 1937, with house meetings and a Sunday school, supported by the Hornchurch Baptists and the Essex Baptist Association.[11] A school-chapel was built in 1938, and the church was formally constituted in 1939. The building was damaged by bombing in 1940. A youth hall was added in 1946. A new church was built in 1963.

A Wesleyan Methodist society, meeting in a house, was reported in 1829.[12] It had a regular congregation of 80, and was under the care of the Romford minister in the Spitalfields circuit. The house may have been Hollies, in North Street, which was being used as a nonconformist chapel about 1835.[13] In 1854 part of a building occupied by Jonathan Diaper of Hornchurch was registered for Wesleyan worship.[14] That society also seems to have been short-lived.

Gidea Park (Wesleyan) Methodist church, Manor Avenue, originated in 1926, when a school-chapel, in the Ilford circuit, was opened.[15] Extensions were carried out in 1931–2. Gidea Park was transferred to the new Romford circuit in 1947. A new church was built in 1958.

Hornchurch (Wesleyan) Methodist church, High Street, originated about 1929 with meetings in the Masonic Hall.[16] A school-chapel, in the Ilford circuit, was opened in 1933. It was transferred to the Romford circuit in 1947. A new church was built in 1958.

Harold Wood (United) Methodist church, The Drive, originated in 1889, when an undenominational mission hall, in Athelstan Road, was registered.[17] That was taken over about 1908 by the United Methodists, and became part of the Forest Gate circuit.[18] In 1929 a church and school were built on a large site at the corner of Gubbins Lane, with the aid of funds from (Sir) William Mallinson (Bt.). Harold Wood was transferred to the Ilford circuit in 1946 and to the Romford circuit in 1947. A new church was built in 1962, and the 1929 building then became a hall.[19]

Grenfell Hall Methodist church, Grenfell Avenue, originated in the early 1930s with house meetings.[20] A site was given by Thomas England, the estate developer, and a two-storey church was opened in 1936. It was in the Ilford circuit until 1947 and then in the Romford circuit.

Elm Park Methodist church, Mungo Park Road, was opened in 1957, in the Romford circuit.[21]

Nelmes United Reformed church, Nelmes Road, Emerson Park, was formed in 1906 as Hornchurch Congregational church.[22] Initial help was given by Romford Congregational church. Meetings were

[96] Cf. Smith, *Eccl. Hist. Essex*, 372.
[97] Cf. *V.C.H. Essex*, v. 297.
[98] *Romford Observer*, 1 March 1973; inf. from L.B. Havering, Engineer's Dept.
[99] G.R.O. Worship Reg. 8640; O.S. Map 6″, Essex, LXXV (surv. 1865–6).
[1] *E.C.U. Reps.* 1869–77; *Cong. Year Bks.* (1866–80).
[2] Unless otherwise stated this paragraph is based on: R. M. Nurse, *Hist. Hornchurch Baptist Ch.* (1953); E.R.O., D/NB 2/1–4.
[3] *Strat. Expr.* 19 July, 1882.
[4] D. Witard, *Bibles in Barrels*, 171.
[5] E.R.O., D/NB 2/3.
[6] Ibid.; Foundation stone.
[7] E.R.O., D/NB 2/3; *Bapt. Handbk.* (1933 and later edns.).
[8] E.R.O., D/NB 2/3.
[9] G.R.O. Worship Reg. 67336.
[10] Foundation stone.
[11] Paragraph based on: E.R.O., D/NB 2/3 and 4; R. M. Nurse, *Hist. Hornchurch Bapt. Ch.*; Witard, *Bibles in Barrels*, 171.
[12] E.R.O., Q/CR 3/2/89.
[13] Perfect, *Village of Hornchurch*, 89.
[14] G.R.O. Worship Reg. 2461; cf. *White's Dir. Essex* (1863), p. 594: Jonathan Draper (*sic*), coachbuilder.
[15] Paragraph based on: E. Barrett, *The Lamp still Burns*, 9, 10, 33–4; *Wesleyan Chapel Cttee. Reps.* (1926–32); inf. from Rev. G. Maland.
[16] Paragraph based on: Barrett, *The Lamp still Burns*, 10, 37–8; inf. from Mr. J. Jenkinson.
[17] G.R.O. Worship Reg. 31855.
[18] Paragraph based on: *Harold Wood Meth. Ch. 21st Anniversary* (1950); Barrett, *The Lamp still Burns*, 48, 55, 81.
[19] Personal knowledge; G.R.O. Worship Reg. 68793.
[20] Paragraph based on: Barrett, *The Lamp still Burns*, 10–11, 40.
[21] Worship Reg. 66196.
[22] Paragraph based on: Perfect, *Village of Hornchurch*, 92–4; W. W. Biggs, *Cong. Ch. Romford*. 25.

held in a hall in Berther Road until 1909, when a permanent building was erected in Nelmes Road, on a site given by Thomas Dowsett of Southend-on-Sea.[23] A new hall was added in 1960.[24]

The Brethren had two congregations at Hornchurch in 1917.[25] One of them was meeting in the Billet Lane hall, and it remained there until 1958, when it built Emerson Park chapel, Butts Green Road.[26] The Brethren also have meeting-places at Bethany hall, Abbs Cross Lane, registered 1935, Athelstan hall, Athelstan Road, Harold Wood (1952), and Hillview hall, Hillview Avenue, Hornchurch (1969).[27]

The Evangelical Free church, Brentwood Road, originated in 1888, when a mission hall was built in Boundary Road, Romford.[28] A free church was formed in 1894. The present church, erected in 1902, was just inside Hornchurch. The Full Gospel church of the Assemblies of God, Frederick Road, south Hornchurch, existed by 1951.[29] Whybridge Evangelical Free church, Rainham Road, south Hornchurch, originated by 1951 as the Whybridge Hall.[30] The church of the Latter Day Saints (Mormons), Ardleigh Green Road, was built in 1964 on a large, wooded site.[31] It is of white brick and timber with part of the front wall in rock-faced brick. The detached spire is of gilded metal in the shape of an arrow. Among several small undenominational missions in Hornchurch[32] is the Craigdale Hall, Craigdale Road, which goes back to the 1920s.[33]

JUDAISM. Elm Park affiliated synagogue was established in 1939, and became affiliated to the United Synagogue in 1948.[34] A permanent building was erected in Woburn Avenue in 1949.

EDUCATION. A school board was formed for Hornchurch in 1889. It took over 4 existing schools and built 2 more. Essex county council built 6 primary and 5 secondary schools between 1929 and 1939. A Roman Catholic primary school was founded in 1933. Under the Education Act, 1944, Hornchurch U.D. was entitled to become an Excepted District, but it waived its right, and remained directly under the county council.[35] Between 1945 and 1965 the county built 3 more primary schools, 4 secondary schools, and a college of further education. A Roman Catholic boys grammar school was opened in 1962. In 1955 many of the schools were renamed, usually with local manor or estate names to replace those of streets.[36] Between 1965 and 1974 the London borough of Havering opened 5 more primary schools in Hornchurch, including 3 previously planned by Essex. By September 1973 all the secondary schools had been reorganized as comprehensive. In the following accounts of individual schools, information, unless otherwise stated, was provided by the Education Department of Essex or that of Havering.

ELEMENTARY SCHOOLS FOUNDED BEFORE 1889. In 1548 poor children in Hornchurch were taught by a priest appointed by Trinity Guild.[37] In the period 1620–2 boys were taught grammar by a curate in the church.[38] The Romford charity school, founded in 1711, was open to Hornchurch children.[39]

Aylett's school was founded in 1731 by the will of Alice Aylett, who gave land in trust to pay £10 yearly to a schoolmaster, appointed by the parish, to teach 10 poor boys. The first schoolmaster, appointed in 1746, was to teach in the church vestry.[40] In 1813 William Jacobs left £200 in trust to Aylett's school. In 1837 ten poor boys were being taught reading, writing, and arithmetic along with several paying pupils in the master's house.[41] Aylett's school never owned a building. It seems to have been amalgamated with the National boys school in 1856.[42] When the National school was taken over by the school board in 1890 a Charity Commission scheme required the income from Aylett's and Jacobs's charities to be used for prizes for Hornchurch children.[43] The rent-charge for Aylett's charity was redeemed in 1904.[44]

Nonconformists founded a small day- and boarding-school in 1830. It still existed in 1833, when there was another nonconformist day-school with 14 children, but both schools had closed by 1839.[45]

Langton's (formerly Village) junior and infants school, Westland Avenue. In 1844 a National school was built next to the Chaplaincy. A new school for girls and infants, with a teacher's house, was built in 1855 in North Street on land given by New College, Oxford.[46] In 1874 the boys moved to a new school for 117 next to the teacher's house, and the infants were transferred to the old building, next to the Chaplaincy.[47] The National school received annual government grants from 1871.[48] The school board took it over in 1889,[49] and in 1902 built a new school for 400 boys and girls in Westland Avenue. The 1855 buildings were used by infants until 1926, when new classrooms were built.[50] The school was enlarged in 1932 and was reorganized in 1935 for juniors and infants. The junior departments were amalgamated in 1951.[51]

Mrs. Skeale's Church infants school, South End

[23] *Cong. Year Bk.* (1910), 147.
[24] Foundation stone.
[25] Perfect, *Village of Hornchurch*, 94.
[26] G.R.O. Worship Reg. 50881, cf. 66668.
[27] Ibid. 55805; 63340; 71909 (9, Hillview Rd.).
[28] Paragraph based on: *Wilson & Whitworth's Romford Almanack* (1902 and later edns.); *Strat. Expr.* 20 Feb. 1892; Worship Reg. 34660, cf. 38884; Foundation stone.
[29] *Hornchurch Official Guide* (1951), 61; Worship Reg. 63545.
[30] *Hornchurch Official Guide* (1951), 61; G.R.O. Worship Reg. 63285.
[31] G R.O. Worship Reg. 69402.
[32] *Havering Dir. Local Organizations* (1971), 5–7.
[33] *Kelly's Dir. Essex* (1929), s.v. Romford; G.R.O. Worship Reg. 53076.
[34] Account based on: inf. from Secretary, United Synagogue; G.R.O. Worship Reg. 62542; Foundation stone.
[35] *Hornchurch Charter Petition* (1956), p. 28.
[36] E.R.O., C/ME 49, pp. 746–7.
[37] E 301/19/19.
[38] E.R.O., D/AEA 32, ff. 106v, 247v.
[39] See p. 92.
[40] *Rep. Com. Char.* [108], p. 728 (1837–8), xxv (1); E.R.O., D/DM T96/20, F27/6.
[41] *Rep. Com. Char.* [108], p. 728.
[42] E.R.O., D/P 115/5/2.
[43] E.R.O., C/ME 1, p. 1748.
[44] Char. Com. Files.
[45] *Educ. Enquiry Abstract*, H.C. 62, p. 279 (1835), xli; E.R.O., D/P 30/28/18.
[46] *Mins. Educ. Cttee. of Council 1857–8* [2380], p. 97, H.C. (1857–8), xlv; Perfect, *Village of Hornchurch*, 94.
[47] Ed. 2/167; Ed. 21/5208.
[48] *Rep. Educ. Cttee. of Council 1871–2* [C. 601], p. 258, H.C. (1872), xxii.
[49] Ed. 21/5208.
[50] Perfect, *Village of Hornchurch*, 95; Ed. 49/2131; E.R.O., C/ME 21, pp. 53, 607.
[51] E.R.O., C/ME 26, p. 749.

Road, South Hornchurch. This school was built in 1864 on Skeale's charity land at West field, apparently with the income of Skeale's charity, savings from the National school funds, and subscriptions.[52] In 1871 sixty-three children were being taught there.[53] The school received annual government grants from 1885.[54] It was taken over in 1890 by the school board, and was replaced by South Hornchurch board school in 1899.[55]

Harold Wood junior and infants school, Recreation Avenue. A National school was opened at Harold Wood in 1882, with the help of John Compton, the main landowner.[56] A permanent building, with 80 places, was opened in 1886 in Gubbins Lane.[57] It had been taken over by the school board by 1890.[58] It was enlarged in 1902 for 207 mixed and infant children[59] and in 1933 was reorganized for juniors and infants. The first part of a new school in Recreation Avenue was opened in 1960.[60] The Gubbins Lane buildings were still in use in 1975.

ELEMENTARY SCHOOLS FOUNDED BETWEEN 1889 AND 1903. Whybridge (formerly South Hornchurch) primary school, Blacksmith's and Ford Lanes, was opened in 1890 as a board school in the building lately used by Mrs. Skeale's school, which it replaced.[61] A new school was built in 1899 in Blacksmith's Lane for 150, and was enlarged in 1912 and 1929.[62] It was reorganized for juniors and infants in 1934, and by 1937 had been enlarged for 450.[63] In 1943 it had 750 children. It was enlarged in 1947 and again in 1964, when a new infants school was built in Ford Lane, and the Blacksmith's Lane buildings became the junior school.[64]

Edwin Lambert[65] junior and infants school, Park Lane. Park Lane board school, opened in 1893, was the first built by the school board. It was enlarged in 1907 for 575.[66] The girls and infants departments were amalgamated in 1926. The school was reorganized in 1930 for juniors and infants, and in 1935 was enlarged for 500.[67]

ELEMENTARY SCHOOLS BUILT BETWEEN 1903 AND 1945. The schools in this and the following sections, unless otherwise stated, were all opened by Essex county council.

Harold Court junior mixed and infants school, Church Road. Harold Court mixed council school was opened in 1929 for 300. It was reorganized in 1934 for juniors and infants. In 1937 it had 400 children, including 128 from the Straight Road area of Romford.[68] It was damaged by bombs in 1940.[69]

Wykeham (formerly Rainsford Way) junior and infants school, was opened in 1932 as a junior council school.[70] It was reorganized in 1933 for juniors and infants.

St. Mary's Roman Catholic junior and infants school, Hornchurch Road, was opened in 1933 for 300.[71] By 1947 it had over 400 children. Temporary accommodation was provided in 1947 at Elm Park chapel and in 1954 at the hall and presbytery of St. Joseph's church, Upminister.[72] The school was granted Aided status in 1951.[73]

Suttons junior and infants school, Suttons Lane. Suttons Lane junior council school was opened in 1933 in temporary buildings for 450. It was closed in 1940. In 1947 it was reopened with an infants department in buildings which had previously belonged to Suttons Institution.[74] It was enlarged in 1949.

Ardleigh Green junior and infants school, Ardleigh Green Road, was opened as a council school in 1933–4.[75] Its senior department was closed in 1938 on the opening of Redden Court school.

Benhurst (formerly Elm Park) junior and infants school, Benhurst Avenue, was opened in 1936 as a council school for juniors and infants.[76]

Ayloff junior and infants school, South End Road, Elm Park, was opened in 1938 for 500. It was closed in 1940 and reopened in 1942.[77]

SENIOR AND SECONDARY SCHOOLS FOUNDED BEFORE 1945.[78] Harrow Lodge school, Hyland Way and Malvern Road, was formed in 1973 by the amalgamation of Hylands and Bush Elms secondary schools. Hylands senior mixed council school, Malvern Road, was opened in 1930 for 400. It was enlarged and reorganized in 1935 for 560 senior boys.[79] Bush Elms senior mixed council school, Hyland Way, was opened in 1933 for 450.[80] It was enlarged in 1963.[81] Redden Court school, Cotswold Road, Harold Wood, originated in 1934 when a senior department was opened at Ardleigh Green school. In 1937 400 seniors were at Ardleigh Green school and in the practical instruction block at Redden Court, where new buildings were completed in 1939 for 480.[82] The school was enlarged in 1974.[83]

Dury Falls school, Wingletye Lane, was opened in 1935 as a senior mixed council school for 500. It was enlarged in 1963–4 and again in 1974.[84]

52 H.R.L., Lewis Scrapbook, iii. 69; Perfect, *St. Andrew, Hornchurch*, 52; Char. Com. Files; O.S. Map 25", Essex, LXXIV. 12 (1896 edn.).
53 Ed. 2/167.
54 *Rep. Educ. Cttee. of Council 1885–6* [C. 4849–1], p. 513, H.C. (1886), xxiv.
55 Ed. 21/5208.
56 Ed. 2/167; *Strat. Expr.* 20 Sept. 1882, p. 5; 17 Oct. 1883, p. 5.
57 *Kelly's Dir. Essex* (1890), 203.
58 *Return of Schs. 1893* [C. 7529], p. 180, H.C. (1894), lxv; *Rep. Educ. Cttee. of Council 1891–2* [C. 6746–1], p. 625 (1892), xxviii; *Kelly's Dir. Essex* (1890).
59 Perfect, *Village of Hornchurch*, 96–7; E.R.O., E/Z 2.
60 *Educ. in Essex* (1956–60), p. 23.
61 Ed. 21/5208.
62 Ibid.; *Educ. in Essex* (1928–35), 118.
63 E.R.O., C/ME 33, p. 503; C/ME 39, p. 297.
64 E.R.O., C/ME 41, p. 827; C/ME 58, pp. 130, 773; *Havering Official Guide* (1966–7), 43.
65 Local councillor, d. 1931: J. Cantwell, *Hornchurch—a political survey*, 3–4.
66 Ed. 21/5207.
67 E.R.O., C/ME 30, p. 180; C/ME 31, p. 618.
68 E.R.O., C/ME 33, p. 353.
69 E.R.O., C/W 1/2/57.
70 *Educ. in Essex* (1928–35), 119.
71 E.R.O., C/ME 28, p. 185.
72 E.R.O., C/ME 41, p. 944; C/ME 47, p. 676; Schools collection.
73 E.R.O., C/ME 46, p. 18.
74 E.R.O., C/ME 28, p. 569; C/ME 29, pp. 26, 223; C/ME 36, p. 320; C/ME 41, p. 6; and see above, p. 45.
75 E.R.O., C/ME 28, p. 429.
76 E.R.O., C/ME 32, p. 554; C/ME 33, p. 352; C/ME 34, pp. 107–8.
77 E.R.O., C/ME 33, p. 37; C/ME 38, p. 12.
78 Frances Bardsley school for girls is described under Romford.
79 E.R.O., C/ME 25, p. 802; C/ME 31, p. 151.
80 E.R.O., C/ME 27, p. 24.
81 *Educ. in Essex* (1960–64), 26; E.R.O., C/ME 58, p. 950.
82 E.R.O., C/ME 33, p. 445; C/ME 34, p. 177.
83 *Havering Official Guide* (1973), 75.
84 E.R.O., C/ME 30, p. 180; C/ME 57, p. 469; C/ME 58, p. 980.

Sanders Draper[85] (formerly Suttons secondary modern) school, Suttons Lane, was opened in 1937 for 1,100 seniors in two departments which became separate schools for boys and girls in 1945.[86] They were amalgamated in 1953. The school was enlarged and renamed in 1973.[87] A unit for deaf seniors was opened in 1974.[88]

Emerson Park (formerly Hornchurch Grammar) school, Wych Elm Road, originated in 1943 when Hornchurch county (mixed) high school was opened in temporary premises at Cedar Avenue (later Branfil) school, Upminster.[89] Permanent buildings were completed in 1954 in Wych Elm Road,[90] and the school was renamed Hornchurch Grammar school. It was enlarged and renamed again in 1973.[91]

PRIMARY SCHOOLS FOUNDED AFTER 1945. Hacton (formerly Hacton Lane) junior and infants school, Chepstow Avenue, was opened in 1948.[92] A unit for deaf children was opened there in 1969.[93] Dunningford junior and infants school, Upper Rainham Road, Elm Park, was opened in 1955.[94] Scargill[95] junior and infants schools, Mungo Park Road, were opened in 1957 and enlarged in 1962, 1970, and 1973. The 1962 extension was gutted by fire in 1973 and was rebuilt in 1975.[96] Nelmes junior and infants school, Wingletye Lane, was opened in 1966.[97]

The following primary schools were built by the London borough of Havering. Towers infants school, Osborne Road, was opened in 1967, and Towers junior school, Windsor Road, in 1969.[98] Newtons infants school, Lowen Road, was opened in 1968, and Newtons junior school, Lowen Road, in 1970. Mitchell[99] junior and infants school, Tangmere Crescent, was opened in 1971. Scotts junior and infants school, Maybank Avenue, was completed before the building of the housing estate it was planned to serve. It was opened in 1974 for children from the burnt-out building at Scargill school.

St. Albans Roman Catholic junior and infants school, Heron Flight Avenue, was opened in 1971.

SECONDARY SCHOOLS FOUNDED AFTER 1945. Brittons school, Ford Lane, south Hornchurch, was opened as a mixed secondary (modern) school in 1952. It was enlarged in 1964.[1] Abbs Cross school, Abbs Cross Lane, was opened in 1958 as a mixed secondary (technical) school. It was enlarged in 1973.[2] Maylands school, Broadstone Road, was opened in 1962 as a secondary (modern) school for girls. Campion Roman Catholic secondary (Aided, grammar) school for boys, Wingletye Lane, was opened in 1962.[3]

FURTHER EDUCATION. Havering technical college, Ardleigh Green Road, developed from the further education centre which was opened in 1947 at Ardleigh House to replace Harold Wood evening institute. A new centre was built in 1958–9 in the grounds of the house. In 1963 it was enlarged and became Hornchurch college of further education.[4] It was enlarged again in 1971.[5] South Havering college of adult education, Wingletye Lane, developed from the Hornchurch evening institute opened at Dury Falls school in the 1930s. The institute's membership greatly increased after the war, and in 1966 it became South Havering college. It was enlarged in 1970.[6]

PRIVATE SCHOOLS. Between 1584 and 1590 John Leche was keeping a school at Hornchurch.[7] In 1590 the Privy Council entrusted to him the education of a boy whose father had unlawfully tried to send him to a Roman Catholic school abroad.[8] In the period 1620–2 a school kept by Joseph Robson was said to hinder the curate's school.[9] A boarding school for girls, started in 1826 and surviving in 1833,[10] had been closed by 1848. Of the two private schools listed in 1848, one may have been conducted by the master of Aylett's school.[11] A girls private school existed 1890.[12] Between 1906 and 1937 ten private schools were listed in directories.[13] Most of them were short-lived but there was a preparatory school at Frome House, Athelstan Road, Harold Wood, for at least 27 years, from *c.* 1906. Hornchurch high school, Walden Road, founded *c.* 1937, seems to have survived as Goodrington school in 1975. In 1966 there were 7 private schools, including 4 nursery schools and a commercial college.[14] Only two private schools appear to have survived in 1972.

CHARITIES FOR THE POOR.[15] Unless otherwise stated the charities treated in this section are thought to have been restricted to the area governed for civil purposes by Hornchurch parish vestry, i.e. the town, North End, and South End wards. In 1837 the poor of Hornchurch were benefiting from 8 bread charities worth £18 a year, and other charitable income of £33, as well as Appleton's

85 An American pilot who, in the Second World War, stayed in his crashing aircraft to avoid the school and was killed in the accident.
86 E.R.O., C/ME 34, p. 399; C/ME 39B, p. 206; *Official Opening of Suttons Senior School* (1938).
87 *Havering Official Guide* (1973), 75.
88 Inf. from the school.
89 E.R.O., C/ME 39, p. 286.
90 *Educ. in Essex* (1952–56), 31.
91 *Havering Official Guide* (1973), 75.
92 *Educ. in Essex* (1945–52), 23. For description see *Hacton County Primary School, Official Opening* (1950).
93 Inf. from school.
94 *Essex Educ. Building Suppl.* May 1955, p. 6.
95 Thos. Scargill (d. 1476): Perfect, *Village of Hornchurch*, 72–3.
96 *Essex Educ. Building Suppl.* July 1958, p. 5; inf. from school.
97 *Havering Official Guide* (1966–7), 41.
98 Inf. from school.
99 R. J. Mitchell, designer of the Spitfire fighter aircraft.

1 *Educ. in Essex* (1945–52), 31; (1960–64), 26.
2 *Havering Official Guide* (1973), 75.
3 *Educ. in Essex* (1960–64), 23; officially opened 21 July 1963: E.R.O., C/ME 58, p. 364.
4 *Essex Educ. Building Suppl.* July 1959, 4; C/ME 41, p. 35; *Educ. in Essex* (1945–52), p. 45; (1956–60), p. 85.
5 *Havering Official Guide* (1973), 86.
6 Inf. from the college; *Educ. in Essex* (1945–52), p. 45.
7 Hale, *Precedents*, 184, 192, 200.
8 *Acts of P.C.* 1590, 87–8.
9 E.R.O., D/AEA 32, ff. 102v., 106v., 107, 132, 147, 247v.
10 *Educ. Enquiry Abstract*, H.C. 62, p. 279 (1835), xli.
11 *White's Dir. Essex* (1848), 376.
12 *Kelly's Dir. Essex* (1890), 203.
13 *Kelly's Dir. Essex* (1906–1937).
14 *Havering Official Guide* (1966–7), 50.
15 Unless otherwise stated this section is based on: *Rep. Com. Char.* [108], pp. 724–31, (1837–8), xxv (1); Char. Com. Files; Perfect, *Village of Hornchurch*, 24, 38, 107–8; inf. from Mr. D. C. Boughton. Aylett's and Jacobs' charities are described above, under Education.

alms-houses in Hornchurch, and Reede's in Romford. Bread was distributed indiscriminately on St. Thomas's day and at Christmas; and small doles on Lady Day and at Michaelmas. By 1862 bread and doles were being given only to the settled poor and to a few large families living outside the parish. A Charity Commission Scheme of 1878 provided that the charities of Webster, Armstead, Rickett, Higgs for bread, H. and J. Richardson, and Page should be administered as the Consolidated bread and poor's gifts.[16] After payments for the repair of Page's tomb, £1 was to be given to the vicar for a sermon on St. Thomas's day, and the remainder in 5*s.* and 6*s.* doles to the Hornchurch poor not receiving parish relief, preferably those whose children attended school most regularly. A Scheme of 1912, varied by Schemes of 1927 and 1939, combined the charities of Appleton, Pennant, Ram, Bourne, Oakley, and Mashiter with the Consolidated bread and poor's gifts as the Consolidated charities. After payment of £1 for the sermon the income was to be used to pay pensions to the alms-people and for the general benefit of the poor in Hornchurch. In 1971 a new Scheme combined the Consolidated charities with the charities of Skeale, Higgs for loans, and Wright, as Hornchurch United charities.

In 1975 the trustees of the United charities built 30 alms-houses, named Skeale's Court, in Abbs Cross Lane. For this they used the proceeds of the sale of property of Appleton's, Pennant's, and Skeale's charities. They also borrowed the capital of the bread and loan charities. In 1976 the income of the United charities, apart from contributions paid by the alms-people, was *c.* £1,600, mainly from ground rents of Oakley's and Ram's charities.

UNITED CHARITIES. Appleton's alms-houses. In 1586 Jane Ayloffe, widow, bought a house on the south side of High Street for conversion into 3 alms-houses. By indenture of 1587 she and her second husband, Henry Appleton, gave the alms-houses in trust for the aged poor who had lived in Hornchurch for at least 7 years. After her death the 3 alms-people were to pay yearly 1*s.* each to the churchwardens for the upkeep of the houses, and 2*d.* each for quit-rent to the lord of the manor. In 1721, after the building of the parish workhouse, Appleton's alms-houses were let on a 61-year lease.[17] By 1837 they were being let to 3 poor families not receiving constant parish relief. They were rebuilt in 1838[18] and continued to be occupied by 3 poor families who paid 1*s.* 2*d.* yearly to the repair fund. In 1967 they were sold and demolished.

Pennant's alms-houses. John Pennant of London, by will proved 1598, gave 4 cottages at the corner of High Street and Billet Lane in trust as free dwellings for Hornchurch poor. He also gave £10 for the upkeep of the cottages.[19] In 1721 a parish workhouse was built on the site of Pennant's alms-houses. In 1837 Thomas Mashiter converted the building, no longer needed as a workhouse, into 4 alms-houses to be let rent-free, and 2 other tenements to be let to provide a maintenance fund. By 1910 the alms-houses had been divided to provide individual rooms for 9 old people. The property, nos. 85–91, High Street and no. 2, Billet Lane, was sold *c.* 1939.

Anthony Ram, a London goldsmith, by will proved 1616, gave his father Francis (d. 1618) £40 in trust for the poor. In 1618 Samuel Ram, Francis's executor, agreed to give a house to the parish instead of the £40. The rent was to be used to employ the poor. In 1621 a deed of settlement confirmed the gift of Poynters (Painters) in High Street to Hornchurch poor. The house was let on lease from *c.* 1623.[20] By 1837 it had been replaced by two cottages, the rent from which was used to maintain charity houses in the parish. In 1862 it was said that the rents had been used to employ the poor on the parish roads, and to provide coal for the poor in the hard winter of 1860. In 1968 the site was let on a 75-year building lease, and in 1971 the annual income was £1,575.

William Armstead, by will proved 1657, left a rent-charge from a farm at Hay Street and other land in Hornchurch, Havering, and Upminster to pay £5 to the poor of Hornchurch, and £1 to the vicar for two annual sermons. By 1830 rent was being received only from the farm at Hay Street. In 1837 the income, after payment for the two sermons, was distributed in small doles twice a year.

Sibell Skeale, by will proved 1679, left £20 to the poor, in trust to be paid from part of the sale of Damons, later Ford Houses, and 2 a. land in West field. In 1682 the parish bought the whole property for £70, with a rebate of £20.[21] In the period 1821–37 the house, then divided into two, and the land, were being let, producing a yearly rent of £17 6*s.*[22] By 1846 the house had been rebuilt as three cottages.[23] After payment of £1 a year to the poor of South End, the income was saved towards the building, in 1864, of a school in West field. Under a Charity Commission Scheme of 1890 the income, then £19 15*s.*, was used to provide pensions for poor people, not receiving poor-relief, who had lived in Hornchurch not less than three years. A Scheme of 1927 reduced the pensioners' qualifying period of residence to two years. The cottages were demolished in 1964, and in 1967 the site was sold to Havering council for £11,250. West field was compulsorily purchased by Havering council in 1973.

By indenture dated 1693, William Oakley, whose cottage on Butts Green had been rebuilt by charitable contributions after a fire, gave the reversion of the cottage, in default of male heirs, to the poor as a parish house. Oakley's last male heir died in 1821. By an indenture of that year Thomas Oakley, unable to prove his lawful succession, quitclaimed to trustees for the poor. From 1823 the house was let, and its rent was used until at least 1910 to maintain the parish's charity houses. It never seems to have housed the poor. Part of the land was let on a building lease *c.* 1911, and in 1971 the annual income was £16 from 6 shops in Butts Green Road.

Thomas Clarke, by will dated 1738, gave an annual rent-charge of £1 to buy bread for the poor on St. Thomas's day. In 1837 the rent was charged on Ford Lodge. David Rickett, by will dated 1787,

[16] For Webster's charity see also p. 96.
[17] E.R.O., D/P 115/8/1A.
[18] Thorne, *Environs Lond.* (1876), 361.
[19] Prob. 11/92 (P.C.C. 81 Lewyn).
[20] Prob. 11/128 (P.C.C. 94 Cope); E.R.O., D/P 115/1/1; 115/5/1.
[21] E.R.O., D/P 115/5/1, ff. 496, 498.
[22] E.R.O., D/P 115/5/2.
[23] I.R. 30/12/177.

gave £100 in trust to buy bread for the poor. John Richardson, by will dated 1797, and Hannah Richardson, by deed of gift 1811, each gave £100 in trust for the same purpose.

John Massu, by will dated 1807, left £1,000 stock, in reversion after the death of his wife, in trust to pay doles to 10 poor men nominated by the vicar and churchwardens. The charity came into effect in 1850.[24] In 1912 the annual income was £50.

William Higgs, by will proved 1811, gave £100 in trust to buy bread for the poor, and £100 in trust to provide four interest-free loans to poor tradesmen or small farmers for terms of three years. In 1829 part of the capital of the loan charity was lost through a churchwarden's bankruptcy. The 3-year term was not always applied and it seems that the loan charity was ineffective for many years. The vestry in 1906 and the parish council in 1910 suggested alternative uses, but a Scheme of 1912 confirmed its application separately from the Consolidated charities, and in accordance with the will.

Thomas Page, by will proved 1815, gave £100 stock in trust to repair his tomb, the remainder to be given to poor widows on St. Thomas's day. By 1820 small doles were distributed yearly according to the will.[25]

John Bourne, by will of 1821, gave £20 in trust to the poor on condition that 2*s.* 6*d.* from the income was used to maintain his grave. In 1822 the trustees received £18 from his executor which, until 1837 or later, was applied to the grave and to provide bread for the poor on St. Thomas's day. By 1894 it was being distributed in cash.[26]

Thomas Mashiter, by will proved 1863, apparently gave £225 stock to Hornchurch poor. There is no early record of the distribution of this charity. In 1912 the income was £5 12*s.* 4d.

Wright's alms-houses. In 1932 Misses E. A. and L. K. Wright conveyed to trustees land in Hacton Lane where 8 alms-houses were built soon after. The houses were damaged by bombs in 1940.[27] In 1969–70 they were converted into 5 flats.

OTHER CHARITIES. Mary Hide, by will proved 1717, gave £200 to buy land producing an annual income of £12 to pay the apprenticeship premiums of two boys from Hornchurch and one from Romford. By indenture of 1722 Mary's brother William Hide retained the £200 and gave in exchange a £10 annual rent-charge from 9 a. near the Gores at the west end of Romford town to apprentice three boys from the Romford charity school according to Mary's will. In 1837 it was reported that the rent-charge was received regularly but that few payments had been made for many years, and that until recently boys had not been chosen from the charity school. About 1835 the premiums were increased to £10. In the 1860s the trustees had difficulty in finding suitable masters for that sum.[28] The income accumulated, and in 1898 four boys were apprenticed.[29] A Board of Education Scheme of 1929 regulated the appointment of trustees and the use of £50 income from stock and the rent-charge from Holm Lodge, London Road, Romford. After an annual payment of £10 for religious instruction the remainder was to be used for apprenticeship and other educational purposes, two thirds being apportioned to Hornchurch and one third to Romford. In 1958 it was said that no applications had been received for some time.[30] Payments were made in 1968, 1969, and 1972. In 1976 Havering education department was considering the future application of this charity.[31]

Burchett Whennell (d. 1780), gave an annual rent-charge of £1 from Albyns farm, Hornchurch, to be distributed in bread to the poor on St. Thomas's day.[32] The rent-charge was paid regularly until 1828, when the owner of the farm claimed that the gift was void by the statute of mortmain. It was reported in 1837 that the rent-charge was not being paid, but in 1859 interest of £5 on Whennell's fund was paid to the Sunday school.[33] In 1917 it was said to be combined with Bearblock's charity,[34] the income from stock being used by the vicar to buy prizes, books, and furniture for the Sunday school.

Under the Havering Inclosure Act, 1811, small allotments of land were made in 1814 to the churchwardens and overseers of Hornchurch for rights of common attached to houses and land belonging to the parish charities.[35] By 1837 the annual income of £1 from 4 r. of land at Noak Hill, Romford, was being paid to the parish houses maintenance fund, and 10*s.* from 1 r. at Harold Wood was being distributed in bread on St. Thomas's day. In 1919 the land at Noak Hill was let for £1 a year.

LOST CHARITIES. Ralph Watson, bricklayer of Hornchurch, by will dated 1594, directed that after his wife's death £20 should be given in trust to provide annual doles for the poor. There is no evidence that the legacy was paid. Mrs. Blackstone, by will dated 1647, apparently gave £40 to the poor. The churchwardens received £20 in 1655, and interest on the remaining £20 in 1659. No more is known of the charity.[36] Samuel Ballard of Orsett, by will dated 1691, gave marsh lands in trust for the repair of his tomb and for the relief of Hornchurch poor. In 1690 the charity was said to be 'not well employed'.[37] The land is thought to have been lost when Dagenham Breach was flooded in 1707.[38]

Shipman's, later Gogney's charity, originally for the poor, but later appropriated for church use, is treated elsewhere.[39]

[24] E.R.O., T/P 114/8.
[25] E.R.O., D/P 115/2.
[26] E.R.O., T/A 521/10, Romford Rural Parish Meetings 28 Mar. 1895.
[27] E.R.O., C/W 1/2/57.
[28] Char. Com. Files.
[29] E.R.O., T/A 521/10.
[30] Char. Com. Files.
[31] Inf. from Havering educ. dept.
[32] E.R.O., D/P 115/1/5.
[33] E.R.O., D/P 115/5/3.
[34] See p. 49.
[35] 51 Geo. III, c. 187 (Local and Personal); E.R.O. T/M 86.
[36] E.R.O., D/P 115/5/1, f. 353; see also below, p. 97.
[37] E.R.O., T/P 195/2.
[38] *V.C.H. Essex*, v. 286.
[39] See p. 49.

ROMFORD

ROMFORD, about 12 miles east of the city of London, is part of the London borough of Havering.[1] During the Middle Ages a small market town grew up here along the main London–Colchester road. Romford market still flourishes, but the old town has been engulfed by commuter suburbs stretching east to Gidea Park and north to Collier Row and Chase Cross. The large Harold Hill housing estate, built by the London county council in 1948–58, forms the north-east corner of Romford.

Romford, or 'Romford side', was a chapelry of the ancient parish of Hornchurch, containing five wards: town, Harold Wood, Collier Row, Noak Hill, and Havering.[2] It remained subject to Hornchurch for church purposes until the 19th century, but for civil purposes was virtually independent by the 16th century. Havering ward became independent for civil purposes in the later 17th century. A local board, later urban district council, was formed for Romford in 1851. The boundary of its district, several times altered, was in 1934 finally enlarged to 9,324 a., an area identical with that of the five ancient wards of Romford side.[3] The district became a municipal borough in 1937. In 1965 it was united with Hornchurch U.D. to form the London borough of Havering.

The old town is about 50 ft. above sea-level, on the upper edge of the gravel terrace that rises from the Thames. Farther north, on the London Clay at Collier Row, the land rises to over 150 ft. The main watercourse is the river Rom, which flows south through Romford and Hornchurch to join the Thames as the river Beam.[4] The old town sometimes suffered from floods, notably that of 1888.[5] By 1936 much of the Rom at the town centre had been culverted.[6] The river Ravensbourne, a tributary of the Rom, flows south and west from Gidea Park. Weald brook, which is the boundary between Romford and South Weald, to the east, flows south into Hornchurch, continuing as the river Ingrebourne to the Thames.[7] Carter's brook, rising at Noak Hill, becomes Paine's brook, as it passes through Harold Hill to join the Ingrebourne.[8] The Loam pond formerly stood at the eastern end of the market-place. In the later 18th century Romford vestry sometimes met the cost of fencing it.[9] The pond was bought by the local board in 1871, and was filled in in 1874.[10]

Schemes for a canal from Romford to the Thames were canvassed several times in the 19th century.[11] Between 1875 and 1880 such a canal was actually started, but it was never finished.[12] Remains of it, near New Road on the Hornchurch–Dagenham boundary, were identified and partly excavated in 1972.[13]

The Roman settlement of *Durolitum* was probably at or near Romford, but its exact site is not known.[14] Most of the Roman remains found there have come from Collier Row, Noak Hill, and Harold Hill.[15] Romford, first recorded in 1153–4,[16] probably means 'wide ford,' from which the river Rom took its name by back-formation.[17] The chapel of St. Andrew, Romford, first mentioned in 1177, stood east of the Rom, on the south corner of Oldchurch Road and South Street.[18] In the 17th century an area of 34 a., extending west of the river for 660 yd. along the south side of Oldchurch Road, was occupied by 6 fields called ruin meadow, lower ruins, great ruins, and three little ruins.[19] There must have been a settlement there, including a number of stone or brick buildings. It is unlikely that it was, wholly or mainly, a medieval site, since masonry was rarely used in Essex between the 5th and 15th centuries, except in churches and other large buildings. Twelfth-century Romford may have stood west of St. Andrew's chapel, amid or beside the ruins of a Roman town[20]; but the Oldchurch site has not been excavated, and no Roman or medieval remains, apart from the chapel, have been recorded there.

If the medieval nucleus of settlement ever was at Oldchurch it had ceased to be there by 1410, when St. Andrew's chapel was abandoned, and the chapel of St. Edward was built about ½ m. to the north, on the present site in the market-place, then a piece of roadside common at the east end of the town.[21] Romford had been given a weekly market in 1247, with an annual fair in 1250,[22] and the growth of the town along the main London–Colchester road probably dates from that period.

Until the 20th century Romford remained a small country town. In *c.* 1618 the urban area was confined to the market-place, High Street, the east end of London Road, and the south end of Woolford (now North) Street.[23] There were hamlets fringing the commons at Collier Row and Noak Hill, and on the main road at Hare Street (now Gidea Park).

[1] O.S. Map 2½", sheets TQ 48, 49, 58, 59. This article was completed in 1976. For a recent air view of Romford see plate facing p. 64.

[2] For Local Government see p. 76.

[3] See maps pp. 2, 80.

[4] For the Beam see: *P.N. Essex*, 3; O'Leary, *Dagenham Place Names*, 5.

[5] *Strat. Expr.* 4, 11 Aug. 1888; T. Robinson, *After the floods at Romford* (1888).

[6] *Romford Charter Petition* (1936): proof of evidence (Engineer), 2.

[7] For the Ingrebourne: *P.N. Essex*, 7.

[8] For Paine's brook: ibid. 9, 116.

[9] E.R.O., T/A 521/1–3.

[10] H.R.L., Romford L.B. Mins. 6 Mar. 1871; 'Notes of Romford Town Centre from Cornell MSS.' (Duplicated TS, 1966), 15.

[11] J. Booker, *Essex and the Industrial Revolution*, 136–7; *Romford Record*, v. 4; E.R.O., Q/SBb 421/9 and D/DCq E2.

[12] Booker, ibid.; Romford Canal Act, 1875, 38 & 39 Vict. c. 155 (local act); E.R.O., Q/RUm 2/233; Lewis, *Rainham*, 121.

[13] Inf. from Mr. R. Sharp, Hornchurch Hist. Soc.

[14] *V.C.H. Essex*, iii. 24.

[15] Ibid. 175.

[16] *Reg. Regum. Ang. Norm.* iii, no. 251.

[17] *P.N. Essex*, 117.

[18] See p. 82.

[19] E.R.O., D/DSa 149 (map, 1696).

[20] Cf. Chelmsford and Kelvedon: *V.C.H. Essex*, iii. 63, 149.

[21] *Cal. Pat.* 1405–8, 175.

[22] See p. 75.

[23] E.R.O., D/DU 162/1; Terry, *Romford*, 113–15.

The face of the parish did not change much in the next 200 years.[24] The population has been roughly estimated as 1,345 in 1580, 1,485 in 1680, and 1,846 in 1735.[25] In 1670 there were 323 houses in Romford, of which 184 were in the town ward, 56 in Collier Row, 50 in Harold Wood ward (the present Gidea Park and Harold Hill), and 33 in Noak Hill.[26]

In 1801 Romford had a population of 3,179, occupying 522 houses.[27] In size and character it was then similar to Epping, another Essex market town with a busy coaching trade on a main road to London.[28] Unlike Epping, however, Romford was linked to a main railway line as early as 1839, and continued to grow steadily throughout the 19th century. The population increased to 5,317 in 1841, to 8,239 in 1871, and to 13,915 in 1901. After the First World War it grew rapidly, from 19,442 in 1921 to 35,918 in 1931, 88,002 in 1951, and 114,584 in 1961.[29]

The first large development in the 19th century was on the old barrack ground, south of London Road. The site comprised about 12 a., extending south to the railway. It was sold *c.* 1840, and during the next 15 years some 200 artisans' cottages and at least two factories were built there.[30] The area, which was known in the 1840s as New Romford, included Waterloo Road, St. Andrew's Road, and Queen Street. Since the Second World War it has been redeveloped with council flats.

At the other end of Romford, east of the market-place, the small middle-class suburb of Laurie town was built *c.* 1850 by John Laurie (d. 1864), a London saddler of Scottish descent who lived at Marshalls, Romford, from 1846 to 1864.[31] It originally included two public halls, St. Edward's hall and the Laurie hall, standing respectively east and west of the Loam pond, in St. Edward's (later Laurie) Square. On the north side of the square were four pairs of semi-detached villas. All those buildings were in existence by 1853.[32] A few more houses were built *c.* 1857 in Park End Road, north of the square.[33] When complete the square included, on its south side, a dwarf wall with ornamental pillars.[34] St. Edward's hall was demolished soon after John Laurie's death.[35] In 1874, when the Loam pond was filled in, the ornamental wall was also removed.[36] The centre of the square was converted into a public garden and war memorial in the 1920s. In 1965 the two pairs of villas on the NE. side of the square were demolished to make way for the new central library. The villas on the north-west side were removed in 1968, when St. Edward's Way was being built, and the Laurie Hall in 1970.[37] The site of the square then became a traffic roundabout, with pedestrian subways named Ludwigshafen Place, from the West German town (Rheinland Pfalz) which is 'twinned' with Romford.

A much larger development was undertaken in 1851 by the National Freehold Land Society, which had acquired the manor of Stewards, comprising some 200 a. on the east side of South Street, near Romford station.[38] By 1854 Western and Eastern Roads, and the southern end of Junction Road had been built, and many plots sold. Victoria Road was laid out *c.* 1855, and the first houses were erected there *c.* 1856–8.[39] Building started in Albert Road *c.* 1860, George Street *c.* 1864, Carlisle, Shakespeare, Milton, and Shaftesbury Roads *c.* 1866, and Richmond Street (now Road) *c.* 1869.[40]

Romford did not grow much in the 1870s, but in 1883 the manor of Mawneys, containing 265 a. north-west of High Street, was sold for building, which by 1889 was proceeding rapidly, and by 1899 stretched from Mildmay Road east to Linden Street, and from Marks Road north to Forest Road.[41] During the 1880s the manor of East House, north of the town, was also cut up for building, but progress there was slower, and as late as 1901 only 50 houses had been built, in Havering, Rosedale, and Hainault Roads.[42] North-east of the town the Hill Park estate, comprising Kingston, Erroll, and Gilbert Roads, was laid out in 1898–9, and at the same time Junction Road was extended to join Main Road.[43]

By 1900 Romford was also expanding westwards. The small Birkbeck estate, comprising Birkbeck, Grosvenor, Wolseley, and West Roads, at Rush Green, was being built by 1885.[44] The Shrubbery estate, lying between London Road and Sheringham Avenue, was developed *c.* 1899–1900.[45] Meanwhile the town was continuing to spread south and south-east. There was more building in Victoria Road, and at its eastern end Manor, Prince's, and King's Roads were laid out *c.* 1886.[46] By 1908 building had extended south to Clydesdale Road, while farther east, beyond the Romford–Upminster railway line, the large Heath Park estate was being developed.[47] The only large area near the town centre which had not yet been built-up was the Marshalls estate, comprising some 120 a. between North Street and Pettits Lane. That came on the market in 1924, and was developed during the following

[24] *Map of Essex* (1777); O.S. Map 1" (Essex), sheet 1 (1805 edn.).
[25] E.R.O., T/P 71/1: calculations based on baptisms and burials in parish registers.
[26] E.R.O., Q/Rth 5.
[27] *Census*, 1801.
[28] *V.C.H. Essex*, v. 114 sqq.
[29] *Census.*
[30] H.R.L., Cornell MSS., *Sale Cat.* (photo.), 19 Sept. 1839; E.R.O., Sage Coll., *Sale Cats.* vol. ix. 2; *White's Dir. Essex* (1848), 378–9; H.R.L., E. Gotto, *Plan of Romford* (1853); E.R.O., T/A 521/4; Romford L.B. Mins. 1853–7. For the factories see below, p. 74.
[31] S. Roberts, *Romford in the 19th cent.* 46–8; C. M. Jones, 'John Laurie of Marshalls and Laurie Town,' *Romford Record*, vii. 12–18; *E.R.* xxxv. 228–9.
[32] E. Gotto, *Plan of Romford* (1853).
[33] Romford L.B. Mins. 15 Aug., 19 and 26 Sept. 1856, 8 May, 11 Sept. 1857.
[34] 'Notes of Romford Town Centre', 15.
[35] For a picture: *Romford in 19th. cent.* 44.
[36] 'Notes of Romford Town Centre', 15.
[37] Inf. from Mr. C. J. Whitwood.
[38] E.R.O., Sage Coll., *Sale Cats.* vol. xi. 12; E.R.O., D/DB T837, 838.
[39] Romford L.B. Mins. 16 Nov. 1855, 13, 27, Feb., 11 Sept. 1857, 11 Feb. 1858.
[40] Romford L.B. Mins. 20 Sept. 1860, 7 July 1864, 7 Sept. 1865, 25 Jan. 1869; E.R.O., Sage Coll., *Sale Cats.* vol. ix. 1.
[41] E.R.O., Sage Coll., *Sale Cats.* vol. x. 14–16; E.R.O., *Sale Cats.* B2869 and A537; Romford L.B. Mins. 6 July 1885 sqq.; Romford U.D. Mins. 18 Apr. 1899; *Strat. Expr.* 1, 22 July 1893, 4 Aug. 1894.
[42] E.R.O., Sage Coll., *Sale Cats.* vol. ix. 11 and 12.
[43] 'Notes of Romford Town Centre', 1; Romford L.B. Mins. 18 Apr., 1 May, 4 Sept. 1899.
[44] Romford L.B. Mins. 9 Apr. 1885, 5 July 1886.
[45] Ibid. 5 June 1899; H.R.L., Cornell MSS.; E.R.O., Sage Coll. *Sale Cats.* vol. xi. 1.
[46] S. Roberts, *Romford in the 19th cent.* 49; *Kelly's Dir. Essex* (1886).
[47] *Romford Handbk.* (1908), 22–3 (map). For Heath Park see E.R.O., Sage Coll., *Sale Cats.* vol. x. 2.

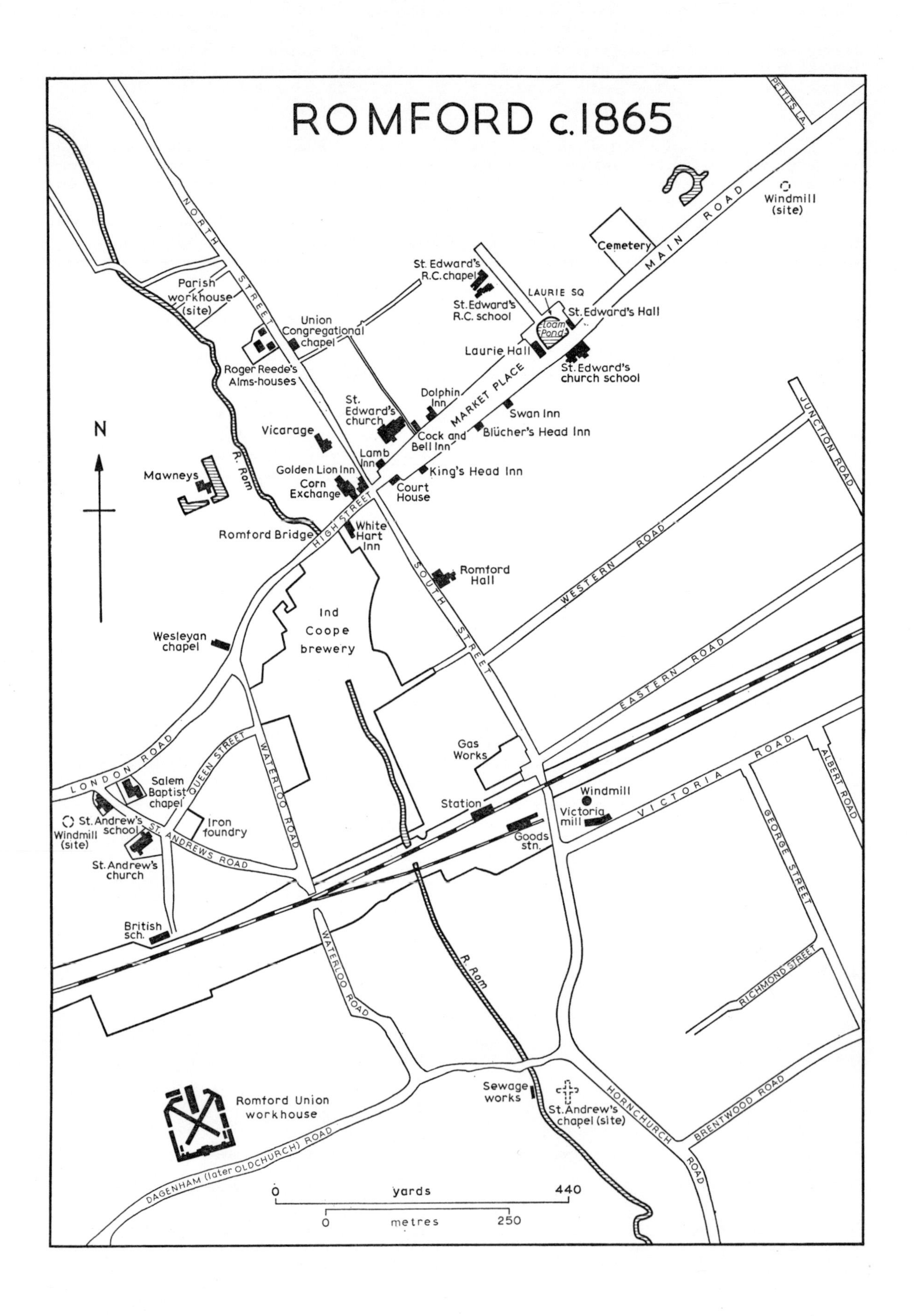
ROMFORD c.1865
N
PETTITS LA.
Windmill (site)
MAIN ROAD
Cemetery
St. Edward's R.C. chapel
St. Edward's R.C. school
LAURIE SQ
St. Edward's Hall
Loam Pond
Laurie Hall
St. Edward's church school
MARKET PLACE
Swan Inn
Blücher's Head Inn
Dolphin Inn
Cock and Bell Inn
King's Head Inn
Court House
St. Edward's church
Lamb Inn
Golden Lion Inn
Corn Exchange
Union Congregational chapel
Parish workhouse (site)
NORTH STREET
Roger Reede's Alms-houses
Vicarage
Mawneys
R. Rom
HIGH STREET
Romford Bridge
White Hart Inn
SOUTH STREET
Romford Hall
JUNCTION ROAD
WESTERN ROAD
EASTERN ROAD
Ind Coope brewery
Wesleyan chapel
Gas Works
Station
Windmill
Victoria mill
Goods stn.
VICTORIA ROAD
ALBERT ROAD
GEORGE STREET
LONDON ROAD
QUEEN STREET
WATERLOO ROAD
Salem Baptist chapel
St. Andrew's school
Windmill (site)
Iron foundry
ST. ANDREWS ROAD
St. Andrew's church
British sch.
WATERLOO ROAD
R. Rom
RICHMOND STREET
Romford Union workhouse
Sewage works
St. Andrew's chapel (site)
HORNCHURCH ROAD
BRENTWOOD ROAD
DAGENHAM (later OLDCHURCH) ROAD
0 yards 440
0 metres 250

years.[48] The growth so far mentioned was nearly all within a mile of the old town and Romford railway station. Beyond that radius there was little urban building in the 19th century. At Prospect Place, in Collier Row Lane, a new hamlet, of about 30 cottages, occupied by artisans, was in existence by 1846.[49] Factory Road (now Elvet Avenue), Squirrels Heath, containing about 50 houses, was built about the same time for workers at the Eastern Counties Railway Co.'s tarpaulin factory.[50] It was redeveloped in 1964 with council flats in towers.[51]

The Gidea Park garden suburb, built in 1910–11, was the most notable development in Romford up to that time.[52] In 1897 the Gidea Hall estate, containing some 480 a., had been bought by (Sir) Herbert Raphael, (Bt.) (1859–1924), of Rose Court, Havering, who earlier in that year had narrowly failed in his second attempt to secure election as Liberal M.P. for the Romford division.[53] He gave a strip on the western edge of the estate for a public park, opened in 1904. On the eastern side of the estate 90 a. were already occupied by Romford golf club, which he had founded in 1894.[54] In 1910 Raphael joined with two other Liberal M.P.s, Charles McCurdy and (Sir) Tudor Walters, to form Gidea Park Ltd., for the purpose of building a garden suburb on the remainder of the Gidea Hall estate. Gidea Park Ltd. had close links with the Hampstead Garden Suburb Co., in which Raphael, McCurdy, and Tudor Walters were all shareholders.[55] As originally planned Gidea Park garden suburb was to occupy about a square mile, extending east to Gallows Corner, and north to the present Rise Park. The company arranged with the Great Eastern Railway for the building of Squirrels Heath (now Gidea Park) station, and bought an additional 60 a. land, south of Main Road, to control access to it.

Gidea Park Ltd. offered to sell building plots or completed houses, to design houses for purchasers' requirements, and to provide 100 per cent mortgages. The foundation stone of the garden suburb was laid in 1910. The designs of the first houses were open to competition, and about 100 architects entered, including such well-known men as Barry Parker and (Sir) Raymond Unwin, M. H. Baillie Scott, T. Gordon Jackson, Philip Tilden, and Clough Williams-Ellis. By the following year 140 houses had been built. The first part of the suburb was laid out around Gidea Hall, between Raphael Park and Heath Drive. Most of the area south of Main Road was not formally included in the suburb, but a few houses were also built there, in Balgores Lane and adjoining roads. Nearly all the houses were detached. The competition was restricted to 'small houses' of 4 bedrooms, costing £500, and 3-bedroom 'cottages', costing £375. Stress was laid on convenient and labour-saving plans. Many of the houses were in Tudor styles, roughcast, colour-washed, or sometimes half-timbered.[56] The area was well landscaped, and the plots were of good size. There was a separate town planning competition for future development.

The Gidea Park garden suburb was not completed as planned. Eastern Avenue, the arterial road built in the 1920s, cut across the northern side of it. In 1934 Gidea Park Ltd. held another competition in an attempt to sell more building plots.[57] By that time Gidea Hall had been demolished. A small area east of the golf course had been laid out as Links Avenue and Hockley Drive. The golf course itself had been considerably enlarged, and a sports ground had been made adjoining Gallows Corner. Most of the plots offered for sale were along Eastern Avenue. Nearly 500 designs were entered for the competition, and 35 houses were built in Brook Road and the adjoining part of Eastern Avenue. The houses were divided into 5 classes, with prices ranging from £650 to £1,475. Those in the two cheapest classes were semi-detached. All were in contemporary styles, some being built of concrete, and most with flat roofs. In promoting the competition Gidea Park Ltd., though stressing architectural innovation, had abandoned the garden suburb idea, and their original town planning designs, referring always to the Gidea Park Estate, and proposing ribbon development along Eastern Avenue. Most of that development did not, however, take place, and there has been little building on the estate since 1934.

By the 1930s the area immediately south of the garden suburb was being rapidly built up, and the name Gidea Park was adopted for a ward of the town, comprising the area round the railway station. Some of the new building was by Gidea Park Ltd., which in 1934 was offering flats to let in Geddy Court, Hare Hall Lane, a large 4-storey block near the station. It was, however, in the north of the town that Romford's main development took place between the two world wars. Collier Row had been growing slowly since *c.* 1900, but was still largely rural until 1929, when 80 a. were released for building. By 1939 more than half the area of the ward had been built up, the peak year being 1937, when some 1,500 house plans were passed.[58] Romford's leading developer between the two world wars was Thomas England (d. 1960), who had started his business career as an assistant in a local chemist's shop.[59]

Schemes for further building in the north of the borough were checked shortly before the Second World War by the Green Belt legislation.[60] Since the war there has been more building, including some large borough council estates, at Collier Row, and farther east at Chase Cross and Rise Park, but the main area of growth has been Harold Hill, where in 1948–58 the London county council built some 8,200 houses, and some factories, on the former Dagnam

[48] E.R.O., *Sale Cat.* A212; *E.R.* xxxv. 230. See also below, p. 71.

[49] E.R.O., T/Z 38/148: L. A. Semple, 'Study of Collier Row and Havering, 1800–1939' (Brentwood Coll. Educ. thesis, 1972), chap. vii; I.R. 29 and 30/12/162.

[50] E.R.O., D/CT 186; *Romford Official Guide* (1936), 130. For the factory see below, p. 73.

[51] *Romford Recorder*, 30 Oct. 1964.

[52] Unless otherwise stated this account of the origin of the garden suburb is based on: H. Anderson, *Squirrels Heath and Gidea Park* (1910); *Exhibition of Houses Romford Garden Suburb, Gidea Park* (1911); Gidea Park Ltd., *The Gidea Park system of Freehold Land and House Purchase* (1911); R. Lonsdale, 'Gidea Park Garden Suburb', *Romford Record*, No. 9 (1977), 14. Miss Lonsdale kindly provided much information before the publication of her paper.

[53] For Raphael see I. G. Sparkes, *Gidea Hall and Gidea Park*, 40–43; *E.R.* iii. 91; vi. 65.

[54] *V.C.H. Essex*, ii. 592–3.

[55] Inf. from Miss R. Lonsdale. [56] See plate facing p. 161.

[57] Gidea Park Ltd., *Gidea Park Modern Homes Exhibition* (1934). For a previous attempt to sell off the estate: P.E.M., *Sale Cat.* (1925).

[58] E.R.O., T/Z 38/148, L. A. Semple, 'Study of Collier Row and Havering, 1800–1939' (Brentwood Coll. Educ. thesis, 1972).

[59] *Romford Times*, 6 Feb. 1963.

[60] e.g. at Havering and Risebridge: see pp. 13, 71.

Park estate.[61] The site had more natural variety than Becontree,[62] and two large areas of park-land were retained. The houses, most of which are of two storeys, semi-detached, or in short terraces, are notable for their restrained design and the frequent use of a dark red facing brick and plain tiles.[63] In the past five years there has been some further building in vacant corners of the estate. In the town centre a new shopping precinct, completed in 1972, has been built between the Market Place and Western Road.

Until the coming of the railways Romford's communications with the outside world depended mainly on the London–Colchester road, that part of which was maintained from 1721 by the Middlesex and Essex turnpike trust.[64] There were also lanes running south to Dagenham and Hornchurch, east via Squirrels Heath to Upminster, and north to Havering and South Weald. In 1814, when the commons were inclosed, new roads replaced the old tracks running east from Collier Row to Noak Hill, and south to Gallows Corner. Eastern Avenue, opened in 1925 as part of the arterial road from London to Southend,[65] ran through Romford about 1 mile north of the town centre. The old London road remained as a busy thoroughfare through the centre until 1970, when St. Edward's Way was opened as the northern section of a projected ringroad.[66]

Romford bridge, which carried the London road (High Street) over the Rom, was presented at the Essex sessions in 1627 as needing repair.[67] It was again presented there in 1648, when it was stated that the king was responsible for repair, but in 1649 the county ceased proceedings after learning that the inhabitants of the liberty of Havering were responsible.[68] In 1650 the tenants of the liberty claimed that the bridge had formerly been maintained by the Crown, and should now pass to the state.[69] It was apparently rebuilt *c.* 1737 at the cost of the Crown.[70] A new bridge, built in 1906, was reconstructed in 1921.[71]

There are also several minor bridges along the London–Colchester road. In 1768 they were recorded as Putwell, Paine's, and Romford Gallows bridges, in Colchester Road, Watermill bridge, in Main Road, Romford Gore and Pigtail Wash bridges in London Road.[72] Putwell (or Delle) bridge is reserved for treatment under South Weald. Paine's bridge was mentioned in 1567.[73] Watermill bridge, styled Watermen's bridge *c.* 1772, was rebuilt to the design of James Paine *c.* 1776, when Gidea Hall park was landscaped.[74] It became known in the 19th century as Black's bridge. In 1893 it was taken over by the county council.[75]

In the 1830s some 30 coaches called at Romford daily, travelling to or from London, Chelmsford, Colchester, Harwich, Bury St. Edmund's (Suff.) and other places.[76] The Eastern Counties railway from London was opened to Romford in 1839, extended to Brentwood in 1840, and Colchester in 1843.[77] Squirrels Heath, later Gidea Park, station was opened in 1910.[78] The line was electrified in 1949. The London, Tilbury, and Southend railway's line from Grays, opened to Upminster in 1892, was extended to Romford in 1893.[79] A separate L.T. & S., later L.M.S., station was built in South Street, opposite and linked with the G.E.R., later L.N.E.R. station. The two stations were amalgamated in 1934, the L.M.S. entrance and booking hall being closed and converted into shops.[80] At the beginning of the present century attempts were made to promote the building of tramways in Romford.[81] They were unsuccessful, but in 1912 the London General Omnibus Co. started services from Mile End to Romford.[82] There was a civil aerodrome at Maylands Farm, Harold Hill, for a few years up to 1937.[83]

Romford was a post town by 1687.[84] In *c.* 1790 the post office was at the Cock and Bell inn, Market Place.[85] It was in the market-place in 1838 and 1848, and in High Street by 1863.[86] In 1870 it was in South Street, where it has since remained.[87] A telegraph line was being installed in 1869.[88]

Little remains in Romford that is older than the 19th century.[89] Even before modern development began there had been much rebuilding. In the Middle Ages there were manor-houses on 12 sites; Mawneys, Stewards, Marshalls, East House, and Gidea Hall were in or near the town, Wrightsbridge at Noak Hill, Dagenhams, Cockerels, and Gooshayes at Harold Hill, Risebridge near Chase Cross, Gobions at Collier Row, and Marks on the north-west boundary. In 1976 there were houses on only three of those sites: Gobions and Risebridge, both rebuilt in the 19th century, and Wrightsbridge, rebuilt in the 18th century and remodelled *c.* 1920. Adjoining Wrightsbridge, however, is the former Little Wrightsbridge, now Angel Cottages, which dates from the late 14th or early 15th century, and is Romford's oldest surviving building.[90] Of the other large domestic buildings known to have existed before the 19th century only five survive. Crown Farm, formerly Pigtails, London Road, is a

[61] Lingham, *Harold Hill and Noak Hill*, 26–7.
[62] *V.C.H. Essex*, v. 270–2.
[63] See H.R.L., Pictorial Coll.
[64] Middlesex and Essex Highways Act, 8 Geo. 1, c. 30; J. Mynde, *Map of Mdx. and Essex Turnpike Roads* (1728); *Map of Mdx. and Essex Turnpike Roads* (1768).
[65] Ministry of Transport, *Arterial Roads in Essex, opening of London–Southend Road* (1925).
[66] L.B. Havering, *Opening of St. Edward's Way* (1970).
[67] E.R.O., Q/SR 256/38.
[68] Ibid. 337/21, 341/23.
[69] E.R.O., D/DSa 63.
[70] *Cal. Treasury Bks.* 1735–8, 386, 557; 1739–41, 325; *E.R.* xxi. 102–3.
[71] *E.R.* xxi. 102–3; H.R.L., *Romford Charter Petition* (1936), Proof of Evidence (Engineer), p. 12.
[72] *Map of Mdx. and Essex Turnpike Roads, 1768.* The modern road names are used for convenience in this sentence.
[73] E.R.O., Q/SR 23/25.
[74] *Map of Essex* (1777). See below, p. 69.
[75] E.R.O., T/A 521/4, 16 Mar. 1893.
[76] *Pigot's Dir. Essex* (1832); *Robson's Dir. Essex* (1839). Cf. *Romford Guide* (1908), 19–20.
[77] E. Carter, *Hist. Geog. Brit. Rlys.* 63.
[78] A. H. Anderson, *Squirrels Heath and Gidea Park* (1910).
[79] K. A. Frost, *The Romford–Upminster Branch*, 13–14.
[80] Ibid. 33, 44; O.S. Map 25", Essex, LXVI. 16 (1895 edn.).
[81] H.R.L., Local Folder 20.
[82] L. A. Thomson, 'Motor omnibus services in . . . Romford and Hornchurch,' *Romford Record*, viii. 34.
[83] Lingham, *Harold Hill*, 22; H.R.L., Pictorial Coll., Maylands.
[84] *Cal. Treasury Bks.* 1685–9, 1677.
[85] *Univ. Brit. Dir.* (1790), 336.
[86] *Robson's Dir. Essex* (1838); *White's Dir. Essex* (1848, 1863).
[87] *Kelly's Dir. Essex* (1870).
[88] H.R.L., Romford L.B. Mins. 20 Dec. 1869.
[89] In preparing the following account of buildings much help was received from the Greater London Council, Historic Buildings Division.
[90] See p. 72.

HAVERING-ATTE-BOWER, ROMFORD, HAROLD WOOD, AND HAROLD HILL 1975

N

HAVERING -ATTE-BOWER
NOAK HILL
HAROLD HILL
HAROLD WOOD
ROMFORD
HORNCHURCH

Pyrgo (site)
Bower Farm
School
North Road
Vicarage
The Green
The Hall
Round House
Broxhill Road
Wellingtonia Avenue
Havering Park Ho. (site)
Blue Boar Hall
Orange Tree Hill
Bower House
Upper Bedfords (Earls)
Bedfords (site)
Bedfords Park
Havering Grange (site)
Havering Rd.
Lower Bedfords Road
Chase Cross Road
Havering Road
Mill (site)
The Lawn House
Rise Park
Risebridge
Public Golf Course
Heaton Grange (site)
Straight Road
Collier Row Lane
Eastern Avenue
Gidea Park Garden Suburb
Romford Golf Course
Raphael Park
Main Road
Balgores Lane
Royal Liberty School
Mawney Park
East Ho. (site)
Marshalls (site)
Victoria Hosp.
Black's Br.
North St.
Factories
Town Hall
Library
Church Ho.
Mawney Road
Shopping Precinct
South St.
Western Rd.
Eastern Rd.
Junction Rd.
Ind Coope Brewery
London Rd.
Romford Stn.
Stadium
To London
Oldchurch Hosp.
Gas Works
Oldchurch Rd.
R. Rom
Oldchurch Park
Crow Lane
Cemetery
Water Works
Roneo Works
Rush Green Rd.
Hornchurch Road
High Street
Victoria Road
Brentwood Road
Heath Park Rd.
Slewins Lane
R. Ravensbourne
Ardleigh Green Road
Butts Green Rd.
Emerson Park Stn.
Billet Lane
North St.
Gidea Pk. Stn.
Balgores La.
Squirrels Heath Lane
Havering Tech. College
Former Railway Factory
Gallows Cnr.
Harold Wood Hall
Colchester Road
Hospital
Gubbins Lane
Stn.
Matthews' Mill (site)
Squirrels Heath Road
Southend Arterial Road
Harold Wood Park
Brock's Fireworks Factory (site)
Mount Pleasant Farm
Cockabourne Bridge
Church Rd.
Brick Works (site)
To Chelmsford
Paines Bridge
Faringdon Avenue
Factories
Hilldene Ave.
Gooshays Drive
Swimming Pool
Central Park
Dagnam Park Drive
Dagnam Park
Dagenhams (site)
North Hill Drive
Carter's brook
Noak Hill Road
Priory (site)
Chequers Road
Wrightsbridge Rd.
Wrightsbridge Farm
Angel Cottages
Weald brook
Church Road
St. Thomas's School
Widdrington Farm

0 yards 880
0 kilometres 1

Parish boundaries c.1865

Churches
+ Anglican
B Baptist
Br Brethren
M Methodist
RC Roman Catholic
UR United Reformed
F Friends' meeting house
Mo Mormon temple
✡ Synagogue
SA Salvation Army

late-16th- or early-17th-century house extended at the back and re-arranged internally in the later 18th century; further additions, for service rooms, were made in the earlier 19th century.[91] Widdrington Farm, formerly Wolves and Joyes, Church Road, Noak Hill, stands on a medieval site.[92] It retains a timber-framed cross-wing of the 17th century, but the main range appears to have been reconstructed in the 18th century, and the whole building was encased in brick and re-roofed in the 19th century. Maypole Cottage, Collier Row Road, is a timber-framed house of the late 17th or early 18th century. The Morris Dancer, formerly New Hall, Melksham Close, Harold Hill, is an early-18th-century brick building now serving as a public house.

Hare Hall, Upper Brentwood Road, Gidea Park, now part of the Royal Liberty school, stands on the site of an earlier house called Goodwins. It is a small Palladian mansion built in 1768–9 by John A. Wallenger to designs by James Paine.[93] The main, north front is of five bays, with a rusticated basement storey, above which the two upper storeys are unified by a giant attached portico and pilasters at the angles. Attached to the south front by short corridors there were pavilions containing service rooms. The principal rooms were on the first floor, and were approached by a central staircase with curved ends and an iron balustrade. The main front was of Portland stone, but the south front was of red brick, and in 1896 the house was considerably enlarged on that side by filling in the space between the pavilions. The Royal Liberty school was opened at Hare Hall in 1921, and in 1929–30 new red-brick buildings were erected to the south of the old house, forming a quadrangle. Nothing remains of the landscape designed by Richard Woods in 1771.

Among the more important old houses which have disappeared in the present century, and of which there are dated descriptions, were Lowland's Farm, London Road, Hawkins atte Well, Pettits Lane North, both of the 17th century, and Bell House, Rush Green Road, of the late 16th.[94] Several other old houses, possibly dating from the 16th century, still survived *c.* 1880. They included Familiarum, later Canons, North Street, and London House, Market Place.[95]

Small houses built before *c.* 1800 have survived in somewhat larger numbers. In the town there are several in North Street and at the east end of the market-place. The oldest of them, now nos. 98 and 100 North Street, is a timber-framed building of the late 17th century. At Gidea Park nos. 202–10 Main Road, also timber-framed, are a group of cottages of the late 18th or early 19th century, surviving from the hamlet of Hare Street. There are a few other cottages of that period in Noak Hill Road, Noak Hill.

As a market town on the main London Road Romford had many inns. In 1686 those in the town contained beds for 139, and stabling for 404 horses, and those at Hare Street 18 beds and stabling for 38.[96] In 1762 there were 22 licensed houses in the town and 3 at Hare Street.[97] Of those in the town only the Golden Lion, formerly known as the Lion or the Red Lion, still functions in its ancient buildings[98] The Lion existed in 1440, and there are later references from 1501.[99] The building, which is largely timber-framed, has a short elevation to High Street, and a much longer one, with a visible jetty, to North Street. It is made up of at least three sections of various dates from the early 16th century to the early 17th. That next to the corner was formerly jettied on both streets, and has a carriageway entrance in High Street. The next section along North Street had a first floor gallery towards the west, where there was an open court. The remaining sections have been much reduced by fire, and much altered internally, but are probably latest in date. In the 18th century the High Street front was raised by one storey and given a new brick elevation, which was remodelled in the 19th century. The south end of the courtyard is now built over. Recent restoration has exposed much of the internal timber framing.

Three other ancient inns in the town continue in modern buildings. The White Hart, High Street, can be traced from 1489.[1] During the Civil War it was used for meetings of the Deputy Lieutenants and Parliamentary Commissioners. In the later 18th century public entertainments were held in the White Hart assembly room.[2] The inn was rebuilt in 1896. The King's Head, Market Place, existed in 1678.[3] It is said to have been rebuilt in 1714 and again in 1898.[4] In 1971 the inn was moved to new buildings in the Liberty.[5] The Lamb, Market Place, mentioned in 1681, was rebuilt in 1852–3 after a fire.[6] The Cock and Bell, formerly the Chequers, Market Place, is no longer an inn, but its 16th-century building survives as Church House.[7]

The Angel, which dated from 1488 or earlier,[8] and the Crown, recorded from 1620,[9] both in High Street, still existed in 1762, but had gone by 1864.[10] The Coach and Bell, also in High Street, was recorded by that name from 1694, and was probably identical with the Bell, mentioned in 1595 and 1631.[11] It was rebuilt in 1895 and demolished in 1956.[12] The Dolphin, Market Place, recorded from 1630, was closed in 1890 and demolished in 1900.[13] The Swan, or White Swan, Market Place, existed in 1468.[14] Its history has been traced from 1598 until 1967, when

[91] Cf. R.C.H.M. *Essex*, ii. 203.
[92] E.R.O., D/DM T46; E.R.O., D/DSa 63.
[93] A. Searle and C. Brazier, *Hist. Hare Hall* (1960) [A full account of the house and its occupants]; Pevsner, *Essex*, 328. See plate facing p. 128.
[94] R.C.H.M. *Essex*, ii. 203–4.
[95] Terry, *Romford*, 113–15; H.R.L., Lithographs by A. B. Bamford, 1889.
[96] *E.R.* liii. 11.
[97] E.R.O., D/DHt T225/6.
[98] See H.R.L., Pictorial Coll.
[99] E.R.O., D/DM M196; D/DMs T12/2, 4; D/DU 70 and 29–42; D/DFr T68; J. Thomas and L. Holder, 'Story of the Golden Lion,' *Romford Record*, iii. 9.
[1] E.R.O., Library Folder, Romford, Annotated summary of history of White Hart (TS).
[2] *E.R.* lx. 31, cf. 37.
[3] E.R.O., T/P 71/1; cf. E.R.O., D/DNe T34.
[4] H.R.L., Cornell MSS., Inns of Romford.
[5] Inf. from manager.
[6] E.R.O., T/P 71/1; H.R.L., Cornell MSS.
[7] New Coll. MS. 4589 (deeds 1847–1909). See also p. 84 below.
[8] E.R.O., D/DCm T45; *E.R.* lii. 123–4.
[9] E.R.O., T/P 71/1; Terry, *Romford*, 190.
[10] E.R.O., D/DHt T225/6; E.R.O., T/A 521/7.
[11] E.R.O., T/P 71/1; ibid. D/DU 297/2, 3; D/DU 651/25.
[12] *Romford Record*, vii. 48; A. B. Bamford, lithograph 1896.
[13] E.R.O., T/P 71/1; *E.R.* lv. 87 n.; H.R.L., Cornell MSS.
[14] E.R.O., D/DU 102/51, m. 6.

it was demolished.[15] The inn signs of the Dolphin and the White Swan are in Havering reference library, Romford. The Duke of Wellington, Market Place, was demolished in 1967.[16] Until 1914 it was the Blücher's Head, a name which had presumably been adopted *c.* 1815.[17] The Queen's Head, Market Place, was mentioned in 1732, but was not among the licensed houses in 1762.[18] The building still existed *c.* 1908 as Charles Ellingworth's dining rooms. A writer at that time thought that it was probably identical with the Queen's Arms, mentioned as the lodging of pretty Bessie in the Elizabethan ballad of the 'Blind Beggar's Daughter of Bethnal Green'.[19] In 1599 the comic actor William Kemp spent two days at a Romford inn, not named, during his morris dance from London to Norwich.[20]

At Hare Street, now Main Road, Gidea Park, the Ship and the Unicorn both existed in 1762.[21] The buildings of the Ship date from the later 16th or 17th century, though much altered.[22] The Unicorn, mentioned in 1679, and later, has been rebuilt in modern Tudor style.[23] In 1762 there were 5 inns at Collier Row and 3 at Noak Hill.[24] The Bear, Noak Hill Road, Noak Hill, was formerly the Goat, and was given its present name in 1715.[25]

During the agrarian boom of the mid 19th century many farm-houses in Collier Row, Harold Wood, and Noak Hill wards were built or rebuilt. At the same time those areas, still rural but within a mile or two of Romford station, were attracting the gentry, and wealthy business men working in London.[26] Notable among the new farm-houses was Heaton Grange, Straight Road, built *c.* 1815 by John Heaton, rebuilt *c.* 1905, and demolished *c.* 1955.[27] Another example, still surviving as a community centre at Harold Hill, is Red House, North Hill Drive, built in 1873.[28] Lawn House, Lawnsway, Collier Row now Lawn social club, was built *c.* 1850, apparently by the owner of the adjoining windmill, and was soon enlarged into a gentleman's residence, in a small park.[29]

Harold Wood Hall, Neave Close, Harold Hill, was built *c.* 1847, perhaps by William Heard, land surveyor, who was living there 1848.[30] Later occupants included Alexander Croll, *c.* 1859–63, William George, *c.* 1876–8, and Edward Bryant, *c.* 1890–1926.[31] Harold Wood Hall is now (1976) a mental health day centre of Havering L.B. It is an Italianate villa of double pile plan with a main front of 5 bays. Late in the 19th century it was extended at both ends, and the interior was extensively refitted. A small building in the grounds, used as an elementary school, *c.* 1859–76, and as a nonconformist chapel, *c.* 1861–82, no longer exists.[32] The Priory, later called Dagnam Priory, Wrightsbridge Road, Noak Hill, was built *c.* 1840 in a curious mixture of Gothic and Tudor styles.[33] It was demolished in 1956.[34]

Until the 19th century Romford's principal public building, apart from the church, was the court house of the liberty of Havering, which stood at the west end of the market-place. It was demolished in 1933.[35] The parish workhouse, North Street (1787), and the Corn Exchange, High Street (1845) have also been demolished, as well as St. Edward's Hall and the Laurie Hall, already mentioned, but Romford union workhouse (1838) survives as part of Oldchurch hospital.[36] Romford county court, South Street, built in 1858, was demolished in 1936.[37] Modern public buildings include the town hall (1937), and the central library (1965), both in Main Road.

During the 17th century military musters were often held at Romford.[38] Troops were stationed in the town during and after the Civil War, and occasionally later.[39] In 1795, during the Revolutionary War with France, barracks for six troops of cavalry were built in London Road.[40] They were demolished *c.* 1825.[41] The Havering company of volunteer cavalry was raised *c.* 1802 for service in the Napoleonic Wars.[42] The Romford rifle volunteers were formed in 1859.[43]

The Liberty of Havering and district association for the protection of property and the prosecution of felons was founded in 1835.[44] Its area was gradually extended, and by 1933, when there were about 50 members, included places as far apart as Woodford and West Thurrock. The association, which met at

[15] *E.J.* iii. 66–8; A. B. Bamford, lithograph, 1889.
[16] H.R.L., Local File 7/6, Notes on D. of Wellington.
[17] H.R.L., Cornell MSS., 'Inns of Romford', *Robson's Dir. Essex* (1838), 87. Perhaps previously the Duke's Head, cf. D/DHt T225/6 (1762).
[18] E.R.O., T/P 71/1; D/DHt T225/6.
[19] Cornell MSS., 'Inns of Romford'; *Percy's Reliques of Ancient English Poetry* (Everyman edn.), ii. 30.
[20] *Kemp's Nine Daies Wonder*, ed. A. Dyce (Camd. Soc. xi.).
[21] E.R.O., D/DHt T225/6.
[22] R.C.H.M. *Essex*, ii. 203; A. B. Bamford, Lithograph of Hare St., 1889.
[23] E.R.O., T/P 71/1; E.R.O., D/DBe T1.
[24] E.R.O., D/DHt T225/6. The Bear is there listed under Harold Wood ward.
[25] Lingham, *Harold Hill and Noak Hill*, 44; E.R.O., D/DNe T11.
[26] For these developments see e.g. E.R.O., T/Z 38/148, I. A. Semple, 'Collier Row and Havering, 1800–1939'. (Brentwood Coll. Educ. thesis, 1972), chaps. viii, ix.
[27] Smith, *Havering*, 122; inf. from Mr. G. J. Clements.
[28] Date plaque on building.
[29] Semple, op. cit. chap. vii; O.S. Map 6", Essex, LXVI (surv. 1862–71); inf. from Mrs. T. Bibbings per Mr. K. G. Farries.
[30] *White's Dir. Essex* (1848), 382: 'Harold Wood House'; cf. I.R. 29/12/162 (tithe map, 1844, which does not show the house); O.S. Map 6", Essex, LXVII (surv. 1866).
[31] *Kelly's Dir. Essex* (1859 and later edns.); *White's Dir. Essex* (1863), 601; E.R.O., Sage Coll., *Sale Cats.* vol. iii. 1 and 2. For the life of a servant at the house during Bryant's time see *Romford Record*, iii. 26, iv. 42.
[32] See pp. 95, 88.
[33] I.R. 29 and 30/12/62 (tithe award, 1846); O.S. Map 6" Essex, LXVII (surv. 1866); H.R.L., Pictorial Coll.; E.R.O., D/DNe T102; Lingham, *Harold Hill and Noak Hill*, 37.
[34] Inf. from Mr. G. J. Clements.
[35] See p. 7.
[36] See pp. 78, 76, 81.
[37] Romford L.B. Mins. 8 Oct. 1857; S. Roberts, *Romford in 19th. cent.* 61; *Romford Guide* (1936), 1.
[38] *Cal. S.P. Dom.* 1631–33, 156; E.R.O., D/DCv 4/1 (date 1661–84).
[39] Hist. MSS. Com. 6, *7th Rep., Barrington*, p. 562; *Cal. S.P. Dom.* 1625–49, 642; ibid. 1648–9, 174, 176, 178; 1653–4, 475; 1679–80, 45, 93; 1695, addenda, 17.
[40] Lysons, *Lond.* iv. 203; Terry, *Romford*, 236.
[41] H.R.L., Cornell MSS., Barracks; E.R.O., T/P 71/1 (memories of J. B. Talbot); T/P 67/7, p. 46: sale of timber etc. from barracks, 1829.
[42] *E.R.* xxviii. 45; *E.A.T.* N.S. xi. 169.
[43] H.R.L., Cornell MSS.
[44] This paragraph is based on: H.R.L., Records of the Liberty of Havering and district association for the protection of property and the prosecution of felons, 1835–1941; *Romford Official Guide* (1936), 23; E.R.O., T/P 212 (Posters and Lists of Members, 1921–37); inf. from Mr. L. C. Symons.

Romford, prosecuted offenders against its members and offered rewards to persons helping to obtain convictions. It eventually became an exclusive club of farmers and tradesmen, popularly known as 'the Felons', but it never entirely abandoned its original aims. It was wound up in 1941 or shortly after.

Romford literary and mechanics' institute, founded in 1848, survived for about 40 years.[45] Romford philanthropic theatre, which in 1831 played for a summer season in the town, contained professional actors as well as amateurs.[46] The Laurie cinema, at Laurie hall, was opened in 1913 and closed in 1939.[47] By 1937 there were two other cinemas in the town, and another was being built.[48] In 1951 there were four in the town and another at Collier Row, but by 1971 only two survived, the Odeon, and the A.B.C. (three-in-one), both in South Street.[49]

Horse races were being run at Romford in 1758.[50] Occasional race meetings were also held there in the 1840s.[51] The Priory polo club, founded in 1887, played at Dagnam Priory, Noak Hill, until 1895, when it moved to Hutton.[52] Romford cricket club, founded 1862, still survived in 1971.[53] Romford football club, founded in 1929, soon became one of the leading amateur clubs.[54] Romford golf club, Gidea Park, was founded in 1894,[55] and Maylands golf club, Harold Park, in 1937.[56] Romford swimming club was founded in 1902.[57] Romford greyhound racing stadium, London Road, was opened near the Crown hotel in 1929.[58] The present stadium, on the opposite side of London Road, was opened in 1933. In 1974 some 70 sports clubs were meeting in Romford.[59] At that date there were also about 50 cultural and recreational societies, with activities ranging from wine-tasting to war games, and from morris dancing to the study of underground railways. That number does not include societies meeting in Hornchurch, many of which were available to Romford people, or religious, political, trade, or professional bodies. Romford historical society, founded in 1956, has since 1968 been publishing an annual journal of local history.

Among persons connected with Romford were Sir Anthony Cooke (d. 1576) of Gidea Hall, politician, religious reformer, and tutor to Edward VI, and his learned daughters, Mildred, wife of William Cecil, Lord Burghley, and Katherine, wife of Sir Henry Killigrew.[60] Seventeenth-century figures included Francis Quarles (d. 1644), of Stewards, poet,[61] Laurence Wright (d. 1657), physician, of Dagenhams, Joachim Matthews (d. 1659), of Gobions, Parliamentary colonel and M.P. for Maldon,[62] and William Mead (d. 1713), Quaker, of Gooshayes. In the 18th century Gloster Ridley (d. 1724) and his son James Ridley (d. 1765), both writers, were successively curates of Romford.[63] Humphry Repton (d. 1818), landscape artist, lived at Hare Street, in a house at the corner of Balgores Lane which was long known as Repton Cottage.[64] Anthony Grant (d. 1883), vicar of Romford, and archdeacon of St. Albans, was for many years an influential local figure.[65] Thomas Bird (d. 1900) was a keen antiquary as well as chairman of the local board.[66] A. Bennett Bamford (d. 1939), topographical artist, lived at Romford for the earlier part of his life.[67] Arthur S. Hunt (d. 1934), papyrologist, was born at Romford Hall.[68] Kenneth Farnes (d. 1941), Essex and England cricketer, was brought up at Gidea Park.[69] Two conspirators are supposed to have plotted at Romford: Thomas Blood (d. 1680), who stole the Crown jewels,[70] and Christopher Layer, Jacobite, who was executed in 1723.[71] John Wilson (d. 1799), butcher of Romford, was notoriously fat.[72]

MANORS AND OTHER ESTATES. All estates in Romford, however styled, were subordinate to the manor of Havering.[73] The manor of *ROMFORD* or *MAWNEYS* lay on the west side of the town, extending north from High Street to Collier Row. It appears to have originated in 1200, when the king granted 'the wood of Romford' to Roger Bigod (d. 1221), earl of Norfolk, in fee for 5*s*. a year.[74] Two later references show that the wood was then held by the serjeanty of providing pasturage for the king's cattle.[75] In 1277 the wood, comprising 100 a., was held of Roger Bigod (d. 1306), earl of Norfolk, by Adam de Creting, whose estate included also 280 a., mostly held in chief, which Adam had bought from Roger de Rolling.[76] In 1280 Creting and his wife Nichola granted the manor of Romford, so styled for the first time, to Henry of Winchester, a Jew, to hold for ¼ knight's fee.[77] Henry, who was a Christian convert, died holding the manor in 1299.[78] He had been married under Jewish law, and there was

45 For its history: *V.C.H. Essex, Bibliog.* 318.
46 *E.J.* ii. 27.
47 *Romford Times*, 31 May 1939; *Romford Guide* (1936), 8.
48 *Romford Guide* (1936), 8; (1937), 46.
49 *Romford Guide* (1951), 47; *Havering Guide* (1971), 54.
50 H.R.L., Local File 86 (extracts from *Lond. Chron.* 29 June–1 July 1758): see *Romford Record*, iii. 29.
51 *V.C.H. Essex*, ii. 587.
52 Ibid. 595.
53 Ibid. 608; *Romford Guide* (1936), 39; (1951), 43; Havering L.B., *List of Organizations* (1971).
54 *Romford Guide* (1936), 40; (1951), 39.
55 *V.C.H. Essex*, ii. 592–3.
56 H.R.L., Pictorial Coll., Maylands Farm.
57 *Romford Guide* (1936), 41.
58 Inf. from Romford Stadium; *Romford Recorder*, 10 Dec. 1976.
59 *Havering L.B. List of Organizations* (1974).
60 *D.N.B.*; M. K. McIntosh, 'Sir Anthony Cooke', *Proc. American Philosophical Soc.* cxix. (1975), 233; Smith, *Havering*, 117–20.
61 *D.N.B.*; *E.R.* viii. 1–12; *E.J.* ii. 140–6.
62 Terry, *Romford*, 170–2; Smith, *Havering*, 154–5; *V.C.H. Essex*, ii. 62, 238.
63 See p. 84.
64 D. Stroud, *Humphry Repton*; Terry, *Romford*, 238; O.S. Map 6", Essex, LXVI (Surv. 1862–71); E.R.O., Sage Coll., *Sale Cats.* vol. x. 7; H.R.L., Local File 16/1; C. Jones, 'Humphry Repton of Hare St.,' *Romford Record*, ii. 17.
65 See pp. 78, 84.
66 See p. 78. His antiquarian notes are E.R.O., T/P 71.
67 C. J. Whitwood, 'Alfred Bennett Bamford', *Romford Record*, vii. 30–8.
68 *D.N.B.*
69 K. Farnes, *Tours and Tests.*
70 Terry, *Romford*, 206–8; *D.N.B.*; C. J. Whitwood, 'Col. Thomas Blood', *Romford Record*, viii. 5.
71 *D.N.B.*
72 *Gent. Mag.* 1799 (2), 997, Terry, *Romford*, 233; *Univ. Brit. Dir.* (1791) names him as John: cf. E.R.O., Q/HF 84 (inf. from Mrs. J. Tarrant).
73 See p. 11.
74 *Rot. Chart.* (Rec. Com.), i. 52.
75 *Red Bk. Exch.* (Rolls Ser.), ii. 508 (list of serjeanties); *Rot. Hundr.* (Rec. Com.), i. 152.
76 *Cal. Inq. Misc.* 1219–1307, p. 322.
77 *Feet of F. Essex*, ii. 25.
78 *Cal. Inq. p.m.* iii. p. 391.

Romford: air view of Town Centre, looking north-east

Romford: Visit of Marie de Medici to Gidea Hall, 1638

Little Warley: Review of Warley Camp by George III, 1778

therefore doubt whether his son Thomas was entitled to inherit the manor. There is no evidence that Thomas did in fact succeed to Romford. Adam de Creting had died in 1298,[79] and by 1303 the tenancy in demesne had been acquired by the earl of Norfolk, who was holding ¼ knight's fee of Adam's son John de Creting.[80] On the earl's death in 1306 Romford passed to the Crown under a previous agreement, by which John Bigod, the earl's brother, had been excluded from the succession.[81]

In the subsequent division of the Bigod estates Romford was assigned to Thomas of Brotherton (d. 1338) earl of Norfolk, on whose death it passed to his elder daughter Margaret (d. 1399) countess of Norfolk, wife of John Segrave, Lord Segrave (d. 1353), and later of Walter de Mauny, Lord Mauny.[82] In *c.* 1355 Mauny's estate, *jure uxoris*, comprised 140 a., held as ¼ knight's fee.[83] He held it until his death in 1372.[84] He was one of the greatest soldiers of his day, celebrated by Froissart,[85] and from him the manor took its alternative name. Margaret, created duchess of Norfolk in 1397, was succeeded in 1399 by her grandson Thomas de Mowbray, duke of Norfolk, who died in the same year.[86] Romford was assigned in dower to the duke's widow Elizabeth (d. 1425) later wife of Sir Robert Goushill (d. 1403) and finally of Sir Gerard Usflete (d. by 1421).[87] In 1412 Elizabeth's Romford estate of 'Moyns' (Mawneys) was valued at £14.[88] It passed on her death to her son John Mowbray (d. 1432), duke of Norfolk.[89] Romford was assigned in dower to John's widow Katherine.[90] She was still living in 1483, having outlived four husbands.[91]

In 1488–9 the manor of Mawneys, held in chief, was settled on William de Berkeley (d. 1492) earl of Nottingham, later marquess of Berkeley, who was a coheir to the estates of the Mowbray earls of Norfolk.[92] He was to hold the manor with remainder to the heirs of his body, and in default to Sir Reynold Bray. After Berkeley's death Mawneys was held by his widow Anne (d. 1497), later wife of Sir Thomas Brandon.[93] When she died the manor appears to have passed under the settlement of 1488–9 to Sir Reynold Bray, to whom Mawneys was quitclaimed in 1499 by Berkeley's brother Maurice, Lord Berkeley.[94] Bray (d. 1503) was an official close to Henry VII, and it is not unlikely that he acquired his interest in the manor by assisting in the transactions, in 1487–9, by which Berkeley obtained his marquessate.[95] Mawneys descended to Sir Reynold's nephew Edmund Bray, later Lord Bray, who was holding it in 1510.[96] Edmund appears to have alienated the manor by 1523, when Thomas Wastell and Edward Barbour conveyed it to Robert Fenrother (d. 1524), alderman and goldsmith of London.[97] Mawneys passed to Fenrother's widow Gillian, and after her death in 1536 to their daughter Gillian and her husband Nicholas Tycheborne.[98] In 1538 Nicholas Tycheborne the younger conveyed it to Robert Dacre.[99]

Robert Dacre was probably identical with the man of that name who died in 1543 leaving George his son and heir.[1] George Dacre conveyed Mawneys in 1573 to John Lennard of Chevening (Kent), who died in 1591, having previously settled it on his son Samuel.[2] In 1612 Samuel Lennard conveyed the manor to Francis Fuller.[3] Fuller (d. 1637), also acquired Easthouse in Romford, as well as Downshall, Loxford, and Wangey in Ilford.[4] Mawneys and Easthouse appear to have descended to Francis Osbaldeston (d. 1648) and then to his brother Henry (d. 1669). Henry Osbaldeston (d. by 1693), son of the previous Henry, sold Easthouse, but Mawneys descended to his daughter Ann, who appears to have carried it in marriage about 1701 to John Milner of London, who was holding it in 1719 and 1722.[5] In 1758 William Lloyd and Elizabeth his wife, who were heirs of the Milners, sold the manor to Richard Newman.[6]

Richard Newman was succeeded by his grandson Richard Harding, who acquired the manor of Nelmes, in Hornchurch, in 1781, and took the surname of Newman in 1783.[7] Mawneys descended with Nelmes until the 1880s.[8] In 1846 Thomas Harding Newman's Romford estate comprised 265 a.[9] Benjamin Harding Newman, who inherited the estate in 1882, put it on the market in the following year, and by 1899 much of it had been developed for building.[10] The name survives in Mawney Road.

The manor-house of Mawneys, sometimes called Great Mawneys, stood on a moated site about 150 yd. north of High Street.[11] About 1618 the house was of considerable size.[12] In the later 19th century it was an irregular building, part of which appears to have been rebuilt in the 18th century.[13] The moat was filled in between 1883 and 1887.[14] The house

[79] Ibid. iii. p. 384.
[80] *Feud. Aids*, ii. 135.
[81] *Cal. Inq. p.m.* iv, pp. 291, 297; *Complete Peerage*, ix. 595–6.
[82] *Cal. Fine R.* 1337–47, 111; *Complete Peerage*, ix. 599–600.
[83] New College MS. 9744, f. 161v.
[84] *Cal. Inq. p.m.* xiii, p. 117; *Cal. Close* 1369–74, 376.
[85] *Complete Peerage*, viii. 571–6.
[86] Ibid. ix. 600–04; C 137/18. In 1399 parts of the manor were said to be held of Adam Karlyl and John Love.
[87] *Complete Peerage*, iv. 604; *Cal. Close*, 1399–1402, 165–6, 381–3; ibid. 1402–05, 211; *Cal. Fine R.* 1399–1405, 134; Morant, *Essex*, i. 65.
[88] *Feud. Aids.* vi. 434.
[89] C 139/160.
[90] *Cal. Close*, 1429–35, 205.
[91] *Complete Peerage*, ix. 607.
[92] *Cal. Pat.* 1485–94, 200; *Feet of F. Essex*, iv. 90; *Complete Peerage*, ii. 133; ix. 610.
[93] *Cal. Inq. p.m. Hen. VII*, i. p. 358; *Complete Peerage*, ii. 135.
[94] *Feet of F. Essex*, iv. 102; *Complete Peerage*, ii. 135.
[95] *Complete Peerage*, ii. 133–4; *D.N.B.*, Bray, Sir R.
[96] *Feet of F. Essex*, iv. 122.
[97] Ibid. iv. 152; C 142/42/122; *E.A.T.* N.S. xiv. 40.
[98] Cf. *V.C.H. Essex*, iv. 255.
[99] *Feet of F. Essex*, iv. 219.
[1] Morant, *Essex*, i. 415; cf. *Visit. Essex* (Harl. Soc.), 78–9.
[2] C.P. 25 (2)/129/1653; C 142/229/143; T. Barrett-Lennard, *Families of Lennard and Barrett*, 8.
[3] C.P. 25 (2)/294 Eas. 10 Jas. I; E.R.O., D/DU 102/105, m.1.
[4] *V.C.H. Essex*, v. 201, 206, 212.
[5] C.P. 25 (2)/830 Trin. 13 Wm. III; E.R.O., T/P 195/2, f. 21*b*; E.R.O., T/A 521/1, Vestry Min. 6 Nov. 1722.
[6] C.P. 25(2)/1125 Mich. 32 Geo. II; Lysons, *Lond.* iv. 185.
[7] *Burke, Land Gent.* (1914), 1395.
[8] See p. 37.
[9] I.R. 29/12/162.
[10] E.R.O., Sage Coll., *Sale Cats.* vol. x. 14–16; E.R.O., *Sale Cats.* B2869 and A537; H.R.L., Romford L.B. Mins. 6 July 1885 sqq.; Romford U.D.C. Mins. 18 Apr. 1889.
[11] E.R.O., D/DU 162/1 (map, *c.* 1618); H.R.L., E. Gotto, *Plan of Romford* (1853).
[12] E.R.O., D/DU 162/1.
[13] H.R.L., Pictorial Coll., Litho. by A. B. Bamford, 1888; A. B. Bamford, *Sketches in Liberty of Havering* (1890).
[14] E.R.O., Sage Coll., *Sale Cats.* vol. x. 14, 15.

was demolished *c.* 1935.[15] The United Services club was later built on the site.

The manor of *DAGENHAMS AND COCKERELS* comprised two adjoining tenements lying north of the Romford–Brentwood road, in the area now called Harold Hill. The tenements appear to have been identical with two held in the earlier 13th century by John of Weald: 3½ virgates, later Dagenhams, and 1 virgate, later Cockerels.[16] These were large virgates, of about 120 a. each.[17] John of Weald (d. 1251) left as heirs his sister Gillian, wife of Roger Cockerel, and his nephew William Shenfield,[18] Sir William of St. Armine, who from 1257 to *c.* 1262 was farmer of the manor of Havering, acquired the lands of both Roger Cockerel and William Shenfield, and in or before 1269 granted them in fee to Robinet Rowley (de Rolee) and his wife Isabel.[19] They later passed to Thomas of Dagenham, who was probably identical with the man of that name who was bailiff of Havering under Edward I.[20] Thomas was apparently succeeded by his son William of Dagenham,[21] whose lands had escheated to Queen Philippa by 1352, when she granted them for life to her clerk Austin Waleys.[22]

About 1355 Dagenhams and Cockerels, with other lands, comprising 606 a. in all, were held by Adam de Holkirk.[23] By 1382 the estate had been acquired by John Organ (d. 1392), a London mercer; he was succeeded by his son Thomas, also a mercer, who made a conveyance of the manor in 1403.[24] The Organs appear to have retained some interest in Dagenhams and Cockerels at least until 1406.[25] In 1420 the manor was held by Humphrey, duke of Gloucester, Edmund de Mortimer, earl of March, and others.[26] They were obviously trustees, but for whom is not clear.

By 1443 the manor had passed to Henry Percy (d. 1455), earl of Northumberland,[27] whose grandfather, Henry Percy (d. 1408), earl of Northumberland, had been keeper of the manor of Havering *c.* 1399–1403.[28] Dagenhams and Cockerels descended to Henry Percy, earl of Northumberland (d. 1461), who fell on the Lancastrian side at the battle of Towton.[29] His estates thus escheated to Edward IV, who in 1464 granted Dagenhams and Cockerels to Henry Bourchier, earl of Essex, and his wife Isabel, to discharge a legacy made to Isabel by her uncle Edmund de Mortimer (d. 1425), earl of March.[30] March's fiduciary interest in the manor, in 1420, has been mentioned above. He is not known to have had any personal interest in it.

The grant of 1464 had no permanent effect. Henry Percy (d. 1489), earl of Northumberland, regained his father's earldom in 1470.[31] He appears to have vindicated his title to Dagenhams and Cockerels in 1474 by a collusive lawsuit against his father's trustees,[32] and in 1482 he sold the manor to Avery Cornburgh.[33] Cornburgh (d. 1487) also held Gooshayes in Romford and Dovers in Hornchurch. Before his death he sold Dagenhams and Cockerels to Sir William Hussey (d. 1495), chief justice of the King's Bench, from whom the manor descended to his son (Sir) John.[34] In 1512 Sir John Hussey conveyed Dagenhams and Cockerels to trustees for the use of his ward Peter Christmas, with remainder, in default of heirs of Peter's body, to the Grocers' Company of London.[35] That transaction had been arranged by Henry VIII to compensate Christmas for the manor of Hanworth (Mdx.), which he had conveyed to the king. Hussey received in exchange two royal manors in Lincolnshire.

Peter Christmas died in 1517.[36] The Grocers' Company duly succeeded to the manor, and held courts there until 1544 or later.[37] Dagenhams and Cockerels was subsequently acquired by Thomas Legatt, who died holding it in 1556.[38] The manor descended in the Legatt family until 1633, when the representatives of Thomas Posthumous Legatt, great-grandson of the last-named Thomas Legatt, sold it to Dr. Thomas Wright, later physician to Cromwell.[39] In 1633 the estate comprised 703 a.[40] Dr. Wright (d. 1657) was succeeded by his son (Sir) Henry Wright (Bt.) (d. 1664), and grandson Sir Henry Wright, Bt. (d. 1681).[41] The younger Sir Henry, who died under age, was succeeded by his sister Ann, who married Edmund Pye and later William Rider. By her will, proved 1732, she devised all her Essex estates to her relative Edward Carteret (d. 1739).[42] She expressed the wish that Carteret would never part with the estate, and would keep it in his family, but in 1749 his daughters and coheirs Ann, widow of Admiral Philip Cavendish, and Bridget Carteret sold it to Henry Muilman.[43]

In 1772 Henry Muilman sold Dagenhams and Cockerels to (Sir) Richard Neave (Bt.), a West India merchant.[44] The manor descended with the

[15] *Kelly's Dir. Essex* (1906 and later edns.); ex. inf. Miss J. M. Davis.
[16] S.C. 11/189 (Survey of Havering Manor, 1250–1); cf. *Cal. Pat.* 1416–22, 301.
[17] *Cal. Pat.* 1416–22, 301.
[18] Morant, *Essex*, i. 62. The original inquisition is missing, and Morant's version of it is probably incomplete and inaccurate. For Cockerel's forename see below, and *Horn. Docs.* (index).
[19] *Cal. Chart. R.* 1257–1300, 119. For St. Armine see also: *Cal. Pat.* 1247–58, 552–3; *Cal. Inq. p.m.* i, p. 126; *Close R.* 1261–4, 65.
[20] *Cal. Pat.* 1416–22, 301; *Horn. Docs.* nos. 194, 344, 363, 368, 404.
[21] *Cal. Inq. p.m.* vii, p. 410; *Horn. Docs.* nos. 163, 423, 516. Thomas and William also held Cockermouth in Dagenham: *V.C.H. Essex*, v. 272.
[22] *Cal. Pat.* 1350–4, 345.
[23] New Coll. MS. 9744, f. 162v.
[24] S.C. 2/172/26; E.R.O., D/DU 102/6, m. 5d.; *Cal. Close*, 1402–5, 155–6.
[25] S.C. 2/172/30 mm. 6d., 8d., 11; *Cal. Close*, 1405–9, 146, 262. Thos. Prudaunce and Simon Bernewell, who figured in those transactions, were trustees appointed by John Organ in 1392.
[26] *Cal. Pat.* 1416–22, 301.
[27] *Cal. Close*, 1441–7, 149.
[28] S.C. 2/172/29 and 30; *Cal. Pat.* 1401–5, 259.
[29] E.R.O., D/DU 102/46, m. 3; C 139/160; *Complete Peerage*, ix. 715–17.
[30] *Cal. Pat.* 1461–7, 321.
[31] *Complete Peerage*, ix. 715–17.
[32] E.R.O., D/DU 102/58, mm. 3d., 5–6d.; cf. 102/46, m. 3 and *Archaelogia Aeliana*, N.S. xvi. 125.
[33] *Arch. Aeliana*, N.S. xvi. 125; S.C. 2/172/33 (13 Mar. 1483).
[34] *Cal. Inq. p.m. Hen. VII*, i, p. 515; *D.N.B.* s.v. Hussey, Sir Wm.
[35] *Cal. Chart. R.* 1427–1516, 277–8; Act for the Assurance of Title of the king's manor of Hanworth, 6 Hen. VIII, c. 32 (Priv. Act): copy in E.R.O., D/DNe T1.
[36] Morant, *Essex*, i. 61.
[37] E.R.O., D/DNe M1.
[38] C 142/105/44.
[39] E.R.O., D/DHt T140/103. For the Legatts see also: *Visit. Essex* (Harl. Soc.), 592–3; E.R.O., D/DU 23/50, 52, 55. For Lawrence Wright see *D.N.B.*
[40] E.R.O., D/DNe P1 (map).
[41] *Complete Baronetage*, iii. 35.
[42] Lysons, *Lond.* iv. 191; E.R.O., D/DNe T2 and 3.
[43] Ibid.
[44] Ibid. Richard Neave was made a baronet in 1795.

baronetcy until 1948.[45] The Neaves put together one of the largest estates in south Essex.[46] Dagnam Park,[47] rebuilt by the first baronet, was their seat until the Second World War. In 1846 the estate included some 1,700 a. in Romford and Havering.[48] By 1876 the total there was over 1,800.[49] In 1919 Sir Thomas L. H. Neave sold 2,200 a. of his Essex lands, of which 1,500 a. were in Romford and Havering.[50] He retained some 500 a. around Dagnam Park, but in 1948 his son Sir Arundell Neave sold that, including the house, to the London county council for the building (1948–58) of the Harold Hill housing estate. For the same purpose the L.C.C. bought from other owners some 850 a., most of which had belonged to the Neaves before 1919.[51]

Dagenhams was listed among important seats in 1594,[52] and was depicted in 1633 as a gabled house, built round a courtyard, within a square moat.[53] Sir Henry Wright, Bt. (d. 1664), rebuilt it on a modest scale *c.* 1660.[54] Pepys, who visited Dagenhams in July 1665, said that it was the most noble and pretty house, for its size, that he had ever seen.[55] It had 23 hearths in 1662 and 24 in 1670.[56] Between 1732 and 1739 the house was altered and enlarged by Edward Carteret.[57] His additions included a private chapel.[58] In 1771 Dagnams had a central block of two storeys with attics, containing eleven bays.[59] That may have been the original house of *c.* 1660. It was flanked at each end by five-bay wings, also of two storeys, but without attics, possibly the additions made in the 1730s. Sir Richard Neave, Bt., who bought Dagnams in 1772, demolished the old house and built a brick house of three storeys. The main front had nine bays, of which the central three bays were bowed.[60] During the Second World War Dagnam Park was occupied by the Army. It was demolished *c.* 1948.[61] The pond immediately south of it still survived in 1976.

Cockerels house was about 800 yd. south of Dagnams. In 1633 it was a substantial gabled building, standing outside a moated site which was by then an orchard.[62] In the 19th century it became known as Dagnam Park Farm.[63] It was demolished *c.* 1948. The moat still survived in 1977.

The manor of *EAST HOUSE* lay east of the river Rom, in Collier Row Lane (North Street). Early in the 14th century it was held by Richard Rous, who granted it for life to Robert William of Havering.[64] About 1332 Robert suffered outlawry and forteiture, and East House, then comprising 167 a., was granted for life to Amy Gaveston, a damsel of Queen Philippa.[65] By *c.* 1355 East House, comprising 60 a., had become part of the Gidea Hall estate,[66] in which it descended until 1613, when Sir Edward Cooke sold it to John Wright.[67] Wright sold East House in 1623 to Francis Fuller (d. 1637), who already held the adjoining manor of Mawneys.[68] East House descended with Mawneys until 1673, when Henry Osbaldeston (d. by 1693) sold it to Francis Hervey Mildmay, owner of Marks.[69] East House descended with Marks until 1878, when it was put up for sale by the Mildmay trustees: it then comprised 143 a.[70] During the next thirty years the estate was developed for building in Havering, Rosedale, and Hainault Roads.[71]

East House manor-house was left standing on the west side of Rosedale Road. It was said in 1908 to be a large building in the style of an early-19th-century farm-house.[72] It had evidently been much altered, and may have been much older than that.[73] Eastern Avenue, built in the 1920s, passed immediately south of the house, which seems to have been demolished about that time.[74]

The manor of *GIDEA HALL*,[75] from which the modern Gidea Park is named, lay north-east of Romford town. In 1250–1 the daughter of Simon of Gidea Hall (Gidiehulle) held two tenements in the manor of Havering, of 1 virgate and ¼ virgate respectively.[76] Since these were large virgates her total holdings were probably about 150 a. In *c.* 1355 Sir John of Havering held Gidea Hall (150 a.), East House, in Romford, and other lands, comprising a total of 501 a.[77] The Gidea Hall section of this estate had previously belonged to John of Abbenach. In 1376 Gidea Hall and East House were held by William Baldwin, saddler of London, to whom they had been granted by Robert of Havering.[78] Robert Chichele, a London merchant, and brother of Henry Chichele, later archbishop of Canterbury, was holding Gidea Hall in 1412.[79] By then the estate also included the manor of Bedfords. In 1441 it was held by Robert Saltmarsh and his wife Christine.[80] They sold it in 1452 to (Sir) Thomas Cooke (d. 1478), a London draper who was lord mayor in 1462.[81] He also bought the manor of Bedfords and Earls in Havering, and that

[45] Burke, *Peerage* (1959), 1650–2.
[46] E.R.O., D/DNe, *passim.*
[47] The foım 'Dagnam' or 'Dagnams' came into use in the 18th century.
[48] I.R. 29/12/162 and 30/12/162.
[49] E.R.O., D/DNe F31.
[50] E.R.O., *Sale Cat.* B2759 (annotated with names of purchasers). The other lands were in south-east Essex.
[51] B. F. Lingham, *Harold Hill and Noak Hill*, 26–7.
[52] Norden, *Essex*, 31.
[53] E.R.O., D/DNe P1.
[54] Lysons, *Lond.* iv. 191: the builder must have been the elder Sir Henry Wright, since his son died under age.
[55] *Diary of S. Pepys*, ed. R. Latham and W. Matthews, vi. 159 and 158 *n.*
[56] E.R.O., Q/RTh 1 and 5.
[57] Morant, *Essex*, i. 62.
[58] E.R.O., D/P 115/28/6: Letters from New Coll. to vicar of Hornchurch *c.* 1734–40.
[59] *Hist. Essex by Gent.* iv. f.p. 290.
[60] A. B. Bamford, *Sketches in Liberty of Havering* (1890), no. 7.
[61] For photographs taken *c.* 1948 see: Valence Libr., Barking, Parish Env., Romford, 1. For the layout of the house see: B. F. Lingham, *Harold Hill and Noak Hill*, 35–6.
[62] E.R.O., D/DNe P1. For the moat see plate facing p. 176.
[63] B. F. Lingham, *Harold Hill and Noak Hill*, 21–2.
[64] *Cal. Inq. Misc.* 1307–49, pp. 314–15.
[65] Ibid.; *Cal. Pat.* 1330–4, 244.
[66] New Coll. MS. 9744, f. 162v.; cf. *Cal. Close*, 1374–7, 332, 341, 461.
[67] E.R.O., D/DU 102/105.
[68] E.R.O., T/A 196.
[69] Ibid. For Marks see *V.C.H. Essex*, v. 275.
[70] E.R.O., Sage Coll., *Sale Cats.* ix. 10.
[71] Ibid. ix. 11 and 12; H.R.L., Cornell MSS.
[72] H.R.L., Cornell MSS.
[73] Ibid. small photo. (1906).
[74] O.S. Map 6″, Essex, LXXIX (rev. 1914; prov. edn. 1938).
[75] The interpretation of this name is obscure: *P.N. Essex*, 117–18. For the manor and its owners see *Gidea Hall and Gidea Park* (Loc. Hist. Reprints, No. 5, 1966), ed. I. G. Sparkes.
[76] S.C. 11/189.
[77] New Coll. MS. 9744, f. 162v.
[78] *Cal. Close*, 1374–7, 332, 341, 461.
[79] *Feud. Aids*, vi. 442.
[80] E.R.O., D/DU 102/30, m. 14.
[81] Ibid. 102/42, m. 10d.; *D.N.B.* Sir Thos. Cooke.

of Redden Court in Hornchurch. During an eventful career he was twice imprisoned, but he retained the estate, which descended in his family until the 17th century. The Cookes became the leading local gentry.[82] Notable among them was Sir Anthony Cooke (d. 1576), tutor to Edward VI and father-in-law of Lord Burghley.[83]

Charles Cooke (d. 1629) was the last of his name to hold Gidea Hall. His heirs were his sisters Ann (d. 1652), wife of Sir Edward Sydenham, and Vere (d. 1685), wife of Sir Charles Gawdy. East House and Redden Court had been alienated before 1629, but the estate still included Bedfords and Earls as well as Gidea Hall itself. In the division of the Cooke property the Gidea Hall estate passed to the Sydenhams.[84] Sir Edward Sydenham suffered sequestration as a royalist in 1642, but his wife and children were allowed to remain at Gidea Hall.[85] In 1658 Sir Edward and his son Charles Sydenham sold the estate to Richard Emes, cooper of London.[86] Emes sold Bedfords and Earls in 1659, but retained Gidea Hall until 1664, when he sold it to John Burch, a West India planter.[87]

Burch (d. 1668) left Gidea Hall to his wife Margaret (d. 1685), for life, with remainder to his sister Rebecca Hothersall, and his nephews Thomas and Burch Hothersall.[88] The Hothersalls duly succeeded to the manor on Mrs. Burch's death, and lived at Gidea Hall at least until 1694.[89] In 1710, under the will of Thomas Hothersall, grandson of Rebecca, the manor was sold to Benjamin Haskins Stiles and John Hunter.[90] Stiles and Hunter were probably agents for Stiles's brother-in-law, (Sir) John Eyles (Bt.) (d. 1745), who certainly acquired Gidea Hall about that time.[91] In 1744 Sir John, as lord of the manor, was receiving quit-rents from 54 tenants in Romford town, Hare Street, Collier Row, and Hornchurch.[92] He was succeeded by his son Sir Francis Haskins Eyles-Stiles, who sold the manor in 1745 to Richard Benyon (d. 1774), governor of Fort St. George (Madras, India).[93]

Gidea Hall descended like Newbury in Ilford[94] until 1802, when Richard Benyon, grandson of the purchaser, sold it to Alexander Black (d. 1835).[95] In 1846 Alice Black, Alexander's widow, was holding the Gidea Hall estate, then comprising 742 a.[96] She died in 1871.[97] The estate had previously been settled on Black's two daughters and their husbands: Anne and William Neave, and Adelaide and Alfred Douglas Hamilton.[98] After Mrs. Black's death the estate was put on the market with a view to development, and in 1883 the main part of it, comprising some 500 a., was bought by the Lands Allotment Co., a member of Jabez Balfour's Liberator group.[99] The company tried to develop the estate, but with little success, and in 1893, after the collapse of the group, Gidea Hall was again put up for sale in one lot.[1] It was not then sold, but in 1897 the house and 480 a. were bought by (Sir) Herbert H. Raphael (Bt.).[2] By then the western edge of the estate (Lake Rise) had been detached. In 1902 Raphael gave some 20 a., including a lake, for the public park (Raphael park).[3] Soon after that he developed the rest of the estate as the Gidea Park garden suburb.[4] The western side, between Raphael park and Heath Drive, has been built over, but most of the eastern side remains open as Romford golf course and Gidea Park sports ground.

The manor-house stood north of Main Road, Gidea Park, about 300 yd. east of Raphael park. In 1466 Sir Thomas Cooke obtained the king's licence to empark the manor, and to rebuild and crenellate Gidea Hall.[5] He left the house unfinished.[6] Sir Anthony Cooke (d. 1576) completed it before 1568, when he entertained Elizabeth I there.[7] The finished building was arranged round three sides of a courtyard, with an open colonnade on the fourth side.[8] In the 17th century Gidea Hall was the largest house in the liberty except for the king's house at Havering.[9] Marie de Medici, mother of Queen Henrietta Maria, stayed there in 1638.[10]

Sir John Eyles, Bt., demolished the old house about 1720, and replaced it with a three-storey mansion.[11] Some stabling from the 16th-century house survived until 1922.[12] Richard Benyon (d. 1796) appears to have altered and enlarged Gidea Hall.[13] In the later 19th century the house was divided into two dwellings.[14] It was used by the Army

[82] Marjorie K. McIntosh, 'The Cooke Family of Gidea Hall, 1460–1661'. (Harvard Ph. D. 1967); *E.R.* xx. 201–11; xxi. 1–9; xxx. 57, 114–16; Smith, *Havering*, 117 sqq.
[83] *D.N.B.*
[84] Morant, *Essex*, i. 67.
[85] B. W. Quintrell, 'The Divisional Committee for Southern Essex during the Civil War'. (Manchester M.A., 1962), ff. 61, 88–9, 92, 100; E.R.O., T/A 196; *Cal. Cttee.* for *Compounding*, p. 1257; *Cal. Cttee. for Money*, pp. 1158, 1386.
[86] E.R.O., D/DHe T1/4. Lady Gawdy joined the Sydenhams in making this conveyance, which suggests that she may still have had an interest in the estate.
[87] Lysons, *Lond.* iv. 185.
[88] Terry, *Romford*, 195–6; E.R.O., T/R 18/2.
[89] E.R.O., T/R 18/2 (Jn. Hothersall died there 25 Aug. 1694).
[90] Lysons, *Lond.* iv. 186.
[91] Morant, *Essex*, i. 67; E.R.O., T/P 195/2, f. 59; *E.R.* vi. 58; G.E.C. *Baronetage*, v. 22.
[92] E.R.O., D/DHt M60.
[93] Lysons, *Lond.* iv. 186; *Gent. Mag.* 1774, p. 494.
[94] *V.C.H. Essex*, v. 208.
[95] Ogborne, *Essex*, 130; *Gidea Hall and Gidea Park*, ed. I. G. Sparkes, 37–8.
[96] I.R. 29/12/162 and 30/12/162.
[97] *Gidea Hall and Gidea Park*, 38.
[98] E.R.O., Sage Coll., *Sale Cats.* vol. ix. 16–18; *White's Dir. Essex* (1848), 377, 382; *Burke Peerage* (1913), 924, 1429.
[99] E.R.O., Sage Coll., *Sale Cats.* vol. ix. 16–20; *The Times* 26 Oct. 1895.
[1] E.R.O., Sage Coll., *Sale Cats.* vol. ix. 17, 19, 20; cf. *V.C.H. Essex*, v. 97, 206 for Balfour's estates at Chingford and Ilford.
[2] E.R.O., Sage Coll., *Sale Cats.* vol. ix. 18.
[3] *Gidea Hall and Gidea Park*, 40–42.
[4] See p. 59.
[5] *Cal. Chart. R.* 1427–1516, 214.
[6] P. de la Serre, *Histoire de L'Entrée de la Reine Mère dans la Grand Bretagne* (1775 edn.), 24 *n.*
[7] Ibid.; *E.R.* xxvi. 192.
[8] *Bk. of Architecture of John Thorpe in Sir John Soane's Museum*, ed. J. Summerson (Walpole Soc. xl), pp. 26, 90; P. de la Serre, op. cit., pl. ii.
[9] E.R.O., Q/RTh 1 (35 hearths in 1662).
[10] P. de la Serre, op. cit.; *E.R.* x. 207. See above, plate facing p. 65.
[11] Lysons, *Lond.* iv. 186.
[12] R.C.H.M. *Essex*, ii. 203; *Romford Recorder*, 14 Nov. 1930.
[13] A. E. Richardson, *Robert Mylne*, 101; Thorne, *Environs Lond.* 513; Berks. R.O., D/EBy A.20: ref. to a chimney piece made 1776–7 to design of 'Mr. Watson architect.' This reference was kindly supplied by Mr. H. M. Colvin. Miss N. R. Briggs points out that Mr. Watson was also working at Belhus, in Aveley, in 1776: E.R.O., D/DL E13.
[14] *White's Dir. Essex* (1863), 596, 602; *Kelly's Dir. Essex* (1870 sqq.).; E.R.O., Sage Coll., *Sale Cats.* vol. ix. 16–18.

during the First World War, and after the war became a club house for the garden suburb.[15] It was demolished in 1930.[16]

The early-18th-century house had a formal arrangement of canals and avenues converging upon it.[17] The northern canal, called the Spoon pond, was the main survivor from that scheme.[18] Its site, now drained, is used as tennis courts. Richard Benyon (d. 1796) enlarged the park, probably to the design of Richard Woods, *c.* 1776.[19] He made it less formal, and introduced a lake in the valley west of the house. The greater width of water at the main road made a new bridge necessary, and that was designed by James Wyatt.[20] It is of three brick arches, forming the north side of the present road bridge. The lake, known from a later owner as Black's canal, is now included in Raphael park. The fishponds also survive farther east. Near them, in Heath Drive, are sections of garden walling from Gidea Hall, probably of the early 19th century. A medicinal spring at Gidea Hall was the subject of a book published in 1783.[21] It was occluded *c.* 1906.

The manor of *GOBIONS* or *UPHAVERING* lay on the south side of Collier Row common, near Marks Gate. It must be distinguished from a house called Gobions on the east side of the same common, and from Gubbins at Harold Wood.[22] The name Uphavering, by which it was usually known before the 16th century, fits its position in the uplands of the parish,[23] but the manor may have been named after the Uphavering family, many of whom are recorded from the 13th century.[24]

John Parker, a servant of the queen, was holding Uphavering in 1387–95.[25] Richard Gobion was holding land in that area in 1440.[26] He may have been the predecessor of John Gobion, who in 1467 conveyed the manor of Uphavering, comprising about 200 a., to (Sir) Thomas Urswick, who already held the neighbouring manor of Marks.[27] Urswick retained both manors until his death in 1479.[28] His heirs appear to have sold them separately, and by 1491 Uphavering belonged to Edmund Worsley.[29] Edmund, son of Edmund Worsley, held it in 1511.[30]

Sir Willaim Roche, a former lord mayor of London, was holding Uphavering and Nelmes when he died in 1549.[31] In 1541 Uphavering had been settled on his wife Margaret, who survived him. Both manors descended to John Roche, son of Sir William, and later to Thomas Roche, probably son of John.[32] Thomas Roche, who had a large estate in the liberty, sold most of it, apparently in the 1620s and 1630s.[33] Gobions was bought from him in 1632 by Sir Richard Minshull, who sold it in 1642 to Joachim Matthews.[34] Matthews, a Parliamentary colonel and commissioner during the Civil War, was succeeded on his death in 1659 by his son (Sir) Philip Matthews (Bt.) (d. 1685).[35]

In 1700 Sir Philip's widow Ann, and his son, Sir John Matthews, sold Gobions to John Blackstone, apothecary of London.[36] In 1720, after Blackstone's death, his estate was divided among his family. Gobions was bought from the executors by William Curwen, another London apothecary, whose son John had married Blackstone's daughter Ann.[37] John and Ann Curwen succeeded to the manor and sold it in 1739 to Sir Philip Hall (d. 1746).[38] Philip Hall, son of Sir Philip, sold it in 1764 to Richard Heighway.[39] Heighway sold Gobions in 1771 to John Gibson, who conveyed it in 1775 to his relative Thomas Gibson.[40] Both the Gibsons were lacemen of London. In 1777 the manor was bought from Thomas Gibson by the executors of William Prior Johnson of Stock, on behalf of Johnson's grandson William Richardson, who himself took the name of William Prior Johnson.[41] Between 1777 and 1796 Gobions was apparently in Chancery, but William Prior Johnson the grandson eventually gained possession of it, and held it until his death in 1839.[42] In 1840 Gobions was settled on his brother James J. W. Prior Johnson, and James's son William.[43] William Prior Johnson was holding it in 1846, when it comprised 183 a., leased to a farmer.[44] He sold it to the Crown in 1854.[45] In 1976 Gobions comprised some 650 a., leased by the Crown to Mr. James G. Fowler, whose family had been tenants since 1895.[46]

The manor-house, called Great Gobions, seems to have been demolished between 1680 and 1700.[47] Another house, Little Gobions, existed in 1715 and later.[48] That was probably the farm-house which in 1840 was said to have been modernized but to need renovation.[49] The present farm-house was built by the Crown in 1899.[50]

The manor of *GOOSHAYES* ('goose enclosure') lay west of Dagenhams, in the area now called

15 *Gidea Hall and Gidea Park*, ed. Sparkes, 48.
16 *Romford Recorder*, 14 Nov. 1930. For pictures of the house see: Engraving (1787) by J. Walker from drawing by H. Repton; E.R.O., Sage Coll., *Sale Cats.* vol. ix. 16–18; A. B. Bamford, *Sketches in Liberty of Havering* (1889); E.R.O., Pictorial Coll., Photos. *c.* 1930.
17 *Map of Essex* (1777), sheet xvi.
18 O.S. Map 6", Essex, LXVI (surv. 1862–71).
19 Lysons, *Lond.* iv. 186; Berks. R.O. D/EBy A2. The latter reference was kindly supplied by Mr. H. C. Prince.
20 *Copperplate Mag.* No. 33 (1794), pl. 66.
21 *Romford Record*, vii. 40.
22 *Map of Essex* (1777). For Gubbins see above, p. 34.
23 *P.N. Essex*, 118.
24 e.g. *Pleas before the King or his Justices, 1198–1202*, (Selden Soc. lxviii), p. 275; *Cur. Reg. R.* iii. 61, 75; iv. 22; *Feet of F. Essex*, i. 37; *Cal. Close*, 1354–60, 320; New Coll. MS. 9744, f. 163v (ten. of Tho. of Uphavering, *c.* 1355).
25 *Cal. Pat.* 1385–9, 382; 1388–92, 257; *Cal. Close*, 1392–6, 327.
26 E.R.O., D/DM M196 (Rental of Marks).
27 E.R.O., D/DU 102/51, m. 3; *V.C.H. Essex*, v. 276.
28 E.R.O., D/DM T12/1; *E.R.* lxiii. 14.
29 *Cat. Anct. D.* ii, C 2366.
30 S.C. 2/173/1, mm. 11d., 12, 14d., 15.
31 C 142/9/91; Morant, *Essex*, i. 63; *Visit. Essex* (Harl. Soc.), i. 477.
32 E.R.O., D/DHt T140/8 and 9.
33 E.R.O., T/A 259/2 (microfilm of Hants R.O., 15 M50/237: Parchment Bk. of Carew H. Mildmay of Marks.); cf. E.R.O., D/DU 162/1 (Map of Havering Liberty *c.* 1618).
34 E.R.O., D/DHt T140/11, 12, 15–23.
35 Ibid. D/DHt T362/3; Smith, *Eccl. Hist. Essex*, 193, 236, 267, 336, 348; G.E.C. *Baronetage*, iii. 249.
36 E.R.O., D/DHt T362/3; D/DU 102/125.
37 E.R.O., D/DHt T362/3.
38 Ibid.; Morant, *Essex*, i. 63.
39 E.R.O., D/DHt T362/3.
40 Ibid.
41 Ibid.; E.R.O., D/DE T61.
42 E.R.O., D/DE T61.
43 Ibid.
44 I.R. 29/12/162 and 30/12/162; cf. E.R.O., D/DSa 156.
45 E.R.O., D/DCm B2; cf. ibid. Sage Coll., *Sale Cats.* vol. 10, no. 13.
46 Inf. from Mr. J. G. Fowler.
47 E.R.O., D/DHt T362/3.
48 Ibid. D/DC 23/392; D/DLo T15/2.
49 E.R.O., D/DSa 156.
50 Date on building.

Harold Hill. It originated, wholly or partly, in a tenement which William Hurel held in 1210–12 by serjeanty of keeping the king's park of Havering.[51] In 1219 and 1227 it comprised ½ hide, which John Hurel (or Parker) held by the same service.[52] John Hurel's widow Gillian was holding it in 1235.[53] The serjeanty seems to have lapsed soon after that. In 1251 John Hurel's daughter Joan, her husband John Mauduit, and her sister Emme sold the tenement, comprising 100 a. land and 1 a. wood, to Richard of Dover (d. by 1254).[54] In 1273–4 John of Dover, Richard's son, held 'Gooseland' of the manor of Havering.[55] He also held, jointly with William Carpenter, land called Hurel.[56] No service was being performed for either tenement. In 1274–5 John of Dover, and William of Felsted, who was probably identical with William Carpenter, held ½ hide in Havering, which John Hurel had once held by custody of Havering park.[57]

John of Dover's lands in Romford appear to have descended like Dovers in Hornchurch at least until *c.* 1355, when Gooshayes comprised a messuage and 120 a., held by Richard of Sutton.[58] At the end of the 14th century Gooshayes passed to Richard Hamme. This probably occurred in 1398, when he acquired two tenements in Havering: a messuage and 60 a. from Joan, widow of John Michel, and 2 messuages and 60 a. from Thomas Hasyll and his wife Katherine.[59] Hamme was a servant of Henry Percy, earl of Northumberland (d. 1408), keeper of the manor of Havering *c.* 1399–1403.[60] In 1405 he bought a field adjoining Gooshayes.[61] His will was proved in 1418.[62]

Richard Hamme was succeeded by his son John, who was apparently holding Gooshayes by 1435.[63] Henry Percy, earl of Northumberland (d. 1455), who held Dagenhams at this period, also had a fiduciary interest in Gooshayes.[64] This suggests that the Hammes were still adherents of the Percies, and may have shared the Percies' forfeiture after Towton. That would explain why Edward IV granted Gooshayes in 1462 to Henry Bourchier, earl of Essex, as well as Dagenhams two years later.[65] At Gooshayes, as at Dagenhams, the grant to Bourchier had no permanent effect. John Hamme retained the manor, and in 1465 sold it to Avery Cornburgh.[66] Cornburgh (d. 1487) also held Dagenhams, and Dovers in Hornchurch.[67] His heirs were his sister Agnes Chambre, and his nephew John Crafford.[68]

By 1512 Gooshayes was in the possession of John Morton,[69] who in 1518 granted a 40-year lease of the manor to John Roper.[70] Thomas Morton, who died holding Gooshayes in 1591, was presumably a descendant of John.[71] He was succeeded by his son George, who in 1600 sold the manor to Richard Humble.[72]

Richard Humble (d. 1616) was a Southwark vintner and alderman of London.[73] His son Peter (d. 1623) left a daughter and heir Martha, who married Reynold Bray.[74] Martha and Reynold both died in 1638, leaving Edmund Bray their son and heir.[75] Edmund appears to have died childless. By 1659 he had been succeeded by his mother's cousin Humble Ward, Lord Ward of Birmingham (d. 1670).[76] Lord Ward's son Edward Ward, Lord Dudley and Ward, sold Gooshayes about 1684 to William Mead (d. 1713), a London linen-draper and a leading Quaker.[77] William's son Sir Nathaniel Mead sold it in 1754 to William Sheldon (d. 1798), who left it to his son William (d. 1817).[78] Thomas Sheldon, son of the younger William, sold Gooshayes in 1829 to Sir Thomas Neave, Bt.[79] It was thus merged in Dagenhams, with which it descended until 1919, when Sir Thomas L. H. Neave, Bt., sold most of that estate. Gooshayes, then a farm of 266 a., was bought by the tenants, R. and H. Watt.[80] Some years later Robert Watt sold the farm to John Mallinson, who already held the neighbouring New Hall farm.[81] In 1948 Gooshayes was compulsorily purchased by the London County Council for the Harold Hill housing estate.[82]

Gooshayes house, described in 1594 as ancient, is said to have been rebuilt by Edward Ward, Lord Dudley and Ward, i.e. between 1670 and *c.* 1684.[83] Gooshayes Chase, which formed the drive to the house from the London Road, may have been made at that time.[84] Most of Ward's house was demolished before 1768, but part of it survived as a farm-house.[85] When the Harold Hill estate was built Gooshayes became a community centre. It was demolished in 1961. Gooshayes Drive follows the line of Gooshayes Chase.

The manor of *MARKS*, in Dagenham and Romford, is treated elsewhere.[86]

The tenement of *MARSHALLS* was in Romford town, on the east side of North Street.[87] It took its name from the Marshall family, which occurs in many local records from the 12th century onwards.[88] About 1618 it comprised about 40 a. land, belonging then to Mr. Thorowgood, and formerly to Edward Carew.[89] Edward was the son of John Carew, deputy steward of the liberty of Havering.[90] Marshalls

[51] *Red Bk. Exch.* (Rolls Ser.), 508.
[52] *Bk. of Fees*, i. 276, ii. 1348.
[53] Ibid. 1361.
[54] *Feet of F. Essex*, i. 190; *Cal. Pat.* 1247–58, 398.
[55] *Rot. Hund.* (Rec. Com.), i. 149.
[56] Ibid.
[57] Ibid. i. 152.
[58] New Coll. MS. 9744, f. 162v.
[59] E.R.O., D/DU 102/10, mm. 2 and 4.
[60] *Cal. Pat.* 1399–1401, 343; 1401–5, 259; S.C. 2/172/29 and 30.
[61] *Cal. Close*, 1405–9, 262.
[62] *E.A.T.* N.S. vi. 316.
[63] *Cal. Close*, 1441–7, 237–8, cf. 80–1, 161.
[64] Ibid. 80–1.
[65] *Cal. Pat.* 1461–7, 145. For Dagenhams see above.
[66] E.R.O., D/DU 102/47, m. 3d.
[67] For Dovers see below.
[68] *Cal. Inq. p. m. Hen. VII*, i. p. 104.
[69] S.C. 2/173/1, m. 21.
[70] C 142/80/135 (inquisition held in 1526: Morton was then mad).
[71] C 142/228/50.
[72] C.P. 25(2)/139/1758.
[73] Morant, *Essex*, i. 63.
[74] *Fragmenta Genealogica*, xiii. 56; C 142/527/13.
[75] C 142/527/13.
[76] E.R.O., T/P 195/2; Morant, *Essex*, i. 63; *Complete Peerage*, xii (2), 342–3.
[77] *Complete Peerage*, xii (2), 343; *D.N.B.*, s.v. Wm. Mead.
[78] E.R.O., D/DNe T28 and 29.
[79] Ibid.
[80] E.R.O., *Sale Cat.* B2759.
[81] B. F. Lingham, *Harold Hill*, 21.
[82] Ibid. 21, 26–7.
[83] Morant, *Essex*, i. 63; Norden, *Essex*, 31.
[84] *Map of Essex* (1777); cf. E.R.O., D/DU 162/1.
[85] B. F. Lingham, *Harold Hill*, 38; Morant, *Essex*, i. 63; *E.R.* iv. 62.
[86] *V.C.H. Essex*, v. 275.
[87] *Map of Essex* (1777).
[88] *Horn. Docs.* nos. 85, 163, 181, 289, etc.; *Feet of F. Essex*, i. 61; E.R.O., D/DM M197; E.R.O., D/DU 202/34, m. 2*d.*
[89] E.R.O., D/DU 162/1.
[90] *Visit. Essex* (Harl. Soc.) i. 371; Terry, *Romford*, 73; E.R.O., Sage Coll. no. 688.

remained in the Thorowgood family until the early 18th century. Simon Thorowgood (d. 1722) was holding it in 1695, when he mortgaged it to Sir William Scawen and his brother (Sir) Thomas Scawen, both of London.[91] The Scawens were friends and business associates of Russell Allsopp, brother of Thorowgood's wife Elizabeth. In 1704 Simon and Elizabeth Thorowgood sold the freehold of Marshalls to Allsopp, in return for an annuity on their joint lives. Allsopp died in 1705 or soon after, leaving the freehold to his sister Katherine, wife of Thomas Baines, for life, with remainder to William, son of John Jerman. (Sir) Thomas Scawen was Allsopp's executor. At the time of his death Allsopp was heavily in debt to Sir William Scawen and others, whose claims on the estate conflicted with the Thorowgoods' right to their annuity, and caused protracted litigation, during part of which Marshalls was in Chancery. In 1725 William Jerman sold the freehold of the estate to Thomas Scawen, heir to his father Sir Thomas and also his uncle Sir William Scawen. Thomas Scawen bought out Elizabeth Thorowgood's life interest in 1729. He mortgaged the estate in 1730 to James Colebrooke, who in 1733 foreclosed and sold it to Onesiphorous Leigh of Tooting. Marshalls later passed to John Leigh of London, who died in 1748, leaving his estates to his mother Elizabeth Leigh for life, with remainder to his sisters Mary Leigh and Mary Frost. In 1748 the remainder to Marshalls was settled on Mary Frost in anticipation of her marriage to John Beesley.

In the late 18th century Marshalls was owned and occupied by Jackson Barwis (d. *c.* 1809),[92] and later by his widow (d. 1816).[93] After Mrs. Barwis's death the estate, comprising a large house and 112 a. land, was put up for sale.[94] Then or soon after Marshalls was acquired by Rowland Stephenson, 'the fugitive banker.'[95] In 1829, after Stephenson's bankruptcy, it was bought by Hugh McIntosh (d. 1840), and it subsequently descended with the Havering manor estate until after the First World War.[96] Marshalls was put up for sale in 1924 and most of the land was soon developed for building.[97]

Marshalls house appears to have been enlarged into a gentleman's residence early in the 19th century, possibly by Jackson Barwis. It was a stuccoed five-bay house with a Tuscan portico and earlier back parts.[98] The Sunday parties held there by Rowland Stephenson were long remembered.[99] Hugh McIntosh lived at Marshalls, but after his death the house was usually let.[1] In 1959 it was demolished and the site was used to extend Romford county technical school.[2]

The manor of *RISEBRIDGE* lay south of Lower Bedfords Road, near the place where an ancient bridge carried that road over a tributary of the Bourne brook.[3] It appears to have originated in a 60-acre tenement which Peter of Romford granted in 1234 to Adam of Lincoln, in exchange for other lands.[4] Lincoln granted it in 1241 to William Dun,[5] who soon afterwards gave it to Hornchurch priory in free alms.[6] In 1315 it was alleged that Dun's gift had been intended as the endowment of a chantry in the parish church, and that the priory had misappropriated it, but the charge failed.[7] Risebridge subsequently descended with Hornchurch Hall and Suttons.[8] In the 17th and 18th centuries it was leased with the tithes from the northern wards of the parish, and was sometimes called Parsonage farm.[9] In 1846 it was a farm of 135 a.[10] New College, Oxford, sold it in 1925 to Mr. C. B. T. Hembry.[11] It seems to have been acquired later by Thomas England, the estate developer, whose widow, Mrs. E. S. England, sold it in 1969 to Havering L.B.[12] In 1976 Risebridge was a municipal golf course, and the farm-house, a mid-19th-century building, was in use as the club house.

The manor of *STEWARDS* lay on the east side of Hornchurch Lane (South Street), Romford. In 1499 John Hotoft of Orsett and his wife Joan conveyed it to William Chapman of Bulphan and others.[13] Chapman conveyed it in 1501 to Edward Hales.[14] Stewards later passed to Marcellin Hales (d. 1561).[15] Thomas Hales, son of Marcellin, sold the manor in 1566 to William Cade.[16] In 1588 Cade sold it to James Quarles (d. 1599), purveyor to the Navy, who was succeeded by his son (Sir) Robert Quarles (d. 1639); Sir Robert's widow Mary held a life-interest in the manor, and was still living in 1659.[17] James Quarles, son of Sir Robert, died in 1642 leaving an infant daughter Hester, who eventually inherited Stewards and married William Holgate.[18] In 1696 the estate comprised 374 a., extending from Hornchurch Lane to Squirrels Heath.[19] William Holgate, son of William and Hester, sold it in 1708 to John Wood.[20] Wood (d. 1761) devised Stewards in equal shares to William Gill and John Leach.[21] The halves were reunited in 1800, when William Tolbut bought them both from the Gill and Leach families.[22] Tolbut (d. 1828) was succeeded by his son William.[23] The Eastern

[91] The descent from 1695 to 1748 is based on E.R.O., D/DNe T34.
[92] *Gent. Mag.* 1788, p. 751; *Universal Brit. Dir.* (1793); E.R.O., Q/RPl 474 sqq. (Land Tax Returns, Romford Town).
[93] Ogborne, *Essex*, 135; *Gent. Mag.* 1816 (1), 88.
[94] E.R.O., *Sale Cat.* B186.
[95] Terry, *Romford*, 233; cf. *V.C.H. Essex*, v. 273.
[96] E.R.O., *Sale Cat.* B186; Smith, *Havering*, 70; E.R.O., Q/RPl 510 sqq. See also above, p. 13.
[97] E.R.O., *Sale Cat.* A212; *E.R.* xxxv. 230.
[98] Pevsner, *Essex*, 328.
[99] Terry, *Romford*, 233.
[1] Smith, *Havering*, 70; *Kelly's Dir. Essex* (1859 and later edns.).
[2] *Romford Times*, 13 Jan., 3 Feb. 1960; inf. from Mr. C. J. Whitwood.
[3] Cf. *P.N. Essex*, 119.
[4] *Horn. Docs.* nos. 522, 523.
[5] *Feet of F. Essex*, i. 139; *Horn. Docs.* 256.
[6] *Horn. Docs.* no. 499.
[7] Ibid. 137.
[8] For leases of Risebridge in the 15th and 16th cents. see E.R.O., D/P 115/28/7.
[9] E.R.O., D/DC 23/387; ibid. D/DDw T268; *Map of Essex* (1777).
[10] I.R. 29/12/162.
[11] Inf. from New Coll.
[12] Inf. from Havering L.B.
[13] S.C. 2/172/39 mm. 4d. and 5d.
[14] Ibid. mm. 22d. and 23; E.R.O., D/P 115/28/3.
[15] C 142/133/136. For the Hales family see also *V.C.H. Essex*, v. 124.
[16] E.R.O., D/DA T287; cf. Terry, *Romford*, 114.
[17] Morant, *Essex*, i. 67–8; Lysons, *Lond.* iv. 188, 199.
[18] C 142/501/19; Lysons, *Lond.* iv. 188, 199.
[19] E.R.O., D/DSa 149 (map).
[20] Lysons, *Lond.* iv. 188; cf. E.R.O., D/DU 102/126, where the conveyance is dated 1710.
[21] Lysons, *Lond.* iv. 188.
[22] Ibid. iv. 188 and *Suppl.* (1811), 353.
[23] *Gent. Mag.* 1828 (2), 573; I.R. 29/12/177.

Counties railway (1839) cut the estate in half, and the station was built at that point. In 1849 Stewards, then comprising some 255 a., was put up for sale by William Tolbut, and during the next 20 years much of it was developed for building in Western Road, Junction Road, Eastern Road, Victoria Road, and South Street.[24]

About 1618 Stewards house stood in a large park.[25] By 1696 the park had been divided up for farming, but the house was still standing.[26] At both dates it was depicted as a substantial gabled building, possibly of the 16th century. The owners lived there from the time of Marcellin Hales at least until the mid 17th century. Francis Quarles the poet (1592–1644), brother of Sir Robert, lived there in childhood.[27] In 1700 an Independent meeting was registered there.[28] Stewards was demolished shortly before September 1717.[29] At that time it was thought unlikely that it would ever be rebuilt, but in fact a new house, called Romford Hall, was built soon after on the same site.[30] It was a large red-brick building which survived *c.* 1914 but was later demolished.[31]

The tenement of *WRIGHTSBRIDGE* lay beside the bridge of that name over Putwell (now Weald) brook at Noak Hill. A small part of it lay east of the brook, in South Weald parish. The Wrights, a prolific yeoman family, had several branches in this part of Essex. The eldest sons were usually called John.[32] About 1355 John Wright was holding Morris's land in Havering, comprising a messuage and 60 a., formerly belonging to Robert Morris.[33] That tenement was evidently in the Noak Hill area, since its tithes were leased along with Newbury in 1378 and 1385.[34] The Wrights were certainly holding Wrightsbridge by the 1550s, and remained there until the later 17th century.[35] John Wright, who was living in 1678, appears to have been at least the fifth holder of the estate, in successive generations, with the same name.[36] In that year Wrightsbridge was mortgaged to John Wood, a London haberdasher. John Wright and John Wood were both dead by 1685, when Wright's mother and sisters conveyed the estate to Wood's daughter Sarah, later wife of George Caldecott. Wrightsbridge was bought from the Caldecotts in 1720 by Sir Robert Abdy, Bt., of Albyns, in Stapleford Abbots.[37] It descended with Albyns until *c.* 1872, when it was bought by Sir Arundell Neave, Bt., and thus became part of the Dagnam Park estate.[38] In 1772 Wrightsbridge farm comprised 80 a.[39] During the next century it was gradually enlarged, to 93 a. in 1818 and 98 a. in 1869.[40] By 1919, when that part of the Dagnam Park estate was put up for sale, Wrightsbridge had been merged in Hill farm, which was bought by the sitting tenents, R. Watt & Sons.[41]

Wrightsbridge house stands immediately north and west of the bridge. About 1618 there was a substantial gabled house there.[42] The present house is a brick building of the early or mid 18th century. It was excluded from the sale of 1919, and was later sold separately. It was remodelled and extended to the rear in 1926, when an earlier service wing was probably replaced. The sundial on the front of the house, dated 1663, was imported at that time.[43]

Angel Cottages, about 150 yd. south of Wrightsbridge, in Wrightsbridge Road, was part of the same tenement in the 17th century, and was probably identical with Malland (1625), and with Little Wrightsbridge (1659).[44] It comprises the northern half of a late-14th- or early-15th-century timber-framed hall house.[45] It is not unlikely that this building was the original house on Morris's land. In the early 17th century the first floor was put into the hall, and the northern end was rebuilt in its present cross-wing form. By 1707 Little Wrightsbridge had been detached from the Wrightsbridge estate, and by 1744 it had become the Angel public house.[46] Sir Thomas Neave, Bt., of Dagnam Park, bought the Angel in 1818 and converted it into two cottages.[47] In 1976 the building belonged to Hill farm.

ECONOMIC HISTORY. The agrarian history of Romford is treated above, along with that of Havering and Hornchurch.[48] In the three rural wards of Romford agriculture continued to be the main occupation down to the present century. The town grew up during the Middle Ages along the main road to London, and its market, established in 1247, became one of the largest in Essex.[49] In the 18th century Romford became also a busy coaching town. The railway, besides maintaining the importance of the town as a commercial centre, stimulated the growth of industry, notably Ind, Coope's brewery. During the present century Romford has become a shopping centre for a populous suburban area, with new light industries developing on the outskirts near the main roads.

There are many references to early corn-mills in Romford; these are treated elsewhere.[50] Romford, like Hornchurch, was an early centre of the leather industry. Tanners are recorded from the 15th century onwards.[51] The making of leather breeches was by the 18th century proverbially associated with Romford.[52] It continued until 1830 or later.[53] There were several curriers and saddlers in the town

[24] E.R.O., Sage Coll., *Sale Cats.* vol. xi. 12; ibid. D/DB T837, 838; O.S. Map 6", Essex, LXVI (surv. 1862–71).
[25] E.R.O., D/DU 162/1 (map).
[26] E.R.O., D/DSa 149.
[27] *D.N.B.*; *E.R.* viii. 1.
[28] See p. 89.
[29] E.R.O., T/A 521/1, Vestry Min. 9 Sept. 1717.
[30] Ibid.; O.S. Map 6", Essex, LXVI (surv. 1862–71).
[31] H.R.L., Cornell MSS.; O.S. Map 6", Essex, LXXIX (rev. 1914).
[32] E.R.O., Sage Coll. No. 762; cf. *V.C.H. Essex*, iv. 66.
[33] New Coll. MS. 9744, f. 163.
[34] *Horn. Docs.* nos. 14, 386.
[35] *P.N. Essex*, 116, *Visit. Essex* (Harl. Soc.), 532–4; E.R.O., D/DDa T12.
[36] E.R.O., D/DDa T12 (abstract of title to Wrightsbridge, 1625–1722).
[37] Ibid.; cf. *V.C.H. Essex*, iv. 226.
[38] E.R.O., D/DNe T65 and F31.
[39] E.R.O., D/DC 27/1122.
[40] E.R.O., D/DDa T12; D/DNe T65.
[41] E.R.O., *Sale Cat.* B2759 (annotated).
[42] E.R.O., D/DU 162/1.
[43] Ex inf. Mrs. Davis of Wrightsbridge house.
[44] E.R.O., D/DDa T12; cf. D/DU 162/1 for a house on the site.
[45] See plate facing p. 161.
[46] E.R.O., D/DNe T5: deeds of Little Wrightsbridge, later the Angel, 1707–1818.
[47] Ibid.; E.R.O., D/DNe E1.
[48] See p. 17.
[49] See p. 75.
[50] See p. 74.
[51] *Cal. Pat.* 1467–77, 78; E.R.O., Q/SR 398/51; Terry, *Romford*, 192.
[52] Salmon, *Essex*, 254.
[53] E.R.O., T/P 71/1, Letter to *Essex Times*, 6 Mar. 1869 Pigot's *Dir. Essex* (1823–4), 64, s.v. Southey, High St.; cf. *Robson's Dir. Essex* (1838), 88.

throughout the 19th century.[54] The Smith family, curriers, traded in the market-place from the 1830s until *c.* 1902.[55] Darke & Sons, saddlers, were in High Street and later in the market-place from the 1880s until 1937 or later.[56]

Cloth-making is indicated by the name Fullers field (*c.* 1233–7), which was probably near Chase Cross,[57] and that of Tayntor Ridden (1616).[58] There are occasional references in the 17th century to weavers,[59] including one engine weaver (1694).[60] Colliers (charcoal burners), recorded in the 15th and 16th centuries, gave their name to Collier Row.[61] Brewing was often mentioned in the 16th and 17th centuries.[62] Metal-workers included a brazier (1667), and a cutler's wife who in 1707 was charged with unlawfully trading as a goldsmith.[63]

A tile-kiln, attached to Wolves and Joys farm, Noak Hill, was mentioned in 1558.[64] In 1775 John Heaton of Bedfords unlawfully built a brick-kiln on land inclosed from the common in Harold Wood ward.[65] That was probably the kiln which then lay south of Noak Hill Road, near its junction with the present Straight Road.[66] In *c.* 1870 the site was occupied by Tilekiln farm.[67] The sites of other brick-kilns are indicated by the field name Brick Kiln mead, which occurs twice in 1846: north of Noak Hill Road, and north of Chase Cross Road, Collier Row.[68] The brickworks of William, later W. & G. Gale, Hainault Road, existed from *c.* 1890 to 1937 or later.[69]

Ind, Coope & Co.'s brewery, which has become Romford's main industry, was established in 1799, when Edward Ind bought the Star inn, with a small brewery attached, beside the river Rom in High Street.[70] It was a fortunate choice of site, for in 1839 Romford railway station was built ¼ mile south of the brewery, and there was plenty of room for expansion in that direction. In 1845, after two changes of partner, Edward Ind was joined by the brothers Octavius and George Coope; two later generations of the Inds and Coopes were associated with the firm. In 1858 Ind, Coope & Co. bought a second brewery, at Burton-on-Trent (Staffs.). The Romford brewery was greatly extended in the later 19th century, becoming a private limited company in 1886, and a public company in 1890.[71] By 1908 it had extensive railway sidings linked to the station, and was employing 450 workers. In 1909, after a financial crisis, it was reconstituted. In 1934 it merged with Allsopp of Burton-on-Trent. After the Second World War Ind, Coope took over several other breweries, and in the 1960s played a leading part in forming Allied Breweries, one of the largest groups of its kind in the world. Since the war the Romford brewery has been greatly extended, and by 1970 it occupied 20 a., with 1,000 workers.[72]

The main engineering works of the Eastern Counties railway were opened in 1843 at Squirrels Heath, a mile east of Romford station.[73] Engineering was transferred to Stratford in 1847,[74] but the Romford building was retained as a factory making railway tarpaulins and sacks.[75] It employed about 100 workers, for whom the railway company built houses in Factory Road. In the later 19th century the factory also produced horse fodder, and in 1900 a separate building was erected for that purpose.[76] The tarpaulin factory continued until *c.* 1960.[77]

The original buildings of 1843 still survived in 1976, when they were occupied as warehouses by Rail Store Ltd.[78] They comprise three blocks. That to the north has a main elevation of three storeys, facing the railway line, behind which there is a single-storeyed workshop with a roof supported on wooden columns. The rear elevation has 13 full-height openings upon a siding, beyond which a similar elevation opens upon a second workshop which has a central hall with side galleries on cast-iron columns and beams. Beyond that is the smaller engine shed.

Fordham Ellis's candle factory, South Street, existed by 1849.[79] In 1872, after complaints about nuisance caused by the factory, Ellis agreed to move it on the payment of compensation by the local board.[80] Joseph Fordham Ellis was trading as a tallow chandler in North Street in 1886.[81]

The Victoria steam flour mill, Victoria Road, seems to have originated in 1851, as an adjunct to the old windmill in South Street,[82] and to have been known at first as the Star mill.[83] The Victoria mill was apparently extended or rebuilt in 1858.[84] Alfred Dockerill, miller in the 1860s, was succeeded *c.* 1870 by Henry Whitmore.[85] The mill was enlarged in 1874.[86] It was closed *c.* 1928.[87] In 1975 the site was occupied by the shops in Old Mill Parade.

Macarthy's mineral water factory, Market Place, existed by 1851.[88] It was the offshoot of a druggist's

[54] *Pigot's Dir. Essex* (1832), 704; ibid. (1839), 144; *Kelly's Dir. Essex* (1854 and later edns.).
[55] *Pigot's Dir. Essex* (1839), 144; *Kelly's Dir. Essex* (1845-1902).
[56] *Kelly's Dir. Essex* (1886–1937).
[57] *Horn. Docs.* nos. 149, 405.
[58] E.R.O., D/DHt T383/1.
[59] E.R.O., Q/SR 322/66; ibid. 500/35.
[60] E.R.O., D/DHt T140/51.
[61] E.R.O., D/DU 102/30 m. 8d.; Q/SR 73/2–6; *P.N. Essex*, 117.
[62] E.R.O., D/DC 27/695; D/DQ 69/6; Q/SR 140/109–12; ibid. 194/65; ibid. 222/75.
[63] E.R.O., Q/SR 532/55.
[64] *Cal. Pat.* 1557–8, 165.
[65] Smith, *Havering*, 122.
[66] *Map of Essex* (1777).
[67] O.S. Map 6″, Essex, LXVI (surv. 1862–71). Later Hilldene farm: O.S. Map 2½ in., TQ 59 (1947 edn.).
[68] I.R. 29 and 30/12/162, nos. 836, and 606–7.
[69] *Kelly's Dir. Essex* (1890 to 1937).
[70] Paragraph based on: Ind, Coope & Co., *Centenary Souvenir* (1899); H.R.L., L.F. 79/1, Allied Breweries, 'History of Ind Coope' (TS, *c.* 1970); ibid. Notes by F. M. Benson (TS, 1961); *Romford Official Guide* (1908), iv–vi.
[71] *Strat. Expr.* 26 July 1890.
[72] *Havering Recorder* 25 Sept. 1970.
[73] E.R.O., T/A 521/3, 13 Oct. 1843.
[74] *V.C.H. Essex*, vi. 85.
[75] I.R. 29 and 30/12/177, no. 1540; *White's Dir. Essex* (1863), 597; *G.E.R. Mag.* x (1920), 96.
[76] *Kelly's Dir. Essex* (1902).
[77] Inf. from Mr. E. Loyd and Havering L.B.
[78] See plate facing p. 112.
[79] I.R. 29 & 30/12/177, no. 1639; cf. *White's Dir. Essex* (1848), 385, which lists Ellis as a grocer and tallow chandler, of High Street.
[80] H.R.L., Romford L.B. Mins. 13 Feb. 1862, 4 Dec. 1871, 1 Jan. 1872.
[81] *Kelly's Dir. Essex* (1886).
[82] See p. 75.
[83] *Kelly's Dir. Essex* (1855).
[84] *Romford Official Guide* (1908), xxiii: photo of mill shows date 1858 on wall; *Havering Expr.* 10 July 1968, photo and caption.
[85] *White's Dir. Essex* (1863), 603; *Kelly's Dir. Essex* (1866, 1870).
[86] H.R.L., Romford L.B. Mins. 20 Apr. 1874.
[87] *Kelly's Dir. Essex* (1926, cf. 1929).
[88] Ibid. (1851).

business which the Macarthy family had carried on in the Market-place at least since 1823.[89] The factory had steam power by 1856.[90] By 1912 it was owned by the Hearn family, who traded there until 1937 or later.[91]

Spencer's comb factory, St. Andrew's Road, *c.* 1851–82, seems to have been the first industry on the site of the Old Barrack Ground, west of Romford station.[92] The next was Alabaster & Wedlake's iron foundry, St. Andrew's Road and Queen Street, opened in 1852.[93] The firm's name suggests that it was associated with one of two Hornchurch iron-founders: Mary Wedlake & Co., or Wedlake & Dendy.[94] By 1855, however, Roger Alabaster, iron- and brass-founder, was apparently trading alone.[95] The foundry was extended in 1869.[96] It apparently continued in the Alabaster family until *c.* 1880, when it was taken over by Frederick Carter.[97] Carter was succeeded *c.* 1913 by B. Rhodes & Son, who traded as brass-founders until 1937 or later.[98] By 1967 Rhodes had moved to Danes Road, off Crow Lane.[99] In 1975 the firm was a subsidiary of British Steam Specialities Ltd., and was manufacturing scientific and industrial instruments.[1]

During the 19th century there were many small workshops in Romford, mostly engaged in metal-working or engineering. Four families of blacksmiths traded for 40 years or more: Staines in Hare Street, *c.* 1832–98, Randall in Collier Row Road, *c.* 1845–1958 or later, Martin in High Street, *c.* 1845–90, and Underwood in the market-place, *c.* 1848–98.[2] Underwood's business was apparently continued in the Lamb Yard, North Street, by the James family, *c.* 1900–08, and later by the Cooks, who *c.* 1937 moved to the yard of the Duke of Wellington, Market Place, and were still there in 1964.[3]

There were several braziers and tinplate workers in the town in the 19th century, but none survived for more than 10 or 15 years. There was a millwright, John Carter, in South Street, later in North Street *c.* 1832–55.[4] Wheelwrights included James Marchant, St. Andrew's Road, *c.* 1855–98, and the Brown family, in Straight Road, Romford Common, *c.* 1878–1926.[5] Among coachbuilders of long standing was Slipper of High Street, later North Street, *c.* 1845–1902.[6] Slipper's business was taken over by Allen Bros., which survived in 1975 as Charles H. Allen, motor engineers, London Road.[7]

The local tradition of light industry, well established by the end of the 19th century, has since then been continued and extended. The largest modern factory is that of Roneo Vickers Ltd., manufacturers of office machinery. It lies at the junction of South Street and Hornchurch Road, now called Roneo Corner. It was on the Hornchurch side of the old parish boundary. During the 1890s part of the site was occupied by a bicycle factory.[8] The Neostyle Manufacturing Co., later Roneo Ltd., opened its works there in 1908.[9] In 1975 Roneo Vickers was a subsidiary of Vickers Ltd.[10]

Factories opened between the two world wars and still surviving include Colvern Ltd., Spring Gardens, manufacturers of wireless components, May's Sheet Metal Works, Danes Road, and Betterwear Products, North Street, brush manufacturers.[11] Since the Second World War several new factory estates have been built on the outskirts of the town. The largest of them is on the G.L.C. housing estate, Harold Hill, which includes the sliding-door factory of P. C. Henderson Ltd., Tangent Road, and the brassière factory of the Lovable Co., Faringdon Avenue. Other estates are in North Street, Lyon Road, Danes and Maldon Roads, London Road, and Spring Gardens. In 1975 there were some 50 factories in Romford.[12] About half of them were engaged in engineering, electrical, or metal work, and most of the others in food, drink, clothing, footwear, textiles, or plastics.

Romford's commercial growth has also been rapid since *c.* 1930, and especially during the past ten years.[13] The new shopping precinct, south of the market-place, has over 100 shops, including branches of the main department stores. One of the largest stores, Debenhams, has grown from a small shop opened in 1864 at 62 Market Place by Denny Stone, and extended by his son Leonard F. Stone.[14] Stones was burnt down in 1945, after a burglary, but it was rebuilt and further extended. L. F. Stone & Sons became a private limited company in 1947. It was taken over in 1960 by Debenhams, which in 1960–63 rebuilt it on the frontage of 60–72 Market Place.

EARLY MILLS.[15] About 1355 and in 1420 the manor of Dagenhams included a windmill near the South Weald boundary.[16] An earlier mill, apparently in the same area, was mentioned in 1222 and 1236.[17] In 1365 there was a windmill called the New Mill on the Havering part of the manor of Marks.[18] There

[89] *Pigot's Dir. Mdx.* (1823–4), 63.
[90] J. Booker, *Essex and Industrial Revolution*, 72.
[91] *Kelly's Dir. Essex* (1912–37).
[92] Ibid. (1851–82); E.R.O., T/A 521/7, Rating Valuation, Dec. 1864, no. 820.
[93] E.R.O., T/A 521/4, 20 June 1852; Romford L.B. Mins. 16 Apr. 1852.
[94] See p. 40.
[95] *Kelly's Dir. Essex* (1855).
[96] Romford L.B. Mins. 4 Oct. 1869.
[97] *White's Dir. Essex* (1863), 604.
[98] *Kelly's Dir. Essex* (1882 to 1937).
[99] *Tel. Dir. Outer London, S.W. Essex* (1967).
[1] *Kompass* (1975), ii. 859.
[2] *Pigot's Dir. Essex* (1832 and 1839); *White's Dir. Essex* (1848 and 1863); *Kelly's Dir. Essex* (1845–1937); *Tel. Dir. Outer Lond. S.W. Essex* (1958).
[3] *Kelly's Dir. Essex* (1902 to 1937); *Wilson & Whitworth's Romford Almanack* (1902), advt.; *Tel. Dir. Outer Lond. S.W. Essex* (1964).
[4] *Pigot's Dir. Essex* (1832), 704; *Kelly's Dir. Essex* (1845–55).
[5] *Kelly's Dir. Essex* (1855–1926).
[6] Ibid. (1845–1902); E.R.O., D/DU 126/331.
[7] *Kelly's Dir. Essex* (1902–37); *Wilson & Whitworth's Romford Almanack* (1906), advt.
[8] *Kelly's Dir. Essex* (1890–98); O.S. Map, 25", Essex, LXXIV. 4 (1896 edn.): St. Andrew's, later New Ormonde, Cycle Works.
[9] *Kelly's Dir. Essex* (1908 sqq.); *Romford Official Guide* (1908), map p. 23; *Havering Official Guide* (1966–7), 163.
[10] *Who owns Whom* (1975–6), i. 672.
[11] *Kelly's Dir. Essex* (1929–37); *Kompass* (1975), ii. 854 sqq.
[12] *Kompass* (1975), ii. 854 sqq.; inf. from Havering L.B.
[13] For a detailed study: H.R.L., C.V. Rolls, 'Development and Current Functions of Romford as a Service Centre.' (Univ. Lond. Teacher's Cert. TS 1972).
[14] For Debenhams, formerly L. F. Stone & Sons, see *One Hundred Years in the Market Place* (1964).
[15] In preparing this section much help was received from Mr. K. G. Farries, who is writing a book on Essex windmills. See also *E.R.* xxxii. 195–200; xxxiii. 53–4.
[16] New Coll. MS. 9744, f. 162v; *Cal. Pat.* 1416–22, 301.
[17] *Feet of F. Essex*, i. 61, 117.
[18] *Cat. Anct. D.* vi, C 6641. For the Marks Gate windmill, in Dagenham, see *V.C.H. Essex*, v. 283.

was a post mill about ¼ mile east of Marks house *c.* 1618.[19] The name of Mill Dam field (1846), which lay about 600 yd. north-east of the site of Marks, indicates that there had once been a water-mill there.[20]

In the mid 17th century there were three windmills in Romford town: one on the manor of Mawneys, one on Stewards, and one in Main Road. The Mawneys mill existed in 1637, but the site is not known.[21] The Stewards mill, mentioned in 1642, was in 1696 in the same position as the later South Street windmill.[22] In 1642 there was also a water-mill, in Stewards park, but that had apparently disappeared by 1696. The Main Road windmill was *c.* 1618 on the north side of the road, near the market-place, where a mound still survived in 1921.[23] East of it, near the present Black's bridge at Raphael park, there seems to have been a water-mill *c.* 1618.[24] Richard Emes (d. 1678) was holding at his death a windmill on Romford Hill, which he had acquired along with the manor of Gidea Hall, but had evidently retained when he sold the manor.[25] It may have been the windmill mentioned *c.* 1618.

There were three windmills in the town in 1777: in London Road, Hornchurch Lane (South Street), and Main Road.[26] The London Road mill, a post mill, was on the south side of the road about 130 yd. west of St. Andrews' Road.[27] In 1751 the owner was Thomas Green.[28] William Gunn was the miller in 1773.[29] From *c.* 1793 the mill was occupied by Stephen Collier, who by his will, proved 1820, left the reversion of it to his nephew Pratt Collier.[30] The Collier family continued to operate the mill until *c.* 1860.[31] It was put up for sale in 1861.[32] There was still a miller in London Road in 1863, but apparently none in 1866.[33] The mill had gone by 1871.[34] The mill-house may survive as Yew Tree Cottage.

The South Street mill was almost certainly the one which from the 17th century to the 19th century descended with the manor of Stewards.[35] It was a post mill on the east side of the street near the corner of the present Victoria Road.[36] The railway embankment, built *c.* 1840, passed within a few yards of the mill, cutting off the wind. A steam-mill was built beside the windmill, *c.* 1850–1.[37] The windmill is said to have remained standing, behind the Rising Sun inn, until the 1880s.[38]

The Main Road mill, a post mill, lay opposite Pettits Lane, on the south side of the road.[39] It may have been the successor to the Main Road windmill mentioned above. Edward Collier, who is said to have been the last miller,[40] was there *c.* 1829–60.[41] The mill had been demolished by 1871.[42]

In the earlier 19th century there was also a post mill at Collier Row, on a site which is now part of Lawns park, Lawnsway.[43] John and Benjamin Miller were occupying it in 1815, when they took William Blakeley as their apprentice.[44] The Millers remained there until 1832 or later.[45] John Collier was there in 1839.[46] William Blakeley, who married into the Collier family, was the owner and occupier by 1846, and was still trading there in 1855.[47] He is said to have built Lawn House, which survives as a social club.[48] The mill had gone by 1871.[49] The site of an earlier mill at Collier Row is indicated by the name Mill field (1846), which lay north of Chase Cross Road and West of Havering Road.[50] Another Mill field (*c.* 1618) was south of Noak Hill Road at Noak Hill.[51]

MARKET, FAIR, AND CORN EXCHANGE. In 1247 Henry III ordered the sheriff of Essex to establish a market at Romford, to be held on Wednesdays.[52] In 1250, by a similar order, he established a fair there, to be held annually throughout Whit week.[53] There seems always to have been a Wednesday market since 1247.[54] A Tuesday market had been established by 1633, and a Monday market also by the later 18th century. The Monday market was discontinued shortly before 1816, and the Tuesday market later in the 19th century. A Saturday market, which existed by 1907, still continues. In 1919 daily markets were inaugurated as a temporary measure. That ended in 1925, but the Friday market was then retained, along with

[19] E.R.O., D/DU 102/1.
[20] I.R. 29 and 30/12/162 no. 1581.
[21] C.P. 43/218.
[22] C 142/501/19; E.R.O., D/DSa 149.
[23] E.R.O., D/DU 162/1 R.C.H.M. *Essex*, ii. 204; O.S. Map 6″, Essex, LXVI (surv. 1862–71).
[24] For Black's (formerly Watermill) bridge see above, p. 60.
[25] E.R.O., T/P 71/1, Will of Ric. Emes.
[26] *Map of Essex* (1777).
[27] I.R. 29 and 30/12/177 no. 1388; H.R.L., Pictorial Coll. Churches, P.p.c. of St. Andrew's school and the mill.
[28] E.R.O., D/DU 461: map of mill fields, depicting the mill.
[29] *Chelmsford Chron.* 17 Dec. 1773.
[30] R. Exch. Insurance Policy no. 134410, 29 June 1793; E.R.O., D/DU 159/16, Will of Steph. Collier.
[31] *Pigot's Dir. Essex* (1823–4, 1832, 1839); E.R.O., T/A 521/5, Rating Assessment 1836; I.R. 29 and 30/12/177, no. 1388; *Kelly's Dir. Essex* (1855). For the Colliers at this period see H.R.L., *List* by A. B. Bamford, *c.* 1906, of mons. in St. Edward's churchyard.
[32] E.R.O., Sage Coll., *Sale Cats.* vol. xi. 4.
[33] *White's Dir. Essex* (1863), 603; *Kelly's Dir. Essex* (1866).
[34] O.S. Map 6″, Essex, LXXI (surv. 1862–71).
[35] C 142/501/19; E.R.O., D/DSa 149; E.R.O., D/DU 102/126, Havering Manor Ct. 16 Feb. 1710; I.R. 29 and 30/12/177, no. 1451.
[36] E.R.O., Sage Coll., *Sale Cats.* vol. xi. 12; E.R.O., Pictorial Coll.
[37] E.R.O., T/A 521/4, 4 Apr. 1851, new buildings rated: Mr. Meritt, Steam Mill (windmill reduced); I.R. 29 and 30/12/177, no. 1451; H.R.L., E. Gotto, *Plan of Romford* (1853); O.S. Map 6″, Essex, LXVI (surv. 1862–71).
[38] *E.R.* xxxiii. 53–4.
[39] I.R. 29 and 30/12/177, no. 1465. For descriptions see: *Chelmsford Chron.* 30 June 1820; E.R.O., Sage Coll., *Sale Cats.* vol. x. 11 (1829).
[40] E.R.O., T/P 71/1, Will of Ric. Emes.
[41] E.R.O., T/A 521/5, Valuation July 1829; *Pigot's Dir. Essex* (1832, 1839); *Kelly's Dir. Essex* (1845, 1850, 1855); *E.R.* xxiii. 53–4.
[42] O.S. Map 6″, Essex, LXVI (surv. 1862–71).
[43] I.R. 29 and 30/12/162, nos. 1250–4; *Essex and Herts Mercury*, 5 Feb. 1833 (sale notice).
[44] Indenture penes Mrs. T. Bibbings (1966): inf. from Mr. K. G. Farries.
[45] *Pigot's Dir. Essex* (1832).
[46] Ibid. (1839).
[47] I.R. 29 and 30/12/162, nos. 1250–4; *Kelly's Dir. Essex* (1855); H.R.L., Cornell MSS., Windmills.
[48] Inf. from Mrs. T. Bibbings.
[49] O.S. Map 6″, Essex, LXVI (surv. 1862–71).
[50] I.R. 29 and 30/12/162, nos. 1045–6.
[51] E.R.O., D/DU 162/1.
[52] *Close R.* 1242–7, 536.
[53] Ibid. 1247–51, 256.
[54] For the market days see: Norden, *Essex*, 13, 24; Hist. MSS. Com. 29, *13th Rep. II, Portland* ii, p. 282; Morant, *Essex*, i. 64; Lysons, *Lond.* (1796), iv. 183; Ogborne, *Essex*, 128; Thorne, *Environs Lond.* (1876), 512; *White's Dir. Essex* (1848), 378; *Romford U.D.C. Mins.* Mkt. Cttee. 19 Feb. 1907, 9 Sept. 1919 sqq.; 18 Feb., 25 Mar. 1925.

Wednesday and Saturday. The annual fair was by the 18th century being held on one day only, 24 June.[55] It was abolished in 1877.[56] It was then stated that in recent years the fair had been held on the last Thursday in June.

The market remained the property of the Crown until 1828. In 1619 James I leased the market tolls for 99 years to trustees for the Prince of Wales, later Charles I.[57] In 1631 the trustees sold the lease to John Edisbury of the Inner Temple (Lond.). During the rest of the 17th century the lease changed hands several times, and sub-leases were occasionally created. As a result of these transactions the control of the market sometimes passed to strangers, who found it difficult to enforce their authority in Romford. The final owner of the 99-year lease, a brewer from Bow (Mdx.) named Mark Frost, between 1710 and 1741 bought from the Crown three consecutive leases running up to 1772. The main lease later passed to Mrs. Anne Freeman of Boreham, who secured its renewal up to 1793. Between 1793 and 1813 the tolls were let from year to year.[58]

In 1828 the market, along with the manor of Havering, was bought from the Crown by Hugh McIntosh.[59] He paid £4,700 for the market, which was then held by Charles Willoughby on a 31-year lease granted in 1813. The market continued to descend with the manor until 1892. Between 1882 and 1887 Romford local board made at least two unsuccessful attempts to lease the tolls from Mrs. McIntosh,[60] and in 1887 they became involved in a legal dispute with her over the installation of a weighbridge in the market.[61] In 1889 they rejected an invitation to lease the tolls, saying that the market was declining, but in 1892, when it was threatened with closure, they bought the freehold from Mrs. McIntosh for £7,000.[62]

The Market Place developed along both sides of the main road to London, on the eastern side of the town. It is about 400 yd. long and 50 yd. wide.[63] At its western end, in the 18th and 19th centuries, lay the court house and gaol of the liberty of Havering, sometimes, but not officially, called the market house.[64] That was demolished in 1933.[65] At the eastern end of the Market Place, until the later 19th century, was the Loam pond.

By the later 17th century Romford was 'a great market town for corn and cattle'.[66] It continued to flourish as an agricultural centre in the 18th and 19th centuries.[67] In 1824 most of the Market Place was reserved for cattle.[68] In 1876 the eastern end was used for pigs and cattle, and the western end for farm tools, clothing, fruit, and vegetables. The market was then thought to be the largest near London for corn and cattle.[69] The cattle trade remained important until the Second World War. After the war it declined rapidly, and the cattle market was closed in 1958.[70] Since then the market has been devoted mainly to food, clothing, and household goods. In 1973 there were about 325 regular traders there.[71] In 1969, after the construction of St. Edward's Way, the Market Place was closed to through traffic by sealing its eastern end.[72]

The Romford corn exchange was opened in 1845 in a converted building adjoining the Golden Lion in High Street.[73] It was enlarged in 1861.[74] It was put up for sale in 1924 and was closed soon after.[75] The corn exchange was used by traders on market days and at other times for public meetings; it was always privately owned.[76]

FOREST. The history of the forest is treated under Havering.[77]

LOCAL GOVERNMENT. The manorial government of Romford is treated above.[78] Romford, like Havering, was originally a chapelry of Hornchurch. By the 16th century Romford chapel vestry was virtually independent for civil purposes, governing Romford town, Collier Row, Harold Wood (or Hare Street), Noak Hill, and Havering wards.[79] By the late 17th century Havering chapel vestry had gained control over Havering ward for civil purposes,[80] and Romford vestry thenceforward governed only the

ROMFORD MUNICIPAL BOROUGH. *Azure, on a fesse wavy, barry wavy of four, argent and azure, between in chief an eagle displayed and in base a Saxon crown, or, a ring also gold, gemmed proper.*
[Granted 1938]

[55] Morant, *Essex*, i. 64.
[56] *Lond. Gaz.* 31 Aug. 1877, 5041.
[57] For the leases, 1619–1828, and disputes arising from them: E 134/24 Chas. I, East./9; *Cal. S.P. Dom.* 1641–3, 42–3; E.R.O., D/DSa 63; D/DFr T66; *Cal. Treasury Bks.* 1669–72, 1253; 1708, 335; 1710, 329; 1739–41, 341; S. J. Madge, *Domesday of Crown Lands under the Commonwealth*, 281, 394; G. A. Selwyn and others, *Manors held by Lease from Crown* (1787), 12; *Hist. Essex by Gent.* iv. 319.
[58] Lysons, *Lond.* (1796), iv. 183 and *Suppl.* (1811), 352; Ogborne, *Essex*, 128.
[59] *Romford Market*, ed. I. G. Sparkes, 22.
[60] H.R.L., Romford L.B. Mins. 5 June, 3 Jly. 1882, 7 Mar. 1887.
[61] *Romford Market*, ed. Sparkes, 23.
[62] Romford L.B. Mins. 4 Mar. 1889; *Romford Market*, 24.
[63] E.R.O., D/DU 162/1 (map *c.* 1618); L.R.R.O. 1/761 (Plan of Market 1624).
[64] Morant, *Essex*, i. 64; Lysons, *Lond.* iv. 183.
[65] For the court house see above, p. 7.
[66] Hist. MSS. Com. 29, *13th Rep. II, Portland* ii, p. 28.
[67] For impressions of the market in the 19th century: E.R.O., T/P 71/1; *Country Life*, 13 Mar. 1897.
[68] L.R.R.O., 1/761.
[69] Thorne, *Environs Lond.* 512. For the market at that period see above, frontispiece.
[70] H.R.L., Christine P. Shaw, 'Past, Present and Future of Romford Market.' (TS thesis, Summerfield Coll. 1966): chaps. 7 and 8 deal with the recent history.
[71] *Havering Official Guide* (1973), 49.
[72] *Havering Expr.* 17 Sept. 1969.
[73] *White's Dir. Essex* (1848), 378; E.R.O., T/A 521/3, Romford Vestry Mins. 1 Jan. 1846; E.R.O., D/DU 126/331.
[74] *White's Dir. Essex* (1863), 597; Romford L.B. Mins. 18th May, 19th Sept. 1861.
[75] E.R.O., *Sale Cat.* A398; *Romford U.D.C. Mins.*, Rep. Mkt. Cttee. 25 Mar. 1925; *Kelly's Dir. Essex* (1926, cf. 1929).
[76] *Romford Official Guide* (1908), 35.
[77] See p. 20.
[78] See p. 1.
[79] E.R.O., T/A 521/1, reverse ff. 16–17.
[80] See p. 21.

town, Collier Row, Harold Wood, and Noak Hill wards.[81]

There are Romford vestry minutes from 1660 to 1924.[82] The oldest surviving book includes a few extracts from earlier parish books going back to 1490. There are also rate books for 1802 and 1829–36.[83]

By 1662 Romford vestry was meeting monthly to deal with poor-relief.[84] There are occasional later references to monthly meetings, although the vestry minutes record only the most important meetings. Attendance, as indicated by signatures to the minutes, was usually between 7 and 14 until after 1810, when figures of 12 to 16 or more were normal. Carew Hervey *alias* Mildmay (d. 1676) and his son Francis Hervey Mildmay (d. 1703), successive owners of Marks, often attended the vestry, and nearly always signed first.[85] Between 1660 and 1769 the chaplain of Romford usually attended. James Hotchkis, 1706–34, and his successors customarily signed first. From 1770 to 1792 the chaplain was hardly ever present, and signatures suggest that one of the churchwardens presided. Between 1793 and 1836, when the chaplains were often non-resident, successive assistant curates usually took the chair.

Romford had two chapelwardens. In the 17th and 18th centuries the vestry customarily elected one warden from the town and one from one of the 'upland' (i.e. rural) wards; each served for two years, with one retiring each year. The chaplains of Romford did not establish their right to appoint one warden until the early 19th century, although they attempted to do so on at least two previous occasions, in 1743 and 1768. Five collectors of the poor, including one for Havering, were appointed by Romford vestry in 1561.[86] In the earlier 17th century there were similarly five overseers of the poor, one for each ward.[87] From 1660 the town ward had two, so that there were six in all. From *c.* 1680 Havering nominated its own overseer. In the 1830s Romford vestry was appointing a paid assistant overseer. In the earlier 17th century there were usually two surveyors of highways, but occasionally one, three, or four.[88] In 1648 the number was fixed at three, and so remained at least until 1689. By the end of the 18th century there were apparently five: two from the town and one each from the other three wards. A high constable for the town, and five petty constables, two for the town and one each for Collier Row, Harold Wood, and Noak Hill, were appointed by ancient custom in the court leet of the manor of Havering.[89] Minor officers included the vestry clerk, beadle, sexton, dog-whipper, and a varying number of sidesmen. There are occasionally references also to a pew-opener, and to a book-keeper.

Here, as at Hornchurch, there seem to have been separate rates for the different parish purposes, though there is little information concerning assessment before the 19th century. In 1660 the vestry adopted a series of resolutions proposed by the senior church warden, Nathaniel Beadle, with the aim of improving the financial administration of Romford. The churchwardens were directed to provide casual relief, presumably out of the church-rates, to relieve the poor-rates. An auditor of accounts was to be appointed, and illiterate churchwardens, if otherwise suitable for office, were to be provided with clerical help. The charity incomes were to be carefully administered, and the parish houses repaired. Beadle's plan was imperfectly realized, for in 1662, when he completed his term of office, his accounts were in confusion, and had to be subjected to a special audit.[90]

By the late 17th century Romford was well provided with charities, including Roger Reede's alms-houses.[91] There were also several poorhouses, which lay near the Loam pond in the market-place. One of them was said in 1660 to have been appropriated by the vestry after the death of its owner, a pauper named Mrs. Greenwood.[92] The others formed the endowment of Simpson's charity as well as accommodating poor people. There was also a pest house, at Collier Row.[93] In 1719 the vestry appointed a committee to prepare a scheme for a workhouse, and at the same time resolved to repair the Half Moon in Romford town, a house belonging to Ann Elsden's charity. These two measures may have been connected, for in 1753 the Half Moon was being used as the workhouse.[94] In 1765 the vestry used £55, part of the capital of Margaret Burch's and Joachim Matthews's charities, to build another poorhouse, possibly the one at Rush Green mentioned below.

The Romford Workhouse Act of 1786 transferred most of the responsibility for poor-relief in the 'parish' of Romford from the vestry to a new body called the directors and guardians of the poor.[95] The directors were, in the first instance, the 30 persons named in the Act, together with the chapelwardens. Vacancies were to be filled by co-option from persons occupying premises rated at £10 a year or more. The directors were to hold quarterly general meetings, and weekly committees. They were empowered to appoint and to pay a clerk, a treasurer, and other officers. The overseers of the poor were still to be appointed, but their functions were limited to levying the poor-rate and relieving the casual poor, and even in those they were under the directors' control. The directors were required to establish a workhouse, and were empowered to borrow up to £3,500. The existing workhouse, and all the poorhouses belonging to the parish, including one recently built for the sick at Rush Green, were to be vested in the directors. The directors were authorized to punish misconduct in the workhouse without recourse to the magistrates, by 'moderate correction', confinement, hard labour, distinction in dress, or abatement in diet.

The directors immediately bought land in Collier Row Lane (North Street) and contracted with

81 In church matters Romford did not abandon its claims over Havering until the 18th century: see p. 23.
82 E.R.O., T/A 521/1–4 (microfilms, from originals with Hunt & Hunt, solicitors, Romford). Unless otherwise stated the following account is based on these vestry minutes, which relate mainly to the work of the churchwardens, and to charities.
83 E.R.O., T/A 521/5.
84 E.R.O., T/A 521/1, 4 Feb. 1662.
85 For the Mildmays see *V.C.H. Essex*, v. 276.
86 E.R.O., T/A 521/1, rev. f. 16.
87 Ibid. ff. 18v., 21v., 22v.
88 Ibid. rev. ff. 17–21v.
89 See p. 5.
90 E.R.O., T/A 521/1, f. 23.
91 See p. 96.
92 E.R.O., T/A 521/1, f. 16.
93 Ibid. 17 Apr. 1666; *N. & Q.* 3rd ser. iii. 84.
94 E.R.O., T/A 521/1, 21 Apr. 1753.
95 26 Geo. III, c. 28. For a similar Act secured by the neighbouring parish of Barking see *V.C.H. Essex*, v. 219.

Abraham Godden and Richard Moore, bricklayers of Romford, to build a new workhouse, completed in 1787.[96] In 1788, they sold to Moore 8 parish houses near the Loam pond.[97] The new workhouse was used until 1836. Apart from a set of rules drafted in 1787[98] there are no records of its administration, or of the other activities of the directors of the poor. It seems likely, however, that the Act of 1786 helped to keep down the costs of relief, which during the following decades rose much more slowly in Romford than in Hornchurch.[99]

In 1836 the chapelry of Romford became part of Romford poor-law union. Romford workhouse was used temporarily by the union from 1836 to 1838.[1] In 1840 it was demolished and the materials and the site were sold.[2]

An Act of 1819 set up a body of commissioners with power to levy rates, not exceeding 2*s.* in the pound annually, for paving, lighting, watching, and cleansing Romford town.[3] The vicar, all resident magistrates, and the surveyors of highways of Romford were to be commissioners *ex officio*. The Act named 24 other commissioners, and provided for the appointment of new ones, subject to a property qualification, to fill vacancies. The commissioners were empowered to employ paid officers, and to borrow on the security of the rates. The Act was to apply only to a small area, corresponding with the present town centre: Market Place, High Street, and adjoining areas of South Street and North Street. These limits were precisely defined, and there was no provision for their extension as the town grew. In 1848 the cmmoissioners' total expenditure was £468, including £108 contributed to the cost of the county police.[4] By that time the growth of Romford had begun to create slums at the west end of the town, and the vicar, Archdeacon Anthony Grant, organized a petition to the government calling for an enquiry into sanitary conditions. The enquiry provided ample evidence of the dangers to public health,[5] and in 1851 a local board of health of 12 members was set up, with responsibility for the whole parish of Romford.[6] In 1855, after complaints against the board, and another public enquiry, the government reduced the area of the board's district to include only the town ward of Romford.[7] The district was slightly extended in 1878.[8]

The local board met at St. Edward's Hall, Laurie Square (1851-3), and later at the old court house of Havering liberty, in the market-place (1853–69).[9] From 1869 until 1883 or later it leased a building in the market-place for offices and to house its surveyor. In 1892 the old court house was bought, with the market, from the lady of the manor, and this was subsequently used for municipal offices.[10]

The first chairman of the local board was the vicar, Grant, 1851–2. Between 1852 and 1873 the chair was successively occupied by six others of whom Edward Collier, miller, 1854–61, and Thomas Haws, farmer, 1861–5 and 1869–71, served longest. Thomas Bird, a manager at Romford brewery and a keen antiquary, was chairman of the board and of its successor the urban district council from 1873 until 1900.[11]

The members of the board served in rotation for three year terms. Most of them were tradesmen or farmers. Among others were William T. Jones, 1852–5, chaplain of Romford union workhouse, and William J. Skilton, 1866–9, rector of St. Andrew's. Both these clergymen joined the board as reformers; Skilton seems to have been the more successful in stirring the board to action.

The local board originally appointed a part-time clerk, a superintendent of roads, and a rate-collector who was also inspector of nuisances. In 1853 roads, rate-collecting, and nuisances were all entrusted to one man, but he was dismissed for embezzlement in the following year, and his duties were again divided between two officers. In 1865 the board first appointed a surveyor as its chief outdoor officer. During the 1870s two successive surveyors were dismissed for embezzlement, and a third for corruption. A part-time medical officer of health was first appointed in 1875, after pressure from the government.

The local board was at first slow and inefficient in dealing with the modest problems of a small town. The first sewage works, opened, after long delays, in 1861, was never satisfactory.[12] In its later years the board was more effective. The purchase in 1869 of Bretons farm, Hornchurch, for a new sewage works, showed foresight in allowing room for expansion. Another decision which proved wise was the purchase of the market rights from the lady of the manor in 1892.[13]

Under the Local Government Act, 1894, the local board was succeeded, in 1895, by an urban district council, also with 12 members. At the same time the parish of Romford was divided into two for civil purposes.[14] The new parish of Romford (Urban) was placed under the U.D.C., while that of Romford (Rural) remained part of Romford rural district. Later in 1895 Noak Hill was taken out of Romford (Rural) as a separate civil parish.[15] In 1900 the civil parish of Romford (Rural) was united with that of Romford (Urban) and included in Romford Urban District, while the U.D.C. was enlarged to 16 members, representing 5 wards.[16] In 1934 the civil parishes of Havering and Noak Hill were added to the urban district, and the number of wards

[96] E.R.O., D/DU 391/2 (title deeds of site, 1786 sqq.); D/DQ 75 (contract with builders, 1786). The site was on the west side of the street, north of Reede's alms-houses: E.R.O., Sage Coll., *Sale Cats.* vol. xi. 9.

[97] E.R.O., D/DGe T90.

[98] E.R.O., D/DBe O3.

[99] See p. 43.

[1] E.R.O.. G/RM 1; T/A 521/3.

[2] E.R.O., Sage Coll., *Sale Cats.* vol. xi. 9

[3] Romford Paving &c. Act, 59 Geo. III, c. 75.

[4] W. Ranger, *Rep. to Gen. Bd. of Health on Sanitary Condition of Romford* (1850), 4–5; B. Tabrum, *Short Hist. Essex Constabulary*, 30.

[5] W. Ranger, op. cit.

[6] Public Health Supplemental Act, 1851 (no. 2), 14 & 15 Vict. c. 98.

[7] H.R.L., Romford L.B. Mins., 17 Nov. 1854 sqq.; Public Health Supplemental Act, 1855, 18 & 19 Vic. c. 125.

[8] Loc. Govt. Board's Provisional Orders Conf. (Bournemouth &c.) Act, 1878, 41 & 42 Vict. c. 162.

[9] Unless otherwise stated the following account of the local board's work is based on: H.R.L., Romford L.B. Mins., 1851–89. The minutes for 1889–95 are missing.

[10] H.R.L., 'Notes of Romford Town Centie, *c.* 1908, from Cornell MSS,' pp. 6, 8.

[11] E.R.O., Libr. Vert. Folder, *Essex Chron.* 23 Mar. 1900 (obit. of T. Bird).

[12] See p. 80.

[13] See p. 76.

[14] E.R.O., T/A 521/10, Mins. Romford (Rural) Parish Mtgs. 1894–1900; E.R.O., Temp. Acc. 917, bdle. 8, Romford Parish Vestry Recs.; H.R.L., Romford U.D.C. Mins.

[15] E.R.O., Temp. Acc. 917, Bdle. 8, Romford Par. Vestry Mins.

[16] Ibid.

was increased to 7, represented by 20 councillors.[17]

The U.D.C. continued to meet in the old court house until 1931, when it moved to temporary premises in South Street. It opened public baths (1900), and joined with Romford R.D.C. to build an isolation hospital (1901). The first public park, part of which was a gift, was opened in 1904. After the First World War, with the town growing rapidly, the U.D.C. expanded its administration and improved its services.[18] A separate finance department was set up in 1932. A full-time clerk of the council was appointed for the first time in 1933, and a full-time medical officer of health in 1934. The U.D.C. acquired several new parks and began to build council houses. It carried out important road works, notably the widening of South Street, and in 1934 combined with Hornchurch U.D.C. in a new sewerage scheme.[19]

Romford became a municipal borough in 1937, with 21 councillors, representing five wards, and 7 aldermen.[20] In the same year a new town hall, designed by Collins & Green of Bournemouth, was opened in Main Road.[21] The council was enlarged in 1952 to 24 councillors, for 8 wards, and 8 aldermen, and in 1953 to 27 councillors (9 wards) and 9 aldermen.[22] Before the Second World War most of the seats on the council were held by Independents or by the Romford Ratepayers' Association.[23] The Labour party, which had begun to win seats in the early 1930s, increased its representation in 1945, and from 1955 to 1965 controlled the council.[24] The Conservatives, who were officially represented for the first time in 1950, were the largest group from 1951 to 1955, and the second largest from 1955 to 1965. During the Second World War Romford suffered much bombing, mainly in 1940–41 and 1944–5. Most of the houses in the borough received some damage and there were 143 deaths.[25] After that war the borough council embarked on a series of major housing schemes, and at the same time provided municipal services for the new L.C.C. estate at Harold Hill.

THE LONDON BOROUGH OF HAVERING. In 1965 the borough of Romford was joined with the urban district of Hornchurch to form the London borough of Havering, with an area of 29,650 a., and a population, estimated in 1976, of 242,000.[26] The borough council consists of 55 councillors, representing 20 wards, and 9 aldermen. Since its formation it has been controlled by a coalition between the Conservatives and the Ratepayers' Association, except between 1971 and 1974, when there was a small Labour majority. It has built a new theatre at Hornchurch, opened in 1975, and a shopping precinct at Romford, completed in 1972, and opened an 18-hole golf course (1972) at Risebridge farm, Chase Cross, and a sports complex (1975) in Lamb's

HAVERING LONDON BOROUGH. *Per saltire argent and azure a gem ring or set with a ruby proper.*

[Granted 1965]

Lane, Rainham. Its main offices are at the town hall, Romford.

PUBLIC SERVICES. Romford's first gas undertaking, with works in South Street, is said to have been established by George M. Bell in 1825.[27] In 1847 the Romford Gas & Coke Co. was formed and took over the works from Bell, who remained manager.[28] In 1892 the company built new works in Nursery Walk, south of the railway station;[29] by 1938 these covered 25 a. The rebuilding and enlargement of the works was begun in 1947. In 1949 the company was taken over by the North Thames gas board.[30]

The County of London Electricity Supply Co. obtained powers in 1913 to supply a large part of south Essex, including Romford, from a power station which was to be built at Barking.[31] This scheme was delayed by the First World War. In 1915, as a temporary measure, the company contracted to buy current from the private generators at Ind, Coope's Romford brewery, and used this to supply a small surrounding area. The company itself took over the operation of the brewery's generators in 1917, and maintained them until 1924, when a new sub-station was opened at Romford. The sub-station received supplies from the generators of Jurgens Ltd., margarine manufacturers, at Purfleet, in West Thurrock, until 1925, when Barking power station was opened. In 1948 Romford was placed under the Eastern electricity board.[32]

Romford had no main water supply until the later 19th century. The Loam pond, and the mineral springs at Havering Well and Gidea Hall, are mentioned elsewhere.[33] In 1859 the local board made a public well, with a pump, at the east end of the market-place.[34] The South Essex Waterworks Co., founded in 1861, began to lay mains in Romford in 1863.[35] The main offices of the company were

[17] Essex Review Order (1934); *Romford Charter Petition* (1936).
[18] H.R.L., *Romford Charter Petition* (1936) and attached TS Proofs of Evidence; *Romford Borough Charter Souvenir* (1937).
[19] See p. 81.
[20] *Romford Borough Charter Souvenir* (1937).
[21] Ibid.
[22] Romford B.C. Mins. 18 June 1952 sqq.; 20 May and 17 June 1953 sqq.
[23] *Romford Official Guide* (1935), [13]; ibid. (1936), 14–15; *Kelly's Dir. Essex* (1933, 1937).
[24] This and the following sentence are based on inf. from Havering Libraries.
[25] G. Richards, *Ordeal in Romford, passim.*
[26] London Government Act, 1963, c. 33. This paragraph is based on: *Havering Official Guide* (1966, 1971, 1973 edns.) and inf. from Havering L.B.C.
[27] This paragraph is based on: *White's Dir. Essex* (1848), 379; Romford Gas Co., *Centenary* (1847–1947).
[28] For detailed records of the company (1848–1949) see E.R.O., D/F 5/11/1–8 and D/DLc B9–14.
[29] *Strat. Expr.* 10 Sept. 1892 (detailed description).
[30] Gas Act, 1948. Areas of Gas Boards, Map A.
[31] This paragraph is based on: F. D. Smith, *Hist. Electricity in Romford and S.W. Essex.* [Duplicated TS. 1956].
[32] *V.C.H. Essex.* v. 76; *Hornchurch Official Guide* (1951).
[33] See pp. 56, 69.
[34] H.R.L., Romford L.B. Mins. 24 Feb. 1859 sqq.
[35] Ibid. 1 Oct. 1863. For this company see: *S. Essex Waterworks Co. 1861–1936; Record of S. Essex Waterworks Co. 1861–1961.*

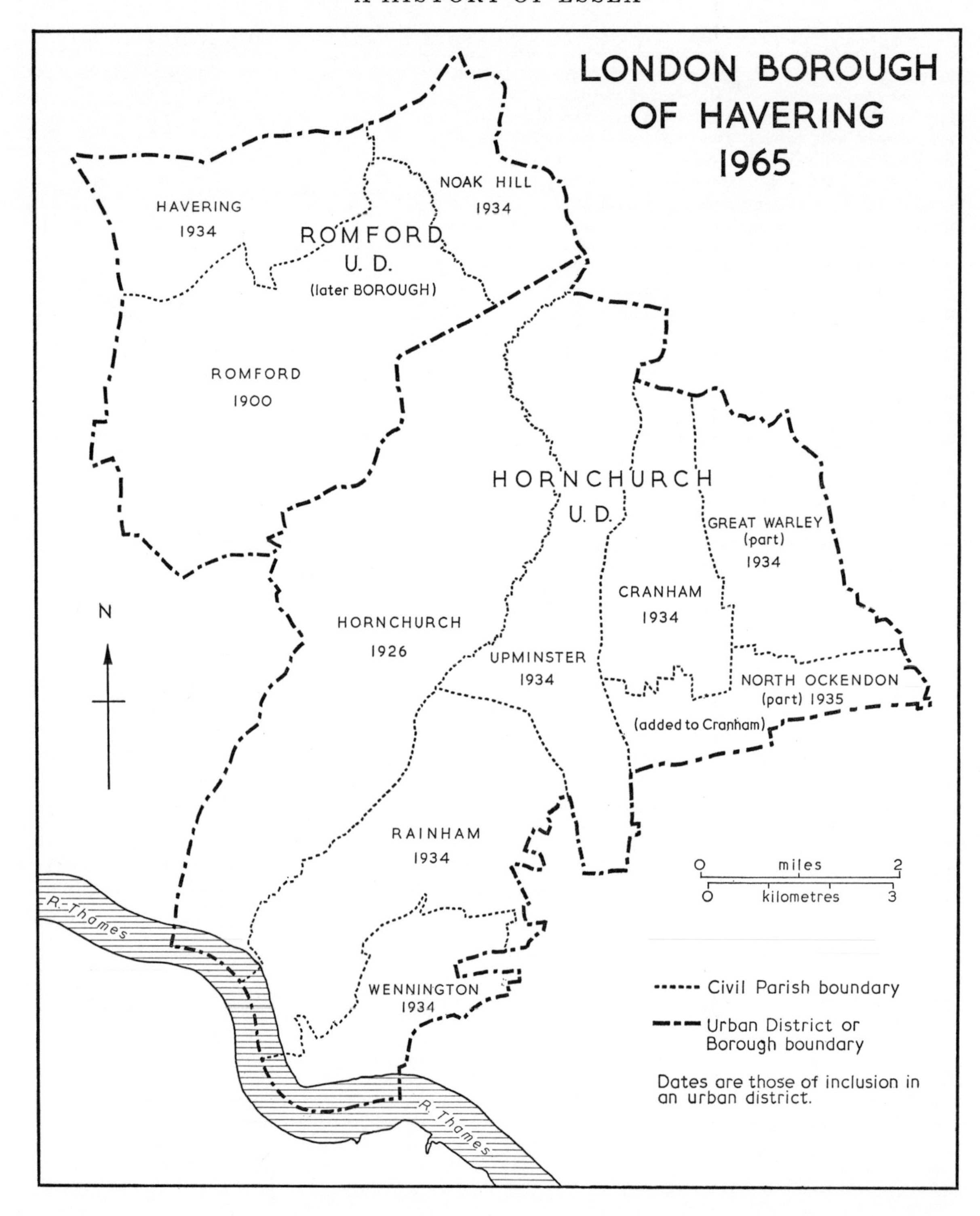

transferred to South Street, Romford, in 1887. By 1905 the mains extended through the town in all directions, to Ilford, Collier Row, Ardleigh Green, Brentwood, and Hornchurch.[36] By 1936 the company had two deep wells in Romford, a covered reservoir at Heaton Grange, and a water tower at Havering.[37] The South Essex Waterworks Co. became part of the Essex Water Co. in 1970.[38]

Romford local board in 1852 drew up plans for main drainage, but took no steps to carry them out until 1858, when Dagenham parish successfully prosecuted them for polluting the river Rom.[39] Sewage works, at Oldchurch, were then put in hand, and were completed in 1862 at a cost of about £7,000.[40] They were badly sited and inefficient, and in 1869, after further complaints about the pollution of the river, the board bought Bretons farm, Hornchurch, and built new works there.[41] By 1881

[36] J. C. Thresh, *Rep. on Water Supply to Rural Districts of Essex*, map after p. 22.

[37] *Romford Charter Petition* (1936), Proof of Evidence (Engineer), p. 26.

[38] Essex Water Co., *Rep. for 1970*.

[39] H.R.L., Romford L.B. Mins. 29 Oct. 1852 sqq.; ibid. 4 Nov. 1858.

[40] Ibid. 30 Mar. 1859 sqq.

[41] Ibid. 9 Nov. 1868 sqq.

nearly all the town was said to be connected to the main sewers.[42] As early as 1886 the local board agreed to allow parts of Hornchurch to drain into the Romford sewers.[43] In 1934 the urban districts of Hornchurch and Romford formed a joint sewerage committee, and during the following years the Bretons farm works were enlarged to serve both districts.[44] In 1965 responsibility for sewage disposal passed to the Greater London council, and the treatment of the sewage from Romford and Hornchurch was subsequently transferred to the Riverside works at Rainham Creek in Hornchurch.[45] The Bretons farm sewage works were closed in 1969.[46]

Raphael park, Main Road, formerly part of the Gidea Hall estate, was opened by Romford U.D.C. in 1904.[47] The original portion of 20 a., given by (Sir) Herbert Raphael, was later enlarged by purchase to 55 a.[48] After the First World War the U.D.C. acquired other parks, including Mawney (1928), of 28 a., Bedfords (1933), of 215 a., and Rise park (1937), of 23 a.; the last was given by Thomas England.[49] In 1937 Romford had some 400 a. of public open spaces.[50] By 1960 the figure had risen to 640 a., which included Oldchurch park and two large parks at Harold Hill.[51]

The public baths, Mawney Road, Romford, were built by the U.D.C. in 1900, and modernized in 1937.[52] They were closed in 1974 and demolished in 1975.[53] The much larger pool in Gooshays Drive, Harold Hill, was planned by Romford borough council and opened by Havering L.B.C. in 1966.[54]

Romford vestry was maintaining a parish fire-engine by 1787.[55] One or two engine masters were regularly employed. In 1805 they were empowered to recruit six firemen when required.[56] An engine house was built in the workhouse garden in North Street, apparently in 1823; this was retained when the workhouse was sold in 1840.[57] In 1852 the fire-engine was taken over from the vestry by the newly formed Romford local board.[58] A volunteer brigade, supported by the local board, was formed in 1890.[59] The founder was Samuel Davis, a local builder. He captained the brigade for many years, and most of the firemen were drawn from his firm.[60] A new fire station was built in Mawney Road, near Davis's premises, soon after the formation of the brigade.[61] It remained in use until 1960, when Essex county council, which had taken over the brigade after the Second World War, opened a new station in Pettits Lane North.[62]

Romford U.D.C. began building council houses after the First World War, at Park farm, London Road, and later at Rush Green.[63] By 1939 the borough council had 358 houses.[64] Between 1945 and 1965 it completed a further 3,929, concentrated mainly at Collier Row, but including several other estates in the borough, and one outside it, at Hutton, in Brentwood urban district.[65] From 1965 Havering L.B.C. continued Romford's building programme and also took over from the Greater London council 2,600 houses at Harold Hill. By 1973 Havering owned over 8,000 houses in the Romford section of the borough.[66]

Victoria hospital, Pettits Lane, was opened in 1888 as a voluntary cottage hospital, on a site given by William Mashiter.[67] By 1937, after three enlargements, it had 31 beds.[68] Oldchurch hospital, Oldchurch Road, occupies the site, and includes the buildings of the former Romford Union workhouse. The original workhouse, designed by Francis Edwards, was built in 1838.[69] A hospital was added in 1893, and was enlarged in 1924.[70] On the dissolution of the poor-law union in 1930 the institution was taken over by the public assistance committee of Essex county council, which in 1935 transferred it to the public health committee.[71] Since 1930 Oldchurch hospital has been greatly enlarged. The original building of 1838 is of two storeys. The plan is a square enclosing a cross set diagonally. The main, south front is of 25 bays with the centre emphasised. There are later 19th-century buildings on the north side, but all these are dwarfed by the 20th-century hospital buildings on the north and east. Rush Green hospital, Dagenham Road, Dagenham, built in 1900 jointly by Romford U.D.C. and Romford R.D.C., as an isolation hospital, has been treated elsewhere.[72]

A parochial cemetery was opened about 1849 on a site of 1 a. in Main Road, originally intended for a new parish church.[73] This soon became full, and in 1871 Romford burial board, which seems to have been formed about two years earlier, opened a new cemetery in Crow Lane, Rush Green.[74] Romford U.D.C. took over the cemeteries in 1900.[75] The old cemetery in Main Road was in 1953 laid out as Coronation Gardens; the Romford war memorial was placed there in 1970 after being removed from

[42] Ibid. 13 June 1881.
[43] Ibid. 14 Sept., 4 Oct. 1886.
[44] *Romford Charter Petition* (1936), 5.
[45] L.B. Havering, *Havering Recreation and Amenities* (1970), Open Spaces.
[46] L.B. Havering, *News Release* (*Bretons farm*), 16 Aug. 1974.
[47] *Romford Handbook* (1908), 52; *Gidea Hall and Gidea Park*, 41–2.
[48] *Romford Borough Charter Souvenir* (1937).
[49] Ibid.
[50] Ibid.
[51] *Romford Official Guide* (1960), 29, 32, See also L.B. Havering, *Recreation and Amenities Division* (1970).
[52] *Romford Borough Charter Souvenir* (1937).
[53] *Havering Exp.* 6 Nov. 1974.
[54] *Havering Official Guide* (1969).
[55] E.R.O., T/A 521/3, Romford Vestry Mins. 24 Apr. and 1 May, 1787. For later refs. to the engine see E.R.O., T/A 521/2 and 3 *passim*.
[56] Ibid. T/A 521/3, 3 Oct. 1805.
[57] Ibid. 8 Oct. 1823, 3 Oct. 1839, 7 Jan. 1841.
[58] H.R.L., Romford L.B. Mins. 8 Oct., 29 Oct., 12 Nov. 1852.
[59] Romford L.B. Mins. 7 Aug., 3 Sept. 1889; *Romford Charter Petition* (1936), Proof of Evidence (Engineer), 21.
[60] Inf. from Miss J. M. Davis.
[61] Ibid.; *Romford Handbk.* (1908), map p. 22–3.
[62] *Essex Co. Co. Mins.* 1960, p. 743.
[63] *Romford Charter Petition* (1936), Proof of Evidence (Engineer), 23.
[64] *Romford Official Guide* (1951), 34.
[65] *Romford B.C. Mins.* 1964–5, p. 455; *Romford Official Guide* (1960), 29; *Havering Official Guide* (1966), 32.
[66] *Romford Official Guide* (1973), 103.
[67] *Wilson & Whitworth's Romford Almanack* (1902); *Nursing Mirror*, 25 Feb. 1911, p. 354.
[68] *Kelly's Dir. Essex* (1937).
[69] Pevsner, *Essex*, 328. See plate facing p. 113.
[70] *Kelly's Dir. Essex* (1898); dates on south blocks.
[71] *Essex Co. Co. Mins.* 1935, p. 1555.
[72] *V.C.H. Essex*, v. 294.
[73] *White's Dir. Essex* (1848), 599.
[74] Romford L.B. Mins. 31 May 1869; E.R.O., T/A 521/4, Romford Vestry Mins. 4 Feb., 2 Apr., 14 and 19 May 1870; *Kelly's Dir. Essex* (1878), 197.
[75] E.R.O., Temp. Acc. 917, Bdle. 8, Order of L.G.B. 24 Mar. 1900.

Laurie Square to make room for the new ring road.[76]

Romford library, the first full-time branch of the Essex county library, was opened in 1930 in the former St. Edward's charity school in the market-place.[77] Temporary branches were established at Havering and Collier Row before the Second World War.[78] After the war the county council built branch libraries at Hilldene Avenue, Harold Hill (1959), Balgores Lane, Gidea Park (1962), and Collier Row Road, Collier Row (1964).[79] It also built a large central library in Laurie Square, Romford. This was designed by the county architect, Mr. H. Connolly, in reinforced concrete clad with Empire stone, and cost £180,000. It was taken over by Havering L.B.C. and was opened in 1965.[80] The old market-place branch was then closed.

PARLIAMENTARY REPRESENTATION. The Romford (or Southern) division, formed in 1885, was a large county constituency comprising the liberty of Havering, Barking, Dagenham, Ilford, and East Ham.[81] John Westlake (Liberal) narrowly won the seat in 1885, but in 1886, standing as a Liberal Unionist opposed by a Gladstonian Liberal, he came bottom of the poll, and lost the seat to James Theobald (Conservative) of Bedfords Park, Havering. The Conservatives held Romford until 1906, when it was recaptured for the Liberals by (Sir) John Bethell (Bt.), later Lord Bethell; he held it in 1910.[82]

In 1918 the Romford division was altered to comprise Romford rural district, and the urban districts of Romford and Barking.[83] At the general election of that year the seat was won by a Coalition Liberal, who held it in 1922 as a National Liberal. Romford was later held in turn by the Conservatives (1923–9, 1931–5) and Labour (1929–31, 1935–45).

The Parliamentary borough of Romford, formed in 1945, was originally coincident with the municipal borough of Romford. It was enlarged in 1948 to include Brentwood urban district, but in 1955 Brentwood was transferred to Billericay county constituency.[84] Romford was held by Labour from 1945 to 1950, and from 1955 to 1970; the Conservatives held it from 1950 to 1955. Boundary changes, which took effect in 1974, created three new constituencies for the borough of Havering: Upminster, Hornchurch, and Romford. The new Romford constituency was won by the Conservatives in February 1974 and held in November 1974.

CHURCHES. The chapel of Romford was first mentioned in 1177, when the pope confirmed it to Hornchurch priory along with the church of Havering i.e. St. Andrew, Hornchurch, and other possessions previously granted by Henry II.[85] Romford remained part of the parish of Hornchurch until the 19th century. The original chapel, also dedicated to St. Andrew, lay at the junction of South Street and Oldchurch Road, on the south side. That spot, immediately east of the river, was still known in the 19th century as Old Church mead.[86] As Romford grew larger its chapel, which was 2½ miles from the parish church, began to seek independence. In 1236 there seems to have been a move to establish a graveyard there. Henry III ordered that this should not be done until he had conferred with the bishop of London, and that seems to have been the end of the matter.[87] By the 15th century the growth of the town along the main London–Colchester road had left the old chapel isolated, and a new one, dedicated to St. Edward the Confessor, was therefore built on the present site in the market-place.[88] When the new chapel was consecrated in 1410 it was at last agreed that there should be a graveyard there, but in other respects the rights of the parish church, and those of New College, Oxford, as owners of the rectory, were strictly reserved. The new chapel was built under the leadership of Robert Chichele, a London merchant, and brother of Henry Chichele, later archbishop of Canterbury.[89] Robert Chichele held the manor of Gidea Hall and other local estates.[90] Henry Chichele, who in 1408 became bishop of St. Davids, was authorized by the bishop of London to consecrate the new chapel.[91] As a graduate of New College he may well have taken part in the negotiations with the college concerning the new chapel.

Under the agreement of 1410 those worshipping at Romford were bound to contribute as before to the repair of the parish church, as well as maintaining their own chapel. They tended to regard that obligation as unfair, and in 1529 joined with Havering to secure an arbitration award under which their total annual payments towards the repair of Hornchurch church were limited to 16*s*. 8*d*., unless the church had suffered catastrophic damage.[92] After 1529 there is no evidence that Romford made any substantial contributions to the repair of Hornchurch church until 1802–3, when the south aisle of the church was being rebuilt. At that time a copy of the agreement of 1410 came to light, and Hornchurch, having taken counsel's opinion, successfully levied a church-rate in Romford.[93] No reference was then made to the award of 1529, which had evidently been forgotten. Romford was still paying church-rates to Hornchurch in 1814.[94]

[76] L.B. Havering, *Recreation and Amenities Division* (1970).

[77] H.R L., Newscuttings, Small bk., f. 58, Reports of opening; *Official Opening of Romford Branch Library (1930)*; *V.C.H. Essex, Bibliography*, 331.

[78] *Hornchurch and Upminster News*, 14 June 1939; *Romford Times*, 5 June 1940.

[79] *Essex County Library Rep.* (1963–4).

[80] G. H Humby, 'Havering's New Library', *Library World*, Sept. 1965.

[81] *E.R.* iii. 86; *Kelly's Dir. Essex* (1886), 5.

[82] For elections to 1910 see *McCalmont's Parliamentary Register*, ed. J. Vincent and M. Stenton, 83.

[83] *Kelly's Dir. Essex* (1922), 5. For elections 1918–66 see *E.J.* iii. 179 sqq.; iv. 9 sqq.

[84] O.S. Maps, Essex, Admin. Areas (1948 and 1955 edns.). For elections 1966–74 see *Dod's Parliamentary Companion*.

[85] *E.A.T.* N.S. vi. 2.

[86] E.R.O., D/DB T1434 (will of Octavius Mashiter, 1864); cf. E.R.O., D/CT 186 (tithe award, 1849), no. 895a and no. 1440. John Finch was Mashiter's tenant in 1849 and 1864. For references to Old Church mead in 1452 and 1457 see *Cat. Anct. D.* iii, C 3723, C 3519.

[87] *Close R.* 1234–7, 314.

[88] *Cal. Pat.* 1405–8, 175; *Horn. Docs.* no. 6 (New Coll. MS. 2941).

[89] *Horn. Docs.* no. 6; *D.N.B.* Hen. Chichele.

[90] *Cal. Inq. Misc.* 1399–1422, p. 159.

[91] New Coll. MS. 2941.

[92] New Coll. MS. 4592.

[93] Ogborne, *Essex*, 148; E.R.O., T/P 71/2.

[94] Ogborne, *Essex*, 148.

While seeking independence from Hornchurch, Romford chapel attempted to gain control over all the northern wards of the parish: Collier Row, Harold Wood, Noak Hill, and Havering, as well as the Town, By the late 15th century Romford was levying chapel-rates in all these wards.[95] The only serious opposition came from Havering, which had its own chapel, and by the late 17th century a graveyard also. In 1650 it was proposed that a new parish should be formed for Romford, comprising the Town, Harold Wood, and Collier Row, and another parish for Havering and Noak Hill; but that came to nothing.[96] By 1750 Havering had at last broken free from Romford, and in 1784 it became independent also of Hornchurch.[97] Romford itself became a separate parish in 1848–9.[98]

The chaplain of Romford chapel was appointed and remunerated by Hornchurch priory from the 12th to the 14th century, and later by New College, until the late 15th century, from which time the college seems usually to have delegated those functions to the vicar of Hornchurch, reserving the right to remove the chaplain.[99] From the later 14th century the chaplain drew his income mainly from the small tithes of Romford, granted to him on long lease.[1] This was a voluntary arrangement similar in effect, though not in law, to that of a normal vicarage.[2] In 1734, when a new chaplain was required, the vicar of Hornchurch considered paying him a fixed stipend, and keeping the small tithes of Romford in his own hands.[3] That may occasionally have been done in the 18th century, but the old practice of leasing the small tithes in kind to the chaplain was probably the usual arrangement until the time of Anthony Grant (chaplain 1838–62).[4] All the parochial tithes were commuted in 1846–9,[5] but Grant's successors continued to be appointed as lessees of the benefice until 1926–7, when New College endowed the vicarage.[6]

The income of the early chaplains is not known, but some idea of it may be inferred from the terms of their leases. A lease granted in 1369 was for 3 years at 9 marks a year.[7] Another, granted to the same chaplain in 1384, was for 14 years at £10.[8] Those two leases included certain great tithes, which no later chaplain is known to have enjoyed. A chaplain appointed in 1615 was granted a 50-year lease at an annual rent of £66 13*s.* 4*d.*[9] In 1650 the chaplain was receiving £45 a year, allowed by the government from the small tithes.[10] During the later years of the Interregnum he was receiving also an augmentation of £30 to £40.[11] By the 17th century the chaplain was receiving a considerable amount from subscriptions.[12] In 1734 it was stated that his total income was never less than £200, including subscriptions of £20 to £50 or more; out of this he had to pay about £80 rent to the vicar of Hornchurch for his lease.[13] In 1849 the small tithes of Romford were commuted for £287, charged entirely on the section of the parish south of the main London road.[14]

By 1384 there was a parsonage, called the Priest's House, which was leased to the chaplain along with the small tithes.[15] It was possibly identical with Priests, a house on the site of the present Priests Avenue, east of Havering Road,[16] and if so it may have been the parsonage as early as 1272, for Ralph of Langley, who was then chaplain, certainly had property in that area, as did one of his successors soon after.[17] If Priests was the parsonage it was inconveniently remote from Romford chapel, and it had passed into lay ownership by 1689.[18] It was rebuilt about 1814 by Octavius Mashiter, whose family held it throughout the 19th century,[19] but it has since been demolished.

The 'old vicarage', adjoining the churchyard, still existed in 1879.[20] It had an 18th-century front, with Ionic pilasters, but the irregular rear portions were probably older. It must have gone out of use by 1846, when the vicarage was a large house, in grounds of 2 a., on the west side of North Street, near the market-place.[21] The North Street vicarage was used until 1909, since when there have been several moves.[22]

The guild of Our Lady in Romford chapel was in existence by 1479, and received several bequests during the following years.[23] At its dissolution in 1548 it had a net annual income of £4 6*s.* 10*d.*, which maintained a priest, John Saunder, and provided 5*s.* for the poor.[24] Its property included a house called the Tilekiln on Harold Wood common, which later formed the endowment of the Tilekiln charity.[25]

Avery Cornburgh (d. 1487), lord of the manors of Dagenhams and Gooshayes, by his will founded a chantry in Romford chapel.[26] The terms of the benefaction were recorded in verse on his tomb, which still survived in the chapel in the early 17th century.[27] The total endowment was £13 a year, of which £10 was for the stipend of the chantry priest, who was to preach not only at Romford, but

95 E.R.O., T/A 521/1 (reverse ff. 15–16).
96 Smith, *Eccl. Hist. Essex*, 249–51, 348.
97 See above, p. 23.
98 E.R.O., T/A 521/3, 11 Sept. 1846, 17 Apr. 1847, 31 Mar. 1848; Romford Vestry Recs. 17 Mar. 1849 (Parish borrows from Public Works Loan Bd.); E.R.O., D/CT 186.
99 Smith, *Havering*, 147–8, 153; E.R.O., T/P 71/2; E.R.O., D/P 115/28/6; *Hist. Essex by Gent.* iv. 327.
1 *Horn. Docs.* nos. 15a, 308; New Coll. MSS. 2941 and 2985; E.R.O., D/P 115/28/6.
2 It was probably the model for the later arrangement at Hornchurch.
3 E.R.O., D/P 115/28/6.
4 *Hist. Essex by Gent.* iv. 327; E.R.O., T/P 71/2; G. Terry, *Romford*, 220.
5 I.R. 29/12/162 and 177.
6 *Kelly's Dir. Essex* (1886 and later edns.); C. Lovett, *Church in the Market Place*, 60; E.R.O., D/CP 16/11.
7 *Horn. Docs.* no. 308.
8 Ibid. no. 15a.
9 New Coll. MS. 2941.
10 Smith, *Eccl. Hist. Essex*, 250.
11 Ibid. 213, 409.
12 E.R.O., D/DXa 31.
13 E.R.O., D/P 115/28/6.
14 I.R. 29/12/177.
15 *Horn. Docs.* no. 15a.
16 E.R.O., D/DB T1434; I.R. 29/12/162. Priests may, however, have been named after the Priest family: *P.N. Essex*, 119.
17 *Horn. Docs.* nos. 73, 307, 329, 503.
18 E.R.O., D/DB T1434; *Kelly's Dir. Essex* (1866 sqq.).
19 Ibid.; Ogborne, *Essex*, 135.
20 H.R.L. Watercolour drawing by A. B. Bamford.
21 I.R. 29/12/162.
22 *Kelly's Dir. Essex* (1866 and later edns.); H.R.L. Cornell MSS.; E.R.O., D/CP 16/12; *Chelmsford Dioc. Y.B.* (1958–9 and later edns.). The North St. vicarage was demolished in 1975: inf. from Mr. C. J. Whitwood.
23 E.R.O., D/AER 1, ff. 10, 18, 120, 150, 152.
24 C 301/30/26.
25 *Cal. Pat.* 1548–9, 312; E.R.O., D/DB T1406. For the Tilekiln charity see below, p. 96.
26 *E.A.T.* iv. 15–20; C 301/30/25 and 26.
27 Terry, *Romford*, 78–81.

at South Ockendon, Hornchurch, Dagenham, and Barking. At the dissolution of the chantry in 1548 the net income was £12 0s. 11*d*.[28] There was a chantry house or 'priest's chamber'. It is thought to have been the building, immediately east of the church, which was a public house for many years before 1908, when it was bought back by the church and re-opened as Church House.[29] It is a timber-framed range of 16th-century character, four bays long, with jetties to the street and the churchyard, and a gallery above a wide jetty on the rear elevation. It may once have formed part of a larger building which extended eastwards along the street, and had an open yard. The building was much altered in the 18th or the early 19th century.[30]

The names of at least 10 chaplains of Romford have been recorded before the Reformation.[31] From the late 16th century the list seems to be fairly complete.[32] By the 17th century, if not earlier, the inhabitants of Romford were choosing, or helping to choose, their own chaplain, though the legal right of appointment still lay with the vicar of Hornchurch as the agent of New College.[33] The most notable 17th-century chaplain was John Morse, 1615–48, a prominent Puritan.[34] Dr. Gloster Ridley, 1748–62, and his son and successor James Ridley, 1762–5, were both successful writers.[35] Between *c.* 1770 and 1848 Romford chapel seems to have been left for long periods in the care of an assistant curate, who usually served also as Sunday afternoon lecturer.[36] In 1792 the chapel vestry complained that the lecturer had delivered 'heavy and pointed denunciations from the pulpit' tending to stir up controversy.[37] His successor, Dr. John Wiseman, was dismissed in 1810, also after a dispute.[38] Dr. George Croly, curate in the 1830s, was a writer, dramatic critic, and later a popular City preacher.[39] Anthony Grant, vicar 1838–62, was a distinguished lecturer who became archdeacon of St. Albans in 1846 and canon of Rochester in 1860.[40] Like many of his predecessors he was a New College man. The parish church was rebuilt during his incumbency.

The former chapel of *ST. ANDREW* has disappeared, and nothing is known of its appearance or construction. The chapel of *ST. EDWARD THE CONFESSOR*, consecrated in 1410, survived until 1849. When new it contained features notable enough to be imitated in the specification (1413) of improvements to the parish church of Halstead, in north Essex.[41] At the time of its demolition the chapel was a large building comprising nave, chancel, north aisle and chapel, west tower, and north and south porches.[42] The north aisle and chapel, which were the same width and height as the nave and chancel, may have been late-15th-century additions, perhaps associated with the guild of Our Lady, or Cornburgh's chantry.[43] From the parish records it seems unlikely that any major external alterations or additions had been carried out after the 15th century except for the rebuilding of the tower in 1790.[44] Repairs carried out in 1641 included the removal of stained glass.[45] Romford celebrated the Restoration by setting up the royal arms, building a chancel screen, inserting new glass in the east window, and repairing the chapel roof.[46] A visitor in 1662 thought the church 'handsomely beautified within.'[47] A (west) gallery was built about 1678.[48] The nave arcade seems to have been rebuilt *c.* 1802.[49] That may have been a botched job, for it was later said that the chapel was 'greatly dilapidated and barbarized' and that 'the masts of ships supplied the places of the stone columns to sustain the aisle and roofs.'[50]

Romford chapel had an organ in 1552.[51] In 1814 there was an organ, erected by voluntary subscription, in the west gallery.[52] During the following years the chapel was employing an organist who was also choirmaster.[53]

There were 6 bells in 1552.[54] One of them, probably dating from the early 15th century, still survives. By the 18th century there were 8 bells, and a society of ringers was active by 1755.[55] All the bells were transferred to the new church in 1850.[56] Before 1552 Romford was well supplied with communion plate, but the earliest surviving pieces date from 1654.[57] In 1552 there were two chests, one of which was allowed to remain in the chapel.[58] An old iron chest existed *c.* 1660, when Nathaniel Beadle, churchwarden, gave another 'great iron trunk coloured blue', standing on iron wheels.[59] Neither of those chests survives.

The original east window of the chapel was placed there by Robert Chichele, and contained an inscription, dated 1407, commemorating Henry IV and his queen as well as Chichele and his wife, and

[28] C 301/30/25.
[29] Terry, *Romford*, 77; *Cal. Pat.* 1549–51, 89; E.R.O., T/P 71/1; *Romford Handbk.* (1908), 28–9; *E.R.* xviii. 166; Lovett, *Church in Market Place*, 45; Char. Com. Files.
[30] R.C.H.M. *Essex*, ii. 204, and pl. f. p. 45.
[31] *Horn. Docs.* 15a, 73, 160, 392, 500; C.C.L., J. L. Fisher, 'Essex Incumbents', f. 201; *Cal. Pat.* 1391–6, 45; E.R.O., D/DU 102/48, m. 1*d.*; *N. & Q.* 5th ser. xi. 285–6; *E.A.T.* N.S. vi. 318.
[32] *N. & Q.* 3rd. ser. ii. 162; Smith, *Havering*, 224; H. Smith, 'Sequence of Parochial Clergy in Essex, 1640–64' (TS. in E.R.O. Libr.), i. 16–17; E.R.O., T/A 521/1–3; Lysons, *Lond.* iv. 197; C. Lovett, *Church in Market Place*, 47.
[33] E.R.O., T/A 521/1 (agreement, 1662, between vicar of Hornchurch and Romford inhabitants on appointment of chaplain).
[34] Smith, *Eccl. Hist. Essex*, 38, 49, 50, 193.
[35] E.R.O., T/A 521/1; Lysons, *Lond.* iii. 457; *D.N.B.*
[36] E.R.O., T/A 521/3.
[37] Ibid. 13 Mar. 1792.
[38] Ibid. 7 Aug. 1810. Wiseman was later curate at Havering.
[39] E.R.O., T/A 521/3; Terry, *Romford*, 241; *D.N.B.*
[40] Terry, *Romford*, 242; *D.N.B.*
[41] L. F. Salzman, *Building in England down to 1540*, 490–1.
[42] C. Lovett, *Church in Market Place*, 18 (illus.); E.R.O., T/P 196 (King MSS.), Eccl. Essex, iv. 97 sqq.; Ogborne, *Essex*, 123 (illus.).
[43] E.R.O., T/P 195/2 (Holman MSS., 1719), Havering Liberty, f. 81; E.R.O., T/P 196, Eccl. Essex, iv. 97 sqq. For 'Our Lady Chapel' see *E.A.T.* N.S. vi. 318.
[44] E.R.O., T/A 521/3, 25 June 1789, 12 Jan. 1790.
[45] E.R.O., T/A 521/1, reverse f. 21.
[46] Ibid. f. 23 (5 June 1660) and f. 37 (acct. for repairs, 1660–1).
[47] *E.A.T.* N.S. x. 1.
[48] E.R.O., T/A 521/1, 27 Mar. 1677, 6 May 1679.
[49] E.R.O., T/A 521/3, 7 Oct., 11 Nov. 1802.
[50] E.R.O., T/P 196, Eccl. Essex, iv. 97 sqq.
[51] *E.A.T.* N.S. iii. 38.
[52] Ogborne, *Essex*, 123.
[53] E.R.O., T/A 521/2, 27 Mar. 1815, 20 Apr. 1835; T/A 521/3, 2 May 1815, 18 May 1826, 5 May 1835.
[54] *Ch. Bells Essex*, 371.
[55] E.R.O., T/A 519.
[56] See below.
[57] Ibid.
[58] *Ch. Chests. Essex*, 180.
[59] E.R.O., T/A 521/1, f. 18.

stating that the chapel was founded in honour of Christ, the Virgin, and St. Edward the Confessor.[60] That window was presumably the one, recorded in the early 17th century, which depicted Edward the Confessor and two pilgrims, with the incomplete inscription 'Johannes per peregrinos misit Regi Edwardo . . .'.[61] It was no doubt removed with the other glass in 1641. In 1661 a new picture of St. Edward was placed in the east window.[62] It was renewed in 1707.[63] It was evidently transferred to the new church in 1850; it still existed *c.* 1876, but must have been removed before 1882, when a new east window was recorded.[64]

The old chapel contained several fine monuments of the 16th and early 17th centuries, which were removed to the new church. Many other monuments in the church and churchyard, including some which have disappeared, are on record.[65]

In 1840 it was decided to demolish the old chapel and build a new one, to the designs of Edward Blore, at the other end of the market-place.[66] The work was started about 1844, but it was abandoned owing to lack of funds, and the site was converted into a cemetery.[67] The new church of St. Edward was at last built in 1850, on the site of the previous one. It is of Kentish ragstone with Bath stone dressings, in the Decorated style, designed by John Johnson.[68] It originally comprised chancel, nave with clerestorey, north and south aisles with north organ chamber and south chapel, west gallery, south porch, and south-west tower with a spire 162 ft. high.[69] In 1885 two vestries were added on the north side.[70]

A new organ, by Walker & Sons, was bought in 1866; it was rebuilt about 1905 by Speechly & Son.[71] In the early years of the 20th century St. Edward's was a musical centre for the churches of the district.[72] The church bells include three by Miles Graye (1636), and one each by John Darbie (1657), John Waylet (1704), Lester & Pack (1756), C. & G. Mears (recast, 1850).[73] The tenor bell was probably by Robert Burford (d. 1418), and would thus have been bought as part of the original equipment of the old chapel of St. Edward.[74] The bells were rehung in 1922.[75] There has been a church clock at least since 1552.[76] A weight-driven clock, made in 1759, served until 1945, when a new electric clock, with a chime of four bells, was given by the London Central Board of Licensed Victuallers, whose chairman was then the mayor of Romford.[77] The dial and hands of the old clock were retained. The church plate includes a silver paten (1654) and silver-gilt cup (1661), both given by Carew Hervey *alias* Mildmay of Marks; a pair of flagons, dated 1640, bequeathed by John Burch (d. 1668);[78] and a silver paten of 1707, given by Thomas Roberts, vicar of Hornchurch.[79] A silver-gilt cup and paten of 1563, listed in 1926, no longer existed in 1976.

The church contains three fine alabaster monuments brought from the old chapel.[80] That to Sir Anthony Cooke (d. 1576) of Gidea Hall, in the north aisle, was restored in 1973 by Miss Inger Norholt under the direction of the Romford Historical Society.[81] Those of Sir George Hervey (d. 1605) of Marks, and Anne (Hervey) wife of George Carew (d. 1605) are in the south porch.

St. Edward's church was the only Anglican place of public worship until the building of St. Thomas, Noak Hill (1842). The church of St. Andrew was built in 1862 for the district west of Romford station, and was given a separate parish in the following year. By 1900 four more churches had been built: two in the town, one at Collier Row, and one at Squirrels Heath. Seven others have been built since the First World War, including two at Harold Hill. Ten new parishes have been formed since 1926.

The church of *ST. THOMAS*, Noak Hill, Church Road, was built in 1842 as a memorial to Frances, wife of Sir Thomas Neave, Bt., of Dagnams.[82] It is a small building of red brick, with transepts and south-west tower, designed by George Smith in the Early English style. The tower was restored in 1971.[83] The church's most notable fittings are collectors' items from elsewhere. They include painted window glass of the 16th–18th centuries, given by Sir Thomas Neave, Bt. Among these pieces are medallions with the badge of Jane Seymour, the arms of Charles II and Queen Anne, and some French and Flemish glass.[84] Three monumental brasses of the 15th to 17th centuries, taken from South Weald church, were given to Noak Hill church early in the present century by John Sands of Dagnam Priory, but were restored to South Weald in 1933.[85] The church remains in St. Edward's parish. From 1882 to *c.* 1895 St. Edward also had a mission in North Street, occupying the former Congregational church.[86]

The church of *ST. ANDREW*, Romford, St. Andrew's Road, was built in 1862 for the new working-class district on the former barrack ground. The building, designed by John Johnson, is of Kentish ragstone in the Early English style.[87] Since

[60] E.R.O., T/P 195/2, Havering Liberty, f. 81 sqq.
[61] Ibid.; Morant, *Essex*, i. 58.
[62] E.R.O., T/A 521/1, f. 58.
[63] E.R.O., T/P 195/2, Havering Liberty, f. 81 sqq; Morant, *Essex*, i. 58.
[64] H.R.L., Pictorial Coll., Churches: copy of drawing by Anderson, 1849; Thorne, *Environs Lond.* (1876), 513; *Kelly's Dir. Essex* (1882).
[65] E.R.O., T/P 195/2, Havering Liberty, f. 81 sqq; Lysons, *Lond.* iv. 192–6; E.R.O., T/P 196, Eccl. Essex, iv, f. 97 sqq.
[66] E.R.O., T/A 521/3, 2 and 4 Jan., 16 Apr. 1840; I.R. 29 and 30/12/62.
[67] *White's Dir. Essex* (1863), 599.
[68] Pevsner, *Essex*, 327.
[69] *Kelly's Dir. Essex* (1866); *Ch. in Market Place*, 33–5.
[70] *Ch. in Market Place*, 34.
[71] Ibid. 49.
[72] Ibid. 52.
[73] *Ch. Bells Essex*, 370–1. From the names of the churchwardens Darbie's bell must be 1657, not 1651: E.R.O., T/A 521/1, reverse f. 22.
[74] *Ch. Bells Essex*, 15, 371, pl. vi, figs 5, 6. In 1595, how ever, Romford levied a rate for 'new casting the great bell': E.R.O., T/A 521/3, reverse f. 16v.
[75] Inscription in south porch.
[76] *E.A.T.* N.S. iii. 38.
[77] *Ch. in Market Place*, 58–9.
[78] *Ch. Plate Essex*, 15; Terry, *Romford*, 196.
[79] E.R.O., T/A 521/3, 5 July 1709.
[80] R.C.H.M., *Essex*, ii. 203–4.
[81] Inf. from Romford Hist. Soc.; *Romford Record*, vi. 58.
[82] *Kelly's Dir. Essex* (1937); Pevsner, *Essex*, 307.
[83] Inf. from vicar of Romford.
[84] R.C.H.M., *Essex*, ii. 197, and pl. f. p. xxxvii; *E.A.T.* N.S. xv. 233 and pl. f. p. 173.
[85] Mill Stephenson, *Monumental Brasses* (1964 edn.), 128, 744; R.C.H.M., *Essex*, ii. 197; *E.A.T.* N.S. viii. 268.
[86] *Strat. Expr.* 22 Nov. 1882; *Kelly's Dir. Essex* (1890–99).
[87] E.R.O., D/CC 9/1; H.R.L., Cornell MSS.; F. T. Wright, *St. Andrew's Romford* (1938). See plate facing p. 49.

the Second World War the district has been redeveloped, but St. Andrew remains, in its small, hedged churchyard. A separate parish, taken from Romford, was assigned in 1863.[88] The benefice, endowed mainly out of the rectorial and vicarial tithes of Romford, was declared a rectory in 1866; the advowson was from 1863 vested in New College.[89] The first rector, William J. Skilton, 1863–85, served with distinction on the local board, and later on the school board, of which he was chairman.[90] The mission church of *ST. AGNES*, Jutsum's Lane, was opened in 1928.[91] The churches of St. Alban, Princes Road (1890), and St. Augustine, Rush Green (1958) also originated as missions of St. Andrew, but were later given their own parishes.

The church of *ALL SAINTS*, Squirrels Heath, Ardleigh Green Road, originated in 1884, when a wooden mission church, in Romford parish, was built in Squirrels Heath Road, at the corner of Upper Brentwood Road.[92] In 1926 a permanent church was completed on the same site, and a separate parish, taken out of Romford (main part), St. Andrew, Romford, and Hornchurch, was formed.[93] The advowson of the vicarage was vested in the bishop of Chelmsford. The church was enlarged in 1933–4, but in 1941 was destroyed by bombing.[94] Services were later held in the Royal Liberty school, and then in a hut on the bombed site.[95] In 1957 a new church, designed by R. C. Foster, was built in Ardleigh Green Road, about a mile farther east, and the parish boundaries were altered accordingly.[96] The church of St. Michael, Gidea Park (1929), which started as a mission of All Saints, was later given a separate parish.

The church of *THE ASCENSION*, Collier Row, Collier Row Road, originated in 1880 as a mission of Romford.[97] Services were held first in the Hainault Forest school, Collier Row Road,[98] and later in a mission hall. The present church was built in 1886. The Crown subscribed £140 towards its erection, no doubt because there were extensive Crown estates in the district.[99] The Revd. J. H. Pemberton (d. 1926) of the Round House, Havering, a noted rose-grower, was curate in charge from 1880 to 1923. He left funds to endow the benefice, and further contributions were made by his sister, Amelia Pemberton. A new parish, taken out of Romford and St. Chad, Chadwell Heath, was formed in 1927, the advowson being vested in Miss Pemberton for life, and then in trustees, including the vicar of Romford; the church was consecrated in 1928.[1] The parishes of the Good Shepherd, Collier Row (1935) and St. James, Collier Row (1955) were both taken mainly from The Ascension.

The church of *ST. JOHN THE DIVINE*, Romford, Mawney Road, originated in 1897, when an iron mission church, in Romford parish, was opened in Willow Street.[2] In 1928, after long delays, the first stage of a permanent church was opened on a new site in Mawney Road. A separate parish, taken out of Romford and St. Andrew, Romford, was assigned to it, the advowson of the vicarage being vested in the bishop.[3] The church, built of brick, was designed by W. D. Caröe in Byzantine style. The first stage comprised the sanctuary, part of the chancel, and a temporary nave. In the second stage (1932), the chancel was completed and five bays of the aisled nave were built. A side chapel was added, as a war memorial, in 1948,[4] and a choir vestry in 1966–7,[5] but parts of the original plan, including the upper part of the tower and the three western bays of the nave, had not been completed by 1975. In that year it was stated that the church was in danger of closure, with a regular congregation of only 9 or ten.[6]

The church of *ST. MICHAEL*, Gidea Park, Main Road, originated in 1929 as a mission of All Saints, Squirrels Heath.[7] An ecclesiastical district, taken out of All Saints, was assigned in 1933.[8] In 1936 the advowson of the vicarage was vested in the bishop of Chelmsford, and in 1938, when a permanent church was completed, a separate parish was formed.[9]

The church of the *GOOD SHEPHERD*, Collier Row, Redriff Road, originated in 1934 as a mission of The Ascension, Collier Row.[10] A separate parish, taken from The Ascension and from St. John, Romford, was formed in 1935. The church (1935), hall, and vicarage were given by Dame Violet Wills, in whom, and in other trustees, the advowson of the vicarage was vested.[11]

The church of *ST. ALBAN*, Romford, Princes Road, was opened in 1890 as a mission of St. Andrew.[12] A conventional district was formed in 1935.[13] A separate parish, taken from St. Andrew, was assigned in 1952, the advowson of the vicarage being vested in the bishop of Chelmsford.[14]

The church of *ST. GEORGE*, Harold Hill, Chippenham Road, originated in 1939, when a mission of Romford was opened in Straight Road, for an area still largely rural.[15] After the Second World War it was well-placed to serve the western side of the new Harold Hill estate. In 1953 a new church was opened on the present site and a conventional district was assigned.[16] A separate parish, taken from Romford, was formed in 1956, the advowson of the vicarage being vested in the bishop of Chelmsford.[17]

[88] E.R.O., D/CP 16/13; D/CE 76; D/CPc 14.
[89] Ibid.; *Lond. Gaz.* 4 May 1866, p. 2761.
[90] For his obituary: *Strat. Expr* 12 Aug. 1893.
[91] F. T. Wright, *St. Andrew's, Romford*, 60; Char. Com. Files.
[92] *Strat. Expr.* 6 Aug. 1884; *Kelly's Dir. Essex* (1886).
[93] E.R.O., D/CC 77/8; D/CPc 201.
[94] C.C.L., Bp. Inskip's Recs., ii. 294.
[95] Ibid. 297; personal knowledge.
[96] E.R.O., D/CC 108/2; D/CPc 356 and 372; Inf from. Church Comm.
[97] Account based on: *Hist. Ascension, Collier Row* (1945); E.R.O., Library Folder (Havering), obit. of Rev. J. H. Pemberton: Cutting from *C. Row Par. Mag.* Jan. 1929.
[98] For the school see *V.C.H. Essex*, v. 300.
[99] For the estates see *V.C.H. Essex*, v. 290 and above, p. 69.
[1] E.R.O., D/CPc 208; E.R.O., D/CP 3/44; D/CC 79/14.
[2] Paragraph based on: St. John, Mawneys, *Souvenir of Stone Laying* (1927) and *Dedication of Extension* (1932).
[3] E.R.O., D/CPc 216; D/CC 79/15.
[4] C.C.L., Bp. Inskip's Recs. iii. 127.
[5] Ex. inf. Rev. D. Dixon.
[6] *Brentwood Review*, 21 Nov. 1975.
[7] *Chel. Dioc. Y.B.* (1929).
[8] E.R.O., D/CPc 257.
[9] E.R.O., D/CPc 275; D/CC 88/6.
[10] Ibid. D/CE 84; C.C.L., Bp. Inskip's Recs. ii. 48; *Chel. Dioc. Y.B.* (1934 and later edns.).
[11] E.R.O., D/CC 85/6; D/CPc 274.
[12] *Kelly's Dir. Essex* (1894); foundation stone.
[13] E.R.O., D/CPc 268.
[14] E.R.O., D/CC 103/6; D/CPc 310; *Chel. Dioc. Y.B.* (1936 and later edns.).
[15] C.C.L., Bp. Inskip's Recs., ii. 266.
[16] Inf. from Church Com.; E.R.O., D/CP 8/26.
[17] E.R.O., D/CPc 342; *Chel. Dioc. Y.B.* (1954 and later edns).

The church of *ST. PAUL*, Harold Hill, Petersfield Avenue, was built in 1953 for the eastern half of the new L.C.C. estate.[18] Churchmen from Harold Wood, in Hornchurch, helped with the work, and in 1954 that part of Harold Hill was transferred to Harold Wood parish.[19] A conventional district was assigned to St. Paul in 1955, and a separate parish, taken from Harold Wood, in 1956.[20]

The church of *ST. JAMES*, Collier Row, Chase Cross Road, which succeeded the Calvary mission of Havering, was built in 1956 and was assigned a separate parish, taken from the Ascension, Collier Row (main part), Romford, and Havering; the advowson of the vicarage was vested in the bishop of Chelmsford.[21]

The church of *ST. AUGUSTINE*, Rush Green, Birkbeck Road, originated in 1946 as a mission of St. Andrew, Romford.[22] In 1948 a hut was erected at the corner of Birkbeck and Rush Green Roads, and in 1953 a conventional district was formed. A dual-purpose church was built in 1958, and a hall was added in 1965. A separate parish, taken from the parishes of St. Andrew, Romford, St. Peter and St. Paul, Dagenham, and Holy Cross, Hornchurch, was formed in 1969. The advowson of the vicarage was vested in the bishop of Chelmsford.

ROMAN CATHOLICISM. In 1852 a cottage in Church Lane was registered for Roman Catholic worship.[23] The church of *ST. EDWARD*, Park End Road, was built in 1856 by William Petre, Lord Petre.[24] A day-school was built in the same year.[25] St. Edward's was one of the first Roman Catholic churches built in south Essex since the Reformation, and for many years it served a wide area. The convent of the Sisters of Mercy, Western Road, was founded in 1908.[26]

At Harold Hill a priest started work in 1949, when the first houses were being built on the L.C.C. estate.[27] A new parish was formed in 1952. In 1953, with Mass attendances averaging about 1,000, a church hall was opened in Petersfield Avenue. The church of the *MOST HOLY REDEEMER*, adjoining the hall, was completed in 1964.[28] It is of variegated brick with roof-line canted up to the tall west front, which is mainly of glass.

A new parish for the western side of Harold Hill was formed in 1954, and the church of *ST. DOMINIC*, Straight Road, was opened in 1956.[29] There is a primary day-school attached to this church.

At Collier Row a new parish was formed in 1952.[30] A church hall was registered in Lowshoe Lane in 1955, and the church of *CORPUS CHRISTI*, adjoining it, in 1965. There is a primary day-school attached to this church.

At Gidea Park a new parish was formed in 1963. The church of *CHRIST THE ETERNAL HIGH PRIEST*, Brentwood Road, was opened in the same year.[31] It is an octagonal building of brown brick with a central spirelet.

PROTESTANT NONCONFORMITY. There have been nonconformists at Romford since the later 17th century. In 1672 Samuel Deakin was licensed to conduct worship in the house of George Locksmith there, and William Blackmore to do so in his own house at Hare Street; at the same time the houses of William Mascall, surgeon, and William Wood, both at Romford, were also licensed for Presbyterians.[32] Deakin (d. 1676) and Blackmore (d. 1684) were both buried at Romford.[33] Nothing certain is known of Deakin's earlier career. Blackmore, a prominent Presbyterian, had been ejected in 1662 from St. Peter's, Cornhill (Lond.).

In 1690 Edward Whiston of Romford, 'aged and poor and no constant meeting', began to receive an annual grant from the Presbyterian and Independent Common Fund.[34] This was continued at least until 1693, and in 1691–3 the Fund also made a grant to Edward Kighley for lecturing to Whiston's congregation.[35] Whiston and Kighley both had connexions also with the Presbyterian congregation at Aldborough Hatch, Ilford.[36] Whiston died in 1697.[37] His work probably led to the foundation of Romford Independent (now United Reformed) church.[38]

In the late 17th century there were also some Quakers at Romford. Among their leaders was William Mead (d. 1713) who about 1684 bought the manor of Gooshayes at Harold Hill, then called Harold Wood, and lived there with his wife Sarah, who was the stepdaughter of George Fox (d. 1691).[39] In his later years Fox visited Gooshayes several times. By 1691 there was a small Friends' meeting at Harold Hill, belonging to the Barking monthly meeting. In 1695 the monthly meeting decided that Harold Hill should be reduced to the status of a 'retired' meeting, attended only by those too infirm to travel to public meetings farther away. The monthly meeting continued to meet occasionally at Harold Hill up to 1701. In 1709 the Friends applied

[18] Inf. from Church Comm.
[19] E.R.O., D/CPc 318.
[20] E.R.O., D/CP 8/27; D/CPc 335; *Chel. Dioc. Y.B.* (1954 sqq.).
[21] E.R.O., D/CPc 329; Inf. from Church Com.; *Chel. Dioc. Y.B.* (1955 and later edns.). For the Calvary mission see above p. 25.
[22] Paragraph based on: S. A. B. Vernon-Penrose, Hist. St. Augustine's (duplicated TS.); *Chel. Dioc. Y.B.* (1948 and later edns.); E.R.O., D/CP 16/24.
[23] G.R.O., Returns Noncf. Mtg. Hos. cert. to Bps. Cts. before 1852, dioc. Rochester, Bps. Ct. Chelmsford, no. 62.
[24] H.R.L., Romford L.B. Mins, 13 July 1855; E.R.O., D/DP E71; G.R.O., Worship Reg. 7370.
[25] See p. 93.
[26] *Brentwood Dioc. Mag.* ix. 61.
[27] Account based on: *Souvenir, New Catholic Church Hall* Harold Hill (1953); G.R.O., Worship Reg. 64111, 69747; *Brentwood Dioc. Yr. Bk.* (1953) 37, 59.
[28] Illustrated in *Universe* (Suppl.), 28 Mar. 1969.
[29] *Cath. Dir.* (1973); G.R.O. Worship Reg. 65854; E.R.O., Libr. Vertical Folder.
[30] Account based on: *Brentwood Dioc. Yr. Bk.* (1953), 37, 59; G.R.O. Worship Reg. 64808, 70271; *Universe* (Suppl.), 28 Mar. 1969.
[31] *Cath. Dir.* (1973); G.R.O. Worship Reg. 69376; *Universe* (Suppl.), 28 Mar. 1969.
[32] G. L. Turner, *Orig. Recs. Early Noncf.*, i. 241, 248, 288–9, 292, 440, 456, 462, 568, 598–9; ii. 931; iii. 501.
[33] A. G. Matthews, *Calamy Revised*, 60, 161; Smith, *Eccl. Hist. Essex*, 403–4.
[34] A. Gordon, *Freedom after Ejection*, 40.
[35] A. G. Matthews, *Calamy Revised*, 307.
[36] *V.C.H. Essex*, v. 231; Smith, *Eccl. Hist. Essex*, 381, 399.
[37] *Calamy Revised*, 524.
[38] See below.
[39] This paragraph is based on: Friends Ho., Mins. Barking M.M. 1691–1734; W. Beck and T. F. Ball, *London Friends' Mtgs.*, 278–9; *D.N.B.* s.v. William Mead.

to quarter sessions to license for meetings the house of William Smith at Romford.[40] Nothing permanent resulted from this. Sarah Mead, who died in 1714, left £100 for building a meeting-house at Romford or Harold Hill. This legacy was an embarrassment to the monthly meeting, which in 1718 declared that the few Friends living in those areas attended the Barking meeting, which was itself small and poor.[41] They asked that the legacy should be made available for the general charitable purposes of the monthly meeting. Sir Nathaniel Mead, Sarah's executor, eventually agreed to this, and the money was handed over in 1732.

For most of the 18th century the Independent church, then in Collier Row Lane (North Street) was the only dissenting place of worship in Romford. Another Independent church, opened in 1798, was merged with North Street in 1818. The first Wesleyan Methodist church in the town was opened in 1827, and the first Baptist church in 1836. By the end of the 19th century there were also Primitive Methodist, Salvation Army, and Catholic Apostolic churches, and several undenominational missions. In 1972 there were 28 registered places of worship. They included 6 Baptist, 4 Methodist, 2 United Reformed, 1 Quaker, and 2 Salvation Army. The remainder belonged mainly to fundamentalist or Pentecostal sects, which accounted for 12 out of the 23 churches opened since the First World War.

BAPTISTS. Salem church, London Road, was founded in 1836 with 13 members, most of whom had previously worshipped at Ilford.[42] Early meetings were held in a schoolroom in the market-place belonging to John R. Ward.[43] Thomas Kendall, from Ilford, was the first pastor (1836–47). In 1840 a small chapel was built on part of the old barrack ground in London Road. Dissension arose, and in 1847 some of the members, led by Kendall, seceded to form a church at Chadwell Heath.[44] In the same year, however, those remaining at Salem built a larger chapel adjoining the earlier building. Another secession took place in 1852. During the ministries of Joseph Davis (1866–79) and J. M. Steven (1879–1913) the church prospered. A hall was added in 1868,[45] and shortly before the First World War Salem opened the Pretoria Road mission, later Mawneys Baptist church. After the war the membership of Salem increased, and in 1934 a new church was built in Main Road. It was originally intended that the old Salem should be retained as the Sunday school of Main Road, but in 1936 it was reconstituted as a separate church, which still survives. Salem is a yellow-brick building with the date 1847 under the roof pediment.

Main Road, now called Romford Baptist church, has grown steadily, and by 1971, with 594 members, was one of the largest Baptist churches in England.[46] It has founded two other churches, at Chase Cross and Dagenham, and helped to form a third, at Harold Hill.[47]

Zoar (Strict) church, Market Place, later North Street, originated in 1849, when Samuel Ford's house was registered for worship by H. W. Tydeman, minister of the New London Road, Chelmsford, church.[48] A chapel seating 40 was opened in 1850 in part of a building at the entrance to Ducking Stool Alley, nearly opposite the Laurie Hall.[49] Zoar is thought to have been joined in 1852 by seceders from Salem.[50] It appears to have moved to North Street by 1871, and to have closed soon after.[51]

Romford Common chapel, Harold Wood Hall, originally Congregational, was taken over about 1866 by the Baptists of the Metropolitan Tabernacle (Lond.).[52] It was still active in 1882.[53] In that year the Baptists opened a church at Hornchurch,[54] and they apparently gave up the Romford Common chapel soon after.[55]

Mawneys church, Pretoria Road, originated in 1910 as a mission of Salem. The original iron hall was replaced by a brick building in 1928, and a separate church was formed in 1931.[56]

Zoar (Strict) church, Carlisle Road, was formed in 1927.[57] It was originally in Hornchurch Road, but had moved by 1936 to Albert Road.[58] The present building was erected in 1953.[59]

Chase Cross church, Chase Cross Road, originated in 1936, as a mission of Romford (Main Road); a permanent building was opened in 1961.[60]

Harold Hill church, Taunton Road, originated in 1950, when the Baptists of Main Road and the Congregationalists of South Street opened a joint Sunday school at Harold Hill.[61] This collaboration continued until 1955, when the Baptists built Taunton Road.[62]

METHODISTS. Trinity (Wesleyan) church, Mawney Road (now Angel Way), originated by 1827 when a chapel was built in High Street.[63] The first resident minister was John Smith (1828–30), whose brilliant career, cut short by death, was long remembered in Romford.[64] By 1829 the church, then in the Spitalfields

[40] E.R.O., Q/SBb 44/50.

[41] For the Barking meeting see *V.C.H. Essex*, v. 231–2.

[42] *Baptist Mag.* 7 July 1836.

[43] Unless otherwise stated this account is based on: Romford Bapt. Ch., *The First Hundred Years*; E.R.O., T/Z 8 (Notes by W. T. Whitley); W. T. Whitley, *Baptists of London*, 162, 170; H.R.L., Cornell MSS., s.v. Salem; E.R.O., D/NB 2/1.

[44] Kendall is also said to have been connected with Ebenezer Strict Baptist church, Ilford: *V.C.H. Essex*, v. 298.

[45] *Wilson & Whitworth's Romford Almanack* (1902), 52.

[46] Romford Bapt. Ch., *First Hundred Years; Bapt. Hndbk.* (1971).

[47] See below, and *V.C.H. Essex*, v. 298.

[48] G.R.O. Returns Noncf. Mtg. Hs. cert. to Bps. Cts. before 1852, Rochester dioc., Ct. at Chelmsford, no.25.

[49] H.O. 129/7/197; H.R.L., 'Notes on Romford Town Centre' (*c.* 1908), 3 (where the church is called 'Zion').

[50] W. T. Whitley, *Baptists of London*, 162.

[51] *Bapt. Handbk.* (1871); *Kelly's Dir. Essex* (1874).

[52] W. T. Whitley, *Baptists of London*, 162; O.S. Map, 6", Essex LXVII (surv. 1866).

[53] *Strat. Expr.* 15 Apr. 1882.

[54] See p. 50.

[55] *Bapt. Handbk.* (1885) is the last to list it. Early in the 20th century the chapel was used for private worship by the owners and staff of Harold Wood Hall: *Romford Record*, iv. 44.

[56] D. Witard, *Bibles in Barrels*, 168–9; E.R.O., D/NB 2/3 and 4.

[57] W. T. Whitley, *Baptists of London*, 258; E.R.O., T/Z 8.

[58] G.R.O. Worship Reg. 56606.

[59] Foundation stone.

[60] Witard, *Bibles in Barrels*, 169; E.R.O., D/NB 2/3 and 4; G.R.O. Worship Reg. 56827.

[61] W. W. Biggs, *Romford Cong. Ch.* 29–30.

[62] *Bibles in Barrels*, 170; E.R.O., D/NB 2/4.

[63] H.O. 129/7/197; Char. Com. Files. Unless otherwise stated this paragraph is based on E. Barrett, *The Lamp still Burns*, 23.

[64] Terry, *Romford*, 239.

circuit, had 80 members and a regular congregation of 260.[65] It was in the Romford circuit 1833–48, and later in the Barking and Romford 1848–77, Romford 1877–1908, Ilford 1908–47, and the new Romford circuit from 1947.[66] The Romford society was affected by the Wesleyan Reform movement. In 1850 John Hornstead, society steward and trustee, was among the delegates to the Reform meeting at Albion chapel, Moorgate (Lond.).[67] He also appears among the local preachers on a plan of the 3rd and 8th London (Wesleyan Reform) circuits for 1852.[68] This indicates that he had seceded from High Street. The nearest Reform chapel on the 1852 plan was at Becontree Heath, in Dagenham.[69] The Romford society, however, remained loyal to the old connexion, and in 1867 built a new schoolroom.[70] In 1887 the old chapel was sold to the Salvation Army, and in 1888 the present Trinity church, seating 600, was built at a cost of £3,400.[71] It was well placed in Mawney Road, on the growing Mawneys estate. A school was built in 1899. In 1906 Trinity was the centre of a free church mission that led to the 'Romford revival.'[72] New vestries were added in 1923, and further extensive alterations were carried out in 1936. At that period one of the church leaders was Thomas England, the estate developer. Trinity was damaged by bombing in 1940.[73] The construction of St. Edward's Way (1970) has left the church awkwardly isolated on the southern edge of that ring road.

Ebenezer (Wesleyan) church, The Lawn, Collier Row, was registered in 1877.[74] In the 1880s it was described as unsectarian. It appears to have ceased about 1890.[75]

Victoria Road (Primitive) church originated about 1873, when missionaries came from Grays.[76] A permanent building was erected in 1875. It was in the Grays and Romford circuit until 1935, the Ilford circuit 1935–47, and then the Romford circuit. It was wrecked by bombing during the Second World War, was rebuilt in 1950, but closed in 1966.[77]

Harold Hill church, Dagnam Park Drive, originated in 1950, when members of the Harold Wood church, under the Revd. Leslie W. Gray, started open air services on the new L.C.C. estate.[78] A school-church was built in 1953 with the aid of 'portable' war damage compensation from the former Grove Methodist church at Stratford, in West Ham.[79] A foundation stone from the Grove (1873) is incorporated in the Harold Hill building.

Collier Row church, Clockhouse Lane, was planned in 1939, when the site was bought with funds from the sale of Chadwell Heath church.[80] About 1950 the Romford circuit started mission work at Collier Row, and in 1954 the church was built.[81]

Havering Road church, Moray Way, Rise Park, originated in 1957, when a hall, in the Romford circuit, was registered.[82] The church was built beside the hall in 1974.[83] It is of snuff-coloured brick, with full-height windows across each corner, giving an octagonal plan; there is a central spirelet.

UNITED REFORMED AND EARLIER CONGREGATIONAL CHURCHES. Romford United Reformed church, Western Road, probably originated in the work of Edward Whiston and other Presbyterians in the late 17th century.[84] In 1700 a meeting at Stewards, Romford, was registered by Independents.[85] Stewards, a manor house in Hornchurch Road (South Street) was demolished shortly before September 1717.[86] In August of that year Peter Goodwin, Independent minister, conveyed to trustees a meeting-house in Collier Row Lane (North Street). William Sheldon, minister 1732–63, took charge also of the Independent meeting at Havering Well, in Hornchurch, which from that time was permanently attached to Romford. During the pastorate of Thomas Ellis, 1771–7, who held unitarian views, the church is thought to have declined, but it was revived by his successor, Thomas Strahan (1777–1825), who as a layman had worshipped with the Calvinistic Methodists at Moorfields Tabernacle (Lond.). By the end of the 18th century the Collier Row Lane and Havering Well churches together had endowments producing £35 a year, mostly for the maintenance of the minister.

In 1819 the Collier Row Lane church united with Bethel chapel, Hornchurch Lane.[87] The Collier Row Lane building was demolished, and the Union chapel was built on the same site in 1823.[88] Samuel H. Carlisle, minister 1827–52, was an unbalanced and quarrelsome Scotsman.[89] His control of the endowments made it almost impossible to dismiss him, and in 1846 a large part of his flock seceded to form Coverdale chapel.[90] After Carlisle's death the two churches re-united. Frederick Sweet, 1864–1902, was an outstanding minister, serving also as chairman of Romford school board, and as a leader of the local Liberal party.[91] In 1877 a new church was opened on a prominent site in South Street.[92] It was built in Early English style, of brick faced with Kentish ragstone, to the design of E. C. Allam of Romford. The 1819 building was later a Salvation Army hall, an Anglican mission, a printing works (*c.* 1900–20), and finally a Peculiar People's chapel; it was demolished about 1934.[93]

[65] E.R.O., Q/CR 3/2/89.
[66] *Hall's Circuits and Ministers*, 178, 256, 400.
[67] Meth. Arch. Dept., Wes. Reform Tracts, *The Delegates Tested*. For Hornstead see also: Char. Com. Files. H.O. 129/7/197.
[68] Meth. Arch. Dept., *Circuit Plans*.
[69] *V.C.H. Essex*, v. 297.
[70] *Wesleyan Chapel Cttee. Reps.* (1867); Char. Com. Files.
[71] *Wes. Chap. Cttee. Reps.* (1890).
[72] S. Roberts, *Romford in the 19th century*, 40.
[73] *Methodist Census* (1940).
[74] G.R.O. Worship Reg. 23690.
[75] Ibid.; *Kelly's Dir. Essex* (1882 and later edns.).
[76] Account based on: Petty, *Hist. P.M. Connexion*, 619; E. Barrett, *The Lamp still Burns*, 39.
[77] Foundation stone; inf. from Revd. G. Maland.
[78] *Harold Wood Meth. Ch. 21st. Anniversary* (1950), 4.
[79] *V.C.H. Essex*, vi. 133; G.R.O. Worship Reg. 64198.
[80] E. Barrett, *The Lamp still Burns*, 42, 45; *V.C.H. Essex*, v. 298.
[81] *Romford Meth. Circuit Plans* (1952–3); Worship Reg. 64494.
[82] G.R.O. Worship Reg. 66461.
[83] Foundation stone.
[84] See above.
[85] G.R.O. Returns. Noncf. Mtg. Hs. cert. to Bps. Cts. bef. 1852, London dioc. no. 123. Unless otherwise stated the following account is based on: J. P. Longstaff, *Hist. Cong. Ch. Romford* (1913); W. W. Biggs, *Cong. Ch. Romford* (1962); E.R.O., D/NC 4/2 (Church Bk. 1779–1857).
[86] See p. 72.
[87] For Bethel see below.
[88] *Evang. Mag.* N.S. i (1823), 113. Illus. in Biggs, op. cit.
[89] G. Terry, *Romford*, 244.
[90] Cf. *Cong. Yr. Bk.* (1847), 172.
[91] Ibid. (1903), 201–2 (obituary).
[92] Ibid. (1877), 488.
[93] *Strat. Expr.* 27 Aug. 1881, 1 Nov. 1882; *Kelly's Dir. Essex* (1886 and later edns.); inf. from Mr. A. E. Searle.

The new church in South Street was gutted by fire in 1883, but was rebuilt in the same year. A hall and schoolrooms were added in 1884, and the old Coverdale building in North Street was then sold. South Street supported the mission at Chadwell Heath, Dagenham, from 1896 to 1901, and in 1906 helped to form a new church at Emerson Park, Hornchurch.[94] In 1910 the hall was enlarged, partly with money given by an American grandson of Samuel H. Carlisle, and was renamed the Carlisle institute. By that time the membership was over 200. During the ministry of T. Sinclair Phillips, 1920–37, it rose to a peak of over 400.[95] After the Second World War mission work was undertaken on the Harold Hill estate, leading to the formation of a new church in Heaton Way. In 1965 the South Street buildings were sold for redevelopment and a new church was built in Western Road.[96] This is a polygonal building of red brick with central spirelet. There are halls behind it. In 1971 the membership was 180.[97]

Bethel Independent chapel, Hornchurch Lane (South Street), appears to have originated in 1792, when John Ping and others registered for worship the house of Hannah Gray in that road.[98] A chapel was built in the same road in 1796.[99] It was joined by a congregation which since 1794 had been meeting in a cottage at Becontree Heath.[1] The first minister, Henry Attely, 1798–*c.* 1805, was active also in Rainham, Upminster, and Dagenham.[2] He established friendly relations with the Collier Row Lane church and in 1819, after the departure of his successor, Bethel united with the older church. After the building of the Union church in 1823 Bethel was sold.

Coverdale Independent chapel, Collier Row Lane (North Street), originated in 1846, in a secession from the Union chapel.[3] With help from the Essex Congregational Union a small chapel was opened in 1847 almost opposite the Union chapel. The split was healed in 1853, when the 20 members of Coverdale re-united with the 28 of the Union chapel. The Coverdale building was retained by the Union chapel, and was used as a Sunday school until 1884. It was sold in 1887 and converted into a dwelling.[4]

Romford Common Congregational chapel seems to have originated in 1861, when a schoolroom at Harold Wood Hall was registered for worship.[5] It was taken over by the Baptists about 1866.[6]

A Congregational meeting existed at Collier Row in the 1870s.[7]

Heaton Way United Reformed church originated in 1950, when the Congregationalists of South Street and the Baptists of Main Road opened a joint Sunday school at Harold Hill.[8] The Baptists departed to Taunton Road in 1955.[9] The Congregationalists, after many setbacks, formed their own church in 1960, and in 1962 completed the building in Heaton Way.

Other Churches and Missions. The Catholic Apostolic church, Manor Road, originated in 1867, when a house in High Street was registered for worship.[10] Meetings were held in the Laurie Hall, Market Place, from 1869 until about 1894, when an iron church was built in Manor Road.[11] In 1962 that church was re-registered as the undenominational Manor Hall.[12]

The Salvation Army opened fire in Romford in 1881. Its missionaries reported a hostile reception in this 'brewery blighted' town.[13] Their headquarters were at first in North Street, in the old Union (Congregational) chapel (1881–2), and its schoolroom, formerly Coverdale chapel.[14] Among their supporters were Mr. and Mrs. C. S. Read, of Holm Lodge, London Road, who are said to have been formerly members of the community of Agapemonites.[15] In 1886 there was a Salvation Army tent at Holm Lodge.[16] In 1887 the Army took over the old Wesleyan chapel in High Street.[17] That remained in use until 1967, when a new citadel was built to replace it.[18] The old building was demolished to make room for the roundabout linking High Street and London Road with St. Edward's Way. The new citadel was built farther east in High Street, to the design of Ernest J. Lipscomb.[19] Its most striking feature is a tall circular building used for the Sunday school. This has windows of coloured glass framed by longitudinal fins of concrete. In North Romford the Salvation Army had a hall in Collier Row Road, 1937–41, and then in Chase Cross Road, registered 1942.[20] In 1963 it built a hall in Oxford Road, Harold Hill.[21]

Brazier's Yard mission, High Street, was opened in 1884 for undenominational religious and temperance work among the poor.[22] Mrs. Read, the founder, was no doubt the friend of the Salvation Army mentioned above. The original mission room was replaced in 1894 by a hall made from three cottages, and two other cottages were later bought for use as classrooms. In 1912 the mission moved to the old Albion Street school. It appears to have closed during the 1920s.

94 *V.C.H. Essex*, v. 298.
95 *Cong. Yr. Bk.* (1910 sqq.).
96 E.R.O., *Sale Cat.* B3891; G.R.O. Worship Reg. 70072.
97 *Cong. Yr. Bk.* (1971).
98 Smith, *Havering*, 279.
99 Ibid.
1 W. W. Biggs, *Cong. Ch. Romford*, 17–18, on which the remainder of this account is based; *Evang. Mag.* iv. (1796), 513. For Becontree Heath see *V.C.H. Essex*, v. 297.
2 At Dagenham Attely was described in one source as a Methodist: *V.C.H. Essex*, v. 297.
3 Account based on: W. W. Biggs, *Cong. Ch. Romford*, 20–1; *Cong. Yr. Bk.* (1847), 172; Char. Com. Files.
4 E.R.O., D/NC 4/4; Romford L.B. Mins., 5 Sept. 1887; J. P. Longstaff, *Hist. Cong. Ch. Romford*, 53.
5 G.R.O. Worship Reg. 11658. For the building, later Baptist, see: O.S. Map 6″, Essex, LXVII (surv. 1866); E.R.O., Sage Coll. *Sale Cats.* vol. i, no. 3, vol. 3, no. 2. For the school see below, p. 95.
6 See above.
7 *Cong. Yr. Bk.* (1872–9.).
8 Biggs, *Cong. Ch. Romford*, 29–30.
9 See above.
10 G.R.O. Worship Reg. 18256.
11 Ibid. 19250 and 39100; *Kelly's Dir. Essex* (1898 and later edns. to 1937); *Wilson & Whitworth's Romford Almanack* (1902); *Romford Official Guide* (1951); E.R.O., D/F 5/11/3, 17 Feb. 1894.
12 G.R.O. Worship Reg. 68638.
13 *Strat. Expr.* 5 Mar. 1881.
14 Ibid. 27 Aug. 1881, 1 Nov. 1882, 21 Feb. 1883; H.R.L. 'Notes on Romford Town Centre', 25.
15 H.R.L., Cornell MSS. (s.v. Holm Lodge).
16 G.R.O. Worship Reg. 29660.
17 Ibid. 30548; E. Barrett, *The Lamp still Burns*, 23.
18 S. Roberts, *Romford in the 19th century*, 42; G.R.O. Worship Reg. 70931.
19 Foundation stone.
20 G.R.O. Worship Reg. 57375, 60047.
21 Ibid. 69012.
22 Account based on: S. Roberts, *Romford in the 19th century*, 43; *Wilson & Whitworth's Romford Almanack* (1902); G.R.O. Worship Reg. 28165; *Kelly's Dir. Essex* (1914 and later edns.).

Romford Town mission was founded about 1886.[23] James Finley, who had been dismissed from his post as a lay missioner at St. Edward's church, continued evangelical work under an undenominational committee whose chairman for many years was J. W. Lasham, a local chemist.[24] Meetings were held at first in a cottage on the Mawneys estate, but by 1895 had been transferred to the Laurie Hall. The mission's aims were similar to those of Brazier's Yard. It was supported for a time by the Country Towns Mission. Finley died in 1906, but his widow Maria carried on the work for several years. The mission met at the Regent Hall, Market Place, *c.* 1913–29, and later at the Ingrave Hall, Ingrave Road. It appears to have ceased about 1933.

Richmond Road Evangelical, formerly Peculiar People's, church originated in the 1920s with meetings in the old Congregational (Union) chapel, North Street.[25] The new church, built in Richmond Road, was registered in 1934.[26] Harold Hill Evangelical Free church, Bridgewater Road, and Collier Row Gospel mission, Mowbrays Road, which belong to the Fellowship of Independent Evangelical churches, were both opened in 1956.[27] The Evangelical church, Brentwood Road, is treated under Hornchurch.

Romford Christian Spiritualist church, St. Edward's Way (formerly Church Lane), originated in 1923.[28] Meetings were held at first in a hall in Brooklands Road (1923–8). A church was built in Church Lane in 1929. The congregation increased, and in 1937 a larger church was built behind the previous one, which became a hall.

The Friends' meeting-house, Balgores Crescent, Gidea Park, originated in 1934, when a particular meeting was formed in Romford.[29] Early meetings were held in Brentwood Road and later, from 1944, in Victoria Road.[30] The present meeting-house was built in 1961.[31] It comprises a range of yellow-brick buildings, including a warden's house in a secluded garden.

The Brethren have five halls in Romford. Ingrave hall, Ingrave Road, was apparently taken over from the Town Mission about 1933.[32] Rush Green hall, Birkbeck Road, and Collier Row hall, Collier Row Road, were both registered in 1936.[33] Rise Park hall, later chapel, Pettits Lane North, was first registered in 1948.[34] The Carlisle room, Carlisle Road, was registered in 1963.[35]

The Jehovah's Witnesses registered premises in Victoria Road 1941–2, in Eastern Road 1951, and in Trowbridge Road, Harold Hill 1959.[36] Only the last was still in use in 1975.

Elim church, Wheatsheaf Road, appears to have originated in 1944, when the British Israel World Federation and Evangelical Church of England registered a hall, later known as Christ Church, in Victoria Road.[37] It was re-registered in 1948 by the Bible Pattern Church Fellowship, which in 1955 moved to Wheatsheaf Road [38] Elim was registered under that name in 1960.[39] The London City Mission registered a hall in Gooshays Drive, Harold Hill, in 1961.[40] Varley Memorial hall, Briar Road, Harold Hill, was registered by the Christian Community in 1962.[41]

JUDAISM.[42] Romford and District synagogue originated in 1933, when a congregation was formed. Temporary burial rights were granted by the United Synagogue in 1934. A synagogue hall in Palm Road was registered in 1938.[43] Activities were suspended during the Second World War. They were resumed after the war at a house in Eastern Road, and a permanent synagogue was built in the garden there in 1954.[44] In 1970 the old house was demolished and a larger synagogue was built on the site.[45]

Harold Hill and District Affiliated synagogue originated in 1953 when a congregation was formed. It became affiliated in 1954. Services were held in hired premises until 1958, when a pre-fabricated building was erected in Trowbridge Road.[46] In 1962 the side walls of the synagogue were rebuilt in brick, making it a permanent structure.

EDUCATION. There was a free school at Romford, kept by Thomas Horrocks, *c.* 1641–6.[47] A charity school, which survives as St. Edward's Church of England primary school, was founded in 1711. In the 1840s and 1850s another Church school, a British school, and a Roman Catholic school were opened in the town, a Church school at Noak Hill, and a railway factory school at Squirrels Heath.

A school board for Romford was formed compulsorily in 1872.[48] It took over the British school and built two new schools. A technical instruction committee was formed for Romford and Havering in 1891.[49] A report prepared for Essex county council in 1906 urged the provision of a secondary school in the town.[50] A county secondary school for

[23] Account based on: H.R.L., Newscuttings, obits. of Jas. Finley (1906); E.R.O., D/DU 681/5; *Wilson & Whitworth's Romford Almanack* (1902 sqq.); *Strat. Expr.* 15 June 1895; H.R.L., 'Notes on Romford Town Centre', 17, 40; *Romford Official Guide* (1908), frontispiece and pl. p. 31; *Kelly's Dir. Essex* (1912 and later edns.). There may have been an earlier town mission: *Kelly's Dir. Essex* (1874) lists R. J. Lavender as missioner.

[24] For Lasham see *Kelly's Dir. Essex* (1878 and later edns.).

[25] *Romford Official Guide* (1935); inf. from Mr. A. E. Searle; G.R.O. Worship Reg. 54111.

[26] G.R.O. Worship Reg. 55109.

[27] Ibid. 65813 and 65523.

[28] Account based on: H R.L., Short Notes on Foundation of Romford Christian Spiritualist church (TS); G.R.O. Worship Reg. 49105, 51485, 56835, 58201.

[29] Inf. from Friends' House, London.

[30] *Kelly's Dir. Essex* (1937); G.R.O. Worship Reg. 60832.

[31] Inf. from Friends' House; G.R.O. Worship Reg. 68462.

[32] G.R.O. Worship Reg. 54671; inf. from Mr. J. Howson; *Romford Official Guide* (1960), 63.

[33] G.R.O. Worship Reg. 46782, 46783, 57057; *Romford Official Guide* (1960), 63.

[34] G.R.O. Worship Reg. 61972, 66487; *Romford Official Guide*, (1960), 63.

[35] G.R.O. Worship Reg. 69089.

[36] Ibid. 59835, 60248, 63161, 67075.

[37] Ibid. 60800, 61214.

[38] Ibid. 61886, 65247.

[39] Ibid. 67904.

[40] Ibid. 68308.

[41] Ibid. 68820.

[42] This section is based mainly on inf. from the Secretary, United Synagogue.

[43] G.R.O. Worship Reg. no. 57819.

[44] Ibid. 62965; personal knowledge.

[45] Inf. from Revd. S. Beck.

[46] G.R.O. Worship Reg. no. 66706.

[47] Davids, *Nonconformity in Essex*, 422–5; Smith, *Eccl. Hist. Essex*, 380.

[48] Ed. 2/171; *Lond. Gaz.* 16 Jan. 1872 (no. 23818), p. 155.

[49] E.R.O., T/A 521/4.

[50] M. E. Sadler, *Sec. and Higher Educ. in Essex*, 380–4.

girls was opened in the same year, but there was no county secondary school for boys until 1921. Between 1906 and 1944 the county opened 5 primary schools, 4 secondary and senior schools, and a special school. Reorganization in line with the Hadow Report was completed by 1937. A church senior school was opened in 1936. Under the Education Acts, 1944 and 1946, Romford borough became an Excepted District. Between 1948 and 1965 one special, 11 primary, and 6 secondary schools were built, including 8 primary and 3 secondary schools on the new L.C.C. estate at Harold Hill. Two Roman Catholic primary schools were opened in 1953. By 1973 the London borough of Havering had reorganized the secondary schools as comprehensive schools, enlarged two of them, built a primary school, and established two special schools.

In the following chronological accounts of individual schools, information, unless otherwise stated, was provided by the Essex education department or that of Havering.

ELEMENTARY SCHOOLS FOUNDED BEFORE 1872. St. Edward's Church of England primary school, Havering Drive, was founded in January 1711 as a charity school for 40 boys and 20 girls.[51] The children were taught reading, writing, and arithmetic by a master and a mistress, and were provided with clothing. The school was supported by subscriptions and an annual sermon.[52] It may have opened in a room above the vestry in St. Edward's chapel, but by the end of 1711 the parish was renting a house for it. Two houses were rented from 1713 until 1726, when the boys moved to the court house and the girls to a room in the master's house.[53] The school attracted gifts and legacies which amounted to about £850 by the end of the 18th century.[54] In 1728 the trustees bought land in the market-place and built a school for 45 boys and 20 girls from Hornchurch and Romford. A master's house was built next to it in 1733. Joseph Bosworth, by his will dated 1730, gave the school a house and land in Hornchurch Lane (South Street). By 1804 the master and mistress were taking private boarding or day pupils as well as the charity children. William Higgs, by will proved 1811, left £50 stock to provide an annual dinner for the charity children; in 1835 the income was added to the general school funds. In 1833 a Chancery order empowered the governors to admit more children, from Romford, Hornchurch, or Havering. In 1834 the school was united with the National Society as St. Edward's school. A new schoolroom for 200 boys, opened in 1835, was added to the charity school by subscription and grants from the government and the National Society. The charity was extended to teach 90 and to clothe 65 children. In 1835 80 girls and 165 boys aged 6 to 13 were being taught on a monitorial system by a master and a mistress. The National school children wore distinctive badges and paid 1*d*. a week.[55] In 1842 a house was built for the mistress.[56] Charity clothing ceased in 1846 for lack of funds. In 1867 the school had 170 boys and 153 girls, of whom 45 boys and 20 girls were taught free.[57] The school was enlarged in 1853 and again in 1869.[58] It received annual government grants from 1866.[59] In 1871 an infants school for 74 was opened in an adjoining building, bought with charity funds. From 1891 girls and infants were taught free; boys paid 1*d*. a week until 1903. The infants school was enlarged in 1891 for 146. A Board of Education Scheme of 1906 required St. Edward's to be conducted as a public elementary school.[60] A Board Scheme of 1915 required the constitution of a higher education fund of £1,600. In 1916 the cottages on Bosworth's land were sold to raise money for a new school.[61] The new building, on land adjoining the original school, was at last completed in 1926. The old school and master's house were sold to Romford U.D.C. and later became a public library.[62] They were demolished in 1968.[63] Both were plain buildings of dark red brick. The school had at first-floor level, facing the street, two niches containing figures of a boy and a girl in 18th century charity school dress. These, and the old school bell, were in 1976 preserved at St. Edward's primary school.

In 1936 the juniors and infants were transferred to new buildings in Mercury Gardens, leaving the senior school in the 1926 buildings.[64] The schools were granted Aided status in 1954.[65] In 1976 St. Edward's primary school moved to new buildings in Havering Drive.[66]

St. Andrew's Church of England school, St. Andrew's Road, seems to have originated in 1835, when a National infants school was opened in the former girls' room at the charity school.[67] In 1843 a permanent infants school was built by subscription on a site later in St. Andrew's Road, to commemorate the baptism of the Prince of Wales.[68] A teacher's house was added in 1857.[69] By 1866 the school was attended by 119 boys and girls, and was receiving an annual government grant.[70] By 1876 it had been enlarged for 234.[71] In 1897 the infants moved to the old Albion Street school, where they remained until the opening of London Road council school in 1908. In 1910 the mixed school in St. Andrew's Road was described as the worst school in Essex; it was closed in 1912, when London

[51] S.P.C.K., Abstracts of letters, vol. 2, no. 2469. For the school see: F. Davis, *Story of St. Edward's schools, Romford* (1950); P. Lloyd, *St. Edward's C. of E. school, Romford* (1960). For the charity school clothing see: M. G. Jones, *The Charity School Movement*, 376, and Lloyd, op. cit. 4, 6.

[52] E.R.O., D/Q 24/1.

[53] E.R.O., T/A 521/1; D/Q 24/1.

[54] *Hist. Essex by Gent*, iv. 323–4; Lysons, *Lond.*, iv. 202.

[55] *Rep. Com. Char.* [108], pp. 731–5, (1837–8), xxv (1); E.R.O., D/Q 24/2, 3. An infants school started in 1835 became St. Andrew's school: see below.

[56] *Applications for grants for educ.* (*1840–43*), H.C. 444, pp. 42–3 (1843), xl.

[57] *Schs. Inquiry Com.* [3966], p. 411, H.C. (1867–8), xxviii (17).

[58] *Mins. Educ. Cttee. of Council 1852–3*, [1624], p. 315, H.C. (1852–3), lxxx; Ed. 49/2190.

[59] *Rep. Educ. Cttee. of Council 1866–7*, [3882], p. 571, H.C. (1867), xxii.

[60] E.R.O., D/Q 24/5, 6.

[61] Char. Com. Files; Ed. 49/2191.

[62] Char. Com. Files; E.R.O., D/Q 24/6. For the library see above, p. 82.

[63] *Hornchurch Hist. Soc. Newsletter*, Sept. 1968.

[64] E.R.O., D/Q 24/6.

[65] Char. Com. Files.

[66] Char. Com. Files; inf. from Vicar.

[67] E.R.O., D/Q 24/4.

[68] H.R.L., Cornell MSS.; Inscription on building.

[69] E.R.O., E/P 102.

[70] *Romford L.B. Mins.* 2 Jan. 1862; *Rep. Educ. Cttee. of Council, 1866–7*, [3882], p. 571, H.C. (1867), xxii.

[71] *Return of Schs. 1875–6*, [C. 1882] pp. 72–3, H.C. (1877), lxvii.

Road school was completed.[72] The 1843 school building still existed in 1976.

The British school, Albion Street. By 1839 Congregationalists had established a Sunday school for 30 children and a dame school for 32 in Angel Yard, High Street.[73] In 1848 a British day-school was opened at Coverdale chapel, North Street.[74] This was transferred in 1851 to new buildings in Queen Street, accommodating 150.[75] The school was supported by subscriptions and children's pence. By 1870 it was admitting only boys. It received annual government grants from 1870. In 1872 it was taken over by the newly-formed school board, which conducted it as a mixed school.[76] The school was enlarged in 1880 for 234.[77] It was replaced in 1896 by Mawney Road school. The old building was later used by St. Andrew's infants school, and in 1912 was sold to Brazier's Yard mission.[78]

St. Thomas's Church of England school, Church Road, Noak Hill, was built in 1848 by subscription and government grant for 96 children.[79] It received annual government grants from 1879.[80] It was reorganized in 1936 for mixed juniors and infants, and was granted Controlled status in 1954.[81]

St. Peter's (formerly St. Edward's) Roman Catholic junior mixed and infants school, Dorset Avenue. In 1852 there was a Roman Catholic school at Romford with 19 children.[82] A permanent school for 58 was built in 1856 in St. Edward's (later Laurie) Square.[83] It was receiving annual government grants from 1880.[84] In 1892 it was rebuilt for 112.[85] Attendance rose slowly from 24 in 1880 to 67 in 1911.[86] The school was granted Aided status in 1951.[87] It was reorganized in 1954 for juniors and infants. In 1968 it was renamed and moved to new buildings in Dorset Avenue.

The Factory Church of England school, Factory Road, Squirrels Heath, was founded in 1858 by the Eastern Counties Railway Co. for the children of its workers at the tarpaulin factory. Two terrace houses were adapted to accommodate 97 pupils.[88] The school was supported by subscriptions and, from 1876, annual government grants.[89] It was enlarged in 1895 for 128. It was closed in 1911 when Salisbury Road school was opened.[90]

ELEMENTARY SCHOOLS FOUNDED BETWEEN 1872 AND 1945. Manor junior mixed and infants school, Albert Road. Albert Road board school was opened in 1884 for 354.[91] It was enlarged in 1890 and 1903.[92] A handicraft centre was opened in 1913. The mixed department was reorganized for juniors in 1930 and amalgamated with the infants department in 1952. The school was renamed in 1956.[93]

Mawney junior and infants school, Mawney Road. Mawney Road board school was opened in 1896 with 740 places, to replace Albion Street school.[94] It was enlarged in 1907.[95] It was reorganized in 1936 for mixed juniors and infants.

Crowlands junior and infants school, London Road. London Road council school was opened in 1908 for 280 infants. The mixed department for 376 was opened in 1912.[96] The school was enlarged in 1931. In 1937 the seniors were transferred to Warren school, Dagenham.[97] The school was renamed in 1956.[98]

Squirrels Heath junior and infants school, Salisbury Road. Salisbury Road council school was opened in 1911 for 276. A separate infants department was built in 1914–15.[99] The school was again enlarged in 1931, and in 1935 was reorganized for mixed juniors and infants. It was renamed in 1956.[1] A new school was built in 1974 on a neighbouring site.[2]

Parklands junior mixed and infants school, Havering Road. Havering Road council school was opened in 1929 in temporary buildings for juniors. A permanent infants department was built in 1931, and a permanent junior department in 1936.[3] The school was damaged by bombs in the Second World War.[4] It was renamed in 1956.[5]

Clockhouse junior and infants school, Clockhouse Lane, Collier Row. Clockhouse Lane council school was opened in 1934 in temporary premises. Permanent buildings for juniors and infants were opened in 1936. The school was enlarged in 1939, 1948, and 1950.[6]

Hilldene junior and infants school, Grange Road and Straight Road. Straight Road council school was opened in 1940 for juniors and infants. In 1949 a new school for juniors was built on an adjacent site in Grange Road to accommodate children from the Harold Hill estate. The school was renamed in 1950.[7]

[72] Ed. 21/5324; 5327; Ed. 2/171.
[73] E.R.O., D/P 30/28/19; H.R.L., Cornell MSS.
[74] Char. Com. Files.
[75] The south end of Queen St. was later called Albion St.
[76] E.R.O., E/MM 40; E.R.O., D/AEM 2/8; Ed. 2/171.
[77] *Reps. Educ. Cttee. of Council 1879–80*, [C. 2562–I], p. 592–3, H.C. (1880), xxii; *1880–1* [C. 2948–I], p. 579, H.C. (1881), xxxii.
[78] Ed. 21/171.
[79] *Mins. Educ. Cttee. of Council 1849–50*, [1215], p. clxxxv, H.C. (1850), xliii.
[80] *Rep. Educ. Cttee. of Council, 1878–9*, [C. 2342–I], H.C. (1878–9), xxiii.
[81] E.R.O., C/ME 46, p. 500; C/ME 49, p. 277; C/ME 53, p. 455; C/ME 59, p. 360; C/ME 48, p. 390.
[82] *Ann. Rep. Catholic Poor Sch. Cttee.* (1852), 80.
[83] *Kelly's Dir. Essex* (1882), 255; *Return of Non-Provided Schs.*, H.C. 178, p. 27, (1906), lxxxvii.
[84] *Reps. Catholic Poor Sch. Cttee.* (1860–69); *Rep. Educ. Cttee. of Council 1880–1*, [2948–I], p. 579, H.C. (1881), xxxii; *Return of Schs. 1893* [C. 7529], p. 172, H.C. (1894), lxv.
[85] Ed. 21/5326.
[86] *Rep. Educ. Cttee. of Council 1880–1* [C. 2948–I], p. 579, H.C. (1881), xxxii; E.R.O., E/Z 2.
[87] E.R.O., C/ME 46, p. 18.
[88] Ed. 21/5323; *Romford Recorder*, 30 Oct. 1964, p. 48; O.S. Map 25", Essex, LXVI. 16 (1896 edn.).
[89] *Return of Schs.* 1893, [C. 7529], p. 172, H.C. (1894), lxv; *Rep. Educ. Cttee. of Council 1876–7*, [C. 1780–I], p. 771, H.C. (1877), xxix.
[90] Ed. 21/5323; E.R.O., C/ME 7, p. 246.
[91] *Kelly's Dir. Essex* (1886), 255.
[92] Ed. 21/5322; *Wilson and Whitworth's Romford Almanack* (1910), 60.
[93] E.R.O., C/ME 9, p. 829; C/ME 49, p. 761; C/ME 50, p. 443.
[94] H.R.L., Cornell MSS.; Ed. 21/5325.
[95] Ed. 2/171; Ed. 21/5325.
[96] Ed. 21/5324.
[97] Cf. *V.C.H. Essex*, v. 301; *Educ. in Essex* (1928–35), 118–9; E.R.O., C/ME 33, p. 501–2.
[98] E.R.O., C/ME 49, p. 761; C/ME 50, p. 443.
[99] Ed. 21/5329.
[1] E.R.O., C/ME 26, p. 337; C/ME 27, p. 476.
[2] *Havering Official Guide* (1973), 73.
[3] E.R.O., C/ME 25, p. 140; C/ME 27, p. 172; C/ME 30, pp. 228, 377–8.
[4] *Ordeal in Romford*, 25–7.
[5] E.R.O., C/ME 49, p. 761; C/ME 50, p. 443.
[6] E.R.O., C/ME 42, p. 385; C/ME 44, p. 307.
[7] E.R.O., C/ME 40, pp. 91–2, 727–8, 824; C/ME 44, p. 211.

SECONDARY AND SENIOR SCHOOLS FOUNDED BEFORE 1945. Frances Bardsley[8] comprehensive school, Brentwood Road and Heath Park Road, was formed in 1973 by the amalgamation of Romford county high school for girls and Heath Park secondary (modern) school for girls.[9] Romford county high school for girls was opened in 1906 at Claughton House, Eastern Road, a former private school. In 1910 it moved to new buildings in Heath Park Road.[10] In 1935 a new school was opened in Brentwood Road.[11] It was enlarged in 1963 and 1973.[12] Heath Park secondary (modern) school for girls was opened in 1935 as a senior council school for girls, in the former county high school buildings in Heath Park Road.[13]

The Royal Liberty school, Upper Brentwood Road, Gidea Park, was opened in 1921 as a county high school for boys at Hare Hall. It soon built up a good academic reputation. New buildings were added in 1929–30. In 1973 the school was enlarged and reorganized as comprehensive.[14]

Marshalls Park comprehensive school, Havering Drive and Pettits Lane, was formed in 1973 by the amalgamation of Romford county technical school and Pettits secondary (modern) school. Romford technical school, Havering Drive, originated in 1927 when Romford intermediate council school was opened at Mawney Road school to provide education with a commercial bias for 280 children aged 11–13. In 1930 it moved to new buildings in Havering Drive.[15] It became a technical school in 1945. In 1947 Marshalls Hall was bought to provide extra accommodation.[16] The school was enlarged in 1960 and 1964.[17] Pettits senior council, later secondary (modern) school was opened in 1936 and enlarged in 1945–6.

St. Edward's Church of England comprehensive school, London Road, originated in 1936 when a senior school was opened in the 1926 buildings at St. Edward's school.[18] The surplus of the higher education fund of the school charity was used to provide extra buildings. The school moved to new buildings in London Road in 1965.[19] It became comprehensive in 1972.[20]

PRIMARY SCHOOLS FOUNDED SINCE 1945. Gobions junior and infants schools, Havering Road North. The infants school was opened in 1952, and the junior school in 1953.[21] Bosworth junior and infants schools, Charlbury Crescent, Harold Hill, were opened in 1951. They were closed in 1974 because of fears of collapse through the use of high alumina cement in their construction. Dycorts junior and infants schools, Dagnam Park Drive and Settle Road, Harold Hill, were opened in 1951 in Dagnam Park Drive. In 1966 the infants school was closed and the junior school was amalgamated with the adjoining Priory school.[22] Mead junior and infants schools, Amersham Road, Harold Hill. The infants school was opened in 1951 and the junior school in 1952. Priory junior school, Settle Road, Pyrgo infants school, Tarnworth Road, and Broadford junior and infants school, Faringdon Avenue, all at Harold Hill, were opened in 1952.

St. Patrick's Roman Catholic junior and infants school, Lowshoe Lane, Collier Row, originated in 1953 with classes in the church hall. In 1960 it moved to permanent buildings and was granted Aided status.[23] St. Ursula's Roman Catholic junior and infants school, Straight Road, originated in 1953 with classes in the church hall in Petersfield Avenue.[24] The new infants department was built in 1955 and the junior department in 1957. The cost of building and staffing the school was undertaken by the Ursuline Sisters of Brentwood.[25]

Crownfield junior and infants schools, White Hart Lane, Collier Row, and Ingrebourne junior and infants schools, Taunton and Ashbourne Roads, Harold Hill, were opened in 1954–5.[26] Rise Park junior and infants schools, Annan Way, Rise Park, and Brookside junior and infants schools, Dagnam Park Drive, Harold Hill, were opened in 1956–7. Pinewood junior and infants schools, Thistledene Avenue, Collier Row, built by the London borough of Havering, were opened in 1967–8.

SECONDARY SCHOOLS FOUNDED SINCE 1945. Chase Cross comprehensive school, Havering Road North, was opened in 1949 as a mixed secondary (modern) school. It originally occupied the building intended for the new Gobions primary school. The boys department was completed in 1950. In 1955, when the girls building was completed, the school was reorganized for boys and girls separately. The schools were enlarged in 1962 and 1964.[27] In 1970 the boys and girls schools were again amalgamated, and in 1973 the school became comprehensive.[28]

Neave comprehensive school, Settle Road, Harold Hill, was formed in 1973 by the amalgamation of Harrowfield and Quarles secondary (modern) schools.[29] Harrowfield school, Settle Road, was opened in 1953–4. Quarles school, Tring Gardens, was opened in 1955. In 1972 Havering technical college began to take over the school buildings, and in 1976 the lower Neave (formerly Quarles) school moved to Settle Road.[30]

Bedfords Park comprehensive school, Appleby Drive and Broxhill Road, was formed in 1973 by the amalgamation of Harold Hill secondary (grammar) school and Broxhill secondary (modern) school.[31]

[8] First headmistress of Romford county high school.
[9] Inf. from school.
[10] S. Roberts, *Romford in the 19th century*, 29; E.R.O., C/ME 5, p. 154; *Wilson and Whitworth's Romford Almanack* (1910), 60, 62.
[11] E.R.O., C/ME 31, p. 136.
[12] *Educ. in Essex* (1960–64), p. 24; *Havering Official Guide* (1973), 75.
[13] E.R.O., C/ME 30, p. 676; inf. from Essex Educ. Dept.
[14] E.R.O., C/ME 16, p. 470; C/ME 17, pp. 181, 537, 749; C/ME 24, p. 193; *Havering Official Guide* (1973), 75; inf. from school. For Hare Hall see p. 62.
[15] E.R.O., C/ME 23, pp. 243–4; *Romford Guide* (1935); *V.C.H. Essex*, v. 299.
[16] E.R.O., C/ME 39A, p. 252; C/ME 39B, p. 383; C/ME 41, p. 703.
[17] *Educ. in Essex* (1956–60), p. 26; (1960–64), p. 26.
[18] E.R.O., D/Q 24/6.
[19] Char. Com. Files; inf. from Vicar.
[20] Inf. from school.
[21] E.R.O., C/ME 42, p. 677; C/ME 46, p. 695; *Educ. in Essex* (1945–52), 23.
[22] *Havering Official Guide* (1966–7), 39.
[23] E.R.O., C/ME 47, p. 461; C/ME 58, p. 473.
[24] E.R.O., C/ME 47, p. 679.
[25] *Harold Hill R.C. Church Souvenir* (1953).
[26] *Educ. in Essex* (1952–56), 21–2.
[27] E.R.O., C/ME 42, pp. 677, 701; C/ME 48, p. 616; *Educ. in Essex* (1945–52), 31; (1960–64), 23–4.
[28] Inf. from Headmaster.
[29] Inf. from school.
[30] Inf. from Mr. B. J. Townsend.
[31] Inf. from school.

Harold Hill secondary (grammar) school originated in 1955, when two grammar school streams were admitted to Quarles secondary (modern) school.[32] Permanent buildings were opened in Appleby Drive in 1958. Broxhill secondary (modern) school was opened in 1958 in temporary premises at Harrowfield and Bosworth schools. Permanent buildings were completed in 1959–60.[33]

Forest Lodge school, Lodge Lane, was opened in 1959 as North Romford Comprehensive school. It was the first comprehensive school in Essex. Permanent buildings were completed in 1960–1. The school was enlarged in 1970–1 and renamed in 1974.[34]

ADULT EDUCATION. Romford evening institute was being held at the intermediate (later technical) school, Havering Drive, by 1935. In 1966 it became North Romford college of adult education.[35]

SPECIAL SCHOOLS. Romford special school, Malvern Road, Hornchurch, originated in 1911 when a special class for mentally deficient children was opened at Salisbury Road school. In 1928 it was moved to a hut in Malvern Road. It was closed in 1934.[36] In 1962–3 four nursery classes for maladjusted children were opened at infant schools in Romford and Harold Hill. Havering Grange school, Havering Road North, was opened in 1963.[37] Dycorts school, Settle Road, Harold Hill, was opened in 1967 in the former Dycorts infants school.[38] Ravensbourne school, Neave Close, Faringdon Avenue, Harold Hill, was opened in 1972 in a former social services training centre. A unit for partially deaf children was opened at Broadford infants school in 1972.[39]

PRIVATE SCHOOLS.[40] In the 1670s Mr. Stonehouse kept a grammar school at Romford.[41] In 1793 there were 2 boarding schools in the town and in 1826 there were three. By 1838 there were at least 6 private schools. The number had doubled by 1870, and 14 are listed in 1886. In the 1970s there were 3 private schools in Romford.

The early schools were in Market Place, High Street, North Street, and London Road. After 1870 some schools were opened in the new roads south of the railway. Many of them were short-lived, but a few survived for more than 30 years. Delamare's Romford academy, Collier Row Lane (North Street), which existed *c.* 1798, survived until at least 1826 and may have been the boarding school listed up to 1870.[42] John Ward, a Baptist, had a private school in Queen's Head Yard in 1836 which was listed as a commercial school in 1838.[43] Albion Cottage school, St. Andrew's Road, which was started by 1848, was a boarding and day school until 1866 and a girls school until at least 1910.[44] Regent House academy, Market Place, existed in 1848 and still survived in 1890.[45] A school which was at Cecil House, Laurie Square, in 1899, may have originated in the school conducted by the Misses Trott in 1838.[46] There was a school at Harold Wood Hall in 1859; in 1876 its buildings were offered to, but rejected by Romford school board.[47] Emma White kept a school in Western Road from at least 1863 until 1899.

Romford grammar school was founded *c.* 1866 in Victoria Road and later moved to Claremont House, Junction Road. In 1886 it was conducted by John Spry, who also had a school in Walthamstow. It apparently closed before 1906. The building was used by Clark's College from *c.* 1937 to 1974, and subsequently by Raphael school.[48]

Romford high school, South Street, was founded in 1881. In 1906, when it had 90 boys, it was the only secondary school for boys in Romford.[49] It had closed by 1910. Mulley's commercial college, Eastern Avenue, which was founded in 1894, still existed in 1966.[50] A girls school at no. 38, Western Road existed in 1902 and survived until at least 1937. St. Mary's convent school, which was listed in 1966–7 as a school for infants and junior girls, was founded in 1908 as a girls high school by Sisters of Mercy from Brentwood.[51]

Gidea Park college, Balgores Lane, appears to have been founded *c.* 1914 in Balgores Square.[52] It was bought in 1919 by James Parkinson (d. 1958) and in 1924 was moved to the present buildings. In 1922 it was recognized as a preparatory school to the Royal Liberty school.[53] In 1976 it had about 200 boys and girls aged 4 to 11. The school was then owned by a private company controlled by the Parkinson family.

EDUCATIONAL CHARITY. The Revd. Frederick Sweet Memorial scholarship was founded in 1911 to provide scholarships for Romford children achieving the highest marks in the local education authority's junior scholarship examination. Sweet (d. 1902) had been a Congregational minister, and chairman of Romford school board.[54] A fund raised in recognition of Sweet's work in education was used to buy property in Golders Green (Lond.) providing an annual income of about £12. The freehold interest was sold in 1956. After the abolition of the exam-

[32] E.R.O., C/ME 49, p. 182.

[33] *Essex Education Bdg. Suppl.* July 1958, p. 5; Sept. 1960, pp. 2, 22–3.

[34] *Educ. in Essex* (1960–64), 22; inf. from school.

[35] *Romford Official Guide* (1935); inf. from college.

[36] E.R.O., C/ME 7, p. 338; C/ME 24, p. 810.

[37] E.R.O., C/ME 57, p. 137; inf. from Havering Educ. Dept.

[38] *Havering Official Guide* (1966–7), 45.

[39] Inf. from Hacton school and Havering Educ. Dept.

[40] Unless otherwise stated this section is based on: *Universal British Dir.* (*c.* 1798); *Pigot's Dir.* (1823–4, 1826–7); *Robson's Dir.* (1838); *White's Dir. Essex* (1848, 1963); *Kelly's Dir. Essex* (1855 and later edns.).

[41] E.R.O., T/A 141. Probably Robert Stonehouse, vicar of Childerditch 1666–83: Newcourt, *Repertorium*, ii. 146; E.R.O., T/P 81/2.

[42] E.R.O., *Educ. in Essex, 1710–1910*, illus. no. 11; *E.J.* ii. 30; *Greenwood's Map of Essex* (1824); E.R.O., D/CT 186.

[43] Romford Baptist Ch., *The First Hundred Years.*

[44] H.R.L., Cornell MSS.

[45] E.R.O., Sage Coll. 606; D/CT 186.

[46] *Strat. Expr.*, 19 Sept. 1883, p. 1; *Romford U.D.C. Mins.* 3 July 1899.

[47] *Kelly's Dir. Essex* (1859); E.R.O., Sage Coll. *Sale Cats.* vol. iii. 1, 2.

[48] *Strat. Expr.*, 23 June 1888, p. 6; 4 Jan. 1890, p. 1, 26 Dec. 1891, p. 6; *V.C.H. Essex*, vi. 296 n; *Daily Telegraph*, 1 Apr. 1974.

[49] *Strat. Expr.*, 28 Dec. 1889, p. 6; *Romford L.B. Mins.* 7 Nov. 1887; M. E. Sadler, *Sec. and Higher Educ. in Essex*, 384.

[50] *Havering Official Guide* (1966–7), 51.

[51] *Brentwood Dioc. Mag.*, ix. 61; *Havering Official Guide* (1966–7), 51.

[52] Account based on: *Kelly's Dir. Essex* (1914 and later edns.); inf. from Headmaster.

[53] E.R.O., C/ME 18, p. 244.

[54] See p. 89.

ination the income was used to support individual school projects. In 1976 the trustees of the United Reformed Church were accumulating the income for award to a project every 5 or 6 years.[55]

CHARITIES FOR THE POOR.[56] In 1837 the poor of Romford were benefiting from 6 charities providing £22 in bread and money given indiscriminately, a loan charity, and two apprenticeship charities, as well as the charity school[57] and Reede's alms-houses. By 1862 the combined income from the dole charities was being distributed in bread on St. Thomas's day. By a Charity Commission Scheme of 1899 the charities of Burleigh, Palmer, Reynolds, Webster, Armstead, Betts, Richardson, and Bourne were combined and administered by the vicar and churchwardens with 5 representative trustees as Romford United charities. In 1948 small doles were paid to 62 old people. A Scheme of 1952, when the income was £43, increased the number of representative trustees to six. In 1974 the income was £63. The charities were then being administered on behalf of the trustees by Havering social services department,[58] which made cash grants to needy persons.

UNITED CHARITIES. Mildred, Lady Burleigh, daughter of Sir Anthony Cooke of Gidea Hall, by her will dated 1588, gave £120 to the Haberdashers' company of London to provide loans of £20 each to 6 Romford husbandmen or tradesmen.[59] By 1660, however, the loans were being administered by the vestry, and from 1737 magistrates of Havering liberty, and the minister of Romford acted as trustees. One loan was lost *c.* 1832 when the recipient became insolvent, and in 1861 the remaining capital was invested to make it up to the original sum. In 1862 it was said that applications for loans were rare, but in 1898 the whole £120 was on loan.

Robert Palmer, glover, by will dated 1624, gave the residue of his chattels in trust for the poor of Romford ward.[60] The legacy was used to buy Hangman's acre, which was let for £2 a year between 1660 and 1790, at £5 in 1800, and £10 10*s.* in 1810. In 1811 the land was exchanged for Townfield, which was let for £7 a year, distributed in bread and money to the poor. The land was sold in 1907 to the county council for the building of London Road (Crowlands) school, and the proceeds were invested in £868 stock.[61]

John Webster, brewer, gave by will *c.* 1629 a house called the Tilekiln on Harold Wood common to provide bread equally for the poor of Romford and Hornchurch. The house had once belonged to the guild of Our Lady but had passed into private hands in 1549.[62] The income was £4 from 1659 to 1846, and £9 in 1862. In the period 1788–90 a pauper was being housed at the Tilekiln, and the lessee then paid only half the usual rent. In 1899 the income was £4 7*s.* from land only. By 1952 the property had been sold and the income from stock was £9 17*s.*

Andrew Reynolds, by will proved 1632, gave to the poor of Romford town the reversion, after his wife's death, of a £3 rent-charge from his house in High Street.[63] In 1837 the income was being distributed in bread and doles. The rent-charge was redeemed in 1954 for £120 stock.

William Armstead, by will proved 1657, gave a rent-charge of £2 to Romford poor. It was redeemed in 1953 for £80 stock.[64]

Lewis Betts, by will dated 1669, gave £4 rent, charged on his house at Collier Row and on Lyon Mead, Hornchurch, to apprentice one poor child from Romford town and one from Collier Row. He also gave £2 rent from the Golden Lion, Romford, for the benefit of four poor husbandmen from Romford town and four from Collier Row, and another rent-charge of £1 to repair the church path. By 1862 the £1 rent had ceased to be used for the path, and had been added to the apprenticing charity, which was being allowed to accumulate to provide larger premiums. The last premium was paid in 1931. A Ministry of Education Scheme of 1952 empowered the trustees to help young persons preparing to enter a profession or trade, The rent-charges were redeemed in 1939, 1951, and 1953.

Hannah Richardson, by will *c.* 1811, gave £90 in trust to provide bread for the poor.[65] In 1895 the income was £2 17*s.* 8*d.*, which was distributed in bread. In 1972 it was £2.60.

The Noak Hill charity. Frances Caroline Neave (d. 1860) expressed a wish to leave £500 to the poor of Noak Hill. Her niece Mary Blanche Neave, on her marriage in 1860 to John R. W. Hildyard, gave the sum to her husband to invest for the poor. The income was distributed in clothes, bedding, and cash. By declaration of trust dated 1900 Hildyard's executors transferred the stock to trustees. Succeeding trustees were to be appointed by the owner of Dagnam Park. In 1976 it was said that the charity had been in abeyance since 1970.[66]

Thomas Bourne, by will proved 1877, gave £100 in trust to provide doles for 6 poor widows and 6 poor widowers at Christmas. In 1972 the income was £2.52.

ROGER REEDE'S ALMS-HOUSES.[67] About 1482 Roger Reede founded alms-houses for 5 poor men in Joyes Mead (Hoo Croft), on the west side of Collier Row Lane, now North Street. By his will, dated 1483, he gave lands in Romford and Dagenham to maintain the alms-houses, to pay 14*d.* a year to a priest and 5 clerks for an obit, 6*s.* 8*d.* a year to the poor, and pensions of 26*s.* and a load of wood to each of the five alms-men, with smaller benefits for their widows. Reede's will laid down detailed

[55] W. W. Biggs, *Cong. Ch. Romford*, 1662–1962, 23; Char. Com. Files; inf. from Revd. K. French.
[56] Unless otherwise stated this section is based on: *Rep. Com. Char.* [108], pp. 735–42, (1837–8), xxv (1); Char. Com. Files; E.R.O., Q/RSr 1; T/A 521/1–3, 9, 10; T/P 195/2, ff. 88–90.
[57] See p. 92.
[58] Ex. inf. Havering social services dept.
[59] *Hist. Essex by Gent.* iv. 324.
[60] E.R.O., D/AEW 17/180.
[61] H.R.L., Cornell MSS.; and see above, p. 93.
[62] *Cal. Pat.* 1548–9, 312; see also above, p. 83.
[63] E.R.O., D/AEW 19/144.
[64] See also p. 54.
[65] Ogborne, *Essex*, 137.
[66] Inf. from Mr. G. Grusin and Havering social services dept.
[67] This account, unless otherwise stated, is based on: E.R.O., T/B 262 (microfilm of the charity's records 1469–1899); D/DBeO 5; Ogborne, *Essex*, 136; S. Roberts, 'Notes on the charity and life of Roger Reede', *Romford Record*, i. 10–16; inf. from Roger Reede's trustees.

regulations for the conduct of the alms-houses. He also gave, in default of his wife's heirs, land in Romford to provide the poor of neighbouring parishes with food in Lent, and petticoats and blankets at All Saints. Later figures show that the charity was endowed with a total of 146 a. land. From 1737 or earlier people from Dagenham, Hornchurch, and Romford were admitted to the alms-houses, and coats and gowns were distributed in the three parishes. The alms-houses were rebuilt in 1784, and in 1786 part of the alms-house land was sold as the site for the new workhouse.[68] In 1789 the number of alms-men was raised to 7, and pensions were increased, but admission to the alms-houses was restricted to those who had paid church- and poor-rates. In 1818 the trustees were charged with mismanagement and misapplication of funds. By a Scheme of 1825, following a Chancery order, 5 alms-men were to receive yearly £26 and a suit of clothes, their widows £20 and a gown and petticoat, and a further £35 was to be shared among the alms-people. From any surplus £30 was to be distributed in clothes and provisions to the poor of the three parishes. In 1837, when the alms-houses consisted of six tenements for men and a centre house for widows, they housed 5 men and 7 women, 3 of them widows. The alms-people received pensions, clothes, coal, and medical aid. From 1838 clothing and provisions were distributed to the poor of Romford, Hornchurch, and Dagenham.[69] A Scheme of 1860 enlarged the number of alms-men to 6, and another of 1890 increased the number of trustees from 10 to 16. By 1940 all the charity land had been sold except the Redyn field, the alms-houses, and neighbouring property in North Street. A Scheme of 1940, amended in 1946 and 1963, required the setting-up of a repair fund, increased the alms-folk stipends and raised to £60 the limit on the yearly payment to the poor of Romford, Hornchurch, and Dagenham. Provision of clothing to the alms-folk was replaced by clothing allowances in 1946. In 1959 the alms-houses and other property in North Street were sold, and 38 new alms-houses, including one bungalow for Hunnable's charity,[70] were built on charity land in Redyn field, Church Lane, in two phases, completed in 1961 and 1973. Payments to the alms-folk ceased in 1973 when a new Scheme introduced payment of contributions by them. The income in 1975 was £17,000.

As rebuilt in 1784 the alms-houses contained a central block of two storeys and three bays having a roof pediment with name plaque, flanked by lower wings of one storey. A 19th-century photograph also shows a pair of detached buildings, on each side of the main block, at right angles to it.[71] It is not clear if these were part of the 1784 rebuilding. The alms-houses accommodated 6 couples and 4 widows. They were damaged by floods in 1888. The side blocks were rebuilt in 1891 and the central block in 1897 in a 'cottage' style.[72] Some of the 1961 alms-houses are illustrated opposite page 113.

Other charities. Mary Hide's apprenticeship charity, founded in 1714, is described elsewhere.[73]

William Mashiter, by deed of 1884, gave land and 4 cottages in Main Road, Romford, in trust to provide doles for the poor. The income accumulated during the First World War. Part of it was used for church purposes and later repaid. The property was sold in 1938. In 1971 the income was £93 from which £80 was distributed to 29 old people.[74]

William Hunnable, a local builder, by will proved 1928, left £1,000 for an alms-house for Romford poor. The money was insufficient to build and maintain an alms-house, and was therefore invested and allowed to accumulate. By a Scheme of 1961 it was used to build one of the alms-houses for occupation by a Romford person in the Redyn Field, and its administration was passed to the trustees of Reede's charity.[75]

Lost charities. John Simpson, by will proved 1504, left the residue of his estate to his wife to dispose of for the good of his soul.[76] It seems that the rent from his house near the Loam pond was given to the poor. In 1660 50*s.* rent was being distributed to 5 poor men. From 1686 the rent of £3 was given to 6 poor men. In 1787 it was said that part of the land had been let on lease for 99 years from 1732, but the rent had not been paid. In 1788 the eight cottages near Loam pond, which had been used as poorhouses for many years, were sold for £198 by the directors of the poor.[77] It was believed that all or some of them had formerly been occupied by James (*sic*) Simpson. The proceeds of the sale may have been put towards the building of the parish workhouse in 1787.[78]

William Ellis, by will proved 1616, gave £20 in trust to be divided equally between the poor of Harold Wood and Noak Hill.[79] The charity seems to have been lost by 1690.

Ann Elsden of Clerkenwell (Lond.), by will dated 1625, left £30 in trust to buy land for the use of Romford poor. The trustees bought the Cross Keys (later the Half Moon) *c.* 1627 and used the income of £3 5*s.* on bread for the poor. The building was being used as the workhouse in 1753. There is no record of the receipt of the rent after 1776.

Elizabeth Parker, by will proved 1630, gave her residuary estate to the poor of the parish.[80] From 1660 to 1685 the interest on £23 was being used for the poor. There is no later record of this charity.

Mrs. Blackstone, by will dated 1647, gave £20 in trust for the poor of Harold Wood. It was on loan in 1660 but seems to have been lost by 1690.

Robert Luckin, by will proved 1652, directed that after his wife's death his heirs should pay 12*d.* each twice a year from his lands in Harold Wood to 10 poor old people of that ward. In 1753 the income was £1. Payment seems to have ceased *c.* 1790.

Col. Joachim Matthews of Gobions, by will proved 1659, left 20 marks in trust for the poor of each of the five Romford wards. The legacy was not received until 1687, after the vestry had taken legal action to recover it. It was put out on loan in the early 18th century. In 1766 part of the capital was

[68] Lysons, *Lond.* iv. 202; E.R.O., T/B 262/1.
[69] E.R.O., T/B 262/2.
[70] See below.
[71] *Romford Record*, i, pl. f. p. 22.
[72] E.R.O., T/B 262/23.
[73] See p. 55.
[74] Char. Com. Files.
[75] Inf. from trustees; Char. Com. Files.
[76] E.R.O., D/AER 2/82.
[77] E.R.O., D/DGe T90.
[78] See p. 77.
[79] E.R.O., D/AEW 15/279.
[80] E.R.O., D/AEW 19/72.

used to build the poorhouse, and the rest had been lost by 1772. In 1776 the churchwardens were charged interest on the capital but nothing more is known of this charity.[81]

Margaret Burch, by will dated 1684, directed that money owing to her should be placed in trust for the poor of Harold Wood and Collier Row. Half the income was to be used for poor widows, and half for apprenticing poor children. In 1689 42*s.* was paid to the churchwardens, who gave 22*s.* to widows and kept the rest for apprenticing. By 1706 the income was £4 2*s.*, and in 1733 the income was from interest on loans of £75. In 1766 part of the capital of Burch's charity was put towards building the poorhouse, and by 1772 the remaining capital was said to be lost.

[81] Smith, *Havering*, 245–7; interest may have been paid on the Havering share until 1778: see above, p. 25.

CHAFFORD HUNDRED

CHAFFORD hundred, with 14 parishes, lies in the south-west of the county, extending from the Thames marshes north for about 13 miles to the clay uplands of South Weald. On the west the Weald brook and the river Ingrebourne formed part of the boundary with the liberty of Havering, while the eastern boundary with the hundred of Barstable included the river Mardyke. There were old towns at Grays Thurrock in the south, and Brentwood, formerly a hamlet of South Weald, in the north. Rainham village was a small port for coastal shipping. At Grays and West Thurrock the chalk outcrop provided materials for an ancient quarrying industry. The other parts of the hundred remained rural until the later 19th century. There are still farms and woods in the centre and north. There have been few great houses. The most notable were South Weald Hall, and Belhus, Aveley, demolished in 1946 and 1957 respectively. South Weald park, Thorndon park, and Upminster common have remained as open spaces.

During the present century an industrial area has grown up along the Thames. West Thurrock is now one of the largest cement-producing areas in Europe. Ferro-alloys are made at Rainham; oil and petroleum are stored at Purfleet in West Thurrock and Grays. The Ford Motor Co. has its British and European headquarters at Little Warley, near Brentwood, and depots at South Ockendon and West Thurrock. In the later 19th century, after the opening of the railway from London, Brentwood town began to spread south into Great Warley. At Rainham there was a little building in the later 19th century, and there has been much more since 1918. At Upminster suburban growth began about 1900. The great housing estate at Belhus, in Aveley and South Ockendon, was built by the London county council after the Second World War.

In 1086 Chafford hundred contained some 112 hides divided between 46 estates in 16 villages distinguished by separate names.[1] Most of the villages later gave their names to the parishes of the hundred, but there were exceptions. The Domesday Warley was later split into the parishes of Great and Little Warley. Thurrock became three parishes, two of which, Grays and West Thurrock, were in Chafford hundred, and the third in Barstable hundred. Part of Ockendon was later included in Cranham, and the remainder became the parishes of North and South Ockendon. Kenningtons became part of Aveley parish. Fingrith and 'Ginga', where the king held estates associated with one at Ockendon, became the parishes of Blackmore and Margaretting.[2] Blackmore and Margaretting were later in Chelmsford hundred, but the order of entries in Domesday Book makes it seem unlikely that they are listed under Chafford hundred by mistake. 'Limpwella' and 'Geddesduna' have not been definitely identified.[3] 'Limpwella', a small estate held of the bishop of Bayeux, may have been Imphy Hall in Buttsbury, later Chelmsford hundred.[4] 'Geddesduna', a one-hide estate held by Westminster Abbey, and recorded elsewhere as Ingeddesdoune, was probably in the northern uplands of the hundred.[5] It may be identical with Englands or Inglondes, an ancient estate in Little Warley which in the 17th century was said to comprise 120 a.

[1] *V.C.H. Essex*, i. 427–574. Occasional ambiguities in Domesday Book make exact totals impossible.

[2] Ibid. 433.

[3] Ibid. 458, 445.

[4] For the etymology: *P.N. Essex*, 244, 583.

[5] C. Hart, *Early Chart. Essex*, no. 72.

or one plough-land, and which was always independent of the surrounding manors.[6]

Chafford was one of the Domesday hundreds with extensive marshland sheep pastures.[7] The pastures were appurtenant not only to the coastal villages of Grays and West Thurrock, but also to the inland villages of Childerditch, South Ockendon, Great and Little Warley, and to 'Limpwella'. Little Warley's marshland was about 8 miles away,

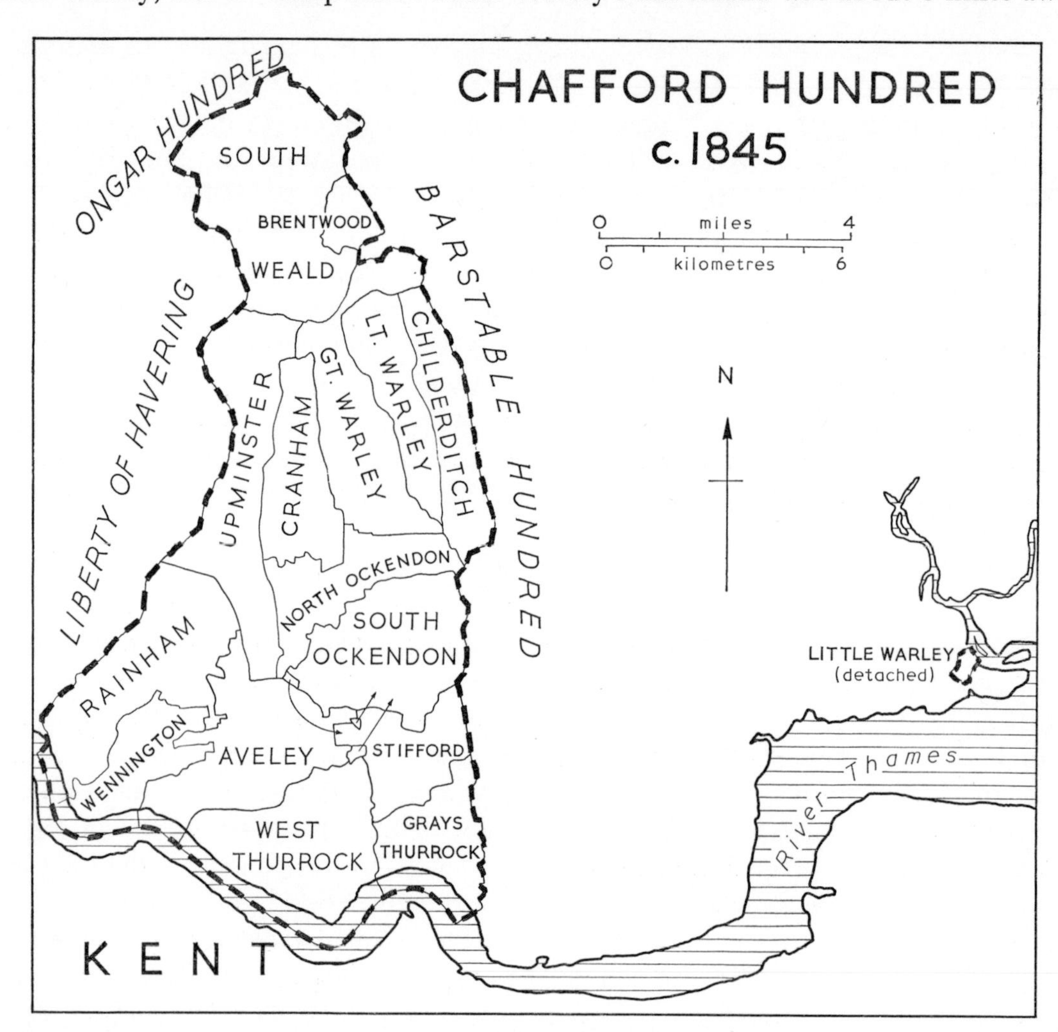

at Corringham, in Barstable hundred, and survived as a detached part of the inland parish until the 19th century. 'Limpwella's' possession of sheep pasture is consistent with its suggested location in Buttsbury, for the main manor of Buttsbury was among the few in Chelmsford hundred possessing sheep pastures.[8]

From the 13th century onwards the hundred comprised the 14 parishes already mentioned.[9] In the Middle Ages the parishes were normally identical with the 'vills', but there were exceptions. The NE. corner of South Weald parish formed part of the Doddinghurst List in Barstable hundred.[10] Chafford hundred sometimes claimed it, as in 1565, when a dispute was heard in the Court of Wards,[11] but the List, which also included part of Kelvedon Hatch, seems to have remained in Barstable hundred down to the 19th century.[12] Brentwood, where a main-road township grew up in the 12th century, remained part of South Weald parish until the 19th century, but by the 16th

[6] See p. 176.

[7] *V.C.H. Essex*, i. 369.

[8] Ibid. 369, 504.

[9] *Rot. Hund.* (Rec. Com.), i. 148; *Feud. Aids*, ii. 194; E 179/108/150.

[10] Morant, *Essex*, i. 192; *Map of Essex* (1777) (hundred boundary).

[11] Wards 3/34; B.L., Add. Ch. 27447.

[12] Q/RPl 1–51 (Land Tax returns, 1781–1832). Kelvedon Hatch was mainly in Ongar hundred. Its connexion with the Doddinghurst List was not noticed when that hundred was dealt with in a previous volume: *V.C.H. Essex*, iv. 1 sqq.

century was being assessed for taxation as a separate vill.[13] Brook Street, another hamlet of South Weald, was also separately assessed in the 16th century and later.[14] In the 14th century Little Warley and Childerditch were sometimes assessed along with Great Warley.[15]

Three parishes in the hundred had detached parts, shown on 19th-century maps.[16] Little Warley has already been mentioned. Two small parts of South Ockendon were locally situated in Stifford, and there was a detached part of Stifford in South Ockendon. The eastern boundary of Grays Thurrock was interlocked with the boundary of Little Thurrock, in Barstable hundred, in a curious layered manner, suggesting ancient intercommoning. West Thurrock had two small salients in Stifford parish.

Chafford hundred remained always with the Crown. In the 13th century it was customarily farmed by the bailiff. In the period 1273–5 it was stated that under Henry III the farm had usually been £5, but that it had been increased to 20 marks by Richard of Southchurch, sheriff in 1265–7,[17] against whom the men of the hundred levelled various charges of extortion and defalcation, and especially that of failing to pay for provisions taken from them in 1267 for the use of the king's troops, then besieging London.[18] In 1292 the hundred was let to farm at £5 6*s.* 8*d.* for half a year.[19] In the later 17th century the profits of the hundred were valued at £2 1*s.* 5½*d.*[20] A hundred bailiff was first mentioned in 1225,[21] and an under-bailiff in the period 1265–7.[22] A high constable was named *c.* 1556 and later.[23]

The ancient meeting-place of the hundred was probably Chafford heath, in Upminster parish.[24] For certain administrative purposes Chafford hundred was grouped with neighbouring hundreds. In 1321 a commission of the peace was issued jointly for Chafford and Barstable.[25] From the 16th century the two hundreds were normally associated for such purposes as musters, taxation, the preservation of game, and poor-relief.[26] In 1586, when the county was split into six administrative divisions, Chafford was included in the southern division, along with Becontree and Barstable hundreds, and Havering liberty.[27] During the Civil War the southern division was placed under a parliamentary committee meeting at Romford.[28]

The competence of the hundred court was affected by liberties granted to the lords of individual manors. By a charter of Henry II, confirmed in 1286, the manor of Costed (Brentwood) in South Weald was quit of suit of the hundred, and of sheriff's and hundred bailiff's aids.[29] During the hundredal inquisitions in the years 1273–5 it was stated that the lords of Aveley, Brentwood, Cranham, North and South Ockendon, Rainham, and South Weald claimed the assize of bread and ale and the right of gallows.[30] The lord of Childerditch was said to have withheld suits at the sheriff's tourn and wardpence for the past 23 years. The view of frankpledge and the assize of bread and ale were being held by the lord of Upminster Hall manor by 1271.[31] Both the manors in Great Warley had the view in the later Middle Ages.[32] The manor of Tillingham in Childerditch was a member of that of West Tilbury, in Barstable hundred,

13 E 179/108/150; E.R.O., Q/RTh 1 and 5.

14 Ibid.; cf. *Norden's Map of Essex* (1594).

15 E 179/107/18 (lay subsidy, 1327).

16 O.S. Map 6", Essex, LXXV, LXXXIII, LXXVII, LXXXV (1881 edn.).

17 *Rot. Hund.* (Rec. Com.), i. 148, 156.

18 Ibid. 148–9; H. M. Cam, *Hundred and Hundred Rolls*, 101.

19 Cam, op. cit. 146.

20 *Cal. Treasury Bks.* 1689–92, 239.

21 *Pat. R.* 1216–25, 524.

22 *Rot. Hund.* i. 148.

23 E.R.O., Q/SR 2/37; 18/64.

24 *P.N. Essex*, 133; *Map of Essex* (1777). See also below, p. 146.

25 *Cal. Pat.* 1321–4, 61.

26 *L. & P. Hen. VIII*, xiv(1), p. 415; E.R.O., D/DP O4 and O5; *Cal. S.P. Dom.* 1627–8, 221; 1628–9, 134; 1631–3, 39; *E.R.* lxi. 63.

27 B. W. Quintrell, 'The Divisional Committee for Southern Essex during the Civil Wars.' (Manchester M.A. thesis, 1962), 2,155.

28 Op. cit. *passim.*

29 *Cal. Chart.* 1257–1300, 333.

30 *Rot. Hund.* i. 148–9, 156.

31 S.C. 2/173/30.

32 See p. 170.

the lord of which had the view and the assize by the year 1274–5.[33] From 1377, when Coggeshall abbey acquired Tillingham, courts leet were held jointly for the manors of Childerditch and Tillingham.[34] Henry III in 1253 granted to the Knights Templars quittance from all hundred pence, and to St. Bartholomew's hospital (Lond.), quittance from shire and hundred courts.[35] Those general grants presumably applied to the Templars' manor of Rainham, and to St. Bartholomew's Elmhouse estate in Rainham.

[33] *Rot. Hund.* (Rec. Com.), i. 154; *Red Bk. Exch.* (Rolls Ser.), ii. 503; *Cal. Inq. p.m.* iv, pp. 148–9.

[34] E.R.O., D/DP M1099 sqq.

[35] *Cal. Chart.* 1257–1300, 237, 368.

CRANHAM

CRANHAM lies about 3 miles south-west of Brentwood and 5 miles east of Romford. The ancient parish was bounded by Upminster on the west, Great Warley on the north and east, and North Ockendon on the south.[1] In the Middle Ages Cranham was more often known as Bishop's Ockendon, since its chief manor was held by the bishop of London, but from the 15th century the parish was usually termed Cranham. The second element in the parish name was originally *hoh* or ridge. It probably referred to the ridge running E–W on which the church and hall were built.[2] Cranham became part of Hornchurch urban district in 1934 and of the London borough of Havering in 1965.

Most of Cranham was in the London Clay belt, with poor loam in the north and valley gravel in the SW. towards Upminster. The ancient parish contained 1,879 a. and was about 3 miles long from north to south; narrow at its northern extremity, it gradually widened to over a mile in the south.[3] From 250 ft. in the north the land fell to below 50 ft. in the south. Until modern changes its road pattern was simple. The road from Brentwood and Great Warley divided just south of Beredens, into Cranham (or Front) Lane and Moor (or Back) Lane further east, both roads being crossed after 1925 by the arterial road to Southend. The two lanes rejoined near the site of Crouches farm and the old Rectory and, as Front Lane, continued south; they crossed St. Mary's Lane from Upminster to Horndon at the 'wants' or cross-roads and ran on southwards, as The Chase, to the church and manor-house. Further east along St. Mary's Lane, Pike Lane led towards North Ockendon.

For transport services Cranham has depended mainly on Upminster and Romford. The railway from Upminster to Southend, opened in 1888, and that from Upminster to Grays (1892) pass through the parish.[4]

Until the 20th century Cranham was a purely agricultural parish, as it remained in 1974 in the north, east, and south. Its population was small until the 19th century. There were 29 men on the two manors in 1086.[5] The tax list of 1327 included 13 Cranham names and that of 1523 had 16.[6] In 1670 there were 24 houses in the parish.[7] In the 19th century the population increased more rapidly, from 240 in 1801 to 437 in 1871; it then fluctuated for 30 years. In the decade 1901–11 it rose from 397 to 489 and in 1921–31 from 519 to 1,240.[8] The earlier increase coincided with an attempt to develop Cranham Park on land between Front and Moor (or Back) Lanes. This scheme, which was presented to the public as an extension of Upminster, ran into difficulties, of which the chief was the supply of water, and ended in failure.[9] In the 1920s and 1930s building fronted mainly on the two lanes.[10] In 1928–30 residents were worried by the presence of gipsies, squatters, and caravan-dwellers, especially when they were reported to be trying to buy plots north of the railway line.[11] In 1931 12 council houses, named Oglethorpe cottages, were opened in Moor Lane.[12] The sale of the Benyon estate in 1937 led to further building in Cranham. North of the railway the area now covered by streets with birds' names represents lot 8; between the railway and St. Mary's Lane the 35 a. of lot 7 was laid out with streets named after bishoprics; south of the Lane F. G. Legg began to develop the 100-acre triangle between St. Mary's Lane, Pike Lane, and the railway to Grays.[13] The Green Belt Act (1938), the Second World War, and the Town and Country Planning Act (1944) eventually thwarted the development of the whole site, but not before sewage pipes had been laid east of Ashvale Gardens in expectation of its extension to Pike Lane.[14] There were plans for a railway station in Cranham, and a plot of land was bought between St. Mary's Lane and the railway line. With the cessation of building, the intention was dropped and in 1959 Judith Anne Court was laid out on the site by a private developer.[15]

Central Cranham became a commuter suburb of London after the Second World War; building took place between Upminster and Cranham in the area bounded on the north by the arterial road and on the south by St. Mary's Lane. In 1971 there were 615 council houses in the parish.[16]

After the First World War Cranham formed a May Day committee (later Cranham Peace Society). It was intended to celebrate the peace and commemorate the dead with a festival and parade, and throughout the 1920s the May Queen placed a wreath under the memorial window in the church. The celebration was consciously modelled on the May Days inaugurated by Ruskin in Chelsea in 1881. In 1929, after the May Day festivities, the society disbanded as a result of parish apathy, debts, and, chiefly, the rector's opposition.[17]

Among the notable people connected with Cranham were the rectors Adam Harsnett (1612–39), a Puritan religious writer,[18] and George Strahan (1786–1819), the editor of Dr. Samuel Johnson's *Prayers and Meditations*.[19] Sir Edward Petre, Bt. (1631–99), Jesuit and confessor to James II, was a son of Sir Francis Petre, Bt., of Cranham.[20] General James Oglethorpe (1696–1785), founder of the colony of Georgia, married the heiress of Cranham Hall in 1743.[21]

[1] O.S. Map 2½″, TQ 58, 59.
[2] For the etymology of Ockendon and Cranham: *P.N. Essex*, 124–6; E. Ekwall, 'Etymological notes on English place names', *Lunds Universitets Arsskrift* NF Aud 1 Bd 53 no. 5, 19–20.
[3] O.S. Map 6″, Essex, LXVII, LXXV (surv. 1865–6).
[4] See p. 148.
[5] *V.C.H. Essex*, i. 440, 458.
[6] E 179/107/13; E 179/108/150.
[7] E.R.O., Q/RTh 5; cf. Guildhall MS. 9557.
[8] *V.C.H. Essex*, ii. 345; Census, 1911–31.
[9] E.R.O., T/P 67/1 p. 225; 67/6 pp. 116–17, 120, 129, 198, 259, 281; 67/7 pp. 95, 167, 173, 190; T/P 181/11/27; *Sale Cat.* A144.
[10] O.S. Map 6″, Essex, LXXX. SW.; LXXXVIII. NW. (3rd edn.; prov. edn.); E.R.O., T/P 181/4/5.
[11] E.R.O., T/P 181/4/5.
[12] Ibid.
[13] E.R.O., *Sale Cat.* B106; D/DBe E71; inf. from Mr. F. W. Legg.
[14] Inf. from Mr. F. W. Legg.
[15] Inf. from L.B. Havering: Judith Anne was the developer's daughter.
[16] *Havering Official Guide* (1971), 97.
[17] E.R.O., T/P 181/4/5.
[18] *D.N.B.*; for his will, *E.R.*, xl. 111. Cf. Davids, *Nonconformity in Essex*, 154 n.
[19] *D.N.B.* s.v. Strahan, Wm.
[20] *D.N.B.*; J. Kenyon, *The Popish Plot*, 126, 140, 142, 157, 160, 201, 205, 207.
[21] *D.N.B.*; *Hist. Parl., Commons 1715–54*, ii. 305–6.

MANORS. There were two manors in Cranham in 1086. Ockendon (Wochenduna), comprising 3 hides and 40 acres, was part of the fee of the bishop of London; it had been held in 1066 by Alvric.[22] Cranham (Craohu), of 1½ hide, was held in chief by Odo, bishop of Bayeux; in 1066 it had belonged to Alwin, a free man.[23] In both manors the under-tenant in 1086 was named Hugh. After the exile and forfeiture of Odo of Bayeux in 1088 his manors were split up. At several places in Essex where the bishop of London held a neighbouring manor, he seems to have taken over Odo's lands.[24] This was probably the case in Cranham, where, after 1088, the bishop of London was the only recorded tenant in chief. The bishop continued to receive rent from Cranham at least until the later 16th century.[25]

The manor of *CRANHAM* (Crawenho), which occurs in the 13th century, possibly represents the estate formerly held by Odo of Bayeux. John de Beauchamp, of Eaton Socon (Beds.) and Beauchamp Roding, first let the manor at farm to Thomas de Haya, and by 1232 had enfeoffed him with it.[26] In 1235 Thomas de Haya in turn enfeoffed Thomas of Stortford; the manor then comprised a carucate of land, 40 a. of wood and 4 a. of meadow.[27] In 1236 Beauchamp's widow Christine claimed dower in the manor.[28] Thomas of Stortford was the precentor of St. Paul's cathedral, and *c.* 1240 he assigned for memorial services rents from properties which he had acquired in Cranham and elsewhere. These properties were then held by William of Fleet.[29] In 1272 William of Cranham acknowledged to the chapter of St. Paul's that he was 5 years in arrear with a yearly rent of 8*s.* and agreed that they might legally distrain on his manor of Cranham.[30] No later reference to the manor has been found; in 1317, however, Meliora, daughter of William of Cranham and John son of Reynold the draper of Barking quitclaimed to Nicholas of Ockendon and his wife Joan 42 acres in Cranham.[31]

The manor of *BISHOP'S OCKENDON* or *CRANHAM* (*HALL*) apparently lay in the north of the parish, and was held from the 12th to the 14th century by the family of Ockendon. To the confusion of historians the family used only the Christian name, William, from 1106 to *c.* 1274.[32] In 1166 William of Ockendon headed the list of the bishop of London's tenants with 4½ knight's fees, 1½ of which were in Bishop's Ockendon,[33] and William of Ockendon still held these fees in 1210–12.[34] The Sir William of Ockendon of *c.* 1230 was not apparently the (Sir) William of 1253–74.[35] Nicholas of Ockendon and his wife Joan held the manor in 1303.[36] Nicholas died in 1319 or 1320; his wife was still alive in 1332.[37]

(Sir) Nicholas de Halughton, who is said to have been heir to Nicholas of Ockendon's daughter Joan, was holding the manors of Bishop's Ockendon and Chadwell along with his wife Margery in 1337.[38] Halughton died in 1338 leaving infant daughters Margaret and Joan.[39] His widow, who married Sir Roger de Northwode, later Lord Northwode, died in 1340.[40] In 1346 Northwode was guardian to Halughton's unnamed heir.[41]

The manor was held in 1363 by Sir Ralph St. Leger and his wife Beatrice with remainder to her heirs.[42] Sir Ralph was alive in 1391 but had died by 1397.[43] Beatrice outlived him, and by 1400 had married Sir John Curzon.[44] Again a widow, she died in 1421, and in 1425 Nicholas Rykhull and his wife Isobel quitclaimed the manor to trustees of (Sir) Lewis John.[45]

John was a successful London merchant and royal official.[46] At his death in 1442 the manor passed for life to his widow Anne (d. 1457) with reversion to his younger son Edmund. It then contained 461 a., and the demesne was farmed out.[47] It is doubtful whether Edmund ever received the manor, for in 1464 his eldest brother (Sir) Lewis FitzLewis (John or FitzJohn) was presenting to the rectory of Cranham.[48] In 1471 (Sir) Lewis was killed at the battle of Barnet.[49] He was posthumously attainted, and late that year his Essex estates, including Cranham, were granted to the king's brother, Richard, duke of Gloucester.[50] Nevertheless FitzLewis's son and heir, (Sir) Richard (d. 1528), seems to have recovered Cranham by 1487 when he presented to the rectory.[51] Sir Richard was survived by his fourth wife, Jane (d. 1535).[52] Cranham was among the estates assigned to her for life, and with her next husband

[22] *V.C.H. Essex*, i. 440.

[23] Ibid. i. 458.

[24] Cf. Little Thurrock, Chadwell, Peldon: ibid. i. 455–8; Morant, *Essex*, i. 225, 229–30, 418.

[25] C 139/111; E.R.O., D/DP M1086.

[26] *Bracton's Note Book*, ii. 531; *V.C.H. Essex*, iv. 198–9; *V.C.H. Beds.* iii. 190.

[27] *Feet of F. Essex*, i. 103.

[28] *Cur. Reg. R.* xv. 459; cf. pp. 395, 453, 455.

[29] *Early Chart. St. Paul's* (Camd. 3rd ser. lviii), 115, 215. The rent from the Cranham land was 8*s.* 4*d.* a year.

[30] *Feet of F. Essex*, i. 283.

[31] Ibid. ii. 172. For Nicholas and Joan, see below.

[32] *Early Chart. St. Paul's* 45, 157, 174, 216–17. Cf. *Dom. St. Paul's* (Camd. Soc. 1st ser. lxix), 125–6, 129, 142 for (the same?) two Williams of Ockendon, father and son.

[33] *Red Bk. Exch.* (Rolls Ser.), i. 186; *E.A.T.* N.S. xvii. 72–3.

[34] *Red Bk. Exch.* ii. 541–2. But cf. *Pipe R.* 1170 (P.R.S. xv), 108 for a claim to these fees by Ralph of Pelham. It is last recorded on the Pipe Roll in 1199: *Pipe R.* 1199 (P.R.S. N.S. x) 88.

[35] *Cat. Anct. D.* i, A 741; v, A 11629; *Close R.* 1253–4, 130, 197; *E.A.T.* N.S. xviii. 18; *Feet of F. Essex*, i. 207; *Cal. Pat.* 1266–72, 283; *Cal. Inq. p.m.* ii, p. 65.

[36] *Feud. Aids*, ii. 151; cf. *Feet of F. Essex*, ii. 127. For Nicholas going to Wales in 1287 and overseas in 1294: *Cal. Pat.* 1281–92, 272; 1292–1301, 68.

[37] *Cal. Pat.* 1317–21, 290, 499; *Docs. Hist. St. Paul's* (Camd. Soc. 2nd ser. xxvi), 66; *Cal. Pat.* 1330–4, 252.

[38] Salmon, *Essex*, 274; *Feet of F. Essex*, iii. 41.

[39] *Cal. Inq. p.m.* viii, p. 153.

[40] *Complete Peerage*, ix. 757.

[41] *Feud. Aids*, ii. 169. Newcourt, *Repertorium*, ii. 125 claims that Northwode presented to the living of Chadwell in 1363, but he died in 1361 according to *Complete Peerage*, ix. 757.

[42] *Feet of F. Essex*, iii. 137.

[43] Newcourt, *Repertorium*, ii. 195; *Cal. Close*, 1389–92, 342; ibid. 1396–9, 244.

[44] *Cal. Close*, 1422–9, 383 for relationships; *Feet of F. Essex*, iii. 233.

[45] Prob. 11/2B (P.C.C. 52 Marche 2); *Feet of F. Essex*, iv. 5, 9–10; *Cal. Close*, 1422–9, 383.

[46] A. D. Carr, 'Sir Lewis John—a medieval London Welshman', *Bull. Bd. Celtic Studies*, xxii. 260–70; *Hist. Parl.* 1439–1509, *Biogs.* 503.

[47] C 139/111; *E.A.T.* N.S. vi. 54–5. For Anne, his second wife: *Complete Peerage*, v. 210–11; E.R.O., D/DP M1081–3.

[48] Newcourt, *Repertorium*, ii. 195; *Cal. Pat.* 1467–77, 344–5.

[49] *Paston Letters and Papers*, ed. Davis, i, p. 438.

[50] *Cal. Pat.* 1467–77, 297; Morant, *Essex*, i. 213.

[51] Newcourt, *Repertorium*, ii. 195. Cranham was not among the manors he had bought back from the duke in 1482: *Cal. Close*, 1476–85, 295.

[52] *E.A.T.* N.S. vi. 44–5.

Sir John Norton, of Milton (Kent), she granted a 40-year lease of the manor from 1531 to Ralph Latham, goldsmith of London.[53] Sir Richard Fitz-Lewis's son and heir John had died *c.* 1525, but John's daughter Ele (d. 1543) survived. By 1526 she had married John Mordaunt, later Lord Mordaunt; their son Lewis succeeded to Cranham in 1571[54] In 1571, after 8 years of negotiation, most of the FitzLewis inheritance, including Cranham, was sold to the Petres of Ingatestone.[55] Cranham then included 540 a. of farm lands and at least 40 a. of woods and 200 a. of common.[56] Sir William Petre died in 1572 and his son (Sir) John, later Lord Petre, succeeded to the family estates.[57] In 1605 he settled Cranham and other properties on his third son Thomas on marriage.[58] Thomas (d. 1625) left as heir his younger son (Sir) Francis Petre (Bt.).[59] Francis sold Cranham for £6,100 in 1647 to Nathan Wright, a London merchant and alderman.[60] He died in 1658 and was succeeded by his son Benjamin who became a baronet in 1660.[61] Cranham descended with the baronetcy until the death in 1738 of Sir Samuel Wright. It then passed to Samuel's sister Elizabeth (d. 1787) who in 1743 married General James Oglethorpe (d. 1785), the founder of Georgia (U.S.A.).[62] By her will Mrs. Oglethorpe devised Cranham to Sir Thomas H. Apreece, Bt., grandson of her half-brother, Sir Nathan Wright.[63]

Sir Thomas (d. 1833) was succeeded by his son Sir Thomas G. Apreece, Bt. (d. 1842), who left his estates to be sold for the benefit of St. George's hospital, Hyde Park Corner (Lond.). His only surviving sister and heir, Amelia Peacocke, contested the will on the ground of his insanity, but in 1848 agreed to a compromise with the hospital. Cranham manor with an estate of 726 a. was consequently sold in 1852 to Samuel Gurney, of Ham Hall, West Ham, a partner in Overend, Gurney & Co., bankers.[64]

Gurney (d. 1856) was succeeded by his son Samuel (d. 1882) who enlarged the estate.[65] Overend, Gurney & Co. failed in 1866, and in 1867 the manor and estate, then 940 a., were offered for sale. The manor, detached from the estate, was then bought by George Rastrick (d. 1905), a solicitor, from whom it passed to his widow Beatrice (d. 1922) and then to his daughter Nora.[66] The greatest part of the estate, 812 a., was bought in 1867 by Richard Benyon, M.P. (d. 1897), of Englefield (Berks.) and descended with the manor of North Ockendon until 1937, when the Benyon estates in Essex were broken up.[67] Cranham Hall Farm and Cranham Lodge, with 415 a., were then sold to the Southend-on-Sea Estates Company who were still the owners in 1974.[68]

In the 18th century Cranham Hall, a brick house which was probably built about 1600, lay near the north-east corner of a walled garden of about 1½ a. Beyond this was a small park on the south and east. Most of the house appears to have been demolished in 1790,[69] but a small part was retained and incorporated in a new house with a main front of five bays facing east. The interior of this house was remodelled and service rooms were added on the west in the earlier 19th century. Further additions were made in 1904. In recent years the garden walls have fallen into decay; the wrought iron gates in the centre of the south side have been removed,[70] but the late-17th-century piers remain. To the west of the garden is a large planned farm of the later 19th century.

The manor of *BEREDENS* or *BERDENS*, which lay in the north of the parish, extending into Great Warley, originated as a free tenement, held of the manor of Cranham Hall.[71] In 1357 and 1362 two daughters of Peter of Ockendon conveyed to John de Berden all their rights in Cranham.[72] In 1363 Berden bought from Sir Ralph St. Leger a house and 52 a. in the parish.[73] A later John Berden of Cranham was living in 1431.[74]

In 1453 Stephen Wylot and his wife Joan sold to John Rand of Barking an estate of 334 a., undoubtedly Beredens, in Cranham and Great Warley.[75] In 1455 Rand also bought Whybridge in Hornchurch.[76] Both manors descended to William Rand, who in 1523 sold them to (Sir) William Roche; Beredens then comprised 213 a.[77] In 1531 Rand's sister and heir, Thomasine, with her husband Ralph Byllopp (Belepe or Belupp) sold a further 49 a. in Cranham and Great Warley to Roche, now an alderman of London.[78] Roche bought more land in Cranham in 1535, and in 1538, with his wife Elizabeth, settled Beredens on their daughter Elizabeth on her marriage with Ralph Latham.[79] Beredens thereafter descended in the Latham family along with the neighbouring manor of Upminster Hall.[80] In 1614 it comprised 272 a.[81] Ralph Latham sold Beredens in 1641 to Stephen Beale (d. 1667), leatherseller of London, who was succeeded by his son Joshua Beale of Tottenham (Mdx.).[82] In 1710, after Joshua's death, his estates were divided, and Beredens passed to his nephew Stephen Jermyn, salter of London. Jermyn (d. 1724) was succeeded by his grandson,

[53] *Cat. Anct. D.* iii, A 4154. For Latham at Upminster and at Beredens in Cranham, see below, pp. 149–50, 105.
[54] C. T. Kuypers, *Thorndon*, 8; *Complete Peerage*, ix. 195.
[55] E.R.O., D/DP T135/3–10, F237–8, E29 ff. 139a-b.
[56] E.R.O., D/DP M1086.
[57] *Complete Peerage*, x. 506.
[58] E.R.O., D/DBe T29.
[59] C 142/418/78; G.E.C. *Baronetage*, ii. 247.
[60] E.R.O., D/DBe T29.
[61] G.E.C. *Baronetage*, iii. 160–1.
[62] Ibid.
[63] E.R.O., D/DBe T30.
[64] G.E.C. *Baronetage*, v. 223–4; E.R.O., D/DBe T30. Gurney paid £28,600 for the manor and estate, £2,550 for the timber and underwood.
[65] E.R.O., D/DBe T30, 35, 37, 44.
[66] E.R.O., D/DVg 3. Nora Rastrick was described in 1929 as 'of Hove spinster'.
[67] E.R.O., D/DBe T30: Benyon paid £27,937 for the land, buildings, and timber on the 670 a. of Lot 1. Lot 3's 142 a. of timber cost him £83 10*s*. The purchase price of the land and buildings is unknown. In 1876 another 112 a. were bought. See p. 112.
[68] E.R.O., *Sale Cat.* B106; D/DBe E71: the Co. paid £53,000 for the estate and £1,075 for the timber on it.
[69] E.R.O., D/AEM 2/6; D/DU 23/139/1, 2 (Little Wakering); *Chelmsford Chron.* 23, 30 Oct., 6, 13 Nov. 1789.
[70] *Essex in 20th Century*, 75; E.R.O., T/P 117/29 (photographs, both 1909, of gates).
[71] C 142/262/103; E.R.O., D/DP M1219, 1224; *Feet of F. Essex*, iii. 115; cf. ibid. 1.
[72] *Cal. Close*, 1354–60, 319; 1360–4, 409.
[73] *Feet of F. Essex*, iii. 137.
[74] Ibid. iv. 17.
[75] Ibid. iv. 48.
[76] See above.
[77] E.R.O., D/DB T586. For Rand, see above, p. 39.
[78] *Feet of F. Essex*, iv. 181; cf. C 1/562/3; C 1/469/16; C 1/517/73.
[79] E.R.O., D/DB T586; C.P. 25(2)/12/66; Prob. 11/274 f. 337. Cf. *Feet of F. Essex*, iv. 225.
[80] See p. 151.
[81] E.R.O., D/DP M1224.
[82] E.R.O., D/DU 434/10; Prob. 11/323 f. 126v. (P.C.C. 16 Carr). Unless otherwise indicated, information in this paragraph derives from the former source.

another Stephen Jermyn, who was declared a lunatic in 1747. On the latter's death in 1795 Beredens passed to George F. Tyson, whose grandmother Martha had been a daughter of Stephen Jermyn the elder. In 1801 Tyson sold the estate, then of 460 a., for £8,230 to Ralph Nicholson of Tottenham (Mdx.). The greater part of the estate was leased to William Rumney,[83] who was succeeded in 1822 by Henry J. Hance. Hance, described in 1858 as the surviving trustee of Ralph Nicholson, was by 1839 both owner and occupier of Beredens.[84] He died in 1863 or 1864.[85]

An agreement of 1865 suggests a family partition of the estate; it divided the lands in Cranham (338 a.), half to the use of Francis Stone and his wife Mary, half to that of trustees for unspecified beneficiaries.[86] Stone farmed Beredens until *c.* 1882.[87] R. T. Stoneham, a London solicitor, appears to have bought Beredens in 1879, and to have lived there from the mid 1880s until about 1910 when he was succeeded by his grandson, R. T. D. Stoneham.[88] In 1918 the Beredens estate of 248 a. was offered for sale in five lots, but only three then found buyers.[89] Over the next 40 years the estate was reconstituted as part of the larger Goldings estate in Great Warley.[90] It was again dispersed, in eight lots, at the Goldings sale of 1971.[91]

In 1886 Beredens was described as an old restored manor-house.[92] In 1920 it was occupied by Ethelreda (Audrey) Petre, Lady Petre.[93] It was destroyed in the Second World War,[94] and in 1945 Lady Petre sold the site with about 36 a. to Mrs. M. E. de Rougemont.[95] In 1971 the G.L.C. bought the site, farm buildings, and 13 a.[96]

ECONOMIC HISTORY. The Domesday figures show Cranham as small and heavily wooded.[97] The manor of (Bishop's) Ockendon had woodland for 500 swine, and that of Cranham (Craohu) for 100 swine. According to J. H. Round's density formula this represents a figure of about 31½ per 100 a. of the whole village.[98] The two manors were both small and poor, but there were considerable differences between them. In 1066 and 1086 the manor of Bishop's Ockendon had the same number of plough-teams (3 on the demesne and 4 belonging to the tenants) but during that period the recorded population increased from 17 (6 villeins, 5 bordars, and 6 serfs) to 27 (8 villeins, 15 bordars, and 4 serfs), and the value of the manor rose from £4 to £6. In 1066 the smaller manor of Cranham had 1 villein, 1 bordar, and 1 plough, and was worth 50*s.* Its recorded population was unchanged in 1086, but there was then only ½ plough, and the value had fallen to 20*s.* The most significent of these figures seem to be those relating to the growth of the population, and especially of bordars, in Bishop's Ockendon. This was probably associated with forest clearance.[99]

By the 15th century the process of forest clearance was far advanced. In 1442 the demesne of Sir Lewis John's manor of Cranham included 264 a. arable and 164 a. pasture out of a total of 461 a.[1] There was a similar pattern of mixed farming, with arable predominating, in the 19th century. In 1808 the parish contained 1,260 a. arable and 298 a. pasture, and in 1839 there were 1,024 a. arable and 556 a. meadow.[2] The pastures were mainly on the northern slopes of the parish: in 1918 Beredens, which lay there, contained 177 a. meadow and pasture out of a total of 247 a.[3] In that part of Cranham, as in neighbouring parishes, livery stables and riding schools have since the Second World War replaced sheep and dairy farming.

By the 19th century only about 80 a. woodland remained in the parish, most of it in the north.[4] There is no evidence of open field farming. About 1565 there were 200 a. common waste, but by 1839 there were only 30 a., lying in the north, at Coombe Green.[5] In the later 18th and early 19th centuries there were some 10 or 12 farms and small holdings, but only 4 of these were over 100 a.[6] The largest were Cranham Hall and Beredens, which in 1839 were 474 a. and 337 a. respectively.[7]

There was a windmill on the manor of Cranham in 1442.[8] It was out of repair in 1463–4[9] and no later reference to it has been found. It was probably in the north-east of the parish: Millfield Hill was said in 1594 to adjoin Cranham Wood, and in 1614 Millfield was part of Beredens.[10]

Cranham, like the neighbouring parishes, possessed brick-earth. In 1839 Brick Field Hollow was one of the Beredens enclosures in the north-east of the parish.[11] The Cranham Brick and Tile Co. had opened a kiln *c.* 1900 west of Franks Wood and north of the railway; it closed in 1920.[12]

LOCAL GOVERNMENT. In 1273–4 the bishop of London claimed the right of gallows in his manor of Cranham.[13] Draft records of the manor's court baron survive for the period 1577–1622, and three court books for 1705–1929.[14]

Parish records include vestry and select vestry

[83] Cf. E.R.O., D/DU 835: the sub-tenant's farming diary.

[84] E.R.O., D/CT 107.

[85] E.R.O., D/P 118/5.

[86] E.R.O., D/DU 434/10: an endorsement of Tyson's conveyance to Nicholson of 1801. Possibly the unnamed beneficiaries were Emma Hance and Arthur Jackson, the second and third parties to the agreement.

[87] *Kelly's Dir. Essex* (1882).

[88] Ibid. (1886–1917); *Essex in 20th Century*, 105, 214; E.R.O., *Sale Cat.* A89.

[89] E.R.O., T/P 181/4/5.

[90] E.R.O., *Sale Cats.* A89, A267, B5742.

[91] E.R.O., *Sale Cat.* B5742.

[92] *Kelly's Dir. Essex* (1886); cf. *Essex in 20th Century*, 105.

[93] E.R.O., T/P 181/12/7; cf. *Kelly's Dir. Essex* (1922–37); *Who's Who* (1938), s.v. Furnivall, Baroness.

[94] Local inf.: perhaps by a flying bomb (E.R.O., C/W 1/2/59: 3 Aug. 1944).

[95] E.R.O., *Sale Cat.* B5742.

[96] Inf. from G.L.C. solicitors, by Mr. Hodson; cf. *D. Telegraph*, 7 Jan. 1975 p. 13.

[97] *V.C.H. Essex*, i. 440, 458.

[98] Cf. *V.C.H. Essex*, i. 375. In applying the formula to Cranham, Round did not include in his calculations Odo of Bayeux's manor of 'Craohu', which had not then been identified.

[99] As, e.g., in East and West Ham at the same period: *V.C.H. Essex*, vi. 14–15, 74.

[1] C 139/111.

[2] E.R.O., D/P 118/8/2; D/CT 107.

[3] E.R.O., T/P 181/4/5.

[4] E.R.O., D/P 118/8/2; D/CT 107.

[5] E.R.O., D/DP M1086; D/CT 107; cf. C/T 388 Deeds.

[6] E.R.O., D/P 118/12/3; D/P 118/11; D/CT 107.

[7] E.R.O., D/CT 107.

[8] C 139/111.

[9] E.R.O., D/DP M1083.

[10] E.R.O., D/DP M1222, 1224.

[11] E.R.O., D/CT 107.

[12] *Kelly's Dir. Essex* (1902); E.R.O., T/P 181/4/5 (15 May 1936).

[13] *Rot. Hund.* (Rec. Com.), i. 148.

[14] E.R.O., D/DP M1219–22, 1235; D/DVg 1–3.

minutes (1643–1800, 1818–23, 1825–9); overseers' accounts (1747–1817), rates (1747–95), and bills (1794–1818); a workhouse order book (1829–36); and surveyors' accounts and rates (1796–1836).[15]

The vestry minutes, up to 1796, recorded only meetings at which parish officers were named or accounts tendered. Signatures were recorded in the minutes between 1669 and 1747 and again in the 1790s. In those periods 3–5 parishioners usually signed. From 1669, when Edward Herbert became rector, the minutes were normally in the handwriting of the incumbent, but from 1731 to 1740 Herbert Tryst, who married Abigail (d. 1741) the widow of Sir Nathan Wright, Bt. (d. 1727), of Cranham Hall, kept the minutes. Thomas Talbot, who was also the vestry clerk of Upminster, was vestry clerk at Cranham from 1795 to 1829 or later.[16]

There were two churchwardens until 1657 but only one between 1659 and 1795. From 1795 there were again two. In 1703, 1704, 1706, 1744, 1760–6, and 1772 the rector chose the warden; in 1796–1800 and 1826–8 he also nominated one. A single overseer was nominated in the period 1646–1764; thereafter there were normally two. In 1778 and 1782 the nominations of voluntary substitutes as overseers were recorded. Between 1791 and 1796 each overseer received two guineas a year. In 1828 a paid assistant overseer was appointed. The appointment, however, was challenged, and it is not known whether it endured.[17] Cranham had two constables in the period 1646–60, one or two between 1660 and 1688, and only one thereafter, until 1800. There seem always to have been two surveyors of highways.

A select vestry was established in 1819. It met twice a month under the chairmanship of the rector. Meetings were held in the church until 1829, and then in the vestry room of the new parish workhouse.

Separate rates were granted to the churchwardens and to the surveyors. The constable also received a separate rate until *c.* 1740, after which he was reimbursed by the churchwardens. From 1761 the highway surveyors received, as well as their rate, allowances or compositions in lieu of statute duty and fines.

In the earlier 18th century Cranham appears to have supported its poor by paying rents and giving doles. From 1770 payments can also be found for various parishioners' club contributions, sometimes as gifts, sometimes as loans. In 1660–1, 1710–11, and 1797, payments were made to those taking apprentices.

A 'parish house' was first mentioned in 1782, when 8*s.* was paid for providing a loom for it. During the following years the vestry alternated between maintaining its own workhouse or poorhouse and sending paupers to workhouses in neighbouring parishes. Between 1786 and 1788 three of Cranham's paupers were in Great Warley workhouse. From 1789 to 1797 Cranham was renting a poorhouse at 1*s.* a week. Between 1797 and 1816 paupers, up to 5 in number, were being sent to Upminster workhouse. From 1817 there was again a Cranham poorhouse with a resident master.

In 1825 Cranham arranged to farm out its poor to South Ockendon,[18] but the arrangement was terminated in 1827 when the vestry decided to build its own workhouse, and meanwhile rented two rooms in a farm-house near the junction of Front and St. Mary's Lanes. The workhouse, completed in 1829, was on the south side of St. Mary's Lane between The Chase and Pike Lane. It had three rooms on the ground floor, one of which was the vestry room. Between 1829 and 1836 there were usually about 12 inmates.

Out-relief continued to be given in some cases, but in 1822 the vestry resolved that such relief should be given to the able poor living in the parish in bread rather than money. Other food was to be earned by labour.

Until 1783 the vestry paid for the medical treatment of paupers on a casual basis. From 1783 regular contracts were made with a succession of local doctors. These contracts usually provided, after 1811, that the doctor should attend the Cranham poor in neighbouring parishes as well as in Cranham itself.

In the later 17th century a 1*d.* rate produced about £3, and the cost of poor-relief averaged about £9. In the period 1698–1700 expenditure was exceptionally high, at over £30 a year, but that level was not again reached until 1719–20. Between 1719 and 1761 expenditure averaged about £36, in 1761–82 over £89, in 1782–95 over £142, and in 1796–1818 almost £336. The product of a 1*d.* rate increased, after revaluation in 1795, to £7.

In 1836 Cranham became part of Romford poor-law union. The parish workhouse was sold in the same year to George Rowe of Upminster.[19]

CHURCHES. The earliest reference to a church in Cranham occurs in 1254.[20] The advowson of Cranham rectory passed with lordship of the manor of Cranham Hall until the 18th century. Three times in the 16th century presentations were granted away.[21] In 1735 Herbert Tryst and his wife Abigail, the widow of Sir Nathan Wright, Bt. (d. 1727), presented John Woodrooffe.[22] Woodrooffe died in 1786, and his successor, George Strahan, presented himself.[23] Strahan sold the advowson in 1818 to Thomas Ludbey (d. 1819), whose son and namesake became rector in the same year.[24] In 1830 the elder Ludbey's widow, Jane, sold the advowson to St. John's College, Oxford, with whom it has since remained.[25]

The value of the rectory was 15 marks in 1254, £8 in 1291, and £13 13*s.* 4*d.* in 1535.[26] In the 18th century the augmented value was £130.[27] The tithes were commuted in 1839 for £560.[28] The glebe, com-

[15] E.R.O., D/P 118/5; D/P 118/8/1–6; D/P 118/12/1–6, 118/11; D/P 118/18/2; D/P 118/21/2–3: information in this section comes from these sources.

[16] For Upminster see E.R.O., D/P 117/8/4–11.

[17] The overseer's account for this period does not survive; the outcome of the dispute is thus unknown.

[18] Payments to S. Ockendon are often concealed behind the names of Mr. or Mrs. Ansell, the master and mistress of S. Ockendon's poorhouse.

[19] George Rowe also bought Upminster's workhouse: see p. 155.

[20] *E.A.T.* N.S. xviii. 18.

[21] Newcourt, *Repertorium*, ii. 195.

[22] Morant, *Essex*, i. 106. This presentation reinforced one of 1734 by Tryst alone.

[23] Guildhall MS. 9557.

[24] C.P. 25(2)/1313/58 Geo. III Hil.

[25] St. John's College, Oxford, muniments lxxv. 15; reference supplied by Mr. H. M. Colvin.

[26] *E.A.T.* N.S. xviii. 18; *Tax. Eccl.* (Rec. Com.), 22; *Valor Eccl.* (Rec. Com.), i. 436.

[27] Guildhall MSS. 9550, 9556–7.

[28] E.R.O., D/CT 107.

prising some 40 a., lay on both sides of Front Lane south of its junction with Moor (Back) Lane.[29] There too was the rectory house, mentioned in 1610.[30] It was rebuilt on the same site in 1790, incorporating material from the recently demolished Cranham Hall, and was a brick building of two storeys and attics, with 7 bays to the front.[31] The house and glebe were sold for development in 1924, and a new rectory was built half a mile south, near the church.[32]

Since Cranham was a small, thinly populated parish, the rectors before the Civil War were often non-resident or pluralist or both.[33] Ignatius Jordan, who became rector in 1639, was sequestrated in 1643. His successor, Robert Watson, was appointed in the same year,[34] and was succeeded *c.* 1652 by John Yardley.[35] In 1660 Jordan petitioned for restoration, but then apparently exercised his right to confirm Yardley as incumbent, for it was not until 1662 that Yardley was ejected for nonconformity.[36] Between the Restoration and 1818 the non-resident and pluralist traditions of Cranham's rectors were revived,[37] but Thomas Ludbey, rector 1818–59, was, like the incumbents of the Interregnum and John Woodrooffe (1735–86), resident in Cranham. There had been no resident landowner since the deaths of General and Mrs. Oglethorpe, and Ludbey was clearly the leader in parish life.[38] It was, however, in the time of his successor Charles Rew (1859–84) that the church was rebuilt.[39]

The names of assistant curates are recorded from 1577.[40] One of the most notable was Ralph Josselin, who was at Cranham briefly in 1640. His income was £44: £24 provided by the rector, £10 by the parish, and £10 in diet by his uncle and namesake, the tenant of Cranham Hall, with whom he lodged.[41]

The church of *ALL SAINTS*, the Chase, was built in 1873–5 on the site of its predecessor, which had the same dedication. The old church, which apparently dated from the 13th century, comprised nave, chancel, south porch, and short weather-boarded west tower.[42] There were three narrow lancets on each side of the chancel, the easternmost window on the south wall being shorter to make room for a round-headed doorway. The east window was of a later date. The nave had a large window with 4 round-headed lights on the north side and another on the south. The timber porch stood on a brick foundation, with weatherboarding below and lattice-work above. The west wall of the nave contained three lancet windows, two below and one above in the gable. These were blocked, apparently in the 15th century, by the west tower.[43] The tower had a semi-octagonal brick base with a tiled pent-roof from which rose a weatherboarded bell-chamber with a low pyramidal slate roof.[44]

In 1638 the high pew was ordered to be removed from the chancel and the altar to be set against the east wall. The latter order was repeated in 1685, when it was added that the altar should be railed.[45] In 1702–3 the north side of the church was 'ripped up and new piled'.[46] No further major repairs have been noted, and in 1871 the church was said to be in a miserable state of dirt and dilapidation.[47]

The present church of All Saints, designed by Richard Armstrong, cost £5,114, most of which was given by Richard Benyon owner of Cranham Hall. It is built of stone in the Early English style and consists of chancel, nave, south porch and north tower.[48]

Of the monuments retained from the old church, the marble tablet to General Oglethorpe (d. 1785) was replaced on the south chancel wall; in the chancel floor were set a brass inscription to Nathan Wright (d. 1658) and a floor-slab to his daughter Susannah (d. 1664), successively the wife of Charles Potts and Francis Drake.

The three bells, all of *c.* 1460, were rehung, for chiming only, in the new church. Two were cast by John Danyell and the third by Henry Jordan.[49]

The church plate includes an undated silver cup of the period 1696–1729 presented by the rector in 1745; a silver paten of unknown date, and another of 1823 inscribed 'Cranham Essex 1745'.[50]

The district of *ST. LUKE*, Cranham Park, was formed in 1957 from Cranham and Upminster, the advowson being vested in the bishop.[51] Services had been held since 1955 in a builder's hut, also used by the Baptists and the Brethren.[52] A dual-purpose church was consecrated in 1957, and a church hall built *c.* 1966.[53]

ROMAN CATHOLICISM. From 1571 to 1647 Cranham Hall was held by the Petres, who were prominent recusants. Sir Edward Petre, Bt. (1631–99), confessor to James II, was a member of the Cranham branch of this family.[54] Cranham (or Crondon) Park, where there was a Roman Catholic congregation in the 18th century, was in Stock parish, not Cranham.[55]

[29] Newcourt, *Repertorium*, ii. 195; Church Register (1558–1812); E.R.O., D/P 118/8/3; E.R.O., D/CT 107.

[30] Newcourt, *Repertorium*, ii. 195.

[31] E.R.O., D/AEM 2/6; E.R.O., T/P 221/2.

[32] E.R.O., D/CP 3/51.

[33] *E.R.* xlvii. 187, l. 36; Newcourt, *Repertorium*, ii. 582, 344.

[34] A. G. Matthews, *Walker Revised*, 157.

[35] Davids, *Nonconformity in Essex*, 378–9.

[36] Smith, *Eccl. Hist. Essex*, 118, 349; Davids, *Nonconformity in Essex*, 378–9. In 1672 Yardley was licensed as a Presbyterian preacher in South Weald.

[37] Guildhall MSS. 9550, 9558; Foster, *Alumni Oxon.* 1715–1886, iv.1363; *D.N.B.* s.v. Strahan, Wm.; E.R.O., T/P 67/7 p. 57.

[38] See p. 105.

[39] See below.

[40] Church Register (1558–1812); Hale, *Precedents*, pp. 168, 202–3,

[41] Foster, *Alumni Oxon.* 1500–1714, ii. 833; *Diary of Revd. Ralph Josselin* (Camd. 3rd ser.), 9–10. The latter makes clear that Jordan was an absentee.

[42] See plate facing p. 17. This paragraph is based on E.R.O., T/P 196 Eccles. Essex, iv. 481*f*; T/P 221/2; Bamford Colln.; D/DU 799; Thorne, *Environs Lond.* 122.

[43] In her will of 1421 (Prob. 11/2B: P.C.C. 52 Marche) Lady Curzon left £5 for bells, and £5 for the bell-tower, of Cranham.

[44] E.R.O., D/AEM 1/5, for 1849 repairs.

[45] E.R.O., D/AEV 7 f.16; *E.A.T.* N.S. xxi. 323.

[46] E.R.O., D/P 118/8/1.

[47] E.R.O., T/P 196 Eccles. Essex, iv. 481*f*.

[48] E.R.O., D/DBe Q5; D/P 118/8/4; V. P. Bowen, *Short Hist. of Cranham and its Parish Church.* Cf. E.R.O., D/DBe Q6.

[49] *Ch. Bells Essex*, 228–9.

[50] *Ch. Plate Essex*, 12.

[51] E.R.O., D/CPc 354; *Chelmsford Dioc. Yr. Bk.* (1958 sqq.).

[52] Inf. from Vicar.

[53] Ibid.

[54] *D.N.B.*

[55] For Cranham (i.e. Crondon) Park, see *Map of Essex* (1777); E. Burton, *Life and Times of Bp. Challoner*, i. 209 inf. from Miss E. R. Poyser, Archivist, Westminster Archives.

In 1973 Sunday mass, served from Upminster, was being celebrated at the Golden Crane, Avon Road.[56]

PROTESTANT NONCONFORMITY. John Yardley, who in 1662 was ejected for nonconformity from the rectory of Cranham, was in 1672 granted a general licence to preach as a Presbyterian.[57] He was then living at (South) Weald, but may well have preached at Cranham, where the houses of John Petchey and Philip Dixon were licensed for Presbyterian worship.[58] In 1676 only one nonconformist was reported in the parish.[59]

In 1835 the house of E. Phillpots at Cranham was registered for worship by Joseph Gray, a Congregational minister at Chelmsford.[60] A mission hall in Lower Road was registered for Christians in 1895.[61] Moor Lane chapel was registered by the Brethren in 1955.[62] Cranham Baptist church, Severn Drive, originated *c.* 1955 when Upminster Baptist church started services in a builders' hut for members who were moving to the new houses in Cranham.[63] The church was completed in 1957.[64] It was extended in 1974.[65]

EDUCATION. The Boyd Church of England school was founded in 1818 by the family of Thomas Boyd (d. 1846) of Cranham Hall.[66] It was held in a cottage where children under 8 years were taught Bible reading, writing, and needlework. Mrs. Sarah Hunwicks was the schoolmistress from 1818 to 1874.[67] In 1836 an evening-school was started at Cranham Hall, supported by Miss Sarah Boyd (1801–97); it was affiliated to Grays technical instruction board in 1897 and transferred to Essex county council in 1901.[68] By 1839 sixteen children were being taught in the day-school. Thomas Boyd, and Thomas Ludbey, rector 1818–59, paid for the teaching of children who could not afford school pence. Good conduct was rewarded by gifts of clothing.[69] In 1846–7 there were 9 boys and 20 girls at the school.[70] When the school cottage was pulled down in 1854, the school moved to a wooden building which had been used by the evening and Sunday schools. It was enlarged in 1861.[71] In 1870 a school for 115 children and a teacher's house were built in St. Mary's Lane as a memorial to the work of Sarah Boyd. Richard Benyon, owner of Cranham Hall, gave the site and paid part of the building costs.[72] The new school contained rooms for Miss Boyd under whose sole control it remained until she moved to Wanstead in 1889.[73] She continued to support the school until her death in 1897, when a voluntary rate was raised to maintain it.[74] It had received an annual government grant since 1890–1.[75] In 1902 the school was reorganized into two departments for mixed and infant children; the infants department was enlarged in 1912 for 40 children. In 1916 it was described as a bad school, needing regular supervision.[76] It was reorganized in 1936 for mixed juniors and infants. In 1938 it was taken over by the county council pending the building of a new school. In 1941 the church hall was also being used for temporary accommodation. The school closed in 1950,[77] but was used temporarily in 1957–8 by children from Oglethorpe primary school.[78] In 1974 it was the village hall.[79]

Oglethorpe county primary school, Ashvale Gardens, opened in 1950 for 320 juniors and 200 infants.[80] Engayne county primary school, Severn Drive, for 320 juniors and 240 infants opened in 1958.[81] Hall Mead county secondary school, Marlborough Gardens, opened in 1960. It was enlarged in 1968 and 1973.[82] All Cranham schools passed to the London borough of Havering in 1965.[83]

CHARITIES FOR THE POOR. It was stated *c.* 1727 that Nathan Wright (d. 1657) gave 'alms-houses for two persons in St. Mary's Lane'.[84] No later references have been found to these alms-houses and they did not exist in 1786.[85]

[56] *Cath. Dir.* (1973).
[57] A. G. Matthews, *Calamy Revised,* 550; Davids, *Nonconformity in Essex,* 379.
[58] G. L. Turner, *Orig. Recs. of Early Nonconformity,* i. 526, ii. 931.
[59] William Salt Libr., Stafford, S. 2112 (Bp. Compton's census, 1676).
[60] G.R.O. Worship Returns, London dioc. Essex and Herts. commissary, no. 708. There was no nonconformist meeting-place in 1829 or 1851: E.R.O., Q/CR 3/1/91; H.O. 129. For Joseph Gray, see *Congr. Yr. Bk.* (1846), 105.
[61] G.R.O. Worship reg. no. 34931 (cancelled 1954 revision). Lower Road may have been the present Moor Lane.
[62] Ibid. no. 65083; it was registered by the name of Moss Hall, amended in 1960 to Moor Lane chapel.
[63] D. Witard, *Bibles in Barrels,* 173–4. See also below p. 160.
[64] Witard, *Bibles in Barrels,* 173–4; E.R.O., D/NB 2/4; G.R.O. Worship Reg. no. 66778.
[65] Local inf.
[66] E.R.O., D/P 30/28/18; D/DU 799.
[67] E.R.O., T/P 67/3, p. 91; D/DU 799.
[68] E.R.O., D/DBe Q4; D/DU 799; *Kelly's Dir. Essex* (1874).
[69] E.R.O., D/P 30/28/18.
[70] *Nat. Soc. Church Schs. Enquiry 1846–7.*
[71] E.R.O., D/DU 799.
[72] E.R.O., D/DBe Q4; D/P 118/28/3, p. 53; *Kelly's Dir. Essex* (1878).
[73] E.R.O., D/DBe Q4; T/P 67/3, p. 91.
[74] E.R.O., D/DBe Q4.
[75] *Rep. of Educ. Cttee. of Council 1890–1* [C. 6438–I], p. 588, H.C. (1890–1), xxvii.
[76] Ed. 21/5077.
[77] Inf. from Essex Educ. Dept.; Ed. 21/28151.
[78] E.R.O., C/ME 51, pp. 233, 735.
[79] Local inf.
[80] E.R.O., C/ME 41, p. 64; inf. from Essex Educ. Dept.; named after Gen. Jas. Oglethorpe (d. 1785).
[81] *Educ. in Essex 1956–60,* pp. 21–23; named after the Engayne family.
[82] Inf. from Essex Educ. Dept. and Havering Educ. Dept.
[83] *Havering Official Guide* (1966–7), p. 33.
[84] E.R.O., T/P 195/2 (Holman MSS.).
[85] E.R.O., Q/RSr 1; Guildhall MS. 9557, f. 57.

NORTH OCKENDON

NORTH Ockendon was a small country parish of 1,709 a.[1] It lay 19 miles east of London, between Brentwood and Grays Thurrock. Its medieval name of Ockendon Setfountayns derived from the lords of the manor. In 1935 the parish was divided between two urban districts: the south-west corner was added to Thurrock, the rest to Hornchurch.[2] In 1965 Hornchurch became part of the London borough of Havering.[3]

North, east, and west of North Ockendon a succession of narrow parishes used to run southwards from a northern wooded slope, but North Ockendon, unlike them, was broader east to west and had a lower and more level terrain with a central plateau whose greatest height, east of Whitepost Farm, was 135 ft. The soil contains deposits of brick-earth and gravel.[4] For a short distance the Mardyke formed the parish boundary in the east. Until 1900 water supplies for the parish came chiefly from wells.[5]

The recorded population of North Ockendon in 1066 was 17; in 1086 it was 23.[6] In 1327 14 householders, and in 1523 26 householders, were named in the tax lists.[7] In 1670 North Ockendon had 33 houses.[8] There were 243 inhabitants in 1801, a number which rose, with fluctuations, to 351 in 1891 and thereafter declined to 291 in 1931.[9]

The pattern of settlement in North Ockendon was established in the Middle Ages and has changed little since; it consists of a nucleated village and outlying farms. Of the latter, Baldwins, in the south-west of the parish and formerly moated, is the oldest. It presumably took its name from the 14th-century lords of the manor, but the present building is a timber-framed house of the 16th century.[10] The main road or street from Brentwood to Grays divided the parish and was crossed by a road running east from Bulphan to Upminster and Romford. At this cross-road the village developed, and it still includes the 15th-century blacksmith's house and a 16th- and 17th-century house, now the post office.[11] From Bulphan to the village the road (Fen Lane) mattered less to the inhabitants of North Ockendon than to those of the parishes eastwards who wished to reach Romford market and London; hence the frequent complaints about its upkeep between 1589 and 1645.[12] A lane ran north from this road[13] past Home Farm to Brasenose Farm, which in 1513 was given to the Oxford college of that name by Sir Richard Sutton.[14] The western stretch of the road from the village towards Upminster was formerly known as Cole Street.[15] From it a lane ran south to the hall and church, and further west Pike Lane crossed it and continued south as Pea Lane.[16] Pea Lane divided at Dennises Corner, and both branches became Dennises Lane. One continued south into South Ockendon; the other turned west towards Aveley, Rainham, and Corbets Tey. In the Middle Ages a green lane may have run south from Cranham past Cranham Hall and Stubbers to Baldwins. The stretch between Cole Street and Dennises Lane survived as a road until 1814, when it was moved west to the parish boundary at the wish of John Russell of Stubbers.[17] In 1974 the lane to Baldwins was a farm-drive.

The only important bridge in the parish carried the road to Bulphan over the Mardyke. It was known as Kennetts (or Kynes or Kinyttes) bridge, and the lord of the manor of North Ockendon was charged with its maintenance.[18] Sir Thomas Littleton (d. 1710) rebuilt it 6 ft. wide, but in 1775 Richard Benyon established public responsibility for any further widening.[19]

In 1848 an omnibus ran daily to Romford to meet the trains.[20] The London, Tilbury and Southend railway's line from Upminster to Grays was opened in 1892; the nearest station was South Ockendon.[21] There was a post office by 1839.[22]

A friendly society at the White Horse was registered in 1818.[23] Richard Benyon built a reading room *c.* 1885 in Church Lane; in 1895 it had 40 ordinary members.[24] Vestry meetings were held there from 1906 to 1910.[25]

Among the notable people connected with North Ockendon were two members of the manorial family: Edward Littleton (b. 1626, fl. 1694), barrister, judge in Barbados 1670–83, and later agent for the island, published economic tracts; his nephew, Sir Thomas Littleton (d. 1710), was Speaker of the House of Commons, 1698–1700, and Treasurer of the Navy, 1701–10.[26] Of the rectors Robert Wilmot (fl. 1568–1608; rector, 1582–5) published a tragedy acted before Elizabeth I; Henry Tripp (d. 1612; rector, 1570–82) was an author and translator.[27] At Stubbers William Coys (d. 1627), the botanist, was renowned for his gardens, in which he grew in 1604 the first yucca in England.[28]

MANORS AND OTHER ESTATES. Before 1066 the manor of (*NORTH*) *OCKENDON*, which comprised the greater part of the parish, was held by Earl

[1] O.S. Map 1/25,000, TQ 58, 68; O.S. Map 6", Essex, LXXV (surv. 1865–6).
[2] *Kelly's Dir. Essex* (1937).
[3] *Havering Official Guide* (1966–7), 9.
[4] *V.C.H. Essex*, i. 16.
[5] W. Whitaker and J. C. Thresh, *Water Supply Essex*, 233.
[6] *V.C.H. Essex*, i. 445.
[7] E 179/107/13; E 179/108/150.
[8] E.R.O., Q/RTh 5, m. 2d.
[9] *Census.*
[10] R.C.H.M. *Essex*, iv. 101.
[11] Ibid.; Thorne, *Environs Lond.* 455.
[12] E.R.O., Q/SR 108/25, 324/34; see TS. index for intervening occasions. For the settlement of a dispute with S. Ockendon in 1789: E.R.O., D/DRu E1.
[13] It ended immediately over the parish boundary in Great Warley at the neighbouring farm, Bolens and Herds.
[14] *D.N.B.*
[15] C 142/531/39; E.R.O., D/DBe E9.
[16] For a diversion of the crossing in 1789: E.R.O., Q/RHi 3/17; Q/SBb 336/18.
[17] E.R.O., D/DRu E1, 4; E.R.O., Q/RHi 3/76. For the diversion in 1679 of the road from Corbets Tey to the unidentified 'Reeves Tie': E.R.O., D/DRu E1; cf. E.R.O., Q/SR 207/38 ('Revstyle green', 1614).
[18] E.R.O., Q/SR 73/58, 100/34, 110/58, 112/45, 121/28, 123/32.
[19] E.R.O., D/DBe E18, 50.
[20] *White's Dir. Essex* (1848).
[21] E. Carter, *Hist. Geog. Rlys.* 477.
[22] *Pigot's Dir. Essex* (1839).
[23] E.R.O., Q/SO 24, f. 626, 25 f. 29.
[24] *Kelly's Dir. Essex* (1886–95): in 1895 the entry emphasized Benyon's continuing ownership; cf. E.R.O., T/P 67/2, p. 46.
[25] E.R.O., D/P 308/8/1.
[26] *D.N.B.*
[27] Ibid.
[28] Pevsner, *Essex*, 308.

Harold as 2 hides less 40 acres.[29] William I took for himself almost all Harold's lands in Essex, but by 1075 he had granted North Ockendon and Feering to Westminster Abbey in exchange for the manor of Windsor (Berks.).[30] In the early 12th century North Ockendon provided 5*s.* towards the support of the monks, and in the 14th century a like sum went to the sacrist.[31] The abbey retained the overlordship of the manor until the Dissolution.[32]

In 1086 one hide of the manor was held of the abbey by William the chamberlain.[33] The manor was granted to Henry son of Wlvred in 1125 for a rent of £10 a year, which in later centuries was assigned to the cellarer.[34] William of Ockendon apparently held the manor *c.* 1155, when he yielded the church to the abbot of Westminster.[35] Between 1201 and 1203 there was litigation over a carucate of land in North Ockendon which Christine of Moulsham claimed as one of an unspecified number of sisters. Her opponent was Ralph of Setfountayns (de Septem Fontibus) of Chelsea (Mdx.). In the settlement Ralph received the carucate; in return Christine and her son Hubert were to hold of Ralph the lands in Ockendon previously held by her husband William son of Osbert.[36] This settlement seems to have been the basis of the Setfountayns possession of the manor, which in the 13th and 14th centuries was named *OCKENDON SETFOUNTAYNS*. Ralph died *c.* 1210.[37] He was succeeded at Ockendon and Chelsea by his son William who was still living in 1230.[38]

The manor descended in the Setfountayns family, until the end of the 13th century. Ralph of Setfountayns, son of William, held the advowson of North Ockendon in 1254 and was still alive in 1286.[39] He was succeeded by his son Thomas, who died in or after 1297 without issue, leaving as heirs his sisters Cecily and Isabel.[40] Isabel had married William (son of) Baldwin (d. 1316) who was in North Ockendon in 1305.[41] She died before the division of the family estates in 1315. Her heir was her son, Baldwin son of William (d. 1323), who took the manor of North Ockendon and the alternate presentation to the rectory.[42] Within two years of Baldwin's death his widow Emme married Nicholas of Brundish, and in 1329 they presented to the rectory.[43] Baldwin's heir was his son John de Baudechon (Bauchon, Bauchun), who seems to have died by 1373, leaving a widow Margaret.[44] She held the manor until her death in 1390 or 1391, when it passed to Poyntz Poyntz of Tockington (Glos.) in right of his wife Eleanor who was probably the granddaughter of William son of Baldwin.[45]

Poyntz Poyntz had died by 1412 when his son John held the manor.[46] John Poyntz (d. 1447) was succeeded by his son, another John (d. 1469 or 1470).[47] The manor then went in turn to the younger John's sons, Thomas and William: Thomas had died by 1481 when William and his father-in-law jointly presented to the rectory.[48]

William Poyntz (d. 1504) was succeeded by his sons John (d. 1547) and Thomas (d. 1562); Thomas's heir was his son (Sir) Gabriel (d. 1607), who devised the manor to (Sir) John Morris *alias* Poyntz of Chipping Ongar, the husband of his late daughter Catherine (d. 1603) and their heirs male, with remainder to Audrey, the daughter of his late son Thomas.[49] North Ockendon descended with the manor of Chipping Ongar until the death in 1643 of Poyntz Poyntz.[50] John Morris, nephew of Sir John Morris *alias* Poyntz then attempted to secure North Ockendon by methods which included forgery and an armed attack on North Ockendon Hall.[51] North Ockendon descended, however, in accordance with Sir Gabriel's will, to his granddaughter Audrey (d. 1648) and her husband, Sir Adam (Poyntz-) Littleton, Bt. (d. 1647). It then passed with the baronetcy until the death in 1710 of Sir Thomas Littleton, Bt., Speaker of the House of Commons, and later Treasurer of the Navy.[52] Sir Thomas, who left no issue, devised his estates to his kinsman, Capt. (later Vice-Admiral) James Littleton (d. 1723).[53] On the admiral's death North Ockendon passed, under the will of Sir Thomas, to Mrs. Elizabeth Meynell (d. 1726), a granddaughter of Sir Adam (Poyntz-) Littleton.[54] From this time the Hall was occupied by tenants.

[29] *V.C.H. Essex*, i. 445.
[30] Ibid. i. 444; Hart, *Early Chart. Essex*, 32–3.
[31] W.A.M. 5670, and Liber Niger Quaternus, f. 141.
[32] *L. & P. Hen. VIII*, xvii, p. 166. In 1542 the overlord's rights were sold by the Crown to the tenant, John Poyntz.
[33] *V.C.H. Essex*, i. 445; W.A.M., Domesday Book, f. 129.
[34] W.A.M., Domesday Book, ff. 129, 446v; W.A.M. 3180, 3221, 29371–2, 29489, 30765, 30767.
[35] A. Saltman, *Theobald Abp. Cant.* 507: 1150 × 1158; *Flete's Hist. Westm. Abbey*, ed. J. Armitage Robinson, 88.
[36] *Feet of F. Essex*, i. 30; *Pleas before King or his Justices*, ii (Selden Soc. lxviii), p. 311; iii (Selden Soc. lxxxiii), pp. 13, 44; *Cur. Reg. R.* ii. 81.
[37] *Pipe R.* 1210 (P.R.S. N.S. xxvi), 75. For Ralph in Mdx., see *Cur. Reg. R.* ii, iii, iv, v *passim.* It is perhaps he who is named *c.* 1155 (*Early Med. Misc. for D. M. Stenton* (P.R.S. N.S. xxxvi), 103) and 1158 × 1173 (W.A.M., Liber Niger Quaternus, f. 125v).
[38] *Pipe R.* 1211 (P.R.S. N.S. xxviii), 247; *Cur. Reg. R.* vi. 306; vii. 153; xiii. 510, 540–1. A Setfountayns claim to the mill and land at Moulsham was settled in 1225–6: *Cur. Reg. R.* vii. 1, 218, 262, 265–6; xi. 517; xii. 58, 267, 427–8, 464; *Feet of F. Essex*, i. 72.
[39] *E.A.T.* N.S. xviii. 18; *Cal. Pat.* 1281–92, 252. In 1274 Ralph was coroner of Mdx. and living in Chelsea: *Cal. Pat.* 1272–81, 61; W.A.M. 3199.
[40] *Cal. Pat.* 1266–72, 87; C.P. 40/352 m. 558; *Cal. Inq. p.m.* iii, p. 259.
[41] *Cal. Inq. p.m.* iv, p. 229.
[42] *E.R.* xxxvii. 52, 57; *Feet of F. Essex*, ii. 172, 179, 204. This family continued to use patronymics rather than surnames throughout its 14th-century existence.
[43] *Cal. Close*, 1323–7, 511; Newcourt, *Repertorium*, ii. 447. Her brother-in-law Bartholomew was exchanging North Ockendon for Cranham; cf. *Feet of F. Essex*, ii. 142, 161.
[44] *Feet of F. Essex*, iii. 99–100, 168, 179; *E.R.* xxxvii. 52; C.P. 40/352 m. 558.
[45] *Feet of F. Essex*, iii. 168. Despite the statement of the fine, Eleanor is more likely to have been the daughter of Baldwin (son of) William rather than of his father William (son of) Baldwin. E.R.O., D/DBe M17; Newcourt, *Repertorium*, ii. 447.
[46] *Feud. Aids*, vi. 444.
[47] B.L., Lansd. MS. 860A, f. 278; for his will, *Genealogist*, vi. 135.
[48] Prob. 11/5 (P.C.C. 29 Godyn); Newcourt, *Repertorium*, ii. 447; E.R.O., D/DBe M18.
[49] Chancellor, *Sep. Mons. Essex*, 181–90, pl. LV–LXII; *E.R.* xxxiii. 22–3; E.R.O., T/R 154/1, p. 108.
[50] *V.C.H. Essex*, iv. 161.
[51] *E.R.* xxxiii. 20–6; *Clarke Papers* (Camd. Soc. 2nd ser. liv), ii. 199. Cf. E.R.O., Q/SR 333/107, 338/23.
[52] Ch. Reg. 1570–1654; Morant, *Essex*, i. 103; E.R.O., T/P 195/2 Ockendons, p. 79.
[53] For the exact relationship, see *Hist. Parl., Commons*, 1715–54, ii. 219.
[54] Morant, *Essex*, i. 103; Burke, *Land. Gent.* (1847), ii. 860; *D.N.B.* (for Edw. Littleton); E.R.O., D/DBe E7.

Mrs. Meynell was succeeded by her son, Littleton Poyntz Meynell, who died in 1751 or 1752.[55] His successor was his son Hugh who sold North Ockendon in 1758 to Richard Benyon, the former governor of Fort St. George, Madras.[56] Benyon was already lord of the manors of Newbury, in Ilford, and Gidea Hall, Romford, and North Ockendon descended with Newbury until 1891.[57] In 1840 the manor comprised 1,135 a.[58]

Richard Benyon (formerly Fellowes) (d. 1897) was succeeded by his nephew, James H. Fellowes, later Benyon (d. 1935).[59] In 1937 Henry, son of J. H. Benyon, sold North Ockendon, together with the other Benyon estates in Essex, to pay death duties.[60] G. Gunary, the tenant, bought the Hall farm with 223 a.[61]

North Ockendon Hall lay within a moated enclosure immediately south of the churchyard. The red-brick house was of 16th-century origin with additions of the early 18th and the 19th centuries.[62] It was damaged by bombing in 1944 and later demolished.[63] The site is now occupied by modern bungalows, one of which incorporates a fragment of an old outbuilding. Several garden walls, probably of the 16th and 18th centuries, also survive. The northern arm of the moat has been filled in and partly built over; the east and outer west moats are little more than ditches; but the south and inner west moats are still wide and water-filled.

The manor of *GROVES*, which is to be distinguished from Groves manor in South Ockendon, lay on either side of Cole Street at the junction with Pike and Pea Lanes. Courts leet were held in 1518 and 1519 and recorded on rolls of the manor of North Ockendon, held of Westminster Abbey by the Poyntz family.[64] In 1570 (Sir) Gabriel Poyntz and his wife Audrey (d. 1594) were said to hold half of Groves manor for her life.[65] In 1608 Groves was regarded as a free tenement of the manor of North Ockendon, with which it descended.[66] In 1650 it was settled on William, the second son of Sir Adam and Lady (Audrey) (Poyntz-) Littleton, but in 1676 Dorothy, William's daughter and heir, sold it back to Sir Thomas Littleton, Bt.[67] Thereafter it remained with the North Ockendon estate, passing to the Meynells and Benyons.[68]

By 1774 the capital messuage of Groves was named Manor Farm.[69] It contained 130 a. in 1725 and 265 a. in 1775.[70] The present (1974) house, built *c.* 1900, stands SW. of the junction of Pea Lane and Ockendon Road.

The estate called *STUBBERS* originated as a free tenement of the manor of North Ockendon.[71] It lay in the north-west of the parish and in Upminster south of Corbets Tey, and took its name from William Stubber, yeoman, who formed the estate in the years between 1439 and his death in 1484.[72] Elements of his estate derived from properties recorded in 1419, 1427, and 1436; and two deeds of 1334 and 1337 presumably indicate, although in a way not now clear, the earliest history of these acres.[73] After Stubber's death the estate passed to Nicholas Davy, who added to it, and then to John Davy (d. 1525).[74] In 1533 the latter's son, another John Davy, sold Stubbers to Robert Warren (d. 1544), merchant tailor of London. The estate then comprised 60 a. and was occupied by Thomas Butler.[75] Warren's son Jasper sold the estate in 1563 for £320 to his Welsh brother-in-law, Roger Coys of London.[76] Roger was succeeded by his son William (d. 1627), the botanist, and he by his son Giles.[77] The estate had grown, and in 1629 comprised 160 a., including 103 a. in North Ockendon.[78] In 1642 Giles Coys sold Stubbers for £2,000 to Bernard Hale, later Master of Peterhouse, Cambridge (d. 1663), and his sister Dionis; in 1647 it passed to her, with other property, on her marriage with Sir Thomas Williamson.[79] Williamson sold Stubbers in the same year to Edmund Hoskins of the Inner Temple, London, and Hoskins sold it in 1660 to Sir Benjamin Wright, Bt., of Cranham Hall, from whom it was bought in 1662 by John Meyrick (d. 1663), merchant of London.[80] In 1689 Meyrick's widow Isabella, with his son Francis, sold the estate to Sir William Russell, alderman of London. It then consisted of 207 a.[81]

Stubbers descended in the direct line from Sir William (d. 1705) to his son William Russell (d. 1727), his grandson William Russell (d. 1754), and great-grandson John Russell (d. 1787).[82] It then passed in turn to John's sons, William (d. 1810), John (d. 1825), and Joseph (d. 1828).[83] Their mother Mary had been the sister of Champion Branfill (II) (d. 1770) of Upminster, and Joseph Russell devised Stubbers, which in 1840 comprised 405 a., to the young Branfill heir, Champion (V), who took the name of Russell.[84] He died in 1887 and was succeeded

55 Prob. 11/798. Meynell's eldest son received only an annuity of £100, enlarged by a private Act of Parliament (26 Geo. II c.42).

56 E.R.O., D/DBe T7, D/DRu T1/162–3; C.P. 25(2)/1125.

57 *V.C.H. Essex*, v. 208; cf. above, p. 68.

58 E.R.O., D/CT 260.

59 *Who's Who* (1924). The Benyons' chief seat was at Englefield (Berks.).

60 E.R.O., *Sale Cat.* B106; E.R.O., D/DBe E57.

61 E.R.O., *Sale Cat.* B106; E.R.O., D/DBe E71: Gunary, as tenant, also bought White Post farm (191 a.) and another 46 a. in the parish.

62 Thorne, *Environs Lond.* 456; O.S. Map 1/2,500, Essex, LXXV. 11 (1895 edn.); cf. E.R.O., D/CT 260B (1841); E.R.O., photos. of B.L., Ord. draft map (1799) for earlier states; R.C.H.M. *Essex*, iv. 100–1; E.R.O., D/DBe E7, 8.

63 E.R.O., C/W 1/2/59 (22 Jan. 1944); Pevsner, *Essex*, 308. For photographs of the Hall: E.R.O., T/P 132/3 (including one of formal E. front annotated 'Stubbers', and 2 of N. front).

64 W.A.M. 3212–13; cf. W.A.M. 3214 (of 1506).

65 C.P. 25(2)/128/1642.

66 C 142/297/163.

67 E.R.O., D/DBe T3, T4; D/DRu T1/159; C.P. 25(2)/550B.

68 See above.

69 *Map of Essex* (1777). The identity of Groves and Manor Farm is indicated by field names: C 142/622/4, 10; C 142/744/39; C 142/745/65 (of 1645); E.R.O., D/DBe P5 (1775).

70 E.R.O., D/DRu T1/159; D/DBe E5.

71 C 142/747/159.

72 E.R.O., D/DRu T1/86–95.

73 E.R.O., D/DRu T1/81–5.

74 E.R.O., D/DRu T1/96–100.

75 E.R.O., D/DRu T1/104–5; Prob. 11/30 (P.C.C. 10 Pynning).

76 E.R.O., D/DRu T1/111; Morant, *Essex*, i. 103. Cf. *Feet of F. Essex*, iv. 227, 269.

77 I. M. Russell, 'Stubbers, North Ockendon', *E.A.T.* N.S. xxi. 49–51.

78 E.R.O., D/DRu T1/114–16.

79 E.R.O., D/DRu T1/118–25; Venn, *Alumni Cantab.* I, ii. 281.

80 E.R.O., D/DRu T1/126, 131–4, 138–41.

81 E.R.O., D/DRu T1/148–52.

82 *E.A.T.* N.S. xxi. 53; Morant, *Essex*, i. 103; H. E. Priestley, *Story of Upminster*, v. 12; Prob. 11/616.

83 E.R.O., T/P 154/2, p. 210; W. Palin, *More about Stifford*, 115–16.

84 Priestley, *Story of Upminster*, v. 12; *E.A.T.* N.S. xxi. 55; ER.O., D./CT 260A; see below, p. 151.

Romford, Gidea Park: Great Eastern Railway Factory, built 1843

Rainham: Murex Ltd. and P.L.A. Lagoons, from the south-east

ROMFORD: Roger Reede's Alms-houses, built 1961

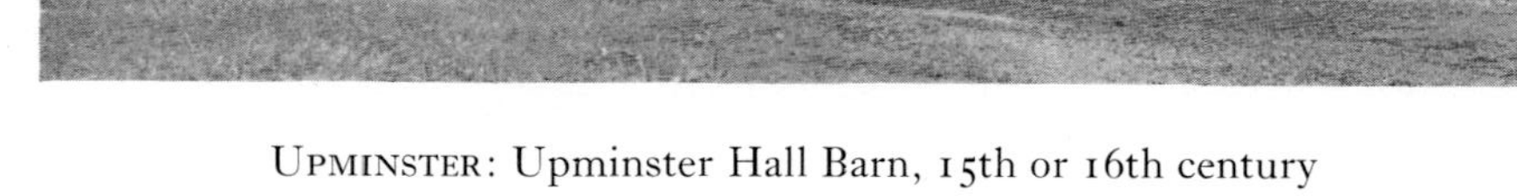

UPMINSTER: Upminster Hall Barn, 15th or 16th century

ROMFORD: Union Workhouse, built 1838, now Oldchurch Hospital

HORNCHURCH: Fairkytes, late-18th century

by his son Champion B. Russell (d. 1945), whose younger son, John N. Russell, lived at Stubbers until the estate was sold to the Essex Education Committee in 1947 for use as a youth centre.[85] In 1965 ownership was transferred to the G.L.C. on the formation of the London borough of Havering.

Stubbers mansion, originally of the 16th century, was several times altered and enlarged in the course of the next 300 years.[86] Major alterations were apparently made in the late 17th century after Sir William Russell's purchase of the estate, and the north hall and main oak staircases of that date were retained in later schemes. In the late 18th century a formal north front was added. This was built of stock brick, with three storeys and seven bays, the central three bays having a raised parapet. It was given an elaborate Doric porch, and the skyline was enlivened by Coade stone urns. About the same time the south drawing-rooms on the ground and first floors were modernized, the latter in Adam style; a stone balcony with iron balustrading was added to the first floor of the south front; and a dairy with vaulted ceiling and Adam decoration was built on the east side. An orangery, a dovecot (dated 1797), kennels, and stables were also built. It was at Stubbers that William Russell (d. 1810) kept the pack of hounds from which originated the Essex Union hunt.[87] The house was in good condition in 1923 but was rapidly decaying in 1954. In 1960 it was demolished.[88]

The gardens of Stubbers were famous among botanists in the time of William Coys, and Coys's walled gardens east and south of the house survived until *c.* 1800. They were then removed on the advice of Humphry Repton, who retained, however, Coys's avenue of limes which ran southwards to the east of the house. The present walled garden beyond the fishpond, with an additional north-south crinkle-crankle wall, presumably dates from this period. Repton's suggestion that the neighbouring road should be diverted further west was carried out in 1814.[89] It is doubtful, however, whether the scheme devised by Repton was completed.[90] The temple indicated by Repton as extant in 1796 south of the house is not to be found on Chapman and André's map or on the tithe map (1841), although they both give the icehouse on the eastern boundary of the estate.[91]

Stubbers cottage, of two storeys, thatched, and timber-framed with stock-brick infilling, dates from about 1800. In 1974 it was derelict.[92]

ECONOMIC HISTORY. North Ockendon has always been a purely agricultural community, increasingly occupied with arable farming. There were eight ploughs on the manor in 1086: two on the holding of William the chamberlain, two on Westminster Abbey's demesne, and four belonging to the men. No meadow or pasture was recorded, but there were 110 sheep on the demesne. There was woodland enough for 300 swine, but in fact the woods held only 30. In 1066 the manor had been worth £4; in 1086, including William the chamberlain's holding, it was worth £12.[93] The Domesday figures must, however, be used with caution. The abbey's estate of 2⅔ hides was exactly a quarter the size of (South) Ockendon manor; yet in the 19th century the parish of North Ockendon was three-fifths of the size of South Ockendon.[94] The most striking figure relating to the abbey's manor is thus that of the swine pastures: in 1086 the abbey's manor, though small, was evidently densely wooded. The woodlands, however, disappeared early. By the 14th century the manor of North Ockendon was usually said to have no more than 10 a. of woods.[95] In 1868 there were less than 11 acres of woods out of 1,709 acres in the whole parish.[96]

No early figures for arable have been found, but in 1731 1,022 a. out of the 1,137 a. of North Ockendon manor were arable.[97] The parish contained 1,257 a. of arable in 1840, 1,482 a. in 1868, and 1,019 a. in 1916.[98] A single landowner controlled most of the parish from the 11th century to 1937; the community therefore consisted largely of tenant-farmers. In the mid 1750s the tenants of the manor estate were said to pay their rents more promptly than any others in Essex. The net annual income was £941; the estate was valued for sale at the high figure of 30 years purchase; and the price suggested was more than £30,500.[99] In 1829, however, 5 of the 6 Benyon farms were in poor condition for lack of manure and from bad cropping. A six-year rotation of crops was therefore recommended: barley or oats; beans or peas; wheat; clover; wheat; a year of fallow ploughed four times, with turnips at the tenant's option.[1] In the later 19th century wheat, beans, and peas were the chief crops.[2]

In 1840 there were 11 holdings over 20 a. held by 9 farmers. Four farms had between 209 a. and 328 a., three between 119 a. and 199 a., the other two about 20 a. each. Only 271 a. out of 1,558 a. in cultivation were meadow or pasture. By 1916 meadow and pasture had increased to 523 a., 162 a. of the arable were market-garden land, and there were 8 farms. Two had about 40 a., the rest between 198 a. and 332 a. Of the 1,550 a. then in cultivation, 666 a. were farmed by members of the Eve family, which then farmed also at Cranham and Rainham. In the 1960s the parish still had no manufacturing industries, but the acreage used for market-gardening had increased, and some gravel-pits had been opened.[3]

The existence of a windmill is first indicated in

[85] E.R.O., T/P 67/1, pp. 181–2, 67/2, p. 4; inf. from Mr. J. N. Russell; E.R.O., C/ME 52, 330.

[86] Unless otherwise specified, this account of the mansion and gardens is based on: R.C.H.M. *Essex*, iv. 101; inf. from Dept. of the Environment; I. M. Russell, 'Stubbers, North Ockendon', *E.A.T.* N.S. xxi. 47–55; E.R.O., D/DRu E5; E.R.O., T/P 132/5, 6.

[87] *V.C.H. Essex*, ii. 567–8.

[88] E.R.O., T/P 135; E.R.O., C/ME 53, 881; inf. from Mr. J. Bush, Warden at Stubbers.

[89] E.R.O., Q/RHi 3/76.

[90] E.R.O., Pictorial Coll.: a pencil sketch (*c.* 1820) of Stubbers from the south; the garden walls have gone, but the recommended planting has not been carried out.

[91] *Map of Essex* (1777); E.R.O., D/CT 260B.

[92] E.R.O., T/P 132/3.

[93] *V.C.H. Essex*, i. 445.

[94] *V.C.H. Essex*, i. 445, 505; O.S. Map 6", Essex, LXXV (surv. 1865–6).

[95] *Feet of F. Essex*, ii. 161; iii. 99–100, 168; but cf. ibid. iii. 179–80.

[96] O.S., 6" (surv. 1865–6) *Map Reference Book*.

[97] E.R.O., D/DBe E7.

[98] E.R.O., D/CT 260; O.S., 6" (surv. 1865–6) *Map Reference Book*; E.R.O., D/Z 45/9.

[99] E.R.O., D/DBe E8, p. 12.

[1] E.R.O., D/DBe E42.

[2] *Kelly's Dir. Essex* (1870 and later edns.).

[3] E.R.O., D/CT 260; D/Z 45/9; 2nd Land Utilization Survey of Britain, Land Use sheets 225–6.

1610 when John Cramphorne paid £20 a year for the mill, a cottage, and 16 a.[4] There are references to millers in 1626 and 1690, and the windmill in 1643.[5] Millers can be identified almost continuously from the 1720s to 1840, but in the latter year the mill, a post mill, was pulled down.[6] In the 18th and 19th centuries it had stood south of Fen Lane.[7]

Agrarian discontent in North Ockendon in the early 19th century has left no clear evidence behind, but in 1830 the tenant-farmers feared incendiaries, and one farmer kept five men on watch nightly.[8]

In the north of the parish there are deposits of brick-earth. There were perhaps brickworks there in 1574, when there is a reference to a brick-maker.[9] In 1840 there were two enclosures called Brick Clamps, a Brick Land field, a Sand Pit field, and four other pits in the parish.[10]

LOCAL GOVERNMENT. The abbot of Westminster in 1273 or 1274 claimed gallows and the assize of bread and of ale in North Ockendon manor.[11] The manor also had view of frankpledge and a court leet, but only a few court rolls for the period 1506–1623 have survived.[12]

Among the parish records are churchwardens' accounts (1787–1922) which include vestry business and parish appointments; overseers' rates (1771, 1828–87) and accounts (1745–1873); and surveyors' rate books (1833–95), accounts, and bills (1828–95).[13] The vestry met in the parish church, and its meetings were normally attended by five or six farmers, who shared the parish offices between them. From 1745 to 1773 and again from 1787 to 1793 there was often a vestry dinner at Easter. There was a vestry clerk in 1791 and from 1796 to 1829.

North Ockendon had two churchwardens in 1637,[14] but there was only one from 1787 to 1823. The assistant curate appointed one of the churchwardens in 1825, 1827, and 1828, and the return to two wardens in 1823 probably marked the introduction of a rector's warden.[15] Normally North Ockendon had one overseer, but in the years 1823–4 and 1825–7 the account was submitted in the name of two. In one year, 1824–5, the overseer claimed a salary. There was a single constable 1788–1813; thereafter there were two, the junior in 1813–15 being termed the headborough. The constables did not submit separate accounts, but recovered their expenses from the churchwardens or overseers. There were normally two surveyors, striking their own rates.

The vestry always provided out-relief for the poor. In addition there was a 'parish house', first mentioned in 1761. In 1769–70 a new house was built south-east of the village, but it was soon too small. In 1786 there were reckoned to be 85 poor within the parish and another 35, belonging to the parish, resident in South Ockendon. Five years later there were 96 in the parish and 47 outside. In 1789 some of the poor were sent to Great Warley workhouse. North Ockendon poorhouse was enlarged in 1791. From that year to 1797 the master of the workhouse and his wife received 4*s*. a day, and the parish paid for the maintenance of the poor. After 1797 the master provided their food and clothing, at first for 3*s*., but by 1813 for 5*s*., a week per head. Numbers in the workhouse between 1797 and 1799 varied from 13 to 21; then they dropped until the period 1808–14, when they were between 14 and 23. From 1819 or 1820 the parish apparently adopted a system whereby several persons received money for the care of the poor. In addition paupers were sent to South Ockendon workhouse between 1823 and 1825. From 1825 there were once again paupers at the North Ockendon workhouse under a master or mistress. When North Ockendon became part of Orsett union in 1835, the parish retained the former workhouse, converting it into six dwellings, one of which was in 1840 assigned rent-free to a pauper family.[16]

The parish also helped the poor in other ways. Between 1746 and 1808 sixteen children of the poor were apprenticed. 'Club' contributions were paid from time to time between 1778 and 1829, and in 1819 the parish therefore received a 'club' payment for a parishioner.

At first the poor received only casual medical aid, but in 1765 and from 1777 a doctor was retained by the parish. Casual payments to doctors continued, however, and in March 1820 the parish doctor received, in addition to his retainer, the large sum of £40 for attending the parishioner whose 'club' payment had earlier gone to the parish.

The cost to the parish of the poor was diminished by the income from a farm in Horndon-on-the-Hill, bought in 1647 with a bequest from Richard Poyntz (d. 1643).[17] In 1745–52 a 6*d*. rate produced a little less than £20 and was enough, with the farm's rent, to take care of the poor. After revaluation, *c*. 1755, 2*s*. rates producing about £95 a year were used for the next 30 years. Thereafter the income from rates rose: for a decade it was about £150, and in the 40 years from 1795 to 1835 it averaged £318 a year.[18]

CHURCH. A church, attached to Westminster Abbey's manor of (North) Ockendon, existed by 1075, and it was then said that the judgment of fire and water was held there by ancient custom.[19] The specification of a particular church is most unusual, and its meaning uncertain.[20] In 1212 the abbot of Westminster acknowledged that the advowson belonged to William of Setfountayns, tenant in demesne

[4] E.R.O., D/DBe M15, 16.
[5] E.R.O., T/R 154/1 burials; E.R.O., Q/SR 252/56, 466/40.
[6] E.R.O., D/DU 651/102; D/DBe E7 p. 13, E6, E8 p. 7, E9 f. 11v., E16, E61; E.R.O., D/P 308/11/2, 3, 5; D/P 308/12/4.
[7] *Map of Essex* (1777); E.R.O., D/DBe P9; E.R.O., D/CT 260.
[8] E.R.O., D/DBe E28.
[9] E.R.O., T/R 154/1, marriages (24 May 1574).
[10] E.R.O., D/CT 260A, items 17 & 139, 237, 110, 58, 95, 186, 242.
[11] *Rot. Hund.* (Rec. Com.), i. 148.
[12] E.R.O., D/DBe M10, 12; W.A.M. 3212–14.
[13] E.R.O., D/P 308/5/1–2; D/P 308/8/1–2; D/P 308/11/1–17; D/P 308/12/1–15; D/P 308/20/1–4; D/P 308/21/1–4; E.R.O., D/DBe E51. Unless otherwise stated, the following account derives from these documents.
[14] E.R.O., T/R 154/1, p. 10.
[15] William Snowden, the curate's nominee, was warden continuously from 1823 to 1856.
[16] E.R.O., D/DBe E52.
[17] See p. 116.
[18] The worst year was 1800–1 (£565). In five other years, 1809–10, 1813–14, 1817–20, the rates also exceeded £400.
[19] *Reg. Regum Anglo-Norm.* i. p. 66; ii. p. 141; Hart, *Early Chart. Essex*, 35–6; and see above, p. 111.
[20] Cf. *Preparatory to Anglo-Saxon England*, ed. Doris M. Stenton, 177.

of the manor.[21] The advowson descended with the manor until 1315. At the partition of the Setfountayns estates in that year, Baldwin the son of Isabel of Setfountayns and William (son of) Baldwin, and his aunt, Cecily of Setfountayns, widow of Richard de Heyle, agreed to present to the rectory alternately. This arrangement was confirmed by the Court of Common Pleas in 1347, and was observed by the descendants of the two sisters, or their nominees, until 1526. Isabel's descendants held the manor of North Ockendon, Cecily's heirs and successors the manor of Chelsea (Mdx.).[22] After 1526 the advowson rested solely with the lords of North Ockendon manor until the 20th century. A presentation was sold in the 18th century, and in the 19th century kinsmen of Richard Benyon de Beauvoir (d. 1854) presented to the rectory.[23] In 1954 the advowson passed from H. A. Benyon to the Bishop of Chelmsford.[24]

The value of the rectory was 15 marks in 1254, and £10 5*s*. in 1291.[25] In 1535 it was £16 13*s*. 4*d*.[26] By the 18th century it had risen to £160.[27] Its gross annual value *c*. 1830, was £557.[28] In 1840 the tithes were commuted for £500.[29] The glebe, reckoned to be 30 a. in 1610, consisted of 39 a. in 1840.[30]

The rectory house, which faces south to the church, was rebuilt *c*. 1750 in brown brick with red dressings.[31] The principal front, of 5 bays with a central doorway, was given 3 storeys but the rear had only two. Additions in the 19th century included a third storey in the rear, a two-storeyed service block to the north, and bay-windows on the west.[32] The house was damaged by bombs in 1944.[33] In 1958 the upper storey of the north wing was removed and the top storey of the main house adapted as a separate flat.[34] The Church Commissioners sold the rectory in 1976.[35]

As a small country parish with only moderate revenues North Ockendon often had non-resident rectors. John Palmer, rector 1526–31, was already rector of Langdon Hills; Henry Tripp, rector 1570–82, was rector of St. Stephen, Walbrook (Lond.), 1572–1601; Robert Wilmot, rector 1582–1608, was also vicar of Horndon-on-the-Hill; and Edward Herbert, rector 1658–97, was also rector of Cranham from 1669. Assistant curates were appointed occasionally in the 16th and 17th centuries, and regularly after 1730.[36]

John Benson, rector 1546–54, was deprived by Bishop Bonner for having married.[37] William Jackson, rector 1619–57, was suspended for flippancy in 1636, but became a member of the Chafford classis in 1645 and in 1650 was described as learned and resident in the parish.[38] A 'register' was appointed in 1653 in accordance with the statute of that year.[39] In 1688 the rector, Edward Herbert, not only read James II's declaration of indulgence but penned a defence of his action.[40]

The church of *ST. MARY MAGDALEN*, Church Lane, comprises chancel with north vestry and Lady chapel, nave with north aisle and south porch, and a west tower.[41] Its walls are of ragstone and flint with dressings of Reigate stone. The nave and chancel were built in the later 12th century but the south doorway is the only surviving feature of that date. A north aisle was added in the mid 13th century; it has the unusual feature of a normal arcade of three bays to the east and a plain arch piercing the nave wall to the west, but the reasons for this are unknown. The north chapel, which has an arcade of two bays to the chancel, was added *c*. 1300. The chancel may have been remodelled at or soon after this time. The north aisle was given a new doorway and windows in the later 14th century. In the 15th century the tower was added;[42] the chancel arch and part of the arcade were rebuilt; at least one new window was put into the nave; and the whole building was reroofed.

In 1840 the church was restored and an organ gallery built. A more complete restoration involving the renewal of much of the exterior stonework including the windows, was carried out in 1858; the vestry was added and probably the porch which replaced a timber-framed structure of unknown date. The cost of the restoration was met by Richard Benyon (formerly Fellowes, d. 1897), lord of the manor, and the work was supervised by Richard Armstrong, the architect who later rebuilt Cranham church for Benyon.[43]

Repairs to the interior were necessary in the earlier 17th century, and in 1685 the communion table was ordered to be set altarwise under the east window and railed off.[44] During the 19th-century alterations some of the monuments and furnishings were lost.[45] The font which dated from *c*. 1200 was replaced by another.[46] The medieval glass, which was at first rejected, was re-set and later replaced in the windows: an unidentified female saint dates from the 13th century, and a Magdalen from the 15th.[47] Their elaborate

[21] *Cur. Reg. R.* vi. 306; cf. A. Saltman, *Theobald Abp. Cant.*, 507.
[22] C.P. 40/352 m. 558; Newcourt, *Repertorium*, ii. 447.
[23] E.R.O., T/A 547; Burke, *Peerage* (1938), 1352–3; Burke, *Land. Gent.* (1914), 138.
[24] *Chelmsford Dioc. Yr. Bks.* 1954, 1955.
[25] *E.A.T.* N.S. xviii. 18; *Tax. Eccl.* (Rec. Com.), 320.
[26] *Valor Eccl.* (Rec. Com.), i. 436.
[27] Guildhall MSS. 9550, 9557 f. 57.
[28] Ibid. 9560.
[29] E.R.O., D/CT 260.
[30] Newcourt, *Repertorium*, ii. 446; E.R.O., D/CT 260; E.R.O., T/A 547.
[31] E.R.O., D/DBe E9.
[32] E.R.O., D/AEM 2/6; Tithe Redemption Office file 2452.
[33] E.R.O., C/W 1/2/59: 22 Jan. 1944.
[34] Inf. from Mr. J. E. L. Cole, churchwarden.
[35] Inf. from Strutt and Parker (Southend); E.R.O., *Sale Cat.* C215.
[36] Newcourt, *Repertorium*, i. 540, ii. 195, 343, 359, 447; Guildhall MSS. 9550–60; *D.N.B.* s.v. Gifford, Ric.; Thorne, *Environs Lond.* 456; W. Palin, *More about Stifford*, 116.
[37] Newcourt, *Repertorium*, ii. 447; H. E. P. Grieve, 'The Deprived Married Clergy in Essex, 1553–1561', *Trans. R.H.S.* 4th ser. xxii. 143.
[38] *E.R.* xlix. 86; Smith, *Eccl. Hist. Essex*, 37, 194, 200, 244; H. Smith, 'Parochial Clergy Essex, 1640–1664' (TS in E.R.O. Libr.), 19; Hale, *Precedents*, pp. 255, 259.
[39] E.R.O., T/R 154/1, p. 150.
[40] E.R.O., D/DM Z11.
[41] The following account, unless otherwise specified, is based on: R.C.H.M. *Essex*, iv. 98–100; Pevsner, *Essex*, 308; E. F. Evans, 'North Ockendon: St. Mary Magdalen', *E.R.* xxxvii, 49–57; E.R.O., T/P 196 Eccles. Essex, v. 1–37.
[42] Prob. 11/5 (P.C.C. 29 Godyn): in 1469 John Poyntz bequeathed money for the new work and steeple.
[43] E.R.O., D/DBe Q5, letter of 20 Mar. 1875 from R. Armstrong to R. Benyon; D/AEM 1/5, 2/9.
[44] *E.A.T.* N.S. xxi. 324.
[45] For the lost monuments, see Holman's MSS.: E.R.O., T/P 195/2 Ockendons.
[46] W. Palin, *More about Stifford*, 116; E.R.O., T/R 154/1; D/AEV 7; *E.A.T.* N.S. xxi. 324
[47] E.R.O., D/CF 78/49, 88/83; St. Helen has often been suggested for the unidentified saint, but she is perhaps St. Audrey: see Prob. 11/5 (P.C.C. 29 Godyn) for a request to be buried before the image of St. Audrey.

canopies are of the 14th century, as are the heraldic shields now in the west window of the tower.

The church has some fine monuments. There are 16th-century brasses to William Poyntz (d. 1504) and his wife Jane (d. 1502), to Thomasyn Ardall (d. 1532), the wife of first Robert Latham and then Roger Badby, and to John Poyntz (d. 1547); a modern brass commemorates Edward F. Evans, rector 1919–30 (d. 1933). Early indents to William (son of) Baldwin (d. 1316) and Baldwin son of William (d. 1323), and a fragment to John Bauchon (d. 1373?) are now concealed by the floors of the chancel and Lady chapel. The other monuments, chiefly to members of the Poyntz and Littleton families, include a series erected by Sir Gabriel Poyntz (d. 1608) to himself, his son (d. 1597), and his Poyntz predecessors at North Ockendon. Larger and more elaborate, but of similar form, was the monument erected by Sir Gabriel to his daughter and son-in-law; its style is virtually duplicated by the monument to Sir James (d. 1623) and Richard Poyntz (d. 1643). Most elaborate and largest of them all is the monument to Sir Gabriel and his wife.[48] The neighbouring monument to Sir Thomas Littleton, Bt. (d. 1710), is of white marble with a bust over a lengthy inscription framed by composite columns; the segmental pediment supports two cherubs and an achievement of arms. The chancel monuments include a bust of John Russell (d. 1825) by William Behnes, and a medallion of his widow Elizabeth (d. 1838) by Thomas Smith.[49]

In 1552 the church had four bells. There are now six: four were cast by Miles Graye in 1621; the fifth was by Philip Wightman in 1695; the treble, by Mears and Stainbank, was hung in 1934. The 15th-century ladder-stairway to the bell-chamber has solid treads and chamfered runners.[50]

The plate includes two chalices and patens. The older pair are of 1561; the newer of 1646. The latter were bought with a bequest for the purpose by Richard Poyntz.[51] The two large flagons, which matched them and were presumably also of 1646, were sold in 1842 to buy 'permanent ornaments' for the church.[52]

The church chest has a panelled lid; the front is inlaid with the initials W.P. and M.P. and the date 1557. The organ, for which a gallery was built in 1840–1, was replaced in 1908.[53]

PROTESTANT NONCONFORMITY. An application was made in 1725 for the house of John Mayes, blacksmith, to be licensed for Presbyterian meetings.[54] There is no later record of organized nonconformist activities in the parish. In 1856 many of the inhabitants were said to be Dissenters;[55] presumably they attended the chapels in South Ockendon.

EDUCATION. In the 1750s the vestry was paying for the education of poor children at a dame school.[56] In 1786 there was a Sunday school for 10 poor children.[57] It seems to have survived until at least 1819, when 30 or 40 attended. There were 5 dame schools in the parish in 1819, with some 70 pupils.[58] A new Sunday school was opened in 1826 by the assistant curate.[59] By 1833 the earlier dame schools seem to have closed, but two others existed in 1839 when the Sunday school, with 37 children, was maintained by local Churchmen.[60] In 1840 there was also a private night-school.[61]

St. Mary's Church of England school, Church Lane, originated in 1842 when a day-school and teacher's house were built by subscription on land in Church Lane owned by Richard Benyon de Beauvoir (d. 1854), lord of the manor.[62] Benyon and his successors remained the owners of the school. By 1846–7 the school had 55 pupils.[63] It received annual government grants from 1871.[64] It was enlarged in 1869 and 1881, and in 1902 was rebuilt by James Benyon for 80 children.[65] In 1936 the school was reorganized for mixed juniors and infants.[66] It was damaged by bombs in 1944.[67] In 1947, when there were only 30 pupils, the county council suggested its closure.[68] It remained open, however, and in 1955 was granted Aided status.[69]

CHARITIES FOR THE POOR.[70] Richard Poyntz of Barningham (Suff.) son of Sir James Poyntz of North Ockendon, by his will proved 1644, left £200 for the poor of North Ockendon.[71] In 1647 the legacy, supplemented by £24 belonging to the parish, was used to buy about 40 a. of land called Steeden (or Sticking) Hills at Horndon-on-the-Hill.[72] The annual income, which fluctuated between £25 in 1787 and £50 in 1877, was used to provide clothing, coal, bedding, and money for the poor.[73] From 1887 to 1890 the land was unlet and uncultivated. In 1912 the land, then 48 a., was sold for £960. In the 1920s the income was distributed in money and coal.

Sir William Russell of Stubbers (d. 1705), by his will, left a £3 rent-charge from a house in Water

[48] Chancellor, *Sep. Mons. Essex*, 181–90, pl. LV–LXII. See above, plate facing p. 33.
[49] R. Gunnis, *Dict. Brit. Sculptors, 1660–1851*, 45–8, 359–60.
[50] *E.A.T.* N.S. ii. 185; *Ch. Bells Essex*, 349–50; E.R.O., D/CF 74/45.
[51] *E.A.T.* N.S. ii. 186.
[52] The chalice and paten are on permanent loan at the Victoria and Albert Museum; E.R.O., D/P 308/5/1 authorized the sale of the flagons; *Ch. Plate Essex* 14–15; *E.A.T.* N.S. xxi. 324 n.
[53] E.R.O., D/P 308/5/1, 308/8/1.
[54] E.R.O., Q/SBb 90/12. The Mayes family were apparently still nonconformists in 1803: see below, p. 124.
[55] E.R.O., D/P 308/8/1.
[56] E.R.O., D/P 308/12/1.
[57] E.R.O., D/DBe E51.
[58] *Returns Educ. Poor*, H.C. 224, p. 264 (1819), ix(1).
[59] *Educ. Enquiry Abstract*, H.C. 62, p. 284 (1835), xli.
[60] Ibid.; E.R.O., D/P 30/28/19.
[61] E.R.O., D/DBe E52.
[62] *White's Dir. Essex* (1848), 193; E.R.O., D/DBe E45–6, P6; E.R.O., D/P 308/8/1. £100 left to the poor by Lady Elizabeth Russell (d. 1838) was used for building the school: E.R.O., D/DBe E57.
[63] *Nat. Soc. Church Schs. Enquiry 1846–7*.
[64] *Rep. Educ. Cttee of Council*, 1871–2, [C.601], p. 259, H.C. (1872) xxii.
[65] *Kelly's Dir. Essex* (1902); *Return Non-Provided Schs.* H.C. 178, p. 24 (1906), lxxxvii; Ed. 21/5294.
[66] Inf. from Essex Educ. Dept.
[67] E.R.O., C/W 1/2/59.
[68] E.R.O., C/ME 41, p. 235.
[69] E.R.O., C/ME 49, p. 282.
[70] Unless otherwise stated this section is based on: *Rep. Com. Char.* [108], p. 717 (1837–8), xxv(1); Char. Com. Files; inf. from Revd. K. M. Briggs, rector.
[71] *Abstracts of Probate Acts*, iii. 249.
[72] E.R.O., D/P 308/5/1.
[73] E.R.O., Q/RSr 1; Q/RSr 2/87; E.R.O., D/P 308/8/1; 308/25.

Lane (Lond.) to provide £1 to the minister of North Ockendon for a sermon on St. Simon's and St. Jude's day, 5*s*. to the clerk, and £1 15*s*. to be distributed to the poor with the advice and consent of Russell's descendants living at Stubbers.[74] In 1835 eight years' income, received in arrears, was used to provide clothing and blankets for the poor. By 1837 the income was being given in bread on the sermon day. The sermon seems to have lapsed during the Second World War, but was revived in 1975.

Daniel Russell (d. 1788) left £500 in trust, the income to be distributed to the poor by the Russell family. By 1837 the annual income of £15 was being used to provide clothing for the poor, and in 1869–70 bread was distributed.[75]

Remembrance Cottages, Church Lane, North Ockendon, were conveyed to trustees in 1930 by Champion Branfill Russell of Stubbers, as alms-houses.[76] Memorial Bungalows, Fen Lane, were built in 1971 as alms-houses by Pamela and John N. Russell in memory of their parents.[77]

In 1937, after local complaints about the administration of the charities, the Charity Commission drew up a Scheme regulating the use of the charities of Richard Poyntz, William Russell, and Daniel Russell. After payment for a sermon, the income was to provide for money and medical care for the poor. In 1975 the income was spent on the upkeep of Remembrance Cottages and Memorial Bungalows, and for gifts of money to the old and needy.

SOUTH OCKENDON

THE ANCIENT parish of South Ockendon lay 20 miles east of London and 8 miles south-east of Romford.[1] The Mardyke stream was its eastern boundary; Stifford lay to the south-east and west, Aveley to the south-west, and North Ockendon to the west and north. In 1868 the parish contained 2,936 acres, including two detached parts, of 2½ a. and 16½ a., lying west of the road from North Ockendon to Stifford, and locally situated in Stifford parish.[2] In 1888 the detached parts were merged in Stifford, in exchange for a detached part (18 a.) of that parish locally situated in the south-west corner of South Ockendon.[3] In 1928 the parish became part of Purfleet urban district, which in 1935 was merged in the newly-formed Thurrock urban district.[4]

South Ockendon lies in a region of valley gravel.[5] The village is about 75 ft. above sea-level, on a ridge running north and south through the centre of the parish. To the east, and to the south at Stifford bridge, the land slopes down to about 15 ft.

The road system of South Ockendon has probably changed little since the Middle Ages, except in the south-west of the parish, where building has been going on since the 1930s.[6] The main road from Brentwood to Grays Thurrock runs along the central ridge, passing through the village, which clusters round a green. From this point a chase runs east to the moated site of the former South Ockendon Hall, and West Road runs through North Ockendon to Rainham and Upminster. East of the main road, both north and south of the village, lanes lead to scattered farms.

Evidence of Romano-British occupation has been found near the sites of the Hall and in the neighbourhood of Little Belhus.[7] In 1086 the recorded population was 66.[8] In 1327 the names of 21, and in 1523 of 43, inhabitants were recorded on the tax lists.[9] In 1670 there were 56 houses in South Ockendon.[10] The population in 1801 was 466; it climbed steadily to 1,267 in 1861, but, after fluctuations, was no more than 1,355 in 1931. Ockendon ward of Thurrock U.D., which was a little larger in area than the ancient parish of South Ockendon, had a population of 4,164 in 1951 and 4,733 in 1961.[11]

Little change occurred in the parish before the 1930s, and even in 1974 several of the farm-houses, with alterations and additions, date from the 16th or 17th century.[12] Of these the most impressive is Little Belhus, a weatherboarded 16th-century building with a walled forecourt and entrance gateway. It was restored and converted into flats by the G.L.C. in 1966.[13] Great Mollands and Grange Farm, in the south of the parish, both date from the late 17th century with later additions. Streets Farm, on West Road, is a 17th-century house with an early-19th-century service wing, and Quince Tree Farm, in South Street, the former Poyntz manor-house, is of the 16th and 17th century.[14]

Of the buildings around the village green, the oldest, apart from the church, is the Royal Oak. The north cross-wing and part of the hall range are late medieval; the rest dates from the 17th century or later. Other 17th-century buildings have been demolished in the 20th century, but two timber-framed houses of that period remain in South Street. They adjoin a symmetrical terrace of brick-fronted early-19th-century cottages, which formerly had semi-circular heads to the doorways and windows but are now mutilated by shop-fronts.

The Red Lion was apparently the hub of village life in the early 19th century. In 1817 a Red Lion friendly society was established;[15] and from the Red Lion a coach left daily in 1839 for London via Romford and Ilford.[16] In 1848 there was a daily omnibus, apparently to Romford.[17] A carrier went daily to London in 1839; in 1863 there was a weekly service

[74] E.R.O., D/P 308/5/1. [75] E.R.O., D/P 308/8/1.
[76] E.R.O., T/P 132/8; O.S. Map 1/25,000, sheet TQ 58.
[77] Inf. from Mr. J. N. Russell and Mr. J. E. L. Cole; plaque on bungalows.
[1] O.S. Map 1/25,000, TQ 58, 68.
[2] O.S. Map 6", Essex, LXXV, LXXXIII (surv. 1863–6).
[3] *Kelly's Dir. Essex* (1899), 282 and 361, citing L.G.B. order, no. 22,350 of 24 Mar. 1888.
[4] W. Thurrock (Constitution of Urban District) Order, 1928; Essex Review Order, 1935.
[5] *V.C.H. Essex*, i. 16.
[6] The roads shown on *Map of Essex* (1777) lead to farm-houses dating from the 16th and 17th centuries.
[7] *V.C.H. Essex*, iii. 165; cf. Thorne, *Environs Lond.* 457; *E.A.T.* 3rd ser. ii. 83.
[8] *V.C.H. Essex*, i. 505.
[9] E 179/107/13, m. 7d.; E 179/108/150.
[10] E.R.O., Q/RTh 5, m. 2d.
[11] *Census* (1801 sqq.).
[12] Statements in this and the next paragraph derive from R.C.H.M. *Essex*, iv. 141–3 unless otherwise specified.
[13] C. Harrold, *Discovering Thurrock*, 22.
[14] See p. 121.
[15] E.R.O., Q/SO 24, ff. 551, 599.
[16] *Pigot's Dir. Essex* (1839).
[17] *White's Dir. Essex* (1848).

to Romford and a daily cart to Grays railway station; and from 1866 to the end of the century a cart went twice weekly to London.[18] The London, Tilbury and Southend Railway line from Upminster to Grays Thurrock was completed in 1892, with a station at South Ockendon west of the village.[19] In 1876 South Ockendon was said to have 'the look of an active and growing place'.[20] The reading room, built *c.* 1885 mainly at the expense of Richard Benyon (d. 1897), had closed by 1898, when the building was being used for parish council purposes.[21]

In the 1930s the pattern of village life changed. Between the railway and South Street the L.C.C. began to build an estate which after the Second World War was greatly enlarged, extending west of the railway into Belhus Park, Aveley.[22] In 1932 the borough of West Ham converted the farm colony established by 1910 at Little Mollands into a colony of mental defectives; in 1948 it passed to the Ministry of Health and is now the South Ockendon hospital.[23] A branch library in West Road was opened by Thurrock U.D. *c.* 1935.[24] In 1937 the Benyon family split up and sold to nine purchasers all its South Ockendon property.[25]

Among the notables of the parish were Sir Richard Saltonstall (*c.* 1521–1601), lord of the manor of Colcarters or Groves, master of the Skinners' Company, lord mayor of London in 1597;[26] and Offspring Blackall, rector 1690–1707, a fashionable preacher and controversialist who became bishop of Exeter.[27]

MANORS AND OTHER ESTATES. The manor of *SOUTH OCKENDON* (or, after 1300, *BRUYNS*) had been held before the Conquest by Frebert, a thegn. It then appears to have contained 11 hides. In 1086 the tenant in chief was Geoffrey de Mandeville, who had acquired the manor by exchange.[28] The overlordship passed to his descendants and remained with the Mandeville and Bohun earls of Essex until the death of Humphrey de Bohun, earl of Hereford and Essex, in 1372. The last earl's daughter, Eleanor (d. 1399) married Thomas of Woodstock (d. 1397) the youngest son of Edward III. Their daughter Anne apparently retained the overlordship of various Essex manors, including South Ockendon, until 1421, when an agreement with her cousin Henry V let him choose the earldom of Essex as part of his share of the Bohun-Mandeville inheritance.[29] Thereafter the overlordship of the manor of South Ockendon was to be found intermittently in the 15th century in the hands of various royal ladies: Philippa (de Mohun) who survived her husband Edward Duke of York (d. 1415) until 1431, and the queens, Elizabeth Woodville and Elizabeth of York.[30]

In 1086 Geoffrey de Mandeville's tenant at South Ockendon was Turold, his steward.[31] In that or the preceding year Turold's son Ralph, who already held many other Essex manors, agreed to his father's grant from the tithes of the manor to the priory of Hurley (Berks.),[32] but no proof of his succession to the manor has been found, and nothing is certainly known of the tenancy in demesne of the manor for almost a century.

By 1187 William Doo (D'Ou) possessed the manor. The witnessing clauses of certain grants to Brook Street hospital, South Weald, in 1163 × 1187 and 1275, with other evidence, suggest that in the 12th century there existed a family, holding the manors of South Ockendon and Willingdale Doe (Essex) and (Market) Lavington (Wilts.), for whom the names of Ou and Rochelle were interchangeable.[33] Godfrey de la Rochelle, who lived under Henry I, was apparently succeeded by his daughter Agnes, she by her son Richard de la Rochelle, who died before 1195, and he by his son William de la Rochelle.[34] William had died by 1198.[35] His heir, also named William de la Rochelle, succeeded as a minor and died *c.* 1226.[36] (Sir) Richard de la Rochelle, heir of the last-named William, was still a minor in 1234, but was married a decade later, and by 1255 had entered on an Irish career, first as deputy to the Justiciar of Ireland, and from 1261 as Justiciar himself.[37] He leased South Ockendon before 1262 to Richard of St. Denis for life, and in 1273 after St. Denis's death he had some difficulty in recovering the manor from the escheator.[38] Sir Richard de la Rochelle himself died at South Ockendon in 1276 and was succeeded by his son Philip.[39]

Philip de la Rochelle (d. 1295) left as heir his daughter Maud, aged 9, whose wardship was granted to Richard de Chigwell, her stepfather.[40] By 1300 she had married Maurice le Bruyn (or Brun).[41] Maurice (d. 1355) was summoned to Parliament between 1313 and 1322, and is thus held to have become Lord Bruyn, but none of his descendants was so summoned.[42] He was succeeded by his son William (d. 1362), who left a widow Alice and infant son, (Sir) Ingram. By 1365 Alice had married Sir Robert Marney of Layer Marney. In 1376 after coming of age, Ingram granted South Ockendon to his mother

[18] *Pigot's Dir. Essex* (1839); *White's Dir. Essex* (1863); *Kelly's Dir. Essex* (1866–1902).
[19] E. Carter, *Hist. Geog. Rlys.*, 477.
[20] Thorne, *Environs Lond.* 457.
[21] *Strat. Expr.* 20 Feb. 1884; *Kelly's Dir. Essex* (1886–98).
[22] *Thurrock Official Guide* [1937], 20; [1959], map. The course of development is suggested by the road names of the area, which, in groups, begin with successive letters of the alphabet, A to I.
[23] *V.C.H. Essex*, vi. 106, 111; cf. *Rep. Cttee. S. Ockendon Hosp.* H.C. 124 (1974).
[24] *Kelly's Dir. Essex* (1937); *Thurrock Official Guide* [1937] and later edns.
[25] E.R.O., *Sale Cat.* B106; E.R.O., D/DBe E71.
[26] *D.N.B.*
[27] Ibid.
[28] *V.C.H. Essex*, i. 505.
[29] *Complete Peerage*, v. 113–37; vi. 467.
[30] *Cal. Inq. p.m. Hen. VII*, i, pp. 378–9; E.R.O., D/DP F305.
[31] *V.C.H. Essex*, i. 505.
[32] *Early Med. Misc. for D. M. Stenton* (P.R.S. N.S. xxxvi), 107.
[33] *Reg. Sudbury* (Cant. & York Soc.), i. 210–11; *Cart. Mon. Sancti Johannis Baptiste de Colecestria* (Roxburghe Club) i. 4; *E.A.T.* N.S. viii. 375; *Feet of F. Essex*, i. 272–3; *Reg. Regum Anglo-Norm.* iii, p. 102; *Cur. Reg. R.* x. 108; E.R.O., T/P 195/2, p. 6; *V.C.H. Wilts*, x. 87.
[34] *Cur. Reg. R.* x. 108. William was already paying scutage for the Lavington manor in 1194–5: *Red Bk. Exch.* (Rolls Ser.), i. 89.
[35] *Pipe R.* 1198 (P.R.S. N.S. ix), 138.
[36] *Cur. Reg. R.* xi. 469; *Bk. of Fees*, ii. 1347, 1349.
[37] *Close R.* 1231–4, 373; 1242–7, 207; 1254–6, 158–9; 1261–4, 11.
[38] Ibid., 1261–4, 124; *Cal. Inq. p.m.* ii, p. 30.
[39] *Cal. Inq. p.m.* ii, p. 133; *Cal. Close*, 1279–88, 343.
[40] *Cal. Inq. p.m.* iii, pp. 163, 495; v. 366–7. Cf. *V.C.H. Essex*, iv. 80, 211.
[41] *Cal. Inq. p.m.* iii, p. 495.
[42] The Brun or Bruyn descent is set out in *Complete Peerage*, ii. 355–8. Information in this paragraph derives from this source, unless otherwise indicated.

and Sir Robert for life.[43] She was still alive in 1386, and Sir Robert in 1398.[44] Sir Ingram Bruyn died in 1400 and his son, Sir Maurice, in 1466. Sir Maurice's son died before his father, in 1461, leaving two daughters, Alice and Elizabeth. Alice (d. 1473) married three times: by her first husband John Berners she had a son John who died without issue between 1475 and 1494; by her second husband, Robert Harleston (d. 1471), another son John (d. *c.* 1496); her third husband was Sir John Heveningham (d. 1499). Elizabeth (d. 1494), her sister, also married three times: by her first husband, Thomas, son of Sir Thomas Tyrell of Heron, she was the mother of Hugh and William Tyrell.[45] The many marriages of the two heiresses, the turbulence accompanying the Wars of the Roses, and the attempt by an uncle, Thomas Bruyn, between 1470 and 1485, to obtain the manor, rendered the descent of the Bruyn inheritance uncertain.[46] In 1494 the heirs to the estate were Hugh Tyrell and John Harleston, but in 1499, when Heveningham died, Hugh's brother William Tyrell and Harleston's 5-year-old son (Sir) Clement were the heirs.[47]

The division of the manor was completed in 1531.[48] Clement Harleston took the hall and most of the lands in the south and south-east of the parish. Thereafter this part of the old manor was termed the manor of *SOUTH OCKENDON HALL.*

At South Ockendon Hall Sir Clement Harleston (d. 1546) was succeeded by his eldest son John (d. 1569), and he by his two sons Robert (d. 1571) and Thomas (d. 1573).[49] Thomas was succeeded by his son John (d. 1624). In 1615 John Harleston and his second wife Jane sold the reversion of the manor after their deaths to William Petre, Lord Petre.[50] In 1625 Jane surrendered her life-interest to Lord Petre, who in 1628 settled the manors of South Ockendon and Stanford Rivers on his third son William.[51] William (d. 1677) settled the manor in 1657 upon his son and heir, another William (d. 1686).[52] In 1692 William and Francis Petre, sons of the last-named William, sold the manor for £6,500 to Jasper Kingsman of Stifford.[53]

Kingsman died in 1704. He had disinherited his son Petre for making an unsuitable marriage, and left his estates to a cousin Josiah Kingsman.[54] Josiah (d. 1719) was succeeded in turn by his sons Josiah (d. 1733) and Jasper (d. 1754), and by Jasper's son, another Jasper.[55] The younger Jasper (d. 1784) left his estates for life to his widow Ann (d. 1789), after whose death they were sold. At the time of the sale in 1789, the manor of South Ockendon Hall, with 671 a., was held by John Cliff.[56] He bought the estate then or in the next year or two, and later enlarged it by buying other South Ockendon properties.[57] There is no reference to the manorial rights after 1789.

John Cliff died in 1833, and his widow Hannah in 1844. The estate was then sold for the benefit of his heirs.[58] South Ockendon Hall, with 668 a., was bought in 1849 by Richard Benyon de Beauvoir.[59] The estate remained in the Benyon family until 1937, when it was sold along with the family's other Essex properties.[60] From 1831 until *c.* 1925 the Hall had been rented by the Sturgeon family.[61]

As late as 1866 the original South Ockendon Hall stood within the moat just over the bridge in the NW. corner.[62] Nothing of it remained in 1974 except the gatehouse wall, the lower part composed of medieval stonework, the upper of early-18th-century brick of similar date to the three-arched bridge. The modern Hall, to the west, was built *c.* 1874.[63]

In the Middle Ages there was a free chapel at South Ockendon Hall. William de la Rochelle made a grant of five marks for the support of its chaplain (1190 × 1225).[64] The chapel was apparently disused by 1471 when Lady (Elizabeth) Bruyn left furnishings from it to South Ockendon church.[65] Her will also mentions her copy of the Canterbury Tales, but there is nothing to suggest that, like Sir Thomas Urswick (d. 1479) at Marks in Dagenham, she kept the book in the chapel.[66]

In 1531 William Tyrell received the manor of *GROVES* or *COLCARTERS* in the division of the Bruyn inheritance.[67] He died *c.* 1534 and was succeeded by his son Humphrey.[68] When the latter died in 1549 the estate included 400 a.[69] Humphrey's heir was his son George who died *c.* 1574.[70] In 1576 George's son Edward Tyrell sold the estate to (Sir) Richard Saltonstall, a London merchant and later lord mayor.[71] From Sir Richard (d. 1601) the manor descended in the direct male line for five generations: to Richard (d. 1618), Richard (d. 1649), John (d. 1658), Philip (d. 1668) and Philip Saltonstall (d. 1694).[72] On the death of the last-named Philip the

43 *Cal. Close*, 1374–7, 340.
44 *Feet of F. Essex*, iii. 205; Newcourt, *Repertorium*, ii. 379, 448.
45 By her second husband, Sir William Brandon, she was the mother of Charles, duke of Suffolk (d. 1545).
46 *Cal. Pat.* 1476–85, 358, 419, 524, 530; C 60 2 Ric. III 18 m.14. The first item refers to the Bruyn heiresses and their first husbands; Alice Bruyn's second husband, Robert Harleston, died in 1471.
47 *Complete Peerage*, ii. 358; *Cal. Inq. p.m. Hen. VII*, ii, p. 236.
48 E.R.O., D/DGe T82.
49 C 142/93/74; C 142/151/51; C 142/157/67; C 142/163/54.
50 C 142/766/68; C 142/778/144; E.R.O., D/DGe T82.
51 E.R.O., D/DGe T82; C. T. Kuypers, *Thorndon*, 20. Cf. *V.C.H. Essex*, iv. 211.
52 Morant, *Essex*, i. 154; E.R.O., D/DP T167/3.
53 E.R.O., D/DGe T82.
54 E.R.O., D/DSq E1; D/DZu 7; E.R.O., T/P 195/2: in 1707 Petre Kingsman was receiving £160 a year.
55 E.R.O., D/DZu 16, 19 for information about the Kingsman family in this paragraph.
56 E.R.O., D/DZu 209. Kingsman's estate received £13,250 for the manor.
57 E.R.O., Q/RPl 116; E.R.O., D/DU 535.
58 E.R.O., D/DU 535.
59 E.R.O., *Sale Cat.* B1531; *White's Dir. Essex* (1848), 192–3; E.R.O., D/DBe T49.
60 For the descent and sale, see p. 112.
61 E.R.O., Q/RPl 156; *White's Dir. Essex* (1848, 1863); *Kelly's Dir. Essex* (1845–1926).
62 O.S. Map 6″, Essex, LXXV (surv. 1865–6); but though *White's Dir. Essex* (1848) refers to the 'fine old moated mansion', *White's Dir. Essex* (1863) is silent.
63 E.R.O., D/DBe E55, 57: the rent, £50 a year, was first paid from Lady Day 1875.
64 E.R.O., D/DP T1 A1688. Cf. *Reg. Baldock* (Cant. & York Soc.), 280.
65 Prob. 11/6 (P.C.C. 2 Wattys).
66 *V.C.H. Essex*, v. 276–7.
67 E.R.O., D/DGe T82; he also took the Lady chapel in the parish church apparently: see p. 123.
68 Guildhall MS. 9531, f. 123(69); *L. & P. Hen. VIII*, xiv (2), p. 68.
69 C 142/88/56.
70 He was alive in 1573: C.P. 25(2)/129/1650.
71 C.P. 25(2)/129/1653; ibid./130/1663; *D.N.B.* The estate may originally have been intended for his son Gilbert (d. 1585) who married Ann Harleston from the neighbouring South Ockendon Hall: Morant, *Essex*, i. 101.
72 C 142/271/175; S. Ockendon ch. reg. I; R.C.H.M. *Essex*, iv. 141.

manor descended to his granddaughter, Philippa Saltonstall, who married John Goodere, younger son of John Goodere of Claybury in Barking.[73]

The estate descended in the Goodere family until 1817.[74] In that year it passed to John H. Stewart, a nephew of the last John Goodere.[75] Stewart died in 1839 and his estates, including 933 a. in South Ockendon, were offered for sale.[76] The bulk of them, containing 643 a. and comprising Street, Colecarters (Groves) and Fen farms, were apparently bought by Samuel Gurney (1786–1856) of West Ham. After the Overend, Gurney bank failure, they were sold in 1867 on behalf of Henry E. Gurney (1821–1905), his third son.[77] Like the Gurney estate at Cranham, they were bought by Richard Benyon (d. 1897), who thus re-united the estates of the old Bruyn manor of South Ockendon. The estate was sold in 1937 along with the other Benyon lands in Essex.[78]

The present (1974) Groves farm-house is a 19th-century building. It stands on the main road from Brentwood to Grays Thurrock on the site formerly occupied by Colecarters farm-house, and at the head of the lane leading east to the Groves Barns. The last named include two timber-framed barns joined by a brick wall with an arched central gateway of *c.* 1600, and they form three sides of the forecourt to the former Groves manor-house of the Saltonstalls. None of that house survives, but its site can be seen in the field, which is partly surrounded by remains of a moat, to the south of the farm buildings. In 1670 the house was the largest in the parish, with 22 hearths.[79] It still existed *c.* 1772, but was demolished soon after.[80]

The estate of *MOLLANDS* lay in the south-east of the parish. It has been suggested that, here as elsewhere, the name denotes land held anciently by a money rent.[81] If so Mollands may have originated in the holdings of the 13 sokemen, who in 1086 paid dues for 8½ hides and 20 acres, within the manor of (South) Ockendon.[82] The name may, however, be derived from the family of Molland (Moland, Molaund) which lived in this part of Essex in the 14th century.[83]

In 1540 Mollands was part of the demesne of the manor of South Ockendon Hall.[84] It descended along with the manor until John Harleston's death in 1624. He had previously settled Mollands on his wife Jane (d. 1626), with remainder to their sons John and Thomas.[85]

The subsequent descent of Mollands has not been traced until 1692, when the estate was sold by William Bayley of Stepney (Mdx.) and his wife Mary to (Sir) William Des Bouverie (Bt.) (d. 1717) for £4,600.[86] Mollands passed with the baronetcy to Sir Edward Des Bouverie (d. 1736) and then to his brother Sir Jacob, who was created Viscount Folkestone and died in 1761. Lord Folkestone's son, William Bouverie, earl of Radnor, sold the estate in 1771 to Guy Bryan (d. *c.* 1775). Mollands passed in succession to Bryan's son Guy (d. 1783), grandson Joseph Bryan (d. 1784) and daughter Mary (d. 1787), before coming to his nephew, another Guy Bryan.

In 1803 Guy Bryan sold part of Mollands to John Cliff of South Ockendon Hall; this became known as Little Mollands.[87] The remainder of the estate, called Great Mollands, was retained by Guy Bryan until 1810 or 1811, when it passed to Campbell Oliphant.[88] Under Oliphant's will, proved 1831, Great Mollands passed to Caroline B. Gray.[89] In 1839 it comprised 307 a.[90] In 1836 Miss Gray had married.[91] After her death, and later that of her husband in 1888, Great Mollands passed to her two surviving children. In 1908 they sold the farm to the tenant, R. A. Manning, who offered it for sale with 309 a. in 1913.[92]

Little Mollands, with 213 a., remained part of the South Ockendon Hall estate until 1845 when the executors of John Cliff sold it to John Aubert of Lower Clapton (Mdx.).[93] John Aubert (d. 1853) left it to his son William, who in 1895, shortly before his death, conveyed it to his daughter Elizabeth, wife of Dr. Francis O. Buckland, of Lower Sloane St. (Lond.). In 1905 she sold Little Mollands to the tenant, R. A. Manning.[94] The same year he sold it to West Ham C.B.C. for use as a farm colony for the unemployed; German prisoners of war were housed there during the First World War; and in 1932 it was converted into a colony for mental defectives.[95] Its successor (1974) is the South Ockendon hospital.[96]

Great Mollands is a late-17th-century farm-house with 18th-century and recent additions. A large brick barn probably dates from the 18th century.[97] Little Mollands farm-house was described as 'new' in 1832.[98]

The manor of *POYNTZ* was first mentioned in 1391, when Poyntz Poyntz and his wife Eleanor held a court for it.[99] It was presumably part of the Bald-

[73] S. Ockendon ch. reg. I; Morant, *Essex*, i. 101; *V.C.H. Essex*, v. 194.

[74] The Gooderes consistently used the name John. The descent is therefore uncertain. John Goodere (d. 1756: S. Ock. ch. reg. I) was probably the husband of Philippa Saltonstall; cf. *V.C.H. Essex*, v. 194.

[75] E.R.O., Q/RPl 141, 142; E.R.O., D/DBe T22: letter of 9 July 1817; W. Palin, *More about Stifford*, 101.

[76] *Gent. Mag.* 1839 (i), 330; E.R.O., D/DBe E34; E.R.O., D/AEM 1/5.

[77] E.R.O., *Sale Cat.* B3894. Old Samuel Gurney also bought the Cranham estate, for his second son, Samuel (d. 1882).

[78] E.R.O., *Sale Cat.* B106; E.R.O., D/DBe E71; Street Farm had been sold a year earlier: E.R.O., *Sale Cat.* B4515.

[79] E.R.O., Q/RTh 5, m.2d.

[80] E.R.O., D/AEM 1/5. *Map of Essex* (1777).

[81] *P.N. Essex*, 126–7.

[82] *V.C.H. Essex*, i. 505.

[83] B.L., Cott. MS. Nero E. vi, ff. 201v., 202v.; *Cal. Inq. p.m.* viii, p. 273; *Cal. Wills Husting*, i. 658.

[84] C 54/424/49.

[85] Prob. 11/54 (P.C.C. 30 Daper); C 142/766/68; C 142/778/144.

[86] E.R.O., D/DU 535: the source of all information in this paragraph.

[87] E.R.O., D/DU 535.

[88] E.R.O., Q/RPl 135, 136 sqq.

[89] Prob. 11/1786; E.R.O., *Sale Cat.* A191: the latter is the source of all information in this paragraph, unless otherwise specified.

[90] E.R.O., D/CT 261.

[91] The name of her husband is not given.

[92] Cf. *E.R.* lxiv. 83.

[93] E.R.O., *Sale Cat.* B1531; E.R.O., D/DU 535. Unless otherwise specified, information in this paragraph derives from the latter source.

[94] From 1902 Manning was also farming, in South Ockendon, Little Belhus, Great Mollands, Glasscocks, Street, and Quince Tree farms.

[95] *V.C.H. Essex*, vi. 106, 111; Inf. from Newham B.C.

[96] See p. 118.

[97] R.C.H.M. *Essex*, iv. 143.

[98] E.R.O., D/DU 535: indenture of 25 Nov. 1846 citing Cliff's will of 13 July 1832.

[99] E.R.O., D/DBe M18 includes certified copies of court rolls 1391–1577.

win inheritance, and descended with the manor of North Ockendon until 1937.[1]

The manorial demesne lay about a half mile south of the village, on the west side of the present South Street. It can be traced from *c.* 1731 as a farm of about 100 a., let to a succession of tenants.[2] In and after the 19th century it was known as Quince Tree farm.[3]

The farm-house is largely of the 17th century, but part of the North wing is of the early 16th century.[4] In 1974 the house was empty; the farmyard was occupied by a building firm, and the farm lands had been built over.

ECONOMIC HISTORY. The Domesday manor of South Ockendon probably occupied the same area as the modern parish.[5] It apparently contained 11 hides, of which 8½ hides and 20 acres were held by 13 sokemen, and another 40 acres by 4 bordars. In 1086 the manor was thriving. Since 1066 the recorded population had risen from 40 to 66; there were 11 ploughs in place of 9; a mill had been built; and the value of the manor had increased from £7 to £16, partly as a result of vigorous stocking. The large number of bordars (34 in 1066, 50 in 1086) may indicate, as at West Ham and Cranham, that forest was being cleared.[6] Certainly this large manor had only woodland enough for 150 swine in 1086, and by 1295 there was apparently none.[7] On the other hand, sheep were being reared in large numbers: in 1066 there had been only 18; in 1086 there were 220. The location of their pastures is nowhere indicated, but the manor was said to have pasture, probably marsh-pasture outside the main manorial holding, for 100 sheep.[8]

From the Middle Ages farming in South Ockendon has been chiefly arable. In 1362 the manor had 360 a. of arable and only 40 a. of field and pasture.[9] This predominance of arable continued in the 16th century, but some land may have been put to grass *c.* 1650 and more in the later 18th century.[10] In 1839 the parish contained 1,874 a. arable and 891 a. meadow and pasture. There were 13 holdings of more than 20 a.; the Hall had 668 a., Groves 526 a., Mollands Hall 306 a., Little Mollands 213 a., and that part of the Grange which lay in South Ockendon 172 a. Three farms had between 130 a. and 150 a., and three more between 90 a. and 100 a.[11]

From 1831 to the 1920s members of the Sturgeon family farmed at the Hall.[12] Thomas B. Sturgeon (d. 1855) kept a notable flock of pure Merino sheep, and also carried on a large business supplying ship's provisions.[13] In 1845 and again in 1864 the family paid increased rents for breaking up pasture, 160 a. in all.[14] From 1895 the Sturgeons also described themselves as millers.[15]

There had been little change by 1916. Cultivated land then comprised 845 a. of meadow and pasture, and 1,848 a. of arable, 485 a. of which were market-garden land. There were still 12 holdings of more than 20 a.: four had about 30 a.; three between 120 a. and 150 a.; the Grange had 172 a., Great Mollands 309 a., Groves 415 a., R. A. Manning's '5 farms' 519 a., and South Ockendon Hall 658 a.[16] By the 1960s, however, there was considerably less land under crops: housing and industry covered the SW. of the parish, and in the NW. and SE. the extraction of gravel, sand, and clay had temporarily withdrawn much land from cultivation.[17]

The presence of a mill in South Ockendon was first recorded in 1086.[18] There was a windmill on the manor in 1295 and 1362, and it may have been one of the two mills mentioned in 1573 and 1576, when property in various parishes including South Ockendon was being conveyed.[19] None of these mills has survived, and their sites are not known.[20] The present smock mill was built *c.* 1800, its earliest known tenant being Samuel Green.[21] It stands on a mill-dam, and the basement housed a small water-mill.[22] Steam-power was added, perhaps in 1870–1 when a complete repair was undertaken.[23] The mill ceased operation in the 1920s, and by 1932 was rapidly decaying, a process which has continued ever since.[24]

In 1254 the lord of the manor secured a grant of a Tuesday market and a yearly fair to be held on the eve, day, and morrow of St. Nicholas (5–7 December), patron saint of the parish church.[25] Neither was apparently established,[26] but there was later a May Day fair at South Ockendon, which was abolished in 1873.[27]

Until recently the only industry in South Ockendon was the quarrying of gravel and clay. In 1789 the gravel-pits on the main road needed fencing, and the tithe award of 1839 names 5 Gravel Pit fields, a Pits, a Great White Pits, and a Brick Clamps.[28] In the 1950s the Ford Motor Company established a depot between Arisdale Avenue and the railway.[29] In 1969 John Lysaght Ltd., a subsidiary of Guest Keen and Nettlefolds, moved their works for the processing of steel sheets from Dagenham to South Ockendon.[30]

[1] See p. 111.
[2] E.R.O., D/DBe E7–9, 42, 54.
[3] E.R.O., D/DBe P5; *Kelly's Dir. Essex* (1845 and later edns.).
[4] R.C.H.M. *Essex*, iv. 142.
[5] *V.C.H. Essex*, i. 505: the source of all statements in this paragraph, unless otherwise specified.
[6] Ibid. vi. 74; and see above, p. 106; below, p. 134.
[7] *Cal. Inq. p.m.* iii, p. 163; cf. *Cal. Close*, 1360–4, 142: the lessee of S. Ockendon may take timber at Beckenham for the repair of S. Ockendon dwellings.
[8] Cf. *V.C.H. Essex*, i. 369–73.
[9] *Cal. Inq. p.m.* xi, pp. 229–30.
[10] C 142/151/51; E.R.O., Q/SR 351/27; cf. *Ag. Hist. Eng.* iv, ed. Joan Thirsk, 214–18; H.O. 67/16; cf. E.R.O., Q/SBb 336/27.
[11] E.R.O., D/CT 261.
[12] E.R.O., Q/RPl 156; *Kelly's Dir. Essex* (1922).
[13] E.R.O., *Sale Cat.* B1531; *Gent. Mag.* 1855(2), 108.
[14] E.R.O., *Sale Cat.* B1531; E,R.O., D/DBe E68 f. 34d.
[15] *Kelly's Dir. Essex* (1895–1922).
[16] E.R.O., D/Z 45/9.
[17] 2nd Land Utilization Survey of Britain, Land Use sheets 225–6.
[18] *V.C.H. Essex*, i. 505.
[19] *Cal. Inq. p.m.* iii, p. 163; xi, p. 229; C.P.25(2)/129/1653 and 130/1663.
[20] The series of mill-ponds, now dried up, suggest that an early mill was a water-mill; for their extent, R.C.H.M. *Essex*, iv. 141
[21] E.R.O., Q/RPl 127–57 (1802–32); so many changes of ownership, tenancy, and assessment occur between 1801 and 1832 that the mill cannot be further traced; but cf. R. Wailes, 'Essex Windmills', *Trans. Newcomen Soc.* xxxi. 179.
[22] D. Smith, *Eng. Windmills*, ii. 60, 64–5; *Trans. Newcomen Soc.* xxxi. 153–80.
[23] E.R.O., D/DBe E68, f. 38d.
[24] *Kelly's Dir. Essex* (1922–6); Smith, *Eng. Windmills*, ii. 65.
[25] *Cal. Pat.* 1247–58, 341.
[26] Inquisitions in 1277 and 1295 are silent (*Cal. Inq. p.m.* ii, p. 133; iii. p. 163), but cf. *Cal. Pat.* 1429–36, 458 for a confirmation of the market and fair in 1435.
[27] *Lond. Gaz.* 14 Nov. 1873, p. 4964.
[28] E.R.O., D/DRu E1; E.R.O., D/CT 261.
[29] *Thurrock Official Guide* [1954, 1959].
[30] Ibid. (1971).

LOCAL GOVERNMENT. The lord of the manor of South Ockendon claimed assize of bread and of ale and the right to a gallows in 1273–4.[31] He had view of frankpledge in 1384 and 1561, but few manorial records survive.[32] In 1561 the court ordered the repair of the ducking stool and appointed a constable.[33] Two rolls of the court baron of Poyntz manor survive for 1574–1647; the earlier includes copies from previous rolls going back to 1391.[34] In 1606 the court was still being held under an elm on South Ockendon Green.[35]

No parish records, except registers, have survived from before 1835. In 1634 there were two churchwardens, and in 1663–4 there were also two constables, and two overseers of the poor.[36] It was stated in 1627 that the parish poorhouse, the site of which was not given, was in danger of collapse, and that a previous house, in North Lane (probably the present North Street), no longer existed.[37] By 1788 South Ockendon had a workhouse.[38] In the early 19th century this sometimes accommodated paupers from North Ockendon and Cranham.[39] In 1835, when South Ockendon became part of Orsett poor-law union, the workhouse was said to have room for 60.[40] It continued to be used by the union until the end of 1838.[41]

In 1776 South Ockendon spent £168 on the poor; in 1783–5 the average expenditure was £196, the gross yield of the rates being almost £239.[42] From 1800 to 1821 South Ockendon spent an average of almost £325 a year on the poor; the worst years were from 1807 to 1810, when the parish paid out in three successive years £416, £748, and £465. Only in 1813–15 did expenditure fall below £200.[43]

CHURCH. There was a church at South Ockendon by the reign of William I.[44] The advowson of the rectory descended with the manor until its division in 1531; thereafter presentations were made alternately by the owners of South Ockendon Hall and Groves, single turns being sold on several occasions.[45] John Cliff bought South Ockendon Hall about 1789, and half the advowson with the next presentation in or after 1806.[46] He died in 1833, and his executors seem to have become the sole owners of the advowson by default, after the death without issue of John Stewart, of Groves, in 1839. Stewart had had no occasion to exercise his right of presentation to the rectory, and his representatives were apparently unaware of it. Cliff's executors offered the advowson for sale in 1845, but did not find a buyer until *c.* 1860 when it was acquired by the Revd. Perceval Laurence (1829–1913), who was himself rector from 1873 to 1879.[47] By 1926 Mrs. W. S. Caldwell had acquired the advowson, and in 1928 she presented W. Somerville Caldwell.[48] In 1958 he and R. H. Caldwell sold the advowson to the Guild of All Souls.[49]

In 1254 the value of the rectory, over and above 20*s.* charged to the abbot of Westminster, was 20 marks. It was 25 marks in 1291 and 50 marks in 1535.[50] A grant of tithes made in 1085 or 1086 to Hurley priory (Berks.) was overlooked in 1254, as was a 12th-century grant of tithes to the Brook Street hospital.[51] The hospital's claim was revived in the later 14th century, but was rejected in 1372 by the bishop of London, who awarded the tithes in question to the rector of South Ockendon.[52] In 1644 the rectory was said to be worth £120; for much of the 18th century it was valued at £200, but by 1790 it had risen to £326 and by the 1820s to £754.[53] The tithes were commuted in 1839 for £828.[54] The glebe was reckoned to be 11 a. in 1610, 13 a. in 1790, and 16 a. in 1839.[55]

The ancient rectory house stood about ¼m. south of the village, on the west side of South Road. The site was originally moated, but only the northern arm remained at the end of the 19th century.[56] In 1975 the outline of the moat was still visible, the island being used as a children's playground.[57] In 1610 the rectory contained 6 rooms. It was almost certainly the nucleus of the much altered 20th-century house, which was timber-framed and of two storeys with a central chimney-stack.[58] The L.C.C. bought the glebe and rectory in 1952, demolished the rectory, and built a housing estate *c.* 1970.[59] In 1954 Sedgewick House, North Road, was bought as a rectory.[60]

Agamund, priest of (South) Ockendon, was living in 1085.[61] The names of several other early rectors have also survived.[62] John Rider, rector 1583–90, was a Latin lexicographer and later bishop of Killaloe (Ireland).[63] Francis Gouldman, rector from 1634, was sequestrated as a royalist in 1644.[64] There were four ministers between this date and the Restoration when Gouldman regained the living and remained rector until his death in 1688.[65] During his years of

[31] *Rot. Hund.* (Rec. Com.), i. 148–9.
[32] E.R.O., D/DP M1149–53: compoti for S. Ockendon in 1318–19 and 1384–5 (M1152–3); S. Ockendon rentals, *c.* 1350 and 1556 (M1150–1); court roll of 1561 (M1149).
[33] E.R.O., D/DP M1149.
[34] E.R.O., D/DBe M18–21.
[35] E.R.O., D/DBe M19; cf. M18 (court of 1567).
[36] E.R.O., Q/SR 399/120; Hale, *Precedents*, p. 256.
[37] E.R.O., D/DBe M19.
[38] E.R.O., Q/SBb 330.
[39] E.R.O., D/P 118/8/3; D/P 308/12/3.
[40] E.R.O., G/Or M1: 22 Oct., 19, 26 Nov. 1835.
[41] Ibid.: 22 Nov. 1838, 10 Jan., 7 Feb. 1839; cf. E.R.O., G/Or Z3, f. 104.
[42] E.R.O., Q/CR 1/1.
[43] E.R.O., Q/CR 1/9/3, 1/12. The gross yield of the rates from 1800 to 1817 averaged £406 14*s.*
[44] Hart, *Early Chart. Essex*, 40.
[45] Newcourt, *Repertorium*, ii. 448–9; E.R.O., T/A 547; Guildhall MSS. 9550, 9552, 9556–8, 9560; C.P. 43/802/35.
[46] E.R.O., D/DU 535; E.R.O., T/P 110/85; cf. E.R.O., D/AEM 2.
[47] E.R.O., *Sale Cat.* B1531; *Clergy List* (1856); Venn, *Alumni Cantab.*, II. iv. 105; *Kelly's Dir. Essex* (1859); *White's Dir. Essex* (1863).
[48] *Chelmsford Dioc. Yr. Bks.* (1925, 1926).
[49] E.R.O., D/CP 14/2.
[50] *E.A.T.* N.S., xviii. 18; *Tax. Eccl.* (Rec. Com.), 22; *Valor Eccl.* (Rec. Com.), i. 36.
[51] Hart, *Early Chart. Essex*, 39; *Reg. Sudbury* (Cant. & York Soc.), i. 210–11.
[52] *Reg. Sudbury* (Cant. & York Soc.), i. 200–2.
[53] Smith, *Eccl. Hist. Essex*, 136; Guildhall MSS. 9550, 9556–8, 9560.
[54] E.R.O., D/CT 261.
[55] Newcourt, *Repertorium*, ii. 448; Guildhall MS. 9558; E.R.O., D/CT 261.
[56] O.S. Map, Essex, 6" LXXV (surv. 1865–6) and 1/25,000, LXXV. 15 (1895 edn.).
[57] Inf. from Thurrock Local Hist. Mus.
[58] Newcourt, *Repertorium*, ii. 448; R.C.H.M. *Essex*, iv. 141; cf. E.R.O., *Sale Cat.* B1531; Acc. 4659 for the rectory in 1845 and 1880.
[59] Papers in church safe; *Thurrock Official Guide* (1968, 1971).
[60] E.R.O., D/CP 14/3.
[61] Hart, *Early Chart. Essex*, 40.
[62] C.C.L., J. L. Fisher, 'Essex Incumbents'; P. H. Reaney, *Early Essex Clergy*, 122–3.
[63] *D.N.B.*
[64] Smith, *Eccl. Hist. Essex*, 116–17, 134–6.
[65] Smith, 'Parochial Clergy, 1640–64' (TS in E.R.O. Libr.), 19–20.

sequestration he had been one of the deprived clergy who prepared *Critici Sacri* (1660), and he was also, like Rider, a Latin lexicographer.[66] His successor was Offspring Blackall, rector 1690–1707, later bishop of Exeter.[67]

In the mid 19th century rector and parish were at odds. As early as 1842 the services conducted by Henry Eve, rector 1819–73, were thought inadequate, and by 1849 the regular congregation had dwindled to 13 or 15 out of a total population of about 1,700. In 1857 there were two factions in the parish; bitterly sarcastic comments had appeared in the press; a church-rate needed for the repair of the crumbling fabric of the church had been refused; and no one was willing to serve as churchwarden. The rural dean appealed to the archdeacon for advice; and it is in this context that the rebuilding of the church in 1866 should be set.[68]

The church of *ST. NICHOLAS*, south-east of the village green, is built of flint and rubble with ashlar dressings. It has a chancel with north chapel and south vestry, a clerestoried nave aisled north and south, a north porch, and a circular west tower.[69]

Only the west wall of the nave survives *in situ* from the 12th-century church. The tower and north aisle were added in the 13th century, the richly-carved 12th-century doorway being reset in the north aisle. The nave roof was probably renewed at the same time and the chancel rebuilt and extended. There is no surviving evidence for alteration in the 14th century but much was done in the 15th century. The north arcade was rebuilt, the wall above it raised to include a clerestorey, and a new nave roof of flattish pitch put on. The north chapel was added or rebuilt and its aisle wall raised to take a new roof with parapets and allow for new and larger windows. New windows were also inserted in the south wall of the nave. The chancel was rebuilt or refenestrated, the chancel arch probably enlarged, and a rood-screen, with a loft approached from a stair turret on the south, was added. There was an altar against its south end. A west doorway was cut into the tower, and the south doorway may have been blocked at the same time; a timber-framed porch was built outside the north door.[70]

In 1471 the north chapel was paved and an alabaster 'table' provided for it.[71] The chapel went with Groves manor and became the responsibility of the Saltonstalls in the 16th century; they probably carried out the alterations in the 17th century which included a new roof, dated 1618, and windows.[72]

In 1652 or 1653 the church was struck by lightning, which apparently destroyed the wooden spire, bells, and nave roof. The parishioners in 1658 obtained a brief to collect for repairs and money was raised by the churchwardens and minister. In 1661, however, after the minister's ejection, the parishioners complained to quarter sessions that all three were refusing to account for the money, and repairs were held up. Quarter sessions intervened, and the repairs were presumably carried out during the following years.[73] The nave roof dates from the later 17th century, and the tower must have been restored by 1678, when a new bell was presented. New fittings at this period included a pulpit, an iron hour-glass stand which survived the restoration of 1866, and altar rails, the last added by the archdeacon's order in 1685.[74]

In 1744 the west side of the tower fell twice. It was rebuilt a second time in 1745, when its height may have been reduced.[75] A gallery formerly at the west end of the nave was probably of the 18th century.

The church was extensively restored in 1866 by Richard Armstrong, largely at the expense of Richard Benyon and Henry Eve, the rector.[76] The south aisle and vestry were added, and the chancel and north porch largely rebuilt. The roofs were renewed, and the tower was heightened. The windows of the chapel were restored, the walls refaced externally, and the ashlar dressings renewed. Inside, virtually all the furniture, including the font and pulpit, was new. The woodwork of the old parish chest was replaced, its medieval ironwork being reset.[77]

The monuments in the north chapel include brasses to Sir Ingram Bruyn (d. 1400), Margaret (d. 1602), wife of Edward Barker of Chiswick (Mdx.) gentleman, and Gilbert (d. 1585), eldest son of Sir Richard Saltonstall, the purchaser of South Ockendon Hall. A large wall-monument, with kneeling figures of Sir Richard and Lady (Suzanne) Saltonstall, dominates the chapel. Less oppressive wall-monuments without figures recall George Drywood (d. 1611), a rector, and Philip Saltonstall (d. 1668). A floor-slab of black marble commemorates Sir William How (d. 1650).

In 1552 the tower contained 4 bells.[78] These were presumably the bells destroyed in 1652 or 1653. They were replaced in 1678 by a single bell, given by Richard Mulford, the sexton. This in turn was replaced by a bell made by Mears & Stainbank in 1865.[79]

The church plate in 1685 consisted of a silver flagon of 1670, a silver plate of 1682, and a silver cup and cover of 1601. They were stolen in the 1860s, and have not been replaced by vessels of comparable quality.[80]

The church possessed in 1552 'a mitre for St. Nicholas' clerks', although the pageantry of the Boy Bishop had been abolished in 1541.[81]

ROMAN CATHOLICISM. Between 1614 and 1677 eighteen persons from South Ockendon were

[66] *D.N.B.* s.vv. Gouldman, Francis, and Pearson, John.
[67] *D.N.B.*
[68] E.R.O., D/AEM 1/5.
[69] See plate facing p. 49. This account is based on R.C.H.M. *Essex*, iv. 140–1; Pevsner, *Essex* (1965), 359; G. Buckler, *Churches of Essex* (1856); W. Palin, *More about Stifford*; Thorne, *Environs Lond.* 457–8.
[70] Perhaps by the terms of Lady (Elizabeth) Bruyn's will of 1471: Prob. 11/6 (P.C.C.: 2 Wattys).
[71] Ibid.
[72] Guildhall MS. 9531, f. 123(69); cf. E.R.O., D/AEM 1/5.
[73] *Cal. S.P. Dom.* 1657–8, 319; *E.R.* xxxii. 13; xxxvii. 166; xxxix. 204; E.R.O., Q/SO 1, p. 240a. Morant, *Essex*, i. 101 follows Salmon, *Essex*, 280 in reporting the spire struck by lightning in 1638. This is apparently a confusion with Upminster: see below, p. 158.
[74] *E.A.T.* N.S. xxi. 104.
[75] E. F. L. Brown, *S. Ockendon Parish Church*, citing 'Old Church records'.
[76] E.R.O., D/AEM 1/5, 2/9; for Armstrong at Cranham and N. Ockendon, see pp. 108, 115.
[77] Palin, *More about Stifford*, 107; *Ch. Chests Essex*, 190–2.
[78] *E.A.T.* N.S. ii. 187.
[79] *Ch. Bells Essex*, 350.
[80] *Ch. Plate Essex*, 28–9; Palin, op. cit., 107.
[81] *E.R.* liv. 108, 139; *Tudor Royal Proclams.* ed. Hughes & Larkin, i. 302.

indicted for recusancy; seven of them, belonging to the yeoman family of Hopthrowe, were repeatedly fined.[82] No papists were reported after 1677.[83]

In 1952 a new Roman Catholic parish of Aveley was created for the L.C.C. estate, and a church hall was opened in Easington Way in 1953. The church of *THE HOLY CROSS*, adjoining the hall, was completed in 1961.[84]

PROTESTANT NONCONFORMITY. Christ Church United Reformed (formerly Congregational) church, Afton Road, originated in 1802, when the Essex Congregational Union appointed James Cover as itinerant preacher in the Grays Thurrock area.[85] In 1803 Cover registered Samuel Mayes's house at South Ockendon for Independent worship.[86] When Cover left the district later in 1803 the E.C.U. asked David Smith, minister of Brentwood Independent church, to preach at South Ockendon whenever possible.[87] In 1806 a 'chapel room' was rented by the E.C.U. and registered by Smith.[88] A chapel was built in North Road in 1812, partly at the expense of John Cliff of South Ockendon Hall, who in 1828 built a manse and in 1832 provided an endowment for the minister's salary.[89] Under the first minister, Anthony Brown (1814–51), daughter churches were formed at Aveley and Grays Thurrock.[90] In 1829 the congregation at South Ockendon numbered about 300.[91]

Joseph Morison, minister 1852–84, also attracted large congregations.[92] During that period the Congregationalists' refusal to pay church-rates caused ill-feeling in the parish.[93] In 1866 the chapel was restored and partly rebuilt at the expense of Richard Benyon, lord of the manor.[94] After the Second World War it was decided to move to the new L.C.C. estate at Belhus Park.[95] A new building, named Christ Church, was opened in Afton Drive in 1965.[96] The cost was met by the sale of the old church and portable war damage compensation.[97] In 1972 Christ Church joined the United Reformed church.[98] In 1975 it had 59 members and shared a minister with Aveley.[99]

South Ockendon (formerly Wesleyan) Methodist church, West Road, apparently originated in 1809, when a house was registered for worship by Henry Smith.[1] Smith and his wife, who are said to have been members of Wesley's Chapel, City Road (Lond.), kept the village shop at South Ockendon.[2] He seems to have led the society at least until 1851.[3] In 1829 South Ockendon, still with a licensed house, was in the Spitalfields circuit.[4] It was placed in the Romford circuit in 1833. A church was built in West Road in 1847. It was enlarged in 1857 and a Sunday school was added in 1891.[5] It was in the Ilford circuit from 1908 to 1947 and in the new Romford circuit from 1947.

Belhus Park chapel, Deveron Gardens, registered for worship by Christians in 1957,[6] was listed as an Evangelical church in 1971.[7] Kingdom Hall, Daiglen Drive, was registered by Jehovah's Witnesses in 1971.[8]

EDUCATION. There is a reference to a schoolmaster in South Ockendon in 1673.[9] In 1714 there was a charity school for 14 boys, which survived until at least 1724.[10] A Congregational Sunday school was founded in 1804.[11] By 1807 there were 4 dame schools where about 80 infants were taught to sew, read, and say their catechism.[12] In 1817 there was a church day and Sunday school which was replaced in 1819 by a Sunday school supported by the rector and local farmers. Ninety children were taught free in a rented school-room by a master and a mistress.[13] By 1839 the school, with 30 children, was supported by the rector alone.[14] By 1846–7 an attempt to build a school had failed, and 17 children were being taught in the church at their parents' expense and 33 in the four dame schools.[15]

South Ockendon British school, North Road. In 1851 winter evening-classes in reading and writing were held in the Congregational chapel vestry. In 1852 Jonathan Birdseye started a day-school in his house on the Green, where he also took private boarders. It moved to the Congregational chapel vestry where, by the end of 1852, 72 children were being taught by day and 35 in the evenings. In 1854 a school for 100 was built, by subscription, adjoining the chapel. Samuel Gurney of West Ham (d. 1856), a large landowner in South Ockendon, gave 100 guineas.[16] The school received annual government grants from 1872, when 59 children attended, until 1878 when it was closed because the managers could not improve the building as required by the govern-

[82] E.R.O., Q/SR 206/117, 325/54, 328/40, 356/26, 428/99, 432/4, 177, 437/25; Q/SBa 5; *Essex Recusant*, i. 29; iii. 83; iv. 16–17, 24, 71–2, 113, 115; v. 29; vi. 92; vii. 37.

[83] *Essex Recusant*, ii. 24; Guildhall MS. 9557.

[84] *Brentwood Dioc. Yr. Bk.* (1952), 29, 59; G.R.O. Worship Reg. nos. 64183 (cancelled 1961), 68281.

[85] E.R.O., D/NC 9/1 (Essex Cong. Union Cttee. Mins. 1798–1807); R. Burls, *Brief Review of the . . . Essex Cong. Union*, 20.

[86] G.R.O. Worship Returns, London Dioc. Essex and Herts. Commissary, no. 131.

[87] E.R.O., D/NC 9/1.

[88] E.R.O., D/NC 9/1; G.R.O. Worship Returns, London dioc. Essex and Herts. comm. nos. 163, 183.

[89] S. D. Challis and J. W. Scamell, *Hist. S. Ockendon Cong. Ch.* 10, f. p. 18.

[90] Ibid. 3; H.O. 129/7/198; *Congr. Yr. Bk.* (1851), 212.

[91] E.R.O., Q/CR 3/2/1, 3/1/202.

[92] *Essex Congr. Union Reps.* (1852) 7, (1858) 13, (1882) 24; I. G. Sparkes, *Hist. Thurrock*, 25.

[93] W. Palin, *More about Stifford*, 102–3, 109.

[94] *Grays and Til. Gaz.* 8 Apr. 1960.

[95] *E.C.U. Reps.* (1958–64).

[96] G.R.O. Worship Reg. nos. 15341 (amended 1964, cancelled 1965), 70136 (replacing 15341).

[97] *Essex Congr. Union Rep.* (1963, 1964); *Essex & Thurrock Gaz.* 8 Apr. 1960, 3 Mar. 1961. The old church still (1975) survives, as a joinery works.

[98] G.R.O. *Official List*.

[99] *Utd. Ref. Ch. Yr. Bk.* (1975), 111.

[1] G.R.O. Worship Returns, Lond. Dioc., Bps. Ct. no. 724.

[2] Unless otherwise stated this account is based on: E. Barrett, *The Lamp still Burns*, 28–30, illus. f. p. 32.

[3] H.O. 129/7/198; cf. *White's Dir. Essex* (1848), 194.

[4] E.R.O., Q/CR 3/2/89.

[5] *Wesleyan Chapel Cttee. Reps.* (1856–7, 1890–1).

[6] G.R.O. Worship Reg. no. 66242.

[7] *Thurrock Official Guide* (1971).

[8] G.R.O. Worship Reg. no. 72710.

[9] E.R.O., Q/SR 426/104.

[10] S.P.C.K. *Reports* (1714, 1724).

[11] E.R.O., D/NC 9/1.

[12] E.R.O., D/AEM 2/4.

[13] E.R.O., D/P 75/28/9; D/P 30/28/19; *Returns Educ. Poor*, H.C. 224, p. 264 (1819), ix(1).

[14] E.R.O., D/P 30/28/19.

[15] *Nat. Soc. Church Schs. Enquiry* 1846–7.

[16] Ed. 49/2205; E.R.O., D/NC 9/1; S. D. Challis and J. W. Scamell, *Hist. S. Ockendon Cong. Ch.*, 20–22; see above, p. 120.

ment.[17] The school was sold to the Congregational Sunday school for £30 in 1908. Under a Board of Education Scheme the annual income from the capital was to be used to provide prizes for South Ockendon schoolchildren.[18]

Benyon county junior and infants school, West Road, formerly South Ockendon National school. In 1863–4 Richard Benyon (d. 1897) built a school and teacher's house on his land at Street Farm, opposite the Green.[19] The school was united with the National Society. A government grant was received from 1866. Attendance dwindled from 95 at the day-school and 45 at the associated evening-school in 1866 to 54 and 21 in 1871. The evening-school was discontinued in 1871 but revived in 1875 and lasted until the end of the decade.[20] In 1878, when the British school closed, Richard Benyon enlarged the National school.[21] By 1893 the school had 204 pupils.[22] Benyon further enlarged it in 1896 and built another teacher's house.[23] In 1911 Essex county council bought the buildings and took over the school.[24] It was again enlarged in 1912–13 for 350.[25] In 1936 it was reorganized for mixed juniors and infants.[26] In 1951 the infants were transferred to a new building, and the school was reorganized in two departments for juniors and infants.[27] It was named Benyon school in 1957.[28]

Dilkes county junior and infants schools, Garron Lane, are named after the adjacent wood.[29] The junior school for 320 was opened in 1952; the infants school was opened for 200 in 1953. Mardyke county primary school, Cruick Avenue, was opened in 1952 for 320 juniors and 200 infants in two departments,[30] which were amalgamated in 1964 in the junior school buildings. The infants building was taken over by Branwood special school.[31] In 1974 the 36 Engineer Regiment built a Perspex shell over the school swimming pool as part of the Army scheme of Military Aid to the Civil Community.[32] Barretts county primary school, Erriff Drive, was opened in 1954 for 560 mixed juniors and infants.[33] The junior department closed in 1965 and the infants department in 1966. The buildings were adapted for use as a youth centre.[34] Shaw county junior and infants schools, Avon Green. The infant school for 240 was opened in 1954 and the junior school for 320 in 1955.[35] West Ockendon temporary county primary school, Faymore Gardens, was opened in 1954 for 320 juniors and 240 infants.[36] The junior department closed in 1957,[37] and the infants department in 1959.[38] Bonnygate county junior and infants schools, Arisdale Avenue, were opened in 1955 for 320 juniors and 240 infants.[39] In 1958 the junior school occupied huts on the site of West Ockendon temporary infants school, with which it was amalgamated in 1959.[40] Somers Heath county junior and infants schools, Stifford Road, were opened in 1956 for 320 juniors and 240 infants.[41]

Courts county secondary school, Fulbrook Lane, was opened in 1951 for 600. It was designed by Denis Clarke Hall.[42] In 1971 it was closed and the buildings sold to the Roman Catholics.[43] Lennard county secondary school, Erriff Drive, was opened in 1954 for 600.[44] It was closed in 1971; the buildings were retained for use by Culverhouse school.[45] Culverhouse secondary comprehensive mixed school, Barle Gardens. The boys department of Culverhouse county secondary school opened for 450 in 1956; a department for 450 girls opened in 1957.[46] The school was enlarged in 1962 to provide extra places for 150 girls and 150 boys.[47] It became a comprehensive school in 1971.[48]

St. Cedd's Roman Catholic voluntary aided secondary comprehensive school for boys opened in 1971 for 600 boys in the former Courts school buildings.[49]

Branwood school, Cruick Avenue. In 1964 Grays Thurrock open-air school, for delicate and physically handicapped children, was moved to the building of the former Mardyke infant school, and renamed.[50] Millards school, Garth Road, named after Millard's Garden,[51] opened in 1971 for 60 educationally sub-normal children aged 5–16. South Ockendon Hospital school, South Road, was opened in 1971 for 120 educationally sub-normal children under 16 years.[52]

In 1839 there was a private school in South Ockendon for 20 boys, and another with about 16 local girls.[53] The girls school was probably identical with the one, near the church, conducted in 1845 by Elizabeth Attwell, who later ran a school in Upminster.[54] Joseph Morison, minister of South Ockendon

[17] *Rep. Educ. Cttee. of Council*, 1872–3 [C.812] p. 409, H.C. (1873), xxiv; Ed. 21/5348.
[18] Ed. 21/5348; Ed. 49/2205.
[19] Ed. 49/2205; *Kelly's Dir. Essex* (1870, 1882); E.R.O., D/DBe Q11; O.S. Map 6″, Essex, LXXV (surv. 1865–6).
[20] *Reps. Educ. Cttee. of Council*, 1866–7 [3882], p. 571; H.C. (1867), xxii; 1871–2 [C.601], p. 259, H.C. (1872), xxii; 1875–6 [C. 1513–I], p. 533, H.C. (1876), xxiii; 1880–1 [C.2948–I], p. 579, H.C. (1881), xxxii.
[21] Ed. 21/5348; *Kelly's Dir. Essex* (1882).
[22] *Return of Schs.* 1893 [C.7529], p. 174, H.C. (1894), lxv.
[23] Ed. 49/2205.
[24] E.R.O., D/DBe Q11; E.R.O., C/TE 209; Ed. 21/5348.
[25] Ed. 21/5348.
[26] Inf. from Essex Educ. Dept.
[27] E.R.O., C/ME 45, p. 15; C/ME 46, p. 543.
[28] E.R.O., C/ME 51, p. 470.
[29] O.S. Map 6″, TQ 58 SE. (1967).
[30] *Educ. in Essex* (1952–6), 20.
[31] E.R.O., C/ME 57, p. 806; C/ME 58, p. 495.
[32] *Reader's Digest*, Nov. 1975, 223–4.
[33] *Educ. in Essex* (1952–6), 21. The school is named after the Barrett-Lennard family of Aveley.
[34] E.R.O., C/ME 57, p. 806; C/ME 59, pp. 195, 200; C/ME 60, p. 451.
[35] Inf. from Essex Educ. Dept.; O.S. Map 6″, Essex, LXXXIII (surv. 1863–6); Shaw and Bonnygate (see below) schools are named from the neighbouring Bonnygate Shaw.
[36] E.R.O., C/ME 47, pp. 256, 509; *Educ. in Essex* (1952–6), 21; inf. from Essex Educ. Dept.
[37] Inf. from Essex Educ. Dept.
[38] E.R.O., C/ME 52, p. 799.
[39] *Essex Educ. Building Suppl.*, July 1956, 3; inf. from Essex Educ. Dept.
[40] E.R.O., C/ME 52, p. 799.
[41] *Educ. in Essex* (1952–6), 21; O.S. Map 6″, TQ 58 SE. (1967).
[42] *Educ. in Essex* (1945–52), 31; Pevsner, *Essex*, 360.
[43] E.R.O., C/ME 64, p. A89; C/ME 65, p. E126; and see St. Cedds school below.
[44] *Educ. in Essex* (1952–6), 31. The school is named after the Barrett-Lennard family of Aveley.
[45] E.R.O., C/ME 64, p. A56.
[46] *Educ. in Essex* (1952–6), 32; inf. from Essex Educ. Dept.
[47] *Essex Educ. Building Suppl.*, July 1963, 50; *Educ. in Essex* (1960–4), 23.
[48] Inf. from Essex Educ. Dept.
[49] E.R.O., C/ME 64, p. A89; and see Courts school above.
[50] *Educ. in Essex* (1960–4), 100; E.R.O., C/ME 58, p. 495; inf. from Essex Educ. Dept.
[51] O.S. Map 6″, TQ 58 SE. (1967).
[52] E.R.O., C/ME 65, pp. D9–10; inf. from Essex Educ. Dept.
[53] E.R.O., D/P 30/28/19.
[54] E.R.O., *Sale Cat.* B1531; and see below, p. 163.

Congregational chapel 1852–84, conducted a private school, possibly the one for 18 boys which existed in 1871.[55]

CHARITIES FOR THE POOR.[56] John Cliff, by will dated 1832, gave an annuity of £5 to provide bread on his birthday for such of the pious poor of South Ockendon, attending the Congregational chapel or the parish church, as the minister of the chapel should select. In the 1970s the income, administered by the United Reformed church, was given to South Ockendon Over-60s club, usually to provide Christmas dinners.

RAINHAM

RAINHAM lies beside the Thames 12 miles east of the city of London.[1] The ancient parish, containing 3,253 a., was bounded west by the river Ingrebourne, north and north-east by Upminster, and east by Aveley and Wennington. Industry reached the parish in 1869, and after the First World War the village became the nucleus of a dormitory suburb. Rainham was included in Hornchurch U.D. in 1934, and Havering L.B. in 1965.[2]

The alluvial marshlands of Rainham are 5–6 ft. above sea-level; the rest of the parish consists chiefly of gravel beds below 60 ft. In the south-east, at Moor Hall, the land rises to 100 ft. Watercourses border the parish: to the west the Ingrebourne is tidal from the Thames to the Red bridge; in the east a stream flows westwards through Aveley and Wennington before turning south to the Thames, forming for part of its course the parish boundary and a common sewer. A third stream flows from Gaynes park, Upminister, to the Berwick ponds, and thence to the Ingrebourne.[3]

A neolithic site has been excavated west of Launders Lane; Iron Age potsherds have been found near Gerpins Lane, and Romano-British sherds at Rainham Ferry, also near the Aveley border, and at Ayletts a half mile south of Gerpins.[4] In 1937 gravel-digging between Gerpins and the Aveley border revealed a rich Anglo-Saxon burial ground of the 6th and 7th centuries, which also yielded evidence of earlier burials.[5] The recorded population of Rainham was 50 in 1066, and 47 in 1086.[6] Those assessed for the taxes numbered 22 in 1327 and 44 in 1523.[7] There were 44 occupied houses in the parish in 1670.[8] The population, which in 1801 was 444, was 868 in 1851, and 1,725 in 1901. It rose to 3,897 in 1931, and to 7,666 in 1951.[9]

The road pattern of the 16th century apparently reflected the medieval one and was unchanged as late as 1865.[10] Two roads from the east met at the village green and crossed the Ingrebourne before dividing to Dagenham and Hornchurch. The northern (Warwick Lane, Upminister Road) came through Upminister from North Ockendon;[11] the southern (Wennington Road) skirted the marshes from Purfleet. In 1349 it was called South Street.[12] A road from Hornchurch to Aveley formed the parish boundary in the north-east, and at Hacton Corner a road (Berwick Pond Road) left it to run south through Rainham. It divided north of Berwick ponds: the eastern branch met Gerpins Lane from the Aveley Road and continued to Warwick Lane; the western crossed Warwick Lane at White Post Corner and continued as Launders Lane to Wennington.[13] Nearer the village Lambs Lane linked the Upminster and Wennington Roads, and by 1531 Manor Way or Ferry Lane ran south from the village to the Thames shore.[14]

Rainham bridge was first mentioned in 1234.[15] It was a broken plank bridge in 1356 when Thomas de Hoggeshawe undertook to repair it, partly at his own costs and partly with voluntary contributions; the king, who often used the bridge when hunting, granted Hoggeshawe a protection for 2 years for his men, carts, and materials.[16] In 1623, when the bridge was again broken, its repair was said to be the duty of the lords of Berwick and South Hall manors in Rainham.[17] In 1641 it was a stone bridge.[18] Termed the Red bridge in 1774, it was said to be wooden in 1834.[19] Its repair was then shared by the marsh bailiff and the lord of Berwick.[20] It was taken over by Essex county council in 1892 and was rebuilt in 1898.[21]

Launders bridge over the brook in Launders Lane was named in 1423–4.[22] In 1576 it was a cart-bridge for which the lord of Launders was responsible, but in 1630 the lord of South Hall was presented for not repairing it.[23] By 1834 it was a brick bridge reparable by the parish.[24] Southall bridge, over the boundary

[55] Challis and Scamell, *Hist. S. Ockendon Cong. Ch.* 22; *Returns Elem. Educ.*, H.C. 201, pp. 112–3 (1871), lv.

[56] Char. Com. Files; inf. from Mr. D. A. Pope, Church secretary.

[1] O.S. Map 1/25,000, TQ 57, 58. This article was completed in 1976. Preliminary work was done by Miss Anne V. Worsley. Much valuable information was provided by the late Frank Lewis, whose scrapbooks are now in Havering Ref. Libr.

[2] Essex Review Order, 1934.

[3] *Map of Essex* (1777) has apparently mistaken its course: see Bd. Ord. surveyor's drawing, 3″ (1799), photo. in E.R.O. Libr.

[4] Lewis, *Rainham*, 2–4; *Med. Archaeol.* viii. 271; the Romano-British villa at Corbets Tey almost certainly spread into Rainham: see below, p. 143.

[5] Lewis, *Rainham*, 4; *Archaeologia*, xcvi. 159–95.

[6] *V.C.H. Essex*, i. 458, 518, 554, 561.

[7] E 179/107/13 m.8; E 179/108/150.

[8] E.R.O., Q/RTh 5 m.3.

[9] *Census*, 1801–1951.

[10] M.P.F. 119 (E.R.O., T/M 145) of *c.* 1575; *Map of Essex* (1777); O.S. Map 6″, Essex LXXIV, LXXV, LXXXII (surv. 1862–8).

[11] Warwick Lane is perhaps named after Thomas Warwick (fl. 1631): E.R.O., Q/SR 275/28.

[12] E.R.O., D/DL T1/143, 146.

[13] White Post Corner may be identical with Bloundelescrouche (1315: B.L. Cott. MS. Nero E. vi, f. 203) or Blundrells crosse (1499: B.L. Lansd. MS. 200, f. 74v.); for a possible origin of the name Lambs Lane: Lewis, *Rainham*, 73.

[14] E.R.O., D/AER 4/91; *Essex and Thurrock Gaz.* 10 June 1966.

[15] *Cur. Reg. R.* xv, p. 300.

[16] *Cal. Pat.* 1354–8, 479; for the King's prey: ibid. 132.

[17] E.R.O., Q/SR 241/26, 242/43.

[18] Ibid. 314/64; cf. 393/11.

[19] *Hist. Essex by Gent.* iv. 350; E.R.O., D/SR 78A.

[20] E.R.O., D/SR 78A.

[21] E.R.O., D/SH 5; E.R.O., C/MH i, ii, iii.

[22] E.R.O., D/DL M32; cf. B.L., Cott. MS. Claud. E. vi, f. 268v.

[23] E.R.O., Q/SR 58/48, 269/120.

[24] E.R.O., D/SR 78A.

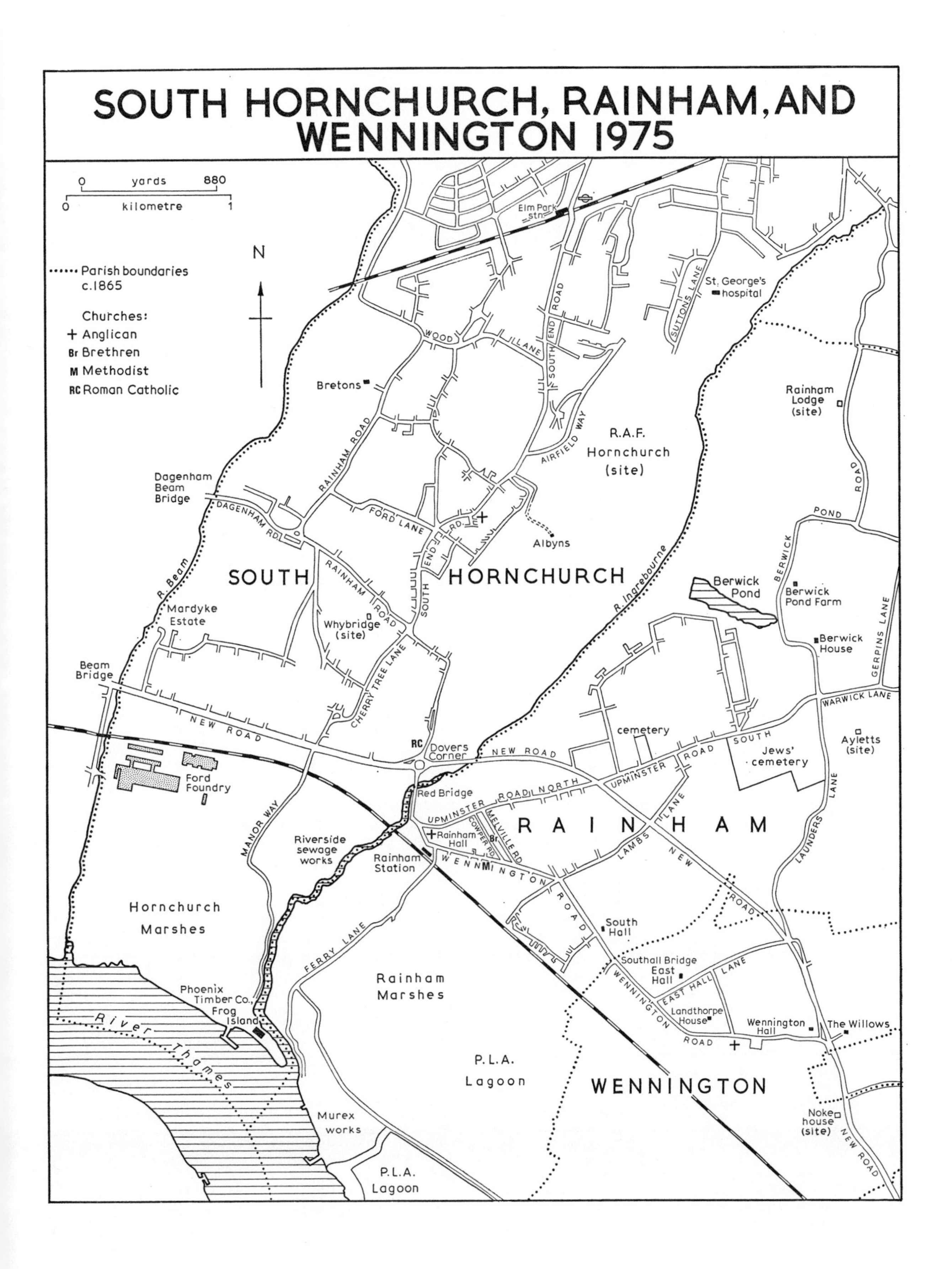
SOUTH HORNCHURCH, RAINHAM, AND WENNINGTON 1975
0 yards 880
0 kilometre 1
N
Parish boundaries c.1865
Churches:
+ Anglican
Br Brethren
M Methodist
RC Roman Catholic
Elm Park stn
St. George's hospital
SUTTONS LANE
SOUTH END ROAD
WOOD LANE
Bretons
Rainham Lodge (site)
RAINHAM ROAD
AIRFIELD WAY
R.A.F. Hornchurch (site)
Dagenham Beam Bridge
DAGENHAM RD
FORD LANE
RD
Albyns
POND ROAD
BERWICK
R. Beam
SOUTH
HORNCHURCH
R. Ingrebourne
Berwick Pond
Berwick Pond Farm
GERPINS LANE
Mardyke Estate
Whybridge (site)
Berwick House
Beam Bridge
CHERRY TREE LANE
WARWICK LANE
NEW ROAD
cemetery
RC
Dovers Corner
SOUTH ROAD
Jews' cemetery
Ayletts (site)
Ford Foundry
UPMINSTER ROAD
UPMINSTER ROAD NORTH
Red Bridge
MANOR WAY
Rainham Hall
COWPER RD
MELVILLE RD
RAINHAM
LAMBS LANE
LAUNDERS LANE
Riverside sewage works
Rainham Station
WENNINGTON ROAD
Hornchurch Marshes
South Hall
FERRY LANE
Southall Bridge
East Hall
EAST HALL LANE
Phoenix Timber Co.
Frog Island
Rainham Marshes
Landthorpe House
Wennington Hall
The Willows
River Thames
P.L.A. Lagoon
WENNINGTON
Noke house (site)
Murex works
P.L.A. Lagoon

stream, was repaired by the lord of South Hall manor until 1908, when the county council agreed to take it over and widen it.[25]

In the Middle Ages settlement appears to have clustered round the church and manor-houses. The church is the only medieval building surviving. Damyns Hall, destroyed by fire in 1965, and Ayletts Farm, demolished in 1968, both had 16th-century elements.[26] South Hall dates from the late 16th and 17th centuries. Berwick House (now Berwick Manor country club) and Berwick Ponds Farm stand on or near sites occupied in the 16th century.[27] The moated Gerpins, west of Gerpins Lane, was probably older than the surviving walls of *c.* 1700.[28] North Lodge, *c.* 1575, was on a site later occupied by Rainham Lodge.[29]

By the 17th century Rainham ferry, across the Thames, and Rainham wharf, were well established, and travellers through the village had the choice of several public houses. Hardly any buildings in the village remain from that period, though Charlotte's Alley, Broadway, survived until 1944, and nos. 2–6, Upminster Road occupy the site of the old Bell tavern, standing in 1702.[30] Opposite the church, in the Broadway, the vicarage is a 17th-century house rebuilt in 1710.

In the early 18th century, as trade increased, the wharf was extended and several new buildings were erected in the village. The most notable was Rainham Hall, Broadway, built by Capt. John Harle (d. 1742), owner of the wharf.[31] The house passed to Capt. Harle's son John (d. 1770), in whose wife's family it remained until *c.* 1887.[32] In 1949 it was transferred to the National Trust.[33] It is a small but sumptuous brick house of 3 storeys on a semi-basement, and has principal fronts of 5 bays. The exterior appears to have been completed by 1729, by which time both plan and elevation were old-fashioned. The interior, which contains many small rooms, is extensively panelled in painted softwoods and has an original staircase with slender twisted balusters. Much of the exterior woodwork was carefully restored *c.* 1920, and an attic floor, with segmental headed dormers, was added in the roof space some years later.[34] The interior was redecorated, partly with marbling and painted enrichments *c.* 1965. South of the Hall there are an early-18th-century coach-house and stables, and a lodge which once served as a counting-house. The small park east of the house has been reduced by recent building but still contains some ornamental stonework.

Nos. 17–21 Broadway, demolished *c.* 1966, were built in the early 18th century; the Phoenix inn was rebuilt in the 1730s and again in 1791; and Redberry House (29, Broadway) is also of the 18th century.[35] Redberry House is associated with a 19th-century wharf and a group of commercial buildings, and has on the ground floor a room probably designed as a counting-house. An oriel window on the first floor overlooks the yard. The house contains fittings and timbers of the later 17th and earlier 18th centuries, and the structure is possibly of the latter date, though its exterior dates from *c.* 1800. An early-19th-century coach-house and stables adjoin the house on the west.

A coach went from Rainham to Whitechapel twice a week in the 1780s and 1820s, and daily by 1838.[36] Another passed through Rainham daily from the 1820s on its way from Tilbury to London.[37] A third ran to Fetter Lane, London, twice a week in 1824 and thrice weekly in 1838.[38] In 1848 and 1850 there was a daily omnibus to London,[39] and from 1824 there are references to waggons and vans going daily to London from Rainham and parishes to the east.[40]

In 1854 the London, Tilbury, and Southend railway was opened as far as Tilbury, with a station at Rainham, linked by ferry to Gravesend (Kent). The line was extended to Southend in 1856.[41] The station was rebuilt after a fire in 1891. In 1961, when the Southend line was electrified, a new station was built nearer the Ferry Lane level crossing.[42] Between the two World Wars buses ran to and from Grays Thurrock.[43]

The Phoenix inn, Broadway, was the post-house in the 1820s and early 1830s, but by 1839 the post office was on a site in Upminster Road South where it remained until 1907.[44] It became a telegraph office in the early 1870s.[45] The National Telephone Company had a call office at the Phoenix inn in 1902; it was later at a draper's but had gone by 1910.[46] The first G.P.O. telephone exchange opened in 1899. In 1928 a new exchange was opened in Wennington Road; it was replaced *c.* 1967 by an automatic exchange at Dovers Corner, South Hornchurch.[47]

Rainham's growth in the later 19th century took place mainly to the east of the Broadway, where Melville and Cowper Roads were laid out *c.* 1880.[48] The houses there were mostly semi-detached or terraced, and in 1908 Rainham was described as an entirely working-class district.[49] At the same period a hamlet grew up at Rainham Ferry, near the Three Crowns public house.[50] In the early 20th century that stretch of the Thames was the resort of day-trippers, but the hamlet declined as the area was industrialized and had disappeared by 1945.[51]

In 1920, when the last of the Crosse estates were

[25] E.R.O., C/MH v. 195, 205, 212.
[26] R.C.H.M. *Essex*, iv. 118; Lewis, *Rainham*, 28; H.R.L., Lewis Scrapbook, iii. 79.
[27] E.R.O., T/M 145.
[28] E.R.O., *Sale Cat.* B 5743.
[29] E.R.O., T/M 145; E.R.O. Library, Rainham folder: *Essex and Thurrock Gaz.* 4 Nov. 1960.
[30] Lewis, *Rainham*, 72; E.R.O., D/DU 650.
[31] See plate on facing page.
[32] *Country Life*, xlvii. 760–8; E.R.O., *Sale Cat.* A361, A615; H.R.L., Lewis Scrapbook, ix. 5; *Essex Countryside*, iv (16), 153; v (17), 15; Lewis, *Rainham*, f. p. 38.
[33] *Essex and Thurrock Gaz.* 30 Apr. 1954.
[34] E.R.O., *Sale Cat.* A615; inf. from Mrs. E. Hussey
[35] Lewis, *Rainham*, 27, 72; E.R.O., D/DB T283.
[36] H.R.L., Lewis Scrapbook, ix. 16; xiii. 6.
[37] *E.R.* xxv. 88; H.R.L., Lewis Scrapbook, xiii. 6; *Pigot's Dir.* (1826); it seems to have been identical with the 'Horndon coach' of *c.* 1840: *Robson's Gazetteer*, 84.
[38] H.R.L., Lewis Scrapbook, ix. 16.
[39] *White's Dir. Essex* (1848); *Kelly's Dir. Essex* (1850).
[40] H.R.L., Lewis Scrapbook, ix. 16; *Robson's Gazetteer* (*c.* 1840), 84; cf. *Kelly's Dir. Essex* (1845).
[41] *Essex and Thurrock Gaz.* 6 Jan. 1956; Lewis, *Rainham*, 67.
[42] Lewis, *Rainham*, 67.
[43] *Kelly's Dir. Essex* (1922–37).
[44] *E.R.* xxv. 88; *Pigot's Dir. Essex* (1832), 704; (1839), 142; E.R.O., D/CT 280; E.R.O., Pictorial Coll.; *Essex and Thurrock Gaz.* 26 Feb. 1965.
[45] *Kelly's Dir. Essex* (1870–4).
[46] Ibid. (1902–10).
[47] Lewis, *Rainham*, 72; H.R.L., Lewis Scrapbook, xii. 36.
[48] E.R.O., D/DB T844.
[49] E.R.O., C/MH v. 211; cf. Lewis, *Rainham*, 69, citing 1896 church restoration fund appeal.
[50] E. A. Bird, *Rainham Village*, 16–17; and *Vanished Hamlet*, 8–12,
[51] Lewis, *Rainham*, 39.

ROMFORD: HARE HALL IN *c.* 1890, NOW ROYAL LIBERTY SCHOOL

RAINHAM: RAINHAM HALL

UPMINSTER: Upminster Court, built 1906

RAINHAM: Houses in Upminster Road, built *c.* 1935

HORNCHURCH: Houses in Avenue Road, Harold Wood, late 19th century

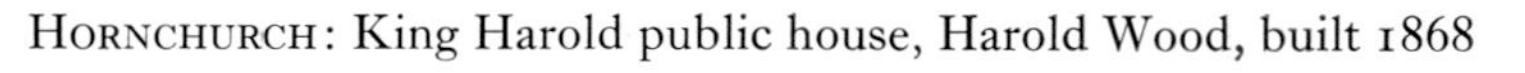

HORNCHURCH: King Harold public house, Harold Wood, built 1868

sold, Brights (262 a.) and Parsonage (102 a.) Farms were bought by Allen Ansell, a developer.[52] New Road, completed by 1926 to by-pass Rainham, ran through Ansell's holding, but he laid out roads on both sides of it, and sold plots which were said to be cheaper per square yard than linoleum.[53] Many of the purchasers were east Londoners who had previously cultivated smallholdings in the eastern fringes of West Ham.[54] Building after 1918 had deprived them of their earlier plots, and the issue at week-ends of cheap day tickets from Plaistow and Bromley-by-Bow brought hundreds to Rainham. In 1921 the South West Ham and Rainham Smallholders association was formed.[55] At first all meetings were held in West Ham, but by 1939 it was a purely Rainham society; in 1936 it became the Rainham Smallholders and Horticultural society, and in 1938 the Rainham Horticultural society. Building on the Brights and Parsonage estate was carried out by individual owners at random; there was no sewer and none of the roads was made up.[56] In 1944 the Greater London Plan recommended that the land should soon be returned to market-gardening, for which it was particularly suited.[57] The Brights and Parsonage estate association, formed to fight this proposal, was successful, and the estate was removed from the proposed Green belt.[58]

In 1958 the association, expanded as the Rainham Residents association, campaigned for the tidying-up of the parish: 21 roads were still unmade in 1961, the Brights and Parsonage Estate was still without a sewer and Rainham was being used as a dump for silt and refuse.[59] Again the association was successful: a sewer system was begun *c.* 1960, and the roads were at last paved by 1972.[60] Between 1961 and 1968 the Port of London Authority filled 200 a. marsh in Rainham and Wennington with 9 million tons of dredged spoil, raising the level of the land by 15 ft. It then leased from the Ministry of Defence 250 a. marsh in the two parishes, lying immediately north, and began to fill this also.[61]

In 1902 a cemetery (2 a.) was consecrated on Upminister Road North, east of the later Allen Road.[62] The Jewish Federation cemetery, dedicated in 1938, contains some 48 a. within its wall and more land outside.[63] By 1891 the South Essex Waterworks Co. had a main pipe in the village.[64] Street lamps lit by oil were replaced by 3 gas lamps in 1914.[65] A volunteer fire brigade of 12 men was formed in 1904; a fire station was built at the corner of Parkway and Upminster Road South in 1914; and in 1933 the brigade replaced its hand-cart with a motor-driven fire-engine. In 1936 Hornchurch brigade took over from the Rainham brigade.[66]

The Rainham Literary society was founded in 1879.[67] It established in 1883 a Workmen's institute and reading room, which continued until 1933, when it was absorbed by Essex county libraries. In 1967 the county library moved from Upminster Road South to its present site in Broadway.[68]

Rainham Working Men's club was founded in 1921, and Rainham Social club and institute in 1928.[69] In 1962 a social centre, later enlarged, was built at Chandler's Corner by Hornchurch U.D.C. to replace a hut built by the Horticultural society in 1950.[70] Rainham Civic society was formed in 1970.[71]

Rainham was the first known centre of coursing in Essex. The first recorded meeting was held there in 1845, and coursing continued intermittently until the marshes were sold in 1906 to the War Office.[72] The Essex Union hunt still met at Rainham in the 1950s.[73] Berwick pond provides good coarse fishing from the Abbey Wood park (9 a.) to its south.[74] Chafford school, Lambs Lane, provides a dual use sports complex, completed in 1975, with a swimming pool and sports hall.[75] Rainham had an association football team in the 19th century; Rainham Town football club was formed in 1945 and in 1948 the club's new ground at Deri Park was opened.[76] Cricket used to be played in a field north of Upminster Road South until the construction of New Road in the 1920s; the Rainham team now plays in Spring Farm recreation ground, Lambs Lane.[77]

MANORS AND OTHER ESTATES. There were four manors in Rainham in 1086.[78] Haghebern held ½ hide which may have become the later manor of Launders. Hugh (de Montfort) held of Bishop Odo 4 hides, later South Hall. Robert, probably Robert Vaizey, held of Robert Gernon 4½ hides, later Berwick. Walter of Douai held in demesne 8½ hides, which became the manor of Rainham.

The manor of *RAINHAM* apparently lay in the west of the parish. Most of Walter's manor had been held in 1066 by Lefstan the reeve, who had 8 hides; 3 free men held the rest.[79] The manor, which formed part of the honor of Bampton, descended from Walter of Douai (d. *c.* 1107) to his son Robert of Bampton (fl. 1136) and to Robert's daughter Gillian.

[52] E.R.O., D/DLc T46.

[53] *Challenge* (Rainham Res. assoc.), Aug. 1959, in H.R.L., Lewis Scrapbook, ix. 20; cf. *Rainham Hortic. Soc. Bull.*, June 1958, and F. Lewis, *Rainham Hortic. Soc. 1920–1970*, 3; *Kelly's Dir. Essex* (1926), map.

[54] Lewis, *Rainham Hortic. Soc. 1920–1970* on which this paragraph is based.

[55] *Rainham Hortic. Soc. Bull.* June 1958.

[56] *Challenge*, Aug. 1959; cf. *Essex and Thurrock Gaz.* 31 July 1959.

[57] P. Abercrombie, *Greater Lond. Plan 1944*, 135.

[58] *Challenge*, Aug. 1959.

[59] *Essex and Thurrock Gaz.* 17 Oct. 1958, 6 Feb. 1959; *Hornch. Recorder*, 12 June 1959; *Hornch. and Upm. News*, 26 Jan. 1961; cf. J. Cantwell, 'Hornchurch, a political survey, 1926–64'. [TS. in H.R.L.], 46–8, 131A–133, for the campaign's effect on local politics.

[60] *Havering Recorder*, 11 Feb. 1972; inf. from L.B. Havering.

[61] *P.L.A. Monthly* (1957), 14, 225; (1958), 271; (1960), 285–8; (1963), 75, 104–5; letter from P.L.A. to F. Lewis, 7 Mar. 1972; cf. *Water City on Rainham marshes* (copy in E.R.O. Libr.).

[62] E.R.O., D/CC 53/11; cf. *Kelly's Dir. Essex* (1914).

[63] Lewis, *Rainham*, 71; local inf.

[64] *Essex and Thurrock Gaz.* 3 Nov. 1961.

[65] Ibid., 10 Apr. 1959; *Challenger*, Feb./Mar. 1963.

[66] *Essex and Thurrock Gaz.* 3 Nov. 1961, 26 Nov. 1964.

[67] H.R.L., Local Coll. LF 77/2; *Strat. Expr.* 27 June 1883; Lewis, *Rainham*, 83.

[68] Lewis, *Rainham*, 83; Bird, *Rainham Village*, 14.

[69] H.R.L., Lewis Scrapbook, xii. 30; Lewis, *Rainham*, 70.

[70] *Essex and Thurrock Gaz.* 5 Jan. 1962.

[71] H.R.L., Lewis Scrapbook, xiv. 16.

[72] *V.C.H. Essex*, ii. 595–8; see below, p. 134.

[73] *Essex and Thurrock Gaz.* 27 Dec. 1957.

[74] Ibid. 3 Jan. 1958.

[75] Inf. from L.B. Havering.

[76] H.R.L., Lewis Scrapbook, xii 4; *Essex and Thurrock Gaz.* 6 Nov. 1948; Lewis, *Rainham*, 72.

[77] Lewis, *Rainham*, 80.

[78] *V.C.H. Essex*, i. 458, 518, 554, 561. The 'Ricingahaam' given to Barking abbey *c.* 687 has not been certainly identified with Rainham: Hart, *Early Chart, Essex*, 9.

[79] *V.C.H. Essex*, i. 554; for Lefstan: C. J. R. Hart, *Early Chart. E. England*, 248–9.

She married William Paynel (d. *c.* 1165) and later Warin de la Haule (d. *c.* 1176).[80] In 1176 Rainham belonged to Gillian's son, Fulk Paynel.[81] He was apparently in financial difficulties from the first. In 1185 he fled the country, and his lands, including Rainham, passed into the King's hand.[82] When they were restored in 1199, Rainham and its advowson were no longer among them. They had been taken into the king's hand late in 1176,[83] and the manor, but not the advowson, had passed, apparently in 1179–80, to Gilbert de Vere; Gilbert gave most of it to the Knights Hospitallers when he entered the order.[84] About 1190 he gave the last virgate, in the tenure of Robert at Elms, to St. Bartholomew's hospital (Lond.); that tenement, the exact location of which is not known, was later called Elmhouse.[85] Gilbert also gave to Buckland priory (Som.) £5 a year from the manor, which was still being paid in 1535.[86]

Rainham manor was valued in 1274 at 10 marks.[87] In 1299 the Hospitallers leased it for life, at a nominal rent, to Joan (d. *c.* 1312) widow of Robert de Grey,[88] and between 1335 and 1341 were selling annuities secured in part by its revenues.[89] The manor remained with the Hospitallers until the Dissolution, being joined to Berwick, with which it subsequently descended.[90]

The site of the manor-house is not known; it was probably near the church. Gilbert de Vere (d. *ante* 1203) built a chapel in his courtyard, and was authorized by the abbot of Lesnes (Kent) to hold services in it.[91]

Elmhouse comprised 50 a. in 1295.[92] It remained in the possession of St. Bartholomew's hospital until the Dissolution.[93] It apparently passed with Rainham and other manors to Sir Robert Southwell, who in 1559 devised it to his servant, Henry Nevill, for life and then to his son Henry Southwell.[94] When Ralph Stint died *c.* 1638 his lands included Elmhouse, also known by then as Ilfords or Normans.[95] In 1676 it was last recorded in the possession of Thomas Hoare of Great Ilford.[96]

Elmhouse was described *c.* 1200 as a house with 2 bedrooms and horse-stalls. Other buildings were a barn, ox-stalls, a brewhouse with oven, and a fowl-house.[97] Nothing more is known of the farm-house or buildings.

The manor of *BERWICK* lay in the NW. of the parish. Before the Conquest it consisted of 3½ hides held by Aluard; in 1086 it was held in chief as 4½ hides by Robert Gernon.[98] The tenancy-in-chief subsequently descended like that of Battles Hall in Stapleford Abbots, and was last noticed in the mid 16th century.[99]

Robert Gernon's tenant in 1086 was Robert, probably Robert Vaizey who deprived Westminster Abbey of an estate at Wennington.[1] The Knights Templars held the manor in the 13th century and perhaps earlier.[2] The order was suppressed in 1308 and the manor taken into the king's hand. Between 1312 and 1314 Berwick was transferred to the Hospitallers.[3]

In the 14th century the manor was leased out, but in the 15th century it was retained for the prior's use, and by 1480 it had been imparked.[4] It remained with the Hospitallers until their dissolution in 1540. In 1545 Berwick was sold with Rainham and Moorhall manors to Sir Robert Southwell, Master of the Rolls (d. 1559), and his wife Margaret (d. 1575), who married secondly William Plumb.[5]

In 1575 Berwick and the other Rainham properties descended to Sir Robert and Lady Southwell's grandson, another Sir Robert Southwell (d. 1598), and then to his son Sir Thomas Southwell.[6] Sir Thomas conveyed it in 1618, with his other Rainham properties, to five prominent Londoners including William Freeman and Humphrey Slaney.[7] Humphrey's son, John Slaney, inherited Damyns farm in the NE. of the parish from his uncle John Slaney in 1632, and from that time Damyns descended separately.[8] The other Rainham lands went to William Freeman (d. 1623), from whom they descended in the direct line to his son, grandson, and great-grandson, all named Ralph Freeman.[9]

The last Ralph Freeman sold his Rainham estates *c.* 1709 to the Hon. George Finch (d. 1710 or 1711).[10] In 1710 they contained 1,546 a.[11] George Finch's son and heir William sold his Rainham estates to the Westminster brewer, Sir Thomas Crosse, Bt. (d. 1738).[12] Sir Thomas's son, Sir John Crosse, Bt., died without issue in 1762. He devised his estates to his widow Mary (d. 1770) for life; next, in tail male to his kinsman Peter Day (Crosse), who died without issue in 1779; and then, ignoring Peter Day Crosse's brother, to his wife's nephew, John Godsalve (Crosse) (d. 1793).[13]

80 *V.C.H. Essex*, i. 554; Sanders, *Eng. Baronies*, 5; *Pipe R.* 1176 (P.R.S. xxv), 142.
81 Sanders, *Eng. Baronies*, 5; *Pipe R.* 1176 (P.R.S. xxv), 8.
82 *Pipe R.* 1185 (P.R.S. xxxiv), 164; Sanders, *Eng. Baronies*, 5.
83 *Pipe R.* 1177 (P.R.S. xxvi), 154.
84 *Pipe R.* 1180 (P.R.S. xxix), 2; 1199 (P.R.S., N.S. x), 191; 1200 (P.R.S., N.S. xii), 227; *Cur. Reg. R.* v. 145.
85 *Cart. St. Bart.'s Hosp.* ed. N. J. M. Kerling, p. 120.
86 B.L. Cott. MS. Nero E. vi, f. 467 v.; *Valor Eccl.* (Rec. Com.), i. 211.
87 *Rot. Hund.* (Rec. Com.), i. 148.
88 *Feet of F. Essex*, ii. 89–90; Morant, *Essex*, i. 88 n.; *Complete Peerage*, vi. 144; *Cal. Fine R.* ii. 147.
89 *Cal. Close*, 1333–7, 363; 1339–41, 649; 1341–3, 110; *Cal. Pat.* 1340–3, 171.
90 See below.
91 *Cur. Reg. R.* v. 145; *Early Chart. St. Paul's* (Camd. Soc. 3rd ser. lviii), pp. 224–5; *Cur. Reg. R.* ii. 175.
92 *Cart. St. Bart.'s Hosp.* ed. Kerling, p. 120.
93 N. Moore, *Hist. St. Bart.'s Hosp.* ii. 106, 125, 150, 154, 159.
94 Prob. 11/43 (P.C.C. 53 Mellershe).
95 C 142/487/156.
96 *Cal. Treas. Bks.* v (1), 340.
97 Moore, *Hist. St. Bart.'s Hosp.* i. 243.
98 *V.C.H. Essex*, i. 518.
99 *V.C.H. Essex*, iv. 227; Sanders, *Eng. Baronies*, 83; C 1/1267/40; E.R.O., D/SH 7, f. 107.
1 *V.C.H. Essex*, i. 445, 518, 520 n.
2 B.L. Cott. MS. Nero E. vi, ff. 199v., 200.
3 Ibid. f. 202v.
4 *Cal. Wills Husting*, ii, p. 39; *Cely Papers* (Camd. Soc. 3rd ser. i), 34, 82, 105.
5 *L. & P. Hen. VIII*, xx (1), p. 124; xxi (1), p. 769; Prob. 11/43 (P.C.C. 53 Mellershe); Newcourt, *Repertorium*, ii. 481.
6 Prob. 11/50 (P.C.C. 13 Babington); Prob. 11/92 (P.C.C. 78 Lewyn); C 142/256/23.
7 C.P. 25(2) /295/16 Jas. I Mich.
8 C 142/465/77; Prob. 11/161 (P.C.C. 42 Audley); E.R.O., D/DL E1, 10 and T1/837; E.R.O., Q/RPl 106–57; *Sale Cat.* B5743.
9 *V.C.H. Herts.* iv. 19; E 331/London 13 (7 Feb. 1627); E.R.O., Q/SR 242/43.
10 E.R.O., D/P 202/9/1; E.R.O., D/DB E14; E.R.O., Sage Coll., no. 280.
11 E.R.O., D/DB E14.
12 E.R.O., D/DB T277; *Hist. Parl., Commons, 1715–54*, i. 596; G.E.C. *Baronetage*, v. 16.
13 *Hist. Parl., Commons, 1715–54*, i. 596; G.E.C. *Baronetage*, v. 16; Prob. 11/874 f. 144; Prob. 11/1066 f. 305; E.R.O., T/B 27/1/29; cf. E.R.O., D/DNe T38/10. 17,

Major John C. G. Crosse succeeded his father in 1793 and died in 1854.[14] In 1838 his Rainham estates had 1,541 a.[15] His son and heir, Henry G. G. Crosse (d. 1865), was followed by John T. G. Crosse (d. 1870), who was probably Henry's son.[16] The family estates were sold piecemeal at that period, and the family's landed connexion with Rainham ended in 1920 when Hector G. G. Crosse, John's son, sold the last 509 a. of the estate in 6 lots.[17]

The earliest manor-house may have stood north of the present Berwick House, but in the 15th and 16th centuries the Hospitallers' mansion was probably situated south of the present Berwick pond.[18] In 1536 the prior of the Hospital was at Berwick when he was summoned to aid in the suppression of the Pilgrimage of Grace.[19] The house was apparently demolished soon after the Dissolution, and *c.* 1575 only an avenue of trees leading north from the Upminster road remained.[20] Within the park there were then two lodges: North Lodge, later known as Rainham Lodge, and South Lodge or Berwick House. Another house stood on the site of Berwick Pond farm-house. Rainham Lodge was built in the 18th century as a three-storeyed, stuccoed building of 5 bays, given a slate roof in the 19th century. It was demolished in 1960.[21] Berwick House dates from the 17th century. It is a substantial timber-framed house with three-roomed plan. It was rendered and given new windows in the early 19th century, perhaps at the same time as a small symmetrically fronted stable-block was built to the SE. There are large modern additions on the north and east.[22] In 1960 the house became an old people's home; since 1970 it has been Berwick Manor country club.[23] Berwick Pond farm-house is a tall narrow-fronted house of the early 19th century with additions of *c.* 1900.[24]

In 1315 there was a chapel on Berwick manor.[25] It was still in use in 1535, when it was called 'the chapel of Our Lady of Berwick'.[26] It probably lay in the field north of Berwick House, where moulded masonry and medieval tiles have been found.[27]

The manor of *GERPINS* (or *GERBEVILES*), in the NE. of the parish, originated in free tenements held of the manors of North Ockendon, Rainham, and Southall. The manor took its name from the family of Jarpeville which was connected with Rainham from the end of the 12th century. When Laurence de Jarpeville died in 1297, he held an estate of some 185 a. in Rainham.[28] He was succeeded by his son William, whose son, another William (d. 1330), left Gerpins to his infant daughter, Joan de Jarpeville.[29] Joan possibly became the wife of Thomas de Bolyngton, and mother of Robert Bolyngton, who with his wife Isabel had a life-tenancy of Gerpins in the early 15th century.[30] Robert and Isabel Bolyngton were still alive in 1416, when Agnes, widow of Clement Symond, had the reversion to the estate.[31] She died *c.* 1433.[32] Katherine Byrt, who died in 1445 holding the manor, was probably her daughter and previously the wife of Richard Merston.[33] In 1462 a granddaughter of Agnes Symond had an interest in the manor.[34]

By 1472 Gerpins had apparently passed to Richard Pasmar (d. 1500) steward and surveyor of all the Hospitallers' lands in England.[35] It was styled a manor in 1507 when Pasmar's son and heir, Thomas, settled it on George Sutton and his wife Joan.[36] In 1510 they conveyed the manor with 160 a. to William Blount, Lord Mountjoy.[37] In 1514 Edward Jordan, a London goldsmith, devised Gerpins to his widow Alice for life and then to his daughters Elizabeth and Katherine; if neither had issue, the manor was to be sold.[38]

In 1551 Sir Thomas and Lady (Katherine) Moyle conveyed the remainder of Gerpins to William Austen and his wife Gillian, who were already holding the manor.[39] Austen died in 1558 or 1559, and in 1559 his widow conveyed Gerpins to John Lowen, a London draper, and his wife Joan.[40] Lowen died the same year, his widow in 1570 or 1571.[41] From them the manor descended to their son John (d. 1588 or 1589), and from him to his son Daniel (d. 1631).[42] When Daniel's son, John Lowen, D.C.L., made his will in 1672, he referred to his manor of Gerpins.[43] In 1685 its owner was his nephew, Daniel Gregory, a London printer.[44]

The ownership of Gerpins for most of the 18th century is unknown. Richard Gregory (d. 1729) and John Gregory (d. 1781) may have been owners.[45] From 1745 or earlier it was farmed by members of the Marden family, and in 1800 William Marden bought the manor from Mr. Baron who had been its owner from 1786.[46]

In 1807 Marden added to the estate Smoke Hall farm, NE. of Gerpins.[47] William Marden owned the estate, containing 211 a., in 1838.[48] He died in 1856,[49] and by 1858 the farm was rented to William Mitchell, a member of whose family was still at Gerpins in 1937.[50] By order of mortgagees, the Marden family

[14] Prob. 11/1232, f. 246; Foster, *Alumni Oxon., 1715–1886*, ii. 533; Lewis, *Rainham*, 13; E.R.O., Q/RPc 276.
[15] E.R.O., D/CT 280.
[16] E.R.O., D/DLc T46; E.R.O., Q/RPc 276; Q/RPr 2/4, 2/7; *Kelly's Dir. Essex* (1870); Lewis, *Rainham*, 13.
[17] E.R.O., *Sale Cat.* A73; Lewis, *Rainham*, 13.
[18] E.R.O., T/M 145.
[19] *L. & P. Hen. VIII*, xi, p. 338.
[20] E.R.O., T/M 145.
[21] *Essex and Thurrock Gaz.* 4 Nov. 1960.
[22] Lewis, *Rainham*, 14.
[23] Ibid.
[24] Ibid. 15.
[25] B.L. Cott. MS. Nero E. vi, f. 203v.
[26] E.R.O., D/AER 4/200 (will of Agnes Smyth).
[27] Lewis, *Rainham*, 15.
[28] *Cart. St. Bart.'s Hosp.* ed. Kerling, p. 120; E.R.O., D/DL T1/25, 38; *Cal. Inq. p.m.* iii. p. 259.
[29] *Cal. Inq. p.m.* iii. p. 259; vii, p. 201; viii, p. 63; *Cal. Close*, 1337–9, 298.
[30] *Feet of F. Essex*, iii. 95, 237, 264; *Cal. Close*, 1399–1402, 400.
[31] *Feet of F. Essex*, iii. 264.
[32] Guildhall Lib., 9171/3 f.373.
[33] Ibid. 9171/4 f.156v.
[34] E.R.O., D/DL T1/446.
[35] *Cal. Pat.* 1467–77, 168, 231, 306; J. Weever, *Ancient Funerall Monuments*, 599.
[36] *Cal. Close*, 1500–9, pp. 309–10.
[37] *Feet of F. Essex*, iv. 122.
[38] *E.A.T.* N.S. xxi. 337–9.
[39] C.P. 25(2)/422/5 Ed. VI Mich.
[40] Prob. 11/42B (P.C.C. 37 Chaynay); C.P. 43/868/40 Geo. III East.
[41] Prob. 11/42B (P.C.C. 45 Chaynay); *E.A.T.* N.S. xxi. 337–9.
[42] Prob. 11/73 (P.C.C. 19 Leicester); C/142/464/66; cf. E.R.O., D/AER 11A/43v (will of Humphrey James).
[43] Prob. 11/356 (P.C.C. 1678 f. 25).
[44] Ibid.; E.R.O., Q/SR 449/1, 22.
[45] Par. regs. in church.
[46] E.R.O., D/P 202/12/2–3; E.R.O., Q/RPl 111–25; cf. C.P. 25(2)/1311/40 Geo. III Eas.
[47] E.R.O., T/P 67/5, p. 120; E.R.O., Q/RPl 131/2.
[48] E.R.O., D/CT 280.
[49] *Gent. Mag.* 1856(1), 323; *Chelmsford Chron.* 1 Feb. 1856.
[50] E.R.O., Q/RPc 276; *Kelly's Dir. Essex* (1937).

in 1891 sold 120 a. of the estate, but not the house.[51] Estate and house were, however, offered together by James S. Vellacott in 1929.[52]

The ancient manor-house of Gerpins was moated and lay west of Gerpins Lane in an angle of the road.[53] It was surrounded by a brick wall of *c.* 1700, part of which survives. The house was probably demolished in the early 19th century when a new one was built on the opposite side of the road.[54] The later Gerpins House was demolished in the 1950s.[55]

The manor of *LAUNDERS* lay in the east of the parish. It may have been the 11th-century estate of ½ hide, held by a priest in 1066, and by Haghebern in 1086.[56] It was named from Richard de Landa, who in 1205 acquired a carucate of land in Rainham on marriage with Maud, daughter of Ralph de Arches (d. *c.* 1206).[57] Richard de Landa apparently died *c.* 1235, but in 1230 he had passed most, if not all, of his estates to Robert de Aundely, king's serjeant, on Aundely's marriage with Richard's daughter Joan.[58] Aundely died in 1247 or 1248; in the latter year Joan de Aundely bought her freedom to marry as she would.[59]

In 1292 Nicholas Malemayns died holding five estates, including Launders, of which four had earlier been held by Richard de Landa and Robert de Aundely.[60] Malemayns' heir was his son (Sir) Nicholas Malemayns (d. 1349).[61] He was apparently holding Launders in 1346, but later that year it was held by Sir John de Staunton (d. *c.* 1355) as ¼ knight's fee.[62]

Thomas Young, who died between 1377 and 1385, held Launders along with Leventhorpes in Wennington.[63] Launders descended with Leventhorpes until 1566, when Richard Heard conveyed Leventhorpes to William Heard, while retaining Launders.[64] At his death in 1578 Richard Heard also owned Ayletts, a free tenement, held of South Hall manor, and lying north of Launders. He was succeeded by his infant grandson Richard Heard.[65] Richard still held Launders in 1598, but by 1621 it had passed to John Heard, probably his brother, who already held Leventhorpes.[66] The two manors again descended together at least until 1672.[67] They were probably separated soon after, in the partition of the Solme family's estates. By 1789 Launders had become part of the Berwick estate, in which it subsequently descended.[68] Nothing is known of the manor-house; it was probably near Launders Barn, which fell down in the 1950s.[69]

By 1790 Ayletts had been detached from Launders and was held by Sir James Esdaile of Upminster.[70] In 1819 it was bought, as a reputed manor with 157 a., by Sir Thomas Barrett-Lennard.[71] In the Second World War the farm was the site of a heavy anti-aircraft battery and after the war it was occupied by gipsies. It was put up for sale, with 50 a., in 1965. Ayletts farm-house, which had been divided, dated from *c.* 1600, with additions in the 18th and 19th centuries. It was demolished in 1968.[72]

The manor of *MOORHALL* or *LA MORE*, which lay in the SE. of the parish, belonged in 1314 to the Knights Hospitallers.[73] Part of it, as Morland, may have been the subject of a dower dispute in 1198.[74] In 1333 the manor was leased to Thomas Kempe of Wennington for 5 years at £5 a year.[75] It subsequently descended with Berwick manor until 1860, when it was sold with 517 a., to Sir Thomas Barrett-Lennard, Bt.[76] Mr. W. Walter Vellacott became the tenant of the Barrett-Lennards in 1933, when the farm had 434 a. In the course of gravel-digging there have been changes in the boundaries and area of the farm, which now comprises *c.* 500 a. and is owned by Mr. Vellacott and his son John.[77] Moor Hall farm-house is an early-19th-century building which was heightened and extended to the rear later in the century. There are some older garden walls and farm buildings to the north, and beyond them are indications of a former moated site.

The *RECTORY* manor or *PARSONAGE FARM* lay in the SW. of the parish between the Upminster road and the river Ingrebourne. In the 12th century it formed part of Rainham manor, but in *c.* 1178 the rectory was granted by Henry II to Lesnes abbey (Kent).[78] The rectory, which was valued at 25 marks in 1254 and £16 in 1291, remained in the possession of the abbey until its dissolution in 1525.[79] In 1526 Cardinal Wolsey received a grant of the rectory, leased it to George Ardyson for 30 years, and transferred the freehold to Cardinal College, Oxford.[80]

On Wolsey's fall the rectory was forfeit to the Crown. It was valued in 1535 at £6, and in 1545 was sold to Sir Robert and Lady Southwell.[81] It was part of their Rainham estate until 1618 when it was conveyed to five Londoners, including Humphrey Slaney.[82] Humphrey apparently was acting for his

[51] E.R.O., Sage Coll., *Sale Cats.* 8/7.
[52] E.R.O., *Sale Cat.* B5743; *Essex Weekly News*, 1 Nov. 1929.
[53] E.R.O., *Sale Cat.* B5743; *Map of Essex* (1777).
[54] Cf. O.S. draft map 3″ (1799) and E.R.O., D/CT 280 (1839).
[55] E.R.O., C/W 1/2/59 (15 Aug. 1944); O.S. Map 1/25,000, TQ 58 (1948 edn.); O.S. Map 1″, sheet 161 (1960 edn.).
[56] *V.C.H. Essex*, i. 561.
[57] *Cur. Reg. R.* iv. 50; v. 37–8, 129–30, 165, 174, 232; *Feet of F. Essex*, i. 34, 36.
[58] *Close R.* 1231–4, 115; *Cart. St. Bart.'s Hosp.* ed. N. J. M. Kerling, p. 120; *Cal. Chart.* i. 119, 138; *Cal. Pat.* 1216–25, 387–8, 417, 446; 1225–32, 411; *Cal. Lib.* i. 39, 90, 137, 140.
[59] *Close R.* 1242–7, 500; *Cal. Inq. p.m.* i, p. 302; *Cal. Pat.* 1247–58, 22.
[60] *Cal. Inq. p.m.* iii, pp. 8–9; cf. *Feet of F. Essex*, i. 36 (Rainham); *Cal. Chart.* i. 119 (Sheppey (Kent) and Stamshaw or Kingston, near Portsmouth (Hants), and 138 (S. Warnborough, Hants)).
[61] *Cal. Inq. p.m.* ix, pp. 319–20.
[62] *Cal. Fine R.* v. 517; *Feud. Aids*, ii. 169; for Staunton's death: *Pub. Wks. in Med. Law* (Selden Soc. xxxii), 77–82 and *Cal. Fine R.* vii. 25.
[63] See p. 184.
[64] E.R.O., D/DU 98/3.
[65] C 142/184/36.
[66] E.R.O., D/DVs 2; C1/382/20; see p. 184.
[67] E.R.O., D/DC 41/449.
[68] E.R.O., Q/RSg 4, f. 74.
[69] O.S. Map 2½″, TQ 58 (1948 edn.); O.S. Map 6″, 58SW (1964 edn.).
[70] E.R.O., D/DHf E183; Ayletts is 'Elliotts' on *Map of* Essex (1777).
[71] E.R.O., D/DU 651/152; D/DL E10.
[72] H.R.L., Lewis Scrapbook, iii. 79; x. 22.
[73] B.L. Cott. MS. Nero E. vi, m. 203v.
[74] *Cur. Reg. R.* i. 244; cf. ibid. 344; vii. 339; *Feet of F. Essex*, i. 16.
[75] B.L. Cott. MS. Nero E. vi, m. 200v.
[76] E.R.O., D/DLc T46.
[77] Inf. from Mr. W. W. Vellacott.
[78] *Cur. Reg. R.* iii. 94.
[79] *Cur. Reg. R.* v. 145; *V.C.H. Kent*, ii. 166; *E.A.T.* N.S. xviii. 17; *Tax. Eccl.* (Rec. Com.), 22.
[80] *L. & P. Hen. VIII*, iv, pp. 849, 888, 971.
[81] Ibid. xx(1), p. 124; *Valor Eccl.* (Rec. Com.), 403.
[82] C.P. 25(2)/295/16 Jas. I Mich.

brother, John Slaney (d. 1632), at whose death various kinsmen received bequests from the Rainham properties: Moses Slaney got Jordans farm and Humphrey himself received Parsonage farm, the former rectory manor.[83] The rectory was valued at £45 in 1650,[84] and was separated from Jordans until 1714 when they were re-united, apparently in the hands of William Blackborne of Hornchurch.[85] Parsonage farm contained about 100 a. when it was leased by him in 1737.[86] He died *c.* 1760, and the farm passed to Levett Blackborne (d. 1781).[87] At Levett's death it was sold to the Crosse family of Berwick manor, who retained it until 1920.[88] It was then bought for development by Allen Ansell.[89] The rectorial tithes were commuted in 1838 for £230.[90]

The manor of *SOUTH HALL*, which lay in the SE. of the parish, contained 4 hides in the 11th century. It was held in 1066 by Alsi, a free man. In 1086 it was held in chief by Odo, bishop of Bayeux.[91] His tenant was Hugh, probably Hugh de Montfort, who was associated with Odo at Dover.[92] After Odo's disgrace some of his manors, including South Hall, were granted to William Peverel (d. *c.* 1132), and became the honor of Peverel of Dover, or Wrinstead, which again escheated to the Crown in 1147 or 1148.[93] The honor was in effect revived in 1336 when (Sir) John de Pulteney (d. 1349) was granted the reversion to the manor of Ospringe (Kent).[94] In 1345 Ospringe was recognized as the *caput* of the barony, and Pulteney's heirs succeeded to it in 1361 on the death of Humphrey de Bohun, earl of Hereford and Essex.[95] The barony appears to have remained with the Pulteneys for a century, but by 1473 it had been taken into the king's hands.[96] From that time its dependant manors were once more held in chief.[97]

For much of the 13th century South Hall was held in demesne by the Cramavill family, which was apparently ruined by a sequence of minorities. Roger de Cramavill, who seems to have been holding the manor in 1204, was last mentioned in 1214.[98] His heir was Henry de Cramavill (I) a minor, who was, however, married and of age in 1219.[99] Henry (I) died, in debt to the Jews, before 1233 when the custody of his heir, Henry de Cramavill (II), was granted to Robert Passelewe, deputy-treasurer of England.[1] In 1267 Robert Waleraund, a royal justice, took over from the Jews rents from South Hall assigned by Henry de Cramavill (II).[2] Waleraund immediately treated the manor as his own, securing a grant of free warren in 1268.[3] Henry de Cramavill (II) died in 1269 or 1270, and in 1272 his son, Henry de Cramavill (III) formally granted the manor to Waleraund.[4]

Waleraund died in 1273, and his widow Maud held the manor until her death, which occurred before 1291.[5] In that year the custody of South Hall was granted to Guy Ferre because Waleraund's nephew and heir, another Robert Waleraund, was an idiot.[6] Robert and his younger brother John Waleraund, another idiot, had both died by 1308.[7] After a dispute Sir Alan de Plugenet, later Lord Plugenet, in 1309 persuaded the courts to accept, incorrectly, his right to the Waleraund inheritance, including South Hall. In 1322 he sub-infeudated the manor to Oliver de Plugenet.[8] Lord Plugenet died in 1325 and his sister and heir Joan Plugenet in 1327.[9] Oliver de Plugenet was also dead by 1329 when the king granted South Hall to his yeoman William Melchet, with reversion to Thomas de Weston, servant to Queen Isabel.[10] Weston soon bought Melchet out, and in 1333 defended his title to the manor against Richard de la Bere.[11] The outcome of that action is not known, but in 1335 (Sir) Walter of Cheshunt, another servant of Queen Isabel, was enfeoffed of the manor, and in 1337 Richard de la Bere released to Cheshunt all his claim to it.[12]

In 1343 the manor was settled jointly on Walter of Cheshunt and his wife Alice.[13] He died in 1344, and by 1346 she had married Sir John de Staunton, Queen Isabel's steward.[14] In 1347 Menaud of Cheshunt, son of Walter, surrendered all claim to the manor and it was settled jointly on Sir John de Staunton (d. *c.* 1355) and his wife Alice (d. 1364), with remainder to Sir John's heirs.[15]

Sir John's son and heir, Ralph de Staunton, did not hold South Hall long, for in 1375 it belonged to John Payn of London, armourer. In that year, just before his death, Payn settled the manor, together with Warley Franks in Great Warley, and the Bridge House lands in Upminster, on his wife Joan.[16] South Hall descended with Warley Franks until 1515. Between that year and 1518 John Godeston's heiresses sold their portions of the manor, which passed to feoffees who included Richard Nix, bishop of Norwich.[17] Nix was described as lord of the manor of South Hall in 1521, but it was probably already held for the benefit of the Bellamy family of Harrow-on-the-Hill (Mdx.).[18] In 1548 William Bellamy (d. *c.* 1565) was lord.[19] His widow, with their son Richard, leased out part of it in 1568, and in 1576 Richard sold

[83] Prob. 11/161 (P.C.C. 42 Audley).
[84] Smith, *Eccl. Hist. Essex*, 245.
[85] E.R.O., D/DB T278–9.
[86] E.R.O., D/DB T279.
[87] E.R.O., D/DB T1447; Venn, *Alumni Cantab.*, I. i. 160.
[88] C.P. 25(2)/1476/22 Geo. III Mich.; E.R.O., *Sale Cat.* A73.
[89] See p. 129.
[90] E.R.O., D/CT 280.
[91] *V.C.H. Essex*, i. 458.
[92] Ibid.; *E.A.T.* v. 113; cf. *V.C.H. Essex*, i. 497.
[93] Sanders, *Eng. Baronies*, 151.
[94] *Cal. Pat.* 1334–8, 273; *D.N.B.*
[95] *Cal. Pat.* 1361–4, 487; cf. ibid. 1330–4, 306; *Complete Peerage*, vi. 471–2. The earl held the manor, but not the honor.
[96] C 139/152/7; *Cal. Pat.* 1467–77, 401.
[97] *Cal. Inq. p.m. Hen. VII*, iii, p. 479.
[98] *Cur. Reg. R.* iii. 170, 264.
[99] *Bk. of Fees*, i. 277.
[1] *Cur. Reg. R.* xv. 262; *Cal. Pat.* 1232–47, 11; cf. *Bk. of Fees*, ii. 677 for Passelewe as guardian in 1242–3.
[2] *Cal. Pat.* 1266–72, 93, 122–3; cf. ibid. 1258–66, 566.
[3] *Cal. Chart. R.* 1257–1300, 92; cf. *Rot. Hund.* (Rec. Com.), 156.
[4] *Cal. Inq. p.m.* i, p. 231; *Feet of F. Essex*, i. 279.
[5] *Cal. Fine R.* 1272–1307, 6; *Cal. Inq. p.m.* ii, pp. 5–9, 63; *Cal. Pat.* 1281–92, 413.
[6] *Cal. Pat.* 1281–92, 413.
[7] *Cal. Inq. p.m.* v, p. 70–9.
[8] *Cal. Pat.* 1321–4, 71; E 179/107/13 m. 8.
[9] *Complete Peerage*, x. 552–6; *Cal. Inq. p.m.* v, pp. 70–9; vii, p. 40; viii, p. 416.
[10] *Cal. Fine R.* 1327–37, 135; *Cal. Pat.* 1327–30, 401
[11] *Cal. Pat.* 1327–30, 567; *Cal. Close*, 1333–7, 11.
[12] *Cal. Pat.* 1334–8, 87; *Cal. Close*, 1337–9, 238.
[13] *Feet of F. Essex*, iii. 61; *Cal. Wills Husting*, i. 276; *Cal. Inq. p.m.* xi, p. 463.
[14] *Cal. Inq. p.m.* viii, p. 367; *Cal. Pat.* 1345–8, 161, 196.
[15] *Cal. Pat.* 1345–8, 218; *Pub. Wks. in Med. Law* (Selden Soc. xxxii), 77–82; *Cal. Fine R.* vii. 25, 301; *Cal. Wills Husting*, ii. 192–3; cf. ibid. i. 276; *Cal. Inq. p.m.* xi, p. 463; S. Thrupp, *Merchant Class Med. Lond.* App. A.
[16] E.R.O., D/DL T1/191; B.L. Add. MS. 38131, ff. 79v.–80; *Reg. Sudbury* (Cant. & York Soc.), i. 276.
[17] *Feet of F. Essex*, iv. 134, 138–9.
[18] Newcourt, *Repertorium*, ii. 482; *Mdx. Pedigrees* (Harl. Soc. lxv), 9–10; E.R.O., D/AER 4, ff. 91–3.
[19] *Cal. Pat.* 1547–8, 346, and 1563–6, p. 333.

the whole manor to Anthony Radcliffe of London.[20]

Radcliffe (d. 1603) was succeeded by his son Edward Radcliffe,[21] and he before 1619 by Anthony Radcliffe, who sold South Hall in 1630 to Giles Fleming (d. 1633) and his son John (d. 1643).[22] By a family settlement of 1642 South Hall passed to John's younger brother Edmund (fl. 1654), and then to John's daughters, who sold South Hall in 1685 to Elizabeth Conaway, widow of an East India Company sea-captain.[23] The manor passed in succession to her son Robert Conaway, barrister of Gray's Inn, and her daughter Katherine Conaway.[24] Katherine went mad and the custody of the manor was granted to her cousin Mary Johnson, who was described as lady of the manor in 1721.[25] On Katherine's subsequent death South Hall was divided between Mary Johnson and another cousin, Frances Howland, each of whom sold her half of the manor to a different purchaser.[26] In the early 1750s the manor was united again by John Hopkins (d. 1772) of Bretons, Hornchurch.[27]

From Hopkins South Hall descended to his grandson, Benjamin Bond (Hopkins) (d. 1794), who died without sons.[28] The manor therefore passed to Hopkins's great-nephew John Hopkins Dare (d. 1805),[29] and descended with the manor of Theydon Bois until 1899 when the South Hall estate, comprising 167 a., was sold in two lots.[30] The manor apparently remained in the Hall-Dare family.

South Hall Farm is a house of hall and cross-wing plan, perhaps of the late 16th century. The principal fronts were encased in brick in the early 19th century when extensive new farm buildings were erected west of the house.

ECONOMIC HISTORY. Until the 19th century Rainham drew its living from farming and the river Thames. The creek gave it a share of the river traffic and provided an outlet for local and inland produce. Cattle and sheep grazed on the coastal marshes; and the upland arable produced grain and from 1850 vegetables for the London market. Industry gradually spread along the creek and river bank after 1870.

The prosperity of Rainham apparently diminished in the generation after the Conquest: manorial values and the number of ploughs and recorded population all dropped.[31] There were 4 freemen, 24 villeins, 11 bordars, and 11 serfs in 1066, but only 25 villeins, 18 bordars, and 4 serfs in 1086. In 1066 there were 8½ demesne and 13½ tenants' ploughs; they numbered respectively 4 and 8½ in 1086. Of the 3 chief manors South Hall fell in value from £6 to £2, and Berwick from £6 to £4. Only Walter of Douai's manor, the largest in Rainham, kept its value. His demesne and the tenants each lost a plough: in 1086 he had 2 ploughs and his tenants 5; but the manor's population had risen. In 1066 there had been 12 villeins, 2 bordars, and 5 serfs; in 1086 the manor had 12 villeins, 9 bordars, and 4 serfs. The later total included 3 men whose holdings had been free in 1066. The most notable difference is the sharp rise in the number of bordars. Their presence often indicates forest clearance,[32] but there were no woodland-pastures for swine in Rainham, and in 1086 there were only 20 pigs on Walter's manor. Perhaps his bordars were reclaiming land along the Ingrebourne. In 1086 Rainham and Berwick manors had 185 sheep, which were presumably kept on the marshes along with the flocks of South Hall, for which no livestock was recorded.

Rainham marshes have always provided grazing. The only change in their extent appears to have occurred with the reclamation of 185 a., probably in the 17th century.[33] In 1309 it was said that 40 a. of marshland were arable, but that was probably a round figure; the amount of marsh arable in 1861 was only 28 a.[34] The livestock of Moorhall in 1333, besides 5 draught animals, comprised 32 head of cattle, and 137 sheep.[35] From the 16th century onwards Rainham wills name butchers, graziers, sheep- and cattle-breeders, and herdsmen.[36] Bequests were often expressed in terms of livestock: William Radley in 1540 bequeathed at least 65 cattle and 164 sheep.[37] By the 19th century the marshes provided pasture for many Welsh, Scottish, Lincolnshire, and Norfolk sheep, as well as cattle for the London market each autumn.[38] In 1838 there were 1,334 a. of pasture; in 1905 there were 975 a.[39] In 1906 the War Office bought 195 a. for use as rifle ranges.[40] Since the Second World War the ranges have been seldom used. Some receive spoil dredged from the Thames, others are once again used for grazing.[41] In 1961 there were 787 a. pasture.[42] The Berwick herd of Friesians was sold in 1961, the Moorhall herd in 1974.[43]

Rainham farming was linked to London from the Middle Ages. St. Bartholomew's hospital drew grain,

[20] E.R.O., D/DYa 1; C.P. 25(2)/130/1662.
[21] C 142/284/39; C 142/398/127.
[22] C.P. 25(2)/295/16 Jas. I Hil.; Prob 11/165 (P.C.C. 19 Seager); Prob. 11/193 (P.C.C. 57 Rivers); E.R.O., D/DHt T210/1.
[23] E.R.O., D/DHt T210/1; C.P. 25(2)/655/36 & 37 Chas. II Hil.; *E.A.T.* N.S. xxi. 100.
[24] Prob. 11/373, f. 54; E.R.O., T/P 195/2; *Grays Inn Admission Reg.* 343.
[25] E.R.O., T/P 195/2; E.R.O., D/P 202/8/1.
[26] Morant, *Essex*, i, 88; C.P. 25(2)/1122/13 Geo. II Mich.; C.P. 25(2)/1124/25 & 26 Geo. II Trin.
[27] E.R.O., Q/RSg 3, f. 31; *Gent. Mag.* (1772), 543.
[28] Prob. 11/982, f. 408; *Gent. Mag.* (1772), 543; (1788), i. 510, ii. 573–4; (1794) i. 183–4; *Hist. Parl., Commons, 1754–90*, ii. 101; Prob. 11/1243, f. 141; W. A. Bartlett, *Antiquities of Wimbledon*, 84–6.
[29] Prob. 11/651, f. 137; *Hist Parl., Commons, 1715–54*, ii. 149; *Visit. Essex* (Harl. Soc.), ii. 739–41.
[30] *V.C.H. Essex*, iv. 252; E.R.O., Sage Coll., *Sale Cat.* vol. i. 8. The South Hall estate had comprised 616 a. in 1838: E.R.O., D/CT 280.
[31] The information in this paragraph comes from *V.C.H. Essex*, i. 458, 518, 554, 561, unless otherwise indicated.
[32] Cf. *V.C.H. Essex*, vi. 74, and above, pp. 106, 121.
[33] See p. 137.
[34] *Cal. Inq. p.m.* v, p. 71; E.R.O., D/SR 77.
[35] B.L. Cott. MS. Nero E. vi, f. 200v.
[36] *Chelmsford Wills*; Prob. 11/13 (P.C.C. 19 Blamyr), 11/38 (P.C.C. 27 Ketchyn), 11/53 (P.C.C. 17 Barrington).
[37] E.R.O., D/AER 4, ff. 91–3; Prob. 11/26 (P.C.C. 17 Crumwell).
[38] Wright, *Essex*, ii. 516; Robson's *Gazetteer* (*c.* 1840), 83; *Steamboat Companion* (1839) cited in H.R.L., Lewis Scrapbook, xii. 26.
[39] E.R.O., D/CT 280; Bd. of Agric., Acreage Returns, 1905.
[40] E.R.O., D/DLc T46; earlier references apparently concern ranges in S. Hornchurch: *Kelly's Dir. Essex* (1874), 175; Thorne, *Environs Lond.* (1876), 481; *Strat. Expr.* 3 Sept. 1881; O.S. Map 1/2,500, Essex, LXXIV. 16 (2nd edn.).
[41] Joan I. Hunt, 'Past, present, and possible future use of the Lower Thames Flood Plain at Rainham' (N.E. Lond. Polytechnic, Dept. Ed. thesis, 1972), 39.
[42] M.A.F. 68/4722; cf. A. Gustard and R. C. Fulcher, 'A Geography of Rainham' (Emmison Prize essay, 1966): E.R.O., T/Z 13/108, fig. 20.
[43] Lewis, *Rainham*, 14; inf. from owner.

beans, and hay from its Rainham estate *c.* 1200.[44] In 1333 Moorhall had 89 a. sown with grain and 14 a. with beans and peas; a further 54 a. were fallow, 14a. of them manured.[45] In 1631 two Rainham farmers were accused of selling cart-loads of hay and straw in London, thus enhancing prices.[46] Capt. Harle's development of the wharf in the 1720s made trade with London even easier; Rainham was probably supplying peas in 1794, and perhaps potatoes in 1807.[47] In 1838 there were 1,705 a. of arable.[48] In the mid 19th century intensive market-gardening reached Rainham from parishes nearer London; arable had increased to 1,995 a. by 1905,[49] and by 1929 almost every major farm in the parish was said to be a market-garden.[50] In 1849 or 1850 Thomas Circuit (d. *c.* 1867), already a market-gardener in East Ham, leased Brick House (84 a.) between Upminster Road and the Ingrebourne.[51] He was succeeded by John Circuit, who at his death in 1876 was farming 413 a. in Rainham, including 227 a. freehold.[52] William Blewitt (d. 1875) was a market-gardener on an even larger scale, as the tenant of Ayletts, Bright's, and Parsonage farms, 664 a. in all.[53]

Rainham's access to the river favoured such a development. The light lands of the parish were suitable for intensive cultivation only if thoroughly manured, and it was by river that barge-loads of London muck were brought to Rainham. Before 1872 the parish was already in bad odour with travellers because of the barges unloading near the railway station,[54] and in that year John Circuit built another wharf on the creek for unloading muck.[55] Rainham produced chiefly vegetables for the London market, especially asparagus and cabbage.[56] The 'Early Rainham' cabbage was first advertised in 1876, and though supplanted by newer varieties was still being grown in 1957.[57] Pickling onions and cauliflowers were widely grown, the latter even giving their name to a public house on the edge of the village in 1878.[58] Since the Second World War the production of greens has been abandoned, temporarily on some farms because of gravel-winning, permanently on others because of the cost of labour.[59] In 1961 there were 825 a. of arable.[60]

The size of farms has diminished in the past century. In 1838 there were 11 farms of 50 a. or more: 3 had between 50 a. and 100 a., and 6 between 150 a. and 500 a. The 2 largest had 581 a. and 664 a.[61] In 1961 only 5 farms had more than 50 a.: 2 had less than 100 a., and 3 between 100 a. and 500 a.[62]

Rainham manor had a windmill in 1248 and perhaps as early as 1219.[63] There was a water-mill on Berwick manor in 1315.[64] South Hall manor had a water-mill in 1270, and in 1838 the manor included a Mill Hill field.[65] St. Katherine's hospital (Lond.) had a water-mill at Rainham in 1335.[66] Moorhall in 1729 included a Mill field but no mill.[67]

In 1270 South Hall manor was granted a weekly market and a yearly fair on the eve, feast, and morrow of St. Giles (31 Aug.–2 Sept.).[68] In 1342 the manor was granted a Tuesday market and a fair on the feast of St. Faith and the two following days (6–8 Oct.).[69] In 1878 an annual fair held in Rainham on Saturday in Whitsun week was abolished.[70]

Alehouses were recorded at Rainham from the mid 16th century,[71] and the first inn may have been established as the result of petitions submitted in 1633.[72] It may originally have been called the White Hart, but in 1716 it was the Phoenix.[73] It was said to be 'new built' in 1739.[74] It was burned down in 1891 and rebuilt with a brick front on the same site in the Broadway.[75] The Ferry house, later the Three Crowns, was first recorded in 1556 and closed in 1951.[76] In 1640 there were 5 licensed houses in the parish.[77] On the north side of the Broadway, the Bell was in existence by 1718. Its site has belonged since 1618 to the Almshouse and Pension Charities of St. Giles-in-the-Fields (Lond.); the house was rebuilt *c.* 1900.[78] The Angel, also in the Broadway, was first recorded in 1730 and last rebuilt in 1907.[79] In 1702 an earlier Bell stood in Back Street (Upminster Road). By 1733 it was the Horseshoe and Can, and by 1769 the Lamb (and Crown). It ceased to be a public house in 1789.[80]

Before the 19th century there was little industry in Rainham, although a boat-builder and two tanners were recorded in the 16th century.[81] From 1869 Rainham Ferry provided a suitable location for obnoxious chemical and fertiliser factories.[82] By 1886 there were 6 works, 2 fronting the creek, and 4 on the Thames.[83] Salamon & Co. occupied a creek site

[44] N. Moore, *Hist. St. Bart.'s Hosp.* i. 240.
[45] B.L. Cott. MS. Nero E. vi, f. 200v.
[46] Assizes 35/73/2, 3 Hil. (Essex).
[47] *Gen. View Essex Agric.* (Bd Agric. 1794), 94; *V.C.H. Essex*, ii. 475. But Rainham had no cherry-orchard: ibid. ii. 477 has misplaced a Hornchurch site.
[48] E.R.O., D/CT 280.
[49] Bd. of Agric., Acreage Returns, 1905.
[50] E.R.O., Sage Coll., *Sale Cats.* vol. i. 8; viii. 7; *Sale Cats.* A73, B2517, B5743.
[51] *Pigot's Dir. Essex* (1832); E.R.O., D/CT 159; E.R.O., D/P 202/5/3; D/P 202/11/10.
[52] E.R.O., D/P 202/11/13, 202/8/2; Lewis, *Rainham*, 83.
[53] E.R.O., D/CT 280; E.R.O., Q/RPl 153–7; E.R.O., D/DB T 843–4.
[54] W. Palin, *More about Stifford*, 136; cf. E.R.O., T/P 67/2, p. 126f for a 'dung craft' in 1801; *Essex and Thurrock Gaz.* 27 Jan. 1956.
[55] E.R.O., D/DDw T278/9; E.R.O., D/P 202/11/12, 13; D/P 202/8/2. In 1976 the wharf was silted up.
[56] Palin, op. cit. 136.
[57] *V.C.H. Essex*, ii. 476; *Rainham Hortic. Soc. Bull.* iv. (Apr. 1957); for the commercial growing of lucerne (1920), rhubarb (1920, 1944), and marrows (1944): E.R.O., *Sale Cat.* A/73; C/W 1/2/59 (20 Aug. 1944).
[58] *Essex and Thurrock Gaz.* 1 Aug. 1958.
[59] Joan Hunt, op. cit. 21–2; cf. Gustard and Fulcher, op. cit. ch. 8.
[60] M.A.F. 68/4722.
[61] E.R.O., D/CT 280.
[62] M.A.F. 68/4722.
[63] J.I. 1/232 m. 3d.; *Feet of F. Essex*, i. 55.
[64] B.L. Cott. MS. Nero E. vi, f. 203; B.L. Cott. MS. Claud. E. vi, f. 240v.; M.P.F. 119.
[65] C 132/37/20; E.R.O., D/CT 280 no. 86.
[66] *Cal. Pat.* 1334–8, 77, 83.
[67] E.R.O., D/DB T277.
[68] *Cal. Chart. R.* 1257–1300, 148–9.
[69] Ibid. 1341–1417, 10.
[70] *Lond. Gaz.* 15 Feb. 1878, 751.
[71] E.R.O., Q/SR 2/22, 25/2, 54/22, 56/28.
[72] D.P.L., Fanshawe MSS., Box 32(5); E.R.O., Q/RLv 21–2; cf. Assizes 35/99/T (21); E.R.O., D/ABR 14, f. 89.
[73] D.P.L., Fanshawe MSS., Box 32(5); E.R.O., D/DB T283.
[74] E.R.O., D/DB T283.
[75] *Essex and Thurrock Gaz.* 18 July 1958.
[76] E.R.O., Q/SR 2/22; see below, p. 137.
[77] E.R.O., Q/RLv 21.
[78] *Hist. Essex by Gent.* iv. 353; *Essex and Thurrock Gaz.* 4 July 1958.
[79] *Essex and Thurrock Gaz.* 26 June 1958.
[80] E.R.O., D/DU 650; E.R.O., Q/RLv 24, 43.
[81] E.R.O., D/AER 4/137, 11/95; D/AEW 3/123.
[82] E.R.O., D/P 202/8/2; *Kelly's Dir. Essex* (1870 and later edns.); *Strat. Expr.* 13 May, 17 June, 15 July, 1882,
[83] *Kelly's Dir. Essex* (1886); cf. O.S. Map, 25" (2nd edn.). LXXXII. 3, 4, 7; E.R.O., *Sale Cat.* A132.

from *c.* 1880 to 1971;[84] the company refined crude tar, but with the introduction of North Sea gas, coal carbonization ceased, and crude tar was no longer available. On the river-front the 3 main firms have been Hempleman & Co., blood- and fish-manure manufacturers (1882–*c.* 1917);[85] J. C. and J. Field Ltd., candle and soap manufacturers (1906–*c.* 1937);[86] and Murex Ltd., iron-founders and ferro-alloy manufacturers. Murex, founded in 1909, moved to Rainham in 1917. Between 1928 and 1937 it bought out the other companies on the water-front, and in 1970, after further land-purchases, owned 63 a. In 1972 Murex was part of the British Oxygen Co.[87] Between 1919 and 1939 there was also a barge-builder at the Ferry.[88]

In the rest of the parish there has been only scattered industry. In 1894 there was a brickfield on an unidentified site;[89] and in the 1930s two sand and ballast companies were operating.[90] Gravel-digging increased after the Second World War,[91] but reclamation has allowed the land to be returned after extraction of the gravel to farming.[92]

CREEK, WHARF, AND FERRIES. Rainham creek was being used as an outlet for local stock as early as 1200,[93] and that use continued until the 19th century.[94] In the later 15th century Rainham ships were also trading in wool to Calais.[95] In the 16th century ships were probably built as well as berthed in the creek, for a Rainham shipwright's will was proved in 1533.[96] Rainham watermen appear regularly in the 16th- and 17th-century records, which from *c.* 1650 also name Rainham lightermen.[97] In 1637 boats were carrying goods and passengers on every tide from Lion quay, London, to Rainham and other Essex river-ports.[98]

In 1526 a wharf and granary, at the west end of the village, were held on lease from the Hospitallers by Thomas Balthrop (d. *c.* 1547).[99] He devised his lease to his wife, with reversion to William Peacock and his wife.[1] In 1574 Richard Peacock (d. 1602) was the wharfinger.[2] Thomas Silvester (d. *c.* 1644) owned the wharf in 1642.[3] In the early 18th century it belonged to William Arnold, a yeoman grazier.[4] The import of coal is first recorded at that time, Arnold having considerable dealings with Thomas Willyford, a coal-factor of St. Botolphs without Aldgate (Mdx.).[5]

In 1718 John Harle, a sea-captain from South Shields (Dur.) married a Stepney widow and about the same time acquired the Rainham wharf.[6] After improving it, he imported building materials as well as coal, and advertised granaries for the storage of corn, and shipments to London twice a week.[7] His business prospered, and by 1729 he had built Rainham Hall.[8]

Capt. Harle (d. 1742) was succeeded by his son, another John Harle (d. 1770), who married Sarah Dearsly (d. *c.* 1824). The Hall and wharf passed to her, and thence successively to two daughters of her second marriage, Miss Susanna Dearsly Chambers (d. 1850) and Mrs. Alicia D. Nicholls (d. 1859).[9] In 1861 the Revd. George M. Platt (d. 1898) owned the wharf and apparently retained ownership until shortly before his death.[10] Lessees of the wharf can be traced from the late 18th century.[11] In 1801 it was described as 'the grand lodging and landing place for the whole mercantile goods of that part of the county.'[12] A series of linked tenancies from 1799 named Messrs. Rose, Pratt, and Daldy, coal-merchants and maltsters. The malting on the wharf was apparently built in the early 19th century; it was demolished after the Second World War.[13] Between 1890 and 1897 Daldy & Co. bought freehold of the wharf piecemeal.[14] The firm continued to trade from the wharf until *c.* 1920.[15] In 1927 it was re-opened as Station Wharf by John Newman Ltd., timber merchants; they closed it in 1969.[16] In 1872 John Circuit built a wharf south of the railway for the unloading of London muck for his market gardening.[17] By 1976 it had silted up.

Two ancient ferries were available to the inhabitants of Rainham: the 'long' ferry from Gravesend (Kent) to London, which made its last stop at the mouth of Rainham creek, and the 'short' ferry across the Thames, from Coldharbour, in Wennington, to Erith (Kent).[18] The way to Coldharbour branched

[84] *Kelly's Dir. Essex* (1882 and later edns.); letter from Salamon & Co. Ltd. to F. Lewis, 24 Aug 1971.
[85] *Strat. Expr.* 13 May, 17 June, 15 July 1882; *Kelly's Dir. Essex* (1917); E. A. Bird, *Vanished Hamlet*, 10.
[86] *V.C.H. Essex*, ii. 458; *Kelly's Dir. Essex* (1906 and later edns.); for the production of T.N.T. and poison gas during the First World War, Bird, op. cit. 9.
[87] *Kelly's Dir. Essex* (1922–37); Bird, op. cit. 10–22; Joan Hunt, op. cit. 35. See plate facing p. 112, above.
[88] *Kelly's Dir. Essex* (1922–37).
[89] Ibid. (1894).
[90] Ibid. (1933–7).
[91] Gustard and Fulcher, op. cit. ch. 9.
[92] Joan Hunt, op. cit. 24, 28–30; letter from Walkers Sand & Ballast Co. Ltd. to F. Lewis, 26 Jan. 1972; inf. from Mr. W. Vellacott; H.R.L., Lewis Scrapbook, xi. 27.
[93] *Cart. St. Bart.'s Hosp.* ed. Kerling, p. 120; *E.A.T.* N.S. xix. 246; cf. perhaps *Pipe R.* 1166 (P.R.S. ix), 130.
[94] *Cal. Pat.* 1324–7, 270; cf. ibid. 1313–17, 582 and *Cal. Close*, 1333–7, 124; D.P.L., Fanshawe MSS. Box 32(5), of 1633; *Cal. S.P. Dom.* 1653–4, 574; 1655, 492; Lewis, *Rainham*, 42; E.R.O., T/P 67/2 p. 126f.
[95] *Cely Papers* (Camd. Soc. 3rd ser. i), pp. 41, 70–2, 75–6, 80; cf. *V.C.H. Essex*, ii. 280 for 3 Rainham ships in James I's reign.
[96] *Chelmsford Wills*, i. 45.
[97] Ibid. 4, 182, 186, 317; ii. 144, 203; E.R.O., Q/SR 53/55, 54/22, 76/21, 160/103, 208/113, 501/1 and 18–20; Lewis, *Rainham*, 61; Prob. 11/225 (P.C.C. 34 Brent).
[98] *E.R.* vii. 30.
[99] B.L. Cott. MS. Claud. E. vi, f. 268v.; E 179/108/150; E.R.O., D/ABW 3/122.
[1] E.R.O., D/ABW 3/122; cf. Prob. 11/10 (P.C.C. 8 Vox).
[2] Lewis, *Rainham*, 41 (citing parish reg.); Prob. 11/100 P.C.C. 51 Montague); cf. E.R.O., Q/SR 153/21a.
[3] E.R.O., Q/SR 318/108; Prob. 11/192 (P.C.C. 22 Rivers).
[4] By 1709 and in 1716: E.R.O., D/HDt T380.
[5] Ibid.
[6] *Country Life*, xlvii. 760–8 (5 June 1920).
[7] E.R.O., Museum Class M1; Salmon, *Essex*, 280.
[8] See p. 128.
[9] Prob. 11/722, f. 357; F. Lewis, *Par. Ch. Rainham* [1960], 24: Lewis, *Rainham*, 42; E.R.O., Q/RPl 106–57; E.R.O., D/P 202/11/9, 10, 9A, 10A; E.R.O., D/SR 51–2, 77; Venn, *Alumni Cantab. II*, v. 137; M.I. Rainham ch.
[10] E.R.O., D/P 202/11/17 (1879); Venn, *Alumni Cantab.* II, v. 137.
[11] E.R.O., Q/RPl 106–57; *Pigot's Dir. Essex* (1823–4, 1826–7); *Robson's Dir. Essex* (*c.* 1840); *Kelly's Dir. Essex* (1845 and later edns.).
[12] E.R.O., T/P 67/2, p. 126f.
[13] E.R.O., D/CT 280; cf. O.S. Map 3" (draft of 1799) and E.R.O., T/P 67/2, p. 126f; Lewis, *Rainham*, 42.
[14] Electoral regs., Essex, SE. division (1890–98).
[15] *Kelly's Dir. Essex* (1917, 1922).
[16] Lewis, *Rainham*, 42; *Hornchurch Echo*, 1 Apr. 1969. The wharf is not used by Gen. Construction & Engineering Co. Ltd., who have occupied the site since 1972.
[17] E.R.O., D/DDw T278/9; E.R.O., D/P 202/11/12, 13; D/P 202/8/2.
[18] For the 'short' ferry, see p. 181.

off Manor Way (Ferry Lane)[19] and ran almost due south across Rainham marsh to the ferry, which was in operation until the late 19th century.[20]

The long ferry from Gravesend to London was first recorded in 1279.[21] The first known reference to Rainham ferry under that name was in 1531.[22] In 1556 there was an alehouse there,[23] and in 1559 the London Company of Watermen and Lightermen issued a tariff of charges which included fares from London to Rainham.[24] In 1580 Thomas Wiseman of Great Waltham devised the alehouse, ferry, and two adjoining marshes to his grandson William Wiseman, who in 1598 sold them to Sir Robert Southwell, the chief landowner of the parish.[25]

With the coming of the railways in the mid 19th century, the long ferry apparently ceased, but pleasure vessels plied up and down the Thames, and from 1850 the Margate paddle steamers called at Rainham ferry.[26] In the 1860s there was a hard leading from the inn to the low water mark, and in the early 20th century a narrow wooden pier surmounted it.[27] In the 1890s there appears to have been for a few years a ferry across the river to Erith marshes.[28]

In 1729 the Ferry house was sold as part of the Berwick and Moorhall estate.[29] It had become the French Horn by 1769 and in 1772 changed its name to the Three Crowns.[30] Edward Ind bought the property from John C. G. Crosse, apparently in 1804, and in 1826 or 1827 sold it to John Wade, the innkeeper.[31] It was burnt down in 1834, and the present structure built.[32] Joseph Lee owned it in 1838.[33] It was sold to Ind, Coope & Co. in 1876 and remained a public house until 1951.[34] It was demolished in 1972.[35]

MARSHES AND SEA DEFENCES. The marshes of Rainham are bounded by Rainham creek on the west and Wennington Road on the north; eastwards they continue as the Wennington marshes. Unlike the marshes to the east and west they seem rarely to have suffered from serious floods, probably because the alignment of the Thames, NW. to SE., protects them from the worst storms driving up the river.

In the Middle Ages responsibility for the marshes' defence rested on the tenants, and there was already a custom and law of the marsh in 1210.[36] The marshes then were probably several feet higher than at present,[37] but they did not always escape flooding. Rainham was flooded at Eastertide 1448, and 3 months later a commission was issued to inspect the walls and ditches from Purfleet to Rainham.[38] In 1452 a more general commission ordered an inquest throughout the county of all lands flooded; it had been provoked by the inhabitants of Rainham, Wennington, and Aveley, who complained at being assessed as usual for a tenth and fifteenth.[39] Their claim that certain lands were still profitless suggests a serious flooding; but whether it caused the 'breach' mentioned in 1524 is not clear.[40]

In 1547 Rainham was under the jurisdiction of a court of sewers whose authority extended from Bow Bridge to Mucking.[41] Aveley 'level', which included Rainham, ran from Rainham bridge to Grays Thurrock.[42] Within the level, Rainham marsh contained 662 a., of which 426 a. had passed from the Hospitallers to Sir Robert Southwell at the Dissolution.[43] About 1680 Aveley level was amalgamated with Mucking level, and the enlarged level was known thereafter as Rainham level.[44]

Between 1563 and 1833 the extent of Rainham marsh under the jurisdiction of the court of sewers increased by 175 a. to 837 a.[45] There is little doubt that the new land came by reclamation, probably in the 17th century at Little Coldharbour, on the SE. edge of the marsh.[46] The Sewers Act, 1833, increased the powers of the court of sewers, and enabled them to bring a further 279 a. under their jurisdiction.[47]

In 1931 Rainham level came under the control of the Essex Rivers catchment board, which in 1952 was merged in the Essex Rivers board.[48] Rainham suffered little damage from the great flood of 1953.[49]

LOCAL GOVERNMENT. In the later 13th century the three manors of Rainham, Berwick, and South Hall had view of frankpledge and assize of bread and ale. In 1274–5 the Hospitallers claimed the right of gallows at Rainham.[50] In 1285 they set up a new gallows there, claiming that they were merely replacing a previous one; the Crown, however, denied their right.[51] Gerpins manor was said to have view of frankpledge in 1800, but no records of a Gerpins court have been found, and the claim must be regarded as doubtful.[52]

The parish records include vestry minutes (1705–1892); churchwardens' rates (1810–16, 1825–60), bills (1683–1890), and accounts (1679–80, 1718–90,

19 O.S. Map 6", Essex, LXXXII (surv. 1862–8).
20 Lewis, *Rainham*, 31; E.R.O., D/DL T1/331.
21 H. Humpherus, *Hist. Co. Watermen*, i. 16; J. R. Hayston, 'The Lower Thames Ferries', *Thurrock Hist. Soc. Jnl.* iv. 9–19; *Cal. Inq. Misc.* i, p. 420.
22 E.R.O., D/AER 4/91; a 1406 ref. to 'Prattysferie' in *Liber Albus* (Rolls Ser.), i. 515–16, has been interpreted as a reference to Rainham ferry: Lewis, *Rainham*, 36.
23 E.R.O., Q/SR 2/22; cf. Lewis, *Rainham*, 32.
24 Humpherus, op. cit. i. 110–12.
25 E.R.O., T/B 62/2; Prob. 11/62 (P.C.C. 49 Arundell); C.P. 25(2)/262 40 Eliz. I Trin. For representations of the Ferry house: E.R.O., D/DU 162/1 (of 1616 × 1627) and 172 (of 1627). Cf. D.P.L., Fanshawe MSS., Box 32(5) for the 'common ferry' in 1633.
26 Lewis, *Rainham*, 35; E. A. Bird, *Rainham Village and Its Ferry*, 16; E. A. Bird, *Vanished Hamlet*, 6–7.
27 Lewis, *Rainham*, 35 and facing p. 39.
28 O.S. Map 1", sheet 257 (2nd edn. revised 1893, 3rd edn. revised 1903); *Essex Countryside*, vii. 288.
29 E.R.O., D/DB T277.
30 E.R.O., Q/RLv 24–6.
31 E.R.O., D/DNe T38/1; E.R.O., Q/RPl 130–1, 151–2.
32 *Romford Times*, 20 Mar. 1963.
33 E.R.O., D/CT 280.
34 Bird, *Vanished Hamlet*, 6, 20.
35 Inf. from Mr. E. A. Bird.
36 e.g. *Feet of F. Essex*, i. 26 (1203); *Cur. Reg. R.* vi. 1; cf. ibid. vii. 289; *E.R.* x. 157; *Feet of F. Essex*, i. 45.
37 Hilda E. P. Grieve, *Great Tide*, 2–3.
38 *Chron. Greyfriars Lond.* (Camd. Soc. 1st ser. liii), 18–19; *Cal. Pat.* 1446–52, 189.
39 *Cal. Pat.* 1452–61, 57.
40 B.L. Cott. MS. Claud. E. vi, f. 240v.; cf. *Cal. Pat.* 1494–1509, 618.
41 *Cal. Pat.* 1547–8, 78; cf. E.R.O., D/DMs 16.
42 E.R.O., D/SH 7.
43 Ibid.
44 E.R.O., D/SR 1–6.
45 O.S. Map 6", Essex, LXXXII (surv. 1862–8) records the antecedent counter-walls.
46 See p. 185.
47 E.R.O., D/SR 78.
48 Cf. *V.C.H. Essex*, v. 238, 285; vi. 17, 94.
49 Grieve, *Great Tide*, 64.
50 *Cal. Inq. p.m.* i, p. 231; *Rot. Hund.* (Rec. Com.), i. 156.
51 B.L. Cott. MS. Nero E. vi, f. 199v; *Rot. Hund.* (Rec. Com.), i. 156 supports the Hospitallers' claim.
52 C.P. 43/868/40 Geo. III East.

1810–16, 1825–60); constables' rates (1708–54), bills (1727–92), and accounts (1720–89); overseers' rates (1745–83, 1792–7), bills (1723–1847), accounts (1685–6, 1706, 1718–97), and apprenticeship papers (1686–1847).[53]

Vestry meetings may have been held monthly, but from 1705 to 1742 only two or three meetings were normally recorded each year; there were seven in 1706 and five in 1710 and 1715. In 1742 the vestry ordered a monthly meeting; but from 1743 to 1769 only the Easter and Christmas vestries were noted, and from 1770 to 1837 only the Easter vestry. The minutes from 1705 to 1807 were signed by those attending; the vicar or curate, when present, normally signed first and presumably took the chair. Until the early 1730s there were usually between 5 and 8 present at meetings; from then until 1807 numbers were between 8 and 14, but only 5 or 6 attended between 1784 and 1796. Before 1719 the meeting place was not stated. From 1719 to 1733 meetings were usually held in the church. Thereafter they were often adjourned to a public house: the Horseshoe and Can was used in 1733, 1736, and 1743, but the list was normally limited to the Phoenix, the Bell, and the Angel. The custom, however, was clearly older: Easter Vestry dinners were held in 1706 and 1707 and often thereafter. In 1742 the vestry, acknowledging that past meetings had often been extravagant, limited expenditure on monthly, Christmas, and Easter vestries by varying amounts. There was a vestry clerk in 1711. In 1719 and 1739 the vicar appointed his successors.

There were two churchwardens, except from 1745 to 1780, and from 1788 to 1822, when there was only one.[54] There were usually two overseers of the poor until 1716, one only from 1716 to 1782, and two again from 1782. A woman was overseer in 1776 and 1777. In 1774 and 1775 the constable acted as the overseer's deputy, and in 1788 the vestry clerk described himself as the overseer's substitute.[55] In 1706, 1711, 1713–15, and from 1804 there were two constables, but for most of the 18th century there was only one. In 1732 there was a headborough as well as a constable.[56] For much of the 18th century separate rates were levied for the churchwardens, overseers, and constables, but after 1782 the constables were reimbursed by the other officers. The names of the highway surveyors are recorded only from 1712 to 1770. There seem normally to have been two. From 1779 to 1791 there was a voluntary association of Chafford and Barstable hundred against robbers, and in 1797 Rainham vestry wanted Aveley and Wennington to join in action against gipsies and vagrants.[57]

In the earlier 18th century poor-relief usually took the form of doles, rent subsidies, and medical care. Those on regular relief numbered only 6 in 1714. In 1723 the vestry ordered parish paupers to wear badges. Strangers, with or without passes, were occasionally given relief. Among them were sailors in 1723 and 1734 who had been Algerian slaves, others in 1759 and 1761 who had been in French prisons, and in 1788 an American refugee.

From 1685 or earlier the parish was renting houses to accommodate the poor. In 1715 a parish house or alms-house was built, in part with a charitable bequest,[58] but in 1721 the house was seized by the lady of the manor of South Hall, who evicted the inmates. The vestry continued to rent houses for the poor until *c.* 1808, when Rainham, Aveley, and West Thurrock established a joint workhouse at Noke House, Wennington. Rainham, like West Thurrock, paid nine twenty-fifths of the cost. Noke House remained in use until 1836, when Rainham became part of Romford poor-law union.

In 1726 the vestry erected stocks, which were repaired in 1757 and 1774. Shortly before 1813 a parish cage was built in Back Street. It was still in use in 1851, but in 1874 its materials were sold.[59]

Medical care for the poor was provided casually until 1811, when a doctor was for the first time employed on a regular contract.[60] Between 1686 and 1821 at least 48 parish orphans were bound as apprentices, two-fifths of them outside the parish but most within Essex.

For much of the 18th century the rateable value of Rainham was about £1,800. In 1791 it was £2,234, and in 1810 £3,152. Before 1740 the overseer's annual expenditure was usually about £30, though it reached £118 in 1720 and £74 in 1723. Between 1741 and 1755 the average was about £50 a year, and in the period 1756–60 over £77. It rose to £115 in the years 1761–79, and to £180 in 1780–97. In 1793, 1795, and 1796 expenditure was over £200 a year. Between 1800 and 1817 the amount spent merely on the relief of the poor varied little from year to year and averaged £346.[61]

CHURCHES. In 1066 a priest held ½ hide freely in Rainham.[62] This suggests the existence of a church there before the Conquest, though the present building dates only from the later 12th century. Warin de la Haule, who held Rainham *jure uxoris*, presented to the rectory *c.* 1170.[63] When Rainham was in the king's hand, *c.* 1178, Gilbert Foliot, bishop of London, presented.[64] About the same time the king gave the advowson of Rainham to Lesnes abbey (Kent) at the request of the abbey's founder, the justiciar Richard de Lucy (d. 1179), and the bishop instituted the abbot as rector.[65] The abbey's right to the advowson of the vicarage was acknowledged in 1204 by Fulk Paynel, formerly lord of Rainham manor, and in 1219 by the Knights Hospitallers, who then held the manor.[66]

The advowson remained in the abbey's possession until its dissolution in 1525; it was then granted to Wolsey, who settled it upon Cardinal College,

[53] E.R.O., D/P 202/8/1–2, 202/5/1–5, 202/9/1–4, 202/12/1–5, 202/14/1–4; the information in this section derives from these sources unless otherwise specified. We are also grateful to Dr. H. E. Priestley for information supplied.

[54] Cf. *E.A.T.* N.S. ii. 172–3 for two churchwardens in 1547 and 1552.

[55] For Rainham's officers the year '1774', e.g., ran from Easter 1774 to Easter 1775.

[56] Moses Marriage, the headborough of 1732, was sole constable in 1730–1, and 1733–38, and again in 1741, 1744–5 and 1755–7.

[57] E.R.O., D/DBe Z1.

[58] See p. 142.

[59] Lewis, *Rainham*, 63.

[60] W. Palin, *More about Stifford*, 136.

[61] E.R.O., Q/CR 1/9/3.

[62] *V.C.H. Essex*, i. 561.

[63] *Cur. Reg. R.* v. 145.

[64] Ibid.

[65] Ibid.; *V.C.H. Kent*, ii. 165–6.

[66] *Cur. Reg. R.* iii. 114, 128; iv. 277; v. 145, 157; *Rot. Chart.* (Rec. Com.), 164; *Feet of F. Essex*, i. 55.

Oxford.[67] On Wolsey's fall the advowson reverted to the Crown and in 1531 was granted to the Hospitallers.[68] It subsequently descended with Berwick manor until 1920. Hector G. G. Crosse, who in that year sold the last of his Rainham estates, retained the advowson until *c.* 1930.[69] By 1933 it had come into possession of the Martyrs Memorial Trust.[70] Rainham was united as a single benefice with Wennington in 1954.[71] In that year South Hornchurch was transferred to Rainham parish.[72]

In 1274 the abbot of Lesnes held the church of Rainham and 20 a. of land which presumably formed the nucleus of Rectory manor, the history of which is traced above.[73]

The demesne of the Hospitallers' Rainham manor was freed of tithes in 1219, but those of their Rainham lands which were tithable were named in 1315.[74] An undated modus, probably of the early 14th century, unequally divided the tithes from the Hospitallers' manor of Moorhall between Aveley church and the chapel of the Hospitallers' Berwick manor in Rainham.[75]

The vicarage was worth £5 gross in 1254 and £10 net in 1535.[76] The vicarial tithes were worth £60 in 1650, and about £90 in the 18th century.[77] About 1800 they began to rise in value, and by 1810 were valued at over £400.[78] In 1838 the tithes were commuted: 166 a. of Berwick House farm were then tithe free; Moorhall (401 a.) paid a modus of £3 10*s.*; Berwick House farm (312 a.) and Berwick Ponds farm (353 a.) a modus of 15*s.* each; and Rainham Lodge (180 a.) one of 10*s.* The rectorial tithes were commuted for £230, the vicarial for £431 10*s.*[79] The vicar's glebe contained 4 a. in 1610 and 1851.[80]

The vicarage house was 'utterly decayed' in 1610, and had vanished by 1650.[81] In 1701 the vicar, Samuel Kekewich, bought a house and garden in the Broadway opposite the church; in 1709, three years after his death, his son formally transferred it to the churchwarden for perpetual use as the vicarage.[82] It was a traditional 17th-century house of three-roomed plan with an internal chimney-stack. In 1710 George Finch, lord of Berwick manor, encased it in purple brick, partly refitted it, and gave it a new staircase in a rear projection.[83] There was some internal remodelling in the early 19th century, and later a wing was added to the SW.[84]

In the 1170s three rectors are known by name.[85] The names of vicars are known from the early 14th century.[86] Twenty can be identified in the 14th and 15th centuries; 4 died while holding the vicarage, but at least 10 resigned it.[87] John Lawrence, vicar *c.* 1523–41, was accused of plotting against the king in 1536.[88] William Talbot, vicar 1544–68, was also rector of Wennington and non-resident in 1560.[89] Leonard Barker, vicar 1569–75 and Samuel Hilliard, 1718–42, were also rectors of Stifford. Hilliard was resident in both parishes.[90] From 1742 to 1897 vicars were usually non-resident and employed assistant curates, the best known being Charles Churchill (1732–64) poet and rake, who assisted his father, 1756–8.[91] In the later 18th century the curate received £30 a year, increased in 1814 to £50 and in 1826 to £120.[92] In 1612 Thomas Frith established an Ascension Day sermon.[93]

The church of *ST. HELEN AND ST. GILES*, a dedication unique in England, consists of chancel, nave with north and south aisles and south porch, and a west tower.[94] The whole church, with the exception of the south porch, was built of septaria and flint-rubble, with ashlar dressings, probably *c.* 1178 when Richard de Lucy the justiciar arranged the grant of the advowson to the abbey of Lesnes (Kent).[95]

The church retains its original dimensions, but has undergone many minor alterations. The 12th-century arcades of three bays north and south of the aisle retain their original round arches and square piers with attached shafts, but 13th-century alterations affected all parts of the church. The upper stage of the tower was built, the clerestory window-splays were recut, and the chancel arch with its chevron decoration was widened. In the chancel the north wall was rebuilt, and three lancet windows were inserted in the south wall. Later in the 13th century blind arches were inserted in the NE. corner of the nave, presumably as a reredos for a side altar. In the 14th century east windows were inserted in both aisles. The nave and chancel roofs were renewed in the 15th century, and the chancel roof with its king-posts survives. Other 15th-century alterations included the building of a north vestry, destroyed at an unknown date,[96] a squint cut in the south wall of the chancel arch, and a large central east window inserted in the chancel below the circular window. About 1500 the upper and lower doorways of the rood-stair were renewed, and it was perhaps then that a ketch at anchor was scratched on the stairway wall.[97] In the 16th century the tower was given buttresses and an embattled parapet of

[67] *V.C.H. Kent*, ii. 166.
[68] *L. & P. Hen. VIII*, v, pp. 286, 732.
[69] *Chelmsford Dioc. Yr. Bks.* (1930–1).
[70] Ibid. (1933).
[71] Ibid. (1955), p. 53.
[72] E.R.O., D/CPc 320; for the mission church of St. John, see above, p. 49.
[73] *Rot. Hund.* (Rec. Com.), 148; and see above, p. 132.
[74] B.L. Cott. MS. Nero E. vi, f. 202v.
[75] Ibid. f. 203v.
[76] *E.A.T.* N.S. xviii. 17; *Valor. Eccl.* (Rec. Com.), 436.
[77] Smith, *Eccl. Hist. Essex*, 246; Guildhall MSS. 9550, 9556–7.
[78] Guildhall MSS. 9557–8, 9560.
[79] E.R.O., D/CT 280.
[80] Ibid.; Newcourt, *Repertorium*, ii. 481; H.O. 129/7/197.
[81] Newcourt, *Repertorium*, ii. 481; Smith, *Eccl. Hist. Essex*, 246.
[82] Salmon, *Essex*, 282; Foster, *Alumni Oxon.* 1500–1714, ii. 840; E.R.O., T/P 195/2; D/P 202/3/1.
[83] Salmon, *Essex*, 282; E.R.O., T/P 195/2.
[84] T. W. Ward, *Guide to Rainham Ch.* (1918).
[85] *Cur. Reg. R.* v. 145.
[86] Newcourt, *Repertorium*, ii. 481; *E.A.T.* N.S. vii. 153; *E.R.* li. 148; E.R.O., T/A 237.
[87] Newcourt, loc. cit.
[88] *L. & P. Hen. VIII*, v, p. 293; xi, p. 587; xii, p. 134.
[89] Corpus Christi Coll., Cambridge, Parker MS.
[90] Newcourt, *Repertorium*, ii. 481, 561.
[91] H. Smith, 'Sequence of Essex Clergy, 1640–68' (TS. in E.R.O.), i, 21; E.R.O., D/P 202/8/1, 202/12/2–3, 202/5/1; *Kelly's Dir. Essex* (1855 sqq.); *D.N.B.*; Venn, *Alumni Cantab.* I, i. 337.
[92] Guildhall MSS. 9551–2, 9557, 9560.
[93] E.R.O., T/P 195/2; D/P 202/8/1.
[94] This account is based on: R.C.H.M. *Essex*, iv. 168; Pevsner, *Essex* (1965), 319; *E.R.* xlv. 140–5, 254; T. W. Ward, *Guide to Rainham Ch.* (1918); F. Lewis, *Par. Ch. Rainham* [1960]; Lewis, *Rainham* (1966); C. R. N. Burrows, *Restoration Rainham par. ch.*; E.R.O., D/CF 35/6; T/P 196 (King MSS.) Eccles. Essex, ii. 1–24; T/P 67/6, pp. 106–7.
[95] *Cur. Reg. R.* v. 145.
[96] Cf. *E.A.T.* N.S. xxii. 346.
[97] It may have been scratched a century earlier: *E.R.* xlv. 143.

brick, and two narrow brick windows were inserted in each wall of the bellchamber.[98]

Thereafter little work was done on the church for over 300 years. In 1719 there was a choir gallery at the west end of the nave.[99] The porch was built after orders given by the vestry in 1738.[1] In 1767 a 1*s.* rate was levied for repairing and beautifying the church, and the repairs probably included the extension of the roof to shelter both aisles as well as the nave.[2] In 1856 the condition of the church was said to be disgraceful, but it was not until 1897 that a major restoration was undertaken.[3] The Revd. Ernest Geldart was appointed architect, and between 1897 and 1910 over £2,600 was raised and spent on the church. The intention was to restore its medieval appearance; the chancel regained its 13th-century fenestration, the clerestory windows were reopened, and the aisles once more had individual roofs.[4]

The font has a 12th-century bowl with a 15th-century octagonal stem.[5] The north door still has an ornamental hinge of *c.* 1200, and the foliated head of a pillar-piscina in the south aisle is of the same date. The south wall of the chancel contains a locker of unknown date, with rebated jambs and triangular head. At the restoration of the church a modern chancel screen made in Antwerp was set upon woodwork incorporating elements of the 15th or early 16th century. In the 1930s the screen was transferred to a Yorkshire church, leaving only the ancient woodwork.[6] The modern oak pews replaced the box-pews of the 18th and 19th centuries; they had replaced 15th-century pews, of which elements are preserved in a chair now in the chancel. The church chest, of oak covered with leather and iron-banded, is probably of the 15th century.[7] The removal of the west gallery during the restoration of 1897–1910 revealed considerable remains of 13th- and 14th-century red wall-designs, similar to traces in the rest of the church. A clock existed in 1687; it often needed repair in the 18th century. It was last mentioned in 1815: the sale of 225 lb. of old iron in 1821 may represent its end.[8]

The church has 3 bells: (i) 1618, Thomas Bartlet; (ii, iii) 1670, John Hodson.[9] The plate includes a cup of 1652 and patens of 1563 and 1713. The earlier paten serves as a cover to the cup of 1652, which may have been made from the Elizabethan one.[10]

The monuments include 2 mutilated brasses with figures, of the late 15th and early 16th century.[11] There are brasses to Kathleen (d. 1612), widow of George Frith and Robert Holden, Mary (d. 1630), wife of Anthony Radcliffe, and John T. G. Crosse (d. 1870).

The names of various fields in the parish appear to indicate lost church endowments: Holy Bread Land, named in 1315, and said in 1499 and 1838 to comprise 26 a.;[12] Goddescroft (1315), Church field (1729),and Giles field (1838).[13] In 1925 Dr. E. H. T. Danaher gave £100 in memory of Mrs. Emily Stoker, the interest to be used for some religious purpose.[14]

The chapel of *ALL SAINTS* stood in Rainham churchyard in 1348.[15] In that year Sir John de Staunton was licensed to found a chantry there with two chaplains.[16] It was endowed with a house, 40½ a., and 20*s.* 10*d.* of Rainham rents.[17] A further 22 a. were settled on the chantry in 1392, but by 1521 the lands had so diminished that the endowment was only 33*s.* 4*d.* a year, and no one would accept the chaplaincy.[18] The right of presentation belonged to the lord of South Hall manor,[19] and with the lord's consent the bishop of London dissolved the chantry in 1521 and reconstituted it as a free chapel to be held by a literate unmarried layman. The right of presentation remained with the lord of South Hall manor, but it was Cardinal Wolsey who appointed Nicholas Lenthall, the only holder of this lay benefice until its dissolution in 1548.[20] Its yearly revenue was then 50*s.*, derived from about 40 a. in the parish.[21] Sir Robert Southwell held half the land as part of Berwick manor, and it was to him that the chantry was sold upon its dissolution.[22]

ROMAN CATHOLICISM. Edward Drury was charged with recusancy in 1641[23] but no papists were found in the parish in reports of 1676[24] and *c.* 1770–*c.* 1812.[25] A temporary iron church was built in Cowper Road, opposite the mission hall, about 1902. It was served at first from Grays Thurrock and after *c.* 1910 from Barking. It closed *c.* 1938 when a parish was founded in South Hornchurch.[26]

OUR LADY OF LA SALETTE, Rainham, Dovers Corner, New Road, was registered for public worship in 1939.[27] A brick barn formerly belonging to Dovers farm served as a temporary church until 1967, when a permanent building, with a steeply pitched roof and a north entrance front mainly of glass, was opened on an adjoining site.[28]

[98] The battlement was replaced in 1959: Bird, *Rainham Village and its Ferry*, 4.
[99] E.R.O., T/P 195/2.
[1] E.R.O., D/P 202/8/1.
[2] Ibid.
[3] E.R.O., T/P 196 Eccles. Essex, ii. 11; D/CF 35/6.
[4] Ibid.; *E.R.* vii. 7; viii. 176; for Geldart: Pevsner, *Essex*, 319; *E.A.T.* N.S. xxv. 116.
[5] *E.A.T.* N.S. xviii. 298 suggests a Saxon origin.
[6] C.C.L., Bp. Inskip's Recs. ii (10 Feb. 1935).
[7] *Rainham Ch. Mag.* (1963); *Ch. Chests Essex*, 175; cf. E.R.O., D/P 202/8/1 for the chest in 1741.
[8] E.R.O., D/P 202/5/1, 2, 4; 202/8/1. Among the clock-makers retained was Yates Thornton, for whom cf. E.R.O., D/AER 34/330.
[9] *Ch. Bells Essex*, 363–4.
[10] *Ch. Plate Essex*, 30; E. Freshfield, *Essex Ch. Plate*, 25.
[11] Mill Stephenson, *Monumental Brasses*, 130; for lost monuments: J. Weever, *Ancient Funerall Monuments*, 599; E.R.O., T/P 195/2; Salmon, *Essex*, 282.
[12] B.L. Cott. MS. Nero E. vi, f. 203; B.L. Lansd. MS. 200, f. 43; E.R.O., D/CT 280 no. 269.
[13] B.L. Cott. MS. Nero E. vi, f. 203; B.L. Cott. MS. Claud. E. vi, f. 240v.; E.R.O., D/DB T277; E.R.O., D/CT 280 no. 112, and cf. no. 328.
[14] Rainham ch., vestry board.
[15] *Cal. Pat.* 1348–50, 133.
[16] Ibid.
[17] *Cal. Pat.* 1348–50, 133; the chapel lands kept their name till the 19th century: B.L. Lansd. MS. 200, f. 74v.; C 142/184/36; E.R.O., D/DVs 2; D/DB T277; E.R.O., D/CT 280 no. 300 (cf. the nearby Paradise field, no. 328).
[18] *Cal. Pat.* 1391–6, 156; Newcourt, *Repertorium*, ii. 482.
[19] *Reg. Sudbury* (Cant. & York Soc.). i. 240, 276; Newcourt, *Repertorium*, ii. 482.
[20] E 301/19/14, E 301/30/82; cf. J. E. Oxley, *Reformation in Essex*, 243.
[21] E 301/30/18.
[22] Ibid.
[23] E.R.O., Q/SR 314/64.
[24] William Salt Libr., Stafford, S. 2112 (Bp. Compton's Census, 1676).
[25] Guildhall MS. 9557.
[26] *Kelly's Dir. Essex* (1902–37); Lewis, *Rainham*, 77–8.
[27] G.R.O. Worship Reg. no. 58639; *Cath. Dir.* (1943).
[28] Lewis, *Rainham*, 77; G.R.O. Worship Reg. no. 71118; *Cath. Dir.* (1973). The church is on the Hornchurch side of the ancient parish boundary.

PROTESTANT NONCONFORMITY. Six nonconformists were enumerated in 1676.[29] They may have been Baptists, for there was a General Baptist church in Rainham by 1697; it was a sister church of the one at Pilgrim's Hatch, in South Weald. Thomas Fowle was its elder.[30] In 1701 some church members were being drawn away by Presbyterian teaching, and there is no record of the church after 1704.[31]

Wesleyan Methodism was introduced *c.* 1767 by John Valton, with the support of John Harle and his wife of Rainham Hall, where meetings were held.[32] Local opposition was violent, led by Harle's father-in-law, who broke into a meeting with a horse-whip, but Valton continued to preach at Rainham until he left Essex in 1775.[33] The society survived his departure. John Wesley visited Rainham in 1784 and 1785, and preached to large congregations there in 1787.[34] Wesleyan preachers from London visited Rainham regularly for some years after Wesley's death in 1791, but eventually gave up.[35] The congregation may have survived a little longer under Independent leadership. In 1798 Henry Attely, minister of Bethel chapel, Romford, registered a building at Rainham for Independent worship.[36] There is no later record of that meeting-house, but private baptisms at Berwick manor were recorded in 1815 by Edward Andrews, Attely's successor at Bethel, and at Moorhall, 1825–9, by Anthony Brown, minister of South Ockendon Independent chapel.[37]

Wesleyan Methodism was revived from *c.* 1831 by preachers of the Spitalfields and Romford circuits.[38] A cottage was rented, probably Joseph Geach's, which was registered in 1831, until local hostility forced the landlord to repossess it.[39] Preaching continued, however, and in 1834 a small chapel was built, in the Romford circuit, probably the one registered that year by William Otter of Romford.[40] It stood in the Broadway opposite Station Approach.[41] Again local hostility led to closure, between 1848 and 1851.[42] The chapel may have been taken over briefly by the Brentwood Primitive Methodist mission in 1847, when Robert Eaglen registered a house.[43] The chapel was converted into 2 cottages which were demolished *c.* 1939.[44]

Methodism was re-established in the late 1920s. Meetings were held in an army hut in Upminister Road until a school-chapel was opened in Wennington Road in 1930, in the East Ham Wesleyan mission circuit. In 1959 a larger church was built beside it.[45]

The Gospel Hall, Cowper Road, originated in 1884 in a small gospel mission in Cowper Road which may have been Providence chapel, attributed that year to Strict Baptists.[46] In 1888 William Spear, of East Hall, Wennington, set up a small iron hall formerly used by Brethren in West Thurrock.[47] The mission was supported by Spear's agricultural partners, the Vellacotts, who were still among its leaders in 1976.[48] The present gospel hall was built later alongside the iron hall.[49]

South View mission hall, Wennington Road, was registered by Brethren in 1902.[50] As it was later known as Maskell's chapel, it may have been founded by Jeremiah Maskell, a village shopkeeper *c.* 1882–1912.[51] It still existed in 1930–5, when the members were described as Exclusive Brethren, but had ceased by 1954.[52]

The Hacton mission at Smokeholes in Rainham, just over the Upminster boundary, is treated under Upminster.

EDUCATION. Rainham junior and infants schools, Upminster Road South, originated in a bequest of £50 by Dr. Lewis Bruce, vicar of Rainham (d. 1779), for teaching children to read. The money was used to establish a day-school[53] which existed by 1785, when John G. Crosse leased to the parish the site in Gravel Pit (or Coney) field, where the school had recently been built.[54] By 1833, when there were also three dame schools in Rainham, the school had 34 pupils and was said to have an endowment for the free education of 6 boys.[55] It was closed from *c.* 1838 to 1846, the building being let to provide alms for the poor. In 1845–6 the vestry used the rent from it to pay for the teaching of 15 children at an infants school which may have been held at the Methodist chapel in the Broadway.

In 1846 the parochial school was reopened and a master and mistress were appointed.[56] A new school for 245 children was built in 1872 next to the old one, which was later demolished.[57] In the 1870s an evening-school was held there. The school re-

[29] William Salt Libr., Stafford, S. 2112 (Bp. Compton's Census, 1676).
[30] W. T. Whitley, *Baptists of London*, 125; *Mins. of Gen. Assembly of Gen. Bapt. Chs. in Eng.* i. 45–83.
[31] Whitley, *Mins. Gen. Assembly*, i. 68, 83.
[32] Thos. Jackson, *Lives of the early Meth. Preachers*, vi. 63–4, 70. For John Harle see above, p. 128.
[33] Jackson, op. cit. vi. 63–4, 70, 78, 84–6; *Jnl. of John Wesley* (ed. Nehemiah Curnock), vii. 345 n.; *Family News* (Rainham Meth. Mag.), Oct. 1959.
[34] *Jnl. of John Wesley*, vi. 471; vii. 45.
[35] *Meth. Mag.* lvii (1834), 775.
[36] G.R.O. Worship Returns, London dioc. bps. ct. no. 451.
[37] Lewis, *Rainham*, 77.
[38] *Meth. Mag.* lvii (1834), 775.
[39] Ibid.; G.R.O. Worship Returns, London dioc. bps. ct. no. 1709. The registration does not state a denomination. Tradition says that the mob burned down the house: Lewis, *Rainham*, 77.
[40] *Meth. Mag.* lvii. 775; G.R.O. Worship Returns, London dioc. bps. ct. no. 1837. No denomination is given.
[41] E.R.O., D/CT 280 (Tithe map, 1838) no. 129.
[42] *Essex and Thurrock Gaz.* 20 May 1955. The chapel was listed in *White's Dir. Essex* (1848), 195, but not in the 1851 census: H.O. 129.
[43] G.R.O. Worship Returns, London dioc. bps. ct. no. 2263.
[44] *Essex and Thurrock Gaz.* 20 May 1955.
[45] Ibid. 20 May 1955, 3 July 1959; *Wesl. Chapel Cttee. Reps.* (1930, 1932); G.R.O. Worship Reg. no. 52430.
[46] Lewis, *Rainham*, 78; E.R.O., T/Z 8.
[47] Wilson and Whitworth, *Grays, Tilbury etc. Dir.* (1928); *Kelly's Dir. Essex* (1890 and later edns.).
[48] Wilson and Whitworth, op. cit. (1928–35); *Hornchurch Official Guide* (1951–62). The farming partnership of Spear and Vellacott Ltd., East Hall, dates from the 1890s.
[49] Lewis, *Rainham*, 78; *Essex and Thurrock Gaz.* 29 Oct. 1965; probably in 1903: G.R.O. Worship Reg. no. 39808.
[50] G.R.O. Worship Reg. no. 39037; E.R.O., T/P 50/14.
[51] Wilson and Whitworth, *Grays, Tilbury etc. Dir.* (1928); *Kelly's Dir. Essex* (1882–1912). It may well have been a secession from the Cowper Road congregation.
[52] Wilson and Whitworth, op. cit. (1930–5); G.R.O. Worship Reg. no. 39037 (cancelled 1954 rev.).
[53] *Proc. Wesley Hist. Soc.* iv. 215.
[54] For this school see: Ed. 21/5310; P. W. Snelling 'Short hist. Rainham school, 1785–1944.' (Barking Coll. Tech. Educ. Dept. thesis, 1970).
[55] *Educ. Enquiry Abstract*, H.C. 62, p. 286 (1835), xli.
[56] E.R.O., D/CT 280; E.R.O., D/P202/8/2. The rent was paid to Mr. Stafford who owned the chapel: E.R.O., D/CT 280.
[57] *Kelly's Dir. Essex* (1890), 281; F. Lewis's photographs; E.R.O., D/CT 280; D/P 202/8/2

ceived annual government grants from 1875.[58] In 1893 a school board was formed, which took over the school.[59] In 1897 a new school for 300 was built behind the 1872 building, which became the infants department.[60] The school was enlarged by Essex county council in 1926. In 1934 it was reorganized for mixed juniors and infants.[61] The 1897 building was destroyed by bombs in 1944 and was not replaced.[62] After the bombing the children were taught in shifts because of lack of accommodation; some went to Arnold Road school, Dagenham. In 1947 four huts were leased and in 1948 the church hall was hired for temporary accommodation. In 1953 the school was reorganized in separate infant and junior departments.[63]

Parsonage Farm junior and infants schools, Allen Road, were planned by Essex county council. The infants school for 240 was opened in 1964 and the junior school for 320 in 1966. The infants school was enlarged in 1967 and again in 1972 and 1973. The junior school was gradually enlarged between 1968 and 1974.[64]

Brady junior mixed and infants school, Wennington Road, was opened in 1969 for 320 children by the London borough of Havering.[65]

The Chafford school, Lambs Lane, was opened in 1934 by Essex county council as Rainham senior, later secondary (modern), school, Upminster Road, for 360 boys and girls.[66] It moved in 1950 to new buildings in Lambs Lane for 450 children.[67] It was enlarged in 1962 and 1971 and was renamed in 1973.[68]

La Salette Roman Catholic junior mixed and infant school, Dover's Corner, New Road, was opened in 1957 as an Aided school for 200. It was enlarged in 1969–70.[69]

In 1965 the administration of the above schools was transferred from Essex county council to the London borough of Havering.

Private schools perhaps included one taught by Wriothesley Danvers, licensed in 1612 to teach in Rainham.[70] The school which Charles Churchill (1731–64) conducted while he was curate at Rainham in 1756–8, may have been at Rainham.[71] In 1823 there was an academy for girls probably at Rainham Hall.[72] Miss M. Swann kept a private school for children aged 5–8½ years for over thirty years until 1958.[73]

CHARITIES FOR THE POOR.[74] John Adgoe (or Adge), waterman, by his will dated 1608, gave a rent-charge of 6*d.* a week from land at Crayford (Kent) to provide bread for the 6 poorest people in Rainham. The rent-charge was redeemed in 1929 for £52 stock.

Thomas Frith of London, scrivener, by deed dated 1612, gave a rent-charge of £5 17*s.* from his estate in South Weald to pay 10*s.* for an annual sermon in Rainham church on Ascension Day, 2*s.* to the minister, 12*d.* to the clerk or sexton, and 2*s.* a week in bread for Rainham poor. In 1966 when it was said that the sermon payment had not been claimed for over 20 years, the vicar agreed to accept it for his discretionary fund.

John Lowen, by will proved 1678, left a rent-charge of £2 12*s.* from his manor of Gerpins to provide six 2*d.* loaves weekly to Rainham poor. In 1938 the rent-charge was redeemed for £104 stock.

Since the 18th century the three bread charities described above have been jointly administered. In *c.* 1750 24 loaves were being distributed each week.[75] During the years 1791–4 only 9 loaves were being given, but from 1795 the number was again 24. In 1811 the income from the three charities was being used to relieve the rates. By 1837, however, it was again being supplied according to the donor's wishes. Bread was still being distributed in 1969.

William Heard, by will proved 1593, gave a rent-charge of 30*s.* from land in Rainham to be distributed at Easter to 15 poor and honest parishioners. By 1620 the charge seems to have been transferred to land in Wennington.[76] It was still being received and distributed in 1818, but had been lost by 1837. John Spicer, by will dated 1598, gave a rent-charge of 6*s.* 8*d.* for the poor. In 1690 the charity was said to be 'abused'. About 1721 an attempt was made to revive it, but there is no later record of payments, which had certainly ceased by 1804. Henry Gabbott, by will dated 1610, gave £5 in trust for the poor. It was in the hands of the vicar in 1613, but nothing further is known about it.[77] Martin Spicer, by will dated 1614, gave 40*s.* stock in trust for the poor. It had been lost by 1690. John Elkin *c.* 1680 gave £20 to the poor. In 1715 this money, with £25 provided by the vestry, was used to build a parish house. In 1721 Mary Johnson, lady of the manor of South Hall, seized the house and evicted the two inmates. There is no evidence that the vestry ever recovered the house.

[58] *Reps. Educ. Cttee. of Council 1874–5* [C. 1265–I], p. 319 H.C. (1875), xxiv; *1875–6* [C. 1513–I], p. 533 H.C. (1876), xxiii.
[59] *Kelly's Dir. Essex* (1894), 270.
[60] *Kelly's Dir. Essex* (1902), 321; Ed. 21/28142; Ed. 21/5130.
[61] Ed. 21/28142.
[62] E.R.O., C/W 1/2/59; inf. from Mr. L. F. Thompson.
[63] E.R.O., C/ME 39A, p. 95; C/ME 41, pp. 7, 319, 716; C/ME 42, p. 769; C/ME 47, p. 558.
[64] Inf. from Essex Educ. Dept. and the school; E.R.O., C/ME 59, pp. 24, 490.
[65] *Romford Recorder*, 25 Apr. 1969. Nicholas Brady was rector of Wennington, 1874–1907.
[66] Ed. 21/28142.
[67] Inf. from Essex Educ. Dept.; *Educ. in Essex* (1945–52), 31.
[68] *Educ. in Essex* (1960–64), 23; *Havering Guide* (1971), 73; inf. from Havering Educ. Dept.
[69] Inf. from Essex Educ. Dept. and the school.
[70] G.L.C., DL/C/340.
[71] *D.N.B.*
[72] *Prospect*, Aug. 1970.
[73] Lewis, *Rainham*, 82; inf. from Mrs. A. G. Swann.
[74] Unless otherwise stated, this section is based on: *Rep. Com. Char.* [108], p. 717 (1837–8), xxv (1); E.R.O., T/P 195/2; E.R.O., D/P 202/8/1; Char. Com. Files.
[75] E.R.O., D/P 202/25/2.
[76] For Heard's Wennington charity see p. 189.
[77] E.R.O., D/P 202/8/2.

UPMINSTER

UPMINSTER lies about 15 miles east of the city of London.[1] It became part of Hornchurch urban district in 1934 and of the London borough of Havering in 1965. The old village at the centre is now a dormitory suburb but there is still farm-land to the north and south. The ancient parish, which contained 3,369 a., was about a mile wide, east and west, and about 6 miles long. Its boundary on the north and west was the Ingrebourne river; ¾ mile south of Hacton Bridge the boundary ran eastwards to the White Hart corner at Hacton, whence it followed the Aveley road south to the stream south of Running Water wood. There it turned east as far as the SE. corner of Little Brickkiln wood before running almost due north for five miles to the SW. corner of Foxberry (or Foxburrow) wood, which it skirted on the west and north. Turning north, the boundary ran through Brick House and continued north for ½ mile or more before turning westwards to rejoin the Ingrebourne.[2]

Upminster's terrain slopes southwards. In the north of the parish, at Upminster Common (formerly Tyler's Common), the ground rises 200 ft. above sea-level, but it drops in the south to 50 ft. Throughout the parish there is a layer of loam, resting in the south on sand and gravel and in the north on London clay. In addition to the Ingrebourne and the Running Water, another stream north of Corbets Tey flowed westwards across the parish. In the late 18th century it was dammed to form a lake in Gaynes Park.[3] Until the 19th century the parish was well supplied with springs; on Tyler's common there was a mineral spring praised in the 18th century but in 1910 said to have little or no medicinal value.[4]

The recorded population of Upminster in 1086 was 39.[5] In 1670 85 houses were listed in the parish.[6] In 1695 there were 370 inhabitants.[7] The number rose to 765 by 1801 and to 1,477 by 1901.[8] The development of the garden suburb after 1906 took the population in 1931 to 5,732. In 1951 the total for the old parish was 13,038, a figure which appears to have altered little since.

A Romano-British farmstead, occupied throughout the 1st century and in the 3rd century, was discovered west of Corbets Tey during gravel-digging in 1962.[9] In medieval Upminster there seem to have been three clusters of settlement: the village itself, and the hamlets of Hacton and Corbets Tey. Then as later the village probably lay along the Hornchurch road (now St. Mary's Lane), and centred on the ancient parish church, which stands at the junction with Corbets Tey Road. South of the Hornchurch road and on the western boundary of the parish Bridge House stood in 1375 on the site of the present Hornchurch stadium.[10] New Place near the eastern boundary was first mentioned *c.* 1475.[11] Hacton and its bridge date from *c.* 1300.[12] Corbets Tey, named in 1461, presumably takes its name from the 13th century family of Corbin or Corvyn or from the 15th-century John Corbyn.[13] Keeling's Cottages, in Ockendon Road, were partly of the 15th century, and with the neighbouring Keelings were demolished after 1958.[14] In addition to the three settlements medieval dwellings were scattered through the parish.[15] Two which dated from the 15th century still survived in 1974: Upminster Hall a mile north of the village on Hall Lane and Great Tomkyns, in Tomkyns (formerly Bird) Lane.[16] Great Tomkyns contains within its exposed timber frame a hall rising the whole height of the house.[17] A 17th-century weatherboarded barn also stands within the partly-dried moat.[18] Pages (formerly Tithe) Farm, Shepherds Hill, is probably late medieval in origin and there are smoke-blackened rafters, now reset, in the central section of the roof. The hall, chimney, and ceiling are 16th-century insertions and the east (service) wing was rebuilt as a parlour in 1663.[19]

Settlement in the 16th and 17th centuries followed the earlier pattern: the village and hamlets continued to expand slowly, and isolated farms were built in the north and south ends of the parish. High House and Hoppy Hall, south of the village on the Corbets Tey road, were built in the late 16th or early 17th century; both were demolished in 1935–6.[20] At Hacton the late-16th-century Park Corner Farm was destroyed by bombing in the Second World War.[21] Great Sunnings, a farm-house of similar date lying south of Corbets Tey, still survives, but its Jacobean panelling and Adam fire-place were removed and sold between 1945 and 1958.[22] In Corbets Tey itself several 17th-century buildings survive. They include the Old Cottage, a timber-framed house at the corner of Corbets Tey Road and Ockendon Road. This was the George inn from 1769 or earlier until 1901. Until 1969 it had an elaborate Jacobean fire-place.[23] Opposite Old Cottage is High House, which has a narrow but elegant late-17th-century brick façade dominating a lower and earlier timber-framed wing.[24] A row of rendered and

[1] O.S. Maps 1/25,000, TQ 58, 59. This article was completed in 1974, and revised in 1976.
[2] O.S. Map 6″ Essex, LXVI, LXXV (surv. 1865–6). The manorial boundaries of 1062 are apparently identical: *P.N. Essex*, 131. Cf. E.R.O., D/P 117/1/1 pp. 6, 205, 211, 3 for perambulations of the parish boundaries in 1700, 1797, 1799, 1812, with slight differences.
[3] See p. 150.
[4] E.R.O., T/P 67/5 p. 205; Morant, *Essex*, i. 110; M. Christy and M. Thresh, *Mineral Waters and Medicinal Springs of Essex*, 6–10, 16–19, 66.
[5] *V.C.H. Essex*, i. 447, 457, 554.
[6] E.R.O., Q/RTh 5 m. 2d.
[7] E.R.O., D/P 117/1/1, p. 195.
[8] *Census*.
[9] *E. Nat.* xxxi. 118–31.
[10] *Cal. Close*, 1374–7, 116.
[11] *Early Chanc. Proc.* ii. 244.
[12] *P.N. Essex*, 132.
[13] Ibid., but Westlake, *Hornchurch Docs.*, 47 mistakenly dates a grant witnessed by Osbert Corbin as 14th-century; it should be dated 1190 × 1209; cf. E.R.O., D/DRu T1/86, 93–4.
[14] R.C.H.M. *Essex*, iv. 162; *Story of Upminster*, ed. H. E. Priestley, iii. 15.
[15] R.C.H.M. *Essex*, iv. 162.
[16] For Upminster Hall see p. 151.
[17] See plate facing p. 161.
[18] Pevsner, *Essex*, 399.
[19] *Story of Upminster*, iii. 24.
[20] R.C.H.M. *Essex*, iv. 162; *Story of Upminster*, iii. 3, 6.
[21] E.R.O., C/W 1/2/57 (6 Oct. 1940).
[22] *Story of Upminster*, iii. 16; R.C.H.M. *Essex*, iv. 162; local inf.
[23] E.R.O., T/P 67/3, p. 83; E.R.O., Q/RLv 24; *Essex Countryside*, x. 156–7; inf. from Mrs. Edwards (owner's wife).
[24] See plate facing p. 17. R.C.H.M. *Essex*, iv. 162; *Story of Upminster*, iii. 12; for its early 19th-century use as a school, see p. 163.

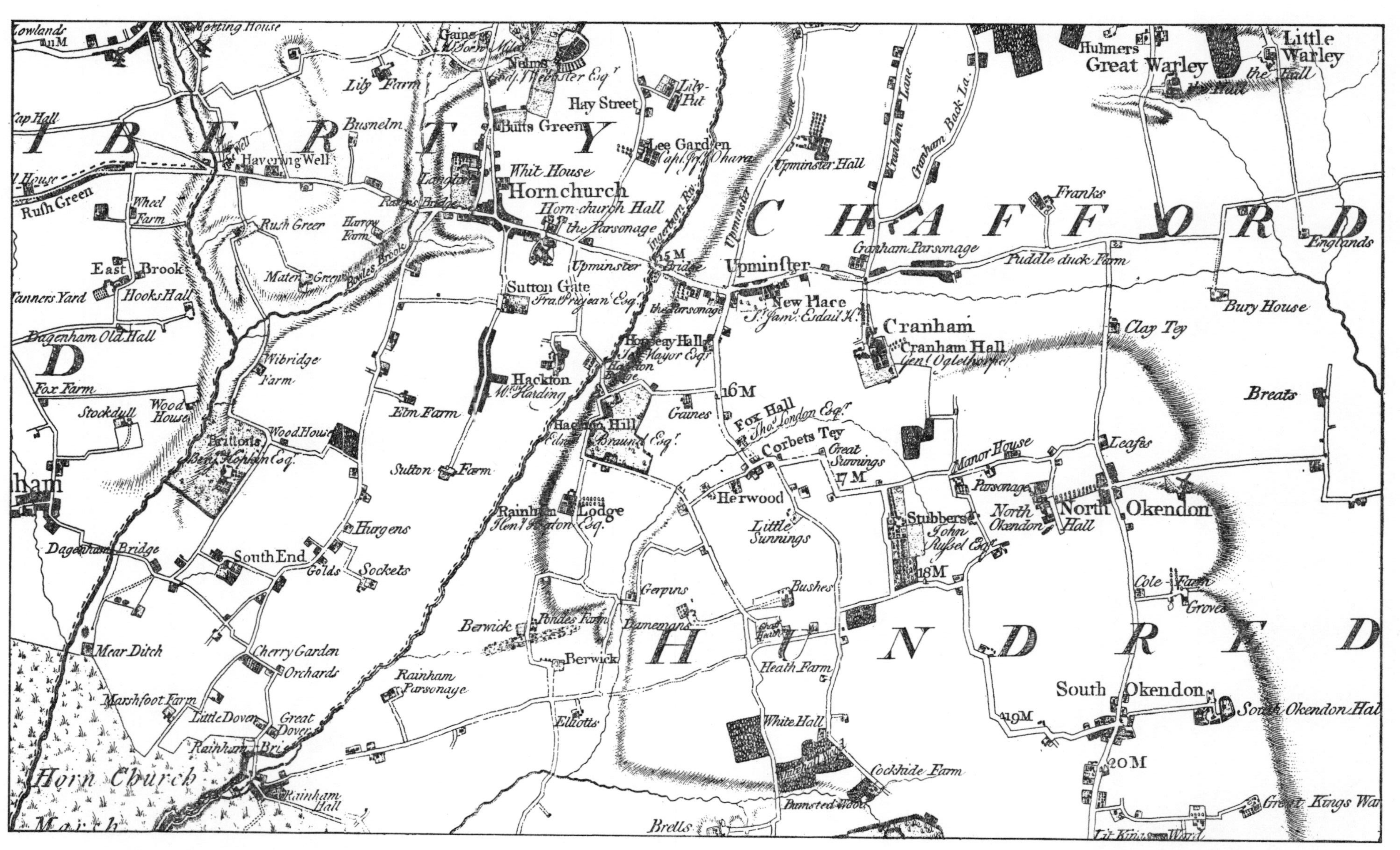

HORNCHURCH AND THE CENTRAL PART OF CHAFFORD HUNDRED, 1777. From Chapman and André's *Map of Essex*, reduced to *c.* $1\frac{1}{2}$ in. to 1 mile.

weatherboarded cottages (nos. 1–8 Harwood Hall Lane) stands to the west. Nos. 1–3 were originally a single dwelling of the early 17th century, but revealing older methods of construction. It was divided when nos. 4–8 were built in the mid 18th century.[25]

From the mid 17th century successful Londoners were buying estates in Upminster, and by 1700 Gaynes, New Place, and Upminster Hall manor had been bought respectively by a brewer, a draper, and a mariner.[26] In his old age Benjamin Braund (d. 1734), a vintner, retired to Corbets Tey, and his bachelor son William (1695–1774), a successful Portugal merchant and City financier, also settled in Upminster.[27] Between 1762 and 1765 William Braund built Hactons at the junction of Little Gaynes and Hacton Lanes. It is a red-brick house with stone quoins and dressings, the main block being flanked by two lower wings containing kitchens and servants' quarters. After military occupation during the Second World War Hactons stood empty until 1954 when it was converted into flats. The brickwork was painted white, and the roof-line of the main block altered to provide windows for an attic storey. The lack of a view from the north front apparently results from planting first undertaken in the 1840s.[28] William Braund was outdone by Sir James Esdaile. After inheriting New Place through his second wife, Esdaile bought Gaynes manor in 1770.[29] He at once undertook a programme of building, renovation, and landscaping which transformed Upminster.[30] In 1771 he began with the Gaynes chapel in the parish church, and he continued with New Place, High House, Hoppy Hall, Gaynes mansion, the West Lodge, Gaynes Cross, Hunts, and the Bell Inn in Upminster, and in Corbets Tey with Londons and Harwood Hall.[31] Of these New Place, Gaynes (or Great Gaynes), Hoppy Hall, and Harwood Hall were occupied by members of his family; Londons took its name from Dr. London, the occupant from 1804 to 1819.[32] In 1974 only two of Esdaile's buildings were still standing: Gaynes Cross (no. 201 Corbets Tey Road) on the site of Gaynes manor pound, and Harwood Hall. The latter, on the lane running from Corbets Tey to Smokeholes on the Aveley road, was built in 1782, enlarged *c.* 1840, and castellated by 1881.[33] Some of Esdaile's programme was carried out by Samuel Hammond, his tenant at West Lodge and the builder responsible for much of the building on Upminster Hill (now St. Mary's Lane) in the later 18th century.[34] Tadlows, no. 251 Corbets Tey Road, is probably another Esdaile building.[35]

North of the village two 18th-century farm-houses still survive: the brick Chapmans or Potkiln farm-house at the corner of Hall Lane and Bird Lane, and the weatherboarded Tylers Hall NE. of Upminster Common. In the late 18th century Tylers Hall consisted of a 'farm end' and a 'family apartment' on which the owner claimed to have spent £1,000; Chapmans was enlarged *c.* 1890.[36] Fox Hall, Corbets Tey Road, is said to have been built in 1718. It originally consisted of a single block with a high-pitched roof and massive flat chimney shafts. A flight of steps led to an ornamental front door. Wings were added at the NW. and SW. corners *c.* 1817. The house was sold in 1923 and demolished soon after.[37] In Ockendon Road, Corbets Tey, is the Huntsman and Hounds public house. It existed as a tavern in 1769, and was rebuilt in 1895–6.[38]

Besides the George and the Huntsman and Hounds in Corbets Tey, there were two other inns in 18th-century Upminster. The Cock at Hacton was the earliest known inn in the parish. It existed in the period 1685–1743, but had closed by 1769.[39] The Bell, on the SE. corner of Cranham Lane and Corbets Tey Road, was in business in 1769, was built or rebuilt in the 18th century, and sold for demolition in 1962.[40]

A late-18th-century map shows a road pattern which remained almost unaltered until the 20th century.[41] From the west three roads entered the parish across the Ingrebourne: the most northerly, Shepherds Hill, skirted the commons on the south and continued as Warley Road; the second, St. Mary's Lane, crossed the waist of the parish from Hornchurch to Cranham;[42] Hacton Lane, the most southerly, entering the parish at Hacton bridge, ran south to Hacton Corner. It continued as Aveley Road, forming the parish boundary with Rainham and Aveley.[43] Nag's Head Lane ran south from Brentwood across the common, continuing as Hall Lane to the village and then as Corbets Tey Road. Bird Lane curved south from the Warley road to join Hall Lane at Chapmans or Potkiln Farm. South of the village Gaynes Lane turned west from Corbets Tey Road at Gaynes Cross to join Hacton Lane north of Hacton Corner. At Corbets Tey the road divided: a lane ran westward to join the Aveley road at Smokeholes, while the main road turned east to North Ockendon. Just east of the hamlet a green lane continued south into Aveley, crossing another

[25] *Story of Upminster*, iii. 14; R.C.H.M. *Essex*, iv. 162. nf. from G.L.C.
[26] See pp. 149, 150, 151.
[27] L. S. Sutherland, *A London Merchant 1695–1774*, 2–7.
[28] E.R.O., D/DRu B3; *Story of Upminster*, iii. 19; E.R.O., T/P 67/5, p. 118.
[29] See pp. 149–50.
[30] E.R.O., T/P 67/3, p. 37; citing an unidentified account of Upminster, *c.* 1789–93.
[31] The order of work after the chapel is unknown. For the chapel, New Place, Gaynes, see pp. 158, 150–1. *Story of Upminster*, iii. 4–7, 10, 17; E.R.O., T/P 67/3, p. 37.
[32] T. L. Wilson, *History and Topography of Upminster* (1881), 131, 134–5; E.R.O., T/P 67/7, p. 32; *Story of Upminster*, iii. 10.
[33] *Story of Upminster*, iii. 17; *V.C.H. Essex*, iv. 68; E.R.O., D/DJn E1. For the interior decoration, V. Body, *Upminster Story*, 26.
[34] *Story of Upminster*, ii. 4–7; iii. 4.
[35] Ibid. iii. 8.
[36] E.R.O., T/P 67/5, p. 145; T/P 67/7, pp. 170–1; *Story of Upminster*, iii. 20–1.
[37] *Story of Upminster*, iii. 9; E.R.O., T/P 67/5, pp. 73, 137; *Essex, historical, biographical and pictorial*, ed. J. Grant; *Country Life*, liv. 297, 550.
[38] E.R.O., Q/RLv 24; E.R.O., T/P 67/3, pp. 83, 87.
[39] E.R.O., Q/SR 446/1; E.R.O., T/P 67/5, p. 119; E.R.O., Q/RLv 24. In 1748 an Upminster will refers to 'the Cock or Skinners and Mealmans' at Hacton Hill: E.R.O., D/DM T16.
[40] E.R.O., Q/RLv 24; E.R.O., T/P 67/3 p. 37; V. Body, *Upminster Story*, 15. The early history of the Bell is obscure. T. L. Wilson's attempts to trace its history from the 17th century are not supported by contemporary evidence.
[41] *Map of Essex* (1777).
[42] The entire length was officially named St. Mary's Lane in 1922: *Story of Upminster*, xiv. 10. Earlier, the western half was known as St. Mary's Lane or Upminster Hill, the eastern as Cranham Lane.
[43] Since the boundary line ran down the middle of the road, Upminster repaired only one wheelrut. In 1714 Upminster agreed with Aveley that each should repair half the length of the common boundary: E.R.O., D/P 117/8/1.

(Bramble Lane) from Rainham to the Ockendons. In 1774 the two roads running east to the Ockendons were connected by a road immediately west of Stubbers; in 1814 this road was closed and a new one opened on the boundary between Upminster and North Ockendon.[44] Chafford Heath, the former meeting-place of the hundred, lay south of Corbets Tey at the junction of Aveley Road and Bramble Lane. It still survived, diminished, in 1799, but by 1842 had been absorbed by neighbouring farms.[45]

The upkeep of the bridges over the Ingrebourne belonged to Upminster alone since Hornchurch, as part of the Liberty of Havering, successfully claimed exemption from responsibility.[46] Upminster bridge (Bridge House bridge, or Lower bridge) on the Hornchurch-Upminster road, existed in 1375, and in 1617 was a horse-bridge in need of repair.[47] Destroyed in the winter of 1709–10, the wooden bridge was replaced by another, the county contributing to the cost.[48] A wooden carriage-bridge was built in 1759, and another in 1827.[49] In 1888 floods made the bridge dangerous for heavy traffic. The county took it over in 1889, and in 1891–2 built a new bridge of brick and iron more than twice the width of the old one.[50] A ford beside Upminster bridge was used regularly until *c.* 1850.[51]

About a mile downstream from Upminster bridge is Hacton bridge. It was originally manorial and already existed in 1299.[52] In the 1630s it was a horse-bridge, but in the 1660s inhabitants of the Barstable and Chafford hundreds persuaded the carpenter in charge of its repair to make it a cart-bridge, since the road was much used by those taking corn to Romford market. Joseph Grave, the younger, absentee lord of Gaynes, objected when he found out, but in 1674 quarter sessions ordered the retention of the cart-bridge with the county paying two-thirds of the cost of its upkeep. A brick bridge was built in 1728. In 1743 the county shared the cost of repair with the lord of Gaynes, but the parish, ignorant of the 1674 ruling, paid for repairs between 1773 and 1820.[53] In 1827 the Solicitor-General nevertheless held that the 1674 ruling still bound the county and the lord of Gaynes, but in 1828 the latter declined responsibility, and by 1857 Hacton Bridge was entirely the county's charge.[54]

The most northerly of Upminster's three bridges is Cockabourne (or Cocklebourne) bridge, which carries the road from Warley and Upminster common to Romford. It was first recorded, as a horse-bridge, in 1613.[55] Damaged in the winter of 1709–10, it was rebuilt in 1714.[56] A brick bridge was built in 1790.[57] By 1892 a new one was needed, and in 1893 the county took over the bridge and rebuilt it with the aid of a contribution from the parish.[58] In 1967 the road was widened and a new bridge was built by Havering L.B.C.[59]

Few large houses were built in Upminster in the 19th and early 20th centuries. Those built by Esdaile satisfied the demand for rented houses from outsiders, most of whom were working in, or had retired from, London. Harold Court, in the far NW. corner of the parish, and Hill Place (sometimes called Hill House) on Upminster Hill, were the two largest houses built in the mid 19th century. In addition Capt. Richard W. Pelly, R.N., the tenant at New Place until 1874, almost wholly rebuilt the east wing *c.* 1867.[60] Harold Court, slated and of white stock brick, was built *c.* 1868 in an Italianate style for W. R. Preston.[61] Preston was a solicitor, farmer, and speculative land developer, who in 1871 undertook to dispose of Brentwood's sewage on 30 a. of adjoining land.[62] He absconded, bankrupt, in 1881, and between 1885 and 1889 Harold Court was occupied by the Shoreditch children's home.[63] A branch of the Essex county lunatic asylum occupied the house from 1892 to 1918, when it became the county's tuberculosis sanatorium. On the introduction of the National Health Service the sanatorium became a hospital in the Brentwood Group. It was sold in 1960 to the Education committee of the Essex county council, and since 1963 it has housed a branch of Brentwood college of education.[64]

Hill Place appears to have been built originally in 1790. Bought in 1827 by Wasey Sterry (d. 1842), a Romford solicitor, it was after his death let to a succession of tenants and sub-tenants until it was bought by the last of them, Temple Soanes, in 1867. Soanes had the house reconstructed in 1871–2 to the restrained Gothic designs of W. G. Bartleet, the architect who had previously remodelled the parish church. In 1927 Hill Place was bought by the Order of the Sacred Heart for use as a convent and school. Bartleet's building survived in 1974: outside, it retained its diapered red brick with stone trim; inside there had been little alteration, and the carving of the marble fire-places, stone corbels, and wooden panelling was well preserved. The windows of the

[44] E.R.O., D/DRu E1; D/DU 35/101. Cf. E.R.O., D/DRu E4, D/P 117/8/11, 12, for disputes between Upminster and North Ockendon in 1819, 1838, 1844, 1847, and 1849 about its upkeep.

[45] *Map of Essex* (1777); O.S. Map 1" (1805 edn., surv. 1799); E.R.O., D/CT 373.

[46] But in 1909 Hornchurch and Upminster shared the cost of a footbridge from Lillyput to Upminster common: E.R.O., T/P 67/6, p. 286.

[47] *Cal. Close*, 1374–7, 116; E.R.O., Q/SBa 1/29; for the later history of this structure, see E.R.O., Q/SR 300/30, 473/66 and D/P 117/8/1 (1692/3, 1701).

[48] E.R.O., Q/SBb 48/32: '. . . and not to be drawn as a precedent'.

[49] E.R.O., T/P 67/5, p. 94; E.R.O., Q/ABp 12; E.R.O., D/P 117/8/3, pp. 45–8; E.R.O., Q/SBb 477/86; 487/11; 479/29, 37; 480/1, 12; 481/21, 52; 482/17, 20, 24; 486/92/2; *Story of Upminster*, x. 11. Cf. E.R.O., Q/SO 28, 30.

[50] E.R.O., T/P 67/2, pp. 15, 20, 110b, 118: 26 ft. 6 in. wide, instead of 11 ft. 5 in.

[51] E.R.O., T/P 67/4, pp. 148–9.

[52] *P.N. Essex*, 132, citing B.L., Add. MS. 37665, a Waltham cartulary of *c.* 1526–40; E.R.O., Q/AB 1 p. 49.

[53] E.R.O., Q/SR 287/14, Q/SBa 2/116, but Q/SR 300/30 calls it a cart-bridge; E.R.O., Q/SBb 487/29; Q/SR 448/106; Q/ABp 12. Unless otherwise stated, this last file provides the information in the rest of this paragraph.

[54] E.R.O., Q/ABz 3/1, pp. 1–2; E.R.O., Q/SO 30.

[55] E.R.O., Q/SR 203/57. It was sometimes called 'Brands Bridge': E.R.O., T/P 67/5, p. 94.

[56] E.R.O., Q/SBb 48/32; E.R.O., D/P 117/8/1 (Dec. 1713).

[57] E.R.O., D/P 117/8/2, p. 1; E.R.O., T/P 67/2 p. 114b.

[58] E.R.O., T/P 67/2, pp. 106a, 107.

[59] Inf. from H.R.L.

[60] Wilson, *Upminster* (1881), 171.

[61] Ibid., 197–8; *Strat. Expr.* 5 Nov. 1881.

[62] The later history of the sewage works is reserved for treatment, under Brentwood, in a later volume. For Preston as land developer, see pp. 26, 28.

[63] Perfect, *Village of Hornchurch*, 128. The home was later at Hornchurch.

[64] *Strat. Expr.* 29 Oct., 5 Nov. 1881; 5 July 1882; 1 Aug. 1883; *Kelly's Dir. Essex* (1886); E.R.O., Q/ALc 9, pp. 138, 276; *Essex Lunatic Asylum, Visitor's Rep.* (1892–3), p. 6; *Essex & Colchester Mental Hosps., Visitors' Rep.* (1918–19), p. 16, and *Chaplain's Rep.* (1918–19), p. 26; E.R.O., C/ME 55, p. 267; *Educ. in Essex* (1960–4), 110.

main staircase were made by William Morris to designs of Burne-Jones.[65]

In the early 20th century only one house comparable to Harold Court and Hill Place was built. This was Upminster Court, Hall Lane, built in 1905–6 for A. E. Williams by Sir Charles Reilly, himself a resident in the parish.[66] The house, with 22 a., was bought in 1946 by Essex county council for use as the education office of the South Essex division. In 1970 it housed the Havering education offices, and the gardens were a borough nursery.[67]

Of the 19th-century inns and beerhouses the Compasses on the south side of Upminster Hill (fl. 1845–70) had a six-day licence, as did the Masons Arms in Cranham Lane, until 1887. The latter, which was already in business in 1848, was rebuilt in 1928.[68] At Hacton the White Hart, opened as a beerhouse in 1854, also survives. The Shepherd and Dog was built *c.* 1848 on Shepherds Hill leading from the Common to Cockabourne Bridge; it was rebuilt after a sale of the property in 1929.[69]

The transformation of Upminster from an Essex village to a London suburb occurred after 1900. The railway had arrived in 1885 but the unwillingness of the major landowners to sell land permitted little development in the next fifteen years.[70] Then in 1901 Dowsing & Davis, of Romford, bought the 10 a. of the Mavisbank property on the north side of Upminster Hill. By 1902 Gaynes, Champion, and Branfill Roads had been laid out, but at the end of 1909 there were only 24 houses on the estate, and it was sold in 1911 to W. P. Griggs & Co.[71]

(Sir) Peter Griggs, who had previously played a large part in the development of Ilford, had turned his attention to Upminster by 1906. He planned to develop 700 a. of the Upminster Hall estate as a garden suburb or 'a new town on an American plan'. North of the railway, houses were to have ½ a. each, south of it would be the shops and smaller houses. Prices were at first intended to range from £455 to £1,145, but leaseholds were soon being advertised from £395, and in 1908 from £295 to £1,250, with freeholds suggested at £395–£1,595.[72] The first brick was laid on 17 November 1906; within a year 44 new houses were built or under construction north of the railway, and by 1909 there were 96. All were private houses except for a 'high-class preparatory school' and a doctor's house. South of the railway, shops were being built by 1907, and by 1909 seventy-nine houses had also been started.[73] North of the railway the new roads were all 'Gardens', named at first after former manorial families of Upminster, except for the substitution of the alien 'Waldgrave' for the less aristocratic 'Latham'; between the railway and Cranham Lane to the south were Howard and St. Lawrence Roads.[74] Development continued in the following years, and even, though at a slower pace, throughout the First World War.[75]

Griggs bought New Place, with about 70 a., in 1909, but it was not until 1924, after the last occupant's death, that the house was demolished, part of the property sold to the parish council for offices, and the rest of the estate laid out for building with frontages at £10 a foot. In 1938 Sunnyside and Argyle Gardens indicated the boundaries of the estate.[76] The death of Henry Joslin in 1927 released more of Upminster for development: an attempt to sell his 400 a. as a single estate failed in 1928, and in 1929 his holdings were offered in 17 lots. Hunts farm, Hoppy Hall farm, the Bridge (House) farm, and Gaynes Park north of the lake had all been built over by 1938, thus completing the development of central Upminster.[77] The area east and north of Upminster Hall was developed in the 1950s and 1960s in a style similar to that of the garden suburb north of the railway.[78] At the corner of Hacton Lane and Little Gaynes Lane the Optimist, the only new Upminster inn of the 20th century, was opened in 1956.[79]

The hamlet of Corbets Tey shrank in population between 1891 and 1911, a fact reflected in the closure of the Anchor public house in 1896 and the George in 1901.[80] Some building N. and NE. of the hamlet occurred in the 1930s, with in-filling in the 1950s. Londons was demolished after 1958 and by 1965 Londons Close had replaced it.[81] The South Essex crematorium, Ockendon Road, was opened in 1957.[82] South of Corbets Tey much of the farm-land east of the Aveley Road and on both sides of Bramble Lane has been given over to gravel-working since 1962. By 1974 the former site of Chafford Heath, and the cottage-chapel and burying-ground there, had been returned to farm-crops, Bramble farm was uninhabited, and Heath Farm no longer standing.[83]

The construction of the Southend arterial road after the First World War cut Upminster in two. The road was officially opened in 1925; the creation of the Hall Lane fly-over in 1965–6 improved communication between the lands north and south of the road, but the renaming of Bird Lane north of the road as Tomkins Lane *c.* 1968 acknowledged indirectly the arterial road's divisive effect.[84]

[65] *Story of Upminster*, ii. 13; E.R.O., D/DSt T40, E15/2–3, 5–7, 9–11; E.R.O., T/P 67/9, p. 17; Wilson, *Upminster* (1881), 175–6; see also pp. 159, 162.

[66] See plate facing p. 129.

[67] Reilly came to High House, Upminster, in 1902: E.R.O., T/P 67/5, pp. 2, 165; 67/4, p. 39; E.R.O., C/ME 40, p. 311; E.R.O., C/TE 648; E.R.O., D/F 8, bdle 454/37; *Havering Official Guide* (1969–70) pp. 34–5, 59.

[68] *Story of Upminster*, x. 25–6; *White's Dir. Essex* (1848); *Kelly's Dir. Essex* (1870); E.R.O., T/P 67/1, p. 168; T/P 67/10, p. 41.

[69] *Story of Upminster*, x. 26.

[70] E.R.O., T/P 67/3, pp. 70, 78, 119; 67/5, p. 135. But E.R.O., D/F 8 bdles 454, 494 contain many drafts, 1885–1900, for the development of the Upminster Hall estate south of the railway.

[71] It was renamed Branfill Park: E.R.O., T/P 67/1 p. 205d; T/P 67/5, p. 53; T/P 67/6, p. 308; T/P 67/7, p. 147.

[72] A. A. Jackson, *Semi-Detached London*, 59–61; *V.C.H. Essex*, v. 189, 198, 251; E.R.O., T/P 67/5, pp. 264–5; 67/6 pp. 59, 77, 91, 148; 67/9, p. 56; *Romford Handbk.* (1908), xix, 60–5.

[73] For the shops see plate facing p. 160.

[74] E.R.O., T/P 67/7, pp. 108, 149, 308.

[75] E.R.O., T/P 67/7, pp. 234, 266; T/P 67/8, p. 51; T/P 67/10, p. 18. Cf. O.S. Map, 6", Essex LXXIX, LXXX (3rd edn., revised 1915). Not all roads authorised were built, For war-time activity: *Essex Countryside*, xiii. 526; E.R.O.. D/F 5/11/5: 30 July 1918.

[76] E.R.O., T/P 67/6, p. 270; T/P 181/11/27; see below, pp. 151, 155; O.S. Map, 6", Essex, LXXIX, LXXX (1938 edn.).

[77] E.R.O., *Sale Cat.*, A314, A1047; O.S. Map, 6", Essex (1938 edn.).

[78] *Hornchurch Official Guide* (1951, 1953, 1960–1).

[79] *Story of Upminster*, x. 26.

[80] E.R.O., T/P 67/3, p. 83.

[81] O.S. Map, 6", Essex (1938 edn.); local inf.; *Story of Upminster*, iii. 10; *Havering Official Guide* (1965–6).

[82] See p. 155.

[83] *E. Nat.* xxxi. 118; see also below, pp. 152, 160.

[84] *V.C.H. Essex, Bibliography*, 53; *Havering Official Guide* (1965–6, 1971). For the arterial road see plate facing p. 160.

A coach service which passed through Upminster on its way to Aldgate from South Ockendon was discontinued in 1846.[85] In 1855 the nearest carriers travelling to London were those of Hornchurch and Romford, and a horse bus plied daily between Romford and Corbets Tey.[86] The Eastern Counties railway's main line from London to Romford, opened in 1839, extended to Brentwood in 1840, and to Colchester in 1843, passed through the northern tip of Upminster parish. The nearest stations were at Romford and Brentwood until 1868, when Harold Wood station was opened. The London, Tilbury and Southend railway's short cut from Barking to Pitsea was opened as far as Upminster in 1885 and from Upminster to Pitsea in 1888.[87] The Romford-Grays branch followed: a single track from Upminster to Grays in 1892 and Romford in 1893.[88] In 1902 the District Line's extension from Whitechapel to Bow made possible a journey without changes from Upminster to Earl's Court, but it was not until 1932, after electrification, that District trains ran regularly to Upminster.[89] The first motor bus service came from Stratford Broadway to Upminster in 1921; the nuisance caused by hundreds of Sunday visitors led the parish council in 1926 to refuse permission to the London General Omnibus Company for a second service.[90]

There were post offices in the village and at Corbets Tey in 1848.[91] From 1889 telegrams were sent through the former, and a public telephone was installed there in 1913.[92] An Upminster telephone exchange was installed in 1922 over Green's Stores in Station Road, and in 1929 a new one was erected in St. Mary's Lane on the south side east of the crossroads.[93]

Of the notables connected with Upminster the earliest was Alice Perrers (d. 1400), the mistress of Edward III, who lived and was buried in the parish.[94] Two 17th-century rectors, John Robotham and John Newton, are remembered by scholars for their writings on religion and mathematics, and a third, William Derham, Canon of Windsor (d. 1735), combined theology and natural science with his pastoral duties.[95] Sir James Esdaile (d. 1793), Lord Mayor of London 1777–8, lived at New Place.[96] Among 19th-century residents were J. W. Benn, M.P., later Sir James Wedgwood Benn, Bt. (1850–1922), and his family, which included his son William, later Viscount Stansgate (1877–1960).[97] F. M. Sir Evelyn Wood, V.C. (1838–1919), rented Upminster properties more than once.[98] T. L. Wilson (1833–1919), carpenter, builder, and undertaker, was the village historian. He published two editions of his work in 1856 and 1881, and from 1881 until within weeks of his death in 1919 he continued to gather in his scrapbooks materials relating to the parish.[99]

A poor club existed in Upminster as early as 1774: between that year and 1797 the vestry paid club money for inhabitants, and in 1820 made an advance to a sick parishioner until his club allowance was paid.[1] In 1814 the Huntsman and Hounds at Corbets Tey started a friendly society, and in 1828 the Upminster Friendly Institution took in no fewer than 26 surrounding parishes.[2] A poor (Women's, or Clothing & Shoe) club existed by 1829; it continued with diminishing support in later years, until 1915, having amalgamated with a Coal club formed in the later 19th century by Miss Rigby, of Hactons.[3] The Bellringers Club, founded in 1889, changed its name to the Loyal Victorian friendly society in 1893 and was still flourishing in 1907.[4] Branches of the United Patriots benefit society and the National friendly deposit society were formed in 1899 and 1907; the latter existed in 1937.[5] A Corbets Tey friendly society, founded *c.* 1895–1900, existed in 1911.[6]

The Upminster cricket club was formed in 1858 and reformed in 1883.[7] It survived the secession of a group of young gentlemen, newcomers to Upminster, who formed under the presidency of W. G. Grace the short-lived Upminster Friars cricket club, 1896–99.[8] Since 1933 the Upminster cricket club has played in the recreation ground (Upminster Park). The Upminster golf club was formed in 1927, with Upminster Hall as its clubhouse.[9] The Capitol cinema, later the Gaumont, was opened in 1929 and demolished in 1974.[10]

MANORS. In 1086 there were three manors in Upminster.[11] Walter of Douai held 6½ hides and 30 a. which became the manor of Gaynes. Waltham abbey held 2½ hides and 40 a. which became the manor of Upminster Hall. The third manor, held by Mauger under Odo, bishop of Bayeux, comprised 1½ hide. It appears to have become part of the manor of Bumpsteads, which is reserved for treatment under Aveley.

The largest of the three Domesday manors, known at first as the manor of *UPMINSTER*, but later

[85] E.R.O., T/P 67/5, p. 11; T/P 95/1, p. 138.
[86] *Kelly's Dir. Essex* (1855).
[87] *V.C.H. Essex*, v. 188; *Essex Weekly News* (7 Feb. 1868); E.R.O., T/P 67/7, p. 208; T/P 67/1, pp. 89, 91, 91b, 207–8; T/P 67/2, p. 71.
[88] E.R.O., T/P 67/2, pp. 124, 131.
[89] *V.C.H. Essex*, v. 26, 71.
[90] C.D.L., W. Marston Acres, 'Upminster Past and Present', (TS *c.* 1940), 161; E.R.O., T/P 181/11/27: 29 Aug., 28 Nov. 1924, 25 Sept. 1925, 1 Oct. 1926.
[91] *White's Dir. Essex* (1848).
[92] E.R.O., T/P 67/2, p. 56; T/P 67/5, p. 20; T/P 67/7, p. 267.
[93] 'Upminster Past and Present', 161.
[94] See p. 149.
[95] *D.N.B.*; for Derham, see also C. K. Aked, 'William Derham and "The Artificial Clockmaker",' *Antiquarian Horology* (1970); the Upminster branch public library has recently acquired a hitherto unknown portrait of Derham in his earlier years.
[96] See pp. 149–50; Wilson, *Upminster* (1881), 134–5; *Hist. Parl., Commons*, 1754–90, ii. 575.
[97] E.R.O., T/P 67/6, pp. 331, 350.
[98] E.R.O., T/P 67/2, p. 121; *Strat. Expr.* 28 May 1881, p. 8.
[99] T. L. Wilson, *Sketches of Upminster* (1856); *History and Topography of Upminster* (1881). 14 scrapbooks and indexes have been deposited in E.R.O.: T/P 67/1–14. Cf. *Story of Upminster*, xiii. 22–7 for details of his life.
[1] E.R.O., D/P 117/12/7–9, 12, 16.
[2] E.R.O., T/P 67/7, p. 24; E.R.O., Q/SO 23, ff. 36, 82.
[3] E.R.O., D/DRu C4/2, F12/4–7, 10–13, 17–21, 23, 25–7, 30, 32, 35, 40; D/DSt E15/5, 7–8; T/P 67/1–3, 5–8.
[4] E.R.O., T/P 67/2, pp. 43, 66–7; T/P 67/3, p. 10; T/P 67/7, p. 7a.
[5] E.R.O., T/P 67/3, p. 123; T/P 67/6, p. 47; *Kelly's Dir. Essex* (1937).
[6] E.R.O., T/P 67/5, p. 245; T/P 67/6, p. 319; T/P 67/7, p. 83.
[7] *Upminster Cricket Club, 1858–1958: Hist. & Centenary programme;* E.R.O., T/P 67/1, pp. 32, 41; T/P 67/2, p. 22; T/P 67/3, p. 110.
[8] E.R.O., T/P 67/3 pp. 71, 73–4, 91, 94, 97, 125–6, 129; 67/6 p. 320.
[9] E.R.O., T/P 187/11/27; see also below, pp. 151, 155.
[10] 'Upminster Past and Present', 161.
[11] *V.C.H. Essex*, i. 447, 457, 554.

styled *GAYNES* or *ENGAYNES*, included the whole parish except the north-eastern and the southern extremities.[12] Before the Conquest the manor had been held by Swein the swarthy.[13] In 1086 it was held in demesne by Walter of Douai, presumably as part of his honour of Bampton, to which it belonged in 1212; it was then appurtenant to Bulwick (Northants.).[14]

In Henry I's reign the tenant in demesne 'by inheritance' was Richard FitzUrse, from whom the manor passed to his son Reynold, to Reynold's daughter Maud, and to Maud's son William de Curtenay. On Curtenay's death without issue in 1215 his lands were claimed by Viel Engaine and Roger Gernet, descendents of Richard FitzUrse's daughters.[15]

During the recent civil war, however, William de Cauntelo had intruded into some of Curtenay's manors. In 1218 Viel Engaine was said to owe the king 10 marks for having seisin of Upminster, saving to Ada, Curtenay's widow, her dower in the manor. In 1221 Viel bought out Ada's interest in Upminster by assigning her an equivalent income, and in 1223 he reached an agreement with William de Cauntelo, whereby Viel secured the Upminster manor, but surrendered Bulwick.[16]

Viel Engaine, from whose family the manor took its name, died in 1248 and was succeeded in turn by his sons Henry (d. 1272) and John (d. Jan. 1297).[17] In July 1297 John Engaine, son of the last and later Lord Engaine, on going overseas, was licensed to enfeoff Simon of Havering with the manor but not the advowson. Simon was to hold the manor in fee farm, the first payment being made 10 years after the licence.[18] The manor was held by Simon in 1303, and by Sir John of Havering in 1346. John was presumably the grandson and heir of Simon mentioned in litigation of 1314.[19] He had died by 1367 and the descent of the manor becomes uncertain.[20] John's widow, Lora, who later married William Morewood, clearly had an interest in the manor until her death on 4 November 1393, but in 1373 and 1378 three kinsmen and next heirs of Robert of Havering quitclaimed the reversion of Gaynes and other manors to feoffees of Alice Perrers.[21] At an unknown date Sir John Deyncourt, a follower of John of Gaunt, was also granted the reversion, but he died a day before Lora Morewood, leaving his son Roger, a minor, as his heir.[22] In 1400 Alice Perrers died, devising 'her' manor of Gaynes to her younger daughter Joan Despaigne or Southerey, but it was entrusted, to Joan's exclusion, to guardians for Roger Deyncourt during his minority.[23] A compromise was later arranged, and by the end of 1406 Joan had surrendered her life-interest in return for an annuity of 40 marks.[24]

Roger Deyncourt held the manor in 1412, was acquiring land in Upminster in 1429, and died in 1455.[25] His son, Thomas Deyncourt of Upminster, can be traced between 1441 and 1464.[26] Anne, the widow of Hugh Cawood, lord of Gaynes, was named as lady between 1504 and 1515.[27] In 1526 Richard Deyncourt of Maidstone sold to Nicholas Wayte, citizen of London, the manor with other properties in Upminster and Bollesworth (Derb.) previously belonging to Anne Cawood and devised by her to Deyncourt.[28] Wayte, who was the husband of Deyncourt's half-sister Ellen, died in 1542, and in 1543 his heirs sold the manor with 1,000 a. of land to Ralph Latham, citizen and goldsmith of London.[29]

Latham (d. 1557) was succeeded by his son William, who in 1587 sold Gaynes to Gerard Dewes (d. 1592).[30] In 1593 Gerard's son Paul re-conveyed the manor to William Latham, with remainder to William Latham his son, husband of Gerard Dewes's daughter Alice.[31] In 1612 Gaynes was settled on Ralph, son of William Latham the younger, on his marriage.[32] Ralph Latham, who became Common Serjeant of London, mortgaged the manor in 1641.[33] By 1650 Joseph Grave, brewer of London, possessed the manor and devised it to his son, the Revd. Joseph Grave.[34] On Joseph's death in 1719 or 1720 the manor passed to his brother Peter, who devised it *c.* 1721 to his wife Jane.[35] Amos White bought the manor from Jane Grave and her son in 1722, and in 1747 sold it to George Montgomerie of St. George's, Hanover Square (Mdx.).[36] Montgomerie died in 1765 or 1766, and in 1770 his trustees conveyed Gaynes with 100 a. to Sir James Esdaile, cooper, and Lord Mayor of London 1777–8, who already held New Place.[37]

Sir James (d. 1793) was succeeded by Peter Esdaile, his son by his first marriage, on whose death in 1817 Gaynes passed to James Esdaile, son of Peter's half-brother.[38] James separated much of the Gaynes estate, which Sir James had increased to some 750 a., from the lordship of the manor. About 540 a. were sold in 1820, but New Place (78 a.) and Hunts farm (130 a.) immediately to the south were retained,

[12] E.R.O., D/DZb 5: the manor boundaries in 1752.
[13] *V.C.H. Essex*, i. 554.
[14] *Bk. of Fees*, i. 122.
[15] *Cur. Reg. R.* viii. 213–15; *E.A.T.* N.S. xi. 98–100; *Complete Peerage*, v. 72–3.
[16] *Pipe R.* 1218 (P.R.S. N.S. xxxix), 75; *Cur. Reg. R.* x. 253; xi. 271–2; cf. ibid. viii. 213–15.
[17] *Cal. Inq. p.m.* i, p. 42; iii, pp. 279–80; iv, pp. 83–4; *Complete Peerage*, v. 72–3.
[18] *Cal. Pat.* 1292–1301, 292. By 1367 a rent of a pair of gilt spurs, worth 6*d.*, was also paid: *Cal. Inq. p.m.* xii. pp. 113–16.
[19] *Feud. Aids*, ii. 151, 169. Simon was still alive in 1306: *Horn. Docs.* 96, 98; *Year Bk. 8 Edw. II* (Selden Soc. xxxvii), 22–3.
[20] *Cal. Inq. p.m.* xii, p. 115.
[21] *Feet of F. Essex*, iii. 169; *Cal. Inq. Misc.* iv, 10; *Cal. Pat.* 1377–81, 503.
[22] *Complete Peerage*, xii(2), p. 879; C 137/31/172; *John of Gaunt's Register, 1379–1383* (Camd. Soc. 3rd ser. lvi, lvii), 9, 70, 407; *Cal. Pat.* 1391–6, 582.
[23] *E.R.* xiii. 177; *Cal. Fine R.* 1399–1405, 179, 205, 216; *Cal. Close*, 1405–9, 39–40.
[24] *Cal. Close*, 1405–9, 227.
[25] *Feud. Aids*, vi. 444; *Feet of F. Essex*, iv. 14; J. Weever, *Ancient Funerall Monuments*, 651.
[26] Hist. MSS. Com. 77, *De L'Isle & Dudley*, i. pp. 18–19; *Cal. Close*, 1461–8, 238.
[27] *Early Chanc. Proc.* iv. 380, 391.
[28] C.P. 40/1052 Carte rott. 2, 4.
[29] Wayte's memorial brass in Upminster church reveals the relationship: Ellen and Richard were children of Robert Deyncourt of Aveley; *L. & P. Hen. VIII*, xviii(1) p. 365. For Latham's purchase of the manor of Upminster Hall, see below, p. 151.
[30] *Cal. Pat.* 1557–8, 302; C 66/1296.
[31] C 142/342/129.
[32] C.P. 25(2)/294/10 Jas. I Hil.; Prob. 11/123 ff. 207v.–209 for date; E.R.O., D/DL T1/770.
[33] E.R.O., D/DA T449.
[34] Ibid.
[35] E.R.O., D/DU 18/30; D/DZb 1; D/DA T449.
[36] E.R.O., D/DU 18/30; D/DZb 2. In 1722 the manor was being offered for £2,400 (*Coll. Top. Gen.* i (1834), 331), roughly a third of the price paid in 1686 for Upminster Hall.
[37] E.R.O., D/DZb 2; Wilson, *Upminster* (1881), 134–5.
[38] E.R.O., D/DU 18/30; T/P 67/1.

together with the lordship. The Esdaile interest in Upminster was virtually ended in 1839 by a sale, at which James Cuddon of Norwich bought the lordship.[39] Cuddon held the lordship as late as 1849; in 1852 Mrs. Branfill, lady of the manor of Upminster Hall, declined to purchase it, being advised that it was valueless.[40] Leopold Leopold was lord of the manor in 1854, Dr. George Rowe following him, 1856–9.[41] Joseph Jackson, a cabinet warehouseman of Shoreditch and Tottenham, (d. 1871) was lord of the manor by 1862; he devised the manor to his older brother John (d. *c.* 1882).[42] John Jackson, after what appears to be a lapse of trustees (1885–95), was succeeded by his nephew, John Atkinson (fl. 1899–1927).[43] In the years 1933–5 Amy Atkinson, widow, was lady.[44]

At the break-up of the Gaynes estate in 1820 the Revd. John Clayton (1745–1843), pastor of the Weigh-House chapel (Lond.), bought Hoppy Hall farm and part of Gaynes Park, the rest of the park being purchased by his second son, the Revd. George Clayton (1783–1862) pastor of York St. chapel, Walworth (Lond.).[45] In 1844 George Clayton bought out the other interests in the park, and his widow Rebecca (d. 1873) thus had a life-interest in the whole 105 a. of Gaynes Park, where after her second marriage in 1865 to Henry Joslin the younger (d. 1927) she and her husband lived.[46] After Mrs. Joslin's death the estate was sold in 1874 to H. A. Gilliat (1852–90), and in the same year Gilliat added to it Londons farm (52 a.).[47] Gilliat attempted to establish a large-scale dairy-farm, but this failed, and in 1878 he sold the Gaynes Park estate to its former occupier, Henry Joslin.[48] By 1887 Joslin had added the whole of Hoppy Hall farm (98 a.) to the estate, and in 1890 he bought Hunts farm (130 a.).[49] In 1929, after his death, the estate was sold for building development.[50]

The manor-house lay in Gaynes Lane. In 1752 it appears to have been no more than a farm-house, but after Esdaile's purchase of the manor in 1770 a new house was built, probably designed by James Paine.[51] Construction had begun in 1771; the house, thought to have cost £22,000, was probably completed by 1774 when Esdaile took the property into his own hands.[52] In 1776 and 1779 Gaynes was advertised as 'a complete residence for either Nobleman or Gentleman'.[53]

In 1856 the building was described, a generation after its demolition, as having had a central mansion with two linked wings. It had a lofty Corinthian portico, and was entered by winding steps on either side. The principal floor, being raised, gave an extended view southwards and the well-proportioned rooms were said to have been elegant rather than large.[54]

Attempts were made to sell the house in 1819 and 1820, but when no buyer came forward, the 'centre mansion' and the west wing were demolished and the remaining east wing and park sold.[55] In 1845 the east wing was also taken down, and in its place a brick house 'in the Tudor style' was erected in 1846 for 'about £7,000'.[56] It was demolished after the sale of the estate in 1929.[57]

Gaynes park was created in the late 18th century. In 1752 the house had been surrounded by fields extending south to a small stream; by 1789 the stream had been dammed and widened to produce a lake, and fields beyond it also brought in to make a park of some 100 a. A plantation with a meandering path closed the view to the west and from the eastern boundary near to the house another plantation looped westward into the park, presumably to cut out a view of Corbets Tey and even the newly-built Harwood Hall. In 1974 only the lake with some grassland immediately to the north survived as Parklands public park.[58]

The manor of *NEW PLACE* lay south of Cranham (now St. Mary's) Lane. For much of its history it was part of the Gaynes estate, and the lord of that manor often lived there. In 1557 it comprised 50 a. of freehold land held of the manors of Cranham and South Ockendon.[59] The house was then the residence of Ralph Latham, owner of Gaynes and Upminster Hall.[60] New Place descended with Gaynes until the 1640s. Serjeant Ralph Latham (d. *c.* 1648) certainly lived at New Place, and Hamlet Latham, his son, was perhaps living there in 1650.[61] The manor appears to have passed to Hamlet's sister Mary (d. 1671), wife of (Sir) Thomas Skipwith (Bt.), of Metheringham (Lincs.), and to have been sold by Skipwith in 1677 to John Rayley, draper of London.[62]

Rayley (d. 1706) left New Place to his widow Hester (d. 1724), from whom it passed to Sarah, wife of Joseph Mayor, and formerly the wife of John Rayley (d. 1718), son of the previous John.[63] Mrs. Mayor (d. 1757) settled New Place on her husband's niece Mary Mayor, on Mary's marriage in 1748 with (Sir) James Esdaile.[64] From 1757 the Esdailes lived at New Place; in 1770 Esdaile acquired Gaynes, and New Place descended with the lordship of that until 1839, when it sold with 63 a. and the rights in St. Mary's (or Gaynes) chapel in the parish church.[65] The purchaser was James Harmer (1777–1853),

[39] E.R.O., T/P 67/1; D/DJn E 1.
[40] E.R.O., D/DZb 3; D/DRu C 4/2.
[41] E.R.O., D/DZb 3.
[42] Ibid.; E.R.O., T/P 67/4.
[43] Ibid.
[44] E.R.O., D/DZb 3.
[45] E.R.O., T/P 67/1, p. 222; E.R.O., Sage Coll. *Sale Cats.* vol. ii. 9; E.R.O., D/CT 373.
[46] E.R.O., T/P 67/1, p. 143a; E.R.O., Sage Coll. *Sale Cats.* vol. ii. 9.
[47] E.R.O., T/P 67/1, p. 222.
[48] E.R.O., T/P 67/2, pp. 62–4.
[49] E.R.O., *Sale Cat.* A314; E.R.O., T/P 67/2, p. 79.
[50] E.R.O., *Sale Cat.* A314, A1047.
[51] E.R.O., D/DZb 5; Wilson, *Upminster* (1856), 75–6; inf. from Mr. P. Leach. Gaynes is not, however, credited to Paine in any edition of the *Ambulator* between 1774 and 1811, nor is it mentioned in Paine's own *Noblemen's and Gentlemen's Houses.*
[52] E.R.O., D/P 117/12/7 (11 July, 6 Oct. 1774); E.R.O., T/P 67/5, p. 116.
[53] E.R.O., T/P 67/7, pp. 25, 50.
[54] Wilson, *Upminster* (1856), 75–6.
[55] E.R.O., D/DU 18/31, 35/77; E.R.O., T/P 67/7, pp. 37, 45.
[56] E.R.O., T/P 67/5, pp. 91, 116; E.R.O., *Sale Cat.* A314; *White's Dir. Essex* (1848).
[57] E.R.O., *Sale Cats.* A314, A1047.
[58] E.R.O., D/DZb 5; Wilson, *Upminster* (1881), 138; O.S. Map 1", (1805 edn., surv. 1799).
[59] C 142/111/29.
[60] Prob. 11/39 (P.C.C. 36 Wrastley).
[61] *Misc. Gen. Her.* 2nd ser., ii (1888), 57; E.R.O., D/DA T449, 450; D/DL T1/783. Born in 1622 or 1623, Hamlet Latham was still alive in 1659: Venn, *Alumni Cantab.* I, iii. 49; E.R.O., D/DL T1/783.
[62] Wilson, *Upminster* (1881), 170; Morant, *Essex*, i. 110; E.R.O., D/P 117/1/1 burials.
[63] E.R.O., D/DU 18/19; E.R.O., D/P 117/1/1 burials; Morant, *Essex*, i. 110.
[64] E.R.O., D/DU 18/19; E.R.O., T/P 67/7, p. 23
[65] E.R.O., D/DU 18/31; D/DJn E1.

alderman of London and owner of the *Weekly Dispatch*. His descendants, the Umfreville family, held New Place until 1909, when they sold it with some 70 a. to W. P. Griggs, the estate developer.[66]

About 1720 it was stated that the 'old seat' of New Place was down and that nothing but the outhouses remained.[67] The house is usually said to have been rebuilt *c.* 1775 by Sir James Esdaile; if so, there was an earlier 18th-century house on the site, for Mrs. Mayor 'died at her seat at New Place' in 1757.[68] Esdaile's house was of red brick, and in 1839 was described as having 'a handsome uniform elevation with wings, ascended by a flight of stone steps under a Gothic Portico . . . '. The east wing was rebuilt and enlarged *c.* 1870.[69] The house was occupied by tenants until 1922, and in 1924 was demolished.[70]

The stable-block of New Place was used as the Upminster council offices from 1924 to 1934, and as a branch of Hornchurch public library from 1936 to 1963. It has since been vacant. Over it is a clock, said to have come from Woolwich arsenal. Its existence led to the alternative style of Clock House being given to New Place.[71]

The manor of *UPMINSTER* or *UPMINSTER HALL* or *WALTHAM HALL* was one of seventeen manors given by Earl Harold to his newly-founded college (later abbey) of Waltham Holy Cross, a gift that was confirmed by the king in 1062.[72] The manor lay in the north and east of the parish; on the south it was bounded by Cranham Lane and on the west by Nag's Head Lane and Hall Lane. Waltham Abbey held the manor until the Dissolution. It was granted to Thomas Cromwell, earl of Essex, but reverted to the Crown on his forfeiture in 1540.[73] It was sold in 1543 to Ralph Latham, goldsmith of London.[74] Ralph (d. 1557) was succeeded by his son William, a minor.[75] William Latham leased most of the manor in 1576 to George Wiseman for 61 years, and in 1594 sold the freehold to Roger James (d. 1596), mercer of London.[76] Roger James, son of the previous Roger, sold Upminster Hall in 1628 to Serjeant Ralph Latham.[77]

In 1642 Latham sold the manor to Elizabeth Hicks, Lady Campden (d. 1643), who settled it on her great-grandson, Henry Noel.[78] On Henry's death in 1677 Upminster Hall passed to his elder brother Edward Noel, later earl of Gainsborough, subject to the life-interest of Henry's widow.[79] Gainsborough sold the manor in 1686 to Andrew Branfill of Stepney (Mdx.), master mariner.[80] It was then occupied, with its two farms, by Francis Seamer and Samuel Springham.[81]

Upminster Hall descended in the Branfill family for over 200 years.[82] In 1842 the estate consisted of 674 a., of which 354 were in hand.[83] On the death in 1844 of Champion Branfill (IV) it passed to his widow Ann Eliza (d. 1873) who was succeeded by her second son Benjamin Branfill (d. 1899).[84] Benjamin's heir was his grandson Champion Andrew Branfill, the last of his family to hold Upminster. By 1906 much of the estate had been sold for development to W. P. Griggs (later Upminster Estates Ltd.).[85] In 1921 the remainder was sold to Godfrey Pike, who in 1927 sold the estate and the lordship separately. The latter was sold to Upminster Estates, and bought from the company in 1938 by Essex county council, which still held it in 1974.[86] The estate was bought by the South Essex Brick and Tile Company which in 1927 leased the Hall itself and 6½ a. to the Upminster Golf Club. In 1935 the club acquired the freehold.[87]

Upminster Hall, Hall Lane, dates certainly from the 16th and probably from the 15th century. To the original plaster and timber house consisting of a central hall with projecting north and south cross-wings, a NW. block was added in the 18th century. Further adaptations and additions have been made since the Hall became the clubhouse of the Upminster Golf Club.[88]

The medieval stone chapel attached to the Hall was still standing *c.* 1720 when it contained a font.[89] The font was given to the parish church later in the 18th century, and in 1790 the chapel was said to have been long taken down.[90]

A thatched timber-framed barn of nine bays stands NW. of Upminster Hall. It is sometimes described without known justification as a tithe barn.[91] It was probably built *c.* 1450,[92] but it is not impossible that it dates from the mid 16th century when Ralph Latham built up his large estate in Upminster. By 1813 three of the barn's nine bays had been floored with oak.[93] The barn was separated from most of the estate in 1935, and in 1937 was bought, with about 30 a., by Hornchurch U.D.C.[94] In 1965 the council re-thatched the barn but vandals fired it in 1973. In 1976 it was opened as an agricultural and folk museum.[95]

[66] E.R.O., C/T 388/4 and 5; *D.N.B.*; E.R.O., T/P 67/3, p. 15, 67/6, p. 270.
[67] E.R.O., T/P 195/2 Upminster, p. 40.
[68] Wilson, *Upminster* (1881), 171; E.R.O., T/P 67/7, p. 23.
[69] Wilson, *Upminster* (1881), 171–2; E.R.O., D/DJn E1.
[70] E.R.O., T/P 181/11/27. A room from New Place is now in the Philadelphia Museum of Art: inf. from Prof. R. B. Pugh.
[71] Wilson, *Upminster* (1881), 172. It is not known when the clock was brought to Upminster. An interior dial bears the date 1774. Cf. Hornchurch Hist. Soc., Newsletter 2 (1974).
[72] Hart, *Early Chart. Essex*, 31.
[73] *L. & P. Hen. VIII*, xvi, p. 139.
[74] Ibid. xviii(1), p. 531.
[75] *Cal. Pat.* 1557–8, 302.
[76] C.P. 25(2)/130/1663; C.P. 25(2)/136/1733. Wisemans were still at Upminster Hall in 1611 (E.R.O., D/AEA 26 ff. 30, 95) but had left by 1619 (E.R.O., Q/SR 192/106, 225/21).
[77] C 142/249/11; C.P. 25(2)/415/4 Chas. I. East.; *Visit. Essex*, i (Harl. Soc. xiii), 68–70; and see p. 149.
[78] C.P. 25(2)/419 18 Chas. I. Trin.; Morant, *Essex*, i. 109.
[79] Morant, *Essex*, i. 109, describing Henry Noel as 'of North Luffenham'.
[80] E.R.O., D/DCq T1.
[81] Ibid.
[82] Burke, *Land. Gent.* (1914), 225.
[83] E.R.O., D/CT 373.
[84] E.R.O., C/T 388/4, 5; E.R.O., T/P 67/2, p. 69.
[85] Champion E. Branfill had died, *v.p.*, in 1890: E.R.O., T/P 67/5, pp. 264–5.
[86] E.R.O., C/T 388 Deeds.
[87] C.D.L., W. Marston Acres, 'Upminster Past and Present', (TS. *c.* 1940), 31; E.R.O., T/P 181/11/27: 28 Oct. 1927.
[88] R.C.H.M. *Essex*, iv. 161; Pevsner, *Essex*, 398.
[89] E.R.O., T/P 195/2 Upminster, pp. 36–7.
[90] *Topographer*, ii. 389; Wilson, *Upminster* (1881), 187–8.
[91] For the rector's tithe barn, dismantled in the 1860s, see p. 156.
[92] C.A. Hewett, *Devt. of Carpentry, 1200–1700*, 123; cf. E.R.O., T/Z 116/4.
[93] E.R.O., T/P 67/7, pp. 71–4, 77.
[94] Inf. from H.R.L.
[95] *Hornchurch and Upminster Echo*, 2 Feb. 1965; Hornchurch Hist. Soc., Annual Rep. (1972), Newsletters 3 (1973) and 2 (1974); inf. from Havering L.B.C.; see above, plate facing p. 113.

ECONOMIC HISTORY. Until the present century most of Upminster's inhabitants were employed on the land or in local trade. In 1066 the two chief manors had 13 ploughs, in 1086 only 12; there was woodland for 500 swine and 14 a. of meadow, the two manors in 1086 actually supporting 30 swine and 160 sheep.[96] In the next century the woodland diminished; Richard I in 1189 acquitted the canons of Waltham of various assarts, including 104 a. at Upminster.[97] An inquiry in 1389 into Essex labour conditions disclosed in Upminster only agricultural labourers and artisans.[98]

Upminster seems always to have been a parish of mixed agriculture. Sheep-farming has been carried on ever since the 11th century. Bequests of sheep are contained in 15th-century Upminster wills, and in 1552 no fewer than 53 sheep were held by the church.[99] The sheep-pastures have been mainly in the north and south ends of the parish. Verses published in 1759 mention 'the fleecy flocks' of Corbets Tey, and *c.* 1830 a writer commented on the acreage in the north end of the parish which was 'chiefly fed by sheep'.[1] Figures relating to the Gaynes estate, in the 15th and 16th centuries, suggest that in the centre of the parish arable farming predominated.[2] In the parish as a whole there was, by the 17th century, a considerable variety of crops and livestock. Tithe disputes of 1618 and 1664 refer not only to acreages of hay, pasturing of wethers, and lambs, calves, eggs, goslings, and piglets, but to cheeses, and fruit: apples and pears on both occasions, plums and cherries as well in 1664.[3]

There were three common wastes in Upminster, of which the two main ones lay north of the Romford-Warley road. In the south Chafford Heath lay east of Aveley Road on either side of Bramble Lane. It had provided 6 a. of common pasture for the tenants of Gaynes manor time out of mind when in 1611 there was an attempt to inclose it.[4] The common still existed north of Bramble Lane in 1772, but had all been inclosed by 1842.[5]

Gaynes (or Mill, or, in recent times, Upminster) common, west of Nag's Head Lane, was extinguished by agreement, 1846–9.[6] To the east of it the 78 acres of Upminster (or Tylers) common was the subject of a bitter dispute in 1951. Essex county council, as lord of the manor, sought to inclose the common.[7] From 1943 to 1950 it had been requisitioned by the Essex War Agricultural committee; on its release the county council fenced and leased it. Opposition to the inclosure was led in Parliament by Mr. Geoffrey Bing, M.P. for Hornchurch, and locally by Mr. Edward Luther, Mr. Edgar Fordham, and a commoner, Mr. Ben Cunningham.[8] The inclosure of Upminster common was declared illegal by the minister of Agriculture in 1951, and in 1952 the Government Auditor surcharged all the members of the county council for the costs of the inclosure, the first occasion on which such a surcharge was imposed. A commemorative stone recording 'the victory of the commoners over Essex County Council' was later erected opposite the common.

In 1795 it was reckoned there were six acres of arable to every one of pasture in the parish.[9] In 1842, out of a total of 3,369 a., there were 1,941 a. of arable, 1,011 a. of meadow, 91 a. of woodland, and 148 a. of common. Roads and homesteads occupied 178 a.[10] By the later 19th century there was a considerable growth of market-gardening in Upminster, as in neighbouring parishes. In 1881 Isaac Gay of Great Sunnings won a prize given by the Royal Agricultural Society for creating a 'new model' in market-gardening.[11] By 1905 arable and woodlands had decreased to 1,578 a. and 63 a. respectively, but there were 1,047 a. of permanent grass.[12] Twenty years later there had been relatively little change, with 979 a. of permanent grass and 1,031 a. available for cultivation.[13] In 1961, although there were fewer than 480 a. of permanent grass, market-gardening occupied 522 a., and there were 1,261 a. available for cultivation.[14]

There were 174 families in Upminster in 1821 and 202 in 1831; of these a local historian reckoned 114 and 134 engaged in agriculture, 46 and 47 in trade.[15]

Of the two mills at Upminster, the older was on Gaynes common. It was a post-mill on a high brick base, and may have existed in 1665, when Thomas Dawson of Upminster, miller, was buried in the churchyard. Certainly it existed in 1670.[16] In 1778 William Pinchon was the miller there and his descendants still possessed the mill in 1846.[17] By 1875 David Pinchon had sold it, and in 1882 it was taken down.[18]

In 1802–3 James Nokes built the other mill on the north side of Upminster Hill (now St. Mary's Lane).[19] It followed the Kentish style, being a smock windmill with boat-shaped cap.[20] From 1818 certainly, and perhaps from 1811 or 1812, it had an auxilliary steam-engine, the earliest recorded for an Essex mill.[21] The Nokes family owned the mill until 1849; and from 1858 to 1934 it was owned by the

[96] *V.C.H. Essex*, i. 447, 554.
[97] W. R. Fisher, *Forest of Essex*, 321.
[98] N. Kenyon, 'Labour Conditions in Essex in the Reign of Richard II', *Ec.H.R.* iv. 444–7.
[99] E.R.O., D/AER 1, ff. 153, 166; *E.A.T.* N.S. ii. 177–8; cf. Assizes 35/58/H, 35/140/H.
[1] E.R.O., T/P 67/7, p. 58; T/P 67/5, p. 203. Cf. E.R.O., D/DRu E6.
[2] *Cal. Close*, 1405–9, 227; *Feet of F. Essex*, iv. 14; C.P. 40/1052 Carte rot. 4.
[3] E.R.O., D/AED 9, ff. 91–4, 82–5v,. 78–9, 87–9v.; D/AXD 3, ff. 1–4.
[4] E.R.O., Q/SR 199/35, 203/44.
[5] *Map of Essex* (1777); E.R.O., D/CT 373b.
[6] E.R.O., D/DZb 2, 3. In 1842 it contained 70 a.: E.R.O., D/CT 373.
[7] *Essex Countryside*, xi. 489; Edward A. Luther, *The Battle of Upminster Common 1951* (in H.R.L.); J. Cantwell 'Hornchurch—A Political Survey, 1926–64' [duplicated TS. in H.R.L.], 26–7.
[8] For Cunningham's father: *V.C.H. Essex*, vi. 106.
[9] C. Vancouver, *Gen. View of Agric. of Essex*, table f. p. 96.
[10] E.R.O., D/CT 373.
[11] Wilson, *Upminster* (1856) 10–11, (1881) 14–15, 162; E.R.O., T/P 67/7, p. 267.
[12] Bd. of Agric. Acreage Returns. (1905).
[13] M.A.F. 68/3240.
[14] M.A.F. 68/4722.
[15] E.R.O., T/P 67/5, p. 206. Cf. *Census Reps.* (1821), 94 and (1831), 182, which differ in some details.
[16] *E.R.* xxxiii. 54; for illus., see E.R O., D/DZb 5, D/DRu P3 and Wilson, *Upminster* (1881), 196; E.R.O., D/P 117/1/1; D/DA T449.
[17] E.R.O., D/DZb 2, pp. 56, 450. In 1772 William Pinchon of Upminster, miller, had married Ann Powtrill of the same: E.R.O., T/P 67/2, p. 2d.
[18] E.R.O., D/DZb 3, p. 71; E.R.O., T/P 67/2, p. 85; E.R.O., Libr., Vertical Folder (Upminster).
[19] E.R.O., T/P 67/4, p. 155, 67/9, p. 76a.
[20] *E.R.* xl. 164–6.
[21] E.R.O., D/F 21/2, p. 165; E.R.O., T/P 67/5, p. 105; J. Booker, *Essex and the Industrial Revolution*, 87.

Abraham family.[22] It was damaged by lightning in 1889.[23] Ten years later the cast-iron shaft to which the sails were attached snapped at the neck and carried away part of the stage as it fell. Since the villagers regarded the mill as their communal weathervane, they raised £150 towards its repair.[24] The mill was sold in 1935 and again in 1937 when Essex county council bought it.[25] It was then in good condition but during the Second World War it decayed rapidly. The county council carried out major repairs in 1962–3. Ownership of the mill passed in 1965 to the London borough of Havering, which completed a major restoration in 1968. Since 1967 the mill has in most years been opened to the public under the management of the Hornchurch and District Historical Society.[26]

There was a tannery on the Corbets Tey road at an undiscovered date but possibly between 1573 and 1635 when Upminster tanners appear in local records.[27] From the 18th century numerous gravel-pits can be traced in southern Upminster.[28] Brickworks also were to be found. On the NE. boundary of the parish Brick House farm in 1881 commemorated a former brickfield, and Tylers farm in 1974 represented a corruption of the Anglo-Saxon *tigelhyrste* (tile-earth wood).[29] In 1708 Samuel Springham had a house at the Brick-kilns.[30] It is possible that this was the site near the junction of Hall and Bird Lanes where there was later a circular brick-kiln 45 ft. in diameter and 70 ft. high.[31] That kiln was said to have been built in 1774 by Matthew Howland Patrick, the lessee of Upminster Hall and husband of the widowed Mrs. Branfill. Here, before his death in 1777 Patrick 'had just brought his sugar-mould-pottery to perfection'.[32] In 1791 Patrick's stepson Champion Branfill (III), spent over £200 on the pot-kiln.[33] Producing bricks, tiles, and pipes, it was worked by a succession of lessees until in 1885 James Brown, of Braintree and Chelmsford and with a head office in London, bought the lease.[34] He enlarged the works, and erected workmen's houses.[35] By 1895 a tramway had been built from the brickworks to Upminster station.[36] Under a variety of titles the brickworks continued to operate until 1933; they were demolished in the 1930s, the tramway track being lifted at much the same time.[37]

LOCAL GOVERNMENT. View of frankpledge was held on the manor of Upminster Hall in 1271 and 1531, but no certain record after the Dissolution reveals a like occurrence.[38] In 1271 the lord enjoyed the assize of ale; in 1531 a constable was chosen. Rolls and books record courts baron of Upminster Hall in 1607, 1608, and 1634 and from 1650 to 1895.[39] No record of a medieval court at the manor of Gaynes has been found, but court books record the meetings of the court baron from 1678 to 1923.[40]

At the cross-roads on the village green, stocks were preserved until the early 19th century, and adjoining the lands of Upminster Hall manor, possibly by the pond on the village green, there existed in the 16th and 17th centuries a ducking-stool. The parish cage, mentioned in 1803, was probably nearby.[41] Gaynes manorial pound, near Gaynes Cross, was repaired by the lord of the manor in 1819. The vestry in 1842 asked him to erect a public pound for the general use of the parish, and in 1864 undertook to pay for re-establishing the old pound if he declined to do so.[42]

Parish records survive from the late 17th century. They include vestry books for 1681–1713, 1721–1826, 1830–66, overseers' rates and accounts 1745–1836, and surveyors' accounts 1790–1810, 1818–36.[43] In 1706 vestry meetings were ordered to be held on the first Monday in the month. They were normally in the church, but in 1798 the vestry voted to meet in future at the Bell Inn opposite the churchyard.[44] Thereafter adjournments thither were frequent. In 1696 those attending vestry meetings were allowed 4*d.* expenses each, but in 1704 the rule was rescinded. Attendance fell, and in 1709 the subsidy was brought back, at the increased rate of 6*d.* for those who arrived at the meeting within two hours of the time announced. In 1739 it was agreed that the parish would spend £2 at each Easter vestry. Nevertheless attendance at meetings was normally small, rarely numbering more than ten, and being restricted to the parish officers, aspirants to office, and a few of the more important tenant-farmers. Occasionally the gentry and other farmers appeared in person or by proxy, as in 1799 when there was discontent over a new rate assessment. No chairman of a vestry meeting was named until 1820. Before that date the rector or curate signed the minutes first when present. From 1820 the rector usually presided at the Easter vestry, the churchwardens presiding at most other times.

The parish was divided by the Hornchurch-Cranham road (now St. Mary's Lane) into two ends

22 E.R.O., D/DJn E1; E.R.O., T/P 67/1, p. 59; A.D. Butler, *Upminster Mill*, 21.
23 E.R.O., T/P 67/7, p. 24.
24 E.R.O., T/P 67/3, pp. 133, 141; G. E. Tasker, *Romford, Hornchurch and Upminster*, 38.
25 E.R.O., T/P 95/2 citing *Upminster Chron.* 21 Nov. 1935; Butler, *Upminster Mill*, 22; *Essex Times*, 29 May 1937.
26 *E.R.* lviii. 217–18; *E. Nat.* xxvi. 119; Butler, *Upminster Mill*, 22–5; Hornchurch Hist. Soc., Newsletter 2 (1963); *E. Jnl.* v. 43. Hornchurch Hist. Soc. newsletters & annual reports (1970 sqq.). See plate facing p. 33, above.
27 E.R.O., T/P 67/3, pp. 74, 186; E.R.O., D/AER 13, f. 11, D/AER 16, ff. 84, 93, D/AEW 15/231, 16/178; E.R.O., D/DU 182/50; E.R.O., Q/SR 128/57, 153/21, 21a, 182/10, 228/80.
28 e.g. E.R.O., D/P 117/8/1: 21 Apr. 1712; D/P 117/8/2: overseer's acct., S. end, 1725–6, Surveyor Highway's acct., 1752–3.
29 Wilson, *Upminster* (1881), 194; *P. N. Essex*, 132–3.
30 E.R.O., Q/SBb 42/15.
31 Wilson, *Upminster* (1881), 190–1.
32 W. Marston Acres, 'Upminster Past and Present', (TS. in C.D.L., *c.* 1940), 151; E.R.O., D/P 117/12/6; E.R.O., D/DU 546/2, pp. 115, 180.
33 E.R.O., T/P 67/5, p. 261. Cf. T/P 67/7, p. 23.
34 E.R.O. has a copy of his trade catalogue, 1900 edn.: James Brown, *Brick Ornament and its Application*.
35 E.R.O., T/P 67/5, p. 146; *Kelly's Dir. Essex* (1886). Cf. E.R.O., T/P 67/5, p. 145, 67/3, pp. 31, 90, 115.
36 O.S. Map 25", Essex LXVII. 14, LXXV. 2 (1896 edn.).
37 *Kelly's Dir. Essex* (1910 sqq.); *Essex Countryside*, xix. (no. 168), 90; inf. from H.R.L.
38 S.C. 2/173/30, 80. In the 17th century the James family was said to be paying a rent to the farmer of Chafford hundred for view of frankpledge in Upminster: *Cal. Treas. Bks.* 1689–92, 239.
39 S.C. 2/173/102; E.R.O., C/T 388/1, 4–6; B.L. Add. Ch. 683.
40 E.R.O., D/DZb 1–4.
41 Wilson, *Upminster* (1881) 57–8; E.R.O., D/DGt 5–7, 10; E.R.O., C/T 388/1, p. 11; E.R.O., T/P 95/1, p. 87.
42 E.R.O., T/P 67/5; E.R.O., D/P 117/8/8, 9, 11, 12.
43 E.R.O., D/P 117/8/1–12; D/P 117/11/1–13; D/P 117/12/1–27; D/P 117/21/1–5. All information in this section, unless otherwise indicated, derives from these records.
44 Joseph Lee had just become landlord of the Bell and overseer of the poor.

or wards, North and South, for each of which was appointed a churchwarden, an overseer of the poor, a constable, and a surveyor of the highways.[45] Despite the administrative division of the parish, differences of opinion only once resulted in a clash of factions exactly representing the two wards: in 1813 the South end stopped the North end from replacing the master of the workhouse by an inhabitant of the North end. Until 1772 and from 1774 to 1791 the vestry elected both churchwardens, but in 1773 and from 1792 the rector appointed one warden. Parish autonomy had first declined, however, *c.* 1730: until 1733 the vestry had nominated a single overseer for each end, but thereafter the justices selected the overseers from four or more vestry nominees. Constables, 1736–63, and highway surveyors from 1729 were similarly chosen, four of the latter being nominated annually 1729–66 and no fewer than ten 1778–1833. The appointment of a salaried vestry clerk was recorded from 1701 onwards; there was apparently a church (or parish) clerk in 1722–3; he was salaried from 1761–2. In 1746–7 the parish paid a dog whipper; from 1784 he was termed the beadle and from 1788 the sexton.[46]

With a population of 370 in 1695, Upminster's rates in 1696–1700 and 1706–10 totalled in each quinquennium 4*s.* and 4*s.* 3*d.* respectively, of which two-thirds was for poor-relief.[47] A century later, with a population in 1801 of 765, the total rates levied in 1796–1800 were 15*s.* 2*d.* and in 1806–10 10*s.*; in 1796–1800, however, the poor-rate represented almost five-sixths, and in 1806–10 all, of the amount raised. In the 18th century the population had doubled and the rateable value had quadrupled: in 1700 it was £1,612, in 1801 £6,451 10*s.*[48] Upminster's annual expenditure on the poor first exceeded £100 in 1739–40, £200 in 1757–8, and £300 in 1773–4. Between 1783 and 1798 it was above £400 in every year but one. It rose to £860 in 1799–1800, £1,200 in 1800–1, and £1,232 in 1801–2. Thereafter until 1836 it was usually between £600 and £900, with expenditure lowest in the years 1820–9 and highest, £982, in 1833–4.[49]

The earliest evidence for systematic parish care for the poor dates from the 16th century. There was a poor-box in the church in 1567.[50] The earliest vestry book regularly records the apprenticing of village orphans, and the earliest surviving apprenticeship agreement dates from 1612.[51] In 1723 recipients of parish relief were to be paid only if they wore badges, a proviso repeated in 1734. Throughout the 18th century the parish rented dwellings for the poor, and even in 1704 contracted with an Upminster carpenter to build 'a sufficient house for any poor man to live in' on the Upminster Hall waste. In 1750 a parish poorhouse was built on Upminster Hill (now St. Mary's Lane) near Upminster bridge. The building was financed by selling the £110 stock held by trustees for the poor.[52] In 1762 its inmates, including six widows, numbered ten. By 1783 the problem of the poor was increasing, and an extension to the workhouse, as it was then called, was reckoned necessary. A grant in 1786 of an adjoining part of the waste of Upminster Hall enabled it to be built. Meanwhile (1784–6) some of Upminster's poor were lodged in the Great Warley workhouse. No record of the capacity of the extended workhouse has been found, but in 1803 the master claimed allowances for 37 inmates, the largest number recorded.

A master of the workhouse was first named in 1787. After frequent changes, a shoemaker was master in the years 1793–1801. He was succeeded by two Colchester weavers, (1803–7 and 1808–10). The former master of the Shenfield workhouse, John Harden (d. 1831), and his widow Mary in turn ran the Upminster workhouse from 1810 until its closure in 1836. At first the parish paid directly for workhouse provisions but in 1788–9, 1794–1801, and 1802–36 it contracted with the master to feed and clothe the inmates.

Agreements in 1801, 1802, and 1813 allowed the Cranham overseers to place a maximum of ten of their poor in the Upminster workhouse. The arrangement apparently ended in 1816, and a request by Cranham for a renewal of the agreement in 1825 was rejected, because there were no places to spare.[53]

The appointment of a weaver as master of the workhouse in 1802 was in part meant to allow the inmates to learn weaving. The weaver received ten guineas for bringing his loom with him, and the vestry built a room for it. In 1807 it was agreed that all the earnings of the poor should belong to the master; and in 1822, when the master's weekly allowance was reduced, his previous half-share of their earnings was increased.

In 1805 the vestry ordered a cell to be built at the workhouse for the solitary confinement of unruly inmates, and in 1806 it arranged for the weekly inspection of the workhouse by parishioners. The vestry's attitude to bastardy was normally limited to the avoidance of financial responsibility, but in 1833 all single women in the workhouse who were pregnant were ordered to wear a distinctive dress.

Besides running the workhouse the parish made regular payments to the poor in their own homes. Litigation over settlement and casual payments also absorbed part of the rates: in September and October 1795 soldiers and their families, *c.* 250 in all and including at least 170 children, received £5 12*s.* 6*d.* as they moved south and north through Upminster. In 1816 and 1821 the parish made bulk purchases of bacon, cheese, butter, and soap for re-sale at cost to the poor outside the workhouse.

Until *c.* 1724 the health of the poor was apparently treated casually by various doctors. Thereafter only one doctor at a time seems to have been retained.[54] In 1767 he attended only those paupers living within 2 miles of the parish church; the whole parish was his responsibility in 1775; from 1797 Upminster's poor in neighbouring parishes were included. Until 1833 the doctor was usually paid separately for inoculations, fractures, amputations, and confinements. These additional fees were surrendered in 1833 when the retainer reached £24 a year.

[45] The overseers were termed 'collectors for the poor' in 1596: E.R.O., D/DA T448. The use of the term 'headborough' 1791–1836 apparently represents the antiquarianism of a vestry clerk. Until 1762 the North and South wards kept separate rate books.

[46] E.R.O., D/P 117/5/3.

[47] Morant, *Essex*, i. 111.

[48] E.R.O., T/P 67/3.

[49] The records are incomplete for 1798–9 and 1809–10, and missing for 1810–12.

[50] Hale, *Precedents*, 150.

[51] E.R.O., D/P 117/14.

[52] See p. 163.

[53] Cf. E.R.O., D/P 118/12/3–6, and above, p. 107.

[54] Dr. Kennedy was first paid in 1725–6, and last in 1746–7. From 1767 there is clear evidence for the exclusive retention of one doctor.

In 1836 Upminster became part of Romford poor-law union. The workhouse was sold and converted into six dwellings.[55]

What parish business remained after 1836 was administered by Jesse Oxley (d. 1877). At the time of his death he was vestry clerk, church clerk, assistant overseer and collector of the poor-rates, and surveyor of the highways.[56] The vestry was still nominating constables in 1866 despite the presence at Upminster from 1843 of members of the new Essex Constabulary. In addition, after a burglary in 1865, some of the leading householders appointed a private night-watchman, still active in 1875.[57] In 1864 a burial board was established.[58]

Under the Local Government Act, 1894, a parish council of nine members was formed for Upminster. The first election was contested by 19 candidates.[59] The electorate was about 250, and the successful candidates polled from 69 to 103 votes.[60] Enthusiasm was never again comparable.[61] The development of Upminster garden suburb began late in 1906, and in 1910 the new council was composed of 5 old and 4 new inhabitants.[62] By 1913 membership of the parish council had been increased to twelve, and Upminster was divided into two wards, north and south of the railway.[63] In 1928 the last member of the original parish council retired, and for the first time a woman was elected.[64] In 1934 Upminster was merged in Hornchurch urban district.[65]

The parish council was served by a salaried clerk, who was also the rate-collector. In 1924 the Clock House, St. Mary's Lane, was bought to provide council offices.[66]

A continual growth of parish council business demanded an increasing number of council committees. By 1910 there were four, and by 1918 six more, of which two were temporary wartime committees.[67] A rate-payers' association existed briefly in 1906; a larger and more effective one was formed in 1915.[68]

PUBLIC SERVICES. In 1872, upon receiving a guarantee from a prospective consumer, the Romford Gas & Coke Company laid gas mains to Upminster. Gas street-lighting was installed in 1905.[69] Electricity became available only in 1926.[70] The South Essex Waterworks Company's mains passed through Upminster on their way from Grays to Romford. They first supplemented the supply of good spring water in 1863, though it was not until 1909 that Upminster Common received piped water.[71] The development of the village after 1906 was attended by none of the problems of water supply which faced Cranham at the same time.[72]

The geography of Upminster made drainage difficult. In 1893, under threat of prosecution, the Romford rural sanitary authority at last piped the Cranham (now St. Mary's) Lane ditch, but it was 1899, nine years after the first complaint, before work on a sewage scheme was begun, restricted to Upminster village and Corbets Tey.[73] In 1900 tenders were invited for a sewer from Hacton, and the development of the Upminster Hall estate necessitated further extensions of the system in 1907.[74] In 1922 new works, to serve both Upminster and Cranham, were completed at Bury farm, Great Warley, on a site where the lie of the land made pumping-stations unnecessary.[75]

The parish adopted the 1833 Lighting and Watching Act for Upminster village south of the railway line in 1904, and north of it in 1910. The Act was extended to the whole parish in 1930.[76]

The first land acquired for recreation by Upminster parish council was rented from the Upminster Hall estate for allotments in 1899. In 1928 alternative land had to be found when the site was reclaimed by the new golf club.[77] Upminster Park, Corbets Tey road, originated in 1929, when the parish council agreed to buy 18 a. glebe adjoining the church.[78] The Upminster Hall playing fields (35 a.) were developed in 1962–3.[79] In 1969–70 there were 93 a. of public parks in Upminster.[80]

A volunteer fire brigade was formed for Upminster in 1909. Its efficiency was greatly improved in 1925 by the appointment as captain of a retired professional fireman, and in 1927 by the purchase of motorized equipment in place of a hand truck.[81]

The Upminster and Cranham Nursing association was formed in 1898. By 1936 the association had over 400 members and its nurses in 1935 had paid over 3,000 visits. From 1933 it was aided by an ambulance of the St. John Ambulance Brigade.[82]

In 1894 the rector said that the churchyard was almost full. The parish bought 2½ a. in 1900, and in 1902 opened the new cemetery at Corbets Tey. In 1957 the South Essex crematorium was opened

[55] *Story of Upminster*, ii. 2. Cf. E.R.O., T/P 67/3, pp. 106a, d; *Rep. Com. Char.* [108], p. 722 (1837–8) xxv(1).
[56] E.R.O., T/P 62/2 p. 144.
[57] E.R.O., Q/APr 8; E.R.O., T/P 67/1, pp. 82, 260; T/P 67/3, p. 14.
[58] In 1895 the parish council wrongly claimed that the Burials Act had never been adopted: E.R.O., T/P 67/3, p. 60.
[59] E.R.O., T/P 67/3, p. 48.
[60] E.R.O., T/P 67/5, p. 271 (1885: 230); T/P 67/3, pp. 138a, c, e (1899: 286).
[61] In 1895 18 votes secured a seat; in 1896, 29; in 1897, 25; in 1899, 40. In 1901 and 1904 there were no contests (E.R.O., T/P 67/3, pp. 58–9, 123, 145; T/P 67/5, p. 4).
[62] E.R.O., T/P 67/6, p. 328.
[63] E.R.O., T/P 67/7, p. 276.
[64] E.R.O., T/P 181/11/27: women had been unsuccessful candidates in 1922 and 1925.
[65] Ibid. As early as 1911 Upminster considered applying for urban status: E.R.O., T/P 67/7, p. 192.
[66] E.R.O., T/P 67/6, pp. 241–2; T/P 181/11/27.
[67] 1910: allotment, cemetery, fire-brigade, and lighting; 1918: finance, footpaths, general purposes, sanitary, and food economy and war charities. For the activities of the first four and of the sanitary committee, see below.
[68] E.R.O., T/P 181/11/27; T/P 67/5, p. 195, 67/8, pp. 96–99, 103, 105, 110.
[69] E.R.O., D/F 5/11/1, 3.
[70] E.R.O., C/DP 225; C.D.L., W. Marston Acres 'Upminster Past and Present' (TS *c.* 1940), 161.
[71] Wilson, *Upminster* (1881), 17; E.R.O., T/P 67/5, p. 205, 67/6, p. 279. In the 1830s the supply of spring water was said to be abundant.
[72] See p. 103.
[73] E.R.O., T/P 67/2, p. 47, 67/3, pp. 22, 125.
[74] E.R.O., T/P 67/3, p. 131, 67/6, pp. 14, 49, 50, 88.
[75] E.R.O., T/P 67/8, pp. 6, 30, 44–5, 53–5, 64, 77, 120; T/P 67/9, p. 11, T/P 67/10, pp. 90–1; T/P 181/11/27.
[76] E.R.O., T/P 67/3, p. 85, 67/5, pp. 2–4, 67/6, pp. 290, 312–13; T/P 181/11/27.
[77] E.R.O., T/P 67/3, pp. 40, 45, 67/5, p. 31; T/P 181/11/27.
[78] E.R.O., T/P 181/11/27.
[79] *Hornchurch Official Guide* (1962–3), 43; Cf. *Hornchurch Charter Petition* (1956).
[80] *Havering Official Guide* (1969–70), 57, 63; L.B. Havering, *Recreation and Amenities Division* (1970).
[81] E.R.O., T/P 67/6, p. 233, 67/7, pp. 258, 275; T/P 181/11/27.
[82] E.R.O., T/P 67/3, p. 120, 67/5, p. 7; T/P 181/11/27.

immediately to the west. It was enlarged in 1961–2.[83]

In 1887 the Upminster district club and reading room was opened at Locksley Villa, Upminster Hill (now St. Mary's Lane). The original intention, to provide lectures, meetings, and reading matter for 'men of every class' as well as occasional evening entertainments, was changed when from 1888 ale was sold and a bathroom and smoking room provided. At first the club flourished but, caught between the paternalism of the founder-president and the resentment of excluded labourers, officials resigned. Membership dropped, and in 1896 the club was dissolved, the assets being shared among the remaining members.[84] At Corbets Tey a reading room and library for working-men existed between 1885 and 1891.[85] A branch of the county library was opened in 1936 at Clock House; in 1963 this was transferred to a new building in Corbets Tey road.[86]

PARLIAMENTARY REPRESENTATION. In 1974 Upminster became one of three parliamentary constituencies in the London borough of Havering; previously it had formed part of the parliamentary borough of Hornchurch.[87] In February 1974 the Conservatives won the seat, retaining it in the election of November 1974.

CHURCH. The name Upminster suggests that an ancient mother church, serving an area wider than the later parish, existed here long before the Conquest.[88] The site of the church, away from the manor-houses but at the centre of the village, is also consistent with an early origin.

In 1223 Viel Engaine, lord of the manor of Gaynes, granted 40*s.* a year from Upminster church to the priory of Worspring (Som.).[89] The advowson descended with Gaynes until 1297, when the manor was sold to Simon of Havering. The advowson was excluded from the sale and remained with the Engaines until the death in 1367 of Thomas Engaine, Lord Engaine. It then passed to Thomas's sister and coheir Elizabeth, wife of Sir Laurence Pabenham, and subsequently passed to her descendents, the Cheynes and the Vauxes of Harrowden.[90] The Cheynes regularly presented, but the Lords Vaux appear to have sold single turns four times, the last in 1562.[91]

The recusant John Wright of Kelvedon Hatch was said at his death in 1608 to possess the advowson of Upminster, but in 1609 the king presented by reason of the minority of Edward Vaux, Lord Vaux.[92] Vaux suffered forfeiture in 1612 for refusing the oath of allegiance. His property was restored in the same year, but in 1614, because of a defect in Vaux's title, the king presented William Halke (d. 1615).[93] William Halke was succeeded by Michael Halke who was presented by Dr. William Harvey (1578–1657), discoverer of the circulation of the blood. Harvey, who was a kinsman of the Halkes, also presented John Halke in 1638; two further presentations, in 1662 and 1679, were made by members of the Halke family.[94] The advowson passed through the hands of the Newman, Bray, Bradshaw and Copestake families until in 1780 it was bought by William Holden of Birmingham.[95] Since 1780 it has continued in the Holden family, five of whom in succession were rectors between 1780 and 1971.[96]

The rectory was valued at £14 13*s.* 4*d.* in 1254, £12 in 1291, and £26 13*s.* 4*d.* in 1535.[97] In 1546 it was farmed to Stephen Heath, cooper of London, for 61 years at £20.[98] In the 18th century the value was said to be about £200.[99] The figure was probably a considerable under-estimate, for in the 1790s the Holdens apparently received about £750 a year.[1] In 1842 the tithes were commuted for £1,052.[2]

In 1610 the rectory house, which was apparently moated, contained 7 upper and 6 lower rooms, in poor repair.[3] Because of the ruinous state of the rectory Dr. Derham, rector 1689–1735, lived at High House, opposite the church in Corbets Tey Road.[4] A new rectory was built before 1740 by Samuel Bradshaw, rector 1735–68.[5] It stands a few yards south of the earlier rectory, and has two storeys of red brick, colourwashed. The projecting wings have hipped old tile roofs and are balanced by a central pediment. The brick porch is modern. A tithe barn formerly stood west of the rectory. It was used for services in 1861–2 while the church was being rebuilt. It was later sold to Dr. Newman of Nelmes, Hornchurch, and before 1870 its materials were used in the construction of Tharp Lodge.[6]

The proximity of Upminster to London and the comparatively high value of the rectory made Upminster a desirable living. In the 15th and 16th centuries pluralist rectors were common, and there were others in the 17th century.[7] Absentee rectors,

[83] E.R.O., T/P 67/3, pp. 118a, 149, 170, 178–9; *E.R.* xi. 172–3; inf. from Superintendent.

[84] E.R.O., T/P 67/1, pp. 189–93; 67/2, pp. 8–9, 54–5, 80, 82–3, 141; 67/3, pp. 48, 40b–43, 66a, 71; 67/5, p. 68.

[85] E.R.O., T/P 67/1, pp. 42, 135–6; 67/2, pp. 43, 89; 67/3, p. 68.

[86] Inf. from Mr. L. Rose, H.R.L.

[87] This section is based on *Dod's Parliamentary Companion* (1970 and later edns.).

[88] *E.R.* lxii. 7.

[89] *Feet of F. Essex*, i. 64.

[90] *Cal. Pat.* 1292–1301, 292. For the descent, see *Complete Peerage*, v. 73–80.

[91] Newcourt, *Repertorium*, ii. 618.

[92] E.R.O., D/DK T190; Guildhall MS. 9531/14, ff. 132v.–133; cf. G.L.C., DL/C/338–9.

[93] *Complete Peerage*, xii(2), p. 224; C 66/1957(15) and 1983(13); Guildhall MS. 9531/14, f. 189; cf. G.L.C., DL/C/340, ff. 132, 159, 202v.

[94] Harvey (1578–1657) was later warden of Merton College, Oxford: K. D. Keele, *William Harvey*, 3. In 1648 John Halke claimed to own the advowson: Hist. MSS. Com. 6, *7th Rep., H.L.* p. 48; Newcourt, *Repertorium*, ii. 618.

[95] Newcourt, *Repertorium*, ii. 618; C.C.L., G. Hennessey, Revision of Newcourt's *Repertorium*: Upminster. The Holden descent is to be found, s.v. Rose, in Burke, *Land. Gent.* (1914), 1628–9.

[96] *Havering Official Guide* (1971), 105.

[97] *E.A.T.* N.S. xviii. 17; *Tax. Eccl.* (Rec. Com.), 23; *Valor Eccl.* (Rec. Com.), i. 436.

[98] Guildhall MS. 9531 pt. i, f. 86v.

[99] Guildhall MSS. 9550, 9553, 9557.

[1] E.R.O., T/P 67/4, pp. 187–8; E.R.O., D/P 117/11/1: 20 Sept. 1799; D/P 117/11/3, 5; D/P 117/3.

[2] E.R.O., D/CT 373.

[3] Newcourt, *Repertorium*, ii. 617; E.R.O., D/AEA 23, ff. 144, 346, D/AEA 25, f. 169; E.R.O., T/P 67/4, pp. 181–2, 186.

[4] Wilson, *Upminster* (1881), 130.

[5] Salmon, *Essex*, 273.

[6] E.R.O., D/CT 373b; E.R.O., D/DRu F 12/33, 34; E.R.O., T/P 67/4, p. 85; *Kelly's Dir. Essex* (1866, 1870), s.v. Hornchurch.

[7] *Cal. Papal Reg.* 1404–15, p. 51; 1431–7, p. 80; *E.A.T.* N.S. vi. 325; vii. 279; H.E.P. Grieve, 'The Deprived Married Clergy of Essex', *Trans. R.H.S.* 4th ser. xxii. 143; Foster, *Alumni Oxon.* iii. 1065; Venn, *Alumni Cantab.* I, i. 38, 192; ii. 352; iii. 1.

held the rectory for 84 years in the period 1492–1678, and exchanges in 1410 and 1482, and the resignation of eight of the eighteen known 15th-century rectors alike suggest that the living was often in the market.[8] The first named assistant curate occurs in 1557, but there appear to have been earlier ones in 1532–5 and 1547–51.[9] Two rectors were deprived of the living, one in 1554 for marriage, another in 1558 for non-residence.[10]

The religious upheaval of the mid 16th century apparently had little effect on Upminster. A guild of the Trinity, which may have existed in 1479, was dissolved in 1552, but in 1573 the church had still not been stripped of all popish features.[11] Such activity as the rector and congregation showed was more secular in spirit. Since 1543 the Lathams had owned both Upminster manors but not the advowson, and in 1574, 1577–8, 1588, and 1600 quarrels between the family and the rector reached the courts.[12] William Washer, rector 1562–1609, was described contemptuously by the Puritans, *c.* 1589, as 'sometime a grocer', but they found nothing more serious to allege against him.[13] John Bowle or Bowles (rector, 1609–13), who was presented by the king, no doubt owed his preferment to the earl of Salisbury, to whom he was household chaplain. He later became dean of Salisbury and bishop of Rochester.[14] In his time (1610) Thomas Frith founded his charities for a St. Mark's day sermon and for reading the Litany.[15]

Michael Halke, rector, 1615–24, was soon embroiled with his parishioners. In January 1617 he was bound to keep the peace; in October he was cited in the archdeacon's court; by November he was engaged in three tithe cases.[16] In 1618 he was accused to getting his maid with child.[17] An assistant curate conducted the services in 1619, and by 1620 Halke was suspended, though he continued to live at the rectory at least until 1624, when he was deprived.[18] In 1641 he was awarded £40 a year from the rectory's profits. It was still being paid in 1650.[19] John Fuller was the parish lecturer from 1631 until his death in 1635.[20]

The tensions of the Civil War did not at first affect Upminster, but there is evidence later of at least two factions in the village. As before, the trouble seems to have begun with a tithe dispute. John Halke, rector from 1638, survived an attempt to remove him in 1644 but was sequestrated in 1646. He regained the living in 1660, but was ejected again, for nonconformity, in 1662.[21] It seems likely that he and a minority of the parishioners supported the Presbyterian or Parliamentary position, but that his successors Marmaduke James (1646–52), Reuben Easthorpe, and John Robotham (*c.* 1657–60) were backed by other inhabitants more in sympathy with the Army and Independents.[22] James and Easthorpe, like Halke, were apparently graduates, but Robotham, ejected in 1660, had a different background. An Independent or Anabaptist from Stepney (Mdx.), he was described by Halke as . . . 'a mean tradesman'.[23]

John Newton, rector 1662–78, and William Derham, rector 1689–1735, were both royal chaplains and scholars. Newton was an absentee, but Derham lived in Upminster for most of his incumbency, and acted also as physician to his parishioners. He became a canon of Windsor in 1716 and employed an assistant curate thereafter, but he continued to visit the parish regularly until his death there.[24] Throughout the 18th century and the earlier 19th century there was usually an assistant curate.[25]

John Rose Holden, rector 1780–99, was the first of five members of that family to hold the cure. He and his son of the same name, rector 1799–1862, engaged in a tithe dispute which alienated many of their parishioners and stimulated the growth of Congregationalism in the parish.[26] The young rector's visit to Rome in 1800 further complicated the affair, and on his return he fell out with the farmer of his tithes and was sued by him.[27] P. M. Holden, rector 1862–1904, nephew of his predecessor, lost his earlier popularity when he married his mistress in 1873, and for 20 years thereafter was engaged in continuous disputes.[28] Once again Congregationalism benefited.[29] After the passage of the 1880 Burials Act a third of those buried in Upminster churchyard between 1881 and 1900 were given 'nonconformist' burial,

[8] *E.A.T.* N.S. vii. 279; Venn, *Alumni Cantab.* I, iii. 1; *Trans. R.H.S.* 4th ser. xxii. 143; E.R.O., D/AEA 25, ff. 169 184v., 202v., 205v., 215; *D.N.B.* s.v. Newton, John; *Bp. Robert Rede's Reg.* (Suss. Rec. Soc. xi), 312; B.L. Add. MS. 5839; Newcourt, *Repertorium*, ii. 618. John Docwra, rector 1492–1535, was in Upminster, however briefly, in 1503, 1506, and 1531: E.R.O., D/AER 2, ff. 19, 80; D/AER 4, f. 111.

[9] *E.A.T.* N.S. vii. 279; E.R.O., D/AER 6, f. 9; Prob. 11/25 (P.C.C. 26 Hogen: will of J. Docwra, clerk); H.R.L., T. L. Wilson, 'Upminster: Religious Hist. (1907)' (xeroxed MS.), 23.

[10] *Trans. R.H.S.* 4th ser. xxii. 143, 155.

[11] *E.A.T.* N.S. ii. 177–8; E.R.O., D/AER 1, f. 26v.; Hale, *Precedents*, 154; see below, p. 158.

[12] E.R.O., D/AEA 8, ff. 61v, 78v; E.R.O., Q/SR 66/24, 38–40; D/AEA 17, ff. 72–72v.; D/AEA 20, f. 235.

[13] Davids, *Nonconformity in Essex*, 95.

[14] *D.N.B.* For the many attempts between 1602 and 1609 to secure the reversion to the rectory: G.L.C., DL/C/338–9.

[15] See p. 163.

[16] E.R.O., Q/SR 216/124–6; E.R.O., D/AEA 30, f. 140; D/AED 9, ff. 91–4, 82–82v.; ff. 83–85v., 78–78v.; 43–43v., ff. 87–89v., 79–79v.

[17] E.R.O., D/AEA 30, f. 201v; cf. E.R.O., D/AEA 31, f. 287v.; E.R.O., Q/SR 234/122. For the child's baptism and that of his full brother in 1633: E.R.O., D/P 117/1/1.

[18] E.R.O., D/AEA 31, ff. 112, 118; D/AEA 34, f. 30; G.L.C., DL/C/341, f. 187v.; cf. G.L.C., DL/C/316, 341–2.

[19] *L.J.* iv. 273–4; Smith, *Eccl. Hist. Essex*, 245.

[20] Hist. MSS. Com. 6, *7th Rep., H.L.*, p. 48. For Fuller, E.R.O., D/P 117/1/1; Prob. 11/199 (P.C.C. 45 Fines: will of Hamlet Clarke); E.R.O., D/AEW 19/314. It is unlikely that Upminster's John Fuller was also the vicar of Stebbing, as is often stated.

[21] Hist. MSS. Com. 6, *7th Rep.* pp. 48, 52–4, 95, 104, 106, 125; *L.J.* x. 460, 498, 507, 527, 547; *Cal. S.P. Dom.* 1653–4, 273. Cf. *Cal. S.P. Dom.* 1657–8, 351, 375; A. G. Matthews, *Calamy Revised*; E.R.O., T/P 95/1 citing B.L. Add. MSS. 15669–71.

[22] Hist. MSS. Com. 6, *7th Rep.* pp. 48, 52, 95, 104, 106, 125; B.L. Add. MS. 15671, p. 151; *E.A.T.* N.S. xviii. 104; xx. 209; E.R.O., T/P 67/3, p. 120b.

[23] *D.N.B.*, s.v. Robotham, John; Matthews, *Calamy Revised*; Hist. MSS. Com. 6, *7th Rep.* pp. 95, 125; Venn, *Alumni Cantab.* I, ii. 82, 284, 461. Despite the assertion in *E.R.* liii. 116, no contemporary evidence has been found to connect Robotham with the nonconformist congregation in Upminster after 1660.

[24] *D.N.B.*; H.R.L., Wilson, 'Upminster: Religious Hist.', 24–5, 34; Hist. MSS. Com. 5, *6th Rep. I*, p. 393; Hist. MSS. Com. 18, *11th Rep. III*, Southampton, pp. 34–9; C. K. Aked, 'William Derham and "The Artificial Clockmaker",' *Antiquariun Horology* (1970).

[25] H.R.L., Wilson, 'Upminster: Religious Hist.,' 25–8; E.R.O., D/DRu F12/10, 18 Jan. 1835.

[26] See p. 160.

[27] E.R.O., T/P 67/4, p. 198.

[28] H.R.L., Wilson, 'Upminster: Religious Hist.', 19–21; E.R.O., T/P 67/4, pp. 121, 196; T/P 67/1, pp. 115–16.

[29] e.g. E.R.O., T/P 67/1, pp. 83, 84, 134.

although far fewer parishioners than a third were nonconformists.[30] Opposition to Holden diminished in the 1890s, and under his kinsman H. H. Holden, rector 1904–43, the church revived. Regular collections at services, a mothers' meeting, annual church fetes, sidesmen, and a parish magazine were started, and the church was repaired and enlarged.[31] The only disturbance in those years was a Kensitite demonstration in 1910 against the rector's ritualism.[32] The growth of Upminster in the 1920s led to the reappointment of an assistant curate.[33] H. R. Holden, rector 1944–71, was the last of his line.[34]

A brick mission used as a Sunday school was built in 1872 at Hacton Corner just across the border in Rainham, probably by the owner of Rainham Lodge with which it was offered for sale in 1891.[35] It appears originally to have been associated with Rainham parish church, but by 1907, and later, was a mission of Upminster.[36] It was closed *c.* 1949 and afterwards demolished.[37]

The church of *ST. LAWRENCE* consists of a nave and chancel, north aisle, two north chapels, two east vestries, a south chapel, south porch, and west tower. With the exception of the tower the church was almost wholly rebuilt in 1861–2, but the 19th-century structure reproduced closely the form of the earlier church with nave and north aisle terminating respectively in a connecting chancel and chapel, and entry to the church being through the south porch. The eastward extensions of the church in 1928 and 1937 considerably enlarged the building.[38]

The earliest part of the church is the stone tower of *c.* 1200. It is capped by a leaded and shingled spire the framing of which dates partly from the 13th century.[39] Internally the weight of three stages is partly borne on a massive frame inserted in the shell of the tower.

The arcade separating nave and north aisle was one of the few elements retained in the rebuilding of 1861–2. It dates from *c.* 1300 and may be contemporary with the construction of the Gaynes (or St. Mary's) chapel at the eastern end of the north aisle. A wooden screen for the chapel was provided in the 15th century, elements of which are incorporated in the present one.[40]

The rood-loft beam and stairs were still standing in 1573 and the monuments had not then been whitewashed.[41] Complaints were made, 1597–1609, concerning the state of the church, churchyard and rectory, and repairs were undertaken.[42] In 1630 Hamlet Clarke, father-in-law and stepfather of Serjeant Ralph Latham of Gaynes, renovated the Gaynes chapel. Some of the dated and painted armorial glass installed then still remains. Clarke also embellished the 15th-century screen but the embellishments did not survive the restoration of 1861–2.[43] In 1638 the church and spire were fired by lightning, but the bells, which happened to have been taken down at that time, were not damaged.[44]

A new pulpit was installed in 1740.[45] In 1771 the north aisle was encased with stock bricks and given circular windows.[46] It contained *c.* 1790 an octagonal 15th-century font from the former chapel of Upminster Hall.[47] In 1782 a western singing-gallery, of mahogany with elaborate Gothic carving, was erected with the aid of a legacy from William Hornby (d. 1780). In 1845 it was replaced by a lower and larger gallery, removed in 1861–2.

From the 17th to the 19th century Gaynes chapel was apparently attached to New Place. In 1685 it belonged to Sir Thomas Skipwith, Bt.[48] Sir James Esdaile, of New Place, rebuilt it in 1771, constructing a family vault below; and in 1839 James Esdaile sold the rights in the chapel along with New Place.[49] At that time the chapel contained a large family pew, and six other pews which later tenants of New Place sometimes rented to other families.[50]

In 1861–2 the church was rebuilt in stone, partly from a gift from the younger J. R. Holden, to the designs of W. G. Bartleet.[51] Additional seating was provided by the wholesale removal of the old fittings.[52]

In 1906 the vestry was rebuilt, the tower repaired, and the spire re-shingled.[53] Choir-stalls were inserted in the sanctuary in 1909, and in 1912 the church was entirely lit by gas for the first time.[54]

In 1928–9 the church was extended eastwards to the designs of Sir Charles Nicholson. A new Lady chapel was erected beyond the Gaynes chapel, the chancel was taken into the nave, and a new one built. A south chapel of St. George was also added, with an adjoining organ chamber.[55] New vestries, east of the south chapel, were built in 1937.[56]

[30] E.R.O., T/P 67/1, pp. 84, 140; T/P 67/2, p. 99; T/P 67/1–3 *passim* for the 'nonconformist' burial certificates; T/P 67/1, pp. 10–12 for numbers in 1873.

[31] E.R.O., T/P 67/5, pp. 57, 195, 247; T/P 67/6, pp. 97, 121, 123, 125, 127, 227; T/P 67/7, pp. 26, 35, 147, 229, 301; T/P 67/10, p. 21; T/P 181/11/27.

[32] E.R.O., T/P 67/6, pp. 310–11.

[33] E.R.O., T/P 67/7, p. 174; T/P 181/11/27.

[34] C.C.L., Bp. Inskip's Rec. iii. 150.

[35] Tasker, *Romford, Hornchurch and Upminster*, 41; E.R.O., Sage Coll. *Sale Cats.* vol. viii. 7 (1891). This C. of E. Hacton mission should not be confused with the nonconformist Hacton Central mission at Smokeholes: see below, p. 161.

[36] Lewis, *Rainham*, 78; E.R.O., T/P 67/6, pp. 206, 218; *Kelly's Dir. Essex* (1912 and later edns.); *Chelmsford Dioc. Yr. Bk.* (1932–49).

[37] It was not listed in *Chelmsford Dioc. Yr. Bk.* after 1949; Lewis, *Rainham*, 78.

[38] Unless otherwise stated, the following account of the church is based on: R.C.H.M. *Essex*, iv. 160–1; Pevsner, *Essex* (1964); R. H. Roberts, *A Little Guide to the Parish Church of St. Laurence, Upminster* (1930); Wilson, *Upminster* (1881).

[39] C. A. Hewett, *Devt. of Carpentry 1200–1700*, 59.

[40] For a detailed description of the screen in 1852: E.R.O., T/P 196 (King MSS.) Eccl. Essex, iv. 448.

[41] Hale, *Precedents*, 154.

[42] E.R.O., D/AEA 15, f. 27v.; D/AEA 23 ff. 144, 284, 346.

[43] E.R.O., T/P 67/3, p. 64a, c; T/P 67/7, p. 239; A. Suckling, *Antiquities of Essex*.

[44] E.R.O., T/P 67/6, p. 8.

[45] E.R.O., D/P 117/8/2.

[46] E.R.O., T/P 67/3, pp. 34–5: from an unidentified description of Upminster (from internal evidence of 1789 × 1793).

[47] Presented in 1777, according to Roberts' *Little Guide*.

[48] For Skipwith's connexion with New Place, see p. 150.

[49] E.R.O., D/DJn E1.

[50] E.R.O., D/DSt E 15/5, 6: letters of 6 Jan., 12 Dec. 1854.

[51] *Kelly's Dir. Essex* (1859, 1862); E.R.O., D/DRu F 12/33–4; E.R.O., D/AEM 2/9; H.R.L., Wilson, 'Upminster: Religious Hist.', 19.

[52] E.R.O., D/AEM 1/2; E.R.O., T/P 67/7, p. 123. All, including many Elizabethan pews, were 'thoughtlessly sold to some promiscuous man for £3'.

[53] E.R.O., T/P 67/6, pp. 71, 97; T/P 67/7, pp. 95, 166.

[54] E.R.O., T/P 67/6, p. 234; T/P 67/7, p. 262.

[55] E.R.O., T/P 181/11/27; *E.R.* xxxix. 49.

[56] E.R.O., T/P 181/11/27; C.C.L., Bp. Inskip's Rec., ii. 329.

An organ was bought by subscription in 1876; a new one, bought in 1911, was rebuilt in 1928.[57]

There were four bells in 1552. There are still four; (i) *c.* 1480; (ii) 1974; (iii) 1583, Robert Mot of Whitechapel (Lond.); (iv) recast 1602. The old (ii) was recast in 1602 and sold in 1823. Its replacement is a memorial gift from the Bowman family.[58]

The plate includes a silver chalice of 1607 or 1608, with the cover missing, a silver paten of 1686, and a silver paten on foot of 1704.[59]

The oldest surviving monuments are 8 brasses. They commemorate, among others, Elizabeth Deyncourt (d. *c.* 1455), Nicholas Wayte (d. 1542) and his wife Ellen (d. 1545), and Gerard Dewes (d. 1591) in armour.[60] There are various Branfill monuments, including a half-figure of Andrew Branfill (d. 1709). An inscription to James Esdaile (d. 1812) by Sir Richard Westmacott, and another to Sir James Esdaile (d. 1793), attributed to Richard Westmacott the elder, are with other Esdaile monuments in the former Gaynes chapel.[61]

In 1961 the rector and churchwardens received £2,600 under the will of Caroline F. Whitehead, to be used for the advancement of religion in the parish. The money was placed in trust and is used for church purposes.[62]

In 1864 the vestry bought the NE. corner of the rectory's kitchen-garden to extend the churchyard, thus giving it a boundary on Upminster Hill (St. Mary's Lane). The 'old' churchyard was closed in 1891, and by 1902 the 'new' churchyard was full.[63] In 1926, with parish sentiment continuing to prefer burial in a churchyard, the rector gave another piece of the rectory garden north of the nave.[64] The present avenues of yew were planted by Mrs. Branfill in 1848; they replaced horse chestnuts given by Champion Branfill (I) before 1735.[65]

ROMAN CATHOLICISM. A cadet branch of the recusant Wiseman family of Felsted and Wimbish was resident at Upminster from 1576 to *c.* 1612.[66] In 1628 there were two Catholic yeoman families in the parish, servants of the Petres of Cranham.[67]

In 1880 or 1881 Helen Tasker, Countess Tasker, bought the Hill Place estate which included Hill House (or Minster House or Upminster House), St. Mary's Lane. Canon J. Kyne (d. 1881) of Brentwood opened a small oratory at Hill House, and services were continued there until 1888, when the property was sold after the Countess's death.[68]

In 1923, through the efforts of the Revd. Julius Van Meenen of Romford and other Romford Roman Catholics, the church of *ST. JOSEPH* was opened; it was served at first from Romford, but by the end of the year a separate parish was formed.[69] The original building, on the corner of St. Mary's Lane and Sunnyside Gardens, was closed in 1932 when a corner site was acquired in Champion Road and a temporary church opened there.[70] In 1934 the adjoining property of Mavisbank, St. Mary's Lane, was bought for use as a school.[71] The present church of St. Joseph was built in 1939.[72]

In 1927 Sisters of the Sacred Heart of Mary bought Hill Place, St. Mary's Lane, as a convent and girls school.[73]

PROTESTANT NONCONFORMITY. Even after the Restoration and the ejection of the rector John Halke in 1662, the influence of Puritanism continued. Five parishioners were charged in 1663 with refusing to attend the parish church.[74] In 1672 the house of Samuel Springham was licensed as a Presbyterian meeting-place.[75] Six nonconformists were reported in the parish in 1676.[76] Some of them may have been Baptists, for in that year a known Baptist, Richard Robinson, was rated in the parish, as well as Springham.[77] Springham's Presbyterian congregation still existed in 1708 when application was made for his house at the Brick-kilns to be licensed, but there is no record of it later.[78]

A general Baptist church drawing its worshippers from Pilgrim's Hatch, Hornchurch, Aveley, and Upminster originated before 1700. One of its members, Richard Robinson of Upminster, was transferred from Pilgrim's Hatch to a sister church at Rainham *c.* 1697.[79] John Pain, whose house at South Weald was licensed for Baptists in 1705, was one of the elders in 1715, the other being Coomes; at that date congregations of 200 were attending meetings at Pilgrim's Hatch and Aveley.[80] From

[57] E.R.O., T/P 67/1, p. 40; T/P 67/7, pp. 104, 138, 293.

[58] *Ch. Bells Essex*, 425; E.R.O., D/AEA 23, f. 284; D/AEA 25, ff. 90v. 96; E.R.O., T/P 67/3, p. 160d; T/P 67/4, pp. 88–9; inf. from Rector.

[59] *Ch. Plate Essex*, 17; the 1686 paten, inscribed 'Upminster', is usually described as an alms-dish, but the visitation of 1685 noted the lack of 'a plate for to administer the bread upon': *E.A.T.* N.S. xxi. 324–5; E.R.O., T/P 67/9, pp. 80–1.

[60] M. Stephenson, *List of Monumental Brasses*, 138–9, 745; for 19th-century losses, *Arch. Jnl.* xiii (1856), 182; *E.R.* v. 205.

[61] Letter to E.R.O., 1974, from Mr. Edmund Esdaile.

[62] Inf. from Rector.

[63] E.R.O., D/P 117/8/12; E.R.O., T/P 67/2, p. 120. See also p. 155.

[64] C.C.L., Bp. Inskip's Rec. i. 245.

[65] E.R.O., D/DRu F 12/22; E.R.O., D/P 117/1/1, preliminary note in the handwriting of William Derham (d. 1735). Cf. H.R.L., Wilson, 'Upminster: Religious Hist.', 28.

[66] C.P. 25(2)/130/1663; *Visit. Essex* (Harl. Soc.), i. 526–8; *Cal. S.P. Dom.* 1591–4, 406; E.R.O., D/AEA 25, ff. 55, 112–13, 119, D/AEA 26, ff. 30, 95.

[67] E.R.O., Q/SR 263/26; 266/15, 43; 269/20; 271/18; 273/18; 274/9. Cf. Q/SR 217/30, 220/26.

[68] H.R.L., Wilson, 'Upminster: Religious Hist.', 61–2; *Kelly's Dir. Essex* (1882); inf. from Rt. Revd. B. Foley, Bp. of Lancaster.

[69] *Brentwood Dioc. Mag.* v. 117–18; x. 72; xii. 115, 118; *Catholic Dir.* (1943), 166.

[70] G.R.O. Worship Reg. nos. 49250 (cancelled 1932), 54123; inf. from Sister Mary, of the Sacred Heart Convent.

[71] *Story of Upminster*, ii. 14; see below, p. 162.

[72] G.R.O. Worship Reg. no. 59001 (replacing 54123); *Cath. Dir.* (1943, 1973).

[73] *Story of Upminster*, ii. 13; *Kelly's Dir. Essex* (1933); *Cath. Dir.* (1943), 166; see below, p. 162.

[74] Wilson, *Upminster* (1881), 117.

[75] G. L. Turner, *Orig. Recs. of Prot. Nonconformity*, i. 568, ii. 931.

[76] William Salt Library, Stafford, S.2112 (Bp. Compton's census, 1676).

[77] Wilson, *Upminster* (1881), 60–1; E.R.O., T/Z 8 (s.v. Pilgrim's Hatch). A Jonathan Pain rated in 1676 may also have been a Baptist. Members of the Pain family were prominent Baptists *c.* 1705–53. See also below.

[78] E.R.O., Q/SBb 42/15. For the house at the Brick-kilns, see the tithe map 1842 (E.R.O., D/CT 373b, no. 150a), called Pot Kilns on O.S. Map 6″, Essex, LXVII (surv. 1866).

[79] W. T. Whitley, *Bapt. London*, 126; E.R.O., T/Z 8 (s.v. Pilgrim's Hatch); see above, p. 141. Richard Robinson was rated in Upminster in 1676 and 1700: Wilson, *Upminster* (1881), 60; E.R.O., D/P 117/8/1.

[80] E.R.O., Q/SBb 32/53, 40/1; Dr. Williams's Libr. MS. 34.4, Evans List, f. 40.

1737 the church, located from 1732 in Hornchurch, was centred on Upminster. Abraham Nelson was named as elder 1732–53.[81] The church died out between 1756 and 1773, perhaps after Nelson's death *c.* 1764.[82] Its meeting-place was probably an old house on Chafford Heath traditionally associated with the Robinson, Nelson, and Wood families, of which part was said to have been used for many years as a chapel by the Wood family.[83] John Wood, a contemporary of Nelson's, died *c.* 1775.[84] A pulpit was removed *c.* 1816 when the house was converted into two cottages, but some chapel fittings still remained in 1856. In a burial ground behind the house were two box trees clipped to form an alcove for the minister and a desk for the bible.[85]

Upminster Baptist church, Springfield Gardens, originated in 1934 with support from North Street Baptist Church, Hornchurch.[86] In 1935 a school-chapel was built and a church of 33 members was formed. The church building was opened in 1959. Membership rose from 133 in 1945 to 257 in 1973.[87] The church initiated the formation of Cranham Baptist church.[88]

The Society of Friends held meetings in 1913 on the initiative of Harry Frizzell (d. 1933), a baker newly arrived in Upminster. After several months the attempt to establish an allowed meeting was discontinued.[89]

Upminster (Wesleyan) Methodist church, Hall Lane, originated in 1910 when a temporary iron church was erected for the developing garden suburb. It was in the Ilford circuit. A permanent church, in the Tudor Gothic style with two low corner towers, was built in 1923 and enlarged in 1935. In 1947 it was included in the new Romford circuit.[90]

A house in Upminster was registered for worship in 1848 by a Primitive Methodist preacher, Robert Eaglen of Brentwood.[91] This society, which was no doubt in the short-lived Brentwood mission circuit, does not seem to have survived.

Upminster United Reformed (formerly Congregational) church, Station Road, originated before 1799 in a weekday lecture given by an unnamed neighbouring minister. He was probably Henry Attely, of Romford Bethel chapel, who registered Thomas Talbot's house in Upminster for Independent worship in 1797 and 1798.[92] In 1799 William Nokes (d. 1846) of Bridge Farm registered his house for Independents, and Hoxton academy was asked to supply students to preach there.[93] Nokes's brother James (d. 1838) of Hunts Farm registered the chapel which was opened in 1800.[94] It stood on the south side of Upminster Hill (St. Mary's Lane) next to Thomas Talbot's house.[95] The strength of local support for the chapel derived partly from the bitterness of local tithe disputes.[96] In 1803 the freehold of the site was bought. Mrs. Elizabeth Fries (d. 1807), who had been a benefactor in 1800, left £100 stock for the maintenance of the chapel and made an equivalent reversionary bequest for poor members of the congregation.[97] In 1819 a plot south of the chapel was bought, the building extended southwards, and a vestry built.[98] In 1824 George Rogers became the first settled pastor.[99] In 1829 the chapel was attracting many members from neighbouring parishes.[1] It was refronted in 1847.[2] In the 1850s the congregation gained an influential if somewhat formidable patron in the Revd. George Clayton (1783–1862), recently retired to Gaynes Park after some fifty years as pastor of York Street chapel, Walworth (Lond.). He had preached his first sermon in the new Upminster chapel in 1800 and preached his last there in 1862.[3] He left £500 stock to the church.[4] A mission was supported at Hornchurch, and Upminster shared with Brentwood the oversight of the chapel at Upminster common.[5]

The disgrace of the rector and the coincidental death of Mrs. Branfill in 1873 left a social and religious void in the parish. It was filled by Congregationalists under the leadership of Henry Joslin of Gaynes Park and his brother-in-law A. M. Carter, minister 1870–1907.[6] In 1885 three, if not four, of the five members of Upminster's first school board were Congregationalists.[7] In 1873 the chapel was restored.[8] In 1911 a larger stone church, designed by T. Stevens in Gothic style, was built in Station Road.[9] The old chapel was sold to the Brethren.[10]

[81] W. T. Whitley, *Mins. of General Assembly of General Baptist Church*, ii. 6 sqq. Abraham Nelson was rated in Upminster 1745–64; no rates survive 1702–44: E.R.O., D/P 117/12/1, 3, 4.

[82] E.R.O., T/Z 8 (s.v. Pilgrim's Hatch). It is not in the Thompson List: Dr. Williams's Libr., MS. 38.5, 38.6. Nelson's executors were rated in his stead in 1765: E.R.O., D/P 117/12/4.

[83] Wilson, *Upminster* (1856), 88.

[84] For Abraham and John Wood from the 1730s: E.R.O., D/P 117/8/2, 117/12/1–4.

[85] Wilson, *Upminster* (1856), 88; E.R.O., T/P 67/5 p. 121. On the tithe map of 1842 (E.R.O., D/CT 373) the two cottages (no. 646) appear on the edge of Chafford Heath (no. 645), with a pightle behind them (no. 647), perhaps the burial ground.

[86] Account based on: E.R.O., D/NB 2/3, 4; D. Witard, *Bibles in Barrels*, 172; *Bapt. Handbk.* (1945–71); R. M. Nurse, *Hornchurch Baptist Church: Souvenir Handbook* (1953), 8; *Bapt. Handbk.* (1936), 363; *Upminster Bapt. Ch., 1935–6*.

[87] *Bapt. Union Dir.*, 1973–4.

[88] See p. 109.

[89] E.R.O., T/P 67/10, p. 33; inf. from Friends House; E.R.O., T/A 568.

[90] E. Barrett, *The Lamp still burns*, 9, 32–3; G.R.O. Worship Reg. nos. 44315 (cancelled 1923), 48916; *Mins. Meth. Conf.* 1946, 1947; *Kelly's Dir. Essex* (1912).

[91] G.R.O. Worship Returns, London dioc. bps. ct. no. 2288.

[92] *Evangel. Mag.* viii. 307 (1800); G.R.O. Worship Returns, London Dioc. bps. ct. nos. 437, 439, 446; see also above, p. 90.

[93] G.R.O. Worship Returns, London dioc. bps. ct. no. 510; H.R.L., T. L. Wilson, 'Upminster: Religious Hist.', 39; *Evangel. Mag.* viii. 307.

[94] G.R.O. Worship Returns, London dioc. bps. ct. no. 525.

[95] Unless otherwise stated, the following account of the chapel is based on H.R.L., Wilson, 'Upminster: Religious Hist.', 38 sqq.

[96] See p. 157.

[97] Wilson, *Upminster* (1856), 102–3.

[98] Wilson, in E.R.O., T/P 67/4, pp. 185, 198, corrected his earlier statement (Wilson, *Upminster* (1881), 119) that the chapel was extended in 1827–8.

[99] Biographical details of all the pastors, 1824–1902, are given in H.R.L., Wilson, 'Upminster: Religious Hist.'

[1] E.R.O., Q/CR 3/1/284. This was probably so from the beginning: William Smith of Hornchurch was one of the original benefactors of the chapel.

[2] See illus. in C. W. Smith, *Upminster Congr. Ch. 1911–61*, 4.

[3] E.R.O., T/P 95, p. 147. See also above, p. 150.

[4] Smith, op. cit. 6, 17.

[5] See p. 50 and below.

[6] e.g. E.R.O., T/P 67/1, pp. 83, 84, 134.

[7] Ibid. pp. 84, 140; T/P 67/2, p. 99.

[8] E.R.O., T/P 67/1, p. 10.

[9] Smith, op. cit. 9–12.

[10] See p. 161.

Southend Arterial Road at Hall Lane, looking west

Station Road: Shops built 1907

UPMINSTER

UPMINSTER: Great Tomkyns, 15th century

ROMFORD: Shops in Balgores Square, Gidea Park, early-20th century

ROMFORD: Angel Cottages, Noak Hill, late-14th or early-15th century

ROMFORD: House in Reed Pond Road, Gidea Park, 1910

The new church had a mission room in St. Lawrence Road, *c.* 1912–26, and also took over the Hacton mission.[11] In 1972 the church joined the United Reformed church.[12] There were 205 members in 1975.[13]

The Hacton Central mission, Smokeholes, opposite Harwood Hall Lane, was founded in 1904 by Mrs. James Strang of Rainham Lodge.[14] It was undenominational and for some years Wesleyan lay preachers helped there. Mr. and Mrs. W. Strang gave the hall to the Upminster Congregational trustees in 1911.[15] It continued as Hacton Congregational mission until 1963 when services ceased, but the hall was in use in 1966, let for undenominational youth meetings at a nominal rent. In 1974 it housed an afternoon Sunday school.[16] The mission has chiefly served Corbets Tey and Hacton, but the site of the hall is just within Rainham.

At Upminster Common there has been a nonconformist congregation, more or less continuously, since the early 19th century. In 1829 about 60 worshippers were meeting in a house there under the superintendence of Samuel H. Carlisle, minister of Romford Congregational church.[17] The connexion with Romford ceased, but for some years, *c.* 1835–40, services were held at the mill-house on the common, in connexion with Upminster Congregational church. Those services seem to have ended with the death of the miller, James Pinchon, in 1840; but in 1850 a chapel was built in Hall Lane on a site given by his sister-in-law, Mrs. Lydia Pinchon of Potkiln Farm.[18] The chapel was under the joint oversight of the Congregational churches of Brentwood and Upminster, and the Brentwood town and village missionary, George Matthews, was in charge of it from 1851 to 1870.[19] An Upminster Common Sunday school existed in 1888.[20] After a period of inactivity the chapel was reopened in 1915.[21] In 1940 the building was re-certified for undenominational worship.[22] The chapel was destroyed by bombing in 1944, and the site was sold.[23] A new undenominational chapel was later built there and was registered in 1953.[24]

The congregation of Open Brethren, St. Mary's Lane, appears to have originated about 1907. In that year Brethren who had been worshipping in a cottage near Hunts Farm built a gospel hall on the south side of St. Lawrence Road.[25] It seems likely that these were the Brethren who took over and registered the former Congregational church and at the same time, perhaps in part-exchange, acquired the gospel hall as a mission.[26] The chapel was bought for the Brethren by Henry Warren of Cranham.[27] In 1971 Open Brethren were still worshipping in the Old Chapel, by then the oldest surviving nonconformist building in the neighbourhood.[28] It has a Tuscan porch and a pediment with a semi-circular window.[29] In 1952 Brethren also registered the Assembly Room, St. Lawrence Road, the original gospel hall.[30]

A meeting-room of unknown denomination in Branfill Road was listed in 1951.[31] Christadelphians were meeting in Clock House Hall, St. Mary's Lane, over the branch library, in 1958.[32]

EDUCATION. There is a reference to a schoolmaster in Upminster *c.* 1580,[33] and another in 1596.[34] For a short time in 1640–1 Ralph Josselin (1616–83) taught school at Upminster, 'which was great trouble'.[35] In 1807 there were two dame schools with 30 children in each.[36] In 1819 there was a dame school for 49 young children.[37] A school for 20 boys and girls was started in 1831, supported by a private person.[38] The efforts of nonconformists and churchmen in the earlier 19th century culminated in the building of a British school and a National school, both in 1851. A non-sectarian evening-school was started and run by Francis Sterry, assistant curate, 1860–64.[39] When a school board was formed in 1885, at least three of its five members were Congregationalists.[40] In 1891 Upminster joined Cranham to provide technical instruction classes.[41]

The British school for 150 children, built on land in Hall Lane (later Station Road), given by Edward Dawson, opened in February 1851.[42] There is evidence of earlier nonconformist schools. There was a Sunday school at the new Congregational chapel where a master from Talbot's private school taught in 1800–1.[43] In 1833 there were two Sunday schools, supported by Independents, for 46 boys and 73 girls.[44] A non-sectarian school for boys and girls, North Upminster school, was founded in 1839 and supported by subscriptions and school pence. A mistress taught spelling, reading, and sewing daily in the schoolroom,[45] which may have been at the mill-house on Upminster common where Congre-

[11] *Kelly's Dir. Essex* (1912–26); and see below.
[12] G.R.O. *Official List*.
[13] *United Reformed Ch. Year Bk.* (1975), 159.
[14] Account based on Lewis, *Rainham*, 78, 86. Cf. G.R.O. Worship Reg. no. 43417. There was also a C. of E. mission at Hacton Corner; see above, p. 158.
[15] Smith, op. cit. 14.
[16] Inf. from Mr. A. Bonnett, sen.
[17] E.R.O., Q/CR 3/2/88. See also above, p. 89. No record of this licence has been found.
[18] H.R.L., Wilson, 'Upminster: Religious Hist.', 46, 60; Wilson, *Upminster* (1881), 196; E.R.O., D/DZb 2, pp. 281–4; *Strat. Expr.* 24 June 1885.
[19] H.O. 129/7/197; Smith, op. cit. 14; J. K. Sigurnay, *A hundred years in a country chapel*, 7–11.
[20] *Strat. Expr.* 25 Apr. 1888.
[21] E.R.O., T/P 67/9, p. 44.
[22] G.R.O. Worship Reg. nos. 25994, 59295.
[23] Smith, op. cit. 14; E.R.O., C/W 1/2/59.
[24] G.R.O. Worship Reg. no. 63941. The foundation stone of 1850 is built into the lecture-room wall of the new chapel.
[25] H.R.L., Wilson, 'Upminster: Religious Hist.', 61.
[26] *Story of Upminster*, ii. 7; G.R.O. Worship Reg no. 44871. See also above.
[27] E.R.O., T/P 67/7, p. 150. Warren lived at Crouch House, Cranham.
[28] G.R.O. *Official List* (1971); *Havering Dir. Local Organizations* (1971), 6.
[29] Pevsner, *Essex*, 398.
[30] G.R.O. Worship Reg. no. 63726: still active in 1974.
[31] *Hornchurch Official Guide* (1951), 61. It was not listed in the 1953 *Guide*.
[32] *Christadelphian Auxiliary Lecturing Soc. Pocket Diary* (1958). There is no mention of this group in *Hornchurch Official Guide* (1951–62).
[33] *D.N.B. s.v.* Salter, Tho.
[34] E.R.O., D/AEA 17, f. 193.
[35] *Ralph Josselin's Diary* (Camd. 3rd ser. xv), 9.
[36] E.R.O., D/AEM 2/4.
[37] *Digest of Returns to Sel. Cttee. on Educ. of Poor*, H.C. 224, p. 274 (1819), ix (1).
[38] *Educ. Enquiry Abstract*, H.C. 62, p. 293 (1835), xli.
[39] H.R.L., Wilson, 'Upminster: Religious Hist.', 30.
[40] E.R.O., T/P 67/1, p. 140.
[41] E.R.O., T/P 67/2, p. 99.
[42] Ed. 21/5404; Wilson, *Upminster* (1881), 126.
[43] E.R.O., T/P 67/4, p. 201.
[44] *Educ. Enquiry Abstract*, H.C. 62, p. 293 (1835), xli.
[45] E.R.O., T/P 67/1, p. 142.

gational services were being held at that period.[46] It may have been the school, supported by subscriptions, where 24 infants were being taught in 1846–7.[47] The British school in Hall Lane was supported by subscriptions and school pence;[48] by 1872 it was receiving a government grant and was attended by 71 children.[49] It was amalgamated with the National school in 1884[50] and was transferred to the school board in 1885.[51] The building was demolished *c.* 1936.[52]

The National school for 100 children, with a school-house, was built by subscription and a government grant on land given by Mrs. Branfill[53] opposite the British school in Hall Lane.[54] It opened in March 1851.[55] It seems to have developed from an earlier parochial school. In 1823 and 1833 John Crowest, vestry clerk (d. 1834), was also schoolmaster[56] and may have taught at the school which existed in 1828.[57] Mrs. Crowest is said to have kept the parochial day-school in two cottages behind the club house and later in Ingrebourne cottage.[58] By 1842 children were required to learn the catechism and to attend church on Sunday wearing pinafores, cloaks and bonnets.[59] A church Sunday school had been founded by 1825.[60] In 1846–7 the Church day- and Sunday school, supported by subscription, had a teacher's house and schoolroom where a master and two mistresses taught 62 boys and girls.[61] By 1872 the National school was receiving a government grant and was attended by 56 children.[62] It was amalgamated with the British school in 1884[63] and transferred to the school board in 1885.[64]

Upminster county primary school, St. Mary's Lane. In 1885 Upminster board school was opened in the buildings of the old British and National schools. The girls and infants department, in the old British school, was enlarged in 1888 for 190 children.[65] By 1911 a hundred girls were being taught there in one room.[66] The old National school was rebuilt in 1897 for 126 boys.[67] In 1927 a temporary school for 150 infants opened in St. Mary's Lane. In 1928 the new school for mixed and infant children was opened and the girls were transferred there from the old British school, which was adapted as a practical instruction centre.[68] The new school was enlarged in 1932 but in 1934, following electrification of the railway and consequent house-building, the 1897 boys school was used again.[69] The school was reorganized for junior mixed and infant children in 1936[70] when the seniors were transferred to Gaynes senior council school. The school was damaged by bombing in the Second World War.[71]

Gaynes county secondary school, Brackendale Gardens. Gaynes senior council school was opened in 1936 on the Cranston Park estate for 480 senior children from Upminster, Cranham, and North and South Ockendon.[72] The school was damaged by bombing in the Second World War.[73] It was enlarged in 1960, 1963, and 1970.[74]

Branfil county infants school, Cedar Avenue, opened in 1943 as a temporary school for 100 infants. Hornchurch county high school used part of the school from 1943.[75] The junior school opened in 1954 when the high school moved to new buildings.[76]

Corbets Tey county special school, Harwood Hall Lane, for sub-normal children aged 5–16 years, was built in 1956.[77]

The Sacred Heart of Mary (known until 1955 as St. Mary's) Roman Catholic secondary school for girls,[78] St. Mary's Lane, opened as a boarding- and day-school in 1927 at Hill Place, and was enlarged in 1930. It was granted Aided status in 1950. In 1966 there were 390 on the roll; in 1974 it was a day-school for about 150.[79]

St. Joseph's Roman Catholic primary school, St. Mary's Lane, opened in a house called Mavisbank after the Second World War.[80] It was recognized by the Ministry of Education in 1953 as a temporary annexe to St. Mary's primary school, Hornchurch, for 110 children.[81] In 1956 it moved to new premises on the site of Mavisbank as a separate Aided school.[82]

The Coopers' Company and Coborn voluntary Aided mixed secondary school, St. Mary's Lane. This school, whose history is described elsewhere, was moved from Bow (Lond.) between 1971 and 1974 owing to the difficulty of recruiting children there.[83]

PRIVATE SCHOOLS. By 1833 there were five private schools in Upminster.[84] Thomas Talbot, who lived in Upminster from 1796 to 1832,[85] kept a boys school in the house which later became the manse, next to Hill Place.[86] It is said that the school was founded there in the 17th century.[87] It was still there in 1833.[88] The house was pulled down in 1872.[89] Upminster House, built by Samuel Hammond in the

[46] See p. 161.
[47] *Nat. Soc. Church Schs. Enquiry 1846–7.*
[48] E.R.O., T/P 67/1, p. 7, items 21, 22.
[49] *Rep. of Educ. Cttee. of Council 1872–3* [C.812], p. 410, H.C. (1873), xxiv.
[50] E.R.O., T/P 67/1, pp. 109–10.
[51] Ed. 21/5404.
[52] *Story of Upminster*, ii. 20; see p. 163.
[53] Wilson, *Upminster* (1881), 126; Ed. 21/5404.
[54] Ed. 21/28149; E.R.O., T/Z 25/123.
[55] Wilson, *Upminster* (1881), 126.
[56] E.R.O., T/P 67/7, pp. 133, 136.
[57] E.R.O., D/DRu F12/3 (9, 15 June, 9, 14, 16 July).
[58] E.R.O., T/P 67/2, p. 61; *White's Dir. Essex* (1848), 207.
[59] E.R.O., T/P 67/2, p. 61.
[60] E.R.O., D/P 117/8/10.
[61] *Nat. Soc. Church Schs. Enquiry 1846–7.*
[62] *Rep. of Educ. Cttee. of Council 1872–3* [C. 812], p. 410, H.C. (1873), xxiv.
[63] E.R.O., T/P 67/1, pp. 109–10.
[64] Ed. 21/5404.
[65] *Kelly's Dir. Essex* (1890).
[66] E.R.O., T/P 67/7, p. 147.
[67] *Kelly's Dir. Essex* (1898); Ed. 21/5404. The building was demolished in 1966: V. Body, *Upminster Story*, 14.
[68] Ed. 21/28149; E.R.O., C/ME 24, pp. 199, 455; E.R.O., T/P 67/7, p. 267.
[69] Ed. 21/28149.
[70] Inf. from Essex Educ. Dept.
[71] E.R.O., C/W 1/2/57.
[72] Ed. 21/28151; inf. from Essex Educ. Dept.
[73] E.R.O., C/ME 47, p. 660.
[74] *Essex Educ. Building Suppl.* (Sept. 1960) p. 2, (July 1963) p. 50; *Havering Official Guide* (1969–70).
[75] E.R.O., C/ME 39, p. 373.
[76] Inf. from Essex Educ. Dept.; see p. 53.
[77] *Havering Official Guide* (1966–7), 45; *Essex Educ. Building Suppl.* (July 1957).
[78] E.R.O., C/ME 49, p. 747.
[79] *Story of Upminster*, ii. 13; E.R.O., C/ME 44, p. 489; local inf.; *Havering Official Guide* (1966–7), 38.
[80] *Story of Upminster*, ii. 14; E.R.O., T/P 221/23 pp. 25–6.
[81] E.R.O., C/ME 47, p. 569; see above, p. 52.
[82] Local inf.; *Story of Upminster*, ii. 13; inf. from Essex Educ. Dept.
[83] Coopers' Co. and Coborn school, official Opening Programme (1974); *V.C.H. Mdx.* i. 290–3.
[84] *Educ. Enquiry Abstract*, H.C. 62, p. 293 (1835), xli.
[85] E.R.O., T/P 95/1, p. 99.
[86] E.R.O., T/P 67/4, pp. 200–1.
[87] Wilson, *Upminster* (1881), 125–8.
[88] *Educ. Enquiry Abstract*, H.C. 62, p. 293 (1835), xli.
[89] Wilson, *Upminster* (1881), 123–4.

1790s for Elizabeth Fries (d. 1807) as a girls school, continued for many years. It was conducted 1848 to 1875 by Elizabeth Attwell who enlarged it twice; it closed in 1878.[90] In 1912 the house, then known as Hill House, was being used as a kindergarten but this had closed by 1929.[91] Another school existed in the house in the 1930s;[92] in the 1950s and 1960s it was occupied by Minster House school.[93]

From 1804 to 1843 John Saunders kept a boarding school at High House, Corbets Tey,[94] where there were 35 children in 1819;[95] in 1833 it was a day- and boarding-school for 37 boys.[96] It was kept by Thomas Freshwater in 1848.[97] Henry Holden (curate 1840–46) kept a preparatory school at Grove Cottage.[98] A high school for girls was opened at Bridge House in 1895, but it closed in 1898.[99] Upminster high school for girls, in Hall Lane, opened in 1907 and by 1918 the numbers taught had risen from 12 to 70;[1] it was later a mixed preparatory boarding-school, and had closed by 1933.[2] In 1966 there were four private nursery schools in Upminster; they had closed by 1972.[3]

EDUCATIONAL CHARITIES. By the gift of Sarah Boyce, *c.* 1855, and by the will of Mary Laycock Boyce, proved 1869, a total of £200 was placed in trust to provide rewards for boys of Upminster, over 11 years old, who habitually attended the parish church and the Sunday and parochial schools.[4] Since the 19th century the trust has provided prizes and study-grants for choir boys.[5]

The old British school in Station Road was sold for redevelopment about 1936. The proceeds accumulated until 1951, when a Ministry of Education Scheme provided that they should be placed in trust for the promotion of education in Upminster. In 1973 grants totalling £485 were paid to various organizations in Upminster.[6]

CHARITIES FOR THE POOR. John Fenick (Fenyx) by his will proved 1587 gave rent from land in Upminster to pay 18*d.* weekly to the poor.[7] In 1596 the rent-charged was redeemed for £40.[8] In the 17th century £15 was added to the stock by the Latham family and £20 by Nathan Sand (Sonds) curate.[9] Other sums also seem to have been added and by 1734 the stock amounted to £110. In 1750 the whole of the capital was used to build a parish poorhouse. This was regarded as a loan secured on the rates and the interest on it was spent on bread for the poor.[10] When the house was sold in 1837 the Poor Law Commissioners directed that the proceeds should be lent to Romford board of guardians towards building the union workhouse. The board paid interest on the loan to Upminster parish officers in 1837. In 1838 the capital was used to liquidate part of Upminster's share in the cost of building Romford union workhouse.[11]

Thomas Frith, by deed dated 1610 and confirmed 1633, granted in trust an annuity of £4 10*s.* out of lands called Cockhides in North Ockendon. Ten shillings were for a sermon on St. Mark's day, 2*s.* for the minister who read the Litany, and the remainder to provide 1*s.* 6*d.* in bread every Sunday to the poor of Upminster. In 1837 the whole income was used to provide twopenny loaves fortnightly for the poor.[12] Distribution of bread continued until 1914. It was withheld during the First World War and for some years afterwards. In 1935, when there was a balance of £40, the parochial church council decided to increase the sum spent because of distress in the district. The income was used to buy bread until at least 1953.[13] In 1964–7 it was combined with the Boyce charity[14] and used for rewards for choir boys. Since 1971 the income has been used for occasional payments by the rector to relieve poverty.[15]

GREAT WARLEY

GREAT WARLEY contains three elements: in the north a suburb of Brentwood, with some light industry; along Warley Road and Great Warley Street a sequence of large houses, several of them designed or adapted by architects of repute; and in the rest of the parish a number of large farms. The first is often styled merely Warley.

The ancient parish lying immediately south of Brentwood, and comprising 2,890 a., was one of several long narrow parishes which sloped from the wooded ridge into the Thames plain; it was about 5 miles from north to south.[1] In 1934 the parish was divided between the urban districts of Brentwood and Hornchurch.[2]

The ground slopes from 375 ft. east of the Horse and Groom public house to less than 20 ft. north of Bury Farm, and the soil consists of London clay with an outcropping of Bagshot sands.[3] Two streams flow south and eventually join the Mardyke: one rises in the west of the parish near Hole Farm; the other for much of its length forms the eastern boundary with Little Warley.

[90] Wilson, *Upminster* (1856), 177–8; E.R.O., T/P 67/5, pp. 128, 143; T/P 67/6, p. 339; Wilson, *Upminster* (1881), 178.
[91] *Kelly's Dir. Essex* (1912, 1929).
[92] *Kelly's Dir. Essex* (1933, 1937).
[93] *Hornchurch Official Guide* (1951, 1964–5).
[94] Wilson, Upminster (1881), 167; *Robson's Gazetteer* (*c.* 1840).
[95] *Digest of Returns to Sel. Cttee. on Educ. of Poor*, H.C. 224, p. 274 (1819), ix (1).
[96] *Educ. Enquiry Abstract*, H.C. 62, p. 293 (1835), xli.
[97] *White's Dir. Essex* (1848), p. 207.
[98] H.R.L., Wilson, 'Upminster: Religious Hist.', 28.
[99] E.R.O., T/P 67/3, p. 40a; T/P 67/6, p. 339.
[1] E.R.O., T/P 67/6, p. 213; T/P 67/8, p. 118.
[2] *Kelly's Dir. Essex* (1922–33).
[3] *Havering Official Guide* (1966), 50; inf. from Havering Educ. Dept.
[4] Ed. 49/2228; E.R.O., C/ME 1 (1905), pp. 1748, 1751: E.R.O., T/P 67/1, p. 67a.
[5] Inf. from Rector.
[6] Char. Com. Files.
[7] Prob. 11/70 (P.C.C. 3 Spencer).
[8] E.R.O., D/DA T448.
[9] Salmon, *Essex*, 273; Prob. 11/388 (P.C.C. 130 Foote).
[10] E.R.O., D/P 117/8/2, 3; D/P 117/12/11, 13.
[11] *4th Rep. Poor Law Com.* H.C. 147, p. 212 (1837–8), xxviii; E.R.O., G/RM 1, pp. 100, 328, 368, 386; E.R.O., D/P 117/19/1.
[12] *Rep. Com. Char.* [108], pp. 721–2 (1837–8), xxv.
[13] Char. Com. Files; inf. from Rector.
[14] See above.
[15] Inf. from Rector.
[1] O.S. Map 1/25,000, TQ 58, 59, 68, 69; O.S. Map 6", Essex, LXVII, LXXV (surv. 1865–6).
[2] Essex Review Order, 1934.
[3] *Hist. Gt. Warley* [W.I., 1957], 5.

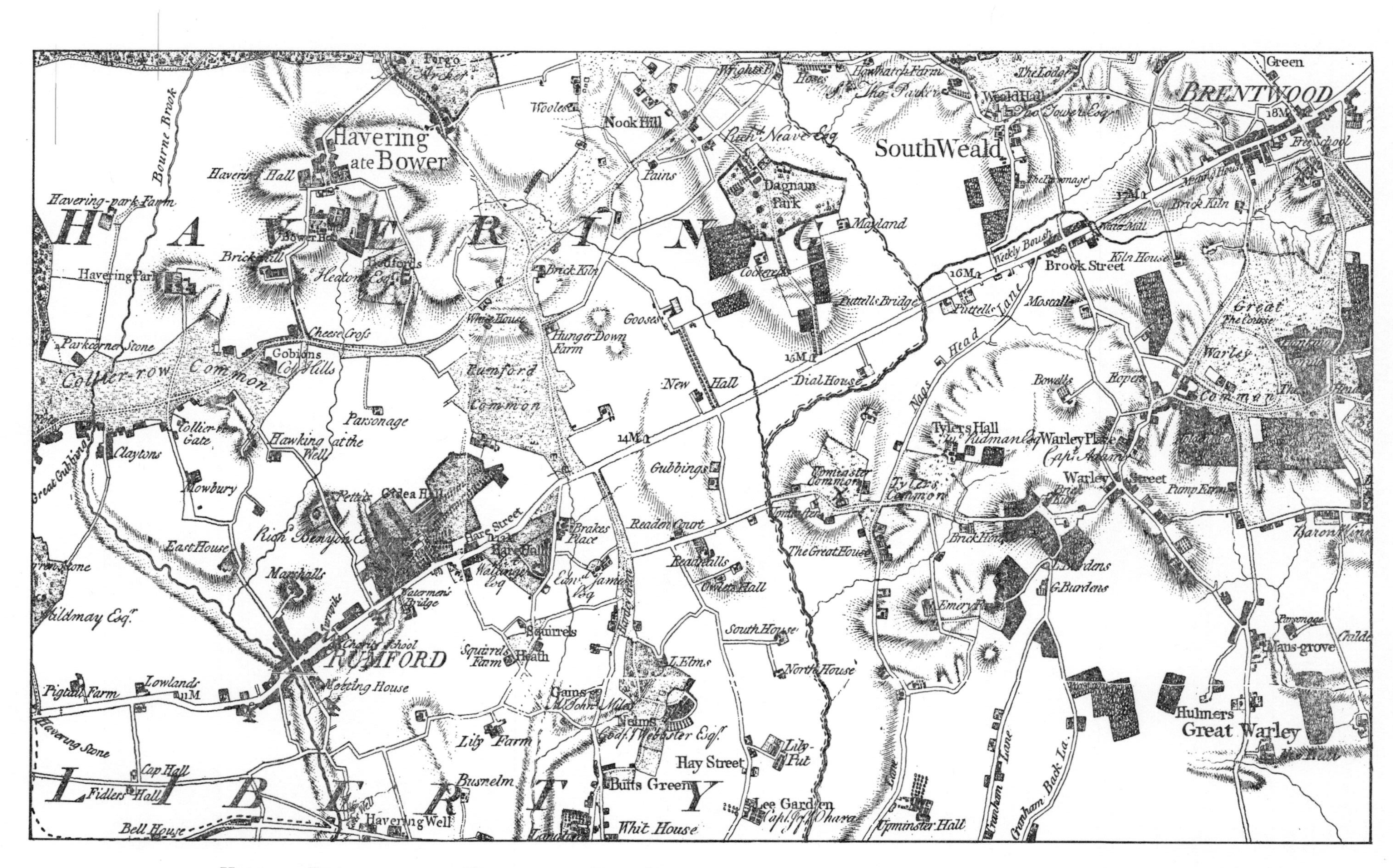

Havering, Romford, and the Warleys, 1777. From Chapman and André's *Map of Essex*, reduced to *c.* 1½ in. to 1 mile.

Great Warley was one of the more populous parishes in Chafford hundred. In 1086 there were 36 recorded inhabitants, and in 1671 fifty-nine occupied houses.[4] The population in 1801 was 430, and after rising in 1811 and 1821 was back to 424 in 1831. In 1841 the population of 596 was swollen by labourers building the Eastern Counties railway. Settlement in the north of the parish followed the extension of the railway beyond Brentwood in 1843: the total population was 952 in 1851, 1,220 in 1861, and 2,051 in 1911. It hardly altered between 1911 and 1921, but in 1931 there were 2,676 inhabitants. The barracks, built in 1805 and re-opened in 1843, were in Little Warley but most of the married quarters were in Great Warley. In 1881 and 1891 they housed some 200 members of army families, and in 1901 and 1911 about 300. After the First World War their population declined: to less than 150 in 1921, and to 202 in 1931.[5]

The road pattern of the late 18th century probably originated in the Middle Ages.[6] A road (Hartswood Road) ran over Warley common from Shenfield to Little Warley. Another ran from Brentwood over Warley Hill along the western edge of the common. It continued as Warley Road to the green, then west to Upminster and Hornchurch.[7] Mascalls Lane, from Brook Street, divided before entering the parish: one branch (now Eagle Way) crossed Warley Hill at the Horse and Groom and continued east across the common; the other (Dark Lane) ran south to the green, where it crossed the Warley Road at the Waylett (Walletts, or cross-roads) on its way south to St. Mary's Lane. Dark Lane probably took its name from the tunnel of elms through which it passed; south of the green most of the trees have been removed, and this stretch is now known as Great Warley Street.[8] In the Middle Ages a second, more westerly road apparently ran south from the green to St. Mary's Lane; it passed Hole Farm, Codham Hall, and Franks manor-house, and still existed in the 19th century as a series of footpaths and lanes known as Pilgrims Way.[9] From Little Warley two lanes ran westwards to the Street; the more northern no longer exists, but at the foot of the hill Bird Lane still runs across the Street to Codham Hall. In the mid 19th century a third lane, Wabbings Lane, lay between them, but by 1895 only the end nearest the Street survived.[10] The derivation of the name is unknown, but it is clearly related to the 8½ a. woodland ¼ mile to the north, known in 1843 as the Wabbings.[11]

This pattern of communication has been little altered since the 18th century. Residential building after the coming of the railway in 1840 led to the creation of a network of streets in the north of the parish. After the closure of the barracks in 1959 more building occurred. In the south the arterial road to Southend, opened in 1925, sliced across the parish between the rectory and the old church; in 1971 a fly-over was built to carry the Street over.[12]

In the Middle Ages Great Warley was a parish of scattered dwellings and farms. Among these was Codham Hall, mentioned in 1276 and perhaps earlier.[13] Bolens, and Herds, in the south of the parish, Hulmers, and Goldings, north of the church, occur in the 15th century.[14] Surviving buildings dating from the 15th century include Wallets, the post office, and a house facing westwards, all around the green, and Franks manor-house.[15] Hole Farm is a small timber-framed house of late medieval type. In the 17th century a chimney and ceiling were inserted in the central room. In the 18th or early 19th century an outshed was built along the north side, and the house was divided into cottages. It has been restored to single occupation and modernized in the present century

By the late 17th century Great Warley possessed a number of large houses: in 1671 sixteen out of sixty had six or more hearths.[16] On the Street, north of the arterial road, the red Brick House has a façade of the early 18th century masking elements of the 16th century, and next to it is Hulmers of the mid 18th century.[17] Warley Elms was built in the early 19th century on the site of an earlier house existing in 1774.[18] North of the green, Warley Place appears to have been built in the late 16th or 17th century; modernized *c.* 1840, the house was enlarged and its gardens were developed between 1875 and the First World War.[19] Warley House, opposite the Horse and Groom, was built in 1805–6 by the Board of Ordnance, apparently for the commandant of the barracks. It was sold in 1820.[20] Sir John English (1788–1840), a former surgeon-general to the Swedish army, owned it from 1826 until his death.[21] In 1921 it became the Marillac hospital.[22] In 1963 the hospital was transferred to the former officers' mess in Eagle Way, and Warley House was later demolished.[23]

Coombe Lodge was built *c.* 1854 for Edward Ind; the house itself lies in Cranham but the lodge, part of the grounds, and much of the original estate of 207 a. are in Great Warley.[24] In 1912 most, if not all, of the estate was sold to Evelyn Heseltine of the Goldings, in Warley Street.[25] Heseltine was a stockbroker who had come to Great Warley *c.* 1875; he bought Goldings in 1881, and throughout his life added to the estate.[26] In the 1880s Ralph Nevill designed cottages, stables, dairy, and alterations and additions to the main house in a style that combined red brick, darkened half-timbering, and shallow plateresque pargetting in a somewhat theatrical style.[27] From Heseltine the estate passed to his

[4] *V.C.H. Essex*, i. 449, 490; E.R.O., Q/RTh 5 m. 1d.
[5] *Census*, 1801–1931.
[6] *Map of Essex* (1777).
[7] The section of Warley Road which bordered the Warley Place estate was moved east from the house, *c.* 1870: O.S. Map 6", Essex, LXVI (1st edn.); E.R.O., *Sale Cat.* B2.
[8] Local inf.
[9] *Hist. Gt. Warley*, 22; O.S. Map 6", Essex, LXVII, LXXV (surv. 1865–6).
[10] O.S. Map 6", Essex, LXVII (surv. 1865–6); O.S. Map 1/2,500, Essex, LXVII. 11 (2nd edn.).
[11] E.R.O., Q/RDc 31.
[12] Inf. from L.B. Havering.
[13] *P.N. Essex*, 135; Hart, *Early Chart. Essex*, 15–16.
[14] *P.N. Essex*, 135.
[15] R.C.H.M. *Essex*, iv. 62.
[16] E.R.O., Q/RTh 5 m. 1d.
[17] R.C.H.M. *Essex*, iv. 62.
[18] *Map of Essex* (1777).
[19] See p. 167.
[20] E.R.O., Q/RPl 130–45.
[21] Ibid. 151–7; *D.N.B.*
[22] E.R.O., T/P 181/12/7 (2 Sept. 1921); see below, p. 173.
[23] *Brentwood Gaz.* 20 Sept. 1963; inf. from hospital.
[24] E.R.O., *Sale Cat.* B1320.
[25] E.R.O., *Sale Cat.* B5742.
[26] Ibid.; *Kelly's Dir. Essex* (1874, 1878); M.I. in church; *Essex in 20th Cent.* (1909), 104, 182; cf. C. Gray, *Peter Warlock*, 286.
[27] E.R.O., *Sale Cat.* B5742; M.I. in church and churchyard.

widow Emily H. (Minnie) Heseltine (d. 1943) and then successively to their grandson, E. R. Denys de Rougemont (d. 1959) and their daughter, Mrs. Muriel E. de Rougemont (d. 1967). In 1971 the estate, then comprising 540 a., was broken up and sold.[28]

Codham Hall, which belonged to the Warley Franks estate, was rebuilt in the later 19th century, after Richard Benyon bought the estate. It is a large building of yellow brick, typical of the Benyon farmhouses. In Benyon times it would have had a uniform trim of dark red paint.[29] Warley Lea, opposite Warley Place, was enlarged for Rose Willmott, perhaps on her marriage in 1891 to Robert Berkeley of Spetchley (Worcs.). The alterations are said to have been designed by Sir Edwin Lutyens. In 1957 a wing of the house was demolished.[30]

In 1769 there were two public houses in Great Warley, the Thatchers Arms and the Magpie. The Thatchers Arms, which stands north of the green, was rebuilt in the early 19th century; the Magpie, on Headley Common, became the Headley Arms *c.* 1846 and was last rebuilt in the 1960s.[31] The Horse and Groom, which stands on the corner of Warley Road and Mascalls Lane in South Weald parish, was built by 1770, probably for the benefit of those attending Brentwood races on Warley Common. It was at first called the King's Head or King Herod, and later (1778–81) the Horse and Jockey, before receiving its present name.[32]

The northern part of the parish remained open common until the 19th century. Warley common, which extended into Little Warley, was sometimes used in the 18th century for military camps,[33] as well as for the races.[34] In 1805 George Winn, who owned the manors of Great and Little Warley, sold 116 a. of the common to the government to build permanent barracks.[35] In 1840 the Eastern Counties railway was extended to Brentwood, looping south of the town, close to the common.[36] In 1843 it was extended to Chelmsford and Colchester.[37] In the same year the remaining 172 a. of Warley common were inclosed, providing a residential area convenient for Brentwood station and later for the staff of the large Essex lunatic asylum, which was opened in 1853 across the parish boundary in South Weald.[38]

This new suburb of Brentwood, usually called Warley to distinguish it from the villages of Great Warley and Little Warley, has grown steadily in the later 19th and 20th centuries. Most of the houses built between 1840 and 1939 are terraced or semi-detached, but there are a few detached houses of the mid 19th century in Warley Hill. One of the main developments has been the Warley Mount estate, begun in 1881;[39] south of it a photographic factory opened in Woodman Road in 1903, stimulated residential building in that area.[40] Considerable private building has taken place at Warley since the Second World War; and in 1959, when Warley barracks were closed, Brentwood U.D.C. bought part of the site, and in the following years built houses, shops, and blocks of flats.[41]

A post office was established at Great Warley in 1858.[42] The South Essex Waterworks Co. first supplied water in 1863; the present pumping-station in the Street bears two dates, 1881 and 1886.[43] Gas was first piped to the parish in 1871–2; electricity, which first became available in Brentwood town in 1902–3, was extended to Great Warley village in 1940.[44]

Notables connected with the parish include the naval administrators, William Gonson (d. 1544), Benjamin Gonson (d. 1577), and Benjamin Gonson (d. 1600), and the diarist John Evelyn (1620–1706).[45] Among the rectors, many of whom were scholars, were William Fulke (d. 1589), master of Pembroke Hall, Cambridge, and chaplain to Robert Dudley, earl of Leicester, and Hastings Robinson (d. 1866), evangelical, classicist, and historian.[46]

MANORS. The manor of *WARLEY*, later known as *WARLEY ABBESS* or *GREAT WARLEY*, was held in 1066 by Barking Abbey as 3 hides.[47] It was probably identical with the 3 hides devised by Leofgifu to her brother-in-law Godwine, *c.* 1040.[48] The manor was assigned to the cellaress and remained with the abbey until the Dissolution. In 1540 it was bought with other properties by William Gonson, Treasurer of the Navy.[49] After his suicide in 1544 it was assigned to his widow Bennett for life, and then to one of his younger sons, Benjamin.[50] Benjamin, also Treasurer of the Navy, died in 1577 and was succeeded at Great Warley by his son, another Benjamin Gonson, who was Clerk of the Ships.[51]

On the death of the younger Benjamin Gonson in 1600 Warley Abbess was assigned for life to his widow Mary, later Lady Bulstrode, with reversion to his sisters Ursula Peterson, Anne Fleming, Bennett Wallenger, and Thomasine Fenton (later Browne).[52] When Lady Bulstrode died in 1627 the estate was divided between the heirs of the sisters. The manorial rights, with land in the north of the parish, went to (Sir) Richard Browne (Bt.), Thomasine's son; Great Warley Hall and the surrounding land went to Bennett's son, Benjamin Wallenger; Clay Tye farm, in the south of the parish, went to Thomas Disney, widower of Ursula, daughter of Ursula Peterson; and Warley Place went to Capt. Arthur Ashenhurst and his wife Ursula, daughter of Anne Fleming.[53]

In 1643 Sir Robert Browne was holding the manor

[28] E.R.O., D/DBe E61.
[29] Inf. from Mr. H. S. Ellingworth.
[30] *Hist. Gt. Warley*, 29; Burke, *Land. Gent.* (1952) 165–6; O.S. Map 1/2,500, Essex, LXVII. 11 (1872 and 1895 edns.).
[31] E.R.O., Q/RLv 24; *Kelly's Dir. Essex* (1845); *White's Dir. Essex* (1848); local inf.
[32] E.R.O., Q/RLv 25–35.
[33] See p. 177.
[34] *Hist. Essex by Gent.* iv. 389; *Map of Essex* (1777).
[35] See pp. 167, 177.
[36] E. Carter, *Hist. Geog. Rlys.* 63.
[37] Ibid.
[38] E.R.O., Q/RDc 31; *White's Dir. Essex* (1863), 576–7.
[39] *Strat. Expr.* 6 Aug. 1881, 5 July, 23 Aug. 1882.
[40] See p. 169.
[41] See p.177.
[42] G.P.O. libr., vol. 197, p. 305.
[43] Inf. from S. Essex Waterworks Co.
[44] Inf. from N. Thames Gas; E.R.O., C/DP 130, 152; inf. from E. Electricity.
[45] C. S. L. Davies, 'Admin. of Royal Navy under Hen. VIII', *E.H.R.* lxxx. 268–88; *D.N.B.*
[46] *D.N.B.*
[47] *V.C.H. Essex*, i. 449.
[48] Hart, *Early Chart. Essex*, 23, 26–7, 44–5.
[49] E.R.O., D/DP L41/74; *L. & P. Hen. VIII*, xv, p. 108. Cf. *E.H.R.* lxxx. 268–88; J. A. Williamson, *Hawkins of Plymouth* (1969).
[50] *L. & P. Hen. VIII*, xx(1), p. 56; C 142/73/50.
[51] C 142/181/50.
[52] C 142/262/13.
[53] C 142/442/42.

and 150 a. land, including the area later called Hart's Wood.[54] He must have acquired more land, for in 1649 he sold the manor with 404 a. for £2,500 to his son-in-law, John Evelyn, the diarist; Evelyn held it only until 1655, when, complaining that heavy taxes ate up the rents, he sold it to John Hart.[55] In 1669 Hart sold it to Roland Wynn.[56]

Roland Wynn (1609–76) was a London merchant, the younger brother of Sir George Wynn (1607–67), the first baronet, of Nostell (Yorks.).[57] At his death Wynn devised the manor first for life to his brother Mark Wynn (d. 1699), and then to Sir George's two youngest sons, Mark and Richard Wynn.[58] The elder Mark Wynn was followed at Warley by another Mark Wynn.[59] This branch of the family died out in 1763, and Great Warley passed to a distant cousin George Winn (1725–98), who was created a baronet in 1776 and Baron Headley in 1797.[60] The manor passed to Headley's second son George Winn (d. 1827), after whose death it was held successively by his sons, Mark (d. 1830) and Charles (d. 1877), Lord Headley.[61] The manor, with 1,011 a. in Great and Little Warley, descended with the barony until the death in 1913 of Charles Winn, Lord Headley. It then passed to his daughter Avis (d. 1936), then the wife of Dr. R. J. L. Llewellyn.[62] In 1919 she offered for sale 794 a. in the two parishes, of which over 500 a. were in Great Warley.[63] From Mrs. Llewellyn the manor and the rump of the estate passed to the daughter of her first marriage, Mrs. Avis Irene Fardell.[64] In 1958, under a family trust, the manor with 432 a. passed to Mrs. Fardell's son George W. Fardell. Most of the estate has since been sold.[65]

Great Warley Hall and the neighbouring land, which in 1627 had been assigned to Benjamin Wallenger, descended in his family until the death of Antony Wallenger in 1728. It then passed to his youngest daughter, who married a London merchant named Harris.[66] In the later 18th century the estate was owned for a time by the Grove family; in 1814 it comprised 229 a.[67] In 1837 it was owned by Samuel Francis, who later bought Warley Franks.[68] Great Warley Hall, the ancient manor-house, stood near the church. It apparently collapsed or was demolished in the 1730s.[69] In 1774 the estate farm-house was Pound House, which stood about a mile north, near the manorial pound.[70] The present Great Warley Hall, of red brick with a slate roof, was built *c.* 1840.

Clay Tye farm, with 212 a. in the south of the parish, was assigned in 1627 to Thomas Disney.[71] In 1705 it was sold by Elizabeth Rothwell to St. Thomas's hospital, London, which, adding to the farm in 1879, sold it with 332 a. in 1927.[72]

Warley Place, which in 1627 fell to the share of Capt. Ashenhurst and his wife Ursula, later passed to her half-brother Giles Fleming (d. 1633) and his son John Fleming, who had 9 daughters.[73] Thomas Jackson (d. 1728) of Gray's Inn devised Warley Place to his son George Jackson (d. 1734) and he to his sister Winifred Jackson (d. 1746). She devised the estate and much other property to David Scott, who retained them after his title was challenged in 1747–8.[74]

In the 1760s and 1770s Warley Place was owned and occupied by Thomas Adams.[75] It was held *c.* 1781–4 by Anthony Merry before passing in 1784 or 1785 to Samuel Bonham (d. 1821), who was succeeded by his son, Lt.-Gen. Pinson Bonham (d. 1855).[76]

Frederick Willmott (d. *c.* 1892) bought Warley Place, with 33 a. in 1875; it passed to his widow and by 1902 to his daughter Ellen A. Willmott (d. 1934).[77] Between 1875 and 1914 the estate was enlarged, but in her last years Miss Willmott sold outlying parts, and in 1935, after her death, the remaining 75 a. were sold in 7 lots.[78] The big house and 45 a. were bought by Mrs. Gray, who sold them in 1938 to Mr. A. J. T. Carter.[79] His attempt to develop the estate in 1938–9 was thwarted by the Green Belt legislation of 1938.[80]

Warley Place was 'an ancient house' *c.* 1725; in 1774 it was said to be of brick, embattled; and 100 years later it was described as a 'good old red-brick embattled mansion modernized'.[81] In 1777 James Gandon exhibited at the Royal Academy an elevation of the principal front, but there is no evidence that this design was carried out.[82] It seems more likely that alterations were made to the east front *c.* 1840. Later views show it as a 7-bay house, of brick, with an Ionic portico.[83] The three central bays were of three storeys, surmounted by a dentilled pediment; the flanking wings were slightly recessed and had only two storeys, their roofs half hidden by a plain parapet. Between 1875 and 1904 extensive additions, including a conservatory, almost doubled the size of the house,[84] which was demolished in 1939.[85]

The gardens were largely developed by Miss Willmott before the First World War and became among the most celebrated in the country.[86] East of the house was an Old English rose-garden with a

[54] E.R.O., D/DU 776.
[55] J. Evelyn, *Diary*, ed. E. S. de Beer, ii. 536, 554; iii. 158–9.
[56] C.P. 25(2)/653 Trin. 21 Chas. II: John and Mary Evelyn and Sir Richard Browne were also joined in the sale.
[57] Burke, *Peerage* (1938), 1273.
[58] E.R.O., D/P 195/1/2; Prob. 11/352, f. 117.
[59] E.R.O., D/DK M5.
[60] Burke, *Peerage* (1938), 1274. From Lord Headley's time the surname was spelled 'Winn'.
[61] Ibid.; E.R.O., Q/RSg 5, ff. 67, 76, 79, 80, 86.
[62] E.R.O., C/TS 75; Burke, *Peerage* (1938), 1274.
[63] E.R.O., *Sale Cat.* B512.
[64] Debrett, *Peerage* (1926), 477; deeds *penes* Barking and Havering area health authority.
[65] Deeds *penes* Messrs. Riders, Lincolns Inn, who kindly arranged access to them.
[66] E.R.O., T/P 195/2; Morant, *Essex*, i. 113.
[67] E.R.O., D/DU 835; *Sale Cat.* B842; cf. D/P 18/28/3.
[68] E.R.O., D/CT 385; see p. 169.
[69] E R.O., T/P 195/2; Salmon, *Essex*, 267.
[70] *Hist. Essex by Gent.* iv. 388.
[71] Morant, *Essex*, i. 113.
[72] E.R.O., *Sale Cat.* A268; *Essex Wkly. News*, 1 July 1927; *Country Life*, lxii (no. 1596), p. xxxviii.
[73] Morant, *Essex*, i. 113; *Visits. Essex*, ii. 569–70.
[74] Morant, *Essex*, i. 113.
[75] *Essex Poll Books* (1764, 1768); *Hist. Essex by Gent.* iv. 388; *Map of Essex* (1777).
[76] E.R.O., Q/RPl 106–57; Burke, *Peerage* (1892), 149; *Gent. Mag.* 1855(1), 642.
[77] E.R.O., *Sale Cat.* B2; *Kelly's Dir. Essex* (1878–1933).
[78] E.R.O., *Sale Cat.* B921; *Hist. Gt. Warley*, 32.
[79] Deeds *penes* Mr. N. Carter, Danbury.
[80] *Essex Chron.* and *Essex Wkly. News*, both of 6 Jan. 1939.
[81] E.R.O., T/P 195/2; *Hist. Essex by Gent.* iv. 388; Thorne, *Environs Lond.* 676.
[82] A. Graves, *Royal Academy of Arts: dictionary of contributors, 1769–1904* (1970), ii. 197.
[83] See plate facing page 177.
[84] E.R.O., *Sale Cat.* B2; *E. Nat.* xvii. 40–60.
[85] Inf. from Mr. N. Carter, Danbury.
[86] Assertions that John Evelyn and Humphry Repton helped to create the gardens are not supported by contemporary evidence.

summer-house; beyond the lawn SW. of the house an alpine ravine-garden ended in a pool; to the NE. the land sloped westwards from a broad terrace with a glazed summer-house to a small tree-sheltered boating lake with a landing-stage and Swiss chalet; further north a group of heated glass-houses contained orchids, ferns, palms, and other exotics. After Miss Willmott's death there was talk of the gardens becoming a branch of the gardens at Kew but the project was dropped on the outbreak of the Second World War.[87] In 1975 the gardens were a wooded wilderness.

The manor of *WARLEY*, later known as *WARLEY FRANKS*, in the SW. of the parish, consisted in 1066 of two hides, held by Godric. In 1086 Swein of Essex held it in demesne.[88] The overlordship of the manor subsequently descended as part of the honor of Rayleigh.[89] In 1285 the manor was said to be held of Laurence of Plumberow in Little Hockley, himself a tenant of the honor of Rayleigh.[90]

Turold is the first known tenant of the manor.[91] By the 13th century the demesne lordship had passed to the Scoland (Estotlond, Escoland, or Scodlaund) family. Osbert was the first member to hold it; Geoffrey was party to a case concerning land in Warley in 1220; and in 1262 Frank Scoland agreed to pay £10 and 1 lb. cummin annually at Christmas to Geoffrey Scoland from whom he was to hold a messuage and 2 carucates of land in Warley.[92] Frank died shortly before 3 April 1285 and was succeeded by his infant son Frank.[93] From one or both of them the manor took its name of Warley Franks.[94]

Frank Scoland (d. 1339) was followed by his son Henry (d. 1367) and grandson Frank.[95] The latter in 1372 sold the manor and advowson to John Payn of London, armourer.[96] In 1375, the year of his death, Payn settled the manors of Warley Franks and South Hall in Rainham, and the Bridge House lands in Upminster, in trust for his wife Joan (d. 1418).[97] In 1389 she transferred the estates to her daughter and son-in-law, Ann and Thomas Newton, probably on their marriage.[98] Newton died, and by 1406 Ann had married John Godeston.[99] Ann died before her mother, but John was still alive in 1428.[1] Their son Robert Godeston (d. 1453) was succeeded by his son John, who was still a minor in 1461, when his guardian leased Franks for £22 a year to Lewis FitzLewis.[2] John Godeston, who in 1498 was declared a lunatic, died in the same year leaving as heirs the five young daughters of his son William.[3] Two of the daughters died without issue: Millicent in 1513 or 1514 and Elizabeth between 1519 and 1529.[4] Of the other three, Joan married Hugh Ellis, Alice John Elton, and Margaret Ralph Holinshed.[5]

In 1529 Margaret and Ralph Holinshed sold their third of the manor to Henry Averell (d. 1540).[6] Averell's son John (d. 1554) devised his lands in Warley Franks to his cousin Elizabeth Clarke, later the wife of Peter Poulton.[7] She disposed of her holding: Henry Billingsley sold two-thirds of it to Anne and Thomas Drywood of Great Warley in 1568, and in 1562 the remaining third was already in the hands of Bartholomew Averell at the time of his death.[8] Averell's posthumous heir, Bartholomew, sold it to Anne and Thomas Drywood in 1584.[9]

Alice Elton died before her husband John (d. 1548).[10] They were followed by their sons John (d. 1550) and Charles (d. 1586) and Charles's son Anthony, who in 1590–1 sold this portion of the manor and estate to Thomas Drywood.[11]

Joan Ellis, the eldest of the Godeston sisters, also died before her husband Hugh (d. 1538).[12] Their son William died in January 1544 and in September his only child, Anne, was born.[13] In 1564 she had livery of her Warley inheritance as Ann Ellis.[14] Nothing more is known of Anne Ellis, but it has been plausibly conjectured that she became the wife of Thomas Drywood, and that the purchases of 1568, 1584, and 1590–1 reconstituted the manor of Warley Franks in its entirety.[15]

Thomas Drywood (d. 1591) devised all his lands to his widow Anne.[16] She died *c.* 1608, and was succeeded by their son William, who in 1611 sold the manor with 252 a. to Nicholas Fuller, Common Pleader and an M.P. for the city of London.[17] Fuller died in 1620, and his son Sir Nicholas Fuller in 1621.[18] The latter left an infant son Dowse, after whose death in 1657 Warley Franks was sold for £5,900 to Thomas Gundrey, an Exchequer official, and a creditor of Fuller for £2,000.[19]

Gundrey (d. 1669) was succeeded by his grandson (d. 1724) and great-grandson (d. 1745) both named Thomas Gundrey.[20] The younger Thomas's heir was his brother John (d. 1749) whose widow, Mary, held the manor at least until 1766.[21] By 1781 she had been succeeded by her husband's nephew, yet

[87] E. Willmott, *Warley Garden in Spring and Summer* (1909); *E. Nat.* xvii. 40–60; *Country Life*, xxxvii. 613; li. 432; D. MacLeod, *Gardener's London*, 312, 314–15; *Gardeners' Chron.* 6 Oct. 1934; *Essex Countryside*, xviii, no. 154, pp. 32–4, xxviii, no. 223, pp. 36–7.
[88] *V.C.H. Essex*, i. 490.
[89] Sanders, *Eng. Baronies*, 139; *V.C.H. Essex*, iv. 276; cf. *Cal. Inq. p.m. Hen. VII*, iii. p. 479; C 142/62/91.
[90] *Cal. Inq. p.m.* ii, p. 335; Morant, *Essex*, i. 288.
[91] Newcourt, *Repertorium*, ii. 640.
[92] Ibid.; *Cur. Reg. R.* viii. 385–6; ix. 180–1, 323; x. 203; *Feet of F. Essex*, i. 259.
[93] *Cal. Inq. p.m.* ii, p. 335; cf. ibid. ii, p. 481; iv, pp. 33–4.
[94] The manor was once (1262) cited as Warley Scoland: *Feet of F. Essex*, i. 259.
[95] *Cal. Inq. p.m.* viii, p. 102; xii, p. 147.
[96] *Cal. Close*, 1369–74, 474–5.
[97] B.L. Add. MS. 38131, ff. 79v.–80; C 138/31.
[98] C 136/95/42; C 138/31.
[99] *Cal. Close*, 1405–9, 167.
[1] C 138/31; *Feud. Aids*, ii. 224.
[2] Morant, *Essex*, i. 110; E.R.O., D/DP T1/1643–4; for FitzLewis see above, p. 104.
[3] *Cal. Inq. p.m. Hen. VII*, ii, pp. 76–7; iii. p. 479; cf. *Cal. Pat.* 1494–1509, 124, and C 142/28/85.
[4] C 142/28/85; *Feet of F. Essex*, iv. 131.
[5] *Feet of F. Essex*, iv. 138–9.
[6] *Feet of F. Essex*, iv. 172; C 142/62/91.
[7] C 142/102/51; Prob. 11/58 (P.C.C. 25 Carew).
[8] *Cal. Pat.* 1566–9, 300; C 142/133/129; C 142/138/37. This Bartholomew was first cousin to John Averell (d. 1554).
[9] E.R.O., D/DSx 307.
[10] C 142/88/43.
[11] C 142/93/66; C 142/213/99; C.P. 25(2)/135/1719.
[12] C 142/61/54.
[13] C 142/71/149.
[14] C 60/380 m. 12.
[15] This suggestion was first made by William Holman in the early 18th century: E.R.O., T/P 195/2 Warleys, pp. 17–18.
[16] C 142/228/69.
[17] Prob. 11/113 (P.C.C. 21 Dorset); E.R.O., D/DU 192/3; Venn, *Alumni Cantab.* I, ii. 184.
[18] Venn, *Alumni Cantab.* I, ii. 184; Foster, *Alumni Oxon.* I, ii. 539.
[19] E.R.O., D/DK T86; E.R.O., T/P 195/2 Warleys, pp. 18–19.
[20] Prob. 11/330; J. Hutchins, *Dorset*, ii. 607.
[21] Ibid.; E.R.O., Q/RSg 3, ff. 20, 48; Q/RSg 4, f. 1.

another Thomas Gundrey, upon whose death in 1805 Francis John Browne (d. 1833) of Frampton (Dors.) succeeded to the property.[22] Browne left all his estates, including Warley Franks, to Lieut.-Gen. Sir Colquhoun Grant, his niece's husband.[23] In 1834 Grant's daughter, Maria Marcia, married Richard Brinsley Sheridan, the grandson and namesake of the dramatist, and on her father's death in 1835, they inherited Frampton and Warley Franks.[24] In 1837 the latter estate contained 640 a., Samuel Francis being the tenant of 349 a.[25] Francis (d. 1874) appears to have bought the estate *c.* 1860.[26] In 1876 his heirs sold it to Richard Benyon, who already owned estates in Cranham and the Ockendons.[27] In 1920 George Seton de Winton, who had been the tenant for about 20 years, bought Franks manor-house and 129 a.[28] The property passed about 1926 to Mrs. Margaret J. de Winton Kyffin, probably his niece, who sold it in 1945.[29] In 1975, after passing through various hands, it was owned by Mr. Andrew Cheale. In 1937 the rest of the estate, then comprising 464 a., with Codham Hall, was included in the sale of the Benyon lands in Essex and bought by Clayhall Park Estates, Ltd.[30] After the passage of the Green Belt (London and Home Counties) Act in 1938, the company sold the estate in 1939 to the present owner, Essex county council.[31]

Franks manor-house is of two storeys. Its two 15th-century wings extend west and north; in the former the hall originally rose the whole height of the house. An east wing with two gables was added in the 17th century, and a single-storey addition along the east front was made probably in the early 19th century.[32]

ECONOMIC HISTORY. Until the 19th century Great Warley was an entirely agricultural parish. In 1086 the two manors contained woodland enough to feed 350 swine.[33] Then, as later, the woodland probably lay in the north and west of the parish. The manor of Warley (Abbess) had 150 sheep. Most of them were probably folded on the manor's marshland pastures, said to be sufficient for 100 sheep. The location of these pastures is not known; they may have been at Corringham, where there was later a detached part of Little Warley.[34] The two manors together had 12½ plough-teams in 1086, compared with 13 in 1066.

In the south-west of the parish the manor of Warley Franks had lost its woods by the 13th century: in 1285 320 a. out of a total of 342 a. were arable.[35] The field names of the manor in 1610 suggest the same predominance of arable over pasture, and the size of the fields hints at the possibility of an open-field system: Hither North Field (47 a.), Hither and Further East field (jointly 54 a.), and Collenowres and Further Collenowres (jointly 48 a.) can be equated with fields on the tithe map of 1838 lying north, east, and south-east of Franks manor-house.[36] Eastwards the manor of Great Warley maintained in 1545 a more evenly mixed acreage of heath, wood, arable, and meadow and pasture.[37] In the late 17th century squatters apparently built on the common waste; in 1670 five named cottagers (*tuguriani*) were said to be without right of pasture.[38] A statement in 1701 of the customs of the manor emphasized the importance of the woodland and waste. Holly, gorse, and juniper belonged equally to the lord and tenants, but tenants might claim herbage in the woods only in areas where the trees had at least seven years growth. The only other custom then stated was the lord's duty to keep a bull and a boar for the tenants' use.[39] The common waste lay in the manor of Great Warley, extending into Little Warley manor. In 1805 116 a. in the two manors were sold for the barracks. The remaining 172 a., of which 160 a. were in Great Warley, were inclosed in 1843.[40]

In 1838 Great Warley contained 1,340 a. arable, 1,025 a. pasture, and 210 a. woodland.[41] There were 24 properties with more than 10 a., belonging to 16 owners and farmed in 18 units. The five largest estates contained 596 a., 330 a., 319 a., 242 a., and 203 a. Three more had between 147 a. and 128 a., and the 8 smallest between 71 a. and 11 a.

Hops were grown at the rectory *c.* 1850, but as elsewhere in Essex their cultivation had died out later in the century.[42] In the 1950s they were reintroduced at Codham Hall, which was then said to be the only farm in the county growing them.[43] Their cultivation was abandoned, however, before 1970.[44] In 1876 wheat, barley, beans, and peas were said to be widely grown in the parish.[45]

In 1916 there were 1,009 a. arable and 1,471 a. pasture, in 14 farms, of which 6 had between 200 a. and 500 a., 2 between 100 a. and 200 a., 5 between 50 a. and 100 a., and one 15 a.[46]

In 1948 Mr. Deaner established a piggery on his smallholding in Warley Street, south of Codham Lane. In 1962, when his son joined him in business, he abandoned the raising of pigs and founded Warley Rose Gardens, which in 1976 covered 22 a.[47]

In 1903 Ilford Ltd., manufacturers of photographic dry-plates, extended their operations, bringing light industry to Great Warley. The company bought 14 a. south of Woodman Road and planned

[22] E.R.O., Q/RSg 4, ff. 34, 48, 131; Hutchins, *Dorset*, ii. 607.
[23] *D.N.B.* s.v. Grant, Sir Colquhoun.
[24] Burke, *Land. Gent.* (1937), 2045–6.
[25] E.R.O., D/CT 385. He had earlier owned Gt. Warley Hall.
[26] *White's Dir. Essex* (1863), 586; E.R.O., C/T 413. Francis is merely 'farmer' in *Post Office Dir.* (1859).
[27] E.R.O., D/DBe E61: letter of 1 Nov. 1876; another letter of 19 March 1897 identifies the 639 a. as the Franks and Codham Hall estate.
[28] *Kelly's Dir. Essex* (1902 and later edns.); *Sale Cat.* (1951), *penes* Mr. Andrew Cheale (E.R.O., T/B 316). For de Winton's presence in the neighbourhood, see E.R.O., T/P 67/3, pp. 71, 91, 93, 97 and T/P 67/5, p. 62.
[29] *Kelly's Dir. Essex* (1926, 1929); *Sale Cat.* (1951), cited above; Burke, *Peerage* (1959), 2396; E.R.O., T/P 181/12/7.
[30] E.R.O., *Sale Cat.* B106; E.R.O., D/DBe E71.
[31] E.R.O., C/T 413.
[32] R.C.H.M. *Essex*, iv. 62.
[33] *V.C.H. Essex*, i. 449, 490: the source of all information in this paragraph, unless otherwise specified.
[34] O.S. Map 6", Essex, LXXVII, LXXXV (1865 edn.).
[35] *Cal. Inq. p.m.* ii, p. 335.
[36] E.R.O., D/DSx 313; D/DU 192/3; D/CT 385A nos. 272–3, 276–7, 286–7, 295–7. Cf. *E. Nat.* xxvi. 8; E.R.O., Q/SR 58/55; W. M. Sturman, 'Barking Abbey', (Lond. Univ. Ph.D. thesis, 1961), 54.
[37] E.R.O., T/P 195/2.
[38] E.R.O., D/DK M3.
[39] E.R.O., D/DK M5.
[40] E.R.O., D/CT 385; E.R.O., Q/RDc 31.
[41] E.R.O., D/CT 385.
[42] *Hist. Gt. Warley*, 6; *V.C.H. Essex*, ii. 369.
[43] *Hist. Gt. Warley*, 6.
[44] Inf. from Mr. H. C. Scott Padfield.
[45] Thorne, *Environs Lond.* 675.
[46] E.R.O., D/Z 45/11.
[47] Inf. from Mr. Deaner the younger.

to provide employment for 350.[48] The works were enlarged in later years, and in the mid 1920s this branch became Selo Ltd.[49] In 1969 Ilford Ltd. became a subsidiary of Ciba, the Swiss chemical company, which in 1970 joined J. R. Geigy S.A. to form Ciba-Geigy Ltd. The company decided to move from Ilford in 1973. Its engineering centre was already at Warley; the adjoining site of the former Christ Church school on Warley Hill was bought in 1974; and in 1975 Ilford's research laboratory opened there.[50]

LOCAL GOVERNMENT. In 1373 the view of frankpledge for the manor of Warley Franks was held by the lord of the honor of Rayleigh, but all the profits of the view, except the common fine, belonged to the lord of the manor.[51] For the manor of Warley Abbess, later Great Warley, there are court rolls and court books for the periods 1483–1544 and 1651–1851. Courts leet were held until the later 17th century, and constables were appointed by the court as late as 1699.[52]

The parish records include vestry minutes (1736–1855), churchwardens' accounts (1792–1844), and overseers' rates (1827–33) and accounts (1800–48).[53] The vestry normally met four or five times a year, but more often in times of distress: from 1793 to 1820 there were never fewer than six meetings a year, and usually eight or nine. The place of meeting, when specified, was the church, but in 1785 the vestry agreed to meet alternately at the Thatchers and the Magpie public houses, spending each time 5*s.* on the overseer's account. The rector or curate normally took the chair when present. Attendance at meetings was occasionally as high as ten, but five or six was a more usual number in the 18th century and three or four in the 19th century. Those who attended were the substantial farmers of the parish, and the parish offices revolved among them.

There were two churchwardens throughout the period. In 1755 one was elected by the parishioners, the other by the rector and parishioners jointly; the following year the same two men were wardens, but the first was stated to be appointed 'by the sole authority of the rector'. Thereafter there was always a rector's warden. Between 1736 and 1749 the vestry nominated two overseers, but after 1749 submitted four names; the duties, however, were usually performed by a single overseer. In 1761–2 Mrs. Hannah Mead was overseer, with William Mead as her deputy. Overseers normally held office for a single year, but John Forster was overseer from 1816 to 1821, and Thomas W. Mayhew held the office from 1822 to 1836, when Great Warley joined the Romford union.[54] Both were salaried. One or two constables were nominated by the vestry in most years up to 1808, but only one seems to have acted. There were also two surveyors of the highways. All the parish officers collected rates, and the vestry minutes until 1781 record summaries of their accounts.

Statute labour on the highways continued in Great Warley in the 18th and 19th centuries. In 1756 composition for services was authorized, but the provision of substitutes was forbidden. In 1834 half the highway duty was to be performed, and half paid by composition; two-thirds of the duty was demanded in 1843: for every £50 rateable value, six days duty with a cart and two horses was required. No one rated at less than £50 might offer less than three days duty.

The rateable value of the parish was about £1,200 in 1737 and £1,811 in 1801. It rose to £2,446 in 1817, just over £3,000 in 1839, and £3,664 in 1842. Expenditure by the overseer of the poor averaged about £60 a year in the four years 1736–40, but in the period 1740–73 was about £110 a year, with more being spent in the last decade than earlier. For the rest of the 18th century the only series of figures available gives the rates voted to the overseer: he appears to have needed about £160 yearly from 1773 to 1786 but only about half that amount from 1786 to 1793. From 1793 the sums needed rose rapidly. In 1800–1 the overseer spent £878, and in the following year £675; for the years 1802–6 his expenditure averaged £432, and for 1816–30 £512. Thereafter expenditure dropped.

In the mid 18th century Great Warley had few poor. Only eight inhabitants received regular weekly allowances in 1746, and only an occasional parish apprentice is named in the records: in 1743 the parish received £10 from an inhabitant who refused to take one. Outdoor relief was given; and the parish also had several poorhouses, including two made in 1757 by converting the former watch-house. By 1783 there was on Headley common a parish workhouse, which seems to have accommodated about 20. In that year Little Warley first rented space in the workhouse;[55] Upminster also used it in the years 1784–6, as did Hutton in 1806.[56] In 1829 it was reckoned unsuitable for future use, and the vestry therefore decided to join nine parishes in Ongar hundred in forming, under Gilbert's Act, a poor-law union with a workhouse at Stanford Rivers.[57] The parish workhouse and 7 poorhouses were sold for £240 in 1830.[58] From 1831 to 1836 Great Warley kept about 10 paupers in the workhouse at Stanford Rivers.

A parish doctor was employed in 1758, and in 1785 it was agreed that the poor might be inoculated at parish expense. No parish doctor is recorded between 1764 and 1800. In 1804 Dr. Butler of Brentwood agreed to attend Great Warley's poor both in the parish and within five miles of Brentwood. In 1816–17 Dr. Richardson was retained as the parish doctor but other doctors received casual payments. Apart from the years 1822–5 Dr. Richardson continued to treat the parish poor until 1836, when Great Warley became part of Romford poor-law union.

CHURCHES. The advowson of St. Mary's rectory descended with the manor of Warley Abbess (or Great Warley) until the death of Benjamin Gonson

[48] E.R.O., T/P 181/12/7 (11 Dec. 1903); cf. *V.C.H. Essex*, v. 254.
[49] *Kelly's Dir. Essex* (1926 and later edns.).
[50] Inf. from Ilford Ltd., and Mr. P. A. Rance.
[51] E.R.O., D/P M1098.
[52] E.R.O., D/DP M76–7, 79–83, 86–8; D/DSg M5, 6; D/DK M2–12; B.L., Cotton MS. App. ii, ff. 4–82.
[53] E.R.O., D/P 195/8/1–3, 195/5, 195/11/1, 195/12/1–6. Unless otherwise noted, all information in this section comes from these records.
[54] E.R.O., G/RM 1.
[55] E.R.O., D/P 66/12/2.
[56] E.R.O., D/P 117/12/10, 195/18.
[57] E.R.O., Q/RSw 1; cf. *V.C.H. Essex*, iv. 221.
[58] The former workhouse was said in 1957 to have been 'recently' demolished. It was then described as thatched weather-boarded: *Hist. Gt. Warley*, 27.

in 1600.[59] For a further sixty years it apparently belonged to the descendants of his sister Bennett, who married Thomas Wallenger of Chelmsford: John Staresmore, rector 1626–36, was husband to Thomasine Wallenger, their daughter; their son Benjamin Wallenger was patron in 1636 and 1650; and the patron in 1660 was John Wells, presumably their son-in-law.[60] Henry Warner, however, who presented David Jenner to the rectory in 1678, has not been identified.[61]

Jenner at his resignation in 1687 owned the advowson, and at his death in 1692 he devised it to his widow Mary (d. 1702).[62] In 1694 and 1698 she presented to the rectory her second and third husbands, and at her death her only child Seth Wigmore inherited the advowson. From him it passed to the Brackenbury Fund and thence in 1718 to St. John's College, Cambridge.[63] In 1906 the college sold the advowson to Evelyn Heseltine (d. 1930), from whom it passed to family trustees.[64] In 1972 Great Warley was united with Childerditch, and the right of presentation to the united benefice vested alternately in the Heseltine trustees and the Martyrs Memorial Trust.[65]

The rectory was valued at 10 marks gross, 7 marks net, in 1254 and 1291, and at £14 in 1535.[66] It was worth about £120 *c.* 1740, £170 *c.* 1770, and £430 in 1800.[67] In 1837 the rectorial tithes were commuted for £523.[68] The leper hospital of Ilford, founded by Adeliza, abbess of Barking, *c.* 1140, received tithes from the manor of Warley Abbess worth 3 marks in 1254; in 1837 they were commuted for £90, paid to the marquess of Salisbury, master and patron of the hospital.[69] In 1254 Prittlewell priory received tithes worth 3 marks from the demesne of Geoffrey Scoland (i.e. the manor of Warley Franks); they had been granted by Turold.[70] In 1513 the priory granted them and a house in the parish to the rector for £1 a year.[71] About 1700 and in 1810 this rent was being paid to the Crown.[72]

There was a rectory house and 6 a. of glebe in the early 17th century.[73] The glebe was said to be 7 a. in 1650 and 10 a. in 1837.[74] In 1777 the rectory house lay ½ mile north of the church in Great Warley Street.[75] It was rebuilt by Edmund Latter, rector 1805–26, and continually enlarged throughout his incumbency by Hastings Robinson, rector 1827–66.[76] It ceased to be used as the rectory *c.* 1892, was sold in 1903, and after passing through various hands was demolished in the 1960s to make way for a haulier's depot.[77] A tithe barn, apparently situated behind the rectory in 1838, was demolished in 1902.[78]

In 1889 Dr. H. Roberson Bailey, rector 1866–1900, commissioned from J. L. Pearson, the architect of Truro cathedral, a large house in Jacobean style, later named Fairstead. It stands in 7 acres a mile north of the old rectory in Great Warley Street. It was Bailey's personal property, and he apparently lived there until his death in 1900.[79] In 1904 a new rectory, of red brick, was built immediately south of Fairstead and almost opposite the new church.[80] It was designed by (Sir) E. Guy Dawber, P.R.I.B.A.[81]

William Fulke, rector 1571–89, Master of Pembroke Hall, Cambridge, from 1578, was presented to Great Warley through the influence of Robert Dudley, earl of Leicester, to whom he was chaplain.[82] He was an absentee, but his successor, John Fabian, rector 1589–1626, lived in the parish.[83] In 1597 Fabian was suspended for playing 'a lord of misrule or Christmas lord among certain yongelings' in Kelvedon.[84] From his time most rectors apparently resided in the parish, but after 1723 there was usually an assistant curate as well.[85] In 1768 the curate was paid £40 a year.[86] David Jenner, rector 1678–87, a royal chaplain, and Henry Cardell, rector 1708–43, were former fellows of Cambridge colleges, and while St. John's College, Cambridge, owned the advowson, former fellows of the college occupied the rectory from 1743 to 1900.[87]

The old church of *ST. MARY* stood immediately south of Great Warley Hall. It consisted of a brick chancel, nave, and west tower, and a wooden south porch.[88] At some time before 1730 the tower, which then held five bells, was wrecked by lightning. It was replaced by a shingled and tile-capped tower set upon the old tower base. It held three bells. In 1681 the arms of the Commonwealth were still visible on the walls.[89] Framed copies of the commandments, Lord's Prayer, and Creed were hung in 1744, and together with the King's arms were still in place in 1810. Repairs to the church walls and tower were carried out in 1803. In 1833 a west gallery was built by Mrs. Robinson, the rector's wife; there was already a north gallery. In 1858–60 the church was remodelled, to the designs of S. S. Teulon, at a total cost of £1,000.[90] The chancel was rebuilt in yellow brick with stone dressings, a north vestry was added, and the west tower reconstructed in red brick. Most of the church fittings were replaced, new open pews

[59] See p. 166.
[60] *Visit. Essex*, i (Harl. Soc.), 516; Lamb., Reg. Laud, pt. i. 348–9; Smith, *Eccl. Hist. Essex*, 244.
[61] Newcourt, *Repertorium*, ii. 641.
[62] E. J. Erith, 'Three Rectors and their Wife', *E.R.* lvii. 187–90.
[63] Ibid.
[64] Inf. from St. John's Coll., Camb.; *Chelmsford Dioc. Year Bks.* (1915 and later edns.).
[65] *Chelmsford Dioc. Yr. Bk.* (1972–3).
[66] *E.A.T.* N.S. xviii. 18; *Tax. Eccl.* (Rec. Com.), 22; *Valor Eccl.* (Rec. Com), i. 436.
[67] Guildhall MSS. 9550, 9556–8.
[68] E.R.O., D/CT 385.
[69] *V.C.H. Essex*, ii. 186–8; *E.A.T.* N.S. xviii. 18; E.R.O., D/CT 385.
[70] *E.A.T.* N.S. xviii. 18; Newcourt, *Repertorium*, ii. 640.
[71] Newcourt, *Repertorium*, ii. 640.
[72] E.R.O., D/P 195/1/2.
[73] Newcourt, *Repertorium*, ii. 640.
[74] Smith, *Eccl. Hist. Essex*, 244; E.R.O., D/CT 385.
[75] *Map of Essex* (1777).
[76] E.R.O., D/AEM 2/6; D/P 195/1/2.
[77] *Kelly's Dir. Essex* (1890, 1894); E.R.O., Accession 4541; *Sale Cat.* A861; T/P 181/12/7 (14 June 1935); inf. from Mrs. Ellingworth.
[78] E.R.O., D/CT 385; St. John's Coll., Camb., Council min. 645; cf. E.R.O., D/CF 44.
[79] E.R.O., *Sale Cat.* B5740; *Hist. Great Warley*, 19, 26. Cf. E.R.O., D/AEM 1/5 (3 Oct. 1872).
[80] E.R.O., D/CP 20/27.
[81] E.R.O., Accession 4541.
[82] *D.N.B.*
[83] E.R.O., D/P 195/1/1.
[84] Hale, *Precedents*, p. 213.
[85] Guildhall MSS. 9550, 9552, 9557.
[86] Guildhall MS. 9552.
[87] Venn, *Alumni Cantab.*
[88] Unless otherwise indicated, this account is based on: E.R.O., D/P 195/1/2 (cuttings and illustrations); 195/5; 195/8/1–3; T/P 195/2; *Hist. Gt. Warley*, 9–10; Thorne, *Environs Lond.* 675; photo. in St. Mary the Virgin, Great Warley.
[89] *Cal. S.P. Dom.* 1680–1, 422.
[90] For the collapse of the chancel in 1858, E.R.O., D/AEM 1/5; for the rebuilding, ibid., 2/9.

were provided, and a new west gallery, apparently reached by an outside stairway on the south of the tower, was erected.[91]

The church ceased to be used for services other than funerals *c.* 1892, the year in which a wooden mission church seating 140 was licensed for use. The mission church stood in the grounds of Fairstead and seems to have been used for about ten years.[92] In 1923 the old church had recently been pulled down; the tower was still standing in 1957, but had fallen by 1975.[93]

In 1904 a new church of *ST. MARY THE VIRGIN* formally replaced old St. Mary's as the parish church.[94] It stands west of Great Warley Street about a mile north of the old church. The site was given in 1902 by Evelyn Heseltine and enlarged by further gifts from him in 1904 and 1927.[95] The church was also his gift, in memory of his brother Arnold Heseltine (1852–97), and was built in Art Nouveau style to the designs of Charles Harrison Townsend and (Sir) William Reynolds-Stephens.[96] It consists of an eastern apse with north vestry and a tunnel-vaulted nave with south chapel and south porch. A small shingled bell-turret surmounts the nave roof towards the west. Harrison Townsend and Reynolds-Stephens designed the fittings, which with their natural forms were intended to symbolize the Resurrection. Only the windows are not original. They now commemorate, among others, Evelyn Heseltine, his son-in-law, and two grandsons, and most replace the first windows by Heywood Sumner, blown out in 1940.[97] In 1975 the windows were damaged by vandals more than once.[98] In the south chapel against the east wall there stands the painted alabaster bust of Giles Fleming (d. 1633), originally part of a monument in the chancel of old St. Mary's.[99]

The church plate includes a cup with cover and a paten of 1700; a cup and cover and alms-dish of 1749, and two flagons of 1872 and 1904, all of silver. There is also a pewter platter, almost certainly of 1678.[1]

In 1851 the parish church was reported to be 'totally inadequate' for the needs of the growing parish.[2] A licensed room on Sunday mornings probably housed the overflow from the Sunday school.[3] In 1862 Sarah Clay, the rector's sister-in-law, gave £1,000 to endow a new church.[4] *CHRIST CHURCH*, Warley, was opened in 1855; it was built by subscription, the rector contributing largely, on a site given by the East India Company, then owners of Warley camp in Little Warley, beside the married soldiers' quarters on Warley Hill.[5] In the same year a new parish was formed from parts of South Weald, Shenfield, and Great Warley.[6] In 1956 the NE. corner of the parish was transferred to Ingrave.[7] The advowson of the vicarage was vested in trustees, always including members of the Clay family, until 1925 when it was transferred to the bishop.[8] The vicarage was worth £135 a year in 1863, derived chiefly from Miss Clay's endowment,[9] but supplemented by an allotment of tithe rent-charges in 1856[10] and a grant of £33 a year from the Ecclesiastical Commissioners in 1861.[11] A vicarage house was built south of the church in 1853. It was sold in 1970, when a new house was provided in Mount Crescent.[12]

Christ Church, built of brick with stone dressings in Early English style to the designs of S. S. Teulon, originally comprised apse, with small north vestry, nave, south porch, and battlemented west tower with pinnacles; a south aisle was added in 1877.[13] In 1891 the apse was replaced by a chancel with an arcade of two bays on the north side opening into a chancel aisle forming a choir vestry and organ chamber.[14] In 1956 the west gallery was taken down and its door way replaced by a window.[15] A new choir vestry, at the west of the south aisle, was formed in 1960.[16]

The church plate includes a silver cup dated 1845, and paten and flagon dated 1850, all by Barnard and the gift of Mrs. Robinson in 1854; a matching silver cup is dated 1882.[17] The original organ was sold in 1915; its replacement, installed in 1916, was rebuilt in 1972.[18]

ROMAN CATHOLICISM. The church of *THE HOLY CROSS AND ALL SAINTS*, Warley, is in Warley Hill, on the South Weald side of the parish boundary. It was built in 1881 by Revd. J. Kyne of Brentwood with money given by Helen Tasker, Countess Tasker, of Middleton Hall, and by Mr. Campbell, who also gave the site.[19] The church, in the Gothic style, originally comprised chancel, nave, south aisle, and small west turret. A second aisle was added in 1888, the gift of the Willmott family of Warley Place.[20]

91 *Ch. Bells Essex*, 439.
92 *Hist. Great Warley*, 26; *Kelly's Dir. Essex* (1898, 1902); for the Rector's attempt to build a mission church in 1876–7, E.R.O., D/AEM 1/5 (30 Dec. 1876, 19 Feb. 1877).
93 *Hist. Great Warley*, 9; cf. *Kelly's Dir. Essex* (1914, 1926, 1933); R.C.H.M. *Essex*, iv. 61.
94 E.R.O., D/CP 20/33.
95 Ibid.
96 This account is based on: *Church of St. Mary the Virgin, Great Warley*: *explanatory memorandum* (1911) [copy in E.R.O.]; Pevsner *Essex*, 213; 'St. Mary the Virgin, Great Warley: illustrated guide'; P. F. Anson, *Fashions in church furnishings, 1840–1940*, 293 and f. pp. 161, 208; J. Malton, 'Art Nouveau in Essex', *Archit. Rev.* cxxvi. 100–3; E.R.O., T/Z 138/1.
97 C.C.L., Bp. Inskip's Recs. ii (6 Oct. 1940); E.R.O., C/W 1/2/11 (21–22 Sept. 1940).
98 Inf. from Rector.
99 E.R.O., T/P 195/2; Thorne, *Environs Lond.* 675.
1 *Ch. Plate Essex*, 69; inf. from Rector.
2 H.O. 129/7/197.
3 Ibid.
4 E.R.O., D/CP 20/29.
5 E.R.O., D/CC 6/6; E.R.O., D/AEM 2/9; cf. O.S. Map 6", Essex, LXVII (surv. 1866); D. W. Coller, *People's Hist. Essex*, 349.
6 E.R.O., D/CPc 3.
7 Ibid. 336.
8 Ibid. 192.
9 *White's Dir. Essex* (1863), 586.
10 E.R.O., D/CP 20/30.
11 E.R.O., D/CPc 11.
12 *Kelly's Dir. Essex* (1855); cf. O.S. Map 6", Essex, LXVII (surv. 1866); date on porch; inf. from Vicar.
13 *Kelly's Dir. Essex* (1870–86); E.R.O., D/CF 30/7; inf. from Mr. P. A. Rance, churchwarden.
14 *E.R.* i. 142; E.R.O., D/CF 30/7, D/CC 42/8. The architect was John Young.
15 E.R.O., D/CF 95/119.
16 Inf. from churchwarden.
17 *Ch. Plate Essex*, 69.
18 *Short Hist. Organs in Christ Church, Warley* (Leaflet, 1971).
19 G.R.O., Worship Reg. no. 25947 (cancelled 1889); *Kelly's Dir. Essex* (1882); *Essex Recusant*, xiii. 116; Essex Cty. Libr., Essex Collection BK 99427; *Brentwood Dioc. Mag.* xii. 113
20 *Brentwood Dioc. Mag.*, xii. 113; *The Builder*, 10 July 1886; *Kelly's Dir. Essex* (1882–94); G.R.O., Worship Reg. no. 31896 (replacing no. 25947).

In 1893, at the request and cost of Mrs. Willmott, Sisters of Mercy from Brentwood rented a small house as a convent and opened a school; they seem to have left *c.* 1911.[21] Marillac hospital was founded in 1921, when the Sisters of Charity of St. Vincent de Paul bought Warley House as a sanatorium for children and nuns with tuberculosis.[22] It later became a hospital for the severely disabled, and in 1963 was transferred to the former officers' mess building in Eagle Way.[23]

PROTESTANT NONCONFORMITY. The house of Charles Halt was licensed for Presbyterian worship in 1672.[24] Five nonconformists were enumerated in the parish in 1676.[25] In 1791 the house of John Cowell was registered for Baptist worship by Thomas Strachan, minister of Romford Independent church.[26] By 1810 the number of dissenters at Great Warley was said to be diminishing and the meeting-house was disused.[27]

Warley Primitive Methodist church originated in 1898, when a Free Baptist church in Cemetery (now Lorne) Road was registered for worship.[28] That church, which lay on the South Weald side of the Great Warley boundary, was originally sponsored by Brentwood and District Free Church council, but it was later taken over by the Primitive Methodists, and in 1912 was placed in Chelmsford circuit.[29] In 1916 a new church was built on the other side of Warley Hill. It was later transferred to the Grays and Romford circuit.[30] It was closed and sold in 1935, when the members united with Brentwood (ex-Wesleyan) Methodist church, also in Warley Hill.[31] The original building in Lorne Road still existed, as a factory, in 1976.[32]

EDUCATION. Great Warley Church of England primary school, Bird Lane, also called the Lower Warley school. In 1807 there were three small day-schools in the parish with a total of about 38 children, and an Anglican Sunday school, founded in 1806, with 46.[33] The three day-schools had a total of 45 pupils in 1819[34] and 54 in 1833.[35] In 1843 the rector and subscribers who had been supporting these schools built a permanent school with the aid of a government grant, on a site in Bird Lane given by Charles Winn, Lord Headley (d. 1877), and John Cross.[36] In 1846–7, when there were 71 pupils, the school was supported by subscriptions, school pence, and grants from the National Society.[37] A teacher's house was added in 1862[38] and the school was enlarged in 1870 for 86 children.[39] Annual government grants were received from 1871.[40] This was always a small school, serving the rural end of the parish.[41] The school was reorganized in 1936 for juniors and infants.[42] It was granted Controlled status in 1952,[43] and was closed in 1968.[44]

Christ Church Church of England, later county primary, school, Warley Hill, also known as Warley Upper school, was built by subscription in 1854–5, on a site, next to the church, given by the East India Company.[45] A teacher's house was added in 1859–60 and an infants classroom in 1868.[46] The school received annual government grants from 1870.[47] In 1872 accommodation was needed for 150 more children, including 79 from South Weald and Shenfield. An infants school was established in 1875 in Crescent Road, Warley, in connexion with Christ Church but maintained by South Weald parish in which it stood.[48] Christ Church school was enlarged by public subscription in 1892, and again in 1910, for 270 children.[49] In 1911 it was a mixed school with 250 children under 6 teachers.[50] It was reorganized in 1936 for mixed juniors and infants,[51] and was granted Aided status in 1951.[52] It was taken over by the county council in 1963 and was subsequently transferred to new buildings in Essex Way (1966) and Chindits Lane (1972).[53] The old school was demolished in 1975. Hastings Robinson, rector 1827–66, by will proved in 1866, left £200 stock in trust to provide annual entertainment and prizes for the children of the school. Under a Chancery order of 1892 the legacy was paid to the trustees. In 1949 the capital fund was £350 stock.[54] In 1975 the income was being used by the rector for the benefit of children in Great Warley parish.[55]

Warley county infants school, Essex Way, was opened in 1966 for 240, and Warley county junior school, Chindits Lane, in 1972 for 320.[56] Holy Cross and All Saints Roman Catholic school, Warley Hill, was opened *c.* 1920 in a hut behind the church. It was closed *c.* 1954, when the children were transferred to St. Helen's school, Brentwood.[57]

Five private schools in Great Warley are listed in

21 *Brentwood Dioc. Mag.*, ix. 61; *Kelly's Dir. Essex* (1894–1912).
22 *Brentwood Dioc. Mag.*, iv. 102, vi. 147; *Kelly's Dir. Essex* (1922 sqq.); *Brentwood Dioc. Yr. Bk.* (1953).
23 *Catholic Dir.* (1973); *Brentwood Gaz.*, 20 Sept. 1963; inf. from hospital.
24 G. L. Turner, *Orig. Recs. Early Noncf.* i. 568; ii. 932.
25 William Salt Libr., Stafford, S. 2112 (Bp. Compton's census, 1676).
26 G.R.O. Worship Returns, London Dioc. Bps. Ct. no. 300.
27 Guildhall MS. 9558.
28 G.R.O. Worship Reg. no. 36931.
29 Inf. from Brentwood Methodist church.
30 E. Barrett, *The Lamp Still Burns*, 27; G.R.O. Worship Reg. no. 46880 (canc. 1935).
31 Barrett, *The Lamp still Burns*, 10, 27. Brentwood Methodist church is reserved for treatment in a later volume.
32 Inf. from Mrs. G. Ward.
33 E.R.O., D/AEM 2/4.
34 *Returns Educ. Poor*, H.C. 224, p. 275 (1819), ix(1).
35 *Educ. Enquiry Abstract*, H.C. 62, p. 294 (1835), xli.
36 Inf. from Min. of Educ.; *Educ. Enquiry Abstract* (1835), p. 294.
37 *Nat. Soc. Church Schs. Enquiry, 1846–7.*
38 Ed. 21/5169.
39 *Kelly's Dir. Essex* (1908), 604.
40 *Rep. Educ. Cttee. of Council, 1871–2* [C. 601], p. 260, H.C. (1872), xxii.
41 E.R.O., E/ML 174/1; E/Z 2; D/DBe Q12.
42 Inf. from Essex Educ. Dept.
43 E.R.O., C/ME 47, p. 10.
44 Inf. from Essex Educ. Dept.
45 *White's Dir. Essex* (1863), 586; *Return Non-Provided Schs.* H.C. 178, p. 491 (1906), lxxxvii.
46 E.R.O., E/P 134; Ed. 49/2103.
47 *Rep. Educ. Cttee. of Council, 1870–1* [C. 406], p. 457, H.C. (1871), xxii.
48 Ed. 2/165; *Return Non-Provided Schs.* H.C. 178, p. 509 (1906), lxxxvii; *Kelly's Dir. Essex* (1878), 267.
49 *Kelly's Dir. Essex* (1894), 370; (1926), 665.
50 E.R.O., E/Z 2.
51 Inf. from Essex Educ. Dept.
52 E.R.O., C/ME 45, p. 328.
53 E.R.O., C/ME 57, p. 228; C/ME 59, p. 664; C/ME 65, A49–50.
54 Char. Com. Files.
55 Inf. from Rector.
56 *Educ. in Essex*, 1964–73, 22, 26.
57 *Reps. Catholic Educ. Council*; inf. from parish priest.

19th-century directories. Of these, a 'ladies' school kept by Susannah Taylor had opened by 1863 and survived until at least 1902. There was a private school in Warley Hill in the 1930s.[58]

CHARITIES FOR THE POOR. Hastings Robinson, rector 1827–66, by his will proved in 1866, gave funds to endow two annual governorships of the London Hospital for the admission to the hospital of the sick of St. Mary's parish.[59] Admission by governorship was abolished in 1896.[60] In 1951 a Scheme provided that the income from £350 stock belonging to the charity should be managed as two separate charities for the sick of St. Mary's and Christ Church parishes.[61] In 1975 the income was being distributed in cash by the rector of St. Mary's.[62]

LITTLE WARLEY

LITTLE WARLEY lies 3 miles south of Brentwood. between Great Warley and Childerditch.[1] The ancient parish comprised 1,691 a.; it included a detached part of 96 a. which lay in Corringham and was transferred to that parish in 1882.[2] The main part was about 3½ miles long, sloping from a wooded ridge to the Thames plain. The parish was rural and thinly populated until the 19th century, when barracks were built at its northern end. They were closed in 1959, but were replaced in 1964 by the new central offices of the Ford Motor Co.[3] In 1934 Little Warley, previously in Billericay rural district, was divided at the railway line between the urban districts of Billericay (later Basildon) and Brentwood.[4] In 1938 the area south of the railway was transferred from Billericay to Thurrock U.D.[5]

The terrain drops from 375 ft. in the north of the parish to 25 ft. in the south, and the soil consists of London clay over a stiff loam.[6] Several streams flow southward: one, which separates Little Warley from Great Warley to the west, joins another stream from Childerditch before flowing into the Mardyke.

Little Warley has always been sparsely populated. Twelve inhabitants were recorded in 1086, and in 1671 there were only 23 houses occupied.[7] There were 169 inhabitants in 1801, 163 in 1831, and 216 in 1841.[8] By 1851 the population of the parish had risen to 988, of whom 644 were soldiers. The other 344 included, however, the officers' and men's families and the permanent population of the parish was probably about 250, the highest figure it ever reached while Little Warley was a separate parish. Between 1861 and 1931 permanent population numbered between 150 and 200.[9]

The road pattern of Little Warley has remained virtually unchanged for the past two centuries and probably for much longer.[10] The village lies in the centre of the parish, along Magpie Lane as it runs westward from Childerditch. At Clapgates Magpie Lane is joined from the SW. by Bird Lane. It then turns north up Warley Gap, swinging west into Great Warley near the Headley Arms, formerly the Magpie, from which the lane took its name.[11] Hall Lane runs south from the village for 2½ miles to Old Englands. Eagle Way, which is now a wide road running across the north of the parish, past the Ford offices, originated as a track over Little Warley common. In the early 19th century, after the inclosure of the common and the building of the barracks, it became Barrack Road. At its western end Eagle Way joins Warley Hill, running down to Brentwood station. At its eastern end it joins Hartswood Road, to Shenfield Common, the Avenue, to Ingrave, and Childerditch Lane, which runs south past Scrub Hill. The Eastern Counties railway from London to Brentwood, opened in 1840, was extended to Chelmsford and Colchester in 1843.[12] The London, Tilbury and Southend railway extension from Upminster to Pitsea, opened in 1886, crossed Little Warley north of St. Mary's Lane, the nearest station being at East (now West) Horndon.[13] The Southend arterial road, opened in 1925, cut the parish in two, isolating the church.[14]

Before the 19th century settlement was scattered through the parish. Old Englands in the extreme south is a 17th-century farm-house.[15] A mile north lie the church, which in its present form dates from the 15th century, and the Hall of the early 16th century.[16] The former rectory, rebuilt in 1858, stands on an older site about a mile north of the church. In Magpie Lane are Little Bassetts, a 17th-century farm-house, and the weatherboarded Blue House Farm of the 18th century.[17] Clapgate Farm, of *c.* 1700, was destroyed by bombing in 1945.[18] In the north of the parish, on an unidentified site, there was a beacon in 1626; its name was preserved in the late 18th century by Beacon House Farm and by the 'cottages at the Beacon' in 1794.[19]

In the 18th century the common was used for military camps.[20] Brentwood races were also held there; the course for the two-day meeting lay partly under the site of the later barracks.[21] In 1746 Denner Bennett, the lord of the manor, kept the Bull on Warley common, the only alehouse in the parish.[22] By 1769 it had been succeeded by the Greyhound, in Magpie Lane.[23]

[58] *White's Dir. Essex* (1848, 1863); *Kelly's Dir. Essex* (1855–1937).
[59] Char. Com. Files.
[60] A. E. Clark-Kennedy, *The London*, ii. 137.
[61] Char. Com. Files.
[62] Inf. from Revd. D. J. Iorns.
[1] O.S. Map 1/25,000, TQ 58, 59, 68, 69.
[2] Divided Parishes Act, 1882, 45 & 46 Vic. c. 58, s.2.
[3] See p. 177.
[4] Essex Review Order, 1934.
[5] County of Essex (Billericay and Thurrock Urban Districts) Conf. Order, 1938.
[6] *V.C.H. Essex*, i. 8–9.
[7] Ibid. i. 439, 445; E.R.O., Q/RTh 5.
[8] *V.C.H. Essex*, ii. 345.
[9] *Census* (1851–1931).
[10] *Map of Essex* (1777).
[11] *Kelly's Dir. Essex* (1845); *White's Dir. Essex* (1848).
[12] E. Carter, *Hist. Geog. Rlys.* 63.
[13] Ibid. 466.
[14] *V.C.H. Essex*, v. 74.
[15] See p. 176.
[16] R.C.H.M. *Essex*, iv. 89–91; Pevsner, *Essex*, 286–7.
[17] R.C.H.M. *Essex*, iv. 91; Thorne, *Environs Lond.* 676.
[18] Inf. from Mr. J. D. Brett.
[19] E.R.O., Q/SR 255/42; E.R.O., D/DB T827.
[20] See p. 177.
[21] D. W. Coller, *People's Hist. Essex*, 349.
[22] E.R.O., T/P 195/2.
[23] E.R.O., Q/RLv 24.

The modern history of the parish began with the sale of 116 a. of Warley common in 1805, and the subsequent building of the barracks.[24] The sale had been made by George Winn (d. 1827), who, *c.* 1820 built (Little) Warley Lodge.[25] This is a large house in stock brick looking over the village from the southern rim of Ellens Wood. It was occupied by a succession of tenants in the 19th and 20th centuries. In 1953 it was bought for use as a mental hospital by the South Ockendon hospital group.[26] The first patients were admitted in 1955. In 1974 the hospital was transferred to the Barking and Havering area health authority.[27]

After the Second World War some bungalows were built in Hall Lane north of the Southend arterial road; and in the 1960s, after the closure of the barracks, the Ford Motor Co. built central offices on part of the site.[28] Almost opposite, Brentwood U.D.C built houses on 31 a. of the barrack ground on a site now bounded by Eagle Way, Warley Hill, and The Drive.[29] In 1975 Brett Essex golf club was opened on 118 a. of the former Clapgate farm.[30] The Warley Sports Centre, Holden's Wood, which was also opened in 1975, includes a golf range and a ski slope.[31]

MANORS AND OTHER ESTATES. In 1066 the manor of *(LITTLE) WARLEY*, which comprised the greater part of the modern parish, was held by Guert as 4 hides less 15 acres, but William I gave the manor to William, bishop of London (d. 1075), as an old possession of his see.[32] In 1507 the manor was still held of the bishop by fealty and the payment of 18*s*. a year.[33]

In 1086 Tascelin the priest held 15 a. of the manor; Humfrey held the rest.[34] The demesne lordship of the manor later passed to the family of Setmels (*de Septem Molis*), which came from Sept Meules in Normandy (Seine Inf.), and from which the manor became known in the Middle Ages as *WARLEY SETMELS*.[35] In 1166 William Setmels held 2¾ unidentified knights' fees of the bishop of London, and *c.* 1210 Robert Setmels held a carucate in Warley as 1 fee.[36] In 1212 Michael of Huntingdon held Warley as guardian of the heir of Ralph Setmels.[37] William Setmels, who was lord of the manor in the mid 13th century, apparently lost his reason and squandered his estates.[38] By 1259 he had surrendered the manor and advowson to the bishop of London in return for nominal sums to his wife and eldest son, and for 20 marks down, 6 marks a year for life, and the bishop's protection for himself. After his death his heirs were to warrant the charter of transfer to the bishop.

John de Belmeis was holding the manor in 1272.[39] Parnel de Belmeis, probably his widow, was holding it at her death in 1295, as tenant of the heirs of Philip Burnel (d. 1294).[40] In other Essex estates Burnel had succeeded his uncle, the acquisitive Robert Burnel, bishop of Bath and Wells and chancellor of England (d. 1292).[41] It therefore seems likely that Philip's rights in Little Warley had also come to him as the bishop's heir; but there is no later reference to their interest in the manor. Malcolm de Belmeis, son and heir of Parnel, granted the advowson of Little Warley in 1301 to Richard of Gravesend, bishop of London; in 1305 he conveyed the reversion of the manor, after his death, to William Cosyn and his wife Emme.[42] Cosyn, apparently of London, was still alive in 1331.[43] In 1346 it was stated that the knight's fee formerly held by Maurice de Belmeis had been split into four: one quarter was held by Thomas of Gravesend and the rector, one by the prior of Thoby and the abbot of Coggeshall, one by the prior of Christchurch (Hants.), and one by William of Bakeswell.[44]

By 1372 John of Fyfield, mercer of London, held the manor.[45] In 1382 he conveyed it to another London mercer, John Lovey, but retained a life-interest for himself and his wife Idony.[46] Fyfield and his wife were still alive in 1390.[47] In 1413 the manor passed to William Parker, son of William Parker deceased, also a London mercer.[48] John Eton, of London, held the manor in 1428.[49] He, or another John Eton, died in 1453, leaving Little Warley to his infant daughter Isabel.[50]

In 1504 Richard Gilmyn and his wife Alice quitclaimed a third of Little Warley manor to Sir Robert Tyrell, Robert Cornwallis, Thomas Glantham, and Cornwallis's heirs.[51] Within the next year or two Glantham and Humphrey Tyrell sued Sir Robert for refusing to complete a sale of the whole manor, a third of which was then said to be held by Anne Petit.[52] Humphrey Tyrell held two-thirds of the manor at his death in 1507, but his son Sir John Tyrell (d. 1541) and grandson John Tyrell (d. 1586) held the whole manor.[53] The latter's daughter and heir Mary married Thomas, second son of Edward Clinton, earl of Lincoln (d. 1585);[54] in 1600 Thomas and Mary Clinton sold Little Warley to Edward Denner.[55]

Denner's daughter and heir Elizabeth (d. 1626)

[24] See p. 177.
[25] See p. 176; E.R.O., Q/RPl 144–5; *Pigot's Dir. Essex* (1826–7), 522; cf. D. Stroud, *Humphry Repton* (1962), 174.
[26] E.R.O., D/DU 353/1; *Kelly's Dir. Essex* (1845 and later edns.); Barking and Havering area health authority deeds.
[27] Inf. from NE. Thames regional health authority.
[28] Inf. from Ford Motor Co.
[29] Inf. from Brentwood D.C.
[30] Inf. from Mr. J. D. Brett. A further 9-hole course was to be opened on 50 a. in 1976.
[31] Inf. from proprietor; *Brentwood Gaz.* 13 Feb. 1976.
[32] *V.C.H. Essex*, i. 339 n, 439.
[33] *Cal. Inq. p.m. Hen. VII*, iii, pp. 484–6.
[34] *V.C.H. Essex*, i. 439. Nothing more is known of Tascelin's holding.
[35] *E.R.* xxix. 212; *Cal. Inq. p.m. Hen. VII*, iii, pp. 484–6; L. C. Loyd, *Origins Anglo-Norm. Fams.* (Harl. Soc. ciii), 97–8.
[36] *Red Bk. Exch.* (Rolls Ser.), i. 186; ii. 542.
[37] *Bk. of Fees*, i. 122.
[38] *Close R.* 1242–7, 357; *Cal. Anct. D.* i, A761, A772; *Close R.* 1259–61, 155–6, Cf. E.R.O., D/DP T1/1158; Morant, *Essex*, i. 114.
[39] E.R.O., D/DP T1/1183, 1177–8.
[40] *Cal. Inq. p.m.* iii, pp. 200–1; *D.N.B.* s.v. Burnell.
[41] Cf. *V.C.H. Essex*, v. 76; vi. 10.
[42] *Feet of F. Essex*, ii. 91, 99; for Belmeis in 1321: *Cal. Pat.* 1321–4, 61.
[43] *Feet of F. Essex*, ii. 119, 123, 169, 232; iii. 19.
[44] *Feud Aids*, ii. 169.
[45] *Cal. Inq. Misc.* iii, 314; *Cal. Close*, 1369–74, 418.
[46] *Feet of F. Essex*, iii. 195; *Cal. Close*, 1381–5, 203–4, 211–12.
[47] *Cal. Close*, 1389–92, 188.
[48] Ibid. 1413–19, 91, 96.
[49] *Feud. Aids*, ii. 224.
[50] C 139/152/5.
[51] *Feet of F. Essex*, iv. 110.
[52] C 1/367/37.
[53] Chancellor, *Sep. Mons. Essex*, 174; *Cal. Inq. p.m. Hen. VII*, iii, pp. 484–6.
[54] Chancellor, *Sep. Mons. Essex*, 174.
[55] C.P. 25(2)/139/1757.

married John Strutt of Hadleigh.[56] Their son and heir, Sir Denner Strutt, Bt. (d. 1661), was survived by two daughters. In the division of his estate Blanch (d. 1671), the wife of Thomas Bennett, took Little Warley, and was succeeded in the direct line by her son (d. 1741), grandson (d. 1742), and great-grandson (d. 1779), all of whom were named Denner Bennett. In 1759 the youngest Denner Bennett sold the manor to John Fisher, who in 1772 sold it to George Winn (d. 1798), later Lord Headley.[57] He already held the manor of Great Warley, with which Little Warley descended until 1919.[58] In that year Essex county council bought Little Warley Hall and 117 a. from Mrs. Llewellyn.[59] The Hall was separated from the estate in 1920 and sold to Mr. J. L. McConnell; in the 1930s it was the home of the actress Mary Clare. It was owned in 1975 by Mr. Jack C. Harris.[60] In 1955 Mrs. Llewellyn's daughter and son-in-law, Mr. and Mrs. K. M. Fardell, sold 140 a. of common to Brentwood U.D.C.[61]

Little Warley Hall stands beside the church south of the arterial road. Fragments of a moat to the south and west of the house suggest that this is an old site. The existing house is probably the product of a partial rebuilding of the early 16th century. It is of red brick, decorated with patterns of black headers, and represents the two-storeyed porch, hall, hall-chamber, and part of the service-end of the 16th-century house. In 1568, when it was attacked by yeomen and others from Little Warley, it was described as 'Little Warley Hall, otherwise Castle Warley.'[62] Until the later 19th century a plaster-fronted range of the 17th century, with two north gables, extended westwards, presumably containing parlours.[63] In the 19th century both the hall and its chamber were partitioned and an early-17th-century stair was reconstructed and reset against the south wall, to the west of the original garderobe. The house has been several times restored in the present century.

The manor or farm of *DAME ELLENS* or *DAME ELYNS* lay in the north of the parish and has left its name in Ellens Wood. It may have been associated with the family of Elyne or Heleyne recorded in the 13th and 14th centuries, but its early decent has not been traced.[64] Henry VIII granted it with other properties to Waltham Abbey *c.* 1536 in exchange for Copped Hall, Epping.[65] In 1540, at the Dissolution, it passed briefly to Thomas Cromwell, earl of Essex, and in 1541 it was among other Essex properties granted to Anne of Cleves for life.[66] The Crown sold the reversion of several of these properties, including Dame Ellens, to Sir William Petre in 1544, and in the same year he leased them from Anne of Cleves.[67] In 1559 Petre transferred Dame Ellens to John Tyrell,[68] and from that time it appears to have descended with Little Warley manor.[69]

In 1586 Dame Ellens contained 20 a. arable, 40 a. pasture, 60 a. wood, and 100 a. heath.[70] It included 140 a. woodland in 1686, and *c.* 1725 was said to be worth £80.[71] It seems to have been held by tenants until 1772, but in that year George Winn, later Lord Headley, bought the estate and took it in hand.[72] Warley Lodge was later built on the wood's southern flank.[73]

The estate called (*OLD*) *ENGLANDS*, or *INGLONDES*, lies in the south of the parish. At his death in 1507 Humphrey Tyrell was holding it of the bishop of London.[74] In 1589 it was held by Richard Luther (d. 1639), of Kelvedon Hatch.[75] By 1601 he had leased it to (Sir) John Morris, son-in-law of Sir Gabriel Poyntz of North Ockendon; it was then reckoned at 120 a., or as 1 plough-land.[76] Luther's son and heir, Anthony Luther (d. 1665), and Anthony's grandson Edward Luther (d. 1734), both enlarged the estate, which in 1729 comprised 180 a.[77] Englands was normally leased to tenants, whose sequence can be established, almost without interruption, from that time.[78]

The estate appears to have descended to Edward Luther's son, Richard (d. 1767), but in 1781 Mrs. Gibson was the owner.[79] She was followed by George Gibson, 1782–1806, and Daniel Pettiward, 1807–32.[80] In 1835 Thomas Cawkwell (d. 1840) owned and occupied the farm.[81] His widow apparently still owned it in 1863, but William Tanner, the tenant from *c.* 1842, later became the owner.[82] He, and his widow from *c.* 1875, farmed Englands until 1885, when mortgagees foreclosed.[83] James Crane, their tenant from 1886, bought the farm with 173 a. in 1911, and it has continued in his family to the present.[84]

Old Englands is a 17th-century farm-house.[85] Its SW. wing, now the kitchen, was formerly open to the roof and may be older than the rest of the house. Having fallen into disrepair, the house was extensively renovated *c.* 1910 when the exterior was weatherboarded.

ECONOMIC HISTORY. Little Warley has always been a mainly agricultural parish. In 1086 there were

[56] E.R.O., T/G 21: unless otherwise stated, the source of information in this paragraph. Cf. *E.A.T.* v. 147; G.E.C. *Baronetage*, ii. 161.
[57] C.P. 25(2)/1262/31 Geo. II Hil.; C.P. 25(2)/1475/12 Geo. III Hil.
[58] E.R.O., C/TS 75; deeds *penes* Barking and Havering area health authority; see p. 167.
[59] E.R.O., C/TS 75.
[60] Ibid.; inf. from Mrs. Harris; *Who's Who in the Theatre* (1925–47).
[61] Inf. from Brentwood D.C.
[62] E.R.O., Q/SR 27/29. For the hall, see also R.C.H.M. *Essex*, iv. 90; Pevsner, *Essex*, 286–7.
[63] E.R.O., Pictorial Coll.
[64] *P.N. Essex*, 135. Reaney correctly assigned Ellens Wood to Little Warley, but mistakenly placed the ancient Dame Elyns in Horndon-on-the-Hill: ibid. 157.
[65] *V.C.H. Essex*, v. 122.
[66] *L. & P. Hen. VIII*, xvi, p. 242; xix (1), p. 494.
[67] Ibid.; F. G. Emmison, *Tudor Secretary*, 266, citing Bodl. MS. D. Phil. d. 1007.
[68] E.R.O., D/DP T1/935–6; cf. *Cal. Pat.* 1550–3, 214.
[69] See above.
[70] C 142/211/184.
[71] E.R.O., T/P 195/2.
[72] Ibid.; E.R.O., D/P 66/12/1–2; E.R.O., Q/RPl 106–57.
[73] See p. 175.
[74] *Cal. Inq. p.m. Hen. VII*, iii, pp. 484–5. It seems possible that Englands was the unidentified Geddesduna of Domesday Book: see above, p. 99.
[75] E.R.O., Q/SR 109/46; cf. ibid. 122/17, 130/27, 135/20; for the Luther family: *V.C.H. Essex*, iv. 67–8.
[76] E.R.O., Q/SR 163/22 and 80, 166/144
[77] E.R.O., D/DFa T21, F6.
[78] Ibid.; E.R.O., D/P 66/1/2; D/P 66/12/1–2; E.R.O., Q/RPl 106–57; E.R.O., D/AER 36/382.
[79] E.R.O., D/DFa F6; Q/RPl 106.
[80] E.R.O., Q/RPl 107–57.
[81] E.R.O., D/DP P109; E.R.O., D/P 66/20.
[82] *White's Dir. Essex* (1863); E.R.O., D/P 66/20. Tanner is said to have been a kinsman of Mr. or Mrs. Cawkwell, and to have bought the property: local inf.
[83] *Kelly's Dir. Essex* (1878, 1882); E.R.O., *Sale Cat.* B3533.
[84] E.R.O., *Sale Cat.* B3533; inf. from Messrs. Crane.
[85] R.C.H.M. *Essex*, iv. 90; inf. from Messrs. Crane.

Wennington: Site of Wharf, Wennington Road, looking south-west

Romford, Harold Hill: Cockerell's Moat, Dagnam Park, looking west

Great Warley: Warley Place and Gardens in the early-20th century, looking west

2 plough-teams on the demesne and 3 belonging to the tenants, woodland for 700 swine, and marshland pasture for 100 sheep.[86] Since 1066 one plough-team had disappeared from the demesne; otherwise there had been no change.

The most striking Domesday figure is that relating to swine-pastures, which shows that Little Warley was one of the most densely wooded places in Essex. At that time the north of the manor probably consisted mainly of woodland and scrub, some of which still survives as Little Warley common.[87] In 1257 Coggeshall Abbey was licensed to inclose 300 a. of heath in Childerditch and Little Warley.[88] Dame Ellens appears to have been won from the common in the Middle Ages.[89] The most northerly parts of the common were sold to the War office in 1805, but in 1838 the parish still contained 140 a. of common, at Warley Gap (44 a.) and Scrub Hill (96 a.), which have never been inclosed,[90] as well as 190 a. of woods, all in the north.[91] In 1946 over 1,000 trees, mostly oak, chestnut, beech, and birch, were felled in Ellens Wood.[92]

The marshland sheep-pasture of 1086 was detached from the main body of the parish.[93] In the 19th century it comprised 80 a. pasture and 16 a. arable, locally situated between Holehaven and Shellhaven creeks in Corringham.[94]

In 1295 the demesne land of Little Warley manor included 283 a. arable and 33 a. meadow and pasture.[95] In the early 16th century there were 340 a. arable, 80 a. meadow, and 10 a. wood.[96] Excluding the detached portion, the parish in 1838 contained 673 a. of arable and 498 a. of pasture in 15 holdings. Two, including the largest (236 a.), belonged to the Petres and were let with Childerditch farms. Three had between 107 a. and 161 a., and another 3 totalling 168 a. were farmed as a single unit. Two holdings of 45 a. and 17 a. were similarly farmed together; 4 of the remaining 5 holdings had between 38 a. and 59 a.; the last had 17 a.[97] In the late 19th century much arable was converted to pasture: in 1916 there were 632 a. of pasture and meadow and only 198 a. of arable.[98] Four farms had between 104 a. and 212 a.; the other 6 holdings, worked as 5, had between 17 a. and 52 a.[99] There was little further change in land use before 1975 when Mr. J. D. Brett began to turn much of Clapgate farm into a golf course.[1]

About 1835 a smock mill was built east of the junction of Magpie and Bird Lanes. It was wrecked by a gale in 1866.[2] There was a brick-maker in the parish in 1605; two fields on the western border of the parish were still styled Brick Kiln field in 1837.[3] There was a tannery at Little Warley from 1652 to 1769. It presumably lay in Tanners meadow NE. of the junction of Warley Gap and Magpie Lane.[4]

When the barracks were closed in 1959 the Ford Motor Co. bought 21 a. of the site of the barracks for their new British central offices opened in 1964. In 1967 the headquarters of Ford in Europe were also opened there. By 1975 the building accommodated 2,000 employees.[5]

WARLEY CAMP. A temporary military camp was set up in 1742 on Warley common, in Great and Little Warley.[6] The common was used for other camps on several later occasions in the 18th century.[7] The 1778 camp was visited by George III and by Dr. Samuel Johnson.[8]

In 1805 the War Office bought 116 a. of the common and built permanent barracks for two troops of horse artillery. From 1806 to 1815 Warley House, formerly on the SE. corner of Eagle Way and Warley Hill, seems to have been the commandant's quarters.[9] Various army units used the barracks until 1832, after which they lay empty for a decade.

The East India Company bought the barracks for £15,000 in 1843, and in the next 15 years greatly altered and added to the buildings, further land being purchased in 1858. In 1861 the India Office transferred the barracks once more to the War Office. From 1873 until their closure in 1959 Warley barracks were the depot of the Essex Regiment.[10] In 1961 Brentwood U.D.C. bought 59 a., and the Ford Motor Company 21 a.[11] The barracks were demolished, and Ford's central office was opened in 1964.[12]

The barracks were of yellow brick in the plain style typical of early-19th-century military buildings. On the main (east) front a central block of 7 bays and 2½ storeys was joined by a single-storeyed wall to 2 wing-blocks, each of 9 bays and 2 storeys, capped with 3-bay pediments. The chapel, which survives, was designed by Sir Matthew Wyatt in 1857 in an Italianate style, in yellow brick trimmed with red.[13]

[86] *V.C.H. Essex*, i. 439.

[87] J. H. Round's figure of 41 swine per 100 a. (ibid. i. 375) should be corrected to 43¾, since the detached portion of the parish is not relevant to the calculation.

[88] *Cal. Chart. R.* i. 466; E.R.O., D/CT 386.

[89] See p. 176.

[90] E.R.O., D/CT 386; J. W. Burrows, *Essex Regiment*, iv. 167–74.

[91] E.R.O., D/CT 386; they were bought by Brentwood U.D.C. in 1955 (inf. from Brentwood D.C.).

[92] Bill of sale *penes* Riders, Lincolns Inn; Mr. T. Murray Mills is thanked for securing access to it.

[93] *V.C.H. Essex*, i. 369, 439.

[94] E.R.O., D/CT 386.

[95] *Cal. Inq. p.m.* iii, pp. 200–1.

[96] *Feet of F. Essex*, iv. 110; *Cal. Inq. p.m. Hen. VII*, iii, pp. 484–6.

[97] E.R.O., D/CT 79, 386.

[98] Or *c.* 832 a. of pasture and *c.* 272 a. of arable, if the two Petre holdings (236 a. and 38 a.), which were farmed from Childerditch, are added. They are most unlikely to have had as much as 90 a. of arable by 1916: E.R.O., D/CT 386, D/Z 45/1.

[99] E.R.O., D/Z 45/1, 11; D/Z 45/1 Little Warley, wrongly includes Clay Tye, Great Warley, but excludes Little Warley glebe, which appears as Church Hill in D/Z 45/11 Great Warley. The two Petre holdings are not included in this description.

[1] 2nd Land Utilization Survey of Britain, Land Use sheets 225–6; inf. from Mr. J. D. Brett.

[2] E.R.O., D/P 66/20; D/CT 386: *Essex Standard*, 12 Jan. 1866. The mill and miller (William Bennett) are absent from the Land Tax returns, 1781–1832: E.R.O., Q/RPl 106–57.

[3] E.R.O., Q/SR 173/32; D/CT 368A, nos. 54, 135.

[4] E.R.O., Q/SR 351/77, 364/25, 479/61; E.R.O., D/ABR 18/334, 26/93; E.R.O., D/DB T827; E.R.O., D/CT 386A, no. 32.

[5] Inf. from Ford Motor Co. See plate facing p. 32.

[6] Burrows, *Essex Regiment*, iv. 167–74: the source of information in this section unless otherwise cited.

[7] *E.R.* xxviii. 42; xxxiv. 57; xlii. 182.

[8] Ibid. xxxiv. 57; O. Hedley, *Queen Charlotte*, 121–2; Chelmsford and Essex Mus. (Essex Regt. Mus.), ER 16; *Chelmsford Chron.* 17 July 1778. Two views of the royal visit, by P. J. de Loutherbourg, are in the royal collection. For one of these see plate facing p. 65.

[9] E.R.O., Q/RPl 131–40; and see above, p. 165.

[10] *E.R.* ix. 105. Cf. *V.C.H. Essex*, ii. 252–4.

[11] *Brentwood Gaz.* 14 July, 29 Sept., 24 Nov. 1961.

[12] Inf. from company.

[13] See plate facing p. 48.

The campanile was added in 1957. The furnishings of the chapel were designed by Sir Charles Nicholson.[14] A few other military buildings survive, including a pair of semi-detached married quarters, of 1892, in Chindits Lane, Great Warley. The 20th-century officers' mess became the Marillac hospital in 1963.[15]

LOCAL GOVERNMENT. No records of manorial courts survive for Little Warley. There are parish vestry minutes for 1718–71 and overseers' accounts and rates for 1749–95.[16]

In the 18th century vestry meetings were held only once or twice a year, and the rector or, usually, the assistant curate took the chair. Five or six of the more substantial farmers normally attended the meetings, and they shared the parish offices among them. There were two churchwardens between 1719 and 1730, and despite a distinction drawn between the 'nominal' one and the one who was 'to act', both submitted accounts of their expenditure. There was only one warden after 1730; from 1733 he was appointed by the rector. From 1718 to 1750 there was a single overseer of the poor; thereafter two were often appointed, but the account was still submitted in the name of one. When Thomas Biggs died in 1757, his widow Elizabeth succeeded him as overseer. She again held the office in the years 1763–5 and 1779–81, but usually acted through her son, John Biggs. Little Warley had a single constable; at the end of the century this office was combined with that of church clerk, a post to which there were appointments in 1725 and from 1763. There were usually two surveyors.

The rateable value of the parish was £570 in 1749. It was continuously revised, and by 1794 was £926. By 1815 it had risen to £1,630, but it later declined, presumably because of the closing of the camp; in 1837 it was £1,122.[17]

In the early 18th century Little Warley had few poor. In 1723 there were only four regular pensioners who were apparently paid monthly. Poor children were sometimes bound as apprentices within the parish, but the practice was unpopular, and in 1768 the vestry resolved to end it. Out-relief was given throughout the century. The homeless poor were boarded out, and since Little Warley had no workhouse of its own, two or three were sent to Great Warley workhouse from 1783. After the closure of Great Warley workhouse in 1830 Little Warley seems to have started using the house belonging to Chappington's charity as a poorhouse.[18]

In the earlier 18th century medical treatment was provided on a casual basis, as in 1719 when Richard Twydell, surgeon, agreed to take 5 guineas if he cured a patient, but only 2 guineas if the patient died under his hand. About 1750, however, the parish appears to have retained a doctor for a decade or more at 2 guineas a year. Thereafter no regular retainer seems to have been paid until 1788.

In the three years 1782–5 approximately 86 per cent of the overseer's expenditure was spent on the poor.[19] If the proportion was constant in the 18th century, about £43 a year was spent on the poor in the period 1749–80, and about £82 in the period 1780–95.[20] From 1804 to 1817 expenditure on the poor averaged £195, in the worst years (1805–6 and 1812–13) reaching £281 and £265 respectively.[21] Comparable figures are not available for later years, but it seems likely that an improvement in 1816–17 was followed by greatly increased distress among the poor in 1817–19.[22] In 1835 Little Warley became part of Billericay poor-law union.[23]

CHURCH. The advowson of the rectory of Little Warley appears to have descended with the manor until 1301.[24] In that year Malcolm de Belmeis ceded it to Richard of Gravesend, bishop of London (d. 1303), as a personal possession.[25] From the bishop the advowson passed to his brother Sir Stephen of Gravesend, and then to Sir Stephen's son, another Stephen, also bishop of London (d. 1338).[26] In 1361 Sewel Michell of Canewdon presented to the rectory; in 1363 he granted the advowson to Sir Thomas Tyrell of Heron, in East Horndon, in whose family it remained for four centuries.[27] On the death of Sir John Tyrell, Bt., in 1766, his daughters Elizabeth, who died unmarried, and Mary (d. 1832) inherited the advowson.[28] Between 1777 and 1837 they, or their trustees, or Mary's husband, Arthur Gore, earl of Arran (d. 1837), made presentations to the rectory.[29] John Pearson, rector 1837–78, owned the advowson by 1848 and kept it until *c.* 1880.[30] It then passed to David Roberts (*c.* 1880 until *c.* 1904) and (Sir) J. Herbert Roberts (Bt.), later Lord Clwyd.[31] By 1932 James F. Hough, headmaster of Brentwood School, held the advowson.[32] In 1940 Little Warley and Childerditch were united, and the advowson of the united benefice was vested in Hough and the Martyrs Memorial Trust alternately.[33] Hough's share of the advowson passed in 1960 to Brentwood School.[34] In 1969 the benefice was vacated, and from 1970 to 1972 it was in the charge of the rector of East and West Horndon. A new union of benefices then occurred: Little Warley was separated from Childerditch, and joined with East and West Horndon, the

[14] Pevsner, *Essex*, 287; *D.N.B.* s.v. Wyatt, Sir M. D.; H.O. 129/7/199; *Essex Churchman*, Nov. 1957.
[15] Inf. from hospital; *Brentwood Gaz.* 20 Sept. 1963.
[16] E.R.O., D/P 66/8/1, 66/12/1, 2: unless otherwise specified, all information in this section comes from those sources.
[17] E.R.O., D/P 66/20. The reopening of the camp and canteen in 1843 added £540 to the valuation of the parish.
[18] See p. 180.
[19] E.R.O., Q/CR 1/1.
[20] In the later period expenditure on the poor averaged a fraction less than £60 a year between 1787 and 1793.
[21] E.R.O., Q/CR 1/9/4. In the years 1812–15, on average, 21 persons received permanent, and 66 occasional, relief: E.R.O., Q/CR 1/10.
[22] E.R.O., Q/CR 1/12.
[23] E.R.O., G/Bi M1.
[24] See p. 175; cf. *E.A.T.* N.S. xviii. 17.
[25] *Feet of F. Essex*, ii. 91; *D.N.B.*
[26] *Cal. Inq. p.m.* iv, p. 130; Newcourt, *Repertorium*, ii. 642; *D.N.B.*
[27] Newcourt, *Repertorium*, ii. 642; *Cal. Close*, 1360–4, 544–5; Chancellor, *Sep. Mons. Essex* [173–5].
[28] Chancellor, *Sep. Mons. Essex* [175].
[29] E.R.O., T/A 547/1.
[30] *White's Dir. Essex* (1848); *Kelly's Dir. Essex* (1878, 1882).
[31] *Kelly's Dir. Essex* (1882–1929); *Chelmsford Dioc. Yr. Bk.* (1915–29).
[32] *Chelmsford Dioc. Yr. Bk.* (1932).
[33] Ibid. (1941); C.C.L., Bp. Inskip's Recs. ii (5 Dec. 1940); cf. E.R.O., T/P 181/12/8.
[34] *Chelmsford Dioc. Yr. Bk.* (1961–2); *Brentwood Gaz.* 22 Jan. 1960.

advowson of the united benefice being vested in Brentwood School and the bishop of Chelmsford alternately.[35]

The rectory was valued at 7 marks in 1254 and 1291, £11 3*s.* 8*d.* in 1535, £80 in 1650, and £100 in the 18th century.[36] In 1837 the tithes were commuted for £287 10*s.*[37] The glebe apparently consisted of 2 a. in the 14th century, about 30 a. in the 17th century, and 38 a. in 1837.[38] In 1601 the rectory house stood about a mile north of the church.[39] It described in 1848 as a small lath-and-plaster building.[40] A new rectory, on the same site, replaced it *c.* 1858.[41] In 1972 it was sold by the Church Commissioners.[42]

The parishes of Little Warley and Childerditch were closely associated: in the second quarter of the 18th century they were described, with Great Warley, as 'one congregation, as it were', and in 1777 the vicar of Childerditch was also the assistant curate of Little Warley.[43] The rectors were usually nonresident, and the parish was served by curates almost continuously from 1718 to *c.* 1870.[44] The curate's stipend in the 18th century was £30 a year, but had risen in the early 19th century to £75 and fees.[45]

The rectors of Little Warley in the reign of Charles I were apparently Puritans. In 1629 Christopher Dennis, rector 1627–32, was among those petitioning the bishop on behalf of Thomas Hooker, and in 1634 Thimbleby Holden, rector 1632–53 appeared before the court of High Commission.[46] In 1649 Holden had to attend the County Committee, but was discharged without penalty, and in 1650 was described as 'an able, godly minister'.[47] His successor stayed at Little Warley only a few months, and at Michaelmas 1653 was followed by William Powell, formerly curate of Brentwood, who was ejected in 1662.[48]

The church of *ST. PETER*, which stands south of the arterial road to Southend, consists of chancel, nave, west tower, and south porch.[49] Frequent rebuilding suggests an unstable site. The nave was rebuilt in the 15th century, when a west tower was probably added. The chancel was rebuilt in brick in the 16th century, and the south porch, of timber on modern brick walls, is probably of the same date. The present brick tower was built in 1718, partly on earlier footings. More recent restorations include the 19th-century east wall of the chancel.

A gallery, no longer extant, contained in 1923 panelling of *c.* 1600, reset. In the nave three seats with moulded rails are of the early 16th century; one panelled back dates from *c.* 1600, as do the box-pews. The present pulpit incorporates elements of a 17th-century pulpit.

The church had three bells in 1552, but *c.* 1725 there was only one, which remains. It was probably cast by William Wodewarde *c.* 1400.[50] The church plate includes a cup of 1564.[51]

A brass commemorating Anne (d. 1592), wife successively of David Hanmer and John Tyrell, has been removed from its indent in the nave and placed in the chancel. The chancel also contains an alabaster monument of Mary (d. 1658), third wife of Sir Denner Strutt, Bt., reclining shrouded on her left elbow on a marble altar-tomb, and a double marble and alabaster monument to Sir Denner (d. 1661) and his first wife Mary (Staresmore, d. 1641). Mary lies on an altar-tomb, revealed by two cherubs drawing back a canopy; on a lower stage, probably added later, Sir Denner lies in plate-armour. An early-17th-century figure of Father Time, formerly in the churchyard, has been set in the blocked north doorway of the nave.

NONCONFORMITY. Four dissenters 'at most' were reported in the parish in 1760,[52] but no record has been found of organized nonconformity at any date.

EDUCATION. Thimbleby Holden, rector, conducted a school at Little Warley *c.* 1640.[53] In 1833 six girls from Little Warley were being sent daily to school at Great Warley by the curate, assisted by the family at Warley Lodge.[54] In 1842 there was a day and Sunday school at Little Warley; in 1846–7 it had 25 pupils and was supported by subscriptions and school pence.[55] In 1858 the house in Magpie Lane belonging to Hugh Chappington's charity was pulled down and replaced by a schoolroom with an almshouse at each end.[56] In 1901, when the building was improved, the school was certified as efficient by the Board of Education, but the certificate was not renewed in 1902 because the teacher was unqualified. In 1904 the school was taken over by the county council, which maintained it until 1907, when a new council school was opened opposite the old one.[57] In 1936 the school was reorganized for mixed juniors and infants.[58] In 1939 there were 64 pupils.[59] The school was closed in 1953; the children were transferred to Oglethorpe county primary school, Cranham.[60]

[35] *Chelmsford Dioc. Yr. Bk.* (1969 and later edns.); *Lond. Gaz.* 2 May 1972.
[36] *E.A.T.* N.S. xviii. 17; *Tax. Eccl.* (Rec. Com.), 23; *Valor Eccl.* (Rec. Com.), i. 436; Smith, *Eccl. Hist. Essex*, 246; Guildhall MSS. 9550, 9556, 9560.
[37] E.R.O., D/CT 386.
[38] *Feet of F. Essex*, ii. 91; Newcourt, *Repertorium*, ii. 641–2; E.R.O., D/CT 386.
[39] E.R.O., Q/SR 154/19, 217/12; cf. Newcourt, *Repertorium*, ii. 641–2; *Map of Essex* (1777).
[40] *White's Dir. Essex* (1848).
[41] *Kelly's Dir. Essex* (1855, 1859).
[42] Inf. from Mrs. David Tee.
[43] Guildhall MSS. 9550, 9557.
[44] Guildhall MSS. 9550–1, 9553, 9557, 9560; *White's Dir. Essex* (1863); *Kelly's Dir. Essex* (1859 and later edns.).
[45] Guildhall MSS. 9550–1, 9553, 9557, 9560.
[46] Davids, *Nonconformity in Essex*, 157; *Cal. S.P. Dom.* 1634–5, 108.
[47] Smith, *Eccl. Hist. Essex*, 166; Davids, op. cit. 506.
[48] A. G. Matthews, *Calamy Revised*, 396–7; Davids, op. cit. 506.
[49] This account of the church is based on: R.C.H.M. *Essex*, iv. 89–90; Pevsner, *Essex*, 286; cf. Hale, *Precedents*, p. 151.
[50] *Ch. Bells Essex*, 24–7, 439; E.R.O., T/P 195/2.
[51] *Ch. Plate Essex*, 68.
[52] Guildhall MS. 9558.
[53] Venn, *Alumni Cantab.* I, ii. 157.
[54] *Educ. Enquiry Abstract*, H.C. 62, p. 294 (1835), xli; in 1832 Warley Lodge was owned by Charles Winn and let to Jacob Hansler: E.R.O., Q/RPl 157.
[55] E.R.O., D/DU 353/1; *Nat. Soc. Church Schs. Enquiry, 1846–7*.
[56] *White's Dir. Essex* (1863), 588; O.S. Map 6", Essex, LXVII (surv. 1866); and see below.
[57] Ed. 21/5256.
[58] Inf. from Essex Educ. Dept.
[59] Ed. 21/50986.
[60] E.R.O., C/ME 47, p. 345.

CHARITIES FOR THE POOR.[61] By the will of Hugh Chappington (d. *c.* 1693) the reversion to an estate in Little Warley with two tenements, called the Blue Ball and the Red Lion, was left, in default of heirs, to the poor of the parish.[62] Chappington's widow Eleanor and her husband Luke King surrendered their interests to the parish in 1706, but the lord of the manor claimed the Red Lion. In 1707 the parish agreed to his claim and in return was allowed to inclose 3 a. alongside the Blue Ball.[63] It was stated in 1837 that the rent of the house and 17 a. land[64] had normally been used to repair the house, pay the parish doctor, and provide money and coal for the poor. Since 1835, however, it had been improperly used to relieve the poor-rates. The house was let with the land until 1830, but in 1837 it was sheltering 6 pauper families. Its use as a poorhouse probably started after the closing of the Great Warley workhouse in 1830.[65] Part of the house was used as a parish school, probably from *c.* 1838 when the trustees started paying annual grants to the school. In 1858 it was replaced by a new school and two rooms for the poor on the same site in Magpie Lane. By 1878 half the £30 annual income was used to support the school.[66] Under a Charity Commission Scheme of 1887 a third of the income of £40 was used to provide prizes and continuation payments to Little Warley children attending public elementary schools. In 1904 this part of the endowment was established as a separate educational foundation. In 1968 the capital of the poor's charity was £1,691 and that of the educational foundation £492. The building was pulled down in 1969 and replaced by three alms-houses, which were opened in 1971.[67] Under a Charity Commission Scheme of 1971 the educational foundation was combined with the poor's charity as the Hugh Chappington alms-house and relief in need charity for residents of Little Warley. After payment of £60 a year to maintain the alms-houses the balance of the income was to be used to provide relief in cash or kind to persons in need. The annual income from the 17 a. of land was £85 in 1971.

WENNINGTON

WENNINGTON is a small marshland village in the London borough of Havering. It lies about 16 miles east of the city of London, within the Green Belt.[1] The ancient parish, containing 1,301 a., was bounded west and north by Rainham, east by Aveley, and south by the Thames.[2] The boundaries of Wennington, Rainham, and Aveley were 'strangely intermixed'.[3] The boundary with Aveley, which was still disputed in the early 19th century, was settled in 1842.[4] Wennington was included in Hornchurch urban district in 1934.[5] It became part of Havering in 1965.

The whole of Wennington lies below the 25-ft. contour except the eastern edge, which rises to 50 ft. near Willows Farm. A broad tract of alluvium stretches from the Thames up to the village, which stands on the edge of the flood plain gravel terrace. The higher land on the east is formed of Woolwich beds of sand and clay.[6] A navigable creek once divided the marshland, running inland for over a mile as far as the gravel terrace, to a wharf beside Wennington Road. Launders brook, which flows south-west from Launders bridge, dividing Rainham and Wennington, formerly turned east near South Hall to flow into the creek as Wennington brook. In the 17th century it was diverted and the creek occluded. A land drain still marks the creek's old course to its former mouth on the Great Salting, and the site of the wharf basin at the head of the creek is still recognizable between Laundry Cottages and New Cottages.[7] The occlusion of the creek and reclamation of salt marsh have much altered the topography of Wennington since the Middle Ages.[8]

The grouping of the village, church, and manor-house along the high road, close to the marsh and wharf, and the elements of the parish name, suggest early sea-borne settlement.[9] The recorded population was 8 in 1066, and only 3 in 1086.[10] In 1327 Wennington was the smallest township in the hundred, with 11 taxpayers,[11] and in 1523 there were only seven.[12] There were 12 houses in 1662, and 15 in 1670.[13] In the late 18th century there were 14 houses.[14] There were 91 inhabitants in 1801.[15] The population rose slowly to 196 in 1881. In the 1880s a small influx of industry, and the prosperity brought to the village by wealthy Rainham industrialists like the Hemplemans and the Salamons, who chose to live there, raised the population to 310 by 1891.[16] It reached a peak of 432 in 1921 but had declined to 359 by 1931.

Wennington Road, on which the village stands, runs alongside the marsh on the margin of the gravel terrace.[17] It leads westward to Southall bridge and Rainham, and eastward past the church

[61] Unless otherwise stated this section is based on *Rep. Com. Char.*[108], pp. 722–3 (1837–8), xxv(1); Char. Com. Files.

[62] Prob. 11/423 (P.C.C. 1694, f. 229).

[63] E.R.O., D/DP T163.

[64] E.R.O., D/CT 386.

[65] E.R.O., D/P 66/8/1; 66/12/1; D/P 195/8/3.

[66] *Kelly's Dir. Essex* (1878), 267.

[67] *Brentwood Official Guide* (1973–5), 71; inf. from Mrs. Bloomfield.

[1] O.S. Map 6", TQ 57 NW and 58 SW (1967 edn.); *County of Essex Devt. Plan, Rep. of Survey (Pt. II): Met. Essex*, Diagram No. 1. This article was completed in 1973 and revised in 1976.

[2] O.S. Map 6", Essex, LXXXII and LXXXIII (surv. 1862–8).

[3] Morant, *Essex*, i. 86.

[4] E.R.O., D/CT 392; E.R.O., D/P 202/28/1.

[5] Essex Review Order, 1934.

[6] *County of Essex Devt. Plan*, Diagrams 3, 4; *V.C.H. Essex*, i. 7; E.R.O., T/P 50/14; R. Allison, 'The changing geographical landscape of SW. Essex from Saxon times to 1600' (Lond. Univ. M.A. thesis, 1958), 16, 33.

[7] See plate facing p. 176. For the creek see E.R.O., D/DL P1; cf. O.S. Map 6", Essex, TQ 57 NW., 58 SW. (1967 edn.).

[8] See p. 185.

[9] Allison, op. cit. 43; cf. *P.N. Essex*, 139.

[10] *V.C.H. Essex*, i. 445.

[11] E 179/107/13 m. 8.

[12] E 179/108/150.

[13] E.R.O., Q/RTh 1 and 5.

[14] Guildhall MSS. 9557, f. 59; 9558, f. 382. Morant's statement (*Essex*, i. 86), following Holman (E.R.O., T/P 195/2 (no. 2)), that Wennington had been depopulated since the 17th century is incorrect.

[15] *Census*, 1801 sqq. In 1841 the total of 281 included 160 Irish migrant workers.

[16] E.R.O., T/P 50/14; *Kelly's Dir. Essex* (1886).

[17] Cf. *Map of Essex* (1777).

to Wennington Hall and Three Wants Corner. In 1557 it was described as the highway from Wennington to London.[18] At the corner the road formerly forked left into Launders Lane leading to north Rainham, Upminster, and Hornchurch. The left fork was modified later by the building of New Road. The right fork led to Purfleet. The street from Wennington Hall to Purfleet was mentioned in 1345 and 1413.[19] The route then taken was probably that shown on a map of 1726, on which the main road to Purfleet lay by Sandy Lane and Mill Lane to Aveley, then south by Ship Lane and Stonehouse Lane to West Thurrock, where it forked west to Purfleet and east to Grays and Tilbury.[20] Only a secondary road led south to Noak Hall, and perhaps on to Purfleet. East Hall Lane, which cuts across the north of the parish from Wennington Road to Launders Lane, may have existed by the 16th century when East Hall was mentioned.[21] Church Lane, leading from East Hall Lane to the church, existed by 1683.[22] The manor way, leading into the marsh near Southall bridge, was mentioned as a 'drove way' or 'defence way for cattle' in 1557.[23] In the 1950s it was still being used to drive cattle into the marsh.[24] It may have led to the ferry.

In the 1760s, when the Royal Ordnance magazines were moved to Purfleet, the government improved the more direct secondary road from Wennington to Purfleet, but local hostility and pilfering led to the erection on the road of a locked and guarded gate, called Purfleet turnpike, south of Noke House in Wennington.[25] The cottage beside the turnpike still existed in 1884, but has since been demolished.[26]

After 1809 Wennington Road became part of Tilbury Fort turnpike road.[27] A toll-bar and cottage were built a few yards east of Southall bridge.[28] The cottage still existed in 1881[29] but was demolished not long afterwards when New Cottages were built on the site. In 1924 the old London road through the village was replaced by a by-pass, New Road, built across the fields north of East Hall Lane to Launders Lane, and continuing down the Purfleet Road.[30] New Road is part of the arterial road to Tilbury and Southend.

Southall bridge, on the boundary between Rainham and Wennington, is treated elsewhere.[31] A 'short' ferry operating from Erith (Kent) to Coldharbour Point (Erehythenasse) existed in the Middle Ages; it ceased about the end of the 19th century.[32] A beacon or lighthouse was built a Coldharbour Point in 1895.[33]

The church is the only medieval building in Wennington, though Wennington Hall, East Hall, and the Willows probably occupy medieval sites. The Willows, formerly Scripps and Otters,[34] is an early-18th-century plastered farm-house of two storeys. In the 1960s its old flint-built barns were replaced by modern buildings.[35] Landthorpe House dates from the early 19th century. Wennington House, built *c.* 1810,[36] was demolished in the 1950s. Most of the cottages in the village date from the late 19th century, including New Cottages, Halldare Cottages (1892), and Laundry Terrace (1891), near the site of the former laundry.[37] A small development at the Green consists of semi-detached council houses, completed *c.* 1924, and privately built houses, *c.* 1928, on three sides of a square green.[38] The only building since the Second World War has been 20 semi-detached houses called Kent View, built in 1956 by the Seven Kings housing association on the site of Wennington House.[39]

In the 1820s, and until about 1838, the landlord of the Lennard Arms, Aveley, operated a daily coach service from Horndon to London via Wennington.[40] From 1838 to 1854 a coach ran to London from the Phoenix in Rainham.[41] The railway from Forest Gate to Tilbury, built across Wennington marshes, was opened in 1854 with a station at Rainham.[42] In 1976 Wennington was served by frequent buses running between Grays Thurrock and Rainham.

There was a sub-post office for Wennington by 1855.[43] The National Telephone Co. were first rated for their posts and wires in 1897.[44] The South Essex Waterworks Co. laid mains about 1891.[45] Wennington was connected to the main sewer draining to Riverside sewage works, south Hornchurch, in 1924.[46] A full-time fire station, to serve the Rainham neighbourhood, was built east of the Green in 1962.[47] A part-time library centre was opened in the school by Essex county council in 1947.[48] It closed, with the school, in 1966.

The great social event at Wennington in the late 18th and early 19th centuries was the vestry feast at the Lennard Arms, when food and drink, including porter for the poor, were charged to the parish rate.[49] In the late 19th century the new school became the centre of the social life of the village, mainly inspired by the rector, Nicholas Brady, and

[18] E.R.O., D/DL T1/645.
[19] E.R.O., D/DL T1/110, 333.
[20] See J. Warburton's *Map of Essex, Middlesex and Hertfordshire* (1726) which shows main roads with junctions of secondary roads; cf. *County Maps of Essex*, ed. F. G. Emmison, 10.
[21] *P. N. Essex*, 139. Though East Hall was in the west of Wennington, it was east of South Hall, Rainham.
[22] E.R.O., D/P 158/5/1–2.
[23] E.R.O., D/CT 392; E.R.O., D/DL T1/645.
[24] Allison, op. cit. 242.
[25] F. Z. Claro, 'Purfleet's Ordnance Magazines', *Thames Topics* (1963); *Map of Essex* (1777); E.R.O., D/DZn 4; ibid. D/P 157/22.
[26] E.R.O., T/P 50/11.
[27] R. Allison, 'The changing landscape of SW. Essex, 1600–1850' (Lond. Univ. Ph.D. thesis, 1966), 210. See also *V.C.H. Essex*, v. 186, 268.
[28] C. and J. Greenwood, *Map of Essex* (1825); O.S. Map 6", Essex, LXXXII (surv. 1862–8).
[29] E.R.O., T/P 50/11.
[30] *Essex and Thurrock Gaz.* 16 Dec. 1955; inf. from Rainham branch libr.
[31] See p. 126.
[32] Lewis, *Rainham*, 30; H.R.L., Lewis Scrapbook, xii. 23; see also p. 136.
[33] *V.C.H. Essex*, ii. 294.
[34] Cf. E.R.O., D/DL T1/484 (1478); D/DL T1/673 (1578).
[35] Lewis, *Rainham*, 109.
[36] E.R.O., T/P 50/14; Q/RSr 2/1.
[37] E.R.O., T/P 50/14; Lewis, *Rainham*, 102.
[38] Local inf.
[39] H.R.L., Lewis Scrapbook, ii. 5; iv. 13.
[40] *Pigot's Dir. Essex* (1826); E.R.O., T/P 50/14.
[41] E.R.O., T/P 50/14.
[42] Ibid.
[43] *Kelly's Dir. Essex* (1855).
[44] E.R.O., T/P 50/14.
[45] Ibid.
[46] Inf. from Riverside sewage works; cf. *County of Essex Devt. Plan, Rep. of Survey (Pt. II), Met. Essex*, Diagram No. 12.
[47] Lewis, *Rainham*, 109; *Essex and Thurrock Gaz.* 24 May, 1957, 14 July, 1961; *Essex C.C. Mins.* (1960), p. 746; (1962), p. 123.
[48] Inf. from Rainham branch libr.
[49] E.R.O., D/P 158/12/2.

supported by a few wealthy residents. Activities included concerts, carols, readings, magic lantern shows, glee club meetings, and choral festivals.[50] In 1923 two army huts were joined together as a village hall. The hall was burned down in 1960 but was replaced in 1962 by a new hall built by local labour.[51]

Henry of Yevele (1320? – 1400), master-mason and architect, held lands in Wennington.[52] Sir John Gildesborough, lord of the manor of Wennington, served as Speaker in two Parliaments of Richard II.[53] Several rectors and curates achieved eminence, including Robert Grove, (1634–96), bishop of Chichester, William Jane (1645–1707), and George Pattrick (1746–1800).[54] Henry Perigal (d. 1898), who claimed to have discovered the geometrical principles underlying the construction of the Great Pyramid, is buried at Wennington.[55]

MANORS AND OTHER ESTATES. In 1066 and 1086 Westminster Abbey was holding Wennington as a manor and 2½ hides.[56] Several pre-Conquest charters, regarded as spurious but possibly embodying an authentic tradition, mentioned land in Wennington given to the abbey.[57] The most specific, *c.* 1042–4, confirmed to the abbey the *burh* at Wennington and 4 hides, with the church and land 'at the lea' (perhaps in Aveley),[58] given by Ætsere the swarthy and his wife Ælfgyth.[59] In 1086 it was stated that ½ hide given to the abbey by a free man had been appropriated by Robert Vaizey, a tenant of Robert Gernon.[60] That holding, later called Wennington Enveyse, probably became part of Leventhorpes manor in the 13th century.

Westminster Abbey's manor was later known as *WENNINGTON WESTMINSTER* or *WENNINGTON* (*HALL*). In the 14th century it was held of the abbey for 100*s.* a year.[61] The abbey's tenancy-in-chief was last mentioned in 1507.[62]

By the later 12th century the manor was held of the abbey by the Marsh family. Graeland Marsh (de Marisco) seems to have been lord in 1198 when Galiena, widow of Geoffrey Marsh, came to terms with him over her dower; Geoffrey's mother was also dowered in Wennington.[63] Graeland was probably dead by 1203.[64] His successor was Gilbert Marsh, son of Geoffrey and Galiena, who had come of age by 1222, and was still alive in 1236.[65] Gilbert's son, John Marsh, held the manor *c.* 1248[66] and in 1293.[67]

In 1313 John de Tany (d. 1315) conveyed the manor of Wennington to Henry Garnet and his wife.[68] It then comprised a house and 114 a. in Wennington, held of Westminster Abbey, and also 26 a. land in Aveley and Rainham, held of Robert Vaizey, and 60 a. in Stifford, held of the archbishop of Canterbury.[69] In 1321 Henry Garnet was imprisoned as a rebel, and the manor was seized by the king.[70] It was still in the king's hands in 1325[71] but was later restored, for Henry died holding it in 1345, leaving as heirs his daughters Maud, Margery, and Margaret.[72]

Margaret Garnet probably died young, for the manor was later divided between Maud and Margery. Margery was the wife successively of John Darcy, John Sawtre, and, by 1361, of Sir John Gildesborough.[73] In 1366 Sir John acquired the other half of the manor from his wife's sister Maud, then widow of Sir Thomas Charnels.[74] Margery died *c.* 1380.[75] Sir John, who re-married, died in 1389, when Henry Sawtre confirmed the manor to Sir John's widow Elizabeth, on whom it had been settled for life.[76] Elizabeth Gildesborough was probably dead by 1399, when Henry Sawtre claimed half of the manor as Margery Gildesborough's son and heir.[77] In 1403 Robert Lytton was holding the manor in right of his wife Maud;[78] he was lord in 1412.[79] By 1475 William Trussell (d. 1481) held the manor.[80] He was followed by his son Edward (d. 1499) and his grandson John Trussell (d. 1499).[81] Elizabeth, sister and heir of John Trussell, married John de Vere (d. 1540), earl of Oxford.[82]

The manor descended in the de Vere family until 1579 when Edward de Vere (d. 1604), earl of Oxford, sold it to William Ayloffe (d. 1585) of Bretons, in Hornchurch.[83] The Ayloffes held it at least until 1664.[84] It then comprised Wennington Hall and 563 a., mainly marshland, let at £565 a year and heavily charged with annuities.[85] It was probably sold by Sir William Ayloffe (d. 1675) or soon after his death. Mrs. Anne Aleyn held it in 1681.[86] She may have been the widow of Thomas Aleyn (d. 1677), rector of Stanford-le-Hope and

50 E.R.O., T/P 50/14.
51 *Essex and Thurrock Gaz.* 5 Jan. 1962; Lewis, *Rainham*, 109.
52 *Essex Jnl.* i. 66–7; *E.A.T.* N.S. xiv. 32; E.R.O., D/DL T1/253, 173. See also *V.C.H. Essex, Bibliography*, 142.
53 *Essex Jnl.* i. 187.
54 *D.N.B.*
55 Lewis, *Rainham*, 97–8. In 1973 Perigal's monument in the churchyard was found broken.
56 *V.C.H. Essex*, i. 445.
57 P. Sawyer, *Anglo-Saxon Charters*, 246, 332, 309, 310; Hart, *Early Chart. Essex*, 14.
58 Cf. *P.N. Essex*, 121.
59 Hart, op. cit. 25.
60 *V.C.H. Essex*, i. 445. See also below.
61 *Cal. Inq. p.m.* vi, p. 455; viii, p. 416.
62 *Cal. Inq. p.m.* Hen. VII, iii, p. 147.
63 *Cur. Reg. R.* vii. 339; *Feet of F. Essex*, i. 16.
64 *Pipe R.* 1203 (P.R.S. N.S. xvi), 132.
65 *Cur. Reg. R.* x. 322; xii. 233; *Feet of F. Essex*, i. 61, 108, 114.
66 *Feet of F. Essex*, i. 175; *Abbrev. Plac.* (Rec. Com.), 128; *Close R.* 1247–51, 537; E.R.O., D/DL T1/1 and 35; B.L. Cott. MS. Nero E. vi, f. 185*v*.
67 *Abbrev. Plac.* (Rec. Com.), 231.
68 *Cal. Inq. p.m.* vi, p. 455 John de Tany was not connected with the main branch of the family: *E.A.T.* N.S. xx. 171 n.
69 *Cal. Inq. p.m.* vi, p. 455.
70 Ibid.; *Cal. Pat.* 1313–17, 688, 693; *Cal. Inq. Misc.* ii, p. 162–3.
71 *Cal. Inq. p.m.* vi, p. 455.
72 Ibid. viii, p. 416.
73 *V.C.H. Herts.* iii. 202; *Feet of F. Essex*, iii. 89, 132.
74 *Feet of F. Essex*, iii. 149; *Cal. Inq. p.m.* x. p. 466.
75 *E.A.T.* N.S. viii. 282; J. Weever, *Ancient Funerall Monuments*, 601.
76 Ibid.; *Cal. Close*, 1385–9, 645, 1389–92, 71.
77 C.P. 40/554 m. 215d.
78 *Feet of F. Essex*, iii. 238.
79 *Feud. Aids*, vi. 438.
80 C 140/78/83.
81 *Cal. Inq. p.m. Hen. VII*, ii, p. 235; iii, p. 147. For the date of Edward Trussell's death cf. ibid. ii. 228, 254–7; iii. 149, 401.
82 *Complete Peerage*, x. 247.
83 Morant, *Essex*, i. 85; E.R.O., D/DL T1/674–8. For the de Vere descent see *Complete Peerage*, x. 247–54.
84 E.R.O., D/DAc 382–4; Morant, *Essex*, i. 70, 85. Morant wrongly states that the manor was alienated by Sir Benjamin Ayloffe.
85 E.R.O., D/DAc 382–4.
86 The descent in the Aleyn family, unless otherwise stated, is based on E.R.O., D/SR 1–3 (sewers presentments.).

lord of Abbots Hall in that parish, for by 1685 Wennington had passed to John Aleyn, nephew of Thomas Aleyn and his successor at Abbots Hall.[87] Wennington and Abbots Hall decended together until about 1771. John Aleyn (d. *c.* 1719) was succeeded by William Ashby, husband of his daughter Elizabeth.[88] Between 1736 and 1740 the manor reverted to Thomas Aleyn, vicar of Cookham (Berks).[89] He was followed by Mrs. Mary Aleyn and Edmund Aleyn, *c.* 1747–50,[90] William Belchier, *c.* 1751–60,[91] Giles Aleyn *c.* 1761–3, and William Aleyn *c.* 1763–9.[92]

After William Aleyn's death Wennington was sold *c.* 1771 to John Hopkins.[93] It decended along with the manor of Theydon Bois to the Dare family.[94] In 1842 the Wennington estate comprised 347 a., held under the will of John Hopkins Dare (d. 1805), and 331 a. acquired separately.[95] In 1858 the Dare trustees sold Wennington Hall farm with 189 a. to Sir Thomas Barrett Lennard, Bt.[96] The War Office bought most of the rest in 1906 and later.[97]

The original manor-house was probably on the site of the present Wennington Hall, at the junction of Wennington Road and New Road, formerly Launders Lane. The *burh* mentioned *c.* 1042–4 may indicate the existence of a fortified house.[98] Certainly there was a 'capital' house by 1198.[99] It was known by 1345 as Wennington Hall,[1] and it was probably one of the manors of Sir John Gildesborough which was plundered by the peasants in 1381.[2] From the late 17th century it was let as a farm-house.[3] It was rebuilt by 1854, when it was described as new.[4] From *c.* 1914 it was occupied by the Gunary family.[5] After the death of S. Gunary, *c.* 1969, the house was sold separately from the farm.[6] It is a red-brick building of the earlier 19th century, considerably altered and refaced.

The manor of *WENNINGTON ENVEYSE* originated in the ½ hide which in 1086 was said to have been taken from Westminster Abbey by Robert Vaizey (*invesiatus*), a tenant of Robert Gernon.[7] The tenancy in chief of this fee, as of Berwick in Rainham, decended along with that of Battles Hall in Stapleford Abbots in the families of Montfichet and Plaiz.[8]

The family of Vaizey (Enveyse, Lenveise) remained under-tenents until the 13th century. Robert Vaizey, who was living *c.* 1200, was succeeded by his son Arnulf (fl. 1235).[9] At least part of Wennington Enveyse had by 1236 been subinfeudated to Gilbert Marsh, tenant in demesne of Wennington Westminster.[10] In 1281 John Vaizey, who was son of Geoffrey Vaizey and brother and apparently heir of William Vaizey, leased all his lands in Wennington and Aveley for three years to William Young, in return for 10*d.* a week for his keep, with 20*s.* and a robe worth 13*s.* 4*d.* once a year.[11] In 1285 John Vaizey, William de Chishull, and Master Ellis de Auxillers gave the Knights Hospitallers 3 messuages and 2½ carucates in Wennington and Aveley.[12] Whether William Young was still lessee in 1285 is not clear, but it seems likely that he continued as the Hospitallers' tenant, and that the Vaizey lands were thus merged in the manor of Leventhorpes.

The *COLDHARBOUR* estate, originally an island, lay in the south-west of the parish. It was reclaimed *c.* 1690–1700.[13] Before that it probably comprised the marshland south of the old counter walls which in the 19th century lay inland of Little Coldharbour, Coldharbour Point, and Great Coldharbour.[14] A small part of it, including Little Coldharbour, lay in Rainham. During the Middle Ages Lesnes abbey (Kent), which held the Rectory manor of Rainham, also had lands on Coldharbour, which passed to the Crown at the abbey's dissolution in 1525.[15] In 1541 Sir Ralph Sadler was licensed to alienate a marsh called Coldharbour to Henry Cooke.[16] It descended in the Cooke family until the 18th century.[17] John Doncastle, who held land at Coldharbour *c.* 1717–66, may have married a Cooke, for his property reverted to William Cooke in 1767.[18] In 1754 William Cooke and his wife sold 42 a. of Coldharbour to Ralph Phillips.[19] This included Kingsland, later Crown, marsh, and was probably the former monastic land. The rest of William Cooke's estate, including Great Coldharbour House, passed *c.* 1778 to John Bourne, possibly his son-in-law. In 1842 Cooke Kemp Bourne owned the house and 124 a., which were occupied by Henry Cooke Bourne, an Independent preacher.[20]

Ralph Phillips's estate passed to Peter Calman (*c.* 1759), Simon Stephenson (*c.* 1767), and then

[87] *E.A.T.* N.S. xxi. 102; E.R.O., Q/SR 449/1; Venn, *Alumni Cantab.* I, i. 19. John Aleyn was not Thos. Aleyn's son, as Morant suggests: *Essex*. i. 240.
[88] E.R.O., T/P 195/2 (2), 195/4 (20); see also E.R.O., D/DL M29.
[89] See also Morant, *Essex*, i. 240 n. [D] correcting ibid. 85.
[90] Cf. also C.P. 25(2)/1123/24 Geo. II Mich.
[91] Cf. also E.R.O., Q/RSg 3, f. 37.
[92] Cf. receipt for quit-rent, signed 'W. Aleyn', 1767: E.R.O., D/P 158/5/2.
[93] E.R.O., Libr. Vertical Folder (s.v. Wennington): newspaper advertisement of sale; Wright, *Essex*, ii. 569; *Hist. Essex by Gent.* iv. 348.
[94] Cf. *V.C.H. Essex*, iv. 252; v. 198.
[95] E.R.O., D/CT 392.
[96] E.R.O., T/P 50/14 (Letter, 1901, to Revd. Nic. Brady from Western & Sons, solicitors); T/P 50/5 (altered tithe apportionment, 1863).
[97] E.R.O., T/P 50/8, 50/10.
[98] Hart, *Early Chart. Essex*, 25.
[99] *Feet of F. Essex*, i. 16.
[1] E.R.O., D/DL T1/110.
[2] E. Furber, *Essex Sessions of the Peace*, 9; *Cal. Pat.* 1381–5, 24. Sir John Gildesborough was assaulted by the rebels while trying to quell the disorders as a J.P. in Brentwood: Furber, op. cit. 7.
[3] E.R.O., D/DAc 382–4; E.R.O., Libr. Vertical Folder (newspaper sale advertisement); *White's Dir. Essex* (1848), 209.
[4] E.R.O., D/DOp B72.
[5] *Kelly's Dir. Essex* (1914–37); *Post Office Tel. Dir.* (1968); H.R.L., Lewis Scrapbook, i. 13; iii. 2.
[6] Local inf.
[7] *V.C.H. Essex*, i. 445.
[8] Ibid. iv. 227; Sanders, *Eng. Baronies*, 83; *Cal. Inq. p.m.* x, p. 466; Morant, *Essex*, i. 86.
[9] E.R.O., D/DL T1/6; *Feet of F. Essex*, i. 53, 104; Morant, *Essex*, i. 86.
[10] *Feet of F. Essex*, i. 114; cf. *Cal. Inq. p.m.* vi, p. 455.
[11] B.L. Cott. MS. Nero E. vi, ff. 189v., 190. For many references to the Vaizeys in the locality see ibid. *passim*, especially ff. 185, 185v., 189v., 190, 340; *Cur. Reg. R.* v. 16.
[12] *Cal. Pat.* 1281–92, 165; B.L. Cott. MS. Nero E. vi, ff. 198, 199v.
[13] See p. 185.
[14] O.S. Map 6", Essex, LXXXII (surv. 1869–72).
[15] *L. & P. Hen. VIII*, iv (2), p. 2244.
[16] Ibid. xvi, p. 279.
[17] Unless otherwise stated the owners have been traced from E.R.O., D/SR 1–3 (sewers records).
[18] Ibid.; E.R.O., Q/RRp 1/19.
[19] E.R.O., D/DB T531.
[20] E.R.O., D/CT 392; Lewis, *Rainham*, 99.

to Nicholas Robinson, who sold it in 1774 to John Corrie.[21] Corrie sold it in the same year to William Allen, whose trustees sold it in 1789 to Nathaniel Brickwood (*d.* 1822).[22] In 1842 Elizabeth Brickwood held the estate, then comprising 45 a.[23] Between 1842 and 1862 a later owner built New Hall, by which name the estate was subsequently known.[24]

The manor of *YONGES*, later *LEVENTHORPES* or *LANDTHORPE*, lying in Wennington, Rainham, and Aveley, was built up in the 13th and 14th centuries by the Young family. It was held mainly of the manor of Wennington Hall, but part of it, held of the Knights Hospitallers, had probably formed the demesne lands of the manor of Wennington Enveyse.[25]

The Youngs were established in Wennington by 1227.[26] In 1327 William Young was one of the three largest taxpayers in the parish.[27] Thomas Young of Wennington, who died between 1377 and 1385, left an estate which included Launders in Rainham to his widow Alice for life, with reversion to William Kelet and his wife Alice.[28] Alice Kelet was probably Thomas Young's daughter. In 1408 she and her husband conveyed the estate, comprising some 500 a. in Rainham, Wennington, and neighbouring parishes, to John Lane.[29] In 1412 Lane held lands worth £20 in Wennington.[30]

About 1418 John Leventhorpe the younger (d. 1484) acquired the estate on marriage with John Lane's daughter Joan.[31] He was the son and heir of John Leventhorpe the elder (d. 1433) of Shingle Hall, Sawbridgeworth (Herts).[32] Thereafter the estate was known as Leventhorpes.[33] In 1434 John Leventhorpe and his wife Joan sold it to William Bismere.[34] They apparently retained the tenancy at least until the 1440s.[35] By 1499 Reynold Bismere (d. 1506) was in possession of the manor of Leventhorpes and Launders.[36] The estate appears to have remained in the Bismere family until 1534, when George Bismere conveyed it to John Bannister.[37] It passed to Sir William Sulyard (d. 1540), whose half-brother and eventual heir Eustace Sulyard sold it in 1545–6 to Sir Robert Southwell (d. 1559).[38] Southwell's son Francis sold it in 1566 to Richard Heard (d. 1578) a London butcher.[39] In the same year Richard Heard conveyed Leventhorpes to William Heard of Rainham, probably his brother, while retaining Launders.[40]

In 1592 William Heard conveyed Leventhorpes to John Heard, who by 1621 also held Launders. By a conveyance of 1621, possibly a marriage settlement, both manors passed to the Solme family.[41] In 1672 George Solme of Gillingham (Dors.) held them both.[42] They were probably separated about that time in the partition of the Solme family's estates among members of the Solme, Davenant, Richardson, Ettrick, and Cheveley families.[43]

About 1768 Thomas Mansfard (d. 1822) acquired Leventhorpes, or what was left of it.[44] He devised the manor, then comprising about 72 a., to his great-nephew Thomas Mansfard for life, with reversion to the heirs of the latter.[45] Thomas Mansfard the younger died in 1859, and the estate was then split up.[46]

A manor-house existed at Leventhorpes in 1443, when it was being thatched, and its gatehouse tiled.[47] That may have been the building called Old Lentrops, which was sold by John Heard in 1620.[48] It stood west of the churchyard, and in the mid 18th century was an alehouse called the Anchor; it was demolished in 1806.[49]

A new manor-house had presumably been built by 1620. It was probably on the site in Wennington Road occupied in 1842 by Thomas Mansfard's manor-house, Landthorpe House.[50] The present Landthorpe (or Lenthorpe) House dates from the early 19th century. After the break-up of the estate in 1859 the house passed through several hands, and a factory was built in its grounds.[51]

The manor of *NOKE*, lying in the east of the parish, was held of the manor of Wennington.[52] It may be identical with Standune *ad quercum*, which was mentioned in the later 12th century.[53] The Noke family held land in that area in the 13th and 14th centuries.[54] Thomas atte Noke (fl. 1313–24) held at least 100 a. in Wennington.[55] In 1327 his son Henry atte Noke was the largest taxpayer there.[56] In the earlier 15th century the manor seems to have been held by the Warner family. John Warner was acquiring land in the area in 1408.[57] In 1456–8 John, son and heir of William Warner, conveyed the manor of Noke to trustees who in 1460 sold it to William Pert.[58] In 1474 Pert conveyed it to William Turke, fishmonger of London, who already had an interest in it.[59] In 1483, shortly after Turke's death, his trustees conveyed the manor to Henry Andrews.[60]

[21] C.P. 25(2)/1308/14 Geo. III Mich; E.R.O., T/P 50/14.
[22] E.R.O., T/P 50/14.
[23] E.R.O., D/CT 392.
[24] E.R.O., T/P 50/14; O.S. Map 6″, Essex, LXXXII (surv. 1869–72).
[25] E.R.O., D/DL M34, cf. 27–8. For Wennington Enveyse see above.
[26] *Feet of F. Essex*, i. 77; cf. E.R.O., D/DL T1 for later 13th-century references.
[27] E 179/107/13 m. 8.
[28] *Cal. Pat.* 1374–7, 468; *V.C.H. Essex*, v. 275; E.R.O., D/DL T1/227.
[29] *Feet of F. Essex*, iii. 250.
[30] *Feud. Aids.* vi. 447. This was equal in value to the manor of Wennington.
[31] *Cal. Close*, 1413–19, 458.
[32] *V.C.H. Herts.* iii. 340.
[33] E.R.O., D/DL M 30–34.
[34] *Feet of F. Essex*, iv. 20.
[35] E.R.O., D/DL M23, 26.
[36] *Cal. Inq. p.m. Hen. VII*, iii, p. 152–3. He also held Dews Hall in Lambourne: *V.C.H. Essex*, iv. 80.
[37] Ibid.; C.P. 40/1083/113, cf. C 1/827/48.
[38] *Feet of F. Essex*, iv. 270; *E.A.T.* iii. 180; Prob. 11/43 (P.C.C. Mellershe); C.P. 25(2)/127/1626; C 142/184/36.
[39] C.P. 25(2)/127/1626; E.R.O., D/DC 41/244.
[40] E.R.O., D/DU 98/1–3; C 142/184/36; E.R.O., D/DC 4/244.
[41] E.R.O., D/DU 98/1–3; C.P. 25(2)/296/19 Jas. I Mich.; E.R.O., D/DVs 2.
[42] E.R.O., D/DC 41/449.
[43] Ibid.; E.R.O., D/DU 160/2.
[44] Mansfard first appears in the parish records in 1768: E.R.O., T/P 50/14. From 1769 he virtually ran the parish.
[45] E.R.O., T/P 50/14 (Notes from title-deeds by Revd. N. Brady, 1899); E.R.O., D/CT 392.
[46] E.R.O., T/P 50/14.
[47] E.R.O., D/DL M24.
[48] E.R.O., D/DC T1/725. See also below, p. 189.
[49] Morant, *Essex*, i. 86; E.R.O., T/P 50/14. See also below p. 186.
[50] E.R.O., D/CT 392; cf. *Map of Essex* (1777).
[51] E.R.O., T/P 50/14.
[52] Morant, *Essex*, i. 86; E.R.O., D/DL M29.
[53] B.L. Cott. MS. Nero E. vi, f. 194 and v.
[54] Ibid. ff. 191, 194, 194v., 340v.
[55] *Feet of F. Essex*, ii. 203, cf. 145, 172, 190, 208. He was buried in the church.
[56] E 179/107/13 m. 8.
[57] E.R.O., D/DL T1/307.
[58] E.R.O., D/DL T1/430–2, 434, 438–9, 460–1; *Cal. Close*, 1454–61, 269.
[59] E.R.O., D/DL T1/460–1, 472.
[60] E.R.O., D/DL T1/484–5, 492, 496, 498–9.

Robert Andrews, Henry's son, sold it in 1499 to John Barrett of Belhus in Aveley.[61] It subsequently descended with Belhus.[62] In 1619 it contained 146 a., lying north of Sandy Lane and extending west to Wennington creek.[63]

Noke (or Noak) House stood ¼ mile SE. of the church on the edge of the marsh.[64] It was described in 1923 as a 17th-century building of two storeys, timber-framed, with cross-wings.[65] From *c.* 1808 to 1836 it was used as a joint workhouse for the parishes of Aveley, Rainham, and West Thurrock.[66] By 1881 it had been converted into 5 cottages.[67] and had been demolished by 1966.[68]

ECONOMIC HISTORY. Wennington has always been a rural parish with agriculture as its main occupation. In 1086 it was assessed as 2½ hides,[69] an estimate so small in relation to the size of the later parish as to suggest that most of the marshland was then unreclaimed salting. There was little land under cultivation, and that had diminished: there was only half a plough-team on the demesne compared with a whole team in 1066. The recorded population had also fallen, from 8 (3 villeins, 3 bordars, 2 serfs) to 3 (2 villeins, 1 bordar). The value of the manor, however, had risen from 40*s.* to 60*s.* That was possibly due to the stock, which included a rouncey, a cow, 4 pigs, and 60 sheep. The sizeable flock of sheep was consistent with a coastal parish of few inhabitants with ample pasture on open saltings.[70]

The inclosure of the saltings is an important feature of Wennington's economic history. Complete reclamation was delayed for several centuries by the existence of the creek, with its long vulnerable frontage, but 'inning' was taking place by the end of the 12th century: 19 a. in 'Newland' are mentioned in 1198.[71] 'New marsh' and 'old marsh' were distinguished in the early 13th century.[72] Land in the 'new marsh', once of Roger atte Fen, was mentioned in 1323.[73] By that date reclamation was far enough advanced to warrant inclusion of the parish in the terms of reference of the commissions of walls and ditches.[74] The value of the new land is reflected in the inhabitants' petition in 1452 for relief from taxation after their meadows had been flooded by a high tide.[75] In spite of such setbacks reclamation continued. In 1500 John Barrett paid 20 marks for the 'inning' of 21 a. marsh at Noke, with a wall 6 ft. high, 14 ft. wide at the base, and 3½ ft. at the top.[76] Another 36 a. was reclaimed *c.* 1560.[77]

From 1532 Wennington was part of the Rainham 'level' for drainage purposes.[78] In 1563 the parish had 331 a. of 'inned' marsh.[79] At that date Coldharbour was still an island. The creek was still navigable in 1614 when Sir Edward Barrett leased the wharf-house and the wharf there, reserving to himself free access to the wharf.[80] Between 1619 and 1652,

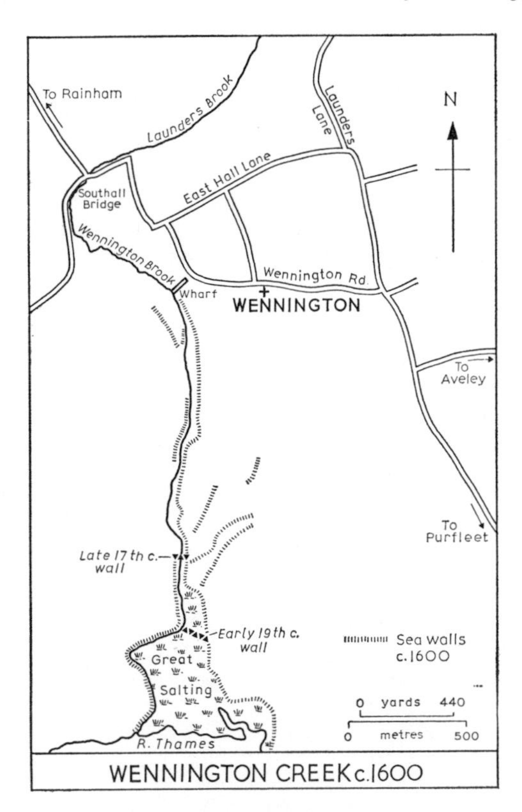

WENNINGTON CREEK c.1600

however, tenants of South Hall, Rainham, diverted the brook which flowed into the creek by a drain which caused it to flow farther west near South Hall bridge, so that the upper part of the creek became 'darved up' or choked.[81] Orders made in 1655 to scour, widen, and deepen the creek from the wharf downwards, were ineffective, while the diversion, which was inadequate to carry away the land water coming down from Launders bridge, sometimes caused flooding. By 1664 the blockage of the creek was accepted as permanent by the court of sewers, which agreed with the local landowners on a scheme to improve the diversion of the brook through Rainham to the Thames west of Little Coldharbour.[82] By 1691 the lords of the manors of Wennington and Noke had built a wall across the former mouth of the creek at the head of the Great Salting. This increased the fresh marsh of Wennington manor alone from 115 a. to 210 a. About the same time Coldharbour Island, containing about 170 a., was reclaimed and joined to the mainland.[83] Between 1799 and 1837 the

[61] E.R.O., D/DL T1/41, 551, 556, 559–60, 562, 564–5; D/DL E4.
[62] Morant, *Essex*, i. 86; *E.R.* xv. 113, 128; E.R.O., T/P 50/14.
[63] E.R.O., D/DL M 14/2; D/DL P1.
[64] *Map of Essex* (1777). Morant, *Essex*, i. 85 gives the location incorrectly.
[65] R.C.H.M. *Essex*, iv. 164.
[66] See p. 138.
[67] E.R.O., T/P 50/11, 14.
[68] Lewis, *Rainham*, 93.
[69] *V.C.H. Essex*, i. 445.
[70] Cf. Hilda E.P. Grieve, *Great Tide*, 5.
[71] *Feet of F. Essex*, i. 16.
[72] B.L. Cott. MS. Nero E. vi, f. 194v.
[73] E.R.O., D/DL T1/95–6.
[74] *Cal. Pat.* 1317–21, 607; see also *Cal. Pat.* 1446–52. 189; 1494–1509, 618.
[75] Ibid. 1452–61, 57.
[76] E.R.O., D/DL T1/566–7.
[77] E.R.O., D/DL T1/654.
[78] E.R.O., D/SR 1 sqq.; see also above, p. 137.
[79] E.R.O., D/SH 7. The following account of the closure of Wennington creek is based on E.R.O., D/SR 1 sqq.
[80] E.R.O., D/DL T1/707.
[81] Cf. E.R.O., D/DL P1.
[82] For its new course see: *Map of Essex* (1777); E.R.O., D/SR 76.
[83] E.R.O., D/SR 1, ff. 81, 103v., 107 (refs. 1692–1701 to walls on the island, to 'the new inset', and to 'the house by the point', i.e. Great Coldharbour.).

head of the Great Salting was also reclaimed.[84] By 1842 Wennington had 858 a. marshland.[85]

Mixed farming, including dairying, was being carried on in the earlier 15th century. When John Leventhorpe acquired the manor of Yonges about 1418 the stock comprised 150 ewes.[86] In the following year he began to buy cows at Braintree, Sawbridgeworth, and Bishop's Stortford (Herts.). and Chelmsford, and to enlarge the flock of sheep. Two rams were bought in 1419, and a bull in 1421. In 1420 78 lambs and 26 calves were sold to a London butcher. Cheese was also sold. By 1422 the dairy comprised 56 cows and 168 ewes, and was farmed out at £25 a year. In 1441 the cows' and ewes' milk was worth £20. The Leventhorpe dairy was apparently sold *c.* 1447, when most of the stock was sent to Shingle Hall, Sawbridgeworth, the family seat. John Leventhorpe's farm also produced wheat, beans, oats, rye, and barley, and sold the surplus in Barking, Dagenham and London. With only a small local population to draw on he was short of labour, and had to hire men by the day for all tasks, including carpenters from Dagenham, and harvesters from Writtle.

In the 17th century and later pasture predominated in Wennington's agriculture. In 1619 Noke manor farm contained 121 a. pasture out of a total of 146 a., and the whole of Wharf House farm, 65 a., was pasture apart from 8a. reeds.[87] In 1801 the area under grass was double that under crops. The main crops were barley, wheat, and turnips, with about 50 a. each, while there were smaller areas of oats, potatoes, peas, and beans.[88] In 1842 the parish had 729 a. pasture and 445 a. arable.[89] The four largest farms ranged in size from 94 a. up to 253 a. Several farmers in neighbouring parishes were leasing parcels of marshland in Wennington. By 1853 some of the arable was exhausted by over-cropping and failure to use manure.[90] The marsh pasture, on the other hand, was in good heart.[91] A visitor in 1856 commented on the large herds of cattle there.[92] In 1953 pedigree Essex pigs were being raised.[93] Large-scale grazing was still being carried out in 1973.

By the mid 19th century Wennington was producing large quantities of vegetables, especially peas, for the London market. Vegetable growing must have been well established in the parish by 1841, when the population was swollen on census day by 160 Irish migrant workers.[94] Two firms played a leading part in developing market-gardening in the parish. Spear & Vellacott grew out of a business run by William Spear at East Hall Farm in the 1880s; by 1922 the firm had been enlarged to include also Coldharbour and Willows farms.[95] In the 1960s it began to cut the production of vegetables in favour of barley for feeding beef cattle.[96] Samuel Gunary & Sons, who also farmed at South Hall, Rainham, were at Wennington Hall from *c.* 1914 to *c.* 1969.[97] In 1933 market crops in Wennington included seakale, rhubarb, and asparagus.[98] Asparagus was still being intensively grown in 1973.[99]

Whatever trade the creek and wharf brought through Wennington in earlier centuries had ceased by 1652, when the inhabitants claimed that its blockage prevented the transport of goods to London.[1] There was little trade in the village. An alehouse which existed in 1630[2] may have been the Anchor, which was named in 1754, and was licensed until 1770.[3] The licence ceased when the building was sold in 1771.[4] The Lennard Arms is reserved for treatment under Aveley. A coffee-house was built *c.* 1882 by John Kidd & Co.[5] It still survived in 1973.

In 1865 the Fresh Meat Preserving Co. built a factory in the grounds of Landthorpe House.[6] The business failed and in 1866 the factory and house were bought by James Ingram & Son, india-rubber manufacturers. They, too, failed and the factory was sold in 1881 to John Kidd & Co., chemical manufacturers. In 1885 Kidd leased the factory to the Camden Marine Steam Laundry, who built a large addition, but in 1891 the factory was burnt down. The derelict buildings, which were used for a time as a mat and rag factory, and later, *c.* 1914, for fish-skin drying, were demolished soon after 1966.[7]

In 1906 William Cunis Ltd. established a lighterage and dredging business at Coldharbour Point.[8] From 1929 the company carried gravel and ballast to London, returning with refuse to fill worked-out gravel-pits. It later undertook land reclamation, building up the marshland with refuse. Since 1956 the company has provided warehousing facilities on the built-up marsh.

Gravel was being extracted in Wennington in 1933 by the Wennington Sand and Ballast Co. Ltd.[9] An extensive tract of land at Willows farm, from which gravel had been extracted by Walker's Sand and Ballast Co., was being restored by the company in 1972 for return to agricultural use.[10] In 1973

[84] Cf. O.S. Map 1″, Essex (surv. 1799); E.R.O., D/SR 82; O.S. Map 6″, Essex, LXXXII (surv. 1869–72).
[85] E.R.O., D/SR 76, 77.
[86] The following details come from the *compoti* of the manor: E.R.O., D/DL M30–4 (dated 1418–24) and M23–8 (1441–50).
[87] E.R.O., D/DL M14/1–5.
[88] R. Allison, 'The changing landscape of SW. Essex, 1600 to 1850' (Lond. Univ. Ph.D. thesis, 1966), figs 81–7, p. 339.
[89] E.R.O., D/CT 392.
[90] E.R.O., D/DOp B72; D/DL E10 (Wennington Hall farm).
[91] Ibid.
[92] E.R.O., T/P 196/2, f. 30; cf. *Kelly's Dir. Essex* (1878).
[93] *Rainham and Wennington Coronation Souvenir (1953).*
[94] *Census,* 1841; cf. Thorne, *Environs Lond.* 683; *Kelly's Dir. Essex* (1870 and later edns.).
[95] *Kelly's Dir. Essex* (1886 and later edns.).
[96] *Essex and Thurrock Gaz.* 30 Aug. 1963; Lewis, *Rainham,* 109.
[97] H.R.L., Lewis Scrapbook, i. 13; iii. 2; *Kelly's Dir. Essex* (1914 and later edns.); local inf.
[98] *Kelly's Dir. Essex* (1933).
[99] H.R.L., Lewis Scrapbooks, i. 13; personal observation.
[1] E.R.O., D/SR 1. f. 15v.
[2] E.R.O., Q/SR 272/18, 273/18.
[3] E.R.O., Q/SBb 200/23; Q/RLv 25. For the Anchor, formerly Leventhorpes Manor-house, see above.
[4] E.R.O., Q/RLv 26.
[5] E.R.O., D/P 158/28/2; E.R.O., T/P 50/14; *Kelly's Dir. Essex* (1882 and later edns.).
[6] E.R.O., T/P 50/14; *Kelly's Dir. Essex* (1866–90). Unless otherwise stated the paragraph is based on these sources.
[7] Lewis, *Rainham,* 109; local inf.
[8] The account of Cunis Ltd. is based on Joan Hunt, 'Past, present, and possible future use of the Lower Thames Flood Plain at Rainham' (Dept. of Ed. thesis, NE. Lond. Polytechnic, 1972), 12, 31–4.
[9] *Kelly's Dir. Essex* (1933).
[10] Inf. from Walker's Sand and Ballast Co. in letter to F. Lewis, 26 Jan. 1972; *Havering Off. Guide* (1966), 84.

Purfleet Timber Storage Ltd, had a depot near the Noak Café, where there was also a scrap-yard.

LOCAL GOVERNMENT. No manor court rolls or books are known to have survived.[11] The lord of the manor was said in 1577 to be responsible for repairing the stocks,[12] but the parish repaired them in 1736 and rebuilt them in 1770.[13]

Most of the earlier parish records were stolen some time before 1837, and only some loose papers and bills survive for the pre-1836 period.[14] Two vestry books, 1762–1831, which existed in 1900, have also disappeared, but extracts from them were made by the then rector, Nicholas Brady.[15]

The oldest surviving vestry book dates from 1832. There were then four vestry meetings a year usually held in the church, with three or four parishioners attending. From *c.* 1769 to *c.* 1837, when there was no resident rector, the chair seems usually to have been taken by successive owners of the manor of Leventhorpes, Thomas Mansfard (d. 1822) and his grand-nephew of the same name. The elder Thomas served as churchwarden *c.* 1769–1822, and the younger from 1825 to 1843.

Wennington was accused in 1579 of having no parish officers.[16] There were two churchwardens in 1569,[17] but only one in 1593[18] and later, until 1822. Two were chosen thereafter. A parish overseer was mentioned in 1734. One was being chosen in 1762, but by 1809 the practice was to choose two, of whom one, termed the acting overseer, was legally regarded as executing the office. As the second overseer named in 1809 was the constable, that officer may have acted also as assistant overseer. The constable, mentioned in 1700, was elected annually but, like all the other parish officers, was usually re-elected several years running. Matthew Turner, also parish clerk, was constable from 1788 to 1834. He had a painted and gilded staff of office. The parish continued to appoint a constable until 1874. A parish clerk was mentioned in 1419.[19] He was being paid £2 a year in 1685, and later was usually tenant of one of the parish cottages. The parish had one surveyor of the highways in 1735. The office was usually held with another. After *c.* 1830 two surveyors were chosen.

The cost of supporting the poor was met by two small charities, the rent of the parish cottages, and occasional rates. In the years 1754–7 two rates of 6*d.* each, producing a total of £46, sufficed to meet the overseer's spending for three years. By 1762 the poundage was usually 1*s.*, levied from one to five times a year as necessary. Poor-relief costs averaged £31 a year in the three years 1783–5, and £83 in the years 1801 to 1817.[20] Between 1829 and 1835 the annual average was about £164. A constable's rate of 3*d.*, producing £10 13*s.* 6*d.*, was levied in 1731. Surveyor's expenses in excess of the sums paid to compound for statute duty were met by special rates, which were levied with increasing frequency after 1800.

In this isolated parish the casual relief of travellers rarely figures in the accounts, but the vestry not infrequently had to recover and bury the bodies of those drowned in the Thames or on the saltings. The number of parishioners in need can never have been large. Five householders were excused payment of hearth tax in 1670.[21] One weekly pension of 5*s.* was paid in 1729; there were two regular pensioners in 1754 and five in 1812. The homeless or helpless poor, including children, were boarded out in the village, sometimes with the constable, or in poor-houses in larger parishes nearby, such as West Thurrock, Aveley, and South Ockendon. The poor were nursed when sick, given medicines, inoculated, and attended by the apothecary, doctor, and mid-wife. In 1764 the parish paid for a family with smallpox to be nursed in Rochford pest-house, and for the survivors to convalesce in the 'airing house'. In the late 1820s an idiot girl was boarded at Bethnal Green asylum, the parish paying extra for hair-cutting, laundry, medicines, and clothing. The overseer's bills include payments for rent, coal, bedding and clothing; for provisions for a wife while her husband was in prison; for a child's writing books and a spinning-wheel; for apprentice-ship indentures; for marriage fees, licence, and ring; and for burial.

The parish had two brick, tarred timber, and thatched cottages,[22] referred to as the parish or poor-houses, or clerk's house.[23] Both were let, one usually to the parish clerk, and the rents applied to parish purposes. The poor were sometimes housed or boarded in them. One of the cottages stood on an acre of land called Merston Set on the west side of Launders Lane. The land was let to the church-wardens in 1569 by Edward Barrett at a nominal rent for so long as it was used for the benefit of the poor and the repair of the church. In 1872 Merston Set was exchanged with Sir T. Barrett-Lennard for a piece of land west and south of the churchyard, on part of which the board school was built. Merston Set was obliterated in 1924 by the building of New Road.[24] The other cottage, built before 1683 on the waste in Church Lane, was a copyhold of Wenning-ton manor.[25] It was later divided into two cottages, one of which was used as the parish school 1866–76. The building, which was standing in 1950,[26] had been demolished by 1973.

Wennington became part of Romford poor-law union in 1836.

CHURCH. Wennington church was said to have been given to Westminster Abbey before the Conquest by Ætsere the swarthy and his wife Ælfgyth.[27] The church certainly existed, in the

[11] The only known manorial records are *compoti*, 1418–22, 1442–50: E.R.O., D/DL M23–8, 30–4.
[12] E.R.O., Q/SR 64/69.
[13] E.R.O., D/P 158/12/2.
[14] *Essex Par. Recs.* 229 and n.
[15] The following account, unless otherwise stated, is based on the parish records, and on Nicholas Brady's notes: E.R.O., D/P 158; E.R.O., T/P 50/12, 14.
[16] E.R.O., Q/SR 73/72.
[17] E.R.O., D/P 158/25/1.
[18] E.R.O., D/ABW 19/230.
[19] E.R.O., D/DL M30.
[20] E.R.O., Q/CR 1/1 and 1/9/3.
[21] E.R.O., Q/RTh 5.
[22] E.R.O., D/CT 392, nos. 109, 142.
[23] This account of the parish cottages is based on: E.R.O., D/P 158/12/2–3 and 158/25/1; E.R.O., D/DL Q4; E.R.O., T/P 50/14.
[24] Cf. O.S. Map 6", Essex, LXXXIII (surv. 1863–6) and O.S. Map 6", sheet TQ 58 SW.
[25] E.R.O., D/P 158/5/1–2.
[26] H.R.L., Lewis Scrapbook, xiii. 30 (*Romford Times*, 25 Oct. 1950, illus.). There is another illus. in *Prospect*, Aug. 1970.
[27] Hart, *Early Chart. Essex*, 25.

abbey's possession, by the time of Richard de Belmeis, bishop of London (1108–27).[28] Gilbert Marsh tried unsuccessfully to claim the advowson in 1222.[29] The abbey held the advowson until 1541.[30] In 1308 and 1385, when the abbacy was vacant, the king presented,[31] and in 1469 and 1491 the bishop of London presented by lapse.[32] In 1541 the advowson was granted to the newly created see of Westminster.[33] When the see was suppressed in 1550 it was granted to the bishop of London.[34] Queen Mary confirmed the grant in 1554,[35] but the abbey, after its restoration by Mary, presented William Talbot, who was instituted in January 1559.[36] The advowson was subsequently held by the bishop of London until 1852. Presentations for one turn were made by Thomas Cole in 1587 and Mark Danvers in 1588.[37] In 1852 the advowson was transferred to the bishop of Peterborough,[38] then in 1867 to the Crown.[39] Since 1958 it has been held by the Martyrs Memorial Trust.[40]

It was stated in 1254 that the church of Wennington, worth 10 marks, was appropriated to Westminster Abbey, and that there was no vicar.[41] Those facts would fit a donative curacy, but the institution of a rector was recorded in 1222,[42] and regularly from the early 14th century. The rectory was valued at £8 in 1291 and at the same figure in 1535.[43] By 1637 there were 4 a. glebe.[44] That may have originated as a toft granted to the rector in 1352 by Sir Thomas Charnels.[45] It lies opposite the church on the north side of the road.[46] The tithes, which were said to be worth £100 in 1650,[47] were commuted in 1842 for £420.[48] There seems to have been no rectory house since *c.* 1600 or earlier.[49] Since 1954 the living has been held in plurality, with Rainham.[50]

From the 17th century to the later 19th century most of the rectors were absentee pluralists.[51] Though some of them became eminent[52] they probably had little personal influence on the parish. Two rectors, William Ashton, 1583–7, and William Danvers, 1588–1616, were deprived of the living.[53] Ashton refused to wear the surplice.[54] Danvers was in prison in 1616, for what reason is not known.[55] He seems to have been a local trouble-maker.[56] Henry Bust, 1616–25, seems to have served the cure himself[57] and probably installed the fine oak pulpit and font cover mentioned below. His successor, John Aylmer, 1626–42, was usually absent,[58] but John Elborough, 1642–52, was described in 1650 as an able minister 'diligently preaching there'.[59] In the 18th and earlier 19th centuries the parish was normally served by a curate, often the vicar or curate of a neighbouring parish, such as Aveley or Rainham.[60] In the late 18th century there was usually one service on each or alternative Sundays.[61] William Hughes, 1865–74, was the first rector to serve the cure himself for over a century. His successor, Nicholas Brady, 1874–1907, who lived at Rainham Hall, restored public baptism, established an evening service, introduced choral celebration, and restored the church.[62] He took the lead in the social life of Wennington and compiled careful notes on the history of the parish.[63] The Revd. Alfred Norton, 1927–37, lived in the parish at a house called the Priory, which he built in 1929.[64]

The church of *ST. MARY AND ST. PETER* stands in Wennington Road, on rising ground above the marshes.[65] It is a restored medieval church of rubble with limestone dressings, comprising nave, chancel, aisles, embattled west tower, north porch, and south organ chamber. The oldest part of the church is a 12th-century round-arched doorway, reset in the vestry.[66] Masoned blocks of limestone, exposed in the foundations of the nave when the floor was renewed in 1960, were attributed to the Norman period, or even earlier.[67] The chancel, nave, and south aisle were apparently rebuilt in the early 13th century. In the early 14th century the north aisle was added. Later in the same century the west tower was built and a new roof was put on to the chancel. In the late 15th or early 16th century the chancel arch and the nave roof were rebuilt, and new furniture was added. The furnishings were further improved in the 17th century. Before 1720,[68] and probably *c.* 1600, the south aisle was demolished, the

[28] *Reg. Regum Anglo-Norm.* ii, p. 216.
[29] *Feet of F. Essex*, i. 61; E.R.O., T/A 172.
[30] Newcourt, *Repertorium*, ii. 651–2.
[31] *Cal. Pat.* 1307–13, 59; 1381–5, 366.
[32] Newcourt, *Repertorium*, ii. 652.
[33] *L. & P. Hen. VIII*, xvi, p. 243.
[34] *Cal. Pat.* 1549–51, 263.
[35] Ibid. 1553–4, 119–20.
[36] Newcourt, *Repertorium*, ii. 652.
[37] Ibid. 653.
[38] *Lond. Gaz.* 4 June 1852, pp. 1583–4.
[39] Ibid. 21 May 1867, p. 2912; E.R.O., D/CP 22.
[40] *Chelmsford Dioc. Year Bk.* (1958).
[41] *E.A.T.* N.S. xviii. 17.
[42] E.R.O., T/A 172.
[43] *Tax. Eccl.* (Rec. Com.), 22; *Valor. Eccl.* (Rec. Com.) i. 436.
[44] Newcourt, *Repertorium*, ii. 652; G.L.C., DL/C/624, ff. 232v., 265.
[45] E.R.O., D/DL T1/158.
[46] E.R.O., T/P 50/14.
[47] Smith, *Eccl. Hist. Essex*, 246.
[48] E.R.O., D/CT 392.
[49] *E.A.T.* N.S. xxi. 102; Morant, *Essex*, i. 87; *White's Dir. Essex* (1848), 209; E.R.O., D/AEM 1/2; G.L.C., DL/C/624, ff. 232v., 265.
[50] *Chelmsford Dioc. Year Bk.* (1955 and later edns.).
[51] Cf. Guildhall MSS. 9556, f. 88; 9557, f. 59. For rectors see Newcourt, *Repertorium*, ii. 652–3; E.R.O., T/P 50/13 (extended list by G. Hennessey); H. Smith, 'Sequence of Essex Clergy, 1640–68' (TS. in E.R.O.), i. 25.
[52] See p. 182.
[53] Newcourt, *Repertorium*, ii. 653.
[54] E.R.O., D/AEA 13, f. 79v.
[55] E.R.O., D/AEV 5 (8 Apr. 1616).
[56] In 1592–3 he accused Wilfred Lutye, one of the Aveley gentry, of treason, in trying to entice him to adhere to Rome: E.R.O., Q/SR 122/36–40; Assizes 35/35/H/40. Lutye was acquitted.
[57] He usually appeared at visitations and does not seem to have employed a curate: E.R.O., D/AEV 5. For his monument see below.
[58] E.R.O., D/AEV 6, ff. 48, 102, 151; Smith, 'Sequence of Essex Clergy, 1640–68', i. 25; G.L.C., DL/C/624, ff. 232v., 265.
[59] Smith, *Eccl. Hist. Essex*, 246.
[60] E.R.O., T/P 50/14 (list of curates compiled by Nic. Brady).
[61] Guildhall MSS. 9557, f. 59; 9558, f. 382.
[62] E.R.O., T/P 50/14. He was son of Sir Antonio Brady of West Ham, for whom see D.N.B.; *V.C.H. Essex*, vi. 64, 119–20.
[63] His notes are now E.R.O., T/P 50/1–14.
[64] C.C.L., Bp. Inskip's Recs., s.v. Wennington.
[65] Unless otherwise stated the description of the church is based on R.C.H.M. *Essex*, iv. 163–4; Pevsner, *Essex*, 415.
[66] See also E. Godman, *Norman Architecture in Essex*, 14, 27.
[67] *Essex and Thurrock Gaz.* 19 Aug., 30 Sep., 21 Oct. 1960.
[68] E.R.O., T/P 195/2 (no. 2): Holman mentions only a north aisle.

two-bay arcade was walled up, two Elizabethan-style windows were inserted, and a south doorway, later blocked.[69] Extensive repairs were carried out in the early 18th century.[70] By 1874 the church was shabby and neglected.[71] Through the efforts of the rector, Nicholas Brady, and under the architectural direction of the Revd. Ernest Geldart, it was restored and enlarged in 1885–6 to accommodate the increasing population.[72] The south aisle was rebuilt on its ancient foundations, with an organ chamber added. New windows were inserted in the chancel. A west gallery of unknown date was removed, and the base of the tower was converted into a vestry.[73] The cost of over £1,000 was met by subscription and from a fund raised earlier to build a rectory.[74] In 1900 the old porch was replaced by a new one of stone, also designed by Geldart.[75]

The fittings of the church include an early-13th-century oak chest.[76] The octagonal Purbeck marble font, also of the 13th century, has an early-17th-century carved oak cover.[77] There is a 13th-century piscina in the chancel and a 14th-century one in the north aisle. An oak bench of the 15th or early 16th century survives, and there are known to have been others. The oak staircase in the two upper stages of the tower is probably of the 15th century. The hexagonal carved oak pulpit dates from the early 17th century.[78] A wrought-iron hour-glass stand of the 17th century is attached to the north-east respond beside it.[79]

In 1552 there were three small bells.[80] The present bell-frame is of the 17th century, and there is one bell dated 1662 by Anthony Bartlet.[81] Two other bells of the same make and date still existed in 1856,[82] but only one bell was in use in 1872,[83] and by 1900 only one survived.[84]

The church plate includes a silver-plated paten dated 1790, with the initials T. M. (Thomas Mansfard), and a silver-plated cup given in 1875 by Nicholas Brady.[85] A silver cup and cover recorded in 1685 no longer survive.

A brass indent on the floor of the south aisle commemorates Thomas atte Noke, who died *c.* 1325.[86] Under the altar is the matrix of another brass, probably that to Margery (d. *c.* 1380), wife of Sir John Gildesborough, lord of the manor of Wennington.[87] In the north aisle is an alabaster tablet to Henry Bust, rector (d. 1625).

NONCONFORMITY. The Wesleyan Methodist John Valton taught and preached at Noke House in 1769.[88] Henry Cooke Bourne (d. 1855), an Independent preacher who lived at Great Coldharbour Farm, was deacon of the Aveley Independent chapel.[89] John Dupray Bourne (d. 1879), of Wennington House, registered it for Independent worship in 1861.[90]

EDUCATION. In the 18th century the vestry sometimes paid for poor children to be taught,[91] but in 1808 the curate reported that the parish was too small to support a school.[92] A Church Sunday school was opened about 1834. It was maintained by subscriptions, and in 1839 was attended by 27 children, who received free schooling and clothing.[93] In 1862 it was amalgamated with a small private day-school kept by Emily Turnpenny.[94] She was appointed mistress at £16 a year, paid by the parish vestry. The school was moved in 1866 from a private house to the parish cottage in Church Lane. After compulsory church-rates were abolished in 1868 the cost of the school, about £30 a year, was met by subscription and children's pence. In 1870 there were 41 children in one small room.[95] A school board was formed in 1875,[96] and a new school and teacher's house, designed by Habershon & Pite, was opened in 1877 on a site, beside the churchyard, acquired by the parish in exchange for Merston Set.[97] Miss Turnpenny, who was uncertificated, then retired. The board school, which had places, for 63 children, was overcrowded by 1906, and the county council therefore reorganized it for mixed juniors and infants. It was closed in 1966, when 42 children were transferred to Rainham. The old building was converted into three dwellings.

CHARITIES FOR THE POOR. William Heard, by his will proved 1593, gave a rent of 10*s.*, charged on his lands in Rainham, to provide doles of 2*s.* each to 5 poor persons on Easter Day.[98] John Heard, heir of William, seems to have transferred the rent-charge to his house in Wennington called Old Lentrops, later the Anchor.[99] In 1837 the rent-charge was still being paid by the owner of Wennington House, which stood on the site of the Anchor.[1] It was then stated that another rent-charge of 10*s.* was due to the parish from the Angel in Rainham. That was presumably Barrett's gift, mentioned in 1719, to buy smocks for poor widows.[2] Its origin and purpose had been forgotten by 1837. The rent-

69 E.R.O., T/P 196/2 (Eccl. Essexienses), f. 27.
70 Salmon, *Essex*, 284.
71 E.R.O., T/P 50/14.
72 Ibid.; E.R.O., D/CF 24/10; D/P 158/6/1–2.
73 E.R.O., T/P 50/4.
74 Ibid.; E.R.O., D/CF 24/10.
75 *E.R.* ix. 173.
76 *Church Chests Essex*, 50–1, 218; Pevsner, *Essex*, 415.
77 R.C.H.M. *Essex*, iv, plate facing p. 104.
78 Ibid. plate facing p. 4.
79 Ibid. plate facing p. 104.
80 *E.A.T.* N.S. ii. 184.
81 *Ch. Bells Essex*, 445.
82 E.R.O., T/P 196/2, f. 30.
83 W. Palin, *More about Stifford*, 137–8.
84 E.R.O., T/P 50/14.
85 *Ch. Plate Essex*, 34; *E.A.T.* N.S. xxi. 102. For Brady's gift see E.R.O., D/P 158/12/3.
86 *E.R.* x. 86; E.R.O., T/P 196/2, f. 33. For Thomas atte Noke see above, p. 184.
87 *E.A.T.* N.S. viii. 282.
88 Thos. Jackson, *Lives of the early Methodist Preachers*, vi. 78. Valton also preached at Rainham.
89 *White's Dir. Essex* (1848), 209; H.O. 129/7/198; Lewis, *Rainham*, 99.
90 G.R.O. Worship Reg. no. 14284 (cancelled 1899 on revision).
91 E.R.O., D/P 158/12/2, e.g. in 1780.
92 E.R.O., D/AEM 2/4.
93 E.R.O., D/P 30/28/19.
94 Unless otherwise stated this account of the school is based on E.R.O., T/P 50/14; E.R.O., D/P 158/12/3; D/P 158/28/1, 3; Ed. 2/175; Ed. 21/5419.
95 E.R.O., D/AEM 2/8.
96 *Lond. Gaz.* 30 Apr. 1875, p. 2342.
97 For Merston Set see p. 187.
98 E.R.O., D/ABW 19/230; cf. *Rep. Com. Char.* [108], p. 718 (1837–8), xxv(1).
99 E.R.O., D/DL T1/725. For Old Lentrops see above, p. 184.
1 E.R.O., T/P 50/14; *Rep. Com. Char.* [108], p. 723; Char. Com. Files.
2 E.R.O., T/P 195/2 (no. 2) (Holman MSS.).

charge had not been paid since 1829. Before that the parish had customarily distributed the income from both rent-charges in doles to poor families. Neither of the charges is known to have been paid after 1837.[3]

The Helen Mary Norton charity was founded in 1937.[4] The Revd. Alfred Norton, rector of Wennington, gave £100 stock in trust to provide relief for the sick and needy in the parish. In 1976 the income was being used to provide Christmas parcels.[5]

Merston Set, let to the parish in 1569, partly for the benefit of the poor, is treated above.[6]

[3] Char. Com. Files.
[4] Ibid.
[5] Inf. from Rector.
[6] See p.187.

INDEX

NOTE. Subjects are indexed mainly under the places to which the references relate, but there are also separate headings for subjects in the following list, and for others to which cross-reference is made under the headings marked in the list with an asterisk: agricultural machinery; *agriculture; airfields; alms-houses; architects; *architecture; barracks; beacons; bell-founders; cages; canals; *Canterbury Tales*; cemeteries; chantries; church-house; coin hoard; *disorder; *entertainment; *epidemics; fairs; fires; floods; gipsies; Green Belt; guilds; hospitals; hundreds; *industry; Jews; judgement of fire and water; Knights Hospitallers; Knights Templars; lakes; libraries; markets; moats; museums; *nonconformity; organ builders; parishes, detached parts of; parks; peculiar, ecclesiastical; *punishment; ritualism; school boards; sculptors; serjeanties; *services, public; spring, mineral; Volunteers; war damage; warren, free; watch-house; workhouses.

An italic page number denotes an illustration on that page or facing it.

The following abbreviations have been used, sometimes with the addition of the letter *s* to form the plural: abp., archbishop; adcn., archdeacon; agric., agriculture; Alb., Albert; Alex., Alexander; Alf., Alfred; anc., ancient; And., Andrew; Ant., Anthony; Art., Arthur; Bart., Bartholomew; bd., board; bdg., building; Benj., Benjamin; boro., borough; bp., bishop; Cath., Catherine; Cathm., Catholicism; ch., church; char., charity; Chas., Charles; Chris., Christopher; cott., cottage; ctss., countess; d., died; Dan., Daniel; dau., daughter; dchss., duchess; dom., domestic; econ., economic; Edm., Edmund; educ., education; Edw., Edward; elec., electricity; Eliz., Elizabeth; ent., entertainment; fam., family; fm., farm; Fran., Francis *or* Frances; Fred., Frederick; gdn., garden; Geo., George; Geof., Geoffrey; Gilb., Gilbert; govt., government; Gt., Great; Hen., Henry; Herb., Herbert; hist., history; ho., house; hosp., hospital; Humph., Humphrey; hund., hundred; inc., inclosure; ind., industry; Jas., James; Jn., John; Jos., Joseph; Kath., Katharine *or* Katherine; Laur., Laurence; Lawr., Lawrence; ld., lord; loc., local; Lt., Little; m., married; man., manor; Marg., Margaret; marq., marquess; Mat., Matthew; mfr., manufacture *or* manufacturer; Mic., Michael; mkt., market; Nat., Nathaniel; Nic., Nicholas; nonconf., nonconformity; par., parish; parl., parliamentary; Pat., Patrick; Pet., Peter; Phil., Philip; pk., park; pop., population; pub., public; rect., rectory; Reg., Reginald; rem., remains; rep., representation; Ric., Richard; riv., river; rly., railway; Rob., Robert; Rog., Roger; Rom., Roman; Sam., Samuel; sch., school; Sid., Sidney; Sim., Simon; soc., society; Steph., Stephen; stn., station; svce., service; Thos., Thomas; vic., vicarage; vct., viscount; w., wife; Wal., Walter; wk., work; Wm., William.